The Chicago Manual of Style

Thirteenth Edition, Revised and Expanded

FOR AUTHORS, EDITORS, AND COPYWRITERS

The University of Chicago Press

CHICAGO AND LONDON

The University of Chicago Press, Chicago 60637
The University of Chicago Press, Ltd., London
© 1969, 1982 by The University of Chicago. All rights reserved
First Edition published 1906. Thirteenth Edition 1982
Printed in the United States of America
95 94 93 92 91 90 89 88 87 86   9 8 7 6 5

Library of Congress Cataloging in Publication Data
University of Chicago Press.
   The Chicago manual of style.

   Rev. ed. of: A manual of style. 12th ed., rev.
c1969.
   Bibliography: p.
   Includes index.
   1. Printing, Practical—Style manuals.
2. Authorship—Handbooks, manuals, etc. I. Title.
Z253.U69 1982   686.2′24   82-2832
ISBN 0-226-10390-0   AACR2

Contents

Preface *page* vii

Part 1   Bookmaking

1. The Parts of a Book 3
2. Manuscript Preparation and Copyediting 37
3. Proofs 87
4. Rights and Permissions 107

Part 2   Style

5. Punctuation 131
6. Spelling and Distinctive Treatment of Words 157
7. Names and Terms 183
8. Numbers 231
9. Foreign Languages in Type 249
10. Quotations 281
11. Illustrations, Captions, and Legends 303
12. Tables 321
13. Mathematics in Type 351
14. Abbreviations 375
15. Documentation: References, Notes, and
    Bibliographies 399
16. Bibliographic Forms 437
17. Note Forms 485
18. Indexes 511

Part 3   Production and Printing

19. Design and Typography 561
20. Composition, Printing, and Binding 585

Glossary of Technical Terms 645
Bibliography 685
Index 695

Preface

Bowing to what has become nearly universal usage, we have made a title change with this edition of the *Manual of Style,* and now call it what everybody else calls it, *The Chicago Manual of Style*— or, for short, *The Chicago Manual.*

Two pervasive features characterize the present edition: it reflects the impact of the new technology on the entire editing and publishing process, and it spells out, in greater detail and with many more examples, the procedures with which it deals. It is, in short, much more a "how-to" book for authors and editors than was its predecessor. In chapter 2, for example, a new section has been added on how to mark a manuscript and how to mark the type specifications on a script. Chapter 12, completely rewritten, begins with advice on how to make a table from raw data. Chapters 15 through 17, reorganized and greatly expanded, offer many more alternative methods of citation—the emphasis being on the most practical—and provide a wealth of examples. In chapter 18, clear step-by-step procedures for the mechanics of index making are set forth. The terminology and methodology of technological advances (in word processing, computerized electronic typesetting, and the like) are reflected most prominently in chapter 20, "Composition, Printing, and Binding" (new to this edition), and in the Glossary, which now emphasizes typesetting and printing terms, excluding many items, formerly included, that were applicable only to the publisher's function. Other notable features of the present edition are chapter 4 ("Rights and Permissions"), rewritten in light of the new copyright law, and chapter 9 ("Foreign Languages"), which includes a new table of diacritics, a pinyin (Chinese) conversion chart, and data on several more languages.

Although this thirteenth edition reflects the publishing arts of our own day, its editors have built upon foundations laid down by their predecessors. The earliest of these foundations were probably coeval with the establishment of the Press itself, in 1891. A single sheet of typographic style fundamentals drawn up by the first proofreader for his—or her—own guidance had by 1901 become a slender "Style Book: Adopted and in Use for University Publications." The first published version of the Press's style rules, no doubt issued in response to demands from outside the university community for such a book, appeared in 1906:

Manual of Style
Being a Compilation of the Typographical Rules
In Force at the University of Chicago Press
To Which Are Appended
Specimens of Types in Use

Since the publication of that first edition of the *Manual of Style* seventy-six years ago much has changed at the Press. Authors are no longer advised that manuscripts "should be either typewritten or in a perfectly clear handwriting." The leaf-entwined art nouveau typographic ornaments and initial letters that graced early Press publications have disappeared, as has also, alas, two-color printing throughout the Press's own *Manual*. Some things, however, have not changed. What was said in the preface to the first edition about the philosophy of a style manual is as true today as it was then, and cannot be said better by the present editors:

> Rules and regulations such as these, in the nature of the case, cannot be endowed with the fixity of rock-ribbed law. They are meant for the average case, and must be applied with a certain degree of elasticity. Exceptions will constantly occur, and ample room is left for individual initiative and discretion. They point the way and survey the road, rather than remove the obstacles. Throughout this book it is assumed that no regulation contained therein is absolutely inviolable. Wherever the peculiar nature of the subject-matter, the desirability of throwing into relief a certain part of the argument, the reasonable preference of a writer, or a typographical contingency suggests a deviation, such deviation may legitimately be made. Each case of this character must largely be decided upon its own merits. Generally it may be stated that, where no question of good taste or good logic is involved, deference should be shown to the expressed wishes of the author.

This revision of the *Manual of Style* was begun some years ago at the urging of John Ryden, then editor-in-chief, and Morris Philipson, then as now director of the University of Chicago Press, who freed the two editors chiefly involved from some of their other responsibilities to give them time for work on the *Manual*. That the revision was completed sooner rather than later may be attributed largely to the efforts of Allen Fitchen, senior editor of the Press, whose involvement, encouragement, and (gentle) insistence on the meeting of deadlines were crucial. Preparation of the volume has been in the general charge of Catharine Seybold and Bruce Young, who wrote the basic text for all of its chapters save one. They are not only editors but authors without peer: their good sense, thoroughgoing knowledge and humane understanding of their craft, and commitment to excellence mark every page of the book. Those colleagues of theirs on the Press staff who deserve special thanks are Joseph Alderfer (for patient assistance on innumerable matters of design and production), Alice M. Bennett (for the Index and many valuable suggestions), Jean Eckenfels, Margaret D. Flack (for wise and witty counsel time and again), John Grossman (for again contributing chapter 5), Jeanne Hopkins (for advice on mathematical and scientific terminology), Jane W. Lightner, John McCudden, Pamela Pokorney (for overseeing details of production and manufacturing), Cameron Poulter (for the design of the book, and for suggestions on chapter 20), Virginia Seidman, Robert Shirrell (for advice on the new copyright law), Estelle Stearn (for exegesis of the new copyright law), Lila Weinberg, and R. Williams (for the illustrations in chapter 20). Others who provided valuable advice on particular chapters or sections of the revision are Robert Berg (chapter 20), Joyce Kachergis (chapter 20), Gwin Kolb (chapters 15–17), and William S. Strong (chapter 4).

Many persons, too numerous to mention by name, have contributed suggestions that are reflected in the final draft of the book. These persons include members of the University of Chicago faculty and staff; authors of books published by this press; our many correspondents throughout the period since the publication of the twelfth edition in 1969; and all of those who responded to our 1975 questionnaire.

The text of this volume was set at the University of Chicago Printing Department by the PENTA system under the direction of Robert Berg. The editors are grateful to him and to his staff for their expert work, and to Beth Garrison for careful proofreading of the entire volume, as well as for many helpful suggestions.

Part 1

Bookmaking

1 *The Parts of a Book*

Outline of Major Divisions 1.1
Preliminaries 1.2
    Half-Title Page 1.2
    Verso of Half-Title Page 1.3
    Title Page 1.9
    Copyright Page 1.14
      Copyright notice 1.14
      Publishing history 1.19
      CIP data 1.23
      ISBN 1.25
      ISSN 1.26
      Permissions 1.27
    Dedication 1.28
    Epigraph 1.29
    Table of Contents 1.31
    List of Illustrations 1.34
    List of Tables 1.37
    Foreword 1.38
    Preface and Acknowledgments 1.39
    Other Front Matter 1.43
      Introduction 1.44
      List of abbreviations 1.45
      Editorial method 1.46
      List of contributors 1.47
      Chronology 1.49
Text 1.50
    Chapters 1.51
    Parts 1.54
    Other Divisions 1.56
      Poetry 1.56
      Letters and diaries 1.57
    Subheads 1.58
Back Matter 1.67
    Appendix 1.67
    Notes 1.71
    Glossary 1.72
    Bibliography 1.73
    Index 1.75
    Colophon 1.76
Running Heads 1.77
    Front Matter 1.78
    Text 1.79
    Back Matter 1.81
    Omission of Running Heads 1.83

Page Numbers 1.84
   Front Matter 1.85
   Text and Back Matter 1.88
   More Than One Volume 1.90
Errata 1.92

OUTLINE OF MAJOR DIVISIONS

1.1   A book usually consists of three major divisions: (1) the *front matter* or *preliminaries* (prelims), (2) the *text,* and (3) the *back matter* or *end matter* or *reference matter.* An appropriate sequence for all the parts is shown in the following outline. Few books have all these parts, of course, and some books have other parts not shown in the outline, for example, a list of abbreviations. Note that front-matter pages here are numbered with lowercase roman numerals (but see 1.86). Note too that each page is counted although no folio (page number) is *expressed* (printed) on display pages or blank pages (i–vi). A *recto* page is a right-hand page; a *verso* page is a left-hand page. Recto folios are odd numbers; verso folios, even numbers.

PRELIMINARIES

Book half title (sometimes called bastard title)	i
Series title or list of contributors or frontispiece or blank	ii
Title page	iii
Copyright notice, publisher's agencies, printing history, country where printed, CIP data[1]	iv
Dedication (or epigraph)	v[2]
Blank	vi
(Table of) Contents[3]	v or vii
(List of) Illustrations	recto[4]
(List of) Tables	recto
Foreword	recto
Preface	recto
Acknowledgments (if not part of preface)	recto
Introduction (if not part of text)	recto

TEXT

First text page (introduction or chapter 1)	1
or:	
Second book half title, or first part title	1
Blank	2
First text page	3

1. See 1.23–25.

2. The dedication may be moved to p. iv to save two pages (v and vi).

3. Placement of the contents page is discussed in 1.31.

4. Any one of the parts marked *recto* in this list may begin on a verso if saving space (by eliminating blank pages) is a consideration.

4

BACK MATTER

Appendix(es) .... recto
Notes .... recto
Glossary .... recto
Bibliography .... recto
Index(es) .... recto

PRELIMINARIES

HALF-TITLE PAGE

1.2 The half title (p. i) normally consists only of the main title. The subtitle is omitted, and the author's name does not appear. The half-title page sometimes carries a series title or an epigraph (see 1.4, 1.29).

VERSO OF HALF-TITLE PAGE

1.3 The verso of the half-title page (p. ii) is often blank, or the designer may wish to make the title page a two-page spread on pages ii and iii.

1.4 If the book is in a series, the title of the series, the volume number, if any, in the series, and the name of the general editor of the series may appear on page ii:

> The Chicago History of American Religion
> A Series Edited by Martin E. Marty

> Negro American Biographies and Autobiographies
> John Hope Franklin, General Editor

A series title may instead appear on the title page or on the copyright page or on the half-title page.

1.5 In a multiauthor book with too many authors (contributors) to be accommodated on the title page, but not more than, say, fifteen, the contributors may be listed, usually in alphabetical order, on page ii. (A longer list of authors or contributors, requiring a full page or pages, should be placed at the end of the prelims or in the back matter preceding the index; see 1.47.)

1.6 If the book is a publication of the proceedings of a symposium, the title of the symposium, the name of the city where it was held, and the date may appear on page ii. Sometimes the committee that planned the symposium and edited the volume may be added here; sometimes also the name of the sponsor of the symposium.

1.7 Some publishers list an author's previous publications on page ii; the University of Chicago Press generally lists these on the jacket, along with a brief biography of the author.

1.8   Page ii often carries an illustration, called a frontispiece. Whether the illustration is actually printed on page ii or is tipped in so that it faces the title page depends largely on the printing process used. The offset process permits either a line cut or a halftone plate (photograph) to appear here and print along with the other prelims; the letterpress process (now seldom used for book printing) will print a line cut on the page, but a halftone must be printed on different paper and tipped in (glued to the next page at the inner margin).

TITLE PAGE

1.9   The title page (p. iii) presents the full title of the book, the name of the author, editor, or translator (if any), and the name of the publishing house. The designer usually specifies a type size or style for the sub-title different from that of the main title; therefore, no colon or other mark of punctuation is needed to separate the two parts of the title.

1.10   If the book is a new edition of a work previously published, the number of the edition ("Third Edition") or "Revised Edition" may also appear on the title page, usually following the title.

1.11   The author's name, or authors' names, may be printed below or above the title (placement and type style are determined by the book designer). Given names should not be shortened to initials unless, like H. G. Wells and others, this is how the author prefers to be known. European authors, many of whom are accustomed to using only one initial and their surnames, may usually be persuaded by their American publishers to permit the spelling out of their given names on the title page. The University of Chicago Press does not print academic degrees or affiliations after an author's name on the title page, with the exception of "M.D.," which may be retained for an author of a book in the field of medicine.

1.12   The usual form for a volume editor's name on the title page is:

Edited by John Doe (*not* John Doe, Editor)

1.13   The publisher's full name (imprint) should be given on the title page, sometimes followed by the name of the city (or cities) where the principal offices are located. The publisher's device (colophon) may appear on the title page as an embellishment. Some publishers give the year of publication on the title page; the University of Chicago Press does not.

COPYRIGHT PAGE

1.14   *Copyright notice.* The most important item on the copyright page (p. iv) is, of course, the copyright notice. The Copyright Act of 1976 does not require the notice to appear on this page or the title page, as the old law did, but most book publishers continue to place it here. The notice consists of three parts: the symbol ©, the year in which the book is published, and the name of the copyright owner. (The law permits the word *Copyright* or the abbreviation *Copr.* to be used instead of the C-in-a-circle symbol, but since the symbol suits the requirements of the Universal Copyright Convention, to which the United States and most European countries belong, it is greatly to be preferred. There is no point in using both symbol and word, as some publishers do.) In addition, most publishers add to the notice the phrase "All rights reserved," as this expression assures protection for the book under the Buenos Aires Convention, to which the United States and most Latin American countries belong.

1.15   A typical copyright notice might then read:

> © 1982 by Samuel Author. All rights reserved

Every effort should be made to assure that the date given is actually the year of publication (this is sometimes troublesome when a book is scheduled for publication near the end or beginning of a year). A date that is no more than a year off is not disastrous, however, and the publisher need take no action except to see that the proper date is recorded when the copyright is registered. A date that is more than a year *later* than the actual publication date requires remedial action. On this, and for other information concerning the copyright notice, see 4.16–19. It is also important that the name of the copyright holder be given correctly; consequently, the person preparing the copyright page for the printer should always consult the publishing contract before completing the copy for the notice.

1.16   Subsequent *editions* (not impressions, new printings) of a book are each copyrighted, and the date of each should appear in the copyright notice (see fig. 1.1).

1.17   The date of copyright renewal or a change in the name of the copyright holder (rights may be assigned to the author or someone else after the initial copyright has been registered and printed in the first impression) should be inserted in the copyright notice if the book is reprinted. If the book is not reprinted, any reassignment of copyright or renewal is legally valid, even though it does not appear on the copyright page.

1.18   If the book is a translation, the original title, publisher, and copyright information should be recorded on the copyright page (fig. 1.2).

1.19   *Publishing history.* The publishing history of a book usually follows the copyright notice, although it may appear elsewhere on the copyright page, or it may be omitted altogether. The sequence of items is as follows: date (year) of first publication; date of second (or other) edition; date of impression if other than the first (but see 1.21). These items may each be on a separate line or may be run together. There should be no period at the end of a line.

1.20 The name of the country where the book was actually *printed* must appear in the book (not just on the jacket) and is usually placed on the copyright page:

> Printed in the United States of America
> Printed in Great Britain

1.21 To avoid resetting in later printings of a book, a publisher may, instead of, for example, "Third Impression, 1979," use a seemingly cryptic line of figures below the publishing history (see, e.g., figs. 1.1, 1.2). The first group of numbers represents, from right to left, successive years after publication; the second group, the possible future impressions of the book. (How many to print of each depends somewhat on the possible future sales of the book; eight dates and five reprint numbers should be adequate for the average book.) When a book is reprinted for the first time, the publisher deletes "1" from the end of the line and, if it has passed, any date earlier than the current year. The knowledgeable reader may thus deduce why one copy of a certain book has a few typographical errors not found in another copy of the same book: the second is a later impression, wherein some typographical corrections have been made.

The University of Chicago Press, Chicago 60637
The University of Chicago Press, Ltd., London

© 1963, 1969, 1976 by The University of Chicago. All rights reserved
Published 1963. Third Edition 1976
Printed in the United States of America
80 79 78   10 9 8 7 6

Library of Congress Cataloging in Publication Data

Turabian, Kate L.
  Student's guide for writing college papers.

  Bibliography: p.
  Includes index.
  1. Report writing.   I. Title.
LB2369.T82   1977   808'.042   76–435
ISBN 0–226–81622–2
ISBN 0–226–81623–0 pbk.

Fig. 1.1. Copyright page of a third edition, sixth printing. Note ISBN for both cloth and paperback.

Originally published as *Quetzalcóatl et Guadalupe,*
© 1974 Editions Gallimard

The University of Chicago Press, Chicago 60637
The University of Chicago Press, Ltd., London

© 1976 by The University of Chicago
All rights reserved. Published 1976
Printed in the United States of America
81 80 79 78 77 76   5 4 3 2 1

Library of Congress Cataloging in Publication Data

Lafaye, Jacques.
  Quetzalcóatl and Guadalupe.

  Translation of Quetzalcóatl et Guadalupe.
  Includes bibliographical references and index.
  1. Mexico—Civilization—History. 2. Mexico—
Religion. 3. Guadalupe, Nuestra Señora de.
4. Quetzalcóatl. I. Title.
F1210.L313   972   75-20889
ISBN 0-226-46794-5

Fig. 1.2. Copyright page of a translation

1.22   The publisher's mailing address—and sometimes the addresses of overseas agents—may also be given on the copyright page. The University of Chicago Press usually puts these above the copyright notice.

1.23   *CIP data.* Since 1971 many publishers have printed the Library of Congress Cataloging in Publication (CIP) data on the copyright pages of their books.[5] This array corresponds to the main card for the book in the Library of Congress catalog, thus enabling libraries to put a book on their shelves as soon as they receive it (see figs. 1.1–6).

1.24   To get the CIP data for a book: As soon as the final title has been decided upon, the contents page is complete, and the ISBN (see 1.25) has been assigned, the publisher fills out a form provided by the Library of Congress and sends it to the Library of Congress, Cataloging in Publication Division, Washington, D.C. 20540, together with either a complete copy of the proofs or enough material from the manuscript to enable the Library to classify it properly (title page, table of contents, preface, summary of text) and the ISBN. The Library requires ten working days after receipt of the material to catalog it and

5. If the copyright page is too crowded, the CIP data may appear elsewhere in the book, but include a note on the copyright page telling where it is to be found (see fig. 1.4). The Library of Congress does not provide CIP data for serial publications.

The University of Chicago Press, Chicago 60637
The University of Chicago Press, Ltd., London

© 1977 by The University of Chicago
All rights reserved. Published 1977
Printed in the United States of America

82 81 80 79 78·77   5 4 3 2 1

Library of Congress Cataloging in Publication Data

Krieger, Leonard.
  Ranke: the meaning of history.

  Bibliography: p.
  Includes index.
  1. Ranke, Leopold von, 1795–1886.   2. History
—Philosophy.   3. Historicism.   4. Historians—
Germany—Biography.
  D15.R3K74   907'.2'024   76-25633
  ISBN 0-226-45349-9

Parts of chapters 7 and 8 of the present work appeared
in a slightly different version in *History and Theory,*
Beiheft 14 (1975): 1–15. © 1975 by Wesleyan University.

Fig. 1.3. Copyright page acknowledging partial earlier publication

send the CIP data to the publisher. The CIP data should be printed line for line as they appear on the card, in whatever typeface is used for the rest of the copyright page. The publisher must not change any facts in the CIP data, or add to or delete from them, without notifying the Library and requesting a revised copy. What appears in the book must be the same as what appears on the Library of Congress card.

1.25 *ISBN.* An International Standard Book Number (ISBN) is assigned to each book by its publisher under a system set up by the R. R. Bowker Co. It uniquely identifies the book, thus facilitating handling orders and keeping track of inventory by computer.[6] The ISBN is included in the CIP data (see figs. 1.1–6). If the CIP data are not printed anywhere in the book, the ISBN should nevertheless be included on the copyright page of the book. The ISBN is usually also printed on the book jacket. If a book is issued in both clothbound and paperback editions, a separate ISBN is assigned to each (see fig. 1.1). When a work comprises two or more volumes, a separate ISBN may be as-

6. For example, in ISBN 0-226-07522-2, the first digit, 0, tells us that the book was published in an English-speaking country; the second group, 226, identifies the publisher (in this instance the University of Chicago Press); the third group identifies the book; and the last is the "check digit," which automatically discloses any error in the preceding group.

The University of Chicago Press, Chicago 60637
The University of Chicago Press, Ltd., London

© 1976 by The University of Chicago
All rights reserved. Published 1976
Printed in the United States of America

83 82 81 80 79 78 77 76   5 4 3 2 1

The following publishers have generously given permission to use extended quotations from copyrighted works: From *Farewell, My Lovely*, by Raymond Chandler. Copyright 1940 by Raymond Chandler and renewed 1968 by the Executrix of the Author, Mrs. Helen Greene. Reprinted by permission of Alfred A. Knopf, Inc. From *Red Harvest*, by Dashiell Hammett. Copyright 1929 by Alfred A. Knopf, Inc. and renewed 1957 by Dashiell Hammett. Reprinted by permission of the publisher. From *I, The Jury* by Mickey Spillane. Copyright 1947 by E. P. Dutton & Co.; renewal © 1975 by Frank Morrison Spillane. Reprinted by permission of the publishers, E. P. Dutton & Co., Inc.

Library of Congress Cataloging in Publication Data will be found at the end of this book.

Fig. 1.4. Copyright page with permissions to quote extensively and notice to libraries of where to find the CIP information.

signed to each volume. If the work is to be sold only as a set, one ISBN may be used for the whole set; it should be printed on the copyright page of each volume.

1.26   *ISSN*. Serial publications (annuals, monthlies, etc.), whether in book or journal form, are given an International Standard Serial Number (ISSN) instead of an ISBN. The ISSN remains the same for each issue of the publication and is printed either on the page containing the copyright notice for the issue or with the instructions for ordering the publication.

1.27   *Permissions*. It is sometimes desirable to include on page iv permissions to publish extensive quotations from previously copyrighted works (see fig. 1.4). But do not duplicate acknowledgments given elsewhere, such as in the preface or acknowledgment section of the prelims (1.39) or in notes (15.70). Photo credits may also appear on the copyright page (fig. 1.6) instead of in the legends to the illustrations.

DEDICATION

1.28   Whether a book includes a dedication at all, to whom it is dedicated, and the phrasing of the dedication are matters for the author to determine. It may be suggested, however, that the word "Dedicated" is superfluous; a simple "To" is sufficient. It is not necessary to identify

The Society for the History of Discoveries and The Newberry
Library wish to acknowledge the help of Mr. Paul Mellon in the
publication of this book.

The University of Chicago Press, Chicago 60637
The University of Chicago Press, Ltd., London

© 1975 by The University of Chicago
All rights reserved. Published 1975
Printed in the United States of America

Library of Congress Cataloging in Publication Data

Cavendish, Thomas, 1560–1592.
  The last voyage of Thomas Cavendish, 1591–1592.

  (Studies in the history of discoveries)
  Includes index.
    1. Cavendish, Thomas, 1560–1592. 2. America—
Discovery and exploration—English. I. Quinn, David
Beers, ed. II. Newberry Library, Chicago.
III. Title. IV. Series.
G246.C38A34   1975   910′.41 [B]   74–11619
ISBN 0–226–09819–2

Fig. 1.5. Copyright page with special acknowledgment

(or even to give the whole name of) the person to whom the work is
dedicated, nor is it necessary to give the life dates of a person who has
died; but both are permissible. Extravagant dedications are things of
the past. A dedication intended to be humorous will very likely lose
its humor with time and so is inappropriate in a serious book destined
to take a permanent place in the literature.

EPIGRAPH

1.29   An author may wish to include an epigraph—a pertinent quotation—
at the beginning of the book. If there is no dedication, the epigraph
may be placed on page v. When there is also a dedication, the epigraph
may follow on a new recto page (p. vii), or, to save space, it may be
put on page vi or on a blank verso page facing the first page of the text.
Less customary but possible in certain books is the placement of an
epigraph on the title page or on the half-title page.

1.30   The source of a quotation used in this way is given on a line following
the quotation and is usually set flush right, with no parentheses or
brackets. Only the author's name (and only the last name of a well-
known author) and, usually, the title of the work need appear. No page
or line numbers and no bibliographical details are necessary or desir-

The University of Chicago Press, Chicago 60637
The University of Chicago Press, Ltd., London

© 1976 by The University of Chicago
All rights reserved. Published 1976
Printed in the United States of America

83 82 81 80 79 78 77 76   5 4 3 2 1

Photo credits: p. ii—Henriette Castex Epstein
(courtesy *Albany Times-Union*); pp. 8, 36,
104, 186—Nate Fine Photo

Library of Congress Cataloging in Publication Data

Pratt, Henry J   1934–
The gray lobby.

  Bibliography: p.
  Includes index.
  1. Aged—United States—Political activity.
  2. Aged—Legal status, laws, etc.—United States.
  I. Title.
HQ 1064.U5P68   301.43′5′0973   75–43232
ISBN 0–226–67917–9

Fig. 1.6. Copyright page with photo credits

able. Since an epigraph is not part of the text, it should never bear a reference number to a note giving its source. Any explanation of an epigraph deemed essential by the author should appear in the preface or other introductory matter.

TABLE OF CONTENTS

1.31   The table of contents (usually titled simply Contents) begins on page v, or, if page v carries a dedication or an epigraph, on page vii. (Some publishers place the table of contents at the end of the preliminary matter, so that it immediately precedes the text.)

1.32   The table of contents should include the title and *beginning* page number of each section of the book: front matter, text divisions, and back matter, including the index. If the book is divided into parts as well as chapters, the part titles should appear in the contents, but their page numbers are not essential if the page number of the chapter following each part title is sufficient indication of where the part begins (see fig. 1.7). Page numbers in the manuscript and first proofs of the table of contents are indicated by "000," the actual numbers being inserted after pages have been made up. Subheads within chapters may be included in the table of contents, particularly in technical books and

Contents

Preface *ix*

Part One: The Theory
    1. The Dubious Legacy *1*
    2. The Unscientific Counterpoint *10*
    3. The Limits of Theory *21*

Part Two: The History
    4. The Preconditions of History (1795–1817) *35*
    5. The Conditions of History (1818–31) *66*
    6. The Incomplete Historian (1819–31) *96*
    7. The First Synthesis: Revolution, Religion, and
       History in the 1830s *128*
    8. The Complete Historian: The Works of the
       Thirties *151*
    9. Conservative Retrenchment and Patriotic
       History in the Forties *180*
    10. The Second Synthesis: Revolution, Politics,
        and History at Mid-Century *202*
    11. The Mature Historian: World History in
        National Perspective (1852–68) *246*
    12. The Third Synthesis: World History in
        German Perspective (1867–79) *290*
    13. The Final Resolution: World History in
        Universal Perspective (1875–86) *320*

Conclusion: The Meaning of History *345*

Notes *359*

Bibliography *388*

Index *393*

Fig. 1.7. Table of contents showing parts, chapters, and preface and back matter.

Contents

BOOK TWO

List of Illustrations   xi
Preface   xv
Introduction   xix

PART I

Portugal and the Learned Community of Europe

Introduction   3

Chapter I: HERALDS OF EMPIRE   5

1. Portuguese Students and Diplomats Abroad   7
2. Damião de Góis, Publicist of Empire   15
3. Foreigners, Returnees, and Jesuits in Portugal   27

Chapter II: BOOKS, LIBRARIES, AND READING   39

1. Portugal and Spain   43
2. Italy   48
3. The Germanies   55
4. The Low Countries, France, and England   63
   Appendix. Books on Asia in Sixty Sixteenth-Century
   Collections   76

· ·

Chapter XII: EPILOGUE   556

General Bibliography   567
Chapter Bibliographies   581
Index   735

Fig. 1.8. Partial table of contents for a historical work divided into books, parts, chapters, and subsections.

Contents

I. INTRODUCTION   1

II. BONE AS A TISSUE   3
   Cells of Bone   5
      Osteoblasts   5
      Electron Microscopy   6
      Mitochondria   7
      Osteocytes   8
      Osteoclasts   8
   Interstitial Substance   11
   Membranes of Bone   11
      Periosteum   11
      Endosteum   12
   Bone Marrow   12
   Blood Vessels of Bone   12
   Nerves of Bone   15
   Lymphatics of Bone   17

III. HISTOGENESIS AND ORGANIZATION OF BONE   18
   Criteria for Designation of Connective Tissue Cells   18
      Morphologic Criteria   18
      Autoradiographic Criteria   18
      Criteria of Location   19
      Criteria of Function   19
   Terminology of Connective Tissue Cells   20
      Precursors of the Cells of Bone   20
      Mesenchymal Cell   21
      Reticular Cell   21

. . . .

XVI. EVOLUTION OF BONE   256
      Origin of Bone   257
      Membrane Phenomena   260
      Physiology: Exoskeletal and Endoskeletal   262
      Bone Tissue and Vitamin D Metabolism   265
      Terrestrial Life, Parathyroids, and Bone Remodeling   267

BIBLIOGRAPHY   269
INDEX   301

Fig. 1.9. Partial table of contents for a scientific work, showing chapter titles, A- and B-level subheads, and back matter.

in books with long chapters divided into sections defined by meaningful subheads. When subheads are included in the contents, they are indented differently from the chapter titles and often set in another type style (see figs. 1.8, 1.9). In a long table of contents they may be run in, each followed by its page number.

1.33   In a volume consisting of papers, or chapters, by different authors, the name of each author should be given in the table of contents with the title of the chapter:

The Supreme Court as Republican Schoolmaster
  Ralph Lerner   127

Self-incrimination and the New Privacy
  Robert B. McKay   193

LIST OF ILLUSTRATIONS

1.34   The list of illustrations (usually titled Illustrations) should match the table of contents in type size and general style. In books containing various kinds of illustrations, the list may be subdivided into sections headed, for example, Plates, Figures, Charts, Maps (see fig. 1.10). Page numbers are given for all illustrations printed with the text and counted in the pagination, even when folios are not expressed on the page (see 1.89). When pages of illustrations are not counted in the pagination—either because they are tipped in between signatures or because they have been added after the book has been made up into pages—their location is indicated by *Facing page 000* or *Following page 000* in the list of illustrations. *Facing page* is used for a single leaf, each side of which faces a page of text. *Following page* is used for four or more pages where inner leaves do not "face" a page of text (see 11.45). *Following page 000* may be set above a group of illustration titles so that the same page number need not be repeated for each (see fig. 1.11). The page indication for a frontispiece is never *ii* but simply *Frontispiece*.

1.35   The titles of illustrations given in the list need not correspond exactly to the legends printed with the illustrations themselves. If the legends are long, shortened forms should be given in the list of illustrations (see 11.46).

1.36   In a book with very few illustrations or one with many illustrations, such as charts and graphs, tied closely to the text, it is not essential to list them in the front matter. Multiauthor books, proceedings of symposia, and the like commonly do not carry lists of illustrations.

Illustrations

Figures

1. A typical organization chart for the Ministry of Agriculture
   in Western Province.   52
2. The relationship between supervisory style and productivity
   in the United States and Kenya.   91
3. Portions of the March and Simon model of the job resignation
   decision.   106
4. Channels by which junior agricultural extension staff receive
   technical information.   130
5. A diagrammatic representation of two hypothetical simple
   acts of communication.   135
6. A diagrammatic representation of a multiple-stage communication process in the Ministry of Agriculture.   137
7. The effect of education on junior agricultural staff's reception
   of technical information.   147
8. The distribution of agricultural extension visits to farmers.   178
9. The distribution of veterinary extension visits to farmers.   185

Maps

1. Kenya: Provincial boundaries.   34
2. Western Province: District and division boundaries and ecological zones.   36
3. Western Province: Location boundaries and research sites.   39

Fig. 1.10. List of illustrations including both figures and maps

LIST OF TABLES

1.37   A list of tables (titled Tables) follows the table of contents or, if there
is one, the list of illustrations. Listing tables in the front matter is
helpful mainly in technical books carrying many tables and with
frequent textual references to them. The titles may be shortened if
necessary.

Illustrations

Following Page 46

1. Josaphat's first outing
2. Portrait of Marco Polo
3. Gold-digging ant from Sebastian Münster's *Cosmographei,* 1531
4. An Indian "Odota" from Sebastian Münster's *Cosmographei,* 1531

. . . .

Following Page 520

84. *Doctrina christam* printed at Quilon
85. First book printed at Macao by Europeans, 1585
86. First book printed in China on a European press, 1588
87. Title page of *Doctrina Christiana* printed at Manila, 1593, in Tagalog and Spanish
88. Final page of above
89. Title page of *Doctrina Christiana* printed at Manila, 1593, in Spanish and Chinese

Fig. 1.11. List of illustrations showing placement of unpaginated plates.

FOREWORD

1.38   A *foreword* is usually a statement by someone other than the author, sometimes an eminent person whose name may be carried on the title page: With a Foreword by ———. The author's own statement about the work is called a *preface*. Both are set in the same size and style of type as the text. A foreword normally runs only two to four pages, and its author's name appears at the end, often in caps and small caps and indented one em from the right. An author's title may appear under the name; or an affiliation may be given, in smaller type and on the left side of the page. If a foreword runs to a substantial length, with or without a title of its own, its author's name may be given at the beginning of it, instead of at the end. For place and date with a foreword, see below, 1.41.

PREFACE AND ACKNOWLEDGMENTS

1.39   Material normally included in an author's preface consists of reasons for undertaking the work, method of research (only if this has some bearing on the reader's understanding of the text), acknowledgments,

19

and, sometimes, permissions granted for the use of previously published material (see 4.54). If the acknowledgments are lengthy, they may be put in a separate section following the preface; or if a preface consists only of acknowledgments, its title should be changed to Acknowledgments. Acknowledgments are sometimes put at the back of a book, preceding the index.

1.40   Material essential to the text, material that should be read before the rest of the book—an account of the historical background of the subject of the book, for example—should not be relegated to a preface but should be printed as an *introduction* at the beginning of the text proper. Text matter should not be mixed with acknowledgments, methodology or history of a research project, or other matter concerning the writing of the book.

1.41   A preface should be signed by its author (name at the end, as described above for the author of a foreword) only when there might be some doubt about who wrote it. The reader logically assumes that an unsigned preface was written by the author whose name appears on the title page. The University of Chicago Press discourages the inclusion of place (city) and date at the end of a preface or a foreword. When these facts are given, they are set flush left with a line space between them and the text.

1.42   When a new preface is written for a new edition, it precedes the original preface, which is usually retitled Preface to First Edition. In a book containing both an editor's preface and a preface by the author, the editor's preface comes first and the editor's name is appended to it.

OTHER FRONT MATTER

1.43   The parts of a book so far described are those found in the front matter of most books. Edited texts and other kinds of scholarly works often require more material in the preliminary pages—biographical information about the author of an edited text, for example, or any explanation of editorial procedures or peculiarities of apparatus that the reader needs to understand before encountering the text proper.

1.44   *Introduction.* A relatively long substantive introduction not part of the subject matter of the text itself should be paginated with the preliminaries. An introduction written by an author to set the scene, however, such as the historical background of the subject, should be part of the text, paginated with arabic folios.

1.45   *List of abbreviations.* In some heavily documented books, especially where there are many references to a few easily abbreviated sources, it may be a convenience to the reader to give a list of abbreviations for these sources before the text rather than in the back matter. If no more than one page long, such a list may be placed on the verso page facing the first page of text. A long list of abbreviations used in notes and bibliography, and sometimes in the text, is generally best placed in the back matter, preceding the notes (see 15.67).

1.46   *Editorial method.* An explanation of an editor's method or a discussion of variant texts, often necessary in scholarly editions, may constitute a large part of an editor's preliminary pages. Any such material is essential for the user of edited texts and is therefore often placed at the end of the prelims, just before the text proper. Short, uncomplicated remarks about editorial method, however—such as the fact that the spelling and capitalization have been modernized—should be incorporated in the editor's preface, not put in a separate section.

1.47   *List of contributors.* In a multiauthor book such as the proceedings of a symposium or a festschrift it is often desirable to list the contributors, with only the editor or editors appearing on the title page (see 1.5). The list may be headed "Contributors," "Participants," or whatever suits the particular work. An alphabetical arrangement of the names is the usual practice (do not reverse the names: Andrew D. White, not White, Andrew D.); in some cases a geographical or other arrangement may be more suitable. In this list academic rank and affiliation may be given for each contributor, and sometimes short biographies may be appropriate. (Such a list is often placed at the back of the book, rather than in the front matter.) For one example see figure 1.12.

1.48   Just because a book has a number of authors, it does not necessarily carry a list of contributors. Often it is enough simply to give the authors' names in the table of contents and at the heads of their respective contributions, with perhaps an unnumbered note at the beginning of each chapter identifying the author (see 1.33, 1.53, 15.71).

1.49   *Chronology.* A chronological list of events important in a person's life or over a certain period of time may be useful in a volume such as a collection of letters or other documents where the sequence of events is not clear in the text itself. For easy reference a chronology should appear immediately before the text. It is possible also to place it after the text, in the back matter, or wherever it will be most helpful (for two examples see figs. 1.13, 1.14).

TEXT

1.50   In general, the preliminary pages of a book serve as a guide to the contents and nature of the book, and the back matter provides refer-

Contributors

DERK BODDE, professor of Chinese at the University of Pennsylvania, has written *China's First Unifier, Peking Diary,* and many other books, including *Law in Imperial China* (with Clarence Morris). He has translated from the Chinese the standard two-volume work, *A History of Chinese Philosophy,* by Fung Yu-lan. He is a member of the American Philosophical Society and the American Academy of Arts and Sciences.

JEROME ALAN COHEN, professor of law at Harvard University, is the author of articles on Chinese law and *The Criminal Process in the People's Republic of China, 1949–1963: An Introduction.*

HERRLEE G. CREEL, the Martin A. Ryerson Distinguished Service Professor of Chinese History at the University of Chicago, is the author of *The Birth of China; Studies in Early Chinese Culture; Confucius, the Man and the Myth;* and *Chinese Thought from Confucius to Mao Tse-tung.*

ROBERT DERNBERGER, assistant professor of economics and chairman of the Committee on Far Eastern Studies at the University of Chicago, is former editor of *Economic Development and Cultural Change* and has contributed articles on China's contemporary economy to *Three Essays on the International Economics of Communist China, Contemporary China,* and *Economic Nationalism in the New States.*

ALEXANDER ECKSTEIN, professor of economics and director of the Center for Chinese Studies at the University of Michigan, has written, among others, *The National Income of Communist China* and *Communist China's Economic Growth and Foreign Trade.*

Fig. 1.12. Partial list of contributors to a multiauthor work. Names here are set in caps and small caps but might be set in caps and lowercase roman or in italic.

ence material.[7] The text proper should contain everything necessary for a reader to understand the author's argument. The organization of the text material can help or hinder comprehension of it. The author who does little more than copy research notes, or who feels compelled

7. In a book containing many preliminary pages a second half title introducing the text proper is helpful to the reader (see 1.88).

MADISON CHRONOLOGY

1787

27 May– 17 September	JM attends Federal Convention at Philadelphia. Takes notes on the debates.
29 May	Virginia Plan presented.
6 June	JM makes first major speech, containing analysis of factions and theory of extended republic.
8 June	Defends "negative" (veto) on state laws.
19 June	Delivers critique of New Jersey Plan.
27 June–16 July	In debate on representation, JM advocates proportional representation for both branches of legislature.
16 July	Compromise on representation adopted.
26 July	Convention submits resolutions to Committee of Detail as basis for preparing draft constitution.
6 August	Report of Committee of Detail delivered.
7 August	JM advocates freehold suffrage.
7 August– 10 September	Convention debates, then amends, report of 6 August.
31 August	JM appointed to Committee on Postponed Matters.
8 September	Appointed to Committee of Style.
17 September	Signs engrossed Constitution. Convention adjourns.
ca. 21 September	Leaves Philadelphia for New York.
24 September	Arrives in New York to attend Congress.
26 September	Awarded Doctor of Laws degree in absentia by College of New Jersey.

Fig. 1.13. First page of a chronology at the end of the prelims in a volume of letters.

Chronological Guide to the Track Chart of Cavendish's Last Voyage

1591

Five ships leave Plymouth, August 26: *Galleon Leicester* ("admiral," namely, flagship), *Roebuck* ("vice-admiral"), *Desire, Daintie, Black Pinnace*

They pass down the Spanish and Portuguese coast

They sight the Canaries, September 14

They probably pass into the ocean by the western Cape Verdes

They are becalmed on or near the equator

They make landfall, November 29, at Salvador, about 36 miles north of Cabo Frio

They arrive at Placencia (Ilha Grande), December 5

They sail December 11

They arrive at Ilha de São Sebastião, December 14

Desire and *Black Pinnace* attack and occupy Santos, December 15

Cavendish in *Galleon Leicester* arrives and occupies Santos, December 16 (or later)

1592

They set sail from Santos and burn São Vicente, January 24

Fleet separated in storm, February 7–8

Daintie loses contact and sails under her master to England; track conjectural

Roebuck and *Desire* arrive at Port Desire, March 6

Black Pinnace reaches Port Desire, March 16

Galleon Leicester arrives, March 18

They leave Port Desire, March 20, and encounter gales

They "fell with" the Strait of Magellan, April 8

They pass through the First Strait, April 14

They pass through the Second Strait, April 16

They double Cape Froward, April 18

They put in to a small cove on the south side of Port Tobias, April 21

They set out on return eastward, May 15

They clear the Strait, May 18

Ships are separated off Port Desire, May 20

Desire and *Black Pinnace* enter Port Desire

In May, Cavendish in *Galleon Leicester* is driven far out to sea and makes for Brazil

Roebuck also driven by storm on course presumably similar to *Galleon Leicester*'s and reaches Brazil somewhat later

Davis quells possible mutiny on *Desire* and *Black Pinnace*, June 2

From May onward (no dates available), Cavendish reaches Baia de São Vicente, near Santos; attempts to raid São Vicente; remains in Canal de Bertioga and is joined by *Roebuck*

The two ships go north to Ilha de Espírito Santo and attempt to attack the town of Espírito Santo

Roebuck returns to England alone, her track being conjectural

Galleon Leicester goes south to Ilha de São Sebastião

Galleon Leicester works up coast from lat. 29° to 20°S on first stage homeward

Desire and *Black Pinnace* leave Port Desire, August 6, to go to Penguin Island to salt food

The two vessels sail southward, August 7

Driven out to sea, they sight unknown islands (Falklands?), August 14

Fig. 1.14. Chronology accompanying a map of a sixteenth-century voyage. Large page of this book suggested two-column format.

to use every relevant fact found in the library, will seldom produce a clearly organized work. The ideal author keeps a prospective audience in mind and presents material in a logical pattern, selecting what is essential and omitting what is nonessential or repetitious. The following paragraphs deal with divisions commonly found in most books, not with substantive organization of text material. Details of handling special elements in the text—quotations, illustrations, tables, mathematics, and notes—are discussed in part 2.

CHAPTERS

1.51   Most prose works are divided into chapters, often, though not necessarily, of approximately the same length. Chapter titles should be similar in tone, if not in length. Each title should give a reasonable clue to what is in the chapter; whimsical titles in a serious book, for example, can be misleading. Many potential readers scan a table of contents to determine whether a book is worth their time (and money). Relatively short titles are preferable to long, ungainly ones, both for appearance on the page and for use in running heads.

1.52   In the printed book, each chapter normally starts on a new page, verso or recto,[8] and its opening page carries a drop folio and no running head. The chapter display usually consists of the chapter number[9] and the chapter title and sometimes an epigraph as well (see 1.30 for treatment of epigraph sources). In titles of two or more lines, punctuation should be omitted at the end of a line unless it is essential for clarity. Footnote reference numbers or symbols should not appear anywhere in the *chapter display* (the type above the beginning of the text proper).

1.53   In multiauthor books (each chapter by a different author) chapter numbers are sometimes omitted. The author's name is always given in the display, but an affiliation, or other identification, is usually not considered part of the display but is put in an unnumbered footnote on the first page of the chapter (see 15.71) or in a list of contributors (1.47). The source of previously published material (e.g., in an anthology) may also be given in an unnumbered footnote on its opening page (see 15.70). When both an author's identification and a source reference appear, the author's identification is given first.

8. When offprints of individual chapters are planned, each chapter in a book should begin on a recto page so that the printer need not reimpose pages for offprints but can simply gather them together.
9. The word *chapter* is usually omitted.

25

PARTS

1.54   When text material may be logically divided into sections larger than chapters, the chapters may be grouped in parts. Each part is normally numbered and given a part title, as in this manual. The part number and title appear on a recto page preceding the part. The back, or verso, of this page is usually left blank. Chapters within parts are numbered consecutively through the book (*not* beginning over with 1 in each part).

1.55   Each part may have an introduction, usually short, and titled, for example, "Introduction to Part 2." A text introduction to an entire book that is divided into parts precedes part 1 and needs no part-title page to introduce it. Also, no part title *need* precede the back matter of a book divided into parts, but part titles may be used for each section of the back matter, e.g., "Appendixes," "Notes," "Bibliography," "Index."

OTHER DIVISIONS

1.56   *Poetry.* In a book of previously unpublished poetry, each poem usually begins on a new page. Any part titles provided by the poet need not be numbered but should appear on a separate page preceding the poems grouped under them.

1.57   *Letters and diaries.* Correspondence and journals are usually presented in chronological order, seldom conducive to division into chapters or parts. Dates, used as guidelines rather than titles, are often inserted above relevant diary entries. The names of the sender and the recipient of a letter may serve the same function in published correspondence. In a collection of letters written by (or to) a single person, however, the name of that person is not used each time. For example, in *The Papers of James Madison,* "To Edmund Randolph" and "From Edmund Randolph" are sufficient. The date of a letter may be included in the guideline if it does not appear in the letter itself. Such guidelines in diaries and correspondence do not begin a new page in the book unless page makeup demands it.

SUBHEADS

1.58   In prose works where the chapters are long and the material complicated, the author (or the editor) may insert *subheads,* or *subheadings,* in the text as guides to the reader. Subheads should be kept short, succinct, and meaningful; and, like chapter titles, they should be similar in tone.

1.59   Many scholarly works require only one degree (level) of subhead throughout the text. Some, particularly scientific or technical works, require sub-subheads and even further subdivisions. Where more than one degree of subhead is used, the subheads are referred to as the *A-level* subhead (the principal subhead), the *B-level* subhead (the secondary subhead), the *C-level,* and so on. Only in the most complicated works does the need for more than three levels arise.

1.60   Subheads, except the lowest level, are each set on a line separate from the text, the levels differentiated by type and placement (specified by the book designer; see 19.28). The lowest level is often set at the beginning of a paragraph, in italics and followed by a period, where it is referred to as a *run-in side head.*

1.61   In some works the number of levels of subheads required may vary from chapter to chapter; that is, one or two chapters may need three levels, the rest only one or two. Some material may require run-in side heads, for example, while the rest of the book is clear, and better off, without them. Again, it is not necessary that the *A*-level heading be used in every chapter. Depending upon the importance and complexity of the material presented in a given chapter, *B*-level headings may well serve to mark the major divisions of one chapter whereas *A*-level headings are required for another, more complex chapter requiring two or more levels of subheads.

1.62   Unless sections in a chapter are referred to in cross-references elsewhere in the text, numbers are usually unnecessary with subheads. Also, in general, subheads are more useful to a reader than numbers alone.

1.63   In scientific and technical works, however, the numbering of sections, subsections, and sometimes sub-subsections makes for easy reference and may be a real convenience to the reader. There are various ways to number sections. The most common of these is the *double numeration* system, in which the number of a section consists of the number of the chapter, a decimal point, and the number of the section within a chapter. The number 4.8, for example, signifies the eighth section in chapter 4. A subsection might be numbered 4.8.3. Another system, used in some monographs, is to ignore the chapter number (which should here be a roman numeral to prevent confusion) and to number *A*-level subheads consecutively through the book, *B*-level subheads consecutively under each *A*-level, and subsections under the *B*-level: 25.10.7 thus might occur in chapter V. This manual employs still another system—chapter number followed by paragraph number to facilitate cross-referencing.

1.64   No reference number to a note should appear in or following a sub-head.

1.65   The first sentence of text following a subhead should not contain a pronoun referring back to a word in the subhead; the word itself should be repeated where necessary. For example:

> SECONDARY SPONGIOSA
> The secondary spongiosa is a vaulted structure . . .
> *not:*
> SECONDARY SPONGIOSA
> This is a vaulted structure . . .

1.66   Instead of subheads, extra space or a type ornament between paragraphs may be used to make text divisions, or changes in subject or emphasis. Usually one blank line of space is enough for this purpose. If such a space falls between pages, however, it will be lost in makeup; an ornament will preserve the division.

BACK MATTER

APPENDIX

1.67   Although an appendix is not an essential part of every book, the possibilities and the uses of the device are many. Some kinds of material properly relegated to an appendix are explanations and elaborations not essential parts of the text but helpful to a reader seeking further clarification; texts of documents, laws, etc., illustrating the text; long lists, survey questionnaires, sometimes even charts or tables. The appendix should not be a repository for raw data that the author was unable to work into the text.

1.68   When more than one appendix appear in a book, they should be numbered like chapters (Appendix 1, Appendix 2, etc.) or designated by letters (Appendix A, Appendix B, etc.), and each should be given a title as well. The first appendix usually, but not necessarily, begins on a recto page; subsequent appendixes may begin verso or recto.

1.69   An appendix may sometimes be placed at the end of a chapter if what it contains is essential to understanding the chapter. Here it may start on a new page, recto or verso, or it may run on at the end of the chapter following a suitable space, perhaps three or four lines. (The interruptive effect of this placement should be carefully weighed, however: most appendixes belong at the end of a book.) In multiauthor books and in any books from which offprints will be required of individual chapters, any appendix *must* follow the chapter to which it pertains.

1.70   The text of appendixes is usually, though not always, set in smaller type than the text proper, often the same as that used for excerpts in the text.

NOTES

1.71   A section of notes or references follows any appendix material and precedes a bibliography. When the notes are arranged by chapters, with references to them in the text, chapter numbers and titles should appear above each relevant group of notes. These are often treated as *A*-level subheads (see 1.59). Each group of notes does not begin a new page, but a line or two of space should be inserted between groups to enable the reader to find the way, and running heads should identify the text pages to which they apply.[10]

GLOSSARY

1.72   A glossary is a useful tool for the reader in a book on a subject necessitating many foreign words or in a technical work intended for the general reader who may be puzzled by words and phrases not in the common vocabulary (such as this manual). Words to be defined in a glossary should be arranged in alphabetical order, each on a separate line and followed by its definition. No period is used at the end of the definition—except where some or all of the definitions consist of more than one sentence. A glossary precedes a bibliography.

BIBLIOGRAPHY

1.73   The form of a bibliography varies with the nature of the book, the inclination of the author, and often the guidance or suggestion of the publisher. It may be a single listing of sources, arranged alphabetically by author. It may be broken into sections, by subject or by kinds of materials (primary and secondary sources, etc.). It may be a selected bibliography (preferable, as a rule, in a published book as opposed to a doctoral dissertation). It may be an annotated bibliography, the annotations sometimes indented under each entry and set in smaller type. Or it may be a discursive "bibliographical essay" in which the author discusses the most useful sources.

1.74   Bibliographies are normally set in a type size smaller than that of the text and in flush-and-hang style (except the essay kind) with extra space between entries. (For examples see chapter 15.)

10. For notes in the back matter as opposed to footnotes see 15.65. For unnumbered back notes and notes keyed to line numbers see 15.73. For running heads to a section of notes see 1.82.

INDEX

1.75   The index, or the first of several indexes, usually begins on a recto page; subsequent indexes begin verso or recto. If there are two indexes, name and subject, the name index precedes the subject index. (For acceptable kinds and forms of indexes see chapter 18.) Indexes are normally set two or more columns to a page and in a type size smaller than that of the text (see 19.42–44).

COLOPHON

1.76   An embellishment sometimes added on the last page of a specially designed and produced book is the colophon, in this sense not simply the publisher's device but an inscription including the facts of production (fig.1.15). This practice is not so common in book publishing today as it once was.

> ### THE CHRISTIAN TRADITION
>
> *Designed by Joseph Alderfer*
> *Composed by Typoservice Corporation*
> *in Linotype Garamond with display lines*
> *in Foundry American Garamond*
> *Printed by Halliday Lithograph Corporation*
> *on Warren's Olde Style*
> *Bound by Halliday Lithograph Corporation*
> *in Joanna Arrestox Vellum and*
> *stamped in purple and gold*

Fig. 1.15. Colophon printed at the end of each volume of a five-volume work.

RUNNING HEADS

1.77   Running heads, the headings at the tops of pages in a book, are signposts telling readers where they are. For this purpose running heads are useful in most scholarly works, textbooks, and the like. They may be omitted where they serve no practical purpose—in a book of poems, for example. (For preparation of running-head copy see 2.151–53.)

FRONT MATTER

1.78   Running heads should never be used on display pages (half title, title, copyright, dedication, epigraph) or on the first page of a table of contents, preface, etc. An element in the prelims that runs more than one page must carry running heads if the design calls for running heads in the text. Each element in the front matter normally carries the same running head on verso and recto pages.

VERSO	RECTO
Contents	Contents
Preface	Preface

TEXT

1.79   Running heads in the text are governed chiefly by the structure and nature of the book. Some acceptable arrangements are:

VERSO	RECTO
Part title	Chapter title
Chapter title	Subhead
Chapter title	Chapter title
Subhead	Subhead
Author [multiauthor books]	Chapter title

Putting the book title on the verso page is no longer common practice. Reasons against it are (1) that the title may be changed while the book is going through production and (2) that most readers know what book they are reading and prefer running heads telling them where they are in it.

1.80   When subheads in the text are used as running heads on the *recto* pages and when more than one subhead falls on a single page, the *last* one on the page is used as the running head. When subheads are used as running heads on *verso* pages, however, the *first* of several subheads to appear on one page is used as the running head. (The principle is the same as that used for dictionary running heads.)

BACK MATTER

1.81   Some acceptable arrangements for running heads in the back matter are:

VERSO	RECTO
Appendix A	Title of appendix
Appendix	Appendix [if no title]
Glossary	Glossary
Bibliography	Bibliography
Bibliography	Section title
Index	Index
Subject Index	Subject Index

1.82   The running heads for a section of notes in the back of the book are especially important. A definite convenience to readers, they should give the inclusive page numbers of the text where the relevant note references are to be found. Thus, two facing running heads might read:

VERSO   RECTO

Notes to Pages 2–10   Notes to Pages 11–25

For a fuller explanation and more examples see 15.56–57, fig. 15.1.

OMISSION OF RUNNING HEADS

1.83   Certain pages do not take running heads. In addition to display pages in the front matter (see 1.78), these include part titles, chapter openings, and any page containing only an illustration or a table. A running head should be used, however, on a page containing both an illustration (or a table) and lines of text.

PAGE NUMBERS

1.84   All modern books are paginated consecutively, and all leaves in a book (except endpapers) are counted in the pagination, whether folios are expressed or not.[11] There are various locations on the page acceptable for the folio. The most common, and perhaps the most easily found, is at the top of the page, flush outside (left on verso pages, right on recto pages). The folio may also be printed at the bottom of the page, and in that location it is called a *drop folio*. Drop folios may appear flush outside or in the center or indented from the outside.

FRONT MATTER

1.85   The preliminary pages of a book usually, especially in United States publications, are paginated with lowercase roman numerals (see outline, 1.1). The practice is due partly to tradition and partly to expedience: some of these pages (those containing the table of contents and the lists of illustrations and tables) cannot be finally made up until the text is in page proofs, and others (those containing the preface, acknowledgments, and dedication) are often heavily revised or even added by the author at the last moment, after the rest of the book is in pages. Thus, separate numeration for the prelims makes good sense.

1.86   In some books, however, arabic numbering begins with the first page (half title) and continues straight through the book. This system, more common in Great Britain than here, should be held in mind as a some-

11. Except full-page illustrations inserted after pages have been made up (see 1.34).

times useful alternative. When prelims are unusually long, use of arabic numerals eliminates the awkwardness of roman folios running up through xlviii, xlix, etc. But since this system affects the pagination of the entire book, the author must understand that there is no possibility of adding a dedication page or an additional page of acknowledgments once paging has begun.

1.87 Whether roman or arabic folios are used, no folio is expressed on display pages (half title, title, copyright, dedication, epigraph), and a drop folio (or none) is used on the opening page of each of the following sections of the prelims.

TEXT AND BACK MATTER

1.88 Following the prelims, arabic numerals are used throughout the book. When roman folios are used in the prelims, the text begins with arabic folio 1. If the text begins with a second half title (same as that on page i) or with a part title, the half title or part title counts as folio 1, its verso page as folio 2, and the first folio to be expressed is the drop folio 3 on the first page of text. If there is no part- or half-title page, the first page of the text proper becomes page 1. Subsequent part titles (1.54) are counted in the pagination but the folios are not expressed.

1.89 The opening page of each chapter and of each section in the back matter carries a drop folio. Folios are not usually expressed on pages containing only illustrations or tables, except in books containing long sequences of figures or tables.

MORE THAN ONE VOLUME

1.90 When a work runs to more than one volume, the publisher must decide how to paginate volume 2: begin with folio 1 on the first page of text or carry on from where the numbering left off in volume 1? The chief consideration is probably the index. When an index to two volumes is to appear at the end of volume 2, it is generally best to paginate consecutively through both volumes so that the index need not include volume numbers as well as page numbers. More than two volumes, however, regardless of index placement, are best paginated separately, both because page numbers in four digits are unwieldy (except in reference works) and because, for the reader's convenience, any reference to a specific page in a work of more than two volumes should include the volume number as well as the page number.

1.91 Note that whether the pagination is consecutive or by volume, the preliminary pages in each volume begin with page i. In rare cases where back matter, such as an index or tabular material, must be added to volume 1 later in the production process, lowercase roman folios may be used; these should continue the sequence from the pre-lims in that volume—if, for example, there are twelve preliminary pages, even though page xii is blank, the back matter would start with page xiii. Again, this is not a common practice but a useful alternative.

ERRATA

1.92 An "errata sheet" is definitely not a usual part of a book. It should never be supplied to correct simple typographical errors (which may be rectified in a later printing) or to insert additions to, or revisions of, the printed text (which should wait for the next edition of the book). It is a device to be used only in extreme cases where errors severe enough to cause misunderstanding are detected too late to correct in the normal way but before the finished book is distributed. Then, the errors may be listed with their locations and their corrections on a sheet that is tipped in either before or after the book is bound, or laid in loose, usually in the front of the book. (Remember that tipping and inserting must be done by hand, thus adding considerably to the cost of the book.) The following form may be adapted to suit the particu-lars:

ERRATA

Page	For	Read
37, line 5	Peter W. Smith	John Q. Jones
182, line 15	is subject to	is not subject to
195, line 8	figure 3	figure 15
23, 214	Transpose legends of plates 2 and 51.	

1.93 The inclusion of an errata page may be fully justified when all or part of a book is photographically reproduced from an earlier publication in which there are a few easily correctable errors. There should be a headnote explaining the matter (see fig. 1.16). Such a page must be prepared in time to be set in type and printed and bound with the book. It may be placed either at the end of the prelims or at the end of the book.

Errata

Chapters 1 through 6 and chapters 8 and 9 have been photographically reproduced from the original journal articles. The following are corrections for typographical errors in those articles.

Chap. 1
P.   43, n. 16: *"wirtschaftmenschen"* should be capitalized.
P.   72, line 12: "1226" should read "1225."

Chap. 2
P.   91, n. 2: "Appendix IV" should read "Appendix III."
P.   91, n. 4: "Appendix IV" should read "Appendix III."
P.   96, line 19: *"stamai uoli"* should read *"stamaiuoli."*
P. 107, n. 3: "Appendix IV" should read "Appendix III."
P. 114, Appendix II: "Vencenzo" should read "Vincenzo."

Chap. 3
P. 130, line 19: *"sopracorpo"* should read *"sopraccorpo."*
P. 134, line 31: *"sovracorpo"* should read *"sovraccorpo."*
P. 155, n. 1: "Accerito" should read "Accerrito"; the date of Folco's death should be 1431.
P. 158, line 24: *"sopracorpo"* should read *"sopraccorpo."*

Chap. 4
P. 198, col. 1, line 21: "enforcible" should read "enforceable."

Chap. 5
P. 201, line 1: *"bancum"* should read *"bancus."*
P. 202, line 1: change "sought" to "found."
P. 203, line 20: "became" should read "become."
P. 208, n. 31: *"Verlagsystem"* should read *"Verlagssystem."*
P. 213, n. 51: *"Tujdschrift"* should read *"Tijdschrift."*
P. 216, n. 64: "Maine" should read "Maino."
P 221, n. 95: "abredged" should read "abridged."
P. 223, n. 107: *"Sicilio"* should read *"Sicilie"*; *"1908"* should read *"1808."*
P. 227, n. 125: "Publication" should read "Publicatiën."
P. 237, line 15: "wors" should read "worse."

Chap. 6
P. 240, line 22: "Masarozzo" should read "Masaiozzo"; insert "Martellini" after "d'Agnolo."
P. 240, n. 3: "wich" should read "wish."

Fig. 1.16. Page of errata printed and bound with photographically reproduced material.

2 *Manuscript Preparation and Copyediting*

Introduction 2.1
The Author's Manuscript 2.3
    Contents 2.3
    Number of Copies Required 2.4
      Manuscript 2.4
      Tape or floppy disks 2.5
      Typescript to be scanned 2.6
    Numbering Pages 2.7
Typing the Manuscript 2.11
    Paper 2.11
    Typewriter 2.12
      Typing for an OCR 2.15
    Spacing 2.16
    Chapter Titles and Subheads 2.18
    Extracts 2.20
    Notes 2.21
    Tables 2.23
    Glossaries 2.27
    Lists of Abbreviations 2.28
    Bibliographies and Reference Lists 2.29
    Indexes 2.31
Machine Copies 2.32
Author's Corrections 2.33
Correlating Parts of a Manuscript 2.37
    Table of Contents and Chapter Titles 2.38
    Cross-References 2.40
    Notes and Their References 2.42
    Notes and Bibliographies 2.43
    Text References and Bibliographies 2.44
    Tables and Text 2.45
    Illustrations, Legends, and Text 2.47
    Abbreviations 2.50
The Editorial Function 2.51
    Mechanical Editing 2.55
    Style 2.56
    Substantive Editing 2.57
Copyediting 2.58
    Preliminary Information 2.59
    Estimating Time 2.60
    How to Mark a Manuscript 2.61
      Insertions and deletions 2.62

Transposition 2.63
Closing up or separating words 2.65
Punctuation changes 2.66
Dashes and hyphens 2.70
Operational signs 2.74
Color of pencil or ink 2.86
Further instructions 2.88
Editing Text 2.89
Style sheet 2.90
Watching for lapses 2.92
Subheads 2.93
Cross-references 2.94
Quotations 2.96
Editing Notes and Footnotes 2.97
Editing Bibliographies 2.104
Editing Tables 2.105
Preparing Illustrations and Legends 2.107
Preparing Front Matter 2.110
Numbering 2.112
Editing Indexes 2.114
Editor and Author 2.116
Queries on Manuscript 2.116
Covering Letter 2.124
Sending Manuscript 2.127
Checking Author's Corrections 2.128
Editor and Typesetter 2.129
Type Specifications 2.131
Identification and Placement of Material 2.145
Numbering Pages 2.147
Other Instructions 2.149
Spine Copy 2.150
Running Heads 2.151
List of Special Characters 2.154
Style Sheet for Proofreader 2.155
Transmittal Sheet 2.156
Preparing Manuscript from Printed Material 2.158
Using Copies of the Original 2.158
Machine Copies 2.161
Source Notes 2.163
Editing 2.166
Handling Symposium Volumes 2.169
Preliminary Planning 2.170
Volume Editor's Responsibilities 2.171
Copyeditor's Responsibilities 2.174
For Further Reference 2.177

INTRODUCTION

2.1   This chapter has two main parts. The first (2.3–50) is addressed to authors of books and articles intended for publication; it points out what publishers expect of authors regarding the physical preparation of manuscripts. The second part (2.51–176) is addressed to publishers' copyeditors, who complete the preparation of manuscripts for the typesetter; this part explains not only what editors do to manuscripts but how they do it. These two operations, author's and editor's, are interrelated because the copyeditor must often perform functions that the author has neglected and because the author's responsibilities for preparing the manuscript are not fully met until he or she has answered all queries on the edited manuscript. The word *editor* in these pages means *copyeditor;* other kinds of editors are subsumed under the umbrella term *publisher.*

2.2 Today, with electronic word processors, scanners (OCRs), and computerized typesetting and page makeup, machines play a significant third role in this author-editor relationship. Because there is, and will continue to be in the near future, wide variation in the requirements of electronic devices developed by different manufacturers, both author and editor must know which process is to be used and how it will affect the preparation of the final typescript or disk (or both). Whatever its final form is to be, however, the manuscript initially submitted to the publisher should be a complete and readable typescript or paper printout prepared according to the rules outlined in the following paragraphs.

THE AUTHOR'S MANUSCRIPT

CONTENTS

2.3 The parts of a book outlined in chapter 1 (1.1) are, in general, what publishers expect to find in manuscripts submitted for publication. The publisher will furnish the half-title page, the copyright page, and the copy for running heads. The author is responsible for providing

> Title page
> Table of contents
> Any other preliminaries (dedication, epigraph, preface)
> All text matter
> Tables, if any, on separate pages
> Notes, or footnotes, in a separate section
> All end matter (appendixes, bibliography, etc.), except index[1]
> All illustrations, and all permissions, in writing, necessary to reproduce them
> Legend copy for illustrations, on separate pages

1. The index is also the author's responsibility, unless other arrangements are made with the publisher. The index manuscript cannot of course be completed until the author has all the page proofs.

NUMBER OF COPIES REQUIRED

2.4   *Manuscript.* Many publishers, including the University of Chicago Press, request two copies of a manuscript submitted for publication— the ribbon, or first, copy and a legible carbon or machine copy.[2] The ribbon copy is marked by the editor and becomes the copy that goes to the keyboard operator, the copy from which the book is made. The second copy goes to the production department for design and estimate. Editorial and preliminary production processes may thus take place simultaneously. Only one set of illustrations—halftones or prepared artwork—is necessary (see chapter 11 for preparation of illustrations). And the publisher normally requires only one copy of the index manuscript, since its probable length has been estimated in advance.

2.5   *Tape or floppy disks.* Publishers who accept manuscripts already keyboarded by authors for computerized typesetting will need, in addition to the disks, two copies of a paper printout. One of these will be read and marked for type specifications by the editor; the other will be used for estimate and design.

2.6   *Typescript to be scanned.* If scanning by an optical character recognition device (OCR, see 20.120) is to be the first step in the production of a book, the publisher will need *three* copies of the typescript. The one to be scanned must be a very clean ribbon copy with no pen or pencil marks on it. The second copy will be edited and marked for type specifications by the editor, and the third copy will be used for estimate and design. (The scanning method is not practicable for a manuscript needing a great deal of editing.)

NUMBERING PAGES

2.7   The author need number preliminary pages only if some element, such as a preface, occupies more than one manuscript page. The sequence of pages within this element may then be indicated by ordinary arabic numerals, e.g., "Preface 2." Before the manuscript goes to the typesetter, the editor will number the preliminaries as they are to appear in the printed book (see 2.112), indicating any verso pages that are to remain blank.

2.8   To facilitate estimating the length of the manuscript, all pages containing text, notes, and back matter should be numbered consecutively from the first page to the last page.[3] The author's page numbers are

2. The author should always retain a copy of the whole manuscript.

3. The University of Chicago Press will also accept manuscript pages numbered by chapter if the chapter number is given with each page number, e.g., 3-25 or III 25 (i.e., chap. 3, p. 25).

best typed in the top center of each page, clearly separated from the text. Pages added after the first typing of the manuscript may be numbered, for example, 55a, 55b, etc., following page 55. After the manuscript has been edited and the author has made all final corrections, the editor will number the pages with a numbering machine just before sending the manuscript to the typesetter.

2.9 Tables and illustrations are estimated separately and therefore are not numbered consecutively with the manuscript pages. The estimate for these is based on the number and complexity of each.

2.10 Index copy, prepared by the author after all the rest of the book has been made up in pages, is numbered separately. And even though an index is in alphabetical order (the sequence of pages presumably obvious), its manuscript pages must be numbered.

TYPING THE MANUSCRIPT

PAPER

2.11 It is essential that the first copy, and desirable that the second copy as well, be on good-quality paper of standard size—in the United States, 8½ by 11 inches. The kind of paper called ''erasable'' (available under various trade names) is *not* acceptable for manuscripts that are to go through the publishing process; the ''erasable'' characteristic of such paper leads to the blurring and sometimes the actual disappearance of the type under the slight pressure of a hand—and many hands touch a manuscript before it becomes a book.

TYPEWRITER

2.12 Whenever possible, the same typewriter or at least the same type size (pica, being larger, is better than elite) should be used for an entire manuscript. The type bars should be clean and the ribbon fresh. When using a typewriter with changeable typefaces, use the same typeface throughout; for example, do not type anything in italic type—if italic is desired, underline the word or words.

2.13 A correct letter should not be typed over an incorrect one; erase or ''white out'' the error and insert the correction, or strike out the incorrect letter and type (or write) the correct one above it.

2.14 A typewriter equipped with diacritical marks and symbols occurring frequently in a manuscript is most desirable. A capital L with a hyphen through it may be used to represent a British pound sign, a double quotation mark may be typed above a letter to indicate a diaeresis or

41

an umlaut (ä), and a comma under a letter may indicate a cedilla (ç). A single quotation mark, however, should not be used to indicate an accent, because it could be either a grave or an acute accent, and the typesetter should not be asked to decide which is correct. These and other diacritical marks or symbols not available on the typewriter must be inserted by the author or typist—in ink and accurately placed. A handwritten Greek letter or a possibly ambiguous symbol should be identified by its name, written and circled in the margin next to the line where it occurs (*alpha, sigma, times* or *mult* for an *x* used as a multiplying sign, etc.; for typing mathematics see chapter 13). Typists should know that if a typewriter lacks the figure 1, the proper substitute is not a capital *I* but a lowercase *l* and that the zero key (0) is different from that for the letter *o*.

2.15 *Typing for an OCR.* Any typewriter that produces a clear image may be used in preparing a manuscript for scanning by an OCR (see 2.6). It is especially important to use a fresh ribbon and to keep the type bars clean. No word should be divided at the end of a line—i.e., no hyphens at ends of lines. Lines may vary considerably in length—i.e., "ragged right" is desirable. Underlining should be used sparingly or not at all (italics may be indicated by symbols or code letters for which the computer can be programmed). Mistakes may be corrected only by whiting out the wrong letter(s) and typing in the correct ones. Neither pen nor pencil should be used on the typed area to be scanned. Before typing, one would be well advised to consult the publisher about other strictures dictated by the process to be used. The author may sometimes be asked to include an input code on the typescript (see 20.118, 20.120).

SPACING

2.16 All copy intended for publication should be typed *double-spaced,* or triple-spaced—never single-spaced. Single-spaced material is not only impossible to edit clearly but difficult to follow in typesetting. The rule about double-spacing applies to the text and also to block quotations and case histories within the text, to notes, to appendix material, to bibliographies and indexes—in other words to all parts of the manuscript.[4] Double space means a full blank line (not a half-line) *between all typed lines,* not just between notes or between items in a bibliography.

2.17 Generous margins—at least an inch—should be left on either side and at the top and bottom of every page. Chapter openings should be at least three inches from the top of the page.

4. A possible exception is tabular material made up of groups of words, where each group may be typed single-spaced with a double space between groups.

CHAPTER TITLES AND SUBHEADS

2.18   Chapter titles and subheads in the text will be printed in a style specified by the book designer, who may decide to put them in full capitals or in capitals and lowercase, in italic or in roman or in boldface type. The typist, not knowing what style will be selected, should type them with initial capitals only—that is, capitalize the first letter of each word except prepositions, articles, and coordinate conjunctions. Chapter titles and subheads should not be underlined. It is easier for the editor who marks the manuscript to indicate capitals or italic type than to delete typed underlining or to lowercase many capitals.

2.19   Subheads of different levels (see 1.59) may be differentiated in typescript by their placement on the page. The most important subhead—the *A*-level subhead—may be centered on the page; the second, the *B*-level, subhead may be typed flush left. A subhead that begins a paragraph should be followed by a period. No period follows a subhead typed on a line by itself.

EXTRACTS

2.20   *Extracts* (block quotations, case histories, poetry, and the like) should be double-spaced and set off from the text by indenting them a few spaces from the left and leaving extra space above and below. Quoted poetry should be centered on the page, the indention of lines and space between stanzas reflecting the original pattern. An omitted line (or lines) of poetry is indicated by a single line of spaced periods approximately the length of the line above it. (For omissions in prose extracts see 10.36–46; for source citations following quotations in the text see 10.54–68.)

NOTES

2.21   Notes, whether they are to appear at the back of the published book or at the foot of the page, should be typed, *all lines double-spaced,* on separate sheets, never at the foot of the page or interlineated with the text. The number and title of a chapter should appear at the head of its notes. Typing footnotes on separate pages is, incidentally, much easier for the typist than trying to fit them in at the bottom of pages.[5] Each note should begin on a new line, with a paragraph indention,[6] and each should end with a period.

5. In dissertations and other academic papers *not intended for publication,* footnotes are commonly typed single-spaced at the foot of the pages for the convenience of the readers. (For typing dissertations, see Kate L. Turabian, *A Manual for Writers of Term Papers, Theses, and Dissertations,* 4th ed.)
6. The design for the printed book may later call for a flush, or unindented, style.

2.22   Notes to the text are numbered consecutively through each chapter (beginning with 1 for the first note in a chapter). Note numbers in the text are typed above the line, with no parentheses, periods, or slash marks. The numbers introducing the notes themselves should be typed on the line and followed by a period. (See 2.42, and examples of notes in chapter 17.)

TABLES

2.23   Tables should be typed on pages separate from the text. The word *Table* and the table number, an arabic figure, are typed on a line above the table. The table title is typed on the line(s) below the number, with only initial capital letters—that is, all words should be capitalized except coordinate conjunctions, prepositions, and articles. Table titles, in other words, should never be typed in full capitals, nor should a period follow a title. Explanatory matter applicable to the entire table, such as "in millions," should be enclosed in parentheses below the title. The table number, title, and subtitle (if any) may be centered or typed flush left. For examples of correctly typed tables, see chapter 12.

2.24   Brief tabular material—not more than, say, four lines and two columns—if it does not include vertical lines or braces, should be typed with the text. Longer lists of one or two columns that may be broken (continued on the next page) should also be typed with the text.

2.25   Columns in a table must be precisely aligned; column headings and stub entries must leave no doubt about what belongs with what. Horizontal rules may be used above and below the column headings, within the body of a table to show totals, and at the foot of a table. But no vertical rules whatever should be used. All typing is double-spaced (but see p. 42, n. 4).

2.26   Table footnotes to a statistical table are typed below the table and indicated by symbols or letters (see 12.48–50).

GLOSSARIES

2.27   Words to be defined in a glossary should be arranged in alphabetical order and typed flush left. They are often followed by a period (sometimes a dash or colon). Definitions begin with capital letters and usually end with periods (see the Glossary in this manual). Whatever style is adopted, punctuation and capitalization must be consistent throughout. Runover lines should be indented three or four spaces.

2.28   Abbreviations and their definitions are typed in two columns, the abbreviations, in alphabetical order, on the left and the definitions on the right. Leave two to four spaces between the longest abbreviation and its definition and align the rest of the definitions accordingly. (For examples, see figs. 15.2, 15.3.)

BIBLIOGRAPHIES AND REFERENCE LISTS

2.29   Each item in a bibliographical list should begin flush left (with no paragraph indention). In entries requiring more than one line, runover lines should be indented three or four spaces. All bibliographical material must be typed *double-spaced,* and it is well to leave two blank lines between items.

2.30   Authors' names in an alphabetical list are typed last name first. If several works by the same author are listed, a dash (three typed hyphens) is used in place of the author's name for each item following the first. If a period follows the author's name in the first item, a period follows the dash as well. (For capitalization, punctuation, and other matters of bibliographical style see chapter 16.)

INDEXES

2.31   After the indexer's cards or slips have been alphabetized and edited (see 18.40–57), the index should be typed double-spaced, and one column to a page, on regular manuscript pages. The author should retain a copy of the index manuscript, and all the index cards, until the index has been printed.

MACHINE COPIES

2.32   Most publishers will accept, as the equivalent of good typescript, machine copies (such as Xerox) made from clean typescript that meets all the other requirements of manuscript preparation (ample margins, double-spaced, etc.). The image must be crisp, not blurred, and the paper of good quality and suitable for marking with the editor's pencil. Machine copies of printed matter—for anthologies or other works containing excerpts from previously published material—are also acceptable, provided the image is clear and the type lines straight (see 2.161) and provided the material is not to be edited. Machine copies of artwork are not acceptable as camera-ready copy.

45

AUTHOR'S CORRECTIONS

2.33   For making corrections on a typescript to be scanned see 2.15. On a typescript to be keyboarded (typeset) by a human operator, corrections may be made by hand provided the author shows consideration for those who must read them—editor and typesetter and proofreader.

2.34   An added or altered word or phrase may be written—with a sharp black pencil (*not* ink) and in a legible hand (*not* printed in capital letters)—directly *above* the line where it is to be inserted. Words, sentences, or whole paragraphs may be deleted by a firm line drawn through them. Pages containing such corrections need not be retyped.

2.35   Corrections too lengthy to be written above the line must be typed and inserted where they belong. The best way to insert such material is to cut the page where the insertion is to be made and paste, or tape,[7] the pieces of text in the desired order on fresh sheets of paper. All pages of a typescript must be the same size but the amount of material on them may vary from page to page. It is not necessary to renumber pages of an entire manuscript as a result of a few added pages, but any added page should bear an indication of where it belongs—two extra pages between pages 24 and 25, for example, should be numbered 24a and 24b (see also 2.147).

2.36   Corrections made on manuscripts in any of the following ways are *unacceptable* to publishers and typesetters:

> Writing or typing on the reverse of pages
> Writing up or down the margins
> Typing inserts on slips attached to pages
> Pasting an addition to the bottom of a page and folding it up
> Directing the typesetter to insert a passage from another page
> Writing illegibly or with a worn-down, blurry pencil
> Drawing lines across the face of the text to show placement of a
>   change written in the margin

CORRELATING PARTS OF A MANUSCRIPT

2.37   References in one part of a manuscript to other parts of the manuscript provide a fertile ground for error, as any copyeditor well knows. The careful author will check the *final* typescript for any discrepancies that may have crept in during the various stages of preparation. The manu-

---

7. It is best to use transparent tape with a dull finish that can be written upon with a pencil; staples, pins, or paper clips should never be used to fasten manuscript material intended for a printer.

script editor should also check all such references and query the author regarding any discrepancies found in them.

TABLE OF CONTENTS AND CHAPTER TITLES

2.38 The table of contents lists the titles of all sections of the book (see 1.31–33) and must therefore be checked against the text to see that the wording is identical in both places and that nothing has been omitted from the table of contents. If a later decision is made to alter a chapter title, to add or delete an appendix, the change must also be made in the table of contents.

2.39 Placing page numbers of the manuscript in the table of contents is helpful to publishers and readers. If the author supplies them, however, the editor must remember to circle them before the manuscript goes to the typesetter so that they will not be set. The printed page numbers will of course be quite different and cannot be added to the table of contents until the pages have been made up. Page numbers to be supplied are normally indicated by zeros (000) in manuscript and galley proofs.

CROSS-REFERENCES

2.40 Any reference in the text to a specific part of the work—a chapter, a section, an appendix, even a sentence of text—should be verified. A chapter number, or its title, may have been changed or an appendix dropped after the author made reference to it. References to tables, figures, or plates must be checked carefully against the actual table or figure. Cross-references in the notes, from one note to another, are especially hazardous because notes are frequently renumbered in the course of preparing a manuscript.

2.41 Cross-references to specific pages in a book should be kept to a minimum. They cannot be filled in until pages have been made up, and then, in many kinds of composition, an entire line must be reset to accommodate each one—a costly process. Wherever possible it is best to refer, if reference must be made, to a chapter or a section. Authors who find themselves including a great many cross-references to other pages might do well to consider (1) whether they have organized the material as efficiently as possible and (2) whether readers would not rather use the index to find related material than be interrupted by frequent admonitions to turn to another page. Where a page reference seems absolutely necessary, it may be indicated by zeros or dashes (e.g., "see p. 000"), not by manuscript page number. Zeros in the text not only alert the proofreader to the fact that a number is to be inserted in final page proof but also reserve space in the printed line for that number. Some typesetters use black en quads for this purpose. If someone other than the author is to insert the page numbers in the page proofs, the author should give the appropriate manuscript page number, and circle it, in the margin of the manuscript next to the line including the reference.

NOTES AND THEIR REFERENCES

2.42   In a work containing numbered notes to the text—either at the foot of the pages or at the back of the book—there must be a number in the text referring to each note and a note corresponding to each number. Obvious as this seems, all notes should be checked against the text to make sure that every note has a corresponding number in the text and that each note is the one intended for that spot in the text. Note numbers are often inadvertently omitted when a manuscript is retyped, and the sequence of notes may be affected by any rearranging of material. Except in certain specialized works and in tabular matter, no note should have more than one text reference to it; when it is desirable to refer to exactly the same material given in an earlier note, the later note may simply give a cross-reference:

> 75. See n. 3 above.

No two notes should bear the same number, such as 15 and 15a. If a note must be added, two notes may be run together to accommodate the addition; otherwise all subsequent notes in the chapter must be renumbered.

NOTES AND BIBLIOGRAPHIES

2.43   In a work containing both notes and bibliography, sources cited in the notes should be checked against the bibliography. If the same source appears in both places, the note citation may be shortened (see 15.77). Author's name and title of the work must be spelled and punctuated the same way in both places.

TEXT REFERENCES AND BIBLIOGRAPHIES

2.44   In a work using the author-date system of citing references, each citation must be checked against the reference list, where it should appear in full. The author's name and the date of publication must agree.

TABLES AND TEXT

2.45   Tables typed or pasted on separate sheets must be marked with the manuscript page number of the text that each is to accompany. The manuscript text page also must have the table number noted in the margin next to the passage where the author wishes it to appear in the printed book. A table usually follows as closely as practicable the first reference to it. Text references to tables must be by table number, not by a phrase such as *the following table* or *the above table*. Nor should a colon be used to introduce a table. In page makeup a table may not fall exactly where the author wants it, but it will be placed as close to the spot as possible.

2.46   A final check of tables in a manuscript will ascertain (1) that they are numbered consecutively (through the entire book or through each chapter), (2) that each bears the manuscript page number of the relevant text, and (3) that the placement of each is accounted for by a marginal direction in the text. If there is a list of tables in the front of the book, this should also be checked against the tables themselves (see 1.37).

ILLUSTRATIONS, LEGENDS, AND TEXT

2.47   Text figures—illustrations that print with the text—and maps are handled in much the same way as tables, described above. Author or editor must insert marginal notes in the text (e.g., fig. 1, fig. 2) indicating where each belongs. Since, unlike table titles, figure legends (captions) are typed on pages separate from the figures themselves, each drawing must bear a penciled notation showing the figure number and the manuscript page number of the text passage where it belongs. Such notations should of course never be written within the boundaries of the drawing itself, but in the upper or lower margins. If the figure is a glossy print, the notation may be written either with a grease pencil in the outside margin or with a plain soft pencil very lightly on the back of the print. Care should be taken that no mark made on the back of a print shows through on the front, for it will mar the finished work.

2.48   Plates—illustrations (usually halftones) that print separately from the text—are gathered in one or more sections within the text. If plates are numbered, they are numbered separately from the text figures, but if they are not referred to in the text, they need not be numbered at all. For identification by editor and printer, however, each illustration and its legend must be numbered—very lightly on the back of each print and a corresponding number, circled, next to each legend. Also, if there is any room for doubt, the word *top* should be written at the top, either front or back, of an illustration.

2.49   A final check of illustrations will ascertain that each has a legend and that each bears a number corresponding to that of its legend. If there is a list of illustrations in the front of the book, this too should be checked against the legends of the illustrations (see 1.34–36). (For a more detailed description of handling illustrations see chapter 11.)

ABBREVIATIONS

2.50   If a list of abbreviations is included in a book (see 1.45), any abbreviation used in notes, bibliography, or elsewhere should be checked against the list. Any abbreviation, such as that for the title of a work, should be consistent throughout a book. Other indications, aside from a list of abbreviations, of intent to abbreviate—such as "hereafter cited as . . ."—should also be checked by the author and the editor: are all subsequent references indeed abbreviated, or shortened, as the author stipulates?

THE EDITORIAL FUNCTION

2.51   By the time the editor begins work on a manuscript a decision on how to produce it will have been made by the publisher (see 2.4–6), and how much copyediting is deemed necessary will have been a factor in that decision. Works that are to be scanned from a clean, well-prepared manuscript and works that are submitted on floppy disks or tape should require minimal attention from an editor.

2.52   A typescript to be scanned should not be touched by an editor except to render it more "scannable" by the particular OCR that is to put it on tape (see 2.15). This could mean adding coding, whiting out underlining and other possibly confusing marks, etc. What editing is necessary should be done on a *second* copy of the typescript, which is then checked by the author. This edited copy, back from the author and marked also for type specifications, goes from the editor to the compositor, who makes the desired editorial changes electronically at the same time as the tape is coded for the type specifications. Some editors now have their own VDTs (video display terminals) on which they can make editorial changes themselves.

2.53   Editing a manuscript received on the author's floppy disks is done on one of the paper printouts of the work. The edited script, approved by the author, is sent to the compositor along with, or following, the disks. The compositor makes the editorial changes from the script when proofreading the output of the floppy disks.

2.54   Editing manuscripts full of complicated material or in need of considerable editorial attention—i.e., most of the works published by university presses—is done on the copy that is to go to a keyboard operator (typesetter, compositor) for typesetting by some one of the various means available (see chap. 20). It is this editorial operation that is described in the following paragraphs.

MECHANICAL EDITING

2.55   The editorial function is in effect two processes. The first, for want of a better term, may be called *mechanical* editing. This process involves a close reading of the manuscript with an eye to such matters as consistency of capitalization, spelling, and hyphenation; agreement of verbs and subjects; beginning and ending quotation marks and parentheses; number of ellipsis points; numbers given as figures or written out; and many other details of style.

STYLE

2.56   The word *style* means two things to an editor. The first meaning is that implied in the title *The Chicago Manual of Style*. Publishers refer to style in this sense as *house style* or *press style*—rules regarding the mechanics of written communication detailed in part 2 of this manual. Authors more often think of style in its other sense, as a way of writing, of literary expression. Editors are of course also aware of this meaning of style when they undertake the second, nonmechanical, process of editing.

SUBSTANTIVE EDITING

2.57   This second editorial process may be called *substantive* editing—rewriting, reorganizing, or suggesting other ways to present material. The editor will know by instinct and learn from experience how much of this kind of editing to do on a particular manuscript. An experienced editor will recognize, and not tamper with, unusual figures of speech and idiomatic usage and will know when to make an editorial change or simply to suggest it, when to delete a repetition or simply to point it out to the author, and many other matters. Since every manuscript is unique in the amount and kind of substantive editing desirable, no rules can be devised for the editor to follow. Except for certain magazine publishers, no publishing house has a *house literary style*.

COPYEDITING

2.58   Copyediting—also, mainly in newpaper offices, called *copyreading*—is the editor's most important and most time-consuming task. It requires close attention to every detail in a manuscript, a thorough knowledge of what to look for and of the style to be followed,[8] and the ability to make quick, logical, and defensible decisions.

8. For rules regarding style see the chapters in part 2 of this manual.

PRELIMINARY INFORMATION

2.59   Most editors prefer to read quickly through a manuscript before they begin editing it. The kind, and amount, of editing to be done depends on the nature of the material, the audience for whom it is intended, and the author's skill in preparing the manuscript—all factors that can be determined by a first reading, or sampling. Also essential to the editor are correspondence between author and publisher and any readers' reports on the manuscript, as well as the author's contract with the publisher. These should be examined for anything pertinent to the editing. The editor should of course know whether the manuscript is part of a series with a particular style of its own. And, certainly, if the manuscript is, say, volume 4 of an author's magnum opus, the first three volumes of which may have been published a number of years before, the editor will, insofar as possible, follow the style of the earlier volumes, regardless of current house style.

ESTIMATING TIME

2.60   In many publishing houses editors are required to estimate the amount of time they will need to complete the editing on each manuscript. No editor should attempt such an estimate before having worked for a while on a manuscript. Until at least twenty-five pages of an average manuscript have been edited and the notes and other apparatus closely examined, the editor cannot, with any degree of accuracy, prophesy how many hours the whole will take.

HOW TO MARK A MANUSCRIPT

2.61   The following paragraphs concern the "mechanics" of mechanical editing—how to make the actual marks on the page. They are addressed primarily to the inexperienced editor unsure of just how to indicate a change and alarmed at the prospect of putting pencil to someone else's paper.

2.62   *Insertions and deletions.* To add a missing letter, word, or phrase, insert a caret ($\wedge$) where the addition belongs and write the correction above the line. To correct a misspelling or to substitute a word or phrase, cross out (draw a line through) precisely what is not wanted and insert the change directly above the line. To delete a phrase, a sentence, or a paragraph, draw a horizontal line through the unwanted words, and through any surrounding punctuation to be deleted as well. To delete a single letter in the middle of a word, draw a vertical line through it and make close-up marks ($\mathcal{C}$) at top and bottom of the vertical line. To delete a mark of punctuation, or a letter at the beginning or end of a word, make a delete mark ($\mathcal{G}$ or $\mathcal{Y}$) through it; be sure

Editing a manuscript from which type is to be set requires a different method from that used in correcting proof. A correction or an operational sign is inserted in a line of type, or above not in the margins as in proofreading. The operator follows each line of the manuscript word for word, and so any editor's change must be in its proper place and clearly written.

Specific marks

A caret between two words shows where additional material is to be inserted. three lines under a lowercase letter tell the typesetter to make it a capital; 2 lines mean a small capital (A.D. 90); one line means *italic*; a wavy line means **boldface**; and a stroke through a capital letter means lowercase. Unwanted underlining in a manuscript is taken out thus. A small circle around a comma changes it to a period. A straight line between parts of a closed compound word will make it two words—to be double sure, use a spacemark as well; two short parallel lines mean a hyphen as in two-thirds or well-done steak.

A circle around an abbrev. or a figure tells the typesetter to spell it out (abbreviations ambiguous or not likely to be recognized by a typesetter should be spelled out by the editor [Biol.=Biology or Biological; gen.=gender, genitive, equal sign or genus], as should figures that might be spelled more than one way [2500=twenty-five hundred or two thousand five hundred].) Dots under a crossed-out word or passage mean stet (let it stand). Whenever it is ambiguous, an end-of-line hyphen should be underlined or crossed out so that the printer's typesetter will know whether to keep the hyphen in the typeset line or to close up the word. Dashes—other than hyphens—should always be marked; otherwise a hyphen may appear between continuing numbers such as 15-25 (see p. 125). (?)

Ink or Pencil

Typesetters prefer ink to pencil for editorial changes: faint pencil marks are indicative of the "timid editor." Green ink is favored by editors who dare to make changes baldly. Editors who use coloured pencil (because erasing is easier than with ink) must write so that the typesetter can see what they have done.

Fig. 2.1. Example of edited manuscript

to put the vertical part of the mark through the bit to be deleted and the hook part above the line, where it can be seen.

```
            k                  e                  a
    picnicing      rapprochment       indispensible

    As I have already noted, Senator Bakers said: "The Ervin Committee
                    quoted                remarks:
                                                           art
    did not invent the leak, but we elevated it to its highest form."

    This was, in effect, the end of the matter.

    In my judgement, you are quite misstaken.

    Dont say that again, ever!

                      s                                   was
    One of her brother-in-laws or her brother were always in
                         n
    the kitchen.
```

Do not write a correction in the margin unless you cannot write it legibly between the lines (as in single-spaced typescript).

2.63   *Transposition.* To change the order of, or transpose, letters, words, or phrases, draw a line over and under the affected elements:

```
    from           sturggle

    She only gave two examples.

    Earth, air, water, and fire
```

2.64   To move a word or phrase to a different line of the typescript, circle it and draw a line to the spot where you want it to be. Do not draw the line through or across any words. And do not forget to adjust any punctuation or capitalization involved in the change.

```
    At first no one wanted to try it. However, after the demonstration
    by the professional actors everyone was eager to do it too.
```

2.65   *Closing up or separating words.* To close up, "pull together," two words or other elements you want the typesetter to set with no space between, use close-up marks:

```
    worth while       any one        "What else ?"
```

To separate, to make a space between, two words or other elements typed without required space, draw a vertical line between them:

```
    for awhile       "No,"she replied.
```

A space mark may be added to the vertical line (although most typesetters will understand the line alone):

```
    post mortem
```

(See also 2.72 on inserting or deleting a hyphen.)

2.66   *Punctuation changes.* Make any change in punctuation right where the punctuation mark occurs, or should be added, and right on the line, not below it. Do not also write it in the margin. For example, to add a comma, insert the mark where you want it and, to make sure the typesetter will see it, put a mark like a caret over it. This symbol, when used over a comma (it is also used to mark subscript letters and numbers), may be referred to familiarly as a roof, a house, even a doghouse. Do not use it over other marks of punctuation:

```
Flopsy, Mopsy, and Cottontail
```

To add a period, make a dot and circle it:

```
All is well⊙
He preferred Chanel No⊙5.
```

2.67 To add quotation marks, an apostrophe, or a missing note reference, use an inverted caret (∨) (the symbol for a superscript letter or figure):

```
The Declaration asserted that Americans were entitled to

"a separate and equal station among the nations of the earth.

states rights         . . . Young's recent work.
```

2.68 Other marks of punctuation (colon, semicolon, question mark, exclamation point) should be inserted without any additional marking. (For the dash, see below, 2.70.)

2.69 To change one punctuation mark to another, either cross out the wrong one and write the correct one beside it or alter the existing one as follows:

A comma to a semicolon, add a dot above the comma: ؛

A semicolon to a comma, make a caret through the dot: ⋏

A comma to a period, circle the comma: ⊙

A period to a comma, affix a tail to the dot and make a caret above it: ⌃

A period to a question mark or exclamation point, leave the dot in place and draw the rest of the mark above it: **?** *!*

A comma to a colon, make the comma into a large period and draw a matching period right above it: **:**

A period into a colon, leave the period in place and draw another right above it: **:**

A semicolon into a colon, make the comma into a larger dot and enlarge the dot above it to match: **:**

A double quotation mark to a single one, make an inverted caret through one of the marks and enlarge the single quote: ∨ —or, to be quite clear, delete the double and write in the single mark: ⌁ ∨

A single quotation mark to a double, add the second mark and put an inverted caret under both: ∨

A parenthesis to a square bracket, or vice versa, make a firm mark through the existing one: [] () or, cross out the existing one and insert the correct one: [( )] ([ ])

55

2.70   *Dashes and hyphens.* After mastering the distinctive uses of dashes of varying lengths (5.82–96), especially how the en dash differs from the hyphen (5.92), remember to mark them when necessary. The em dash, being a common mark of punctuation, need not be marked after its first occurrence in the text, but many editors mark it every time anyway. The typesetter will understand any of the following:

M   !   em
     M̄

Longer dashes in the text should always be marked:

2   2-em ;   3   3-em
M̄   M̄

Editors should watch spacing around dashes. Em dashes within sentences should be set with no space on either side. If they have been typed incorrectly, with spaces, put close-up marks with the first occurrence of the dash and write a note in the margin to the typesetter:

. . . subjects⌒-⌒math, French . . . *Typesetter: No space with em dashes*

For spacing around 2- and 3-em dashes see 5.95–96.

2.71   Where a hyphen in the typescript is to be set as an en dash in print, it should be marked:

pre-Civil War;   1978-80

If it is to be used between numbers throughout a section of a book, such as the index or the notes, you can save a lot of writing by marking only the first two or three and giving an instruction to the typesetter on the first page of the section:

Typesetter: en dash between numbers throughout

2.72   To insert a hyphen use two short parallel lines:

two⹀thirds   cross⹀eyed

To delete a hyphen and make two words, use a vertical line and a space mark:

fellow#students

To delete a hyphen and make one word, put a vertical line through the hyphen and add close-up marks:

four⌒fold

2.73   When a hyphen appears at the end of a line in the typescript dividing a word that might be so hyphenated, the editor should indicate whether to keep the hyphen (underline it) or to close up the word (line through the hyphen and close-up marks; see fig. 2.1). But do not insult the typesetter's intelligence by underlining every hyphen in the text or deleting every end-of-line hyphen where it is obvious that the word should be closed up.

2.74   *Operational signs.* To change a capital letter to lowercase, draw a slant line through it:

To lowercase a whole line of capitals, or all letters except the first, draw a slant through the first letter you want to lowercase and extend it horizontally across the top of the letters until the next capital or the end of the line:

STORIES FROM THE UNDERWORLD

To make doubly sure of the correct result, many editors also mark the capitals (see 2.75):

STORIES FROM THE UNDERWORLD

2.75   To indicate *full* capitals (i.e., regular capital letters), draw *three* lines under the letters:

the middle ages   Gatt

To indicate *small* capitals,[9] draw *two* lines. For words to be set in small capitals with an initial full capital (caps and small caps), draw three lines under the initial and two under the rest of the word:

46 B.C.   Lady Bracknell

2.76   To indicate *italics,* draw *one* line:

Tolkein's The Hobbit

2.77   To indicate *boldface* type, draw a *wavy* line:

Section 3

Do not mark for boldface unless your type specifications (book design or journal format) call for it.

2.78   To delete underlining in the typescript, make several short vertical lines through it:

As Publius said

In deleting a full line or more of underlining, two or three vertical lines under each word is enough:

To read is not always to understand.

9. Small caps have specific uses (see Index) and are not available in some kinds of typesetting.

For longer underlined passages that are to be set in roman type (not italicized), write a note to the typesetter in the margin:

2.79 To tell the typesetter to spell out an abbreviation or a number draw a circle around it:

When you circle an abbreviation or a number, be sure that there is only one way to spell it out; do not ask the typesetter to choose between alternative spellings. For example, 10-fold might be tenfold or ten-fold; 100 might be one hundred or a hundred; 7,500 might be seven thousand five hundred or seventy-five hundred. If there is any ambiguity about the abbreviation you want to spell out, cross it out and write the spelled-out version above it. If the same abbreviation occurs frequently, you may spell it out the first time it appears and circle it thereafter; but if a number of pages have elapsed since its last occurrence, spell it out again. Similarly, if the abbreviation is an uncommon one or in a foreign language, spell it out.

2.80 To indicate a paragraph opening where the manuscript does not show one, use a paragraph mark ($\mathcal{G}\!\!\!/$) right before the first word (see fig. 2.1, second paragraph). Use the paragraph mark also to break a long paragraph into two or more shorter ones. Be sure to put it right before the sentence you select to start a new paragraph:

> . . . tempo and volume.⁋One of the musically important aspects . . .

To "run in" a paragraph to the one preceding it (i.e., "no paragraph"), draw a line from the last word of one paragraph to the first word of the next (see fig. 2.1).

To show that you want a paragraph to start flush left (i.e., with no indention), make a mark like a square bracket where the paragraph should start and draw a line from it to the first word (see fig. 2.1, first paragraph).

If you want to indicate that something should be set flush right, use the same mark in reverse:

A straight line, instead of a square bracket, also works if done carefully:

> ⊢Editing . . .   (396) ─────────────┤

2.81 To center a heading or other unit on the page, use marks that look like reverse square brackets on either side and, to be doubly sure, write "ctr" and circle it (see heading of fig. 2.1).

2.82 To indicate lateral positions other than flush left, flush right, and center, use em quads (see Glossary under "Quad" and "Spacing"), to the number desired, one quad: ☐ ; two quads: ☑ or ☐☐ ; three quads: ☒ or ☐☐☐ ; etc. A quad mark to the left of the typed line tells the typesetter to indent it one em from the left margin (see fig. 2.1, first subhead); a quad mark to the right will indent it one em from the right margin (often used with signatures following material such as a foreword, or in correspondence):

    I. F. Stone ☐

2.83 If two or more lines in succession are to be indented, as in a set-off quotation, put a quad by the first line and draw a vertical line from its inner side the length of the passage to be indented (see 2.134 for marking extracts):

    What Betsey was like . . . is told by Ebenezer:

    Though not strikingly beautiful, her person and manner were
    infinitely engaging; her natural understanding of the first
    class; her conversation and attainments beyond her age, her
    station, and her instruction.

2.84 Vertical spacing in the text—spaces above and below subheads and set-off quotations and spaces showing division between sections of text—is measured by *points* (see Glossary). In text set in 10-point type, a line space equals 10 points. To indicate a line space in the text, write "blank line" or "line space" or "10 pt. #" (or "11 pt. #" if the text is set in 11 point) in the middle of the space in the text, or in the margin, with an arrow showing between which two lines the space should be inserted. Space above and below set-off quotations is usually 6 points but may be otherwise specified by a designer. When in doubt, simply make a space mark (⧣) in the center of the space and leave the exact amount to the typesetter. Most typesetters have good judgment about spacing in printed material—above and below tables, equations, quotations, etc. If your typesetter has poor judgment (i.e., inserts either no space or widely varying amounts of space), you will have to correct it in proofs. In general, however, it is wise not to overspecify vertical spacing in the manuscript.

2.85 Vertical spacing of more than a line or two, such as at chapter openings, is measured in *picas* (see Glossary). Editors, unless they are also designers, are not usually required to mark such spacing.

2.86 *Color of pencil or ink.* All editorial changes should be made in a color distinct from that used by the author for alterations. If there will be any reason to make a machine copy of all or part of a manuscript after it has been edited, remember that the traditional *blue* editorial pencil will be lost in many photographic processes; it is therefore best to experiment with your copying process before marking a manuscript. Many editors prefer to use a colored pencil that can be easily erased; others prefer colored ink. Whatever you use, write firmly, neatly, and legibly at all times. Typesetters have little patience with "timid" editors.

2.87 Some editors use different colors to distinguish three functions: (1) text alterations, (2) queries to author, and (3) directions to typesetter. Except in some circumstances, this distinction is not really necessary because queries to the author are crossed out before the typesetter sees the manuscript and directions to the typesetter are circled, indicating they are not to be set in type. For color-coding extracts see 2.136.

2.88 *Further instructions.* Rules for inserting authors' corrections given in 2.33–36 apply also to the editor's emendations. For marking type specifications following a designer's layout, see 2.129–44 and 19.72 with accompanying illustrations.

EDITING TEXT

2.89 An editor will usually edit one kind of material at a time, beginning with the text. (Notes should be edited together, tables together, legends together, because to edit similar matter in a manuscript in a continuous process lessens the chance of variations in style.)[10] To check spelling and meaning in editing the text the editor must have a dictionary and other reference works close to hand. The spelling of unfamiliar names and words should be checked, as well as some commonly misspelled familiar ones (e.g., Apennines, Pyrenees, stratagem, improvise, consensus, supersede).

2.90 *Style sheet.* No style book will provide rules covering all matters of style encountered by the editor, and no editor worth the title will apply identical rules to every book manuscript. Therefore, to ensure consistency in the style used in a particular manuscript, and to aid the editorial memory, it is helpful if not imperative to keep for each manuscript a running account of special words to be capitalized, odd spellings, compound words with or without hyphens, and the like. For easy reference this style sheet should be in rough alphabetical order, and the manuscript page number of at least the first occurrence of a word should be noted beside it. If there is any chance that the editorial mind will change late in the manuscript—say, about hyphenating a partic-

10. This system is of course impractical for a long manuscript such as a book of readings or a collection of papers that goes through the publishing process in separate sections.

ular compound—it is well to note the page number of each occurrence. One, and perhaps the tidiest, way to keep such an editor's style sheet is to rule off a blank page allowing enough space (a guess) for each letter of the alphabet. The abbreviated sample style sheet shown in figure 2.2 may serve as an example. The editor should consult and add to the style sheet throughout the copyediting process, remembering that a word added from the middle or end of a manuscript may well have escaped attention in earlier pages. A final, quick rereading of the entire manuscript is desirable to catch any such slips. The style sheet should also be consulted in editing discursive notes and figure legends and in checking names on maps, words in figures, tables, and the like.

2.91   A style sheet not only aids the editor's memory as editing progresses but may be indispensable in the later stages of production. Few editors can give their time exclusively to one manuscript. An editor may be responsible for as many as twenty or so manuscripts in various stages of production. It is difficult to remember the particular style for each when checking manuscript returned from the author, galley proofs, page proofs, index, months after editing the original. Also, another editor may have to take over at some stage of production, and that editor will need to know the style followed. Therefore, the style sheet should remain in the editor's file until the book is bound.

2.92   *Watching for lapses.* In addition to regularizing details of style, the editor is expected to catch errors or infelicities of expression that mar an author's prose. Such matters include dangling or misplaced modifiers, unclear antecedents, redundancies, split infinitives (a debatable "error"), lack of agreement of verb with subject, faulty attempts at parallel construction, overuse of an author's pet word or phrase, unintentional repetition of words, racial or sexist connotations,[11] and so on. The editor should also consider, insofar as possible, the logical flow of argument and suggest moving a sentence or a paragraph, deleting irrelevant material, or adding a transitional sentence where such emendations would improve the sequence of thought. Also, special terms or little-known persons should usually be defined or identified the first time they appear in the book; and first names of persons should normally be given the first time they are mentioned. It is well to remember, however, that a term unfamiliar to the editor may be commonly accepted in the author's field and thus need no definition for prospective readers. And first names of well-known persons (e.g., Disraeli, Shakespeare) should not be inserted by an editor.

11. For useful and sensible suggestions on how to avoid sexist connotations see Casey Miller and Kate Swift, *The Handbook of Nonsexist Writing.* For more general advice on usage see Fowler, Bernstein, and others listed at end of this chapter and in the Bibliography.

ABCD
city-state 5
balance of power diplomacy 15
air force 16
Co-Prosperity Sphere 30
drillmaster 32
breech-loading 36

MNOP
macroeconomics 6
Peace of Paris 12
Napoleonic Wars 21
manpower 29
Ottoman empire 38
map reading 50

EFGH
firepower 7
esprit de corps 10
Hellenistic age 20
great-power (adj.) 25
Hsiang-yang 39
Genghis' 40

QRST
sine qua non 16
trans-regional 17
riverboat 23
troublemakers 25
sea power 27
shortfall 40

IJKL
industrial revolution 6
Kublai Khan 11
levée en masse 20
Jürchen 25

UVWXYZ
war-horse 18
victuallers 31
Western Front 42
Zeitgeist 43

Fig. 2.2. Manuscript editor's style sheet

2.93 *Subheads*. Subheads in the text should be checked for uniformity and pertinence. Does each give an accurate indication of what is in the following text? Are they too long and can they be shortened? Does the first sentence of text following a subhead refer to a word in the subhead without repeating it? (See 1.65.)

2.94 *Cross-references*. All references in the text to tables, charts, figures, maps, appendixes, lists of references, or other parts of the book should be verified by the editor, even if the author has also done so (see 2.37–50). If the author, for example, mentions the gross national product for 1965 in the text and refers the reader to table 4, which the editor finds gives figures only through 1964, the editor should query the author about the discrepancy. Again for example, place names on a map intended to illustrate the text must be spelled as they are in the text. When an author uses an excessive number of cross-references to specific pages, the editor should suggest eliminating most of them (see 2.41).

2.95 Some authors need to be discouraged from distracting the reader and interrupting the subject matter by frequent remarks on the structure of their work—the "this is what I did earlier in my book, this is what I am doing now, and this is what I will do later" syndrome. A clear organization of material, a good index, and, where absolutely necessary, a note giving a reference to relevant material elsewhere in the book will obviate the need for most such remarks in the text.

2.96 *Quotations*. Aside from adjusting quotation marks and ellipsis points to conform to house style (see 10.24–29, 10.36–48), the editor must do nothing to material quoted by an author from another source. Interpolations (in square brackets) by the author and translations by the author of foreign language material, however, may be edited for style. Misspelled words and apparent errors in transcribing a quotation (obvious omission of a word, for example) should be queried to the author. Frequent errors, or apparent errors, of this kind, including inconsistent punctuation, may indicate that the author has been careless in transcribing quoted material. The editor should then be especially firm in requesting the author to check all quotations for accuracy, including punctuation.

EDITING NOTES AND FOOTNOTES

2.97 In editing manuscripts with many citations it is helpful to keep a separate list, arranged by chapter and note number, of the first citation of each work. The last name of the author is usually sufficient here. To provide a shortened form for subsequent citations to a work it is often necessary to check its first appearance, which is easy to find if the editor has noted it on the list.

2.98   The editor must be sure that every reference to a work is given the same way. Shortened titles or abbreviations, for example, once decided upon, must be the same every time they appear. If a volume number is given with one or more references to a journal, the volume number should be given for every reference to that journal.

2.99   Before making sweeping changes affecting the style of an author's notes, the editor is often well advised to consult the author, giving reasons for wishing to make such changes and asking for the author's concurrence. An author who has prepared notes with meticulous care, with the necessary information in each citation and consistency of style throughout, is likely to be dismayed by editorial efforts to force house style upon them. In such cases the author's style should be kept (unless the work is part of a multiauthor volume that is being edited to a uniform style). In other cases the author and editor may work out a compromise system acceptable to both.[12]

2.100   Discursive material in notes is edited like the text and should be read as carefully as the text. When the notes are to be printed at the bottom of the page, the author should be asked to shorten any excessively long note, either by deleting material in it or by adding parts of it to the text. The chief reason for shortening long footnotes, apart from the reader's possible annoyance and the effect on the printed page, is to avoid the makeup problem caused by a footnote that won't fit and must be continued on the next page. Long notes create no such problem when all notes are printed at the back of the book instead of at the foot of the page. Whichever way the notes are to be printed, however, long lists, long tables, and the like are better placed in the text or an appendix.

2.101   The editor should always check note reference numbers in the text against the notes themselves. Checking the numbers, or renumbering notes, should be a separate operation. An attempt to renumber notes while editing the text or the notes increases the risk of skipping or repeating a number. When renumbering is necessary, the old number should be crossed out and the new one inserted simultaneously in the text and before the note.

2.102   An editor's judgment is sometimes helpful to an author unsure or careless about the use of citations. The source of any direct quotation in a scholarly text should be made clear to the reader, either in what the

12. For detailed rules about the style of notes and footnotes, and examples, see chapter 17.

author says about it in the text or in a note. Paraphrases of other writers' ideas should be acknowledged and sources of little-known facts given. Well-known facts, easily ascertainable from many sources, need no documentation. The editor, however, must be cautious and entirely confident of the facts before asking an author to alter documentation.

2.103   In a work containing a bibliography as well as notes, each citation in the notes should be checked against the bibliography. Any discrepancy in spelling, date of publication, and the like should be either resolved by the editor or queried for the author's attention. Since works peripheral to the subject of the manuscript may be cited in a note but, quite properly, not listed in the bibliography, the editor should not question the omission of such items from the bibliography but simply make certain that a source not in the bibliography is given with full bibliographical details in the note. Nor should an editor try to determine whether every entry in a bibliography is cited somewhere in the notes, even when the author titles the bibliography "Works Cited." (See also chapter 15.)

EDITING BIBLIOGRAPHIES

2.104   The editor's task in editing a bibliography or reference list is to make each entry conform to the same style: order of the items in each entry, capitalization of titles, abbreviations, punctuation.[13] Alphabetically arranged lists should be checked to see that every entry is in the right place. If the list is chronological, the dates should be checked, and so on. Discrepancies or omissions found in correlating source citations in the text or notes with the bibliography should be queried and the manuscript page number of the citation in question given so that the author can easily compare the two.

EDITING TABLES

2.105   If the author has typed the tables on pages with the text, the editor should cut them out and paste them on separate pages, making sure that the text page number is inserted on the new page containing the table and the number of the table is in the margin of the text page. An alternate, less time-consuming method is to make machine copies of the text pages containing tables, crossing out table copy on the text pages and text copy on the table pages. If the author has prepared the tables on separate pages, the editor need only check to see that the author has noted the placement of each in the text (see 2.45–46).

13. For specific bibliographical styles see chapter 16.

2.106   The editor will then check for uniformity of style in tables containing similar material: wording in titles, column headings, and stub entries; abbreviations; use of leaders or dashes in empty cells; and other matters.[14] The sequence of symbols or letters referring to footnotes should be checked (see 12.48–49). Commas may need to be added in figures of four or more digits, columns brought into proper alignment, rules drawn or deleted, and so on. And sometimes the editor will find it necessary to recast an entire table to provide a clearer presentation of its material.

PREPARING ILLUSTRATIONS AND LEGENDS

2.107   When an author fails to identify illustrations or to type legends on separate sheets, the editor must do so (see 2.47). The editor will often find it convenient to have a copy of the legends in the file for future reference; in some instances engraver's proofs of the illustrations may have to be checked before the printer's proofs of the legends have been delivered.

2.108   The editor should examine the illustrations themselves, primarily to see that the spelling of any words in them conforms to the text spellings. The editor may also work with the production department on cropping and scaling illustrations, arranging them on a page, and so on.

2.109   If a map or other illustration containing words to be set in type must be redrawn, the editor will usually provide a typed list of all such words. Place names on a map should be arranged by category—countries, states, cities, rivers, mountains, etc.—since each category will be set in a different type size or style.[15]

PREPARING FRONT MATTER

2.110   The editor normally provides copy for the half-title page of a book, the series title, if any, and the copyright page. To prepare the copyright page, the editor needs to read the contract to determine the copyright holder and to examine any correspondence between author and publisher relating to such matters as permissions, translation, or new edition. Any oversight or inaccuracy on the copyright page is attributable to the editor, not to the author.[16]

2.111   Often the editor will need to retype (or supply) copy for the title page, table of contents, and list of illustrations. The editor should always

---

14. For various styles used in setting tables see chapter 12.
15. For further suggestions on preparing illustrations and legends see chapter 11.
16. See chapter 1 for sequence and form of preliminaries and sample copyright pages.

check the table of contents carefully to see that it lists all parts of the manuscript (including the index) and that the wording of titles matches that of the text.

2.112 *Numbering*. The manuscript pages of front matter (prelims) should be arranged in the order in which they will appear in the printed book (see 1.1–49, 1.85). To indicate page number and placement of each element in the front matter, the editor should number each page up to and including the first page of the table of contents with lowercase roman numerals, usually at the *foot* of the page and circled, since these numerals are not intended to be printed (expressed). Blank pages are noted also; if, for example, page ii is blank, the half-title page would be marked "p. i (p. ii blank)," or a dedication page marked "p. v (p. vi blank)." If the editor cannot determine what page an element (such as the preface) will fall on when the pages are made up, the words "recto page" (or just "recto") on the first manuscript page will tell the typesetter how to paginate it. (Traditionally, each element following the copyright page begins on a recto page.) The manuscript pages of a preface or foreword may be numbered serially with arabic numerals, but with some flag to prevent their being taken for text pages (e.g., "Pref.-1, Pref.-2, Pref.-3, etc.") and "roman folios" written on the first page to alert the typesetter.[17]

2.113 In place of any material not yet received from the author, the editor should insert a sheet indicating what is to come and, if possible, when (e.g., "Dedication to come," "Preface approx. 3 MS pp. to come, ca. 4/12"). Front matter usually goes straight into pages, even when the rest of the book is to go through the galley proof stage.

EDITING INDEXES

2.114 When the index manuscript arrives, the editor should edit and mark it for the typesetter at once. The rest of the book is now in pages, some of it perhaps even being printed, and the index must be set in type as soon as possible. If the author has prepared the index in a logical fashion, the editor need only verify cross-references and check alphabetization of main entries, arrangement of subentries, sequence of page numbers (such errors as "74–74" or "85, 50, 97" obviously require consulting the pages cited), and punctuation in each entry (see also 18.126–129). If the index is excessively long or so illogically planned that it would be difficult to use, the editor must either repair the matter as quickly as possible or again consult the author. Specific

17. Editors at the University of Chicago Press often number (with a numbering machine) all the pages of a manuscript beginning with the half-title page as 1. This can be done only when the manuscript is complete, in order, and ready for the typesetter. Preliminary pages in the *printed book* are paginated with roman folios (see 1.85).

instructions given an author *before* he or she prepares an index will usually, but not always, prevent such traumatic editorial experiences.

2.115 To aid the compositor, the editor should note, on the first page of the index manuscript, the page in the book on which the index begins, usually the recto folio following the last number of the page proofs; the index may start on a verso, but should always begin a new page.

EDITOR AND AUTHOR

QUERIES ON MANUSCRIPT

2.116 What to ask an author about a manuscript—and how and when to query the author—is an important part of editing. First, the editor should not usually query matters of house style—capitalization, spelling, etc. If, however, the editor has found it necessary to lowercase words consistently capitalized by the author, it might be well to explain why in the covering letter (see 2.124–26); and if there are many such editorial changes, the editor may want to send the author a copy of the style sheet (see 2.90). But where the editor has not changed the author's pattern of capitalization, etc., but has only tried to bring consistency to the manuscript, no mention need be made of these details.

2.117 Second, the editor should avoid writing long notes explaining editorial changes. Most authors readily understand, and appreciate, corrections of dangling modifiers, misplaced pronouns, repeated words or phrases, misalliances between subject and verb, and the like. An editor should of course know why any such emendation has been made but need not explain it unless challenged by the author.

2.118 Third, no query to an author should sound stupid, naive, or pedantic. Nor should a query be phrased so that it seems to reflect upon the author's scholarly ability or powers of interpretation. Humorous remarks, even when addressed to an author the editor knows will appreciate them, are generally better omitted. Every author has a right to expect conscientious, intelligent help from an editor. Unintelligent queries, as well as sloppy editing, will quite rightly make any author lose faith in an editor and may prejudice that author against the publisher as well.

2.119 The editor should call the author's attention to any discrepancies in statements of fact. For example, if a meeting is said, on page 13, to have taken place on 10 May 1896, and the same meeting is mentioned on page 87 as occurring in 1897, the editor (if sharp-eyed enough to catch it) will lightly circle each date and will write "1897? see p. 87" in the margin of page 13, and, on page 87, "1896? see p. 13." Similarly, possibly unintentional repetition of material, sometimes on widely separated pages, should be pointed out: "Repetition intentional? see p. 25." A missing quotation mark or note reference number: "Where does quote begin?" "Where is n. 87?" Or, if the editor inserts the missing item where it seems to belong and wants the author to verify it: "OK?"

2.120 Some editors prefer to write queries not in the margins of the manuscript but on separate slips, or fliers, that are gummed on one end so that they can be attached to the underside of the edge of a manuscript page. The slips are detached by the editor after the author returns the edited manuscript and before it goes to the typesetter. The advantage of this method is that the margins of the manuscript remain clean; thus, in a manuscript requiring many queries or many suggestions for sentence revision, it is usually better to use separate slips (pins, *not* paper clips or staples, may be used if the slips are not gummed). The disadvantage is that the author may detach the slips, with or without answering the questions, and the editor thus has no record of what was queried. A second possible disadvantage is that, after the editor has removed the slips and sent the manuscript to the typesetter, a proofreader may ask the same question on the proofs, not knowing that the author has already given an answer.

2.121 Whichever method of querying an author is used—slips or marginal notes—the editor should always ask the author *not* to detach slips or *not* to erase any queries. When the manuscript is returned by the author, the editor, while checking the author's answers, will detach any slips or cross out any marginal queries before releasing the manuscript for typesetting.

2.122 Manuscripts requiring extensive revision—heavy rewriting, deleting, rearranging—that has not been agreed upon by the author before the editor begins work demand a more cautious approach. The editor may send a preliminary letter explaining proposed editorial changes and how they might improve the manuscript. The editor may then send one or two edited chapters and wait for the author's approval of these before proceeding with the entire manuscript.

2.123 To save time later, as the editing progresses the editor may note on a separate piece of paper any general questions, suggestions, or explanations appropriate for inclusion in the letter to the author accompanying the edited manuscript.

COVERING LETTER

2.124 The contents of the editor's letter to the author, sent with the manuscript or separately (but timed to reach the author no later than the manuscript itself), will depend on the nature of the manuscript, how much telephone or personal contact the editor has had with the author while editing the manuscript, and how much experience the author has had in publishing books. No form letter could ever serve the purpose.

2.125 Most such letters will include the following points, not necessarily in this order:

1. What the editor has done to the manuscript; in brief, the reasons for doing it (e.g., "I have rephrased, reworded, here and there to eliminate dangling modifiers, inadvertent repetition of words, too many passive verbs, or to clarify your meaning, etc."); and what the author is expected to do now (answer all queries in the margins of the manuscript and read carefully any editorial change to make sure the meaning has not been altered). In the absence of specific objections, the author's approval of all editorial markings is assumed. To avoid possible unpleasantness at the proof stage and to encourage a more thorough reading of the edited manuscript, some publishers ask authors to sign a statement agreeing to emendations made by the editor or decided upon through consultation between author and editor. The editor may also want to advise the author about how to make corrections on the manuscript pages, or caution how *not* to make them (see 2.33–36).

2. A warning that now is the time for the author to make any last-minute changes, additions, or deletions in the manuscript and that, if it has not already been done, all the quotations should now be checked for the last time. Most publishers today do not permit extensive, sometimes even minor, author's alterations after type has been set (see 3.14, 3.35–37).

3. A specific date by which the editor expects the manuscript to be returned. The author should be made aware of the importance of keeping a schedule, particularly if it is the author's first book; experienced authors know, or should know, that a delay of a week on their part may result in a much longer delay in the production of the book.

4. An approximate date for the arrival of proofs, and an inquiry about whether the timing will cause problems for the author. Although the editor will probably not be able to give a precise date at this time, consultation with the production department should make an educated guess possible. A busy author's availability to read proofs must be considered, as well as the typesetter's schedule, when planning the final production schedule (see 3.4). To ensure the most expeditious handling of proofs, the editor should confirm the address to which the author wishes proofs sent. It goes without saying that the editor is responsible for knowing the author's whereabouts at all stages of the publishing process.

5. What kind of proofs the author may expect: galleys or pages or both. If only pages are to be sent, the author should be strongly fore-warned against making alterations in proofs, because of the added cost not only of resetting lines but of remaking pages and changing relevant index entries. Now is the time, too, to inquire whether the usual two sets of proofs will be sufficient; if the author has hired an indexer, for example, a third set may be required.

6. An inquiry about the index: Does the author plan to prepare it per-sonally or to have someone else prepare it; or does the author expect the publisher to provide an indexer?[18] Does the author need advice on index making? The University of Chicago Press sends reprints of chapter 18 of this manual to its authors who request advice,[19] and the editor usually supplements this with suggestions about number and kind of entries, subject and name indexes, etc., appropriate to the individual book. Although the index cannot be completed until page proofs are ready, all preliminary planning about its nature and prepa-ration should be done well in advance.

2.126 An editor must give careful thought to the style and tone of a covering letter and must never forget that it is the author's book, not the edi-tor's. The tone should be firm, businesslike, and gracious. A well-writ-ten and informative letter accompanying a carefully edited manu-script will assure an author of the editor's ability and concern for the book and therefore make for easy cooperation between editor and author throughout the publishing process.

SENDING MANUSCRIPT

2.127 An edited manuscript is a unique copy of that manuscript, represent-ing a considerable investment of editorial time and thought. It must not be lost. A manuscript sent by mail should be carefully wrapped with cardboard and strong wrapping paper, sealed, marked for first-class mail, and insured or registered. When in doubt about the relia-bility of the postal service, the editor should retain a machine copy of the edited manuscript (see 2.86).

CHECKING AUTHOR'S CORRECTIONS

2.128 When the manuscript comes back to the editor from the author, the editor must go through it again to see what the author has done to it and whether all queries have been answered. This task may be short and pleasant (the author has agreed to all suggestions, made emen-dations neatly and legibly, and introduced no new problems) or an

18. As a rule, the University of Chicago Press prefers that an author prepare his or her own index. When the Press hires a free-lance indexer to do it, the cost is taken out of the author's royalties.
19. The Press also sells copies of the reprint to anyone who writes for it.

editor's nightmare (the author has scribbled all over the manuscript with a pen or a dull, blurry pencil, has added material on slips clipped to the pages, has inserted new notes without renumbering, and has been thoroughly disagreeable about the editor's efforts) or somewhere in between. Whatever the situation, the editor must clean up the manuscript so that the typesetter can read it; retype heavily marked-up or barely legible parts and tape them or paste them in place; edit any new or revised material to match the original; renumber notes if necessary. In cases of disagreement over wording, the author's version should now prevail, unless editor and author can reach a compromise. And the editor should refrain from further word changing unless the author can be consulted before the manuscript goes to production. The editor's next task is to mark the manuscript for the typesetter according to the book design (see 2.129–44). (This is sometimes done in conjunction with the initial editing, but more often with the checking of the manuscript returned from the author.)

EDITOR AND TYPESETTER

2.129   In many publishing houses, including the University of Chicago Press, the editor marks the manuscript with type specifications indicated on the designer's layout (see chap. 19) or from a list of specifications furnished by the designer. Care must be exercised to follow the specifications exactly and to mark like parts alike. The layout does not show all parts of a book but does give samples of all type sizes and spacing to be used in text and display matter.

2.130   In electronic typesetting, type specifications must be translated into symbols or codes that can be read by the machine; this coding is usually done by the typesetter, not the editor.

TYPE SPECIFICATIONS

2.131   Each item in a chapter or section opening (number, title, etc.) should be marked for its particular type size and placement, and any ornamental rule or other device used in the design should be noted on the manuscript. At least for the first chapter in a book, the editor may also specify the *sinkage*—the vertical space from the top of the type page to the bottom of the first print line of text—as well as the amount of space between chapter number and title and between title and text; for these measurements of vertical space in chapter openings, however, it is usually best to refer the typesetter to the designer's layout: "See layout."

2.132   A design often calls for the first line of a chapter to begin flush left or with a special indention or with a display initial, any of which should be indicated in each chapter opening. If small caps are specified for the initial word or phrase of a chapter, the editor must indicate how much is to be set in small caps:

the beginning of 1937 Germany was increasingly . . .

2.133   The type size, leading (see Glossary), typeface, and type width to be used in the text proper should be written in the left margin next to the first paragraph of each chapter or other division of text. In computerized typesetting, once for a whole book is enough. For example:

Here "10" is the type size (10 point); "12" means a space between lines of two points, i.e., 2-point leading; "Times Roman" is the name of the typeface; and " × 26" means "by 26 picas," i.e., the width of the print line.

2.134   The type size, leading, and amount of indention, if any, should be placed beside the first extract (block quotation) in each chapter, or often only the first extract in a book. For example:

10/10 Times Roman
Indent 2 ems from left

Here "10/10" means 10-point type with no leading, i.e., 10 point solid. (For marking indentions with em quads, see 2.83.)

2.135   Poetry extracts, unless the design specifies otherwise, are generally marked "center on longest line" (shortened to "ctr" after first time in each chapter), regardless of the indention of the prose extracts. Poems with relatively long lines, however, such as blank verse, are all set to the same indention, specified by the designer. The placement of a source citation following a poetry extract should be specified. "Drop one line & ctr on last letter of longest line above" is the formula used successfully by the University of Chicago Press journal editors. In some works the editor and book designer may find it more feasible to place the source citations flush right or indented one or two ems from the right.

2.136   Indicate *all* extracts, and any other passages with the same type specifications, by drawing a colored vertical line to the left of each one. All vertical lines indicating the same type specifications should be in the same color; the University of Chicago Press favors red for extract lines. To draw colored lines indicating type specifications is called

73

color-coding. Even when type specifications are also written next to the passage, draw the colored line as well because it shows the exact beginning and end of the passage. Be sure to draw the line precisely to the bottom of the last line (see example, 2.83). In material with a variety of type specifications, a different color may be used for each, and the typesetter provided with a key to the color system.

2.137 Like extracts, subheads generally need be marked for type specifications only at the first occurrence in each chapter. All set-off subheads should be marked *A, B,* etc.—the letter circled—to indicate which level is intended (see 1.58). And if the subheads are to be set in small caps, italics, or boldface, each should be underlined accordingly at least the first time (see 2.75–77).

The Editorial Function

Mechanical Editing

2.138 An italic subhead that begins a paragraph (run-in side head) need not be marked either with a letter or with type specifications, if it will be set in the same type size and typeface as the text.

2.139 In marking the type specifications and designating the levels of sub-heads, the editor should also do the following:

1. Check the capitalization of each subhead to see that it follows the design specifications and, if it is to be caps and lowercase or caps and small caps, that it is capitalized according to the rules for capitalizing titles (7.123). Run-in side heads should have sentence capitalization.

2. Delete a period or other punctuation following a subhead set on a line by itself (use a period after a run-in side head).

3. Mark the placement of each subhead (center, flush left, etc.; see 2.81–82) and the amount of space above and below it (2.84).

4. Mark the first line of text following a subhead if the design calls for it to begin flush left or with an indention other than that used for a regular paragraph.

2.140 The first page of each section of back matter in a book should be marked with the type specifications for that section. Appendixes are often in the same type size as extracts in the text proper, but it is unnecessary to color-code them like the extracts, unless there are several type sizes required in the same section.

2.141 In a note section the type specifications may be given at the beginning of each chapter's notes or just at the beginning of the section. The editor should indicate whether note numbers are to be superior or on the line, whether each note begins with a paragraph indention or flush left, and whether any extra space is to be inserted between notes. The University of Chicago Press sets note numbers on the line rather than superscript, and both the indention and the space between notes depend on the designer's specifications. An unnumbered footnote to be set on the first page of the chapter should be labeled as such and placed at the foot of the first manuscript page of the chapter. (For a full description of notes and footnotes, see chapter 15.)

2.142   A bibliography or reference list arranged alphabetically, chronologically, or by some other system is customarily set "flush and hang." This means that the first line of each item is set flush left and any runover line is indented under it. Therefore, in addition to the type specifications for the bibliography, the editor should note the amount of indention specified for the runovers, the "hang":

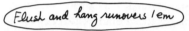

2.143   An index, like a bibliography, is set flush-and-hang style. If there are no indented subentries, runover lines are indented one em; if there is one level of indented subentry, indent all runovers two ems. Mark the subentries with em quads (see 2.82), and specify the amount of indention for the runovers along with the type specification note at the beginning of the index.

2.144   An index is usually set in two columns, the width of which must be specified. If the designer has not provided specifications, you can determine the width of one column by subtracting 1 from the pica width of the print line and dividing by 2. This will give 1 pica for the space between columns. Specifications for an index of a book with a 26-pica print line might read:

IDENTIFICATION AND PLACEMENT OF MATERIAL

2.145   Before the manuscript goes to the typesetter, where it will very likely be separated into parts for both typesetting and proofreading, the editor should identify each part in the top right corner of the first page. The author's last name and the part are usually sufficient: "Jones, chap. 3," "Jones, Bibliog." At the bottom of the last page of text of a chapter or other part the editor may write "End chap. 3." At the end of the last chapter the editor should tell the typesetter what is to follow in the book (not always the same as what follows in the manuscript): "End chap. 10. Appendix A follows," for example. Each section of the back matter should be so marked, and the last page of the last section of a book should indicate whether an index is to come: "End Bibliog., Index to follow," or, for example, "End chap. 15 & book. *No* index." All such notes to the typesetter should be circled, indicating that they are not to be set in type.

2.146 Any material that is separate from the text in the manuscript but is to be printed with the text—tables, figures, illustrations—must be identified with the author's name or the title of the work or both, and each item must be marked with the manuscript page number indicating where it belongs (see 2.105, 2.107). When figures or other illustrations are not included with the text but are to be inserted later, either the editor or the designer must specify the exact amount of vertical space to be left in the pages to accommodate each one.

NUMBERING PAGES

2.147 If the author has not numbered the manuscript pages consecutively, the editor must do so (see 2.7–10). If the author has numbered the pages, the editor should check the numbers and indicate to the typesetter any added or missing page numbers. For example, two pages added after page 54 are numbered 54a and 54b; on page 54, next to the page number, the editor notes: "54a–b follow." Similarly, if, say, pages 22–24 have been deleted, a note should be written on page 21: "p. 25 follows." (If there are many of these, and there usually are, the editor should renumber the whole manuscript.)

2.148 In addition to indicating the *roman* folios of the front matter (see 2.112), the editor should always note on the manuscript where the *arabic* folios are to begin in the book. A part title or a second half title preceding the text counts as page 1, and page 2 is normally blank. The editor will therefore mark the part title with a figure 1 at the bottom of the page, circling the number to indicate that it is not to be set, and will also, on the same page, note "p. 2 blank." The first page of the text will then be marked "folio 3," or "p. 3," indicating to the typesetter that 3 is the first folio to be set. If there is no part title or half title, the editor should indicate the beginning of the arabic folios by writing "folio 1" on the first page of text. The proofreader should transfer such notations to galley proofs.

OTHER INSTRUCTIONS

2.149 In addition to the manuscript edited and marked with type specifications, the editor should supply on separate sheets any special information or parts needed in the production of a particular manuscript. Such material includes spine (and cover) copy, running heads, list of special characters, style sheet for the proofreader, and a transmittal sheet telling what is included and what is yet to come (see 2.156 and fig. 2.3).

SPINE COPY

2.150   The layout should be consulted for what the designer has specified for the spine of the cloth cover and for what, if anything, is planned for the front cover. The editor then prepares copy accordingly.[20] Copy must also be prepared for the spine and cover of the book jacket. Normally the editor furnishes copy only for the author's name, title of the book, and the publisher's name. The marketing department provides flap copy and any other material for the front and back of a jacket. If the layout gives no specification for the spine, the editor will supply copy anyway, giving the full name of the author, the main title of the book, and the publisher's name, usually in shortened form ("Chicago" instead of "The University of Chicago Press").

RUNNING HEADS

2.151   The editor must provide copy from which running heads will be set.[21] This is usually typed in two columns, one for verso, the other for recto running heads. A running head for any preliminary matter that will occupy more than one printed page must be included, as well as the running head for the index. Since, except in special cases provided for by the designer, a running head must be short enough to fit in a single line, usually containing the page number (folio) as well, the editor must often shorten a title to fit. To do this it is necessary to determine from the designer's layout how many characters (letters, punctuation marks, and spaces between words) are allowed for the running head. Second, the most meaningful words in a title, considering the subject of the entire book and the significance of the chapter title within it, must be selected. (If titles must be drastically shortened as running heads, it is best to submit the list to the author for approval before type is set.) In shortening foreign language titles the editor must avoid omitting a word governing the case ending of another word included in the running head. Third, the editor will mark the running-head copy with the type specifications and will note also the specification for the folios. For example:

20. *Never* should the designer's layout be used as copy for typesetting.
21. For selection of material to be used in running heads see 1.78–80.

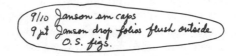

"Flush outside" means flush left on verso pages and flush right on recto pages. "O.S." means old style; see Glossary.

2.152 Running-head copy is usually sent with the edited manuscript to the production department and the typesetter. It may, in some cases, be sent with galley proofs returned to the compositor for page makeup.

2.153 In a work where the running head reflects what is on a given page, running heads cannot be prepared and set in type until pages have been made up (see 1.80).

LIST OF SPECIAL CHARACTERS

2.154 The typesetter usually needs to know what special characters have to be provided for a particular manuscript. Special characters normally are Greek letters, isolated mathematical or other symbols, letters bearing diacritical marks (except French accents and the German umlaut). The editor should prepare a separate list of such characters, including the manuscript page number where each first appears, the type size in which it is to be set, and whether it is italic or roman, capital or lowercase.

STYLE SHEET FOR PROOFREADER

2.155 Professional proofreaders, either in the printing house or in the publishing establishment, find it helpful to have a copy of the editor's style sheet (see 2.90). When thus advised of the editor's intentions, a proofreader will not query any of these particular points on proofs.

TRANSMITTAL SHEET

2.156 The last thing an editor usually does before turning an edited manuscript over to the production department for typesetting is to make a list of what is in the package. The University of Chicago Press has a form called "Editor's Checklist" (fig. 2.3) for this purpose, which the editor fills out in triplicate—one for the editor's file, two to go with the manuscript (one for the production department, the other for the typesetter). In addition to the author's full name, the correct title of the work, and the editor's name, this form lists all possible parts of a book, followed by two blank columns, one headed "Herewith," the other

UNIVERSITY OF CHICAGO PRESS
5801 S. Ellis Ave. / Chicago, Illinois 60637

AUTHOR:
TITLE:

Date:
Manuscript Editor:
House Editor:

GENERAL INFORMATION	EDITOR'S CHECK LIST	TRANSMITTAL INFORMATION		
	Items to be transmitted for this publication (√)	Here-with	To come (date)	For printer's use
Number of chapters				
Total number of MS pages				
Front matter				
Text				
End matter	**GENERAL**			
Notes print at:	Spine & cover layout			
Foot of page	Prelim layouts			
End of book	Text layouts			
Subheads (how many levels?)	Spine copy (2 copies)			
Reduced material	Running head copy			
Halftones	List spec. characters			
Print as figures on text paper				
Print as plates in special section(s)	**PRELIMS**			
Text figures				
	Half title			
	Series title			
HANDLING OF PROOF	Frontispiece			
	Title			
Editor's Proofs	Copyright			
	Dedication			
Galleys____sets	Epigraph			
Pages____sets	Contents			
	List of illustrations			
Author's Proofs	List of tables			
	List of abbreviations			
Galleys____sets	Foreword			
Pages____sets	Preface			
Allow____wks for galleys out & back	Acknowledgments			
Allow____wks for pages out & back	Introduction			
Allow____wks for index after last pages out				
	BODY OF BOOK			
SPECIAL INSTRUCTIONS				
	Second half title			
	Part half titles			
	Text (all or part?)			
	Tables (how many?)			
	Plates (how many?)			
	Figures (how many?)			
	Legend copy			
	Footnotes			
	END MATTER			
	Appendix(es)			
	Notes			
	List of Abbreviations			
	Glossary			
	Bibliography			
	Index			

Fig. 2.3. Transmittal sheet to accompany a manuscript from editor to production department.

"To Come." The editor checks the relevant items in the proper column and crosses out items irrelevant to the work concerned. The form also lists items not part of the work itself but necessary to its production and so provided by the editor where necessary. These include layout, spine copy, running-head copy, list of special characters, and editor's style sheet for the proofreader. Space is provided for instructions about the number of sets of proof needed by the author and the editor and, if the editor is not to mail proofs, the author's address and any special mailing instructions.

2.157   If a manuscript goes to production in piecemeal fashion (an uneconomical practice, but sometimes necessary), a complete transmittal sheet should accompany the first batch released, indicating what is yet to come. Successive batches should each be accompanied by a partial transmittal sheet (listing only what is being transmitted) so that the editor has a record of when all parts of the manuscript were released.

PREPARING MANUSCRIPT FROM PRINTED MATERIAL

USING COPIES OF THE ORIGINAL

2.158   Manuscript for anthologies, collected works, and other books containing previously published material should not be retyped unless the material has been substantially rewritten. The editor, compiler, or author of the volume must have *two* clean copies of the printed material to make one copy of the manuscript. Each page should be pasted or taped (not stapled) to a standard sheet of paper (8½ by 11 inches), so that the "manuscript" pages are of uniform size and the typesetter can follow the copy as if it were a typed manuscript. A Xerox or other machine copy may be made of the pasted-up pages to provide a second copy of the manuscript. (If the machine copy is clearer than the pasted-up copy, it may be used as the first copy; see 2.161.)

2.159   If footnotes on the original pages are to remain as footnotes (not endnotes), they may sometimes be left at the foot of the pasted-up pages, because to cut them apart and paste them on separate pages is to run the risk of losing some of them. If much editing must be done on the notes, if an editor's notes are intermingled with the original notes, or if footnotes are to be converted to endnotes, all notes should be pasted, or typed, on separate sheets. And all notes should be retyped and placed in a separate section for the typesetter when the original type is very small (e.g., 8/8) or faint.

2.160   Unless there is ample space to insert corrections above printed lines in the original, any corrections made in the original should be put in the margins, the method used in correcting proofs (see 3.15). Corrections squeezed between closely set lines are usually hard to see and often quite illegible.

MACHINE COPIES

2.161   When two clean copies of the original are not available for making the manuscript copy to be used by the typesetter, clear Xerox or other machine copies will serve the purpose, provided:

1. The lines of type do not turn up at the ends, reflecting the curve of a book's page as it is being copied.

2. All words at the ends of lines are present and clearly decipherable.

3. The image is not blurred and is neither too dark nor too light.

4. The paper on which the copy is made can be written upon with pencil.

2.162   Machine copies of original illustrations are unacceptable for reproduction. The editor or compiler should make every effort to procure glossy prints of the original illustration. Failing that, the publisher can usually have a reproduction made from the illustration in the original publication—without destroying the book or journal in which it appears.[22]

SOURCE NOTES

2.163   Each selection of previously published material should be accompanied either by a headnote before the text begins or by an unnumbered footnote on the first page of text giving the source of the selection (see 1.53) and the name of the copyright holder (see chap. 4). If the title has been changed, the original title should appear in the note.

2.164   Some selections in anthologies may have been previously published in several places and in several versions. The source note should give as much of the publishing history as necessary and, where there are several versions, should state which version is used.

2.165   Many complications may arise in seeking permissions from copyright holders and in phrasing source notes, and the compiler of an anthology may well need the advice of an expert. The matter should never be ignored or left to the last minute (see 4.38–58).

22. For a more detailed description of acceptable illustrations see chapter 11.

EDITING

2.166 Usually only certain alterations are permissible, without explanation, in editing material previously published. Notes may be renumbered consecutively throughout a selection or a chapter in a selection. Cross-references to parts of the original work not reprinted should be deleted. Obvious typographical errors, inadvertent grammatical slips, and unintentional inconsistencies in modern works may be corrected. Single quotation marks may be changed to double quotation marks, and double to single, following American practice (see 10.24), and periods and commas may be put inside a quotation mark (see 5.10). Words set in full capitals in the text may be marked for small capitals. Other typographical oddities should not be reproduced unless they contribute to the sense of the original. An old title page, for example, should not be set in type approximating the original typeface. (If desirable, it may be reproduced as an illustration.)

2.167 Unless the editor or compiler explains—in the preface or elsewhere—what kinds of changes have been made in the original text, all other matters of style should be retained: British or archaic spelling; excessive punctuation, or lack of punctuation; capitalization in the text and notes; style of footnotes (in some instances this may need slight modification for clarity). Any internal deletion in a selection should be indicated by ellipsis points (see 10.36).

2.168 The copyeditor should read all material for sense; there is always the chance that material has been pasted up out of order, that something has been omitted, that meaningless cross-references have not been deleted. Ambiguous hyphens at the ends of lines should be marked so that the typesetter will know when to keep the hyphen and when to close up the word. Discrepancies and apparently incorrect sentences should be queried, but no changes made without calling the volume editor's attention to them.

HANDLING SYMPOSIUM VOLUMES

2.169 Volumes in which each chapter is by a different author usually multiply, often magnify, the problems a publisher encounters in producing a one-author book. Even when the copyeditor does not have to deal directly with each author, to cope with from five to sixty-five or more styles—not only of the writing itself but of spelling and capitalization, footnotes or references in text, bibliographies, subheads, and tables, graphs, charts, or other artwork—can be a nightmare. Symposia, particularly papers read before a conference of scholars learned in a highly specialized subject, usually require the most time and effort.

And because the proceedings of a particular conference reflect the current state of research in that subject, it is highly desirable that they be published as soon after the conference as possible. A sense of urgency must be maintained through all stages of publishing the book.

PRELIMINARY PLANNING

2.170 Many problems and delays may be avoided and costs reduced through careful planning by the publisher (including the copyeditor) and the volume editor together before the manuscript has been submitted for publication. The functions and responsibilities of each should be clearly defined and understood.[23] The publisher, having agreed to publish the manuscript, will draw up the contract, arrange for the physical production of the volume, and send offprints and complimentary copies to contributors. Some of the functions listed below, as ideally the responsibility of the volume editor, may in particular cases be undertaken by the publisher, and these are the decisions to be made in the planning stage.

VOLUME EDITOR'S RESPONSIBILITIES

2.171 The term *volume editor* as used here refers not to a member of the publisher's staff but to the scholar selected, usually by the contributors to the symposium or the sponsors of it, to collect the papers for the volume and to work with the publisher. The competence and availability of the volume editor can affect the publication process at every stage. Ideally, the volume editor will undertake, and carry out, the following responsibilities, where applicable:

1. Getting manuscripts, including illustrations, from all contributors well before the date set for submitting the volume to the publisher

2. Sending a publishing agreement (a legal form provided by the publisher) to each contributor (see 4.30)

3. Getting written permission from copyright holders to reproduce any material previously copyrighted: papers published elsewhere, illustrations, tables, and the like taken from another work, as well as long quotations from secondary sources, which may require permission to use (see chap. 4)

4. Editing each paper, especially those written by foreign-born authors, for sense and grammar, and checking lists of references and other apparatus for uniformity of style

23. If there is more than one volume editor, the exact responsibilities of each editor must be spelled out in advance. Two or more editors attempting to perform the same functions during the publication process will delay production and may easily frustrate the copyeditor with conflicting directives.

5. Sending edited or rewritten manuscripts to the contributors for their approval *before* the volume goes to the publisher

6. Editing any discussions to be included in the volume and getting any necessary approvals from the discussants

7. Providing a list of contributors, with their affiliations, to be printed in the volume, or an identifying note for each contributor to be printed as an unnumbered footnote on the first page of the paper

8. Providing copy for the title page and the table of contents and writing, or providing, any necessary prefatory material

9. Sending the manuscript to the publisher, either complete or chapter by chapter, in a form acceptable for publication

10. Checking the manuscript after it has been edited by the publisher's copyeditor and answering the copyeditor's queries

11. Reading the master proofs

12. Sending all contributors copies of their proofs (*if* the contributors are to see proofs), *setting a strict deadline for the return of the proofs,* and transferring corrections from contributors' proofs to the master proofs before returning the master proofs to the publisher

13. Preparing the index

14. Determining how many offprints (reprints) each contributor will want (the publisher usually has a form for this) and providing the publisher with a list of mailing addresses to which offprints should be sent

2.172   In general, the volume editor should take responsibility for keeping the production schedule set by the publisher and for seeing that each contributor returns edited manuscript or proof by the date stipulated; one dilatory contributor may delay the entire project. The volume editor should also answer any questions and settle any complaints from individual contributors.

2.173   Since the volume editor is usually a busy professor for whom the task of editing the proceedings of a symposium is an added chore, he or she will seek to lighten the burden. A competent secretary is of course invaluable. Notifying contributors ahead of time about what is expected of them may save time. If possible, the volume editor should inform the contributors, before they prepare their papers, of the publisher's requirements concerning manuscripts acceptable for publication, including a uniform style for listing references, and should also notify them of what they may expect to see in the way of proofs (or, sometimes, edited manuscript) and approximately when. And the volume editor must know where the contributors can be reached at all times during the publication process.

COPYEDITOR'S RESPONSIBILITIES

2.174   The publisher's copyeditor may find it necessary to perform some of the functions outlined above, if the volume editor is unable or unwilling to do so. It is very important, therefore, that the exact division of responsibility for a particular volume be decided at the preliminary planning stage. The copyeditor should be fully aware of everyone's responsibilities, since the copyeditor must see that the volume goes through the publication process as quickly as possible and thus must know what is happening to all parts of the volume at all times.

2.175   The copyeditor must also copyedit the entire manuscript. The volume editor cannot usually be expected to bring about consistency in capitalization, spelling, abbreviations, and so forth. Rewording or substantive editing should be kept to an absolute minimum, especially when contributors are not to see copyedited manuscripts. Queries, also kept to a minimum, should be addressed to the volume editor, to whom the copyedited manuscript should be sent unless other arrangements have been made in advance.

2.176   Such volumes often come to a copyeditor not complete but chapter by chapter and not necessarily in sequence. To keep track of matters, the copyeditor will need to prepare a schedule sheet of some kind. The left-hand column should list the chapters in the order in which they will appear in the finished volume. Columns are then provided in which to record the specific dates when (1) copy is received, (2) edited copy goes to volume editor, (3) edited copy returns from volume editor, (4) manuscript goes to printer, (5) proofs are received and sent to volume editor, and (6) proofs are returned from volume editor. Where pertinent, it is helpful also to note the number of illustrations and tables in each chapter. Both illustrations and tables are numbered consecutively in each chapter, not throughout the volume—that is, the first figure in each chapter is figure 1, the first table is table 1.[24] In some volumes a double numeration system is used for tables and figures: chapter number, period, table number. In chapter 2, for example, tables are numbered 2.1, 2.2, 2.3, etc.

FOR FURTHER REFERENCE

2.177   Nearly all the works listed in the Bibliography of this manual are helpful to editors and authors. Among the most generally useful are H. W. Fowler, *A Dictionary of Modern English Usage,* 2d ed. revised by Sir

24. All illustrations and separate tables should be identified by the name of the author of the chapter as well as by the name of the volume editor and the number of the item, to avoid confusion in makeup.

Ernest Gowers, for refined distinctions regarding English usage, with entertaining and informative examples; Theodore M. Bernstein, *The Careful Writer* and *Miss Thistlebottom's Hobgoblins,* for modern idiom and for avoiding jargon and other forms of bad writing; Porter G. Perrin, *Writer's Guide and Index to English,* or the survey in *Words into Type,* for grammar and syntax. All authors and their editors should be familiar with Strunk and White's little classic, *The Elements of Style,* now in its third edition.

3 *Proofs*

Introduction 3.1
Schedules 3.4
First Proofs 3.6
    Master Proofs 3.7
    Dead Manuscript 3.8
Reading Proofs 3.9
    Typographical Errors 3.9
    Word Division 3.11
    Coding 3.12
    Type Fonts 3.13
    Sense 3.14
Correcting Proofs 3.15
    Proofreaders' Marks 3.19
        Operational signs 3.20
        Typographical signs 3.32
        Punctuation marks 3.34
    PE and AA 3.35
Second Proofs 3.38
Page Proofs 3.40
    Running Heads and Folios 3.41
    Adjusting Page Length 3.44
    Table of Contents 3.45
    Preliminary Pages 3.48
Index Proofs 3.49
Illustrations 3.50
Other Proofs 3.53
    Reproduction Proofs 3.54
    Blueprints 3.55
Case and Jacket 3.56
Press Sheets 3.57
Finished Book 3.58
For Further Reference 3.59

INTRODUCTION

3.1   The previous edition of this manual, published in 1969, presupposed the tidy progression of a finished, edited manuscript through galley proof to page proof to book. Hot-metal typesetting, principally Linotype or Monotype, was the usual method of composition in the printshop. All proofs showed typefaces as they would be in the finished book, with lines justified and headings in place; italics, diacritical marks, math symbols, illustrative material (except halftones) were all book-ready. The advent of electronic and computerized typesetting equipment has altered many features of these older printing systems and has introduced new methods and increased capabilities. For an account of these operations see chapter 20, especially 20.126–29. For unfamiliar terms see the Glossary.

3.2   In today's streamlined and economy-minded "printshops" proof is rarely read as carefully as it was in the days when a trained *printer's proofreader* scrutinized every word on the proofs while a *copyholder* read aloud from the manuscript. Now proofs are likely to be checked by the compositor who set the type or by a single proofreader who can only glance at the manuscript from time to time while reading rapidly through the proofs before sending them back to the compositor for correcting and returning to the publisher. Eliminating typographical errors, pointing out the omission or misplacement of material, even rectifying poor page makeup and other printing lapses—all have become in varying degrees the responsibility of the publisher and also of the author concerned for accuracy in the printed work.

3.3   Although the new technology with its different procedures and different kinds of proofs has changed many aspects of the traditional book production process, proofreading terms and the method of marking paper proofs in whatever form remain essentially the same. All editors and authors should therefore have a thorough knowledge of standard proofreaders' terminology and should be proficient in marking proofs correctly. These skills, and their place in the production of printed works, are the subject of this chapter.

SCHEDULES

3.4   After an editor has transmitted a manuscript to the production department for typesetting, a schedule is prepared stipulating dates for receipt and return of proofs and index and, depending on the typesetting process to be used, any further steps in the production process requiring the publisher's attention. The final date on the schedule is the *delivery* date, the day finished books are to be delivered by the printer or binder to the publisher's warehouse. The schedule is affected by various factors, chief among them the compositor's and printer's workloads—when the typesetting will take place, when the book will go on press, and finally when the bindery can finish the job. Among other factors are the proximity of the author to the publisher (mailing time must be taken into account), the complexity of the book, and the date on which the publisher wants to issue it (*publication* date, some weeks after delivery date).

3.5 Most publishers interpret the production schedule for the author in terms of deadlines, basically the dates (1) when proofs will go to the author and (2) when the author will be expected to return them to the publisher and (3) when the index manuscript will be expected. An author who cannot meet the specified deadlines should inform the editor at once. Proofs returned even a few days late may delay production of the book for weeks. A busy typesetting house schedules its work far ahead and when a certain time has been allotted for making up or revising pages of a book and the author's proofs have not been returned in time, the process must be rescheduled for a later (sometimes much later) date. When the delivery date (and therefore the publication date) is put off, the marketing department is also affected, since plans for announcing, advertising, and distributing the book must be timed to reflect its actual appearance. Production schedules are therefore very important; they are not to be filed and forgotten.

FIRST PROOFS

3.6 The term "first proofs" is used here to mean the first set of proofs, either galley proofs or page proofs, sent by the compositor to the publisher, and by the publisher to the author. Publishers sometimes ask authors to read both galleys and pages (i.e., galleys as first proofs, pages as second proofs), sometimes only one or the other, usually pages (because the author needs pages to make the index).

MASTER PROOFS

3.7 Normally two copies (sets) of the proofs are sent to the author, along with the manuscript from which type was set. One set, called *master proofs,* or *marked proofs,* carries the compositor's or proofreader's queries, if any, and is the copy to be returned to the publisher with the author's corrections marked on it. The second set is to be retained by the author for reference and, if proofs are page proofs, for indexing. The author may wish to transfer corrections to this copy. Some publishers do not send master proofs to authors, partly for safety's sake and partly because authors sometimes correct their proofs in such a way that the typesetter has difficulty in deciphering the author's intentions. Instead, the editor transfers the proofreader's corrections to another copy—the author's copy—and sends this, along with an unmarked copy, for the author to read. When the author returns corrected proofs, the editor then transfers the author's corrections to the master copy. Only *one* copy of proofs—the master copy with *all* corrections on it—should be returned to the compositor.

DEAD MANUSCRIPT

3.8   The manuscript from which type has been set is called *dead manuscript,* or *dead copy.* The University of Chicago Press—as do most other publishers—sends the dead manuscript to the author along with the first proofs and requests that it be returned with the master proofs. The author is expected to read proofs against the manuscript and to put corrections only on the proof sheets. No correction—no mark at all—should ever be made on the dead manuscript by the author or the editor. The manuscript must be kept, for the record, exactly as it went to the typesetter.[1]

READING PROOFS

TYPOGRAPHICAL ERRORS

3.9   The most effective, the ideal, way to catch "typos" in first proofs is for two people to read together, as printers' proofreaders used to do. One follows the proofs while the other, the copyholder, reads aloud from the manuscript. The copyholder should speak clearly and at a steady pace. In addition to reading the text the copyholder signals the beginning of paragraphs (par, pronounced pair), all punctuation marks (names are usually abbreviated: com [,], sem [;], query [?], bang or screamer [!], quotes ["], close quotes ["], poz [']), italics in the text, capitals or lowercase where there might be some question about which is used. All figures in text, tables, mathematical copy, and so forth should receive special attention.

3.10   The reader following the proof should have a good grasp of spelling in order to spot errors; regardless of education or intellectual capacity, a poor speller is a poor proofreader.

WORD DIVISION

3.11   When a word must be divided at the end of a printed line, the way it is divided has become more important in proofreading than it used to be. In hot-metal and typewriter composition, and in some photocom-

1. Publishers usually keep manuscripts, and corrected proofs, for a certain length of time after the book has appeared—a year, or until the printer's bill has been received—in case of controversy over charges or to check errors found in the printed book. The University of Chicago Press returns manuscripts to its authors if they want to keep them.

posing methods, the keyboard operator decides where a word should be divided. Hence, accuracy is chiefly a meeting of minds between operator and proofreader. When copy is "set" electronically, however, end-of-line hyphenation is often performed by computer. While computers can be programmed to divide words according to one system or another (hyphenation routines), and some have compendious "exception dictionaries" stored in their data banks, not all computers are yet able to handle every problem of word division. It is wise therefore to check end-of-line hyphens carefully, not only in first proofs but in any revised proofs as well (3.39). For example, when an error in a single word is corrected, only that word is reset, but when such a correction changes the length of the line in which it occurs, that line and all the following lines in the paragraph will end differently after running through the computer again. The result may be new word divisions to be checked. For guidance in dividing words see 6.33–47.

CODING

3.12   When type is to be set by computer, the tape or disk that drives the typesetting device is usually coded to indicate matters such as where and how to set headings, excerpts, tables, etc., when italics (or boldface) are to begin and end, and how much spacing to insert where needed. Mistakes in inserting code symbols may result in errors on proofs seldom or never encountered in hot-metal typesetting. A heading may be in the wrong place or the wrong type size, for example, or several words following an italic title in the text may also be set in italic. Such errors are usually caught and rectified before proofs are sent to a publisher, but not always.

TYPE FONTS

3.13   Broken type and wrong fonts, hazards of hot-metal typesetting, are usually spotted by a printer's proofreader trained to recognize such errors. Photocomposition proofs sometimes show only part of a letter or a word, not because type is broken but because a piece of foreign matter (dust, a scrap of paper) has got onto the repro proofs (camera-ready copy) or film negative; this rare "error" should be marked so that the printer can correct it by removing the obstructing object. Blurred or fuzzy type and spotty paper do *not* indicate errors, however, and should not be marked.

SENSE

3.14   In addition to reading proofs for mechanical aberrations discussed in the preceding paragraphs, authors understandably wish to read their

91

works for sense. Ideally such a reading should take place after the initial word-for-word proofreading. Since all source checking and final substantive and stylistic changes should have been made on the edited manuscript (2.125), authors must refrain from rewriting in proofs in any way except to correct the most flagrant error of fact (see 3.35–37).

CORRECTING PROOFS

3.15 Unlike corrections on the manuscript, corrections on proofs must always be put in the margin, left or right, next to the line of type in which the correction is to be made. A mark within the line—a caret for an addition, a line through a letter or word to be deleted—will indicate where the correction is to be made. Never should a correction, or addition, be written above a line of type. The typesetter responsible for making corrections scans the margins only and will not see writing buried between lines of type. Where more than one alteration is to be made in a line, corrections should be marked in the margin in the order they are to be made in the line, reading from left to right; a vertical or slant line separates one correction from the next. Remember that in proofreading every mark in the margin requires a mark in the line, and vice versa. Guidelines (lines drawn from the point in the line where the correction is to be made to the explanation of it in the margin) are unnecessary, and undesirable, unless the correction cannot be put next to the line. When guidelines are used, they should never cross each other; if they must cross—as in transposing several items in an index, for example—a different color should be used for each.

3.16 Where many errors occur in a line or two, it is best to cross out the whole passage containing the errors and write it all correctly in the margin because the typesetter will need less time to read the rewritten passage than to figure out where each of many small corrections should be made. A longer correction, or addition, should be typed on a separate slip and fastened (with gummed tape or straight pin, not paper clip) by one end to the proof. A note in the margin, circled, reading "Insert attached," and a caret in the line to show where it goes, will alert the typesetter (don't forget to cross out a passage being replaced). A circled note on the slip itself will tell the typesetter where it belongs should the slip become detached from the proof—for example, "Insert gal. 4," "Insert p. 10." If more than one such insert must be made on a single proof (page), each should be identified by letter: Insert A, gal. 4; Insert B, gal. 4; etc. The note in the margin of the proof then reads: Insert A attached, etc. To save resetting type, any such addition should be a separate paragraph or should be added to the end of an existing paragraph. In page proofs every effort must be made to adjust spacing so that pages will not have to be remade (see 3.37). (Remaking pages affects the index and often also the placement of illustrations.)

3.17 In correcting proofs, authors and editors should use a color different from that used by the proofreader. Either a clear, sharp pencil or a pen is acceptable; soft, easily blurred pencil marks and barely legible handwriting are two undesirable ways to make corrections on proofs.

3.18 Master proofs to be returned to the typesetter must never be cut apart for any reason. Material to be transposed from one galley or page to another should be so marked in the margin; for example, a paragraph on galley 4 to be moved to galley 5 would be marked "tr to gal. 5," and the place where it is to be inserted on galley 5 would be marked "tr from gal. 4."

PROOFREADERS' MARKS

3.19 With the first set of proofs sent to the publisher some typesetters include elaborate instructions on how to make corrections. These should be followed if possible; they will differ little from the instructions given here. Symbols and marks explained in the following paragraphs and illustrated in figure 3.1 are commonly understood by printers of publications in the English language. For purposes of discussion and for easier comprehension by those unfamiliar with them, proofreaders' marks may be classified as (1) operational signs, (2) typographical signs, and (3) signs clarifying certain punctuation marks to be inserted.

3.20 *Operational signs.* The *delete* sign is used only when something is to be removed from a line—a letter, a word or more, a whole line—without substitution. It is *not* used when another letter, word, or line is to be inserted in place of the deleted matter. A diagonal line through a letter to be deleted, a straight line through a word or more to be deleted, indicates where the deletion is to be made. Matter to be deleted from a typeset line should not be obliterated to the extent that the compositor cannot see what to take out; a comma or period or single letter likely to be totally covered by the in-line delete mark may be circled instead, so that it is still visible. The form of the delete sign written in the margin need not be exactly as shown in figure 3.1, but it should be made in such a way as not to be confused with any handwritten letter, such as *d, e,* or *l.* Where a letter is to be deleted from the middle of a word, the delete sign may be written within close-up marks (*delete and close up*), although this is not necessary unless there might be some doubt in the typesetter's mind, such as what to do with a word from which a hyphen has been deleted.

93

PROOFREADER'S MARKS

OPERATIONAL AND TYPOGRAPHICAL SIGNS

ℱ	Delete	*ital*	Set in *italic* type
◡	Close up; delete space	*rom*	Set in roman type
ℱ	Delete and close up (use only when deleting letters *within* a word)	*bf*	Set in **boldface** type
stet	Let it stand	*lc*	Set in lowercase (uncapitalized)
#	Insert space	*cap*	Set in CAPITAL letters
eq #	Make space between words equal; make leading between lines equal	*sc*	Set in SMALL CAPITALS
hr #	Insert hair space	*wf*	Wrong font; set in correct type
ls	Letterspace	X	Reset broken letter
¶	Begin new paragraph	∨	Insert here *or* make superscript (N²)
□	Move type one em from left or right	∧	Insert here *or* make subscript (Nₜ)
⊐	Move right		PUNCTUATION MARKS
⊏	Move left	⌄,	Insert comma
⊐⊏	Center	⌄⸜	Insert apostrophe (or single quotation mark)
⊓	Move up	⌄⌄	Insert quotation marks
⊔	Move down	⊙	Insert period
fl	Flush left	⎬⎭ ?	Insert question mark
fr	Flush right	⌖|	Insert semicolon
=	Straighten type; align horizontally	:|	Insert colon
‖	Align vertically	|=|	Insert hyphen
tr	Transpose	⊥/M	Insert em dash
sp	Spell out	⊥/N	Insert en dash
		(|)	Insert parentheses

Fig. 3.1

EXAMPLE OF MARKED PROOF

⌐ Authors As Proofreaders ⌐

⌐ "I don't care what kind of type you use for my
book," said a myopic author to the publisher, but please
print the galley proofs in large type. Perhaps in the
future such a request will not sound so ridiculous ⌐
to those familar with the printing process. Today,
however, type once set is not reset exept to correct
errors.

1. Type may be reduced in size, or enlarged photographically when a
book is printed by offset.

Proofreading is an Art and a craft. All authors
should know the rudiments thereof, though no
proofreader expects them to be masters of it. Watch
proofreader expects them to be masters of it. Watch
not only for misspelled or incorrect works (often a
most illusive error, but also for misplace dspaces, "un-
closde" quotation marks, and parenthesjs, and im-
poryper paragraphing; and learn to recognize the
difference between an em dash—used to separate an
interjectional part of a sentence—and an en dash, used
commonly between continuing numbers, e.g., pp.
5–10; q.d. 1165/70) and the word, dividing hyphen.
Sometimes, too, a letter from a wrong font will creep
a mathematical formula. Whatever is underlined in
into the printed text, or a boldface k, or ⓓ turn up,
in a MS. should, of course, be italicized in print.
Two lines drawn beneath letters or words indicate
that these are to be reset in small capitals, three
lines indicate full capitals. To find the errors over-
looked by the proofreader is the authors first problem in proof reading. The sec/ond problem is to
make corrections, using the marks and symbols,
devized by proffesional proofreaders, than any trained
typesetter will understand. The third—and most
difficult, problem for authors proofreading their own
works is to resist the temptation to rewrite in proofs.

Manuscript editor

3.21   Too much space between letters is corrected by the *close-up* sign, used in the line as well as in the margin. Sometimes the last letter of a word appears at the beginning of the next word; when this happens, the close-up mark followed by a space mark is written in the margin, and a close-up mark and a vertical line indicating the space are inserted in the line.

3.22   The *space* mark is used to call for more space between words; a vertical line or caret shows where the space is to be inserted. The space mark may also be used to show where extra space (leading) is needed between lines. Words in the same line should be separated by the same amount of space. When the word spaces in a single line are unequal, the *equal-space* sign is written in the margin and carets are inserted in the line to mark the difficulty. Note that spacing between words in two successive lines is not necessarily equal in justified composition (see 19.26). Hair spaces, thin spaces, and letter spaces are generally matters of design and need not concern an author unless there appears to be some inconsistency in the setting of similar material.

3.23   A *paragraph* sign in the margin tells the typesetter to begin a new paragraph; in the line either another paragraph sign before the first word of the new paragraph or, more common, an L-shaped mark to the left and partly under the word will show the typesetter where to begin the paragraph. To run two paragraphs together, a *no paragraph* sign is written in the margin and a line drawn from the end of one paragraph to the beginning of the next.

3.24   Indention of a line one em from the left or right margin is indicated by a small, open square drawn in the left or right margin next to the line to be moved; another square, or a caret, is drawn next to the material itself. An indention of two or more ems may be indicated either by the desired figure written inside one square or by a rectangle divided into two or more squares.

3.25   The signs for *moving* type *right* or *left* or for *centering* are used when a line of type is printed too far to the left or right—when a subtitle, an item in a table, or a letter has been set in the wrong place horizontally. Signs for moving type *up* or *down* are used when something has been set on the wrong line—is vertically out of place. All these signs are used in the line as well as written in the margin.

3.26   The sign for *aligning horizontally*—marked in the line as well as in the margin—is used when one or more letters have slipped slightly above or below the line. In machine-copy proofs uneven or wavy type is likely to be the fault of the copying machine (not the composition) and should be ignored in proofreading.

3.27   The sign for *vertical* alignment should be used sparingly in correcting proof; the left and right type margins are often slightly irregular in proofs from hot-metal typesetting because the type itself has not yet been locked in place for printing. In photocomposition vertical mis-alignment is rare. The sign should be used mainly to indicate inaccurate alignment in tabular matter.

3.28   The sign for *transposing* is used for letters, words, phrases, lines, paragraphs, or any other material to be moved from one place to another. The indication of where the transposition is to be made in the line is drawn in the same way as in editing a manuscript (see 2.63–64), but *tr* must appear in the margin in proofs so that the typesetter will see the change.

3.29   When abbreviations or figures set in type are to be spelled out, they should be circled in the line and the *spell-out* sign written in the margin. Note that to spell out something in the text means that the line will be longer, possibly making the paragraph and the page longer unless compensation is made for the extra space (see 3.37). Also, the full word should be written in the margin, instead of the sign, if there is any ambiguity about spelling (see 2.79).

3.30   The word *stet* is used to tell the typesetter not to take out something earlier marked for deletion. Dots under the crossed-out material indicate what is to remain. Where a note in the margin is also crossed out, *stet as set* will clarify what to let stand.

3.31   The direction to "push down type" applies to hot metal, where a letter is occasionally raised higher than the others and therefore prints darker or where a space quad between words is too high and turns up printed as a black rectangle. The mark may be used in photocomposition proofs to indicate a line of type much darker than the others on the page (for various mechanical and climatic reasons a line that has been reset to make a correction and then pasted back in place on a repro proof may be darker than the type set originally).

3.32   *Typographical signs*. Letters set in the wrong kind of type are corrected as follows. To make a capital letter lowercase, draw a diagonal line through the letter and write *lc* in the margin. To capitalize a lowercase letter, draw three lines under the letter (or letters) and write *cap* (*caps*) in the margin. Indicate small capitals by two lines under the letter and *sc* in the margin. To italicize, draw one line under the word and write *ital* in the margin. To have italicized words reset in roman type, circle the words and write *rom* in the margin. Indicate boldface type by a wavy line under the letter or word and *bf* in the margin.

3.33   Errors occurring in proofs from hot-metal typesetting are wrong font (*wf*), broken type (x), or a letter turned upside down; for these, circle the error and write the appropriate symbol in the margin. The mark x is used in photocomposition proofs to indicate a blemish on the repro proof or film negative.

3.34   *Punctuation marks*. To change a punctuation mark—from a comma to a semicolon, for example—draw a vertical line through or circle the mark and write the correct one in the margin. To supply a mark where none appears, place a caret at the spot and the correct mark in the margin. Since a handwritten comma, apostrophe, and parenthesis may be confused one with another, a comma written in the margin should have a caret mark over it; an apostrophe, or quotation mark, should have a reversed caret under it, indicating its superior position; a parenthesis should simply be made large enough not to be taken for one of the smaller marks. Hyphens and en and em dashes should be differentiated by their appropriate symbols (see fig. 3.1). A period, being small, should be circled. Semicolons, colons, question marks, and exclamation points, if written clearly, need no further identifying marks, except that a question mark that might be mistaken for a query should be followed by *set* with a circle around it.

PE AND AA

3.35   The typesetter's job is to *follow copy* exactly. Any deviation from the manuscript found on the proofs, such as a misspelled, wrong, or missing word, is attributed to the typesetter. In times gone by, typesetter and printer were the same person or firm, and such an error is still called a printer's error (PE). Any change made by an author (or editor) in proofs, including cross-references that must be filled in on page proofs, is called an author's alteration (AA). When authors are to be charged for their alterations, PE or AA (*or* pe, aa) should be written and circled in the margin next to each proof correction. When an editor makes a change that should not be attributed to the author, some other signal may be used, such as EA or a line under AA. Another way to distinguish between printer's errors and author's alterations is to use a different color for each. (Always use a different color from that used by the typesetter or printer's proofreader for corrections or other marks on the master proofs.)

3.36   Many authors do not realize how costly alterations can be. An allowance of 5 percent stipulated by an author's contract does *not* mean 5 percent of the number of lines, or words, in a book! It refers instead to the typesetter's charges for time necessary to make the changes. This is often considerably more than the time spent in, and therefore the charge for, setting the material in the first place. The processes involved in making simple corrections in proofs may cost an average of $60 per hour. Changes made in proofs also often result in further errors—a line may be reinserted in the wrong place, for instance—and many changes will delay production and throw off schedules all along the production line. Clearly, it is extremely important for both author and publisher to keep proof corrections of any kind to a minimum.

3.37   Sometimes disaster strikes, however, and a change must be made at the last minute. Then author or editor should rewrite enough to compensate for space added or deleted by the change. Some cooperative and knowledgeable authors even compensate for typesetter's errors that could require substantial resetting. Authors should keep in mind that additions may be made more easily in galley proofs than in pages. Any addition of more than, say, one line in page proofs will throw off not only pagination but index entries as well.

SECOND PROOFS

3.38   The term "second proofs" is used here to mean a new set of proofs sent by the printer to the publisher after corrections have been made on the first proofs (see 3.6). If they are page proofs and are to be sent to the author, two sets are sent, marked as were the first proofs (3.7). The first proofs, now called *foul galleys* or *foul proofs,* are sent to the author with the second proofs and should be returned to the publisher with the master copy of the second proofs. As with dead manuscript (3.8), authors and editors must make no mark whatever on foul proofs. If the second proofs are revised galleys or revised pages, they are usually checked only by the publisher.

3.39   Second proofs are not read against manuscript but only checked against the first proofs to see that all corrections have been made and no further errors introduced. To do this most expeditiously, put the two proofs side by side and check to see that each correction has been made. In hot-metal composition and in some kinds of photocomposition, making one correction means resetting an entire line and putting it back in its place, either of which operations can produce another error: a new typographical error in the line may appear, and the line may be reinserted in the wrong place. In proofs from these methods of composition, therefore, each reset line, or lines, must be proofread carefully, and lines above and below must be checked to make sure the line has been put back in the right place. In computerized typesetting, individual corrections are made without resetting whole lines but end-of-line word divisions must be checked in paragraphs where corrections have been made (see 3.11).

PAGE PROOFS

3.40   Page proofs may be either first proofs or second proofs (see 3.6). They must be looked upon by author and editor as complete *pages* in the book or article and checked as such. The top and bottom lines of text on each page should be checked to make sure nothing has been dropped. Any footnote must be checked to make sure it begins on the page that carries its reference; the note itself may run over to the next page. Any table, equation, excerpt, figure, or other illustrative matter must appear where it belongs, or the correct amount of space must have been provided for its later insertion. Other matters to be checked—running heads and folios, page length, preliminary pages—are taken up in the following paragraphs.

RUNNING HEADS AND FOLIOS

3.41   Running heads and folios on every page must be checked, usually by the editor when page proofs are returned from the author. It is best to do this as a separate operation, not while checking the text pages. A running head may be missing altogether, the wrong running head may have been inserted through part of a chapter, a word may suddenly turn up misspelled in a running head halfway through a chapter. Running heads and folios should be deleted by the editor from any page containing *only* a table or an illustration (see 1.83, 1.87). Careful, undivided attention is thus required to check running heads. Folios are usually accurate but sometimes one is omitted or set in the wrong place; and, in very rare instances, folios may somehow have got out of sequence (if this should happen, the indexer must be notified of the correct pagination).

3.42   When a section of notes at the back of a book requires page numbers in the running heads (see 1.82, 15.56–57), the editor should insert the numbers or should check all numbers supplied by the author.

3.43   For running heads made up of subheads or other subdivisions of a chapter, as in this manual, see 1.80. These, like all running heads, are primarily the editor's responsibility (see 2.151–53).

ADJUSTING PAGE LENGTH

3.44   The length of the type page, specified by the book designer and carefully observed by the compositor, need concern the author or the editor only when the makeup process runs into difficulties. In regular text material it is permissible to let *facing pages* (verso and recto; pp. 68 and 69, for example) each run one line long or one line short to avoid a widow (short line at the end of a paragraph) at the top of a page or to fit footnotes and their references on the same page (see 20.35–37). It is also permissible—indeed necessary—to let one page run short if a subhead or only one line of an excerpt would fall at the bottom of the page. Sometimes, however, the compositor is unable to make a page come out right and will ask the author or the editor to *save a line (lose a line)* or to *make a line*. To save a line, one looks for the paragraph with the shortest last line—preferably only a word or two—on the page and deletes enough characters from the paragraph to accommodate the last line at the end of the line above. To make a line is to add a phrase or a longer word so that the last line of a paragraph will run over to a new line. In hot-metal composition such changes should be made as close to the end of the paragraph as possible, because all subsequent lines must be reset in consequence of the change. In computerized composition, it makes no difference where in the paragraph the change is made.

TABLE OF CONTENTS

3.45   Page numbers are inserted, usually by the editor, in the table of contents after all pages (except the index) have been received from the typesetter. The page on which the index will start is the first recto page after the end of the text pages and any back matter preceding the index. If more than one index is to be included, the page numbers for any index other than the first cannot be determined until index page proof has been received. When someone other than the editor—the typesetter or the author, for example—has inserted page numbers in the table of contents, the editor should check each number carefully against the page proofs.

3.46   The wording of chapter titles and other parts of the book in the table of contents should also be checked carefully once more in page proofs. In checking the table of contents, the editor should look at each page of the page proofs to make sure nothing has been omitted from the table of contents that should be in it; this is particularly important in checking tables of contents that include subheads as well as chapter titles.

3.47   Any list of illustrations, figures, or tables should be carefully checked in the same way as the table of contents, and page numbers supplied when they are missing. Although some typesetters do supply page numbers in contents and lists in the preliminary pages, no typesetter should be expected to do so, and certainly not after corrected page proofs have been returned by the publisher.

PRELIMINARY PAGES

3.48 Display preliminary pages (pp. i–iv; see 1.1–27) should be checked carefully by production department and designer for fidelity to the design specified; by the person in charge of contracts (permissions secretary or other) for information on the copyright page; and by the editor and author for typographical errors of any kind. A misspelled word in these pages—the author's name for instance—is an inexcusable catastrophe in a printed book.

INDEX PROOFS

3.49 The urgency of preparing and editing indexes on schedule has been pointed out elsewhere (2.114). Most typesetters also feel a sense of urgency about setting type for and proofreading an index when they receive manuscript copy. Except in rare instances, the University of Chicago Press sends neither the edited manuscript nor the proofs of an index to the author. The editor reads the index proofs carefully, with a copyholder, as soon as they are received; they are usually returned to the typesetter in less than twenty-four hours.

ILLUSTRATIONS

3.50 Black-and-white text figures (which for offset printing may include halftone reproductions of photographs) print along with the text and may therefore be placed anywhere in the book, rather than tipped in or grouped in unpaginated plate sections. This means that the correct amount of space, either part of a page or a full page, must be allowed for each illustration when pages are made up. Consequently, before that time comes, the designer (if necessary, the editor) must crop and scale all illustrations (see 11.15–20) and make a record of the vertical space each will require on the page.

3.51 When first proofs are to be pages, explicit instructions about placement and size of illustrations must go to the typesetter with the manuscript. When first proofs are galleys, instructions must be returned with corrected galleys to the typesetter, including (1) a list of all illustrations and their finished sizes, together with the galley numbers of the passages they are to accompany, and (2) circled notes in the appropriate galley margins: e.g., "fig. 2 about here."

3.52   The editor bears chief responsibility for seeing that correct spaces are left in proofs for all illustrations, for proofreading the legends, and for inspecting the illustrations at whatever stage they turn up, usually in blueprints of the offset negatives (see 3.55), to see that they are printed right side up, that they have not been flopped (turned over, resulting in a mirror image), and that each is accompanied by its proper legend. If authors are to see illustrations in place, they should be reminded that any alteration at this stage means remaking the drawing, rephotographing, and restripping, with heavy expense and serious delay.

OTHER PROOFS

3.53   Page proofs are normally the last proofs seen by an author. If the book is to be printed by offset lithography, as most books are now, the publisher will usually see further proofs before printing. The editor should check these to see that all corrections in page proofs have been made, that all material is there and in the correct order.

REPRODUCTION PROOFS

3.54   Reproduction proofs, or "repros" as they are usually called, are the actual camera copy from which the book will be photographed and printed. Repros from metal type are printed on special coated paper, and from photocomposition on high-quality photographic paper; they represent the quality of image to be achieved in the final printing. The editor should not make any changes on repros except to correct typographical errors (and then only serious ones). Any such corrections should be made in the margin with a *light blue* pencil, a color that the camera does not pick up. Only the faintest of blue marks should be made on the type area itself. A list of page numbers on which such corrections have been made should go to the production department with the corrected repros. If two sets of repros are available, the art department can often make corrections by cutting letters from another set of repros and pasting them carefully in place on the set to be used as camera copy. Unwanted marks can be whited out at the same time. Further resetting of type at this stage should be avoided if humanly and mechanically possible.

BLUEPRINTS

3.55   Blueprints (*blues*), vandykes (brown prints), silver prints, Ozalids (white prints), are all different forms of photographic prints made from negatives to be used in offset printing. They do not show the quality of image to be attained in the final printing, but they provide a means of checking the accuracy of the contents. As with repros, the editor should check to see that all parts are in place and all corrections made. Corrections made on these prints mean type must be reset by the compositor, pages made up again, and new repros made and photographed. Such prints should be checked by the editor the moment they arrive from the printer, who is often waiting for a final OK by telephone from the production department. In rare cases, authors are allowed to see blues to confirm placement of illustrative material (see 3.52). The publisher, and the printer, must be notified at once of any error.

CASE AND JACKET

3.56   The editor should always check proofs of the *die copy*—names, titles, and ornaments to be stamped on the spine of a book and (sometimes) on the cover. Later, when dies have been made, the binder submits a sample case for approval—an actual cover, stamped as it will be for the finished book. The production department checks the quality of the casemaking and stamping; the editor, the placement of the various type elements. Normally the editor also sees proof of copy for the jacket—front, back, spine, and flaps—at some stage in the production of the jacket. The author usually sees copy written for the jacket flaps but is not asked to check proofs of the jacket.

PRESS SHEETS

3.57   Folded and gathered sheets (familiarly, "f and g's") are not proofs but the first printed sheets of a book. By the time the publisher sees them, the book is off the press. The production department checks the quality of the press work, and the editor runs through all pages to make sure that none are missing or out of order and that no damage has occurred to the negatives since blues were checked (3.55). Any previously unnoticed typographical errors that turn up at this point must be ignored, to await correction in a second printing of the book. The only exception would be an error so egregious as to cause real harm to the author or publisher if the book were issued in this form. A serious flaw in the copyright notice, a misspelling on the title page of the author's name or the book title, or a statement in the text suddenly found to be clearly libelous would qualify for correction at this point, but nothing less grave. The only way to make such a correction is to reprint all or (sometimes) part of the signature in which it occurs—a wasteful, time-consuming, and very expensive business. The publisher's OK on the f and g's (often given initially by telephone) authorizes the binder to go ahead with binding and shipping the book.

FINISHED BOOK

3.58   When the folded sheets reach the bindery, one or two copies of the bound book from the first part of the run are sent to the publisher's production department, where the book is checked for flaws in binding or assembling. Normally, neither author nor editor sees the book at this stage, but if they happen to be present they may be allowed to hold it for a while. When books arrive in the warehouse on the delivery date. the courteous publisher will send the author the first copy at once and by the fastest courier available. The rest of the free copies stipulated in the author's contract will be sent from the warehouse at a somewhat later date. Any typographical errors discovered by the author in the finished book should be noted on the flyleaf against the day the author is notified that a second printing is imminent.

FOR FURTHER REFERENCE

3.59   Some publishers have their own manuals of style containing instructions for proofreading, and some typesetters send instructions with proof. Marshall Lee's *Bookmaking* (2d ed., 1979) gives lucid descriptions of the various processes used in bookmaking and explains how to deal with many of the different kinds of proofs available.

4 *Rights and Permissions*

Copyright 4.3
    Duration under the Old Law 4.4
    Duration under the New Law 4.5
        Joint works 4.8
        Works made for hire 4.10
        Anonymous and pseudonymous works 4.12
    Termination of Copyright Transfer 4.13
    The Copyright Notice 4.16
        Placement 4.17
        Correcting mistakes 4.18
        Public domain materials 4.19
    Deposit and Registration 4.20
    Fair Use 4.22
        Library copying 4.24
        Copying for classroom use 4.25
Publishers' Responsibilities 4.26
    The Publishing Agreement 4.26
        New book 4.27
        Journal article 4.29
        Contribution to a symposium 4.30
    Copyright Tasks 4.31
    Handling Subsidiary Rights 4.33
    Granting Permission 4.35
Authors' Responsibilities 4.36
    Guarantee of Authorship 4.36
    Obtaining Permissions 4.38
        Material requiring permission 4.41
        Deciding whether use is fair 4.45
        How to ask permission 4.48
        Acknowledging permissions 4.53
        Fees 4.55
        Permissions for an anthology 4.57
For Further Reference 4.59

4.1   When anyone, acting on his or her own initiative, writes a book, article, play, story, or poem, prepares an outline or report, or indeed creates any written work or work of art, however great or trivial, he or she is the author under the law and automatically possesses certain *rights* in the work. If a written work is to be published, the author normally transfers some or all of these rights, by formal agreement, to the publisher. Two of the rights are, from the publisher's point of view, basic: the right to make copies of the work (usually, but not exclusively, by printing) and the right to distribute such copies to the public—that is, to publish the work. A third important right is the right to make what the law terms "derivative works"—that is, works based on the original work, such as a translation, an abridgment, a dramatization, or other adaptation of the work. Taken together, these rights (along with others not discussed here, such as the right to perform a dramatic work and to display a work of the visual arts) constitute what are known as the *copyright rights* in a work. They exist from the time the work is created—that is, put in tangible form—and they belong to the author, who can sell, rent, give away, will, or transfer them in some other way, individually or as a package, to whomever the author wishes.

4.2   Whoever controls the rights to a work, whether author or publisher, may not only exercise those rights directly but empower others to exercise them. If for example the author of a book has transferred the whole package of rights to a publishing house (as is often, though not always, done), the publishing house will probably itself exercise the *basic rights* of printing and publishing the book, compensating the author by paying a percentage of the sales receipts (a *royalty*) from each book sold. *Subsidiary rights* (most of which spring from the right to make "derivative works" based on the author's book) are more likely to be exercised by someone else, whom the publisher licenses to do so. Part of the publisher's responsibility to the author is to see that subsidiary rights are exploited as effectively as possible. Another part of the publisher's responsibility to the author is to handle *permissions,* that is, to respond to requests from others—authors, editors, or publishers—for permission to use small parts of the author's work in works of their own creation.

COPYRIGHT

4.3   Underlying all rights and permissions work is the body of law known as copyright law, and some knowledge of it is essential for both authors and editors. For most publishing purposes the relevant law is the Copyright Act of 1976 (Public Law 94-553), a sweeping revision of prior law, which took effect on 1 January 1978, superseding the older federal law and eliminating (though not retroactively) the body of state law known as common-law copyright. Anyone involved with publishing should understand the chief differences between the old and the new laws as they affect printed matter.

DURATION UNDER THE OLD LAW

4.4   Until the new law was promulgated, a dual system of copyright existed in the United States. *Common-law copyright,* created by the individual states of the Union, protected works from the time of their creation until publication, however long that might be. A personal letter written in the eighteenth century but never published was protected as effectively as a manuscript completed the day before it was submitted to a publisher for consideration. In neither case could the document be copied and distributed (that is, published) without the express permission of the creator of the work or his or her legal heirs. *Statutory copyright,* a creation of federal law, in general protected works for a period of twenty-eight years from the time they were published, provided that a proper copyright notice appeared on the published work; thereafter, copyright in the work could be renewed for another twenty-eight years if the original copyright claim had been registered with the Copyright Office (a department of the Library of Congress) and if renewal was asked for by appropriate claimants during the final year of the first term of copyright. Thus in the normal course of things copyright in a work was intended to last for a total of fifty-six years from the date of publication, after which time the work went into the public domain. In 1962, however, Congress, thinking ahead to the new and presumably more generous law it expected to pass some day, began to extend the length of copyright for works then in their second term, and succeeding Congresses followed suit. The result was that any work published on or after 1 January 1906, in which copyright was later validly renewed, was still protected on 1 January 1978.

DURATION UNDER THE NEW LAW

4.5   The new law is both simpler and more complex as regards the duration of copyright. For works created on or after 1 January 1978 the provision is simple: copyright runs from the time of the work's creation, throughout the life of the author, and for another fifty years thereafter. (There are a few exceptions to this rule, which will be discussed later.) Publication does not affect the duration of copyright under the new law, and no renewal is necessary.

4.6   For works that were still under common-law copyright when the new law went into effect there is another, transitional, rule. They are given the same copyright term as post-1977 works, but with the proviso that copyright in them will last at least until 31 December 2002, and if they are published prior to that date, expiration is postponed at least until 31 December 2027. Thus, these works have a copyright term of not

109

less than fifty years from the date the new law went into effect, and (of course) longer if their authors were still living at that time.

4.7 For works published before the new law went into effect, the provisions are a bit more complicated. For these the potential duration of copyright is seventy-five years: copyrights still in their first term must be renewed, but the second term now runs for forty-seven years, not twenty-eight, and for works already in their second term, the duration of that term is automatically extended to forty-seven years.

4.8 *Joint works.* Many works covered by copyright law involve the efforts of more than one author. Some of these are what are called *joint works.* As defined by the statute a joint work is "a work prepared by two or more authors with the intention that their contributions be merged into inseparable or interdependent parts of a unitary whole." The authors of a joint work are considered to be co-owners of the copyright, which runs throughout the lives of the authors and for fifty years after the death of the last author to die.

4.9 Not all works in which the contributions of two or more authors are combined are joint works. Many, such as anthologies and issues of a periodical, are considered *collective works.* Copyright in them, which covers the selection and arrangement of materials, belongs to the compiler or editor.

4.10 *Works made for hire.* The new law makes special provisions for copyright in the category of works long known as "works made for hire." These are works created by someone who is paid by another person to create them. In law the employer is regarded as the "author" of any such work, and hence the owner of the copyright. The 1976 law defines much more stringently than the earlier law the conditions that must be met for a work to be considered a work made for hire. Such a work may be (1) prepared by an employee within the scope of his or her employment, such as an article written for use in an encyclopedia by a person on the encyclopedia's paid staff. Or it may be (2) any of several kinds of works that are ordered or commissioned for use by another person, if the employer and the person doing the work both agree in writing that the work is to be considered a work made for hire. Not all commissioned works qualify to be so considered. Some that do are a contribution to a collective work such as a paper presented at a conference or symposium, a translation of another work, an instructional text, a compilation of existing materials, or a "supplementary work" such as a foreword, a bibliography, an index, textual notes, or illustrations for another work. (Clearly, many kinds of works that could conceivably be commissioned do *not* qualify for consideration as works made for hire, no matter what agreement might be made between a writer and a publisher—a biography or a novel, for example.)

4.11   Since the owner of the copyright in a work made for hire is not the actual creator of the work (often, indeed, is a corporate entity), the law specifies a fixed term of years for the duration of copyright. This is seventy-five years from the date of publication or one hundred years from the date of creation, whichever is the shorter.

4.12   *Anonymous and pseudonymous works.* As in the case of works made for hire, the regular rule for duration of copyright cannot be applied if an author publishes anonymously or under a pseudonym. Again, the law prescribes the same fixed term of copyright for these works—seventy-five years from the date of publication or one hundred years from creation, whichever is the shorter. If after publication, however, such an author's name is revealed and recorded in the documents of the Copyright Office, the regular rule is made to apply.

TERMINATION OF COPYRIGHT TRANSFER

4.13   Under the new law it is usual, as it was under the old, for an author to transfer copyright in a work to the prospective publisher of the work as a condition of publication. The new law, however, provides that the author or certain of the author's heirs (surviving spouse and children, and in some cases, grandchildren) may demand return of the rights transferred after a certain number of years, no matter how the publishing contract reads. For works published in 1978 and later the term will be thirty-five years from the date of publication or forty years from the date of the contract, whichever is the shorter period of time. If the provision is exercised, the notice of termination must be served two years before the effective date and will have to be registered in the Copyright Office. This is an important provision of the 1976 law and will undoubtedly be of great value to authors and their families as time goes on.

4.14   For works published before 1978 the provisions are of course much more complicated. Unless a termination clause was written into the original publishing contract (which was very unusual), there was and still is no way that anyone can terminate the grant of rights during the first twenty-eight-year term of copyright—or indeed during the first twenty-eight years of the renewal term, if renewal-term rights were preassigned to the publisher (which was *not* unusual).

4.15   What the new law can and does do for authors of pre-1978 works and their heirs is to give them the privilege of terminating any assignment of rights for the final nineteen years of the renewal period. (Remember that the old maximum copyright term of fifty-six years was extended to seventy-five by the new law, and therefore the new law can make regulations applicable to this extended renewal period.) Under the new law, termination can be effected by the same persons and in the same way as that provided for later works. This provision of the 1976 law is of course of immediate benefit to many people profiting from works published more than fifty-six years ago.

THE COPYRIGHT NOTICE

4.16 The law requires that a notice of copyright be included in any published work in which copyright is claimed. Under the new law, as under the old, the notice consists of three parts: (1) the symbol © (preferred because it also suits the requirements of the Universal Copyright Convention), the word *Copyright,* or the abbreviation *Copr.,* (2) a date—the year of first publication, and (3) the name of the copyright owner. Most publishers also add the phrase *All rights reserved* because it affords some protection in Central and South American countries that are not signatories to the Universal Copyright Convention.

4.17 *Placement.* The copyright notice is to be placed where those looking for it can find it easily. The old law was very specific about its location: for books, either on the title page or the page immediately following, and for journals and magazines, on the title page, the first page of text, or the front cover. The 1976 law simply states that the notice should be so placed "as to give reasonable notice of the claim of copyright," but most publishers continue to place the notice in the traditional locations required by the old law.

4.18 *Correcting mistakes.* The new law is also more liberal concerning the consequences of accidental omission of a copyright notice or of including a defective notice—a notice lacking one of the three required elements. Under the old law such errors were difficult, sometimes impossible, to correct and often resulted in loss of copyright in the work. The new law makes correcting them much easier if they are caught within a reasonable time. If the notice is omitted from only a few copies, nothing need be done. If it is omitted from all the copies in the press run, the copyright proprietor should make sure the copyright is registered (see 4.20–21), either before publication or within five years after publication, and should make a "reasonable effort" to add the notice to all copies distributed to the public. (In many instances, pasting the omitted notice in unsold copies of a book would answer the latter requirement.) If the name or date is omitted from a notice or if the date given is later than the actual publication date by more than a year, the work is considered to be published without a notice, and the error is corrected as described above.

4.19   *Public domain materials.* When a work consists "preponderantly" of materials created by the United States government, and hence in the public domain, the law specifies that the parts of the work in which copyright is claimed be identified in the notice. This may be done either positively (e.g., "Copyright is claimed only in the Introduction, Notes, Appendixes, and Index of the present work") or negatively (e.g., "Copyright is not claimed in 'Forest Management,' a publication of the United States government reprinted in the present volume").

DEPOSIT AND REGISTRATION

4.20   For any work published with a notice of copyright the law requires the copyright holder to send two copies to the Copyright Office for use of the Library of Congress. The deposit is to be made within three months of publication, and no fee is required. Failure to make this required deposit does not forfeit any rights under the law, but the copyright holder may be fined for noncompliance if a specific request from the Register of Copyrights is ignored. When sending the deposit copies to the Copyright Office, publishers usually make application for registration of the copyright as well. Registration also requires deposit of two copies, and if application is made at the same time as the original deposit, no additional copies need be sent. To register a work the author or other claimant obtains and fills out the appropriate application form (there are several—see fig. 4.1: TX is the one used for literary works, including scholarly books) and sends the ten-dollar fee currently required (publishers may keep funds on deposit at the Copyright Office for this purpose). In return, if the Copyright Office approves the application, it sends the applicant a certificate of registration (which is also a public record), giving the name and address of the copyright owner, the dates of completion of the work, of publication, and of registration of copyright, as well as other information supplied by the applicant, such as a list of those parts of the work on which copyright is claimed, if the entire work is not new.

4.21   Registration, it should be noted, is not necessary to "obtain" a copyright (which exists in the work from the moment it is created) or to assure its validity, but responsible publishers seldom publish without registering copyright because of the added protection registration affords. Unlike the copyright notice, registration puts on public record the exact details of a copyright claim. In cases of infringement registration is a prerequisite to bringing suit, and if registration has been made within three months of publication, or before the alleged in-

113

Copyright Office Registration Forms	
TX	"Application for Copyright Registration for a Nondramatic Literary Work."
SE	". . . for Serials" (includes periodicals, newspapers, annuals, journals, and proceedings of societies).
VA	". . . for a Work of the Visual Arts."
PA	". . . for a Work of the Performing Arts."
SR	". . . for a Sound Recording."
GR/CP	"Adjunct Application for Copyright Registration for a Group of Contributions to Periodicals." (For a collection of works by the same author previously published with notice of copyright—used only in conjunction with one of the foregoing, such as TX.)
CA	"Application for Supplementary Copyright Registration: To Correct or Amplify Information Given in the Copyright Office Record of an Earlier Registration." (Useful for correcting errors made in the initial, basic registration.)
RE	"Application for Renewal Registration." (To register claim for renewal of copyright in works published between 1 January 1950 and 31 December 1977.)

Fig. 4.1

fringement, the copyright owner, instead of going through the difficulties of proving actual damages, can sue for statutory damages—and for attorney's fees as well. Also, as noted above, registration is necessary if a missing, defective, or erroneous notice is to be corrected.

FAIR USE

4.22 One final aspect of the 1976 copyright law that is of importance to both authors and publishers is its contribution to the doctrine of *fair use*—the licit employment of copyrighted material in another work. Although copyright law exists to protect the exclusive right of the copyright owner to copy the work, the law has long been interpreted as allowing others to copy brief portions of the work for certain purposes—as when a reviewer quotes from a work being reviewed or when a scholar buttresses an argument by quoting from the work of another scholar.

4.23 The current law does not attempt to define the exact limits of the fair use of copyrighted work. It does state, however, that in determining whether or not the use made of a work in any particular case is fair, the factors to be considered must include the following:

1. The purpose and character of the use, including whether such use is of a commercial nature or is for nonprofit educational purposes
2. The nature of the copyrighted work
3. The amount and substantiality of the portion used in relation to the copyrighted work as a whole
4. The effect of the use upon the potential market for, or value of, the copyrighted work

These are, of course, among the criteria that have long been used, by courts and by private individuals, in trying to decide whether or not the fair-use principle applies. So the chances are good that if a particular use would have been considered fair before 1978, it may be considered so now (see also 4.45–47).

4.24 *Library copying.* The new law does attempt to define minimum fair-use limitations on machine copying by libraries, in a long section with many exemptions and caveats too complex to discuss here. In general, it allows libraries to make single copies of copyrighted works, provided that the copies bear a notice of copyright, under certain circumstances, including the following:

> If the copy is made for a library's own use, because the library's own copy of the work is damaged or missing and a replacement cannot be obtained at a fair price.

> If the copy is made for a patron's use, and is limited to an article or small part of a larger work—or the whole of a larger work if a printed copy cannot be obtained at a fair price—and only if the copy is intended for use by the patron in "private study, scholarship, or research."

The law specifically forbids "systematic" copying by libraries. Presumably this means (1) making copies of books or periodicals as a substitute for buying them and (2) making copies for a patron without regard to the patron's intended use of the material.

4.25 *Copying for classroom use.* The 1976 law does not include similar guidelines pertaining to machine copying by teachers for classroom use. But it is clear from congressional reports published at the time the law was being written that a certain very limited amount of such copying was thought to constitute fair use of copyrighted material. Selections were to be brief and include a notice of copyright. Multiple copies were not to exceed the number of pupils in the class. They were not to substitute for anthologies or regular school purchases. The same items were not to be copied from year to year or semester to semester. Workbooks and other consumable materials were not to be copied, and the pupils could not be charged more than the actual copying cost. Furthermore, in every case copying was to be "spontaneous"—that is, at the instance of a particular teacher for immediate use in the classroom.

PUBLISHERS' RESPONSIBILITIES

THE PUBLISHING AGREEMENT

4.26 No publishing house can legally publish a copyrighted work unless it first acquires the basic rights of copying the work and of distributing it to the public. In most instances these rights are acquired from the owner by means of a contract called the *publishing agreement*.

4.27 *New book.* In book publishing the publisher typically draws up the contract for a new book, to be signed by both the publisher and the author. In it publisher and author agree to certain things. For the publisher these include publishing the book and (usually) paying the author a stipulated royalty out of the proceeds. For the author they include guaranteeing that the work is original and never before published, assigning some or all of the copyright rights to the publisher, and (usually) agreeing to correct and return proofs. Book-publishing agreements are generally fairly lengthy documents—too long to reproduce here—and include many other points of agreement and variations on the basic points. For a joint work (see 4.8) the contract is between the publisher and all the joint authors, not just one of them.

4.28 In scholarly publishing, in addition to contracts with the authors of new books, several other types of agreement are in use for special kinds of works. Two of the common ones cover contributions to scholarly journals and to symposia.

4.29 *Journal article.* Contributors to a journal possess exactly the same rights in their work as authors of books. Consequently, when an article has been accepted for publication in a scholarly journal, the author is usually asked to sign a formal transfer of rights in the contribution to the publisher. In the absence of such an agreement (since an issue of a periodical is considered to be a "collective work"—see 4.9), all that the publisher is assumed under the law to have acquired is the privilege of printing the contribution in that and subsequent printings of the journal issue. The agreement is a legal contract between publisher and contributor wherein the contributor assigns some or all of his or her rights in the contribution to the publisher, and the publisher agrees to publish the contribution under specific conditions and (sometimes) to furnish the contributor with offprints of the contribution as published. In the agreement currently in use at the University of Chicago Press, the publisher at the same time returns to the contributor the right to reprint the article in other scholarly works (see fig. 4.2).

4.30   *Contribution to a symposium.* Other collective works, made up of papers by different authors, may present legal situations similar to those of a scholarly journal, but often such a collection can be considered a commissioned work. In that instance the individual contributions may qualify as "works made for hire" (see 4.10–11), and a different form of agreement is appropriate. This is usually the case with a volume of conference papers. The publisher of such a volume first negotiates a contract with the general editor or sponsor of the proposed work and at some later appropriate time supplies the volume editor with enough commission forms for all contributors (see fig. 4.3). When these have been signed, they are returned to the publisher and filed with the contract for the volume.

COPYRIGHT TASKS

4.31   When publishers accept the author's assignment of rights in a publishing contract, they normally assume the responsibility of performing all the tasks associated with copyright. These include preparing an appropriate copyright notice (for examples see chap. 1) and seeing that it is included in the published work, supplying and forwarding the deposit copies of the book to the Copyright Office, registering the copyright, and (for books published before 1978) assisting the author or the author's heirs to renew it.

4.32   Since the assignment of rights in most instances includes subsidiary rights as well as the basic right to publish the work, publishers thereby take on the tasks of licensing other publishers who wish to produce other versions of the work and of granting permission to other authors and publishers who wish to use parts of the work in their own publications.

HANDLING SUBSIDIARY RIGHTS

4.33   In book publishing subsidiary rights are usually thought of as including the following categories:

> *Foreign rights*—whereby a foreign publisher may be licensed to sell the book in its original version in that publisher's own territory or to translate the book into another language and sell that version.
>
> *Serial rights*—whereby a magazine or newspaper publisher may be licensed to publish the book in a series of daily, weekly, or

PUBLICATION AGREEMENT

FROM: *The University of Chicago Press*
Journals Division
5801 South Ellis Avenue
Chicago, Illinois 60637

TO: DATE:

The University of Chicago Press is pleased to undertake the publication of your contribution to its journal,
entitled:

(the "Contribution"). We ask you to assign the copyright, thus granting us all rights for the Contribution,
so that you as author and we as sponsor of the Journal may be protected from the consequences of un-
authorized use. You will have the right, however, after publication in the Journal, to reprint the Contribution
without charge in any book of which you are the author or editor.

Accordingly, the following terms of publication are submitted for your consideration.

Copyright Assignment: Whereas The University of Chicago, acting through its Press, is undertaking to publish
the Contribution in its journal, named above, and whereas you desire to have the Contribution so published,
now therefore you grant and assign the entire copyright for the Contribution to the University for its exclusive
use. The copyright consists of any and all rights of whatever kind or nature now or hereafter protected by the
copyright laws of the United States and of all foreign countries, in all languages and forms of communication,
and the University shall be the sole proprietor thereof. The University, in turn grants to you the right to
reprint the Contribution in any book of which you are the author or editor, subject to your giving proper
credit in the book to the original publication of the Contribution in the Journal. To protect the copyright
in the Contribution, the original copyright notice as it appears in the Journal should be included in the
credit.

Warranty: You warrant that the Contribution is original with you; that it contains no matter which is
defamatory or is otherwise unlawful or which invades individual privacy or infringes any proprietary right
or any statutory copyright; and you agree to indemnify and hold the University harmless against any claim
to the contrary. Further, you warrant that you have the right to assign the copyright to the University and
that no portion of the copyright to the Contribution has been assigned previously. It is understood that the
copyright to the Contribution has not been registered with the Library of Congress, but that in the event
such registration has taken place you will promptly transfer the copyright to the University.

Previous Publication and Permission: You warrant that the Contribution has not been published elsewhere in
whole or in part (except as may be set out in a rider annexed hereto and signed by the University) and that
no agreement to publish is outstanding. Should the Contribution contain material which requires written
permission for inclusion in the Contribution, such permission shall be obtained at your own expense from
the copyright proprietor and submitted for review to the editor of the Journal with the manuscript.

Proofhandling: You will be given an opportunity to read and correct the edited manuscript and/or proofs,
but if you fail to return them to the editor of the Journal by the date set by the editor, production and
publication may proceed without your corrections.

Subsidiary Rights and Compensation: It is understood that you will receive no monetary compensation from the
University for the assignment of copyright and publication of the Contribution in the Journal. However,
fees received from licenses to reprint the Contribution in readers, anthologies, and/or textbooks will be
divided equally between you and the Press. You will receive no monetary compensation for other licenses
which may be granted for the use of your Contribution, nor will you receive any share of fees amounting
to less than $20.00. Your share of fees collected by the Press will be paid to you (in the case of joint authors,
to the first named) within three months of receipt.

If the foregoing terms are satisfactory, please sign and date this agreement. (All joint authors should sign,
and every author's Social Security number and year of birth should be included. Use the other side of this
page, if necessary.) Please return the white copy to the editor immediately and retain the yellow copy for
your own files.

For The University of Chicago

Morris Philipson

MORRIS PHILIPSON, *Director*
The University of Chicago Press

Author:...   Date:.............................

U.S. Social Security Number (where applicable):...

Year of Birth:..

Address:...

....

Fig. 4.2. Agreement for publication of a journal article, currently in use by the
University of Chicago Press journals department. Here the author transfers
all copyright rights to the publisher of the journal, and the publisher transfers
back to the author the right to reprint the article in other scholarly contexts.

The University of Chicago Press
5801 Ellis Avenue, Chicago, Illinois 60637

The University of Chicago, acting through its Press, is pleased to commission you to prepare material as follows, hereinafter referred to as the Work,

to be included in a Volume now entitled

edited by
which we contemplate publishing. This Agreement is intended to set forth all the terms and conditions under which our commission to you is made and which you accept.

1. You agree to prepare a Work which preliminarily must be acceptable for publication to the Editor of the Volume and which also meets the editorial standards of the Press. Nevertheless, the suitability of your Work for publication shall be finally determined by the Press in our own best judgment.

2. You warrant that the Work will be original with you and that no part of it will have been previously published, and that the Work will contain no matter that is defamatory or otherwise in violation of law and of the rights of others. Should the Work contain any copyrighted material of others, you undertake to obtain written permission from the copyright proprietor and include the permission with your material when you send it to the Editor on the date agreed upon between you. Similarly, appropriate releases should be obtained from persons appearing in photographs, and all photographs should be fully identified.

3. You understand that the Work will be the exclusive property of the University of Chicago, and recognize that the Work shall be considered a work made for hire, specially commissioned for use as a Work supplementary to, or as an adjunct of, the Volume. All copyright rights to the Work shall be owned by and be in the name of the University of Chicago.

4. As is customary, after publication of the Volume and upon your written request, we will freely grant permission for the republication of your Work in any recognized scholarly or professional journal, subject only to full credit appearing in the journal with an acknowledgment of first publication by the Press in the present Volume.

5. As may be agreed among you, the Editor, and the Press, you will have the opportunity to read and correct edited manuscript and/or galley proofs, and/or page proofs, but if you fail to return any of this material to the Editor by the date the Editor has set, production and/or publication may proceed without your further correction.

6. You will receive no royalty or other monetary compensation for your Work, but in lieu thereof the Work will be printed by us, and you will receive one free copy of the published Volume. You may purchase additional copies of the Volume for your own use at a discount from list price.

6. As total monetary compensation for your preparation of the Work you will receive
payable on publication of the Volume, and we will send you one free copy of the Volume. You may purchase additional copies of the Volume for your own use at a discount from list price.

7. If the foregoing terms and agreements are satisfactory to you, please indicate your acceptance by signing and dating this Agreement below. The white copy should be returned to the Press, marked "Attention   " The blue copy is for your files.

_____
Contributor's signature   date

For The University of Chicago

_____
Federal tax identification (social
security) number

Morris Philipson

_____
Citizenship

Morris Philipson, Director
The University of Chicago Press

Fig. 4.3. Agreement for publication of an article commissioned as a contribution to a collective work—symposium or conference papers. Other "works made for hire," such as translations, forewords, or indexes, require somewhat different forms of agreement. Note the two paragraphs numbered 6: one or the other will be struck out, depending upon whether or not a fee is to be paid.

monthly installments. *First serial rights* refers to publication before the work has come out in book form, *second serial rights,* to publication afterwards.

Paperback rights—whereby a publisher is empowered to produce and sell a paperback version of the book. *Quality,* or *trade, paperbacks* are normally sold in bookstores, like clothbound books. *Mass-market paperbacks* are typically marketed through newsstands and supermarkets, although some find their way into bookstores. The publisher of the paperback may be either the original publisher or someone else, or indeed the book may be an *original paperback,* with no previously published clothbound version.

Book club rights—whereby a book club is given the right to distribute the book to its members at a lower price than the regular trade price.

Reprint rights—whereby another publisher is licensed to reprint the work, in whole or in part, in an anthology or some other form of collection.

Motion-picture rights—whereby a movie studio is given the right to make a motion picture based on the book.

4.34   This list by no means exhausts the various forms of subsidiary rights in a work that may be handled by the publisher, but it includes the major ones. Depending upon the administrative structure of the publishing house, and upon the importance and marketability of the book involved, various persons or departments may handle different aspects of subsidiary-rights work—a special rights and permissions department, the sales or marketing department, the acquiring editor, or even the chief executive officer. When the publisher sells or licenses rights to others, money is paid, either in the form of a lump sum or in the form of a royalty, and these proceeds are normally split between the publisher and the author, according to whatever terms are specified in the publishing contract.

GRANTING PERMISSION

4.35   A publisher with a relatively large backlist of books and journals, such as the University of Chicago Press, may receive an average of thirty letters a day requesting permission to use material from one or another publication. These requests range from whole books or journal articles to snippets of prose from a scholarly monograph. At this press all permissions are granted subject to the author's approval, which the requester is asked to obtain. Before any request, large or small, can be granted, however, the material requested must be checked to make sure that the publisher does indeed hold the copyright to *all* of it. And to be unequivocally sure of this the publisher needs to have had the author's full cooperation when the book or article was first published.

AUTHORS' RESPONSIBILITIES

GUARANTEE OF AUTHORSHIP

4.36   In signing a contract with a publisher an author guarantees that the work is original, that the author owns it, that no part of it has been previously published, and that no other agreement to publish it or part of it is outstanding. If a chapter or other significant part by the same author has been published elsewhere—as a journal article, for example—written permission to reprint it must be secured from the copyright owner and sent to the publisher to be filed with the contract of the book in which it is reprinted. Notice of the original copyright in any previously published material, and permission to reprint it, will then appear either on the copyright page of the book, in a footnote on the first page of the reprinted material, or in a special list of acknowledgments. In the future, then, when handling permissions requests for the author, the publisher will refer any requests for permission to reprint this material to the original copyright holder.

4.37   If the original copyright is held by the author of the book, written permission to reprint is not necessary, but the fact of prior publication should be noted in the book. (It should be realized that in some cases copyright may be in the author's name, but the original publisher may still control publication rights.)

OBTAINING PERMISSIONS

4.38   It is the author's responsibility to request any permission required for the use of material owned by others. When all permissions have been received, the author should send them, or copies of them, to the publisher, who will note, and comply with, any special provisions contained in them. The publisher will file all permissions with the publishing contract, where they may be consulted in the event of future editions or of requests for permission to reprint from the work. The publisher is not usually given the right to grant future requests to reprint separately from the author's book any items—illustrations, charts, diagrams, poems, long prose passages, or whatever—taken from another, copyrighted work or procured from a picture agency, library, or museum. The author must therefore provide accurate information regarding the source of any such material used.

4.39 Permission for the use of such items, even when no fee is charged, is often granted only for the first edition of a book. New editions, paperback reprints, serialization in a periodical, and so forth, will then require renewed permissions.

4.40 In the course of writing a book or article, the author will do well to keep a record of any copyright holder whose permission may be necessary before the work is published. For a book containing many illustrations, long prose passages, or poetry, the process of obtaining permissions may take weeks, even months, to complete. For example, the author may find that an American publisher holds rights only for distribution in the United States and that European and British Commonwealth rights are held by a British publisher. The author, wishing worldwide distribution for the book ("world rights"), must then write to the British publisher requesting permission to reprint, mentioning that permission has already been obtained from the American publisher. Again, if the author of copyrighted material has died, a voluminous correspondence may ensue before anyone authorized to grant permission can be found. The author, therefore, should begin requesting permissions as soon as the manuscript is accepted for publication. Most publishers wisely decline to start setting type for a book until all of the author's permissions are in hand.[1]

4.41 *Material requiring permission.* To use anyone else's copyrighted work, whether published or unpublished, an author must have the copyright owner's permission, unless the intended use is a "fair use." To be on the safe side, and to meet the publisher's requirements, the author should obtain all permissions in writing. No permission is required, of course, to quote from works in the public domain—works on which copyright never existed (such as works of the United States government) or on which copyright has expired. Although the original text of a classic reprinted in a modern edition may be in the public domain, recent translations and abridgments, as well as editorial introductions, notes, and other apparatus, are protected by copyright. Whether permission is needed or not, of course, the author should always credit any sources used.

4.42 In determining whether a work published in the United States is still in copyright, an author should assume that the copyright has been renewed, whether or not the renewal date is specified in the copyright notice. Anything published in the United States before 1906 can safely

---

1. It is possible to engage professional help in obtaining permissions for a large project. Specialists in this work are listed in the annual publication *LMP (Literary Market Place)*, under Permissions.

be assumed to be in the public domain (see 4.4). The same cannot be assumed of British or Continental works, however: copyright law in the United Kingdom and many other countries has long protected works for the same period as the U.S. Copyright Act of 1976—that is, for fifty years after the death of the author—and in some countries the term may be longer.

4.43 Authors who wish to include unpublished material in their works should be aware that public regulations or private restrictions, unrelated to copyright, may limit its use. The keeper of a collection, usually a librarian or an archivist, is the best source of such information, including what permissions must be sought and from whom. Archives consisting of public records are usually in the public domain, but an author using them should check to make sure this is true.

4.44 As for personal correspondence, the law has always held that the recipient owns the physical letter itself but that the writer of the letter controls the right to reproduce it. The new law has made no change in this distinction. Of course the letter itself and the ownership of the copyright may well have been given, willed, or sold to other persons or institutions. Also, the author of an unpublished, unregistered dissertation (or any other paper) is equally the owner of the right to reproduce it, not the library or collection where it is housed.

4.45 *Deciding whether use is fair.* The doctrine of fair use was originally a concept of the common law, and even with the criteria enumerated by the new federal law (4.22–23), the limits of fair use are nowhere spelled out exactly. Essentially the doctrine implies that authors may quote from other authors' work to illustrate or buttress their own points. They should transcribe accurately and give credit to sources. They should not quote out of context, making the author of the quoted passage seem to be saying something opposite to, or different from, what was intended. And quotations should not be so long that they diminish the value of the work from which they are taken. In the latter instance proportion is more important than the absolute length of a quotation: to quote five hundred words from an essay of five thousand is bound to be more serious than to quote the same number of words from a work of fifty thousand.

4.46 Although neither the Copyright Act nor the courts define fair use of quoted material in terms of length, some publishers tend to do so. One publisher may wish to be asked for permission to quote as few as a hundred words scattered through several passages from a publication; another may set upper limits of five hundred or a thousand words. Still another publisher may try to be more strict about the use of some well-known author's work than about that of a lesser-known

123

writer. It should be remembered that no such rules have validity outside the publishing-house walls: courts, not publishers, adjudicate fair use. The rules exist in part to give an overworked permissions department, which often cannot tell whether or not a proposed use of a quotation is actually fair, something to use as a yardstick and also, perhaps, to intimidate unscrupulous would-be users of their authors' works.

4.47   Fair use is use that is fair—simply that. Uses that are tangential in purpose to the original, such as quotation for purposes of criticism, will always be judged more leniently than uses that are parallel, such as relying on quotations to prove one's point rather than putting it in one's own words. Use of anything in its entirety—a poem, an essay, a chapter of a book—is hardly ever acceptable. Use of less than such a discrete entity will be judged by whether the second author appears to be taking a free ride on the first author's labor. As a rule of thumb, one should never quote more than a few contiguous paragraphs or stanzas at a time, or let the quotations, even if scattered, begin to overshadow the quoter. If by these guidelines a use appears to be fair, the author should probably *not* ask permission for use. The right of fair use is a valuable one to scholarship, and it should not be allowed to decay through the failure of scholars to employ it boldly. Furthermore, excessive caution can be dangerous if the copyright owner proves uncooperative. Far from establishing good faith and protecting the author from suit or unreasonable demands, a permission request may have just the opposite effect. The act of seeking permission establishes that the author feels permission is needed, and the tacit admission may be damaging to the author's defense.

4.48   *How to ask permission.* All requests for permission to reprint should be sent to the copyright holder (1) in writing and (2) in duplicate. In granting permission the copyright holder will sign and return one copy of the request to the author, noting any fee demanded for the proposed use and any special conditions under which the grant is made. The second copy of the request will be retained in the copyright holder's files. (Naturally, the author making the request will keep a third copy for reference.)

4.49   The request must contain explicit information:

The title of the original work and exact identification, with page numbers, of what is to be reprinted (include table or figure number, title of a poem, or for prose passages, the opening and closing phrases).

Information about the publication in which the author wishes to reproduce the material: title, approximate number of printed pages, form of publication (book—clothbound or paperback?—or journal), publisher, probable date of publication, approximate print run and list price (if available).

The kind of rights requested (the most limited acceptable rights would be "nonexclusive world rights in the English language, for one edition," the broadest—which could well be cut back by the granting publisher—might be "nonexclusive world rights in all languages and for all editions"").

4.50 The University of Chicago Press supplies authors or editors of books requiring many permissions with a model request letter (fig. 4.4) but suggests that they write on their own personal or (when appropriate) institutional letterhead.

4.51 Permission to reproduce original photographs, paintings, and drawings (unlike charts or diagrams from a published work) must be obtained from the owner or (sometimes) the artist. Formerly, it was usual for the owner of such a piece to control the reproduction rights as well. But the new copyright law has made it easy for photographers and artists to retain the reproduction rights to a piece while selling the piece itself and the right to display it. Consequently, for works produced or sold since 1977 careful inquiry may be needed before permission to reproduce is requested.

4.52 Such a permission request is sent to the picture agency, museum, artist, or private individual controlling reproduction rights. Again, the request should be as specific as possible regarding the identity of what is to be reproduced, the form of publication in which it will appear, and the kind of rights requested. If the author making the request knows that the illustration will also be used elsewhere than in the text proper (as on the jacket or in advertising), this fact should be noted. Any additional fee for such use is the responsibility of the publisher, however, not the author.

4.53 *Acknowledging permissions*. Whether or not the use of others' material requires permission, an author should give the exact source of such material: in a note or internal reference in the text, in a source note to a table, in a credit line with an illustration. In instances where formal permission has been granted the author should, within reason, follow any special wording stipulated by the grantor. For a text passage complete in itself, such as a poem, or for a table, the full citation to the source may be followed by:

> Reprinted by permission of the publisher.

A credit line below an illustration may read:

> Courtesy of the Newberry Library, Chicago, Illinois.

[Author's letterhead]

Reference:
Date:

[Addressee]

I am writing to request permission to reprint the following
material from your publication:

[Author, title, date of publication]

[Pages on which material appears or other
identifying information]

This material is to appear as originally published [or with
changes or deletions as noted on the reverse side of this
letter] in the following work, which the University of Chicago
Press is currently preparing for publication:

[Author or editor, title, approx. no. pages]

This book is scheduled to be published in [month, year] in
[clothbound/paperbound] form at an approximate list price of
[$00.00] in a press run of [0,000] copies.

[Additional remarks, if needed]

I am requesting nonexclusive world rights to use this material
as part of my work in all languages and for all editions.

If you are the copyright holder, may I have your permission to
reprint the material described above in my book. Unless you
request otherwise, I shall use the conventional scholarly form
of acknowledgment, including author and title, publisher's name,
and date.

If you are not the copyright holder, or if for world rights I
need additional permission from another source, will you kindly
so indicate.

Thank you for your consideration of this request. A duplicate
copy of this letter is enclosed for your convenience.

Yours sincerely,

The above request is approved on the conditions specified below
and on the understanding that full credit will be given to the
source.

Approved by: Date:

Fig. 4.4. Suggestions for a letter seeking permission to reprint material in a
scholarly book. Some of the information about the proposed book may be
lacking when the author begins to request permissions, but as much as possible
should be supplied. Note that spaces are left so that the person addressed can
use the letter itself for granting or denying the request or for referring the
author elsewhere.

Examples of various kinds of credit lines may be found elsewhere in this volume by consulting the index.

4.54   In a work necessitating many permissions, acknowledgments may be grouped in a special Acknowledgments section at the front or back of the book. Citation to the source should, however, be made on the page containing the relevant material.

4.55   *Fees.* The author is responsible for any fees charged by grantors of permission to reproduce, unless other arrangements are made, in writing, with the publisher. A publisher may agree to pay the fees and to deduct them from the author's royalties or—in rare instances—to split the fees with the author. If it appears that a book would be enhanced by illustrations not provided by the author, the publisher may (with the author's consent) undertake not only to find the illustrations but to pay any fees involved.

4.56   Fees paid for reproducing material, especially illustrations procured from a picture agency, normally cover one-time use only—in, say, the first edition of the book. If an illustration is to be used also on the jacket or in advertising, a higher fee is customary. Also, if a book is reprinted as a paperback or goes into a second edition, another fee is usually charged.

4.57   *Permissions for an anthology.* A book made up entirely of other authors' copyrighted materials—stories, essays, poems, documents, selections from larger works—can be brought into being only by permissions granted by copyright holders. The compiler of such a volume, therefore, must begin seeking permissions at the earliest possible date. This is normally as soon as a contract for publication of the volume has been executed—or at the earliest, when a "letter of intent" has been received from the prospective publisher. Informal inquiries among copyright holders may be initiated before that time, but no sensible publisher of material to be anthologized is likely to grant permission for its use or to set fees without knowing the details of eventual publication.

4.58   Once a publication contract has been signed, the need for dispatch is obvious. Permission for a selection may be refused, or the fee charged may be so high that the compiler is forced to drop that selection and substitute another. And until all permissions have been received and all fees agreed upon, the table of contents cannot be final.

FOR FURTHER REFERENCE

4.59   An excellent short analysis of the 1976 law and practical guide to its application is *The Copyright Book,* by William S. Strong. Longer standard works on the subject are *The Copyright Law,* by Alan Latman, and *Nimmer on Copyright* (4 vols.), by Melville B. Nimmer. Publishing agreements are well covered by Richard Wincor in *Literary Rights Contracts* and the subject of libel in communications work generally by Paul P. Ashley in *Say It Safely.*

Part 2

Style

5   *Punctuation*

Introduction 5.1
Multiple Punctuation 5.5
Period 5.6
    Terminal Punctuation 5.6
    Lists 5.8
    Periods with Quotation Marks, Parentheses, and Brackets 5.10
    Display Lines, Headings, and Legends 5.11
    Faltering Speech 5.12
Exclamation Point 5.13
Question Mark 5.16
Comma 5.24
    Compound Sentences 5.25
    Adverbial Clauses or Phrases 5.29
    Adjectival Phrases or Clauses 5.36
    Introductory Participial Phrases 5.37
    Parenthetical Elements 5.38
    Interjections, Transitional Adverbs, and Similar Elements 5.39
    Direct Address 5.41
    Display Lines 5.42
    Appositives 5.43
    Coordinate Adjectives 5.45
    Complementary or Antithetical Elements 5.46
    Series 5.50
    That is, Namely, and Similar Expressions 5.54
    Mistaken Junction 5.55
    Separating Identical or Similar Words 5.56
    Titles, Addresses, and Dates 5.57
    Elliptical Constructions 5.61
    Quotations 5.63
    Questions 5.66
    Use with Other Punctuation 5.67
Semicolon 5.68
Colon 5.74
    Relating Clauses 5.74
    Introducing Statements, Quotations, or Lists 5.75
    Use with Other Punctuation 5.81
Dash 5.82
    Sudden Breaks and Abrupt Changes 5.83
    Amplifying, Explanatory, and Digressive Elements 5.84
    Use with Other Punctuation 5.88
    En Dash 5.92
    2- and 3-em Dashes 5.95
Parentheses 5.97

Brackets 5.102
Quotation Marks 5.107
Hyphen 5.108
For Further Reference 5.109

INTRODUCTION

5.1   Punctuation should be governed by its function, which is to make the author's meaning clear, to promote ease of reading, and in varying degrees to contribute to the author's style. Although there is inevitably a certain amount of subjectivity in punctuation, there are some principles that the author and editor should know, lest the subjective element become so arbitrary as to obscure the sense or make the reader's task difficult or unpleasant.

5.2   The tendency to use all the punctuation that the grammatical structure of the material suggests is referred to as close (klōs) punctuation. It is a practice that was more common in the past, and though it may be helpful when the writing is elaborate, it can, when misused, produce an uninviting choppiness. There is a tendency today, on the other hand, to punctuate only when necessary to prevent misreading. Most contemporary writers and editors lean toward this open style of punctuation yet preserve a measure of subjectivity and discretion.

5.3   The punctuation guidelines offered in this chapter apply largely to running text. For the special punctuation recommended in notes, bibliographies, indexes, and so on, see the appropriate chapters in this manual.

5.4   Punctuation marks should generally be printed in the same style or font of type as the word, letter, character, or symbol immediately preceding them:

> Luke 4:16*a;*   **Point:** one-twelfth of a pica

Italic or boldface parentheses or brackets, however, are often not used in such situations:

> (*a*)   (see paragraph 6*a*)   (see **12b**)   [*Continued*]   [*sic*]

MULTIPLE PUNCTUATION

5.5   The use of more than one mark of punctuation at the same location in a sentence (multiple punctuation) is, for the most part, limited to instances involving quotation marks, parentheses, brackets, or dashes (see 5.10, 5.15, 5.23, 5.89, 5.90). An abbreviating period, however, is never omitted before a mark of sentence punctuation unless the latter is the period terminating the sentence:

> O. D., who had apparently just heard the report, came over to our table in great agitation.
> The study was funded by Mulvehill & Co.

When two different marks of punctuation are called for at the same location in a sentence, the stronger mark only is retained:

> Who shouted, "Up the establishment!"
> "Have you read the platform?" asked Williams in distress.

PERIOD

TERMINAL PUNCTUATION

5.6   A period is used to indicate the end of a declarative or an imperative sentence:

> The two men faced each other in silence.   Wait here.

5.7   A period should be omitted at the end of a sentence that is included within another sentence:

> The snow (I caught a glimpse of it as I passed the window) was now falling heavily.
> Gilford's reply, "I do not trust the man," was unexpected.

LISTS

5.8   Use a period without parentheses after numerals or letters used to enumerate items in a vertical list:

> 1. strigiformes   *a*. the Bay of Pigs
> 2. caprimulgiformes   *b*. the Berlin airlift

Numerals or letters enumerating items in a list within a paragraph should be enclosed in parentheses and should not be followed by a period (see 5.100).

5.9   Omit periods after items in a vertical list unless one or more of the items are complete sentences. If the vertical list completes a sentence begun in an introductory element, the final period is also omitted unless the items in the list are separated by commas or colons:

> The following metals were excluded from the regulation:
> molybdenum
> mercury
> manganese
> magnesium

133

>After careful investigation the committee was convinced that
>1. Watson had consulted no one before making the decision;
>2. Braun had never heard of Watson;
>3. Braun was as surprised as anyone.

PERIODS WITH QUOTATION MARKS, PARENTHESES, AND BRACKETS

5.10   Periods should be placed within the quotation marks except when single quotation marks are used to set off special terms (see 6.56, 6.63). When parentheses or brackets are used to enclose an independent sentence, the period belongs inside. If the enclosed matter is part of an including sentence, the period should be placed outside the parentheses or brackets:

>Emerson replied nervously, "There is no reason to inform the president."
>
>From then on, Gloria became increasingly annoyed by what she later referred to as Sidney's "excessive discretion."
>
>"I was dismayed," Roger confided, "by the strange exhilaration she displayed after reading 'The Metamorphosis.' "
>
>He had not defined the term 'categorical imperative'.
>
>Florelli insisted on rewriting the paragraph. (I had encountered this intransigence on another occasion.)
>
>From time to time the driver glanced at his rearview mirror to observe the passenger (the latter had now removed his derby and was twirling it ostentatiously on the end of his index finger).

DISPLAY LINES, HEADINGS, AND LEGENDS

5.11   Omit the period after display lines, running heads, centered headlines, sideheads set on separate lines, cut-in heads, column heads in tables, one-line superscriptions and legends, date lines heading communications, and signatures.

FALTERING SPEECH

5.12   Authors and editors are not always consistent in the way they use ellipses and dashes in interrupted speech, but an attempt should perhaps be made to establish a distinction. Ellipsis points seem to suggest faltering or fragmented speech accompanied by confusion, insecurity, distress, or uncertainty, and they should be reserved for that purpose. The dash, on the other hand, suggests some decisiveness and should be reserved for interruptions, abrupt changes in thought, or impatient fractures of grammar without the confusion or indecisiveness suggested by ellipses.

>"I . . . I . . . that is, we . . . yes, *we* have made an awful blunder!"

The binoculars . . . where the devil did I put them?

"The ship . . . oh my God! . . . it's sinking!" cried Henrietta.

Felicia sat down suddenly, almost as though she had fallen into her chair, and said, "I don't understand. We were beginning . . . I had thought . . ."

"But . . . but . . . ," said Tom.

Notice that in the last example a comma is used after the closing series of dots to separate the speech from the words identifying the speaker.

For examples of the use of dashes to denote sudden breaks or changes in thought see 5.83.

EXCLAMATION POINT

5.13 An exclamation point is used to mark an outcry or an emphatic or ironical comment. In order not to detract from its effectiveness, however, the author should use it sparingly.

> Look out!
>
> Your comment was certainly lacking in tact!
>
> How can you say that!
>
> The emperor, it seemed, had forgotten to notify his generals!
>
> Suddenly the ambassador perceived that all was lost!

5.14 The use of an exclamation point as an editorial protest in quoted matter is strongly discouraged. The expression *sic* (in brackets) is preferred (see 10.51).

5.15 The exclamation point should be placed inside the quotation marks, parentheses, or brackets when it is part of the quoted or parenthetical matter; otherwise, it should be placed outside:

> The woman cried, "Those men are beating that child!"
>
> Her husband replied—calmly—"It is no concern of mine"!
>
> Mrs. Laslow (I could have died!) repeated the whole story.
>
> "I offered to drive him to her flat, you know, but he became abusive and said, 'To hell with you, Drake!' "
>
> "Look here, Wellington, the duchess had no right to say, 'We're not at home'!"

QUESTION MARK

5.16 The question mark, or interrogation point, is used to mark a query or to express an editorial doubt:

> Who will represent the poor?
>
> The subject of the final essay was Montezuma II (1480?–1520), the last Aztec emperor of Mexico.

5.17   A question mark should be used at the end of an interrogative element that is part of a sentence:

> How can the two women be reconciled? was the question on every-one's mind.
> What for? he wondered.
> As she asked herself, How am I going to pay for this? she looked thoughtfully at John.

5.18   Whether or not a question should begin with a capital letter when it follows an introductory element is usually a matter for the author to decide. Generally, the more formal the question, the more usual it is to begin with a capital letter:

> He wondered, what for?
> Before deciding, ask yourself, will it work?
> Pausing with his hand on the doorknob, Stetson bit his lip and won-dered, What if I have been mistaken?
> The question still to be decided was, Which of the two strategies would be less likely to provoke opposition?

5.19   When the question consists of a single word, such as *who, when, how,* or *why,* within a sentence, neither question mark nor capital letter need be used. In this case the word is often italicized:

> The question was no longer *how* but *when.*
> He asked himself why.

(See also 10.33.)

5.20   A sentence essentially declarative or imperative in structure may be-come interrogative by the substitution of a question mark for the pe-riod:

> This is your reply?   Wait here?

5.21   A request courteously disguised as a question should not be termi-nated by a question mark:

> Will you please rush the manuscript to the publisher.
> Will the audience please rise.

5.22   Indirect questions should not be followed by a question mark:

> Plimpton was thoughtful enough to ask whether we had eaten.
> How the two could be reconciled was the question on everyone's mind.

5.23   The question mark should be placed inside the quotation marks, pa-rentheses, or brackets only when it is part of the quoted or parenthet-ical matter:

> The ambassador asked, "Then why, sir, are these maneuvers occurring so close to our border?"

Why was Farragut trembling when he said, "I'm here to open an inquiry"?

When Crichton was introduced to the agent (had he met him before?), he turned to his host and winked.

If that was the case, why did she delay answering the governor until the morning of his departure (18 March)?

"What do you suppose he had in mind," inquired Newman, looking puzzled, "when he said, 'You are all greater fools than I thought'?"

"He looked at me for a long time," said Grant, "and then he said, 'Why have you bothered to tell me this, Peter?' "

COMMA

5.24 The comma indicates the smallest interruption in continuity of thought or sentence structure. There are a few rules governing its use that have become almost obligatory. Aside from these, the use of the comma is mainly a matter of good judgment, with ease of reading as the end in view.

COMPOUND SENTENCES

5.25 When the clauses of a compound sentence are joined by a conjunction, a comma should be placed before the conjunction unless the clauses are short and closely related:

> The two men quickly bolted the door, but the intruder had already entered through the window.
>
> Everyone present was startled by the news, and several senators who had been standing in the hall rushed into the room to hear the end of the announcement.
>
> Are we really interested in preserving law and order, or are we only interested in preserving our own privileges?
>
> Charles played the guitar and Betty sang.

5.26 In a compound sentence composed of a series of short independent clauses the last two of which are joined by a conjunction, commas should be placed between the clauses and before the conjunction (see also 5.50, 5.71):

> Harris presented the proposal to the governor, the governor discussed it with the senator, and the senator made an appointment with the president.

5.27 If the coordinate clauses themselves contain commas, semicolons may be used to separate them. (See the example in 5.70.)

5.28 Care should be taken to distinguish between a compound sentence (two or more independent clauses) and a sentence having a compound predicate (two or more verbs having the same subject). Preferably, the comma should not be used between the parts of a compound predicate:

> He had accompanied Sanford on his first expedition and had volunteered to remain alone at Port Royal.
>
> Mrs. Chapuis has been living in the building for over thirty years and is distraught over the possibility of now having to move.
>
> On Thursday morning Kelleher tried to see the mayor but was told the mayor was out of town.

ADVERBIAL CLAUSES OR PHRASES

5.29 If a dependent clause following a main clause is restrictive—that is, if it cannot be omitted without altering the meaning of the main clause— it should not be set off by a comma. If it is nonrestrictive, it should be set off by a comma:

> We shall agree to the proposal if you accept our conditions.
>
> Paul was astonished when he heard the terms.
>
> Paul voted for the proposal, although he would have preferred to abstain.
>
> I did not go to the piazza until after eight o'clock because I was afraid that Babs might still be there.
>
> Babs remained on the beach with her dark glasses and her fashion magazine, while Charlotte and I returned to the hotel.
> > *But:*
> Babs looked steadily at me while she sipped her daiquiri.

5.30 A dependent clause that follows the conjunction between two coordinate clauses of a compound sentence is usually followed, but not preceded, by a comma:

> Brighton examined the documents for over an hour, and had not Smedley intervened, he would undoubtedly have discovered the forgery.

In close punctuation, the dependent clause is both preceded and followed by a comma:

> In the morning, twenty angry parents assembled in Effingham's waiting room, and, unless I am mistaken, Effingham took the occasion to depart through a back door.

In open punctuation, both commas might be omitted:

> Babs had gone to Naples with Guido, and when Baxter found out about it he flew into a rage.
> > *Or even:*
> Babs had gone to Naples with Guido and when Baxter found out about it he flew into a rage.

5.31 A dependent clause that precedes the main clause should usually be set off by a comma whether it is restrictive or nonrestrictive:

> If you accept our conditions, we shall agree to the proposal.

> Although he would have preferred to abstain, Paul voted for the proposal.

5.32 An adverbial phrase at the beginning of a sentence is frequently followed by a comma:

> After reading the note, Henrietta turned pale.
> Because of the unusual circumstances, the king sent his personal representative.

5.33 The comma is usually omitted after short introductory adverbial phrases:

> On Tuesday he tried to see the mayor.
> After breakfast the count mounted his horse.
> For thirty years the widow had refused to move.

5.34 A comma should not be used after an introductory adverbial phrase that immediately precedes the verb it modifies:

> Out of the automobile stepped a short man in a blue suit.
> In the doorway stood a man with a summons.

5.35 An adverbial phrase or clause located between the subject and the verb should usually be set off by commas:

> Wolinski, after receiving his instructions, left immediately for Algiers.
> Morgenstern, in a manner that surprised us all, escorted the reporter to the door.

ADJECTIVAL PHRASES OR CLAUSES

5.36 An adjectival phrase or clause that follows a noun and restricts or limits the reference of the noun in a way that is essential to the meaning of the sentence should not be set off by commas; but an adjectival phrase or clause that is nonrestrictive or is purely descriptive, which could be dropped without changing the reference of the noun, is set off by commas:

> The report that the committee submitted was well documented.
> The report, which was well documented, was discussed with considerable emotion.
> McFetridge, sitting comfortably before the fire, slowly and ceremoniously opened his mail.
> The elderly woman sitting beside McFetridge was his nurse.

INTRODUCTORY PARTICIPIAL PHRASES

5.37 An introductory participial phrase should be set off by a comma unless it immediately precedes (and forms part of) the verb:

Having forgotten to notify his generals, the king arrived on the battle-field alone.

Exhausted by the morning's work, the archaeologists napped in the shade of the ancient wall.

Judging from the correspondence, we may conclude that the two men never reached accord.

Running along behind the wagon was the archduke himself!

PARENTHETICAL ELEMENTS

5.38   Parenthetical elements that retain a close logical relationship to the rest of the sentence should be set off by commas. Parenthetical elements whose logical relationship to the rest of the sentence is more remote should be set off by dashes or parentheses (see 5.83–87, 5.97–98):

Wilcox, it was believed, had turned the entire affair over to his partner.

The Hooligan Report was, to say the least, a bombshell.

The members of the commission were, generally speaking, disposed to reject innovative measures.

Bardston—he is to be remembered for his outspokenness in the Wainscot affair—had asked for permission to address the assembly.

The Wintermitten theory (it had already been dropped by some of its staunchest early supporters) was dealt a decisive blow by the Kringelmeyer experiments.

INTERJECTIONS, TRANSITIONAL ADVERBS, AND SIMILAR ELEMENTS

5.39   Commas should be used to set off interjections, transitional adverbs, and similar elements that effect a distinct break in the continuity of thought (see also 5.38):

Well, I'm afraid I was unprepared to find Virginia there.

Yes, I admit that Benson's plan has gained a following.

This, indeed, was exactly what Scali had feared would happen.

That, after all, was more than Farnsworth could bear.

On the other hand, the opposition had been conducted clumsily.

All the test animals, therefore, were reexamined.

Babbington, perhaps, had disclosed more than was necessary.

We shall, however, take the matter up at a later date.

Their credibility, consequently, has been seriously challenged.

When these elements are used in such a way that there is no real break in continuity and no call for any pause in reading, commas should be omitted:

The storehouse was indeed empty.

I therefore urge you all to remain loyal.

> Wilcox was perhaps a bit too hasty in his judgment.
> Palmerston was in fact the chairman of the committee.

5.40 A comma is usually used after exclamatory *oh* or *ah,* but not after vocative *O:*

> Oh, what a dreadful sight!
> Ah, how charming!
> O mighty king!

So nearly have such expressions as *oh yes* and *ah yes* become irreducible units, that they are now, especially in dialogue, rendered without a comma:

> "Oh yea? Who says?"
> "Ah yes," she said, arching an eyebrow. "Your mother!"

DIRECT ADDRESS

5.41 Use commas to set off words in direct address:

> Friends, I am not here to discuss personalities.
> The evidence, good people, contradicts my opponent.

In the following, *no sir* is treated almost as a single word, not as a negative followed by direct address:

> He looked at Sylvia in disbelief and said, "No sir! You're mistaken, my love!"

Sir may still, of course, be used in direct address:

> "No, sir, you must allow me to disagree!"

DISPLAY LINES

5.42 For aesthetic considerations, commas are usually omitted at the ends of display lines, such as titles, centered headings, signatures, and date lines.

APPOSITIVES

5.43 A word, phrase, or clause that is in apposition to a noun is usually set off by commas (dashes or parentheses might also be used):

> The leader of the opposition, Senator Darkswain, had had an unaccountable change of heart.
> We were unable to locate Marsden, the committee member who had written the report.
> His second novel, a detective story with psychological and religious overtones, was said to have been influenced by the work of Dostoevski.
> My wife, Elizabeth, had written to our congressman.

141

Sometimes an appositive is disguised by the conjunction *or:*

> The steward, or farm manager, was an important functionary in medieval life.
>
> A "zinc," or line engraving, will be made from the sketch.

5.44   If the appositive has a restrictive function, it is not set off by commas:

> My son Michael was the first one to reply.
>
> Jeanne DeLor dedicated the poems to her sister Margaret.
>
> O'Neill's play *The Hairy Ape* was being revived.
>
> The statement "The poor have much patience" is attributed to Count Précaire.

COORDINATE ADJECTIVES

5.45   Separate two or more adjectives by commas if each modifies the noun alone:

> Shelley had proved a faithful, sincere friend.
>
> Rocco had said that it was going to be a long, hot summer.

If the first adjective modifies the idea expressed by the combination of the second adjective and the noun, no comma should be used:

> He had no patience with the traditional political institutions of his country.
>
> Blanche stood beside a tall blue spruce.

COMPLEMENTARY OR ANTITHETICAL ELEMENTS

5.46   When two or more complementary or antithetical phrases refer to a single word following, the phrases should be separated from one another and from the following word by commas:

> This harsh, though at the same time logical, conclusion provoked resentment among those affected.
>
> The most provocative, if not the most important, part of the statement was saved until last.
>
> This road leads away from, rather than toward, your destination.
>
> He hopes to, and doubtless will, meet Caspar in Madrid.

5.47   An antithetical phrase or clause beginning with *not* should usually be set off by commas if the phrase or clause is not essential to the meaning of the modified element:

> The delegates had hoped that the mayor himself, not his assistant, would be present.
>
> White, not Thurgood, was the candidate to beat.
>
> Baum attended the lecture, not to hear what Morgan had to say, but to observe the reaction of his audience.

But:

> Baum attended the lecture not so much to hear what Morgan had to say as to observe the reaction of his audience.

5.48   If an open style of punctuation is preferred, commas may be omitted between antithetical elements joined by *not . . . but* or *not only . . . but also:*

> Baum attended the lecture not to hear what Morgan had to say but to observe the reaction of his audience.
>
> Fournier had been appointed to the committee not only because of his experience but also because of an alliance he had formed with the chairman's cousin.

5.49   Interdependent antithetical clauses should be separated by a comma:

> The more he read about the incident, the greater became his resolve to get to the bottom of it.
>
> Say what you will, Senator Watson's bill leaves much to be desired.
>
> The higher Fisher climbed, the dizzier he felt.

Short antithetical phrases, however, should not be separated by commas:

> The more the merrier.
>
> The sooner the better.

SERIES

5.50   In a series consisting of three or more elements, the elements are separated by commas. When a conjunction joins the last two elements in a series, a comma is used before the conjunction (see also 5.26):

> Attending the conference were Farmer, Johnson, and Kendrick.
>
> We have a choice of copper, silver, or gold.
>
> The owner, the agent, and the tenant were having an acrimonious discussion.

5.51   When the elements in a series are very simple and are all joined by conjunctions, no commas should be used:

> I cannot remember whether the poem was written by Snodgrass or Shapiro or Brooks.

5.52   When the elements in a series are long and complex or involve internal punctuation, they should be separated by semicolons (see 5.71).

5.53   Although the use of *etc.* in running text is to be discouraged, it should, when used, be set off by commas:

> The firm manufactured nuts, bolts, nails, metal wire, etc., in its plant on the Passaic River.

"THAT IS," "NAMELY," AND SIMILAR EXPRESSIONS

5.54   A comma is usually used after such expressions as *that is, namely, i.e.,* and *e.g.* The punctuation preceding such expressions should be determined by the magnitude of the break in continuity. If the break is minor, a comma should be used. If the break is greater than that signaled by a comma, a semicolon or an em dash may be used, or the expression and the element it introduces may be enclosed in parentheses:

> He had put the question to several of his friends, namely, Jones, Burdick, and Fauntleroy.
>
> The committee—that is, several of its more influential members—seemed disposed to reject the Brower Plan.
>
> Keesler maneuvered the speaker into changing the course of the discussion; that is, he introduced a secondary issue about which the speaker had particularly strong feelings.
>
> Bones from a variety of small animals (e.g., a squirrel, a cat, a pigeon, a muskrat) were found in the doctor's cabinet.

MISTAKEN JUNCTION

5.55   A comma is sometimes necessary to prevent mistaken junction:

> To Anthony, Blake remained an enigma.
>
> Soon after, the conference was interrupted by a strange occurrence.
>
> She recognized the man who entered the room, and gasped.

SEPARATING IDENTICAL OR SIMILAR WORDS

5.56   For ease of reading, it is sometimes desirable to separate two identical or closely similar words with a comma, even though the sense or grammatical construction does not require such separation:

> Let us march in, in twos.
>
> Whatever is, is good.
>> *But:*
> He gave his life that that cause might prevail.

Similarly, a comma should be used to separate unrelated numbers:

> In 1968, 248 editors attended the convention.

Better still, revise the sentence to avoid conjunction of unrelated numbers:

> Attending the convention in 1968 were 248 editors.

5.57   Although they are not necessary, commas may be used to set off a phrase indicating place of residence immediately following a person's name:

> The first speaker was Andy Porkola, of Toronto.
> Mr. and Mrs. Osaki of Tokyo were also present.

The commas should always be omitted, however, in those cases, historical or political, in which the place name has practically become a part of the person's name or is so closely associated with it as to render the separation by comma artificial or illogical:

> Clement of Alexandria
> Philip of Anjou

5.58   Use commas to set off words identifying a title or position following a person's name (see also 5.43):

> Merriwether Benson, former president of Acquisition Corporation, had been appointed to the commission.

5.59   Use commas to set off the individual elements in addresses and names of geographical places or political divisions:

> Please send all proofs to the author at 743 Maret Drive, Saint Louis, Missouri.
> The plane landed in Kampala, Uganda, that evening.

5.60   In the date style preferred by the University of Chicago Press, no commas are used to mark off the year:

> On 6 October 1966 Longo arrived in Bologna.
> The meetings were held in April 1967.

In the older style, however, commas must be used before and after the year:

> On October 6, 1966, . . .

ELLIPTICAL CONSTRUCTIONS

5.61   A comma is often used to indicate the omission, for brevity or convenience, of a word or words readily understood from the context:

> In Illinois there are seventeen such institutions; in Ohio, twenty-two; in Indiana, thirteen.
> Thousands rushed to his support in victory; in defeat, none.

5.62   When, in spite of such omissions, the construction is clear enough without the commas (and the consequent semicolons), the simpler punctuation should be used:

> One committee member may be from Ohio, another from Pennsylvania, and a third from West Virginia.
> Ronald adored her and she him.

QUOTATIONS

5.63 A direct quotation, maxim, or similar expression should ordinarily be set off from the rest of the sentence by commas:

> Vera said calmly, "I have no idea what you mean."
> "The driver refused to enter the bus," retorted Eberly.
> "I am afraid," said Kroft, "that I can offer no explanation."
> You know the old saying, Politics makes strange bedfellows.

5.64 If the quotation is used as the subject or the predicate nominative of the sentence, however, or if it is a restrictive appositive, it should not be set off by commas:

> "Under no circumstances" was the reply he had least expected.
> Morgenstern's favorite evasion was "If only I had the time!"
> Rushmore had grown weary of the watchword "Less is more."

If the predicate nominative is actual dialogue, however, the usual comma is employed:

> When Babs asked Morgenstern to drive her to the piazza, his reply was, "Ah my dear, if only I had the time!"

5.65 A colon should be used to introduce a long, formal quotation. (For a detailed discussion of quotations see chapter 10.)

QUESTIONS

5.66 A comma is frequently necessary to set off a question from the clause that introduces it (see also 5.17):

> Suddenly he asked himself, why shouldn't I?
> What troubled Babs was, when had Anselm discovered that the key was missing?

USE WITH OTHER PUNCTUATION

5.67 When the context calls for a comma at the end of material enclosed in quotation marks, parentheses, or brackets, the comma should be placed inside the quotation marks but outside the parentheses or brackets (see also 5.63):

> See Brighton's comments on "political expedience," which may be found elsewhere in this volume.
> Here he gives a belated, though stilted (and somewhat obscure), exposition of the subject.

> Although he rejected the first proposal (he could not have done otherwise without compromising his basic position), he was careful to make it clear that he was open to further negotiations.

Commas should not be used with dashes except when necessary to separate quoted material from the words that identify the speaker (see 5.88–89).

SEMICOLON

5.68   Though the semicolon is less frequently employed today than in the past, it is still occasionally useful to mark a more important break in sentence flow than that marked by a comma. It should always be used, of course, between the two parts of a compound sentence (independent, or coordinate, clauses) when they are not connected by a conjunction:

> The controversial portrait was removed from the entrance hall; in its place was hung a realistic landscape.

5.69   The following words are considered adverbs rather than conjunctions and should therefore be preceded by a semicolon when used transitionally between clauses of a compound sentence—*then, however, thus, hence, indeed, accordingly, besides, therefore:*

> Partridge had heard the argument before; thus, he turned his back on Fenton and reiterated his decision.
>
> Mildred says she intends to go to Europe this summer; however, she has made no definite plans.

In contemporary usage, clauses introduced by *yet* and *so* are preceded by a comma:

> Elizabeth was out of the office when I called, so I left a message.
>
> Frobisher had always assured his grandson that the house would be his, yet there was no provision for this in the will.

5.70   If the clauses of a compound sentence are very long or are themselves subdivided by commas, a semicolon may be used between them even if they are joined by a conjunction:

> Margaret, who had already decided that she would ask the question at the first opportunity, tried to catch the director's attention as he passed through the anteroom; but the noisy group of people accompanying the director prevented him from noticing her.

5.71   When items in a series are long and complex or involve internal punctuation, they should be separated by semicolons for the sake of clarity:

> The membership of the international commission was as follows: France, 4; Germany, 5; Great Britain, 1; Italy, 3; the United States, 7.

> The defendant, in an attempt to mitigate his sentence, pleaded that he had been despondent over the death of his wife; that he had lost his job under particularly humiliating circumstances; that his landlady—whom, incidentally, he had once saved from attack—had threatened to have him evicted; that he had not eaten for several days; and that he had, in this weakened condition, been unduly affected by an alcoholic beverage.

5.72   A semicolon may be used before an expression such as *that is, namely, i.e., e.g.,* if the break in continuity is greater than that signaled by a comma. For comparative examples see 5.54.

5.73   The semicolon should be placed outside quotation marks or parentheses. When the matter quoted ends with a semicolon, the semicolon is dropped:

> Curtis assumed that everyone in the room had read "Mr. Prokharchin"; he alluded to it several times during the discussion.
>
> Ambassador Porkola had hoped that the committee would take up the question (several members had assured him privately that they favored such a move); but at the end of August the committee adjourned without having considered it.

COLON

RELATING CLAUSES

5.74   The colon is used to mark a discontinuity of grammatical construction greater than that indicated by the semicolon and less than that indicated by the period. It may thus be used to emphasize a sequence in thought between two clauses that form a single sentence or to separate one clause from a second clause that contains an illustration or amplification of the first:

> The officials had been in conference most of the night: this may account for their surly treatment of the reporters the next morning.
>
> Many of the policemen held additional jobs: thirteen of them, for example, doubled as cabdrivers.

In contemporary usage, however, such clauses are separated more frequently by a semicolon than by a colon (see 5.68) or are treated as separate sentences:

> The officials had been in conference most of the night. This may account for their surly treatment of the reporters the next morning.

INTRODUCING STATEMENTS, QUOTATIONS, OR LISTS

5.75   A colon is used to introduce a formal statement, an extract, or a speech in a dialogue:

> The rule may be stated thus: Always . . .
> We quote from the address: "It now seems appropriate . . .
> MICHAEL: The incident has already been reported.
> TIMOTHY: Then, sir, all is lost!

5.76 A colon is commonly used to introduce a list or a series:

> Binghamton's study included the three most critical areas: McBurney Point, Rockland, and Effingham.

If the list or series is introduced by such expressions as *namely, for instance, for example,* or *that is,* a colon should not be used unless the series consists of one or more grammatically complete clauses.

> Binghamton's study included the three most critical areas, namely, McBurney Point, Rockland, and Effingham.
> For example: Morton had raised French poodles for many years; Gilbert disliked French poodles intensely; Gilbert and Morton seldom looked each other in the eye.

5.77 A colon should not be used to introduce a list that is a complement or object of an element in the introductory statement:

> Madame Mirceau had taken care to (1) make facsimiles of all the documents, (2) deliver them to the foreign minister's office, and (3) leave the country.
> The metals excluded were
>   molybdenum
>   mercury
>   manganese
>   magnesium
> Dr. Brandeis had requested wine, books, bricks, and mortar.

5.78 The terms *as follows* or *the following* require a colon if followed directly by the illustrating or enumerated items or if the introducing clause is incomplete without such items:

> The steps are as follows:
> 1. Tie the string to the green pole and . . .

If the introducing statement is complete, however, and is followed by other complete sentences, a period may be used:

> An outline of the procedure follows. Note that care was taken to eliminate the effect of temperature variation.
> 1. Identical amounts of the compound were placed . . .

5.79 A colon should follow a speaker's introductory remark addressed to the chairman or the audience:

> Mr. Chairman, Ladies and Gentlemen:

5.80 If the element introduced by a colon consists of more than one sentence, or if it is a formal statement, a quotation, or a speech in dialogue, it should begin with a capital letter. Otherwise it may begin with a lowercase letter:

> To Henrietta, there seemed no possibility of waking from her nightmare: If she were to reveal what was in the letter, her reputation would be ruined and her marriage at an end. On the other hand, if she were to remain silent, her husband would be in mortal danger.
>
> Henrietta's distress seemed insupportable: not only had her lover abandoned her at the last moment, but she had already sent a note to her husband announcing her intention of leaving him.
>
> I wish only to state the following: Anyone found in possession of forged papers will immediately be arrested.

USE WITH OTHER PUNCTUATION

5.81 The colon should be placed outside quotation marks or parentheses. When matter ending with a colon is quoted, the colon is dropped:

> Kego had three objections to "Filmore's Summer": it was contrived; the characters were flat; the dialogue was unrealistic.
>
> Herschel was puzzled by one of the changes noted in the behavior of the experimental animals (rhesus monkeys): all the monkeys had become hypersensitive to sound.

DASH

5.82 There are several kinds of dashes, differing from one another according to length. There are en dashes, em dashes, and 2- and 3-em dashes. Each kind of dash has its own uses. The most commonly used dash is the em dash. In the following material, the em dash is referred to simply as "the dash." The other dashes are identified.

SUDDEN BREAKS AND ABRUPT CHANGES

5.83 A dash or a pair of dashes is used to denote a sudden break in thought that causes an abrupt change in sentence structure (see also 5.12, 5.38, 5.97–99):

> "Will he—can he—obtain the necessary signatures?" Mills said pointedly.
>
> The Platonic world of the static and the Hegelian world of process—how great the contrast!
>
> Consensus—that was the will-o'-the-wisp he doggedly pursued.
>
> The chancellor—he had been awake half the night waiting in vain for a reply—came down to breakfast in an angry mood.
>
> There came a time—let us say, for convenience, with Herodotus and Thucydides—when this attention to actions was conscious and deliberate.

AMPLIFYING, EXPLANATORY, AND DIGRESSIVE ELEMENTS

5.84 An element added to give emphasis or explanation by expanding a phrase occurring in the main clause may be introduced by a dash (see also 5.74):

> He had spent several hours carefully explaining the operation—an operation that would, he hoped, put an end to the resistance.
>
> Marsot finally conceded that the plan was bold and unusual—bold and unusual in the sense that . . .

5.85 A defining or enumerating complementary element that is added to or inserted in a sentence may be set off by dashes. Such an element may also, however, be enclosed in parentheses (see 5.97) or—at the end of a sentence—be introduced by a colon (see 5.74–78):

> He could forgive every insult but the last—the snub by his former office boy, Tim Warren.
>
> It was to the so-called battered child syndrome—a diverse array of symptoms indicating repeated physical abuse of the child—that he then began to turn his attention.
>
> The influence of three impressionists—Monet, Sisley, and Degas—can clearly be seen in his early development as a painter.

5.86 A dash may be used before an expression such as *that is, namely, i.e., e.g.,* if the break in continuity is greater than that signaled by a comma. For comparative examples see 5.54.

5.87 In sentences having several elements as referents of a pronoun that is the subject of a final, summarizing clause, the final clause should be preceded by a dash:

> Ives, Stravinsky, and Bartók—these were the composers he most admired.
>
> Klingston, who first conceived the idea; Barber, who organized the fund-raising campaign; and West, who conducted the investigation—these were the men most responsible for the movement's early success.
>
> Broken promises, petty rivalries, and police harassment—such were the obstacles he encountered.
>
> Winograd, Burton, Kravitz, Johnson—all were astounded by the chairman's resignation.

USE WITH OTHER PUNCTUATION

5.88 If the context calls for a dash where a comma would ordinarily separate two clauses, the comma should be omitted:

> Because the data had not yet been completely analyzed—the reason for this will be discussed later—the publication of the report was delayed.

151

5.89   A comma should be used after a dash, however, to separate quoted material from the words that identify the speaker:

> "I assure you, there will never be—," Sylvia began, but Mark interrupted her.

5.90   When a parenthetical element set off by dashes itself requires a question mark or an exclamation point, such punctuation may be retained before the second dash:

> All at once Cartwright—can he have been out of his mind?—shook his fist in the ambassador's face.
>
> Later that night Alexandra—what an extraordinary woman she was!—rode alone to Bucharest to warn the duke.

5.91   To avoid confusion, no more than a single dash or single pair of dashes should be used in a sentence.

EN DASH

5.92   The en dash is one-half the length of an em dash and is longer than a hyphen:

> em dash: —   en dash: –   hyphen: -

(In typing, a hyphen is used for an en dash, two hyphens for an em dash; in preparing a manuscript for the printer, the editor will indicate where en dashes are to be set.) The principal use of the en dash is to indicate continuing, or inclusive, numbers—dates, time, or reference numbers:

> | | |
> |---|---|
> | 1968–72 | 10:00 A.M.–5:00 P.M. |
> | May–June 1967 | pp. 38–45 |
> | 13 May 1965–9 June 1966 | John 4:3–6:2 |
>
> *but:*
>
> from 1968 to 1972 (*never* from 1968–72)
> from May to June 1967
> between 1968 and 1970 (*never* between 1968–70)
> between 10:00 A.M. and 5:00 P.M.

When the concluding date of an expression denoting a duration of time is in the unforeseeable future, the en dash is still used:

> In Professor Lach's magnum opus, *Asia in the Making of Europe* (1965–) . . .
>
> John Doe (1940–); *better:* John Doe (b. 1940)

5.93   Periods or seasons extending over parts of two successive calendar years may be indicated by the use of a solidus (slant line) or an en dash:

> winter 1970/71   fiscal year 1958–59   362/361 B.C.

5.94   The en dash is also used in place of a hyphen in a compound adjective one element of which consists of two words or of a hyphenated word:

> New York–London flight
> post–Civil War period
> quasi-public–quasi-judicial body
> *but:* non-English-speaking countries

(For hyphenated compounds see 6.24–32 and table 6.1.)

5.95   A 2-em dash is used to indicate missing letters. No space appears between the dash and the existing part of the word, but where the dash represents the end of a word, the normal word space follows it:

> We ha—— a copy in the library.
> H——h [Hirsch?]

5.96   A 3-em dash (with space on each side) is used to denote a whole word omitted or to be supplied; it is also used in bibliographies to indicate the same author as in the preceding item (see 15.94).

> A vessel which left the ——— in July . . .

PARENTHESES

5.97   Parentheses, like commas and dashes, may be used to set off amplifying, explanatory, or digressive elements. If such parenthetical elements retain a close logical relationship to the rest of the sentence, commas should be used. If the logical relationship is more remote, dashes or parentheses should be used (see 5.38, 5.83–87):

> The disagreement between the two men (Westover has discussed its origins in considerable detail) ultimately destroyed the organization.
> The final sample that we collected (under extremely difficult circumstances) contained an unexpected impurity.
> The Williamsport incident (Martin still turns pale at the mention of it) was unquestionably without precedent.
> Wexford's analysis (see p. 84) was more to the point.
> He had long suspected that the inert gases (helium, neon, argon, krypton, xenon, radon) could be used to produce a similar effect.

5.98   A combination of parentheses and dashes may be used to distinguish two overlapping parenthetical elements each of which represents a decided break in sentence continuity:

> The Whipplesworth conference—it had already been interrupted by three demonstrations (the last bordering on violence)—was adjourned without an agreement having been reached.

> He meant—I take this to be the (somewhat obscure) sense of his speech—that . . .

5.99 An expression such as *that is, namely, i.e., e.g.,* and the element it introduces, may be enclosed in parentheses if the break in continuity is greater than that signaled by a comma. For comparative examples see 5.54.

5.100 Use parentheses to enclose numerals or letters marking divisions or enumerations run into the text (see also 5.8):

> He had, in effect, discovered a remarkable similarity among (1) strigiformes, (2) caprimulgiformes, and (3) psittaciformes.
>
> A hyphen is used to show (*a*) the combination of two or more words into a single term representing a new idea; (*b*) the division of a word at the end of a line; (*c*) a part of a word (prefix, suffix, or root); and (*d*) the division of a word into syllables.

5.101 All punctuation except terminal punctuation (periods, question marks, and exclamation points) should be dropped before a closing parenthesis (see 5.10, 5.15, 5.23). No punctuation should be used before an opening parenthesis unless the parentheses are used to mark divisions or enumerations run into the text (see 5.100). If required by the context, other nonterminal punctuation should follow the closing parenthesis. For more regarding the use of other punctuation with parentheses, and for examples, see under individual marks. For use of the single parenthesis with figures and letters in outline style, see 8.75.

BRACKETS

5.102 Brackets are used to enclose editorial interpolations, corrections, explanations, or comments in quoted material:

> "These [the free-silver Democrats] asserted that the artificial ratio could be maintained indefinitely."
>
> "Despite the damaging evidence that had been brought to light [by Simpson and his supporters], Fernandez continued to believe in his friend's innocence."
>
> "As the Italian [*sic*] Dante Gabriel Ros[s]etti is reported to have said, . . ."
>
> [This was written, it should be remembered, before Zantoni's discovery of the Driscoll manuscript.—EDITOR]

For further discussion of the use of brackets with quoted material see 10.50–51.

5.103 Brackets should be used as parentheses within parentheses (but see also 5.98):

This thesis has been denied by at least one recognized authority (see William B. Davis, *The Second Irrawaddy Discoveries* [New York: Babbington Press, 1961], pp. 74–82).

During a prolonged visit to Australia, Glueck and an assistant (James Green, who was later to make his own study of a flightless bird [the kiwi] in New Zealand) spent several difficult months observing the survival behavior of cassowaries and emus.

For their use in mathematics see 13.27.

5.104   Brackets may also be used to enclose the phonetic transcript of a word:

He attributed the light to the phenomenon called gegenschein [gā′-gən-shīn′].

5.105   Such phrases as *To be continued* and *Continued from . . .* may be placed within brackets and set in italics and in reduced type:

[*Continued from page 138*]
[*To be concluded*]

5.106   For the use of brackets with other punctuation see under individual marks.

QUOTATION MARKS

5.107   The use of quotation marks to set off direct discourse and quoted matter is discussed in chapter 10, and their use with single words or phrases to signal some special usage is discussed in chapter 6. Foreign quotation marks are discussed in chapter 9.

HYPHEN

5.108   The hyphen, sometimes considered a mark of punctuation, is discussed in chapter 6, especially 6.24–32, 6.33–42, and table 6.1.

FOR FURTHER REFERENCE

5.109   The interested reader will find related information on punctuation in the English language in Perrin's *Writer's Guide,* a full listing for which appears in the Bibliography.

6 *Spelling and Distinctive Treatment of Words*

Spelling 6.3
    Preferences of Special Groups 6.3
        British versus American spelling 6.3
        Spellings peculiar to particular disciplines 6.4
    Plurals 6.5
        Proper names 6.5
        Italicized words 6.8
        Letters, noun coinages, numbers 6.9
        Choice of plurals 6.11
    Possessives 6.12
        Proper names 6.15
    Compound Words 6.24
        Definitions 6.25
        General principles 6.30
    Word Division 6.33
        General principles 6.34
        Compound words 6.40
        Words with prefixes 6.41
        The ending *-ing* 6.42
        Personal names 6.43
        Figures 6.44
        Abbreviations 6.45
        Divisional marks 6.46
        Word breaks in ragged-right style 6.47
    O and Oh 6.48
    "A Hotel" 6.49
    Use of Ligatures 6.50
Distinctive Treatment of Words 6.51
    Emphasis 6.53
    Foreign Words 6.54
        Proper names 6.55
        Translation appended 6.56
        Ethnological studies 6.57
        Familiar words 6.58
        Scholarly abbreviations 6.59
    Special Terminology 6.60
        Technical terms 6.61
        Technical terms in special senses 6.62
        Philosophical terms 6.63
    Quoted Phrases 6.64
    Words Used as Words 6.66
    Irony 6.68

Slang 6.69
Use of "So-called" 6.70
Letters Used as Words 6.71
  Letters as letters 6.72
  Named letters 6.73
  Letters as musical notes 6.74
  Letters as names 6.78
  Letters as shapes 6.79
  Letters indicating rhyme schemes 6.81
Table 6.1: A Spelling Guide for Compound Words, p. 176

6.1   For general matters of spelling the University of Chicago Press rec- ommends use of *Webster's Third New International Dictionary* and its chief abridgment, *Webster's New Collegiate Dictionary*. If two or more spellings of a word are given, the first listed is the one preferred in Press publications, and if the *Collegiate* disagrees with the *Third International* (as sometimes happens), the *Collegiate* spelling is the one to follow, as it represents the latest lexical research. This said, a chapter on spelling in a style manual can disregard most of the dozens or hundreds of questions about spelling that arise in the course of writing or editing a serious book. "Look it up in Webster." But there are still spelling matters that a dictionary does not cover or upon which its guidance is obscure, and it is to these that the present chapter addresses itself.

6.2   The first part of the chapter is concerned with actual questions of spelling; the second part, with related questions about distinctive ways of treating words and phrases, especially the use of italics and quotation marks.

SPELLING

PREFERENCES OF SPECIAL GROUPS

6.3   *British versus American spelling.* The practice of the University of Chicago Press is generally to change British spelling to American (e.g., *colour* to *color*) in books published under its imprint and com- posed in the United States. This is done not out of chauvinist attach- ment to American ways but because American compositors, American proofreaders, and American editors are far more likely to catch incon- sistencies when they are departures from normal American spellings than when they are departures from less familiar British spellings. Retaining British spelling is particularly perilous when heavy editing is called for. Transatlantic authors seldom mind this kind of change, especially as Press editors seldom presume to change peculiarly British *usage,* even when it sounds odd to American ears.

6.4   *Spellings peculiar to particular disciplines.* Although Press practice, as noted above, is to follow Webster's first-listed form for words with variant spellings, the variant may carry special connotations within certain disciplines, and these should be respected. For example, although *archaeology* is the first spelling given for the name of that science, and the one generally preferred, some specialists in North American studies insist on the spelling *archeology* when it is used in connection with their work. So, too, many bankers, as well as students of the banking and home-loan businesses, traditionally spell the word *installment* with one *l—instalment—*an acceptable variant that editors should feel no compulsion to change.

PLURALS

6.5   *Proper names.* Names of persons and other capitalized names form the plural in the usual way, by adding *s* or *es:*

> five Toms, four Dicks, and three Harrys
> the Pericleses of modern times
> keeping up with the Joneses
> six Hail Marys
> two cold Januarys

Note that the apostrophe is never used to denote the plural of a personal name: "The Schumachers left for London on Friday" (not "The Schumacher's . . .").

6.6   Exceptions to the general rule on adding *s* or *es* sometimes have to be made when the ending would suggest a false pronunciation. French names ending in an unpronounced *s, z,* or *x,* for example, are best left uninflected in the plural:

> the six King Georges of England and the sixteen King Louis (*not* Louises) of France
> the two Dumas, father and son
> There are Charlevoix both in Michigan and in France.

6.7   Also, when following the general rule for plurals results in awkward formations—as, for instance, with polysyllabic Spanish names ending in sibilants—it is often best to recast the sentence to avoid the plural forms. Instead of "four El Grecos and seven Velasquezes" one could probably just as well write "four paintings by El Greco and seven by Velasquez." Sometimes it is better to sidestep difficulties than face them head on.

6.8   *Italicized words.* If names of newspapers, titles of books, foreign words, or other italicized names are used in the plural, the inflectional ending preferably is set in roman type:

> He had two *Tribune*s and three *Times*es left.
> FitzGerald actually wrote three *Rubaiyat*s.
> The Egyptian *faddan* is divided into twenty-four *qirat*s.

If the foreign plural is used for an italicized word, the entire word, of course, is then set in italics:

> *kolkhoz, kolkhozy*   *halakah, halakoth*

6.9   *Letters, noun coinages, numbers.* So far as it can be done without confusion, single or multiple letters used as words, hyphenated coinages used as nouns, and numbers (whether spelled out or in figures) form the plural by adding *s* alone:

> the three Rs   several YMCAs and AYHs
> thank-you-ma'ams   CODs and IOUs
> in twos and threes   the early 1920s

6.10   Abbreviations with periods, lowercase letters used as nouns, and capital letters that would be confusing if *s* alone were added form the plural with an apostrophe and an *s:*

> M.A.'s and Ph.D.'s   *x*'s and *y*'s   *S*'s, *A*'s, *I*'s   SOS's

6.11   *Choice of plurals.* When Webster gives two different plurals for the same word, the first is the one generally preferred by the University of Chicago Press:

> memorandums (*not* memoranda)   appendixes (*not* appendices)
>   *but:*
> symposia (*not* symposiums)   millennia (*not* millenniums)

Note, however, that different senses of the same word may have different plurals. Thus a book may have two *indexes* and a mathematical expression two *indices*.

POSSESSIVES

6.12   The possessive case of singular nouns is formed by the addition of an apostrophe and an *s,* and the possessive of plural nouns (except for a few irregular plurals) by the addition of an apostrophe only:

> the horse's mouth   the puppies' tails   the children's desks

There is one notable exception to the rule for common nouns, a case wherein tradition and euphony dictate the use of the apostrophe only:

> for appearance' (conscience', righteousness', etc.) sake

6.13 Closely linked nouns are often considered a single unit in forming the possessive, when the entity possessed is the same for both:

> my aunt and uncle's house
> the skull and crossbones' symbolic meaning
> *but:*
> our son's and daughter's playthings

6.14 Analogous to possessives, and formed like them, are expressions of duration based on the old genitive case:

> an hour's delay   in three days' time

6.15 *Proper names.* The general rule covers proper names as well as common, including most names of any length ending in sibilants:

> Burns's poems   General Noguès's troops
> Marx's theories   Jefferson Davis's home
> Berlioz's opera   Dickens's novels
> the Rosses' and the Williamses'   the Joneses' reputation
>   lands

6.16 Like common nouns, closely linked proper names may be treated as a unit in forming the possessive:

> Fraser and Squair's French grammar
> Minneapolis and Saint Paul's transportation system

6.17 When a proper name is in italic type, its possessive ending is preferably set in roman:

> the *Saturday Review*'s forty-fifth year of publication
> *Boris Godunov*'s impact upon the audience

6.18 For names ending in silent *s, z,* or *x* (see 6.6, above) the possessive, unlike the plural, can generally be formed in the usual way without suggesting an incorrect pronunciation:

> Josquin Des Prez's motets   Margaux's bouquet
> Vaucouleurs's theorems

6.19 Traditional exceptions to the general rule for forming the possessive are the names *Jesus* and *Moses:*

> in Jesus' name   Moses' leadership

6.20 Names of more than one syllable with an unaccented ending pronounced *-eez* form another category of exceptions. Many Greek and hellenized names fit this pattern. For reasons of euphony the possessive *s* is seldom added to such names:

> Euripides' plays   Xerxes' army
> Demosthenes' orations   R. S. Surtees' novels
> Ramses' tomb   Charles Yerkes' benefactions

161

6.21   The question of how to form the possessive of names of more than one syllable ending in the sound of *s* or *z* probably occasions more dissension among writers and editors of good will than any other orthographic matter open to disagreement. Some hold with the rule espoused for many years by a highly respected learned association: "In words of more than one syllable ending in a sibilant, only the apostrophe is added . . . except for names ending in a sibilant and final *e* (e.g., Horace's odes)" (*MLA Handbook,* 1977). "Sibilant," of course, won't do. According to the usual definition, *sh* is a sibilant, and so in place of "Parrish's cartoons" one would have to write "Parrish' cartoons," clearly absurd. If the definition of sibilant is restricted to the sounds of *s* and *z,* the rule produces fewer oddities, but it still would outlaw such spellings as "Dylan Thomas's poetry," "Roy Harris's compositions," and "Maria Callas's performance," in favor of *Thomas', Harris',* and *Callas',* none of them spellings that would commend themselves to many.

6.22   Other writers and editors simply abandon the attempt to define in precise phonic or orthographic terms the class of polysyllabic names to which only the apostrophe should be attached and follow a rule both more subjective and more pragmatic. In essence this is, "If it looks and sounds like a plural, treat it like a plural." Thus they would write *Dickens', Williams', Hopkins',* etc., but also *Harris's, Angus's, Willis's,* and the like.

6.23   The University of Chicago Press prefers its own rule as enunciated above (6.12, 6.15)—which is essentially a restatement of William Strunk's "Rule no. 1" in the famous *Elements of Style.* The Press is willing to accept other ways of handling these situations, however— if they are consistently followed throughout a manuscript. Often a logical consistency is easier to attain than the appearance of consistency, and the latter is important in good writing. Most sensitive writers and editors would be distressed, for instance, by the logical consistency of the possessives in a sentence like "Grinling Gibbons' wood carvings adorn some of Inigo Jones's and James Gibbs's London churches," and would wish to take some sort of corrective action.

COMPOUND WORDS

6.24   Of ten spelling questions that arise in writing or editing, nine are probably concerned with compound words. Should it be *selfseeking* or *self-seeking?* Is the word spelled *taxpayer, tax-payer, or tax payer?*— solid, hyphenated, or open? Most such questions are readily answered by the dictionary. If the compound is used as a noun, the chances are good that it will appear in the columns of the unabridged Webster, in one of the three possible spellings. If it is used as an adjective, the chances of finding it are still fair. But there will yet be some noun forms and a great many adjective forms for which no "authoritative" spelling can be found. It is then that general principles must be applied. Before these are outlined, however, some definitions are in order.

6.25   *Definitions.* By *open compound* is meant a combination of words so closely associated that they constitute a single concept but are spelled as separate words. *Examples:* settlement house, lowest common denominator, stool pigeon.

6.26   By *hyphenated compound* is meant a combination of words joined by a hyphen or hyphens. *Examples:* kilowatt-hour, mass-produce, ill-favored, love-in-a-mist.

6.27   By *solid* (or *close*) *compound* is meant a combination of two or more elements, originally separate words but now spelled as one word. *Examples:* henhouse, typesetting, makeup, notebook.

6.28   Not strictly compounds but often discussed with them are the many coined words consisting of a word-forming prefix (such as *non-* or *re-* or *pseudo-*) and another word.

6.29   In addition to such classification by form, compounds are also classified by function as *permanent* or *temporary.* A permanent compound is one that has been accepted into the general vocabulary of English and can (or should) be found in dictionaries. A temporary compound is a joining of words, or words and particles, for some specific purpose. A writer may employ the word *quasi-realistic,* for example, assigning some specific meaning to it appropriate to the work in hand. (One can think of contexts in which such a term might be useful.) The word *quasi-realistic* is not to be found in Webster, and probably not in other dictionaries either, and so would be considered a temporary compound. Having made its appearance, however, if it were picked up and used by other writers, it could acquire the currency and status of a permanent compound.

6.30   *General principles.* For some years now, the trend in spelling compound words has been away from the use of hyphens; that is, there seems to be a tendency to spell compounds solid as soon as acceptance warrants their being considered permanent compounds, and otherwise to spell them open. It should be emphasized that this is a trend, not a rule, but it is sometimes helpful, when deciding how to spell some new combination, to remember that the trend exists.

6.31   A second helpful principle to remember is this: When a temporary compound is used as an adjective before a noun, it is often hyphenated to avoid misleading the reader. *A fast sailing ship,* for example, is ambiguous. Does the phrase mean a sailing ship with the general characteristic of fleetness or a ship that at the moment is sailing fast? Since the latter construction is intended, we write *a fast-sailing ship,* and our reader does not have to pause over it. So, too, not *a free form sculpture* but *a free-form sculpture.* Even though *form sculpture* has no rational meaning (as *sailing ship* does), it could cause a moment's hesitation for the reader: after an adjective like *free* we almost instinctively expect a noun, and there is indeed one there—*form*—but it is intended to hook up with *free* as a kind of adjective to modify *sculpture,* the real noun in the phrase. So to bypass this confusion we insert a hyphen between *free* and *form* and thus make its adjectival function clear:

> A free-form sculpture stood on the terrace.

Note that this device is appropriate only before the noun. If the compound adjective occurs after the noun, the relationships are usually perfectly clear, and the hyphen is not needed:

> A piece of sculpture, free form, stood on the terrace.
> The sculpture on the terrace was free form.

6.32   There are, quite literally, scores of other rules for the spelling of compound words. Many of them are nearly useless because of the great numbers of exceptions. To give authors and editors a few firm stepping-stones through the slough of compound-word spelling, table 6.1, printed at the end of the chapter, has been prepared in an attempt to reduce a few of the dependable rules to systematic form.

WORD DIVISION

6.33   When type is set in justified lines, it is inevitable that words be *divided* (*broken,* or *hyphenated*) at the ends of lines. (Even in unjustified setting it is desirable to break some words: see 6.47, below.) Such divisions are made between syllables, which should be determined in doubtful cases by consulting Webster. Not all syllable breaks, however, are acceptable end-of-line breaks. The paragraphs that follow are intended to offer editors and proofreaders a brief guide to conservative modern practice in word division. For word division in foreign languages see chapter 9.

6.34   *General principles.* Most words should be divided according to pronunciation (the American system, reflected in Webster), not according to derivation (the British system):

> democ-racy (*not* demo-cracy)   knowl-edge (*not* know-ledge)
> aurif-erous (*not* auri-ferous)
> antip-odes (*still better* antipo-des; *not* anti-podes)

Consequently, words such as the following, in which the second "syllable" contains only a silent *e,* are never divided:

aimed	helped	spelled
climbed	passed	vexed

Nor are word endings such as the following, which despite occasional use in verse as disyllables are for all practical purposes monosyllables:

-ceous	-geous	-sion
-cial	-gion	-tial
-cion	-gious	-tion
-cious	-sial	-tious

And by a similar principle final syllables in which the liquid *l* sound is the only audible vowel should not be carried over to the next line:

convert-ible (*not* converti-ble)	pos-sible (*not* possi-ble)
en-titled (*not* enti-tled)	prin-ciples (*not* princi-ples)
people (*not* peo-ple)	read-able (*not* reada-ble)

6.35 Division should be made after a vowel unless the resulting break is not according to pronunciation. Where a vowel alone forms a syllable in the middle of a word, run it into the first line. Diphthongs are treated as single vowels:

aneu-rysm (*not* an-eurysm)
criti-cism (*not* crit-icism)
liga-ture (*not* lig-ature)
physi-cal (*not* phys-ical *or* physic-al)
sepa-rate (*not* sep-arate)
preju-dice (*not* prej-udice)

6.36 Two consonants standing between vowels are usually separated if the pronunciation warrants:

ad-van-tage	foun-dation	moun-tain
ex-ces-sive	im-por-tant	profes-sor
finan-cier	In-dian	struc-ture
fin-ger		

6.37 Words that have a misleading appearance when divided should be left unbroken if at all possible:

women   often   prayer   water   noisy

6.38 One-letter divisions are not permissible. Such words as the following must not be divided:

acre	enough	item
again	even	oboe
amen	event	onus
among	idol	unite

6.39   Two-letter divisions are permissible at the end of a line, but two-letter word endings should not be carried over to the next line if this can be avoided:

> en-chant   di-pole   as-phalt
>   *but:*
> losses (*not* loss-es)   stricken (*not* strick-en)
> money (*not* mon-ey)   fully (*not* ful-ly)

6.40   *Compound words.* Hyphenated compounds should not be broken except at the hyphen if this is possible:

> court- / martial (*not* court-mar- / tial)
> poverty- / stricken (*not* pov- / erty-stricken; *much less*
> pover- / ty-stricken)

Words originally compounded of other words but now spelled solid should be divided at the natural breaks whenever possible:

> school-master *is better than* schoolmas-ter
> clearing-house *is better than* clear-inghouse
> handle-bar *is better than* han-dlebar
> *never:* passo-ver, une-ven, etc.

6.41   *Words with prefixes.* By the same principle, division after a prefix is preferred to division at any other point in the word:

> dis-pleasure *is better than* displea-sure
> pseudo-scientific *is better than* pseu-doscientific *or*
> pseudoscien-tific

6.42   *The ending "-ing."* Most gerunds and present participles permit division before the *-ing:*

> certify-ing   giv-ing   pranc-ing
> chang-ing   improvis-ing   revok-ing
> dwell-ing   intrigu-ing   tempt-ing
> enter-ing   learn-ing   twin-ing
> entranc-ing   picnick-ing   whirl-ing

When the final consonant is doubled before the addition of *-ing,* however, the added consonant is carried over:

> abhor-ring   dab-bing   run-ning
> bid-ding   pin-ning   trip-ping
> control-ling   occur-ring   twin-ning

And when the original verb ends in an *-le* syllable in which the only audible vowel is the liquid *l* (for example, *startle, fizzle*), one or more of the preceding consonants are carried over with *-ing:*

> bris-tling   gig-gling   ruf-fling
> chuck-ling   han-dling   siz-zling
> dwin-dling   ram-bling   twin-kling

6.43   *Personal names.* Personal names ought not to be divided if there is any way to avoid it. Since this is often a counsel of perfection, however, some guidelines may be in order: (1) Try to break after a middle initial. The following breaks are in descending order of desirability:

> Frederick L. / Anderson
> Frederick L. An- / derson
> Frederick / L. Anderson
> Fred- / erick L. Anderson

(2) When initials only are used in place of given names, again try not to break at all, but if necessary break after the second (or last, if there are more than two):

> *if necessary:* A. E. / Housman
> *but never:* A. / E. Housman

(3) Avoid breaking before a numeral suffix, as in Henry VIII or in John D. Rockefeller 3d. (Breaking after the comma preceding the suffix in a name like John D. Rockefeller, Jr., is permissible.)

6.44   *Figures.* When large numbers are expressed in figures, they should be kept intact if possible; if this is impossible, they may be broken after a comma—but not a decimal point. Do not break after a single digit. Slant lines show permissible breaks:

> 1,365, / 000, / 000 $24, / 126.83   £36, / 520, / 000

6.45   *Abbreviations.* Abbreviations used with figures should not be separated from the figures:

> 345 mi.   24 kg   55 B.C.   A.D. 1066   6:35 P.M.

6.46   *Divisional marks.* A divisional mark, such as (*a*) or (1), even when it occurs in the middle of a sentence, preferably should not be separated from what follows it. When such a mark occurs at the end of a line, carry it over to the next line if possible.

6.47   *Word breaks in ragged-right style.* A good deal of typesetting nowadays is done in what is called *ragged-right* style: all lines are left unjustified, so that the right-hand margin of the type column is irregular. If copy is intended for ragged-right setting, the editor should not simply mark it (for example) "Set 10/12 × 25 ragged right," or the typesetter will probably not break any words at all. Then there are likely to be ludicrously long spaces at the ends of some lines. The editor (in conference with the designer, if appropriate) should add "minimum length of line 23 picas"—or whatever. This will ensure that long words will be broken whereas short ones need not be.

167

O AND OH

6.48   The vocative *O* is capitalized, but not the interjection *oh* unless it begins a sentence or stands alone:

> Why, O Lord, did you not help him?
> I don't know, oh, truly I don't know why I did it.
> Oh! What have I done?

"A HOTEL"

6.49   Such forms as "an historical study" or "an union" are not idiomatic in American English. Before a pronounced *h,* long *u* (or *eu*), and such a word as *one,* the indefinite article should be *a:*

a hotel	a euphonious word
a historical study	such a one
but: an honor, an heir	a union

USE OF LIGATURES

6.50   The ligatures *æ* and *œ* should not be used either in Latin or Greek words or in words adopted into English from these languages:

aes	aetatis	poena
Encyclopaedia Britannica		*Oedipus tyrannus*

For most English words derived from Latin or Greek words containing *ae* or *oe,* the preferred spelling is now *e:*

coeval	ecumenical	maneuver
economy	enology	medieval
but: aesthetics, archaeology		

The digraph *æ* is needed for spelling Old English words (along with other special characters) in an Old English context:

Ælfric	Ælfred	wes hæl

And the ligature *œ* is needed for spelling modern French in a French context (but not for French words in an English context):

> *Œuvres complètes* de Racine
> le nœud gordien
> un coup d'œil
> *but:*
> a tray of hors d'oeuvres
> a circular window, or *oeil-de-boeuf*

DISTINCTIVE TREATMENT OF WORDS

6.51   Writers have probably always felt the need for devices to give special expression—emphasis, irony, or whatever—to the written word, to achieve what gesture and vocal intonation achieve for the spoken word. One old device, the use of capital letters to lend importance to certain words, is now totally outmoded and a vehicle of satire:

> When John came to the throne he lost his temper and flung himself on the floor, foaming at the mouth and biting the rushes. He was thus a Bad King.[1]

6.52   Other devices, notably the use of italics and quotation marks to achieve special effects, are not outmoded but are used less and less as time goes on, especially by mature writers who prefer to obtain their effects structurally:

> The damaging evidence was offered not by the arresting officer, not by the injured plaintiff, but by the boy's own mother.

In the sentence above, for example, there is no need to set the words *boy's own mother* in italics: the structure of the sentence gives them all the emphasis they need. Obviously, an effect of emphasis cannot always be achieved so easily. But writers who find themselves underlining frequently for emphasis might consider (1) whether many of the italics are not superfluous, the emphasis being apparent from the context, or (2) if the emphasis is not apparent, whether it cannot be achieved more gracefully by recasting the sentence. The same reservations apply to frequent use of quotation marks to suggest irony or special usage. Often the quotation marks offend an intelligent reader who is quite capable of detecting the irony or the oddness of the expression without having it pointed out. (Apart from these stylistic uses, of course, italics and quotation marks find purely technical uses, discussed later in the chapter, which are not to be called in question.)

EMPHASIS

6.53   A word or phrase may be set in italic type to emphasize it if the emphasis might otherwise be lost:

> Let us dwell for a moment upon the idea of *conscious* participation. How do we learn to think in terms of *wholes?*

Seldom should as much as a sentence be set in italics for emphasis, and never a whole passage.

FOREIGN WORDS

6.54   Isolated words and phrases in a foreign language may be set in italics if they are likely to be unfamiliar to readers:

1. Walter C. Sellar and Robert J. Yeatman, *1066 and All That: A Memorable History of England* (New York: E. P. Dutton, 1931), 24.

> The *grève du zèle* is not a true strike but a nitpicking obeying of work rules.
>
> *Honi soit qui mal y pense* is the motto of the Order of the Garter.
>
> a deed of endowment (*vakfiye*)

As with matter italicized for emphasis, a full sentence in a foreign language (as the second example above) is only occasionally set in italics, and a passage of two or more sentences should never be italicized but should be treated as a quotation (see 10.1).

6.55 *Proper names.* Proper names are not italicized, even when cited as foreign terms:

> Moscow (in Russian, Moskva) has been the capital of the Russian national state since the late fourteenth century.

6.56 *Translation appended.* If a definition follows a foreign word or phrase, the definition is enclosed in parentheses or quotation marks:

> The word she used was not *une poêle* (frying pan) but *un poêle* (stove).
>
> Volition is expressed by the infix *-ainu-*, as in the phrase *ena tuainubo,* "I would like to eat," or *ena tuainu-iai,* "I wanted to eat."

In linguistic and phonetic studies a word under discussion is often set in italics (as above) and the definition enclosed in *single* quotation marks, with no intervening punctuation:

> French *le cheval* 'the horse' represents a replacement for Latin *equus.*
>
> The gap is narrow between *mead* 'a beverage' and *mead* 'a meadow'.

6.57 *Ethnological studies.* Scholarly work in cultural anthropology is full of words drawn from the languages of the societies studied, and these are usually italicized only on first occurrence. In a kinship study, for example, once it is made clear that a married woman's mother-in-law's sister is her *aiku* and her father-in-law's sister is her *aiku-esu,* the terms appear thereafter in roman type. (A glossary at the end, however, is helpful.)

6.58 *Familiar words.* Familiar words and phrases in a foreign language should be set in roman type (note the lowercase style for the two German nouns):

effendi	mea culpa
pasha	fazenda
élan	ménage
barranca	weltschmerz
remuda	kapellmeister
trattoria	a priori

The problem, of course, is deciding how familiar a word is, and this depends partly on how we think about the word when we use it. When we write that the atmosphere of Restaurant X is gemütlich, we are not thinking of the word as peculiarly German but simply as the most appropriate adjective to use for what we mean. And the chances are good that our audience will find the word equally familiar and equally unforeign. On the other hand, if we write that Playwright Y never misses a chance to *épater les bourgeois,* we are probably thinking of the expression as peculiarly French, no matter how familiar it is to us or to our audience (and of course if it is at all probable that the expression is *not* familiar to our particular audience, it would be bad manners to use it without a translation). In deciding whether or not to italicize, the author's and editor's task is to place the word on the spectrum of usage stretching from foreign-and-unfamiliar at one end to unforeign-and-familiar at the other. And for doing this there are no guides but sensitivity and common sense. In doubtful cases the choice should always be for roman.

6.59 *Scholarly abbreviations.* It is now the custom at the University of Chicago Press to use roman type also for scholarly Latin words and abbreviations such as:

    ibid.   et al.   ca.   passim

But because of its peculiar use in quoted matter, it seems wise to retain italics for *sic:*

    They are furnished "seperate [*sic*] but equal facilities."

SPECIAL TERMINOLOGY

6.60 Key terms in a discussion, terms with special meaning, and, in general, terms to which the reader's attention is directed are often italicized on first use. Thereafter they are best set in roman:

    As will appear in the following pages, *obstructionism* and *delaying tactics* have been the chief weapons of this group.

    What is meant by *random selection?*

In the last example note the italic question mark. This illustrates the printer's rule that punctuation is set in the style of the immediately preceding word (see 5.4).

6.61 *Technical terms.* A technical term, especially when it is accompanied by its definition, is often set in italics the first time it appears in a discussion, and in roman thereafter:

    Tabular matter is copy, usually consisting of figures, that is set in columns.

    Ground and polished *thin sections* permit microscopic examination of the cellular structure of some fossils.

6.62   *Technical terms in special senses.* Often it is better to apply a standard technical term in a nonstandard way than to invent a new term. In such instances the term is often enclosed in quotation marks:

> In offset printing "proofs" of illustrations come from the darkroom, not the proof press.
>
> the "Levalloisian" culture complex of Tanzania [application of a European term to an African site]

6.63   *Philosophical terms.* By convention in works of philosophy and theology, terms having special philosophical or theological meaning are often enclosed in single quotation marks. Following punctuation is placed outside the quotation marks:

> If such procedure is justifiable, 'agrees with' must carry the sense of 'is consistent with'.
>
> 'being'   'nonbeing'   'the divine'

QUOTED PHRASES

6.64   Words and phrases quoted from another context, of course, are usually set in quotation marks:

> The "pursuit of happiness" is an end more often mentioned with approbation than defined with precision.

Such uses are discussed in chapter 10.

6.65   Often, however, an author wishes to single out a word or phrase, not quoting it from a specific document as in the example just given but referring it to a general background that will be recognized by the reader. Here quotation marks are also appropriate:

> Myths of "paradise lost" are common in folklore.
>
> In Tate's "alteration" the ending of *Lear* is changed so that Cordelia survives and marries Edgar.

WORDS USED AS WORDS

6.66   References to words as words are commonly italicized, as are terms singled out as terms:

> Use of the word *desuetude* when *disuse* will serve is often pretentious.
>
> The term *gothic* means different things to typographers and paleographers.

6.67   When use of the spoken language is implied, quotation marks sometimes serve better:

> In Elizabethan dialogue a change from "you" to "thou" often implies studied insult.

6.68   Words used in an ironic sense may be enclosed in quotation marks:

> Five villages were subjected to "pacification."
> The "debate" resulted in three cracked heads and two broken noses.

Such use of quotation marks should always be regarded as a last resort, to be used when the irony might otherwise be lost. Skillfully prepared for, an ironic meaning seldom eludes the reader even though quotation marks are not used.

SLANG

6.69   Words classed as slang or argot may be enclosed in quotation marks if they are foreign to the normal vocabulary of the speaker:

> Alfie was accompanied by his "trouble and strife" as he strolled down the Strand.
> Had it not been for Bryce, the "copper's nark," Collins would have made his escape.

USE OF "SO-CALLED"

6.70   When the expression *so-called* is used with a word or phrase, implying that something is popularly or (sometimes) mistakenly given such-and-such designation, the designation itself should not be enclosed in quotation marks or set in italics. *So-called* is sufficient to mark off the usage as a special one:

> The so-called shadow cabinet was thought to be responsible for some of the president's more injudicious decisions.
> A so-called right of sanctuary was offered in justification of the minister's failure to surrender the escaped felon.

LETTERS USED AS WORDS

6.71   Letters used as words demand varied treatments depending upon the kind of letter and its context.

6.72   *Letters as letters.* Individual letters of the Latin (English) alphabet and combinations of letters are italicized:

> the letter *q*   a lowercase *n*   a capital *W*
> The normal sign of the plural in English is a terminal *s* or *es*.
> He signed the document with an *X*.

In some proverbial expressions the distinction is ignored:

> Mind your p's and q's.

6.73   *Named letters.* The name of a letter, as distinct from the letter itself, is usually set in roman type:

> from alpha to omega
> daleth, the fourth letter of the Hebrew alphabet
> an aitch   a dee   an ess

6.74   *Letters as musical notes.* Letters standing for musical tones are usually set as roman capitals:

> middle C   440 A
> the key of G major   the key of F-sharp minor
> the D-major triad   an E string

6.75   In technical works dealing with keyboard instruments differing systems are used to designate the various octaves. In one system tones in the octave below middle C are designated by lowercase letters, that is, c, c$\sharp$, d, . . . , a$\sharp$, b. Octaves above are designated with lowercase letters bearing superior numbers or primes: c^1, c^2, etc., or c', c'', etc. Lower octaves are designated, in descending order, by capital letters, double capital letters, etc.: C, CC, CCC. Technical works on the modern piano usually designate all tones with capital letters and a subscript, from A_1 at the bottom of the keyboard to C_{88} at the top.

6.76   In works on musical subjects where many keys are mentioned, it is common practice to use capital letters for major keys and lowercase for minor. If this practice is followed, the words *major* and *minor* are omitted:

> the key of G
>
> the e triad: E–G-natural–B
>
> The second movement of Beethoven's Sonata in c (op. 13) is in the key of A-flat.

6.77   In analyzing harmony, chords are designated by capital roman numerals indicating the note in the scale upon which the chord is based:

> V [a chord based on the fifth, or dominant, note of the scale]
> V⁷ [dominant seventh chord]

Step progressions are indicated, for example: IV–I$^6_4$–V–I.

6.78   *Letters as names.* A letter used in place of a name in a hypothetical statement and an initial used alone or with a 2-em dash to stand for a name are set as roman capitals:

> If A sues B for breach of contract . . .
> Admiral N—— and Lady R—— were guests.
> Mr. D. is the one to whom to address your request.

6.79   *Letters as shapes.* Gothic (sans serif) letters are preferred, when possible, for indicating shape:

> A V-shaped valley becomes U-shaped by glaciation.
> an S curve   an A frame

Roman capitals may always be used for this purpose when a gothic font is not available, and sometimes a roman letter suggests a particular shape better than gothic:

a steel I-beam

6.80 The spelled-out names of letters are also used as the names of particular objects, with reference to their shapes:

an ell (of a house)   a tee, a wye (road intersections, pipe fittings)

6.81 *Letters indicating rhyme schemes.* Lowercase, spaced italic letters are used to indicate rhyme patterns:

The Italian sonnet consists of an octave and a sestet: *abbaabba, cdcdcd.*
The English, or Shakespearean, sonnet: *abab, cdcd, efef, gg.*

Type Compound	Similar Compounds	Remarks
	Noun Forms	
master builder	master artist, master wheel *but:* mastermind, masterpiece, mastersinger, masterstroke	Spell temporary compounds with *master* open.
fellow employee	brother officer, mother church, father figure, foster child, parent organization	*Type:* word of relationship + noun. Spell all such compounds open.
decision making	problem solving, coal mining, bird watching	*Type:* object + gerund. Spell temporary compounds open. Many closed permanent compounds (e.g., *bookkeeping, dressmaking*) will be found in the dictionary. See also under Adjective Forms, below.
quasi corporation	quasi contract, quasi scholar, quasi union	Spell *quasi* noun compounds open. But see under Adjective Forms, below.
attorney general	postmaster general, surgeon general, judge advocate general	Safe to spell all similar compounds open.
vice-president	vice-chancellor, vice-consul *but:* viceroy, vicegerent, vice admiral	Temporary compounds with *vice-* are best hyphenated: *vice-manager, vice-chief.*
scholar-poet	author-critic, city-state, soldier-statesman	*Type:* noun + noun, representing different and equally important functions. Hyphenate.
grandfather	grandniece, grandnephew	Close up all *grand-* relatives.
brother-in-law	mother-in-law, sisters-in-law	Hyphenate all *in-laws.*
great-grandson	great-great-grandmother	Hyphenate all *great-* relatives.
self-restraint	self-knowledge, self-consciousness	Hyphenate all *self-* compounds. See also under Adjective Forms, below.
Johnny-on-the-spot	light-o'-love, Alice-sit-by-the-fire, stay-at-home, stick-in-the-mud *but:* flash in the pan, ball of fire	*Type:* combination of words including a prepositional phrase describing a character. Hyphenate any new creations.

TABLE 6.1—*Continued*

TYPE COMPOUND	SIMILAR COMPOUNDS	REMARKS
	Noun Forms—*Continued*	
one-half	two-thirds, four and five-sevenths *but:* thirty-one hundredths, three sixty-fourths	*Type:* spelled-out fractional number. Connect numerator and denominator with a hyphen unless either already contains a hyphen.
president-elect	senator-elect, mayor-elect *but:* county assessor elect	Hyphenate *-elect* compounds unless the name of the office is in two or more words.
headache	toothache, stomachache	Spell compounds with *-ache* solid.
checkbook	notebook, textbook, pocketbook, storybook *but:* reference book	Permanent compounds with *-book* are solid except for a few unwieldy ones. Temporary compounds should be spelled open: *pattern book, recipe book.*
boardinghouse	boathouse, clubhouse, greenhouse, clearinghouse *but:* rest house, business house	Permanent compounds with *-house* are solid; temporary ones, mainly open.
ex-president	ex-husband, ex-mayor, ex–corporate executive	Compounds with *ex-* meaning *former* are hyphenated (en dash when the second part is an open compound). Seldom used in formal writing, where *former* is preferred.
	Adjective Forms	
highly developed species	poorly seen, barely living, wholly invented, highly complex	*Type:* adverb ending in *-ly* + participle or adjective. Always open.
long-suffering	much-loved, ever-fruitful, still-active	*Type:* adverb other than the *-ly* type + participle or adjective. Now usually hyphenated before the noun.
Central European countries	Old English, Scotch Presbyterian, New Testament, Civil War, Latin American	*Type:* compound formed from unhyphenated proper names. Always open. (Do not confuse with such forms as *Scotch-Irish, Austro-Hungarian.*)

TABLE 6.1—*Continued*

TYPE COMPOUND	SIMILAR COMPOUNDS	REMARKS
	Adjective Forms—*Continued*	
sodium chloride solution	sulfuric acid, calcium carbonate	*Type:* chemical terms. Leave open.
grand prix racing	a priori, post mortem, Sturm und Drang *but:* laissez-faire	*Type:* foreign phrase used as an adjective. Leave open unless hyphenated in original language.
bluish green paint	gray blue, emerald green, coal black, reddish orange	*Type:* color term in which first element modifies the second. Leave open.
blue-green algae	red-green color blindness, black-and-white print	*Type:* color term in which elements are of equal importance. Hyphenate.
self-reliant boy	self-sustaining, self-righteous, self-confident, self-effacing *but:* selfless, selfsame, unselfconscious	Hyphenate *self-* compounds whether they precede or follow the noun. See also under Noun Forms, above.
decision-making procedures	curiosity-evoking, dust-catching, thirst-quenching, dissension-producing, interest-bearing	*Type:* object + present participle. Hyphenate all before the noun and a few permanent compounds (e.g., *thought-provoking*) after the noun.
twenty-odd performances	sixty-odd, fifteen-hundred-odd, 360-odd	*Type:* cardinal number + *odd*. Hyphenate before or after the noun.
ten-foot pole	three-mile limit, 100-yard dash, one-inch margin, 10-meter band, four-year-old boy *but:* 10 percent increase	*Type:* cardinal number + unit of measurement. Hyphenate compound if it precedes noun.
well-known man	ill-favored girl, well-intentioned person *but:* very well known man; he is well known	Compounds with *well-, ill-, better-, best-, little-, lesser-,* etc., are hyphenated before the noun unless expression carries a modifier.
high-, low-level job	high-class, high-energy, low-test, low-lying *but:* highborn, highbrow, lowbred	With few exceptions, *high-* and *low-* adjectival compounds are hyphenated in any position.
matter-of-fact approach	devil-may-care attitude, a how-to book, everything is up-to-date	*Type:* phrase used as adjective. Hyphenate in any position.

TABLE 6.1—*Continued*

Type Compound	Similar Compounds	Remarks
	Adjective Forms—*Continued*	
quasi-public corporation	quasi-judicial, quasi-legislative, quasi-stellar	Hyphenate adjectival *quasi-* compounds whether they precede or follow the noun. But see under Noun Forms, above.
half-baked plan	half-asleep, half-blooded, half-cocked, half-timbered *but:* halfhearted, halfway	Hyphenate adjectival *half-* compounds whether they precede or follow the noun.
two-thirds majority	The project is three-fourths completed. He was one-fourth white.	Common fractions used as adjectives or adverbs are hyphenated.
cross-referenced entries	cross-country, cross-fertile, cross-grained *but:* crossbred, crosscut, crosshatched, crosstown	Any temporary adjectival *cross-* compounds can be safely hyphenated.
all-inclusive study	all-around, all-powerful, all-out	Hyphenate *all-* compounds whether they precede or follow the noun.
coarse-grained wood	able-bodied, pink-faced, straight-sided, even-handed	*Type:* adjective + past participle derived from a noun. Hyphenate such compounds when they precede the noun. After the noun they can generally be left open.
catlike movements	fencelike, gridlike, saillike (*or* sail-like), basilicalike (*or* basilica-like) *always:* Tokyo-like, gull-like, vacuum-bottle-like	The suffix *-like* is freely used to form new compounds, which are generally spelled solid except for those formed from proper names, words ending in *ll,* and word combinations. Some also prefer to hyphenate when the base word ends in a single *l* or consists of three or more syllables.
a **tenfold** increase	twofold, multifold *but:* 25-fold	Adjectival compounds with *-fold* are spelled solid unless they are formed with figures.
a **statewide** referendum	worldwide, boroughwide, parishwide, archdiocese wide (*or* archdiocese-wide)	*Type:* word denoting a geographical, political, or social division + *-wide*. Close up unless the compound is long and cumbersome.

TABLE 6.1—*Continued*

Words Formed with Prefixes

A few words that might be considered word-forming prefixes appear in the columns above, and most of the adjectival forms are there hyphenated. The word-forming prefixes listed below (the list is not exhaustive) generate compounds that are nearly always closed, whether they are nouns, verbs, adjectives, or adverbs. The chief exceptions to the closed-style rule are the following:

Compounds in which the second element is a capitalized word or a numeral, as *anti-Semitic, un-American, pre-1914, post-Kantian, Anti-Federalist.*

Compounds that must be distinguished from homonyms, as *re-cover, un-ionized,* sometimes *re-create.*

Compounds in which the second element consists of more than one word, as *pre-latency-period* therapy, *non-English-speaking* people, *pre–Civil War.* (In the last, note the en dash, used with an open compound.)

A few compounds in which the last letter of the prefix is the same as the first letter of the word following. Examples of these appear below.

Newly invented compounds of the last type tend to be treated in hyphenated style when they first appear and then to be closed up when they have become more familiar. This may happen, for example, to coinages like *infra-area* and *meta-analysis,* as it already has to *intraarterial.* (For *meta-analysis,* however, a better choice would be *metanalysis,* since the combining prefix also exists in the form *met-.*) In addition to familiarity, appearance also influences the retention of hyphens, and it is never wrong to keep a hyphen so as to avoid misleading or puzzling forms (e.g., *non-native, anti-intellectual*).

Note also that when a prefix stands alone, it carries a hyphen: *over- and underused, macro- and microeconomics.*

Prefix	Examples
ante-	anteroom, antediluvian, antenatal
anti-	anticlerical, antihypertensive, *but* anti-inflammatory, anti-utopian, anti-hero
bi-	bivalent, biconvex, binomial
bio-	bioecology, biophysical
co-	coauthor, coordinate, coeditor, *but* co-edition, co-opt, co-op, co-worker
counter-	counterclockwise, countermeasures, countercurrent, counterblow
extra-	extraterrestrial, extrafine
infra-	infrasonic, infrastructure
inter-	interrelated, intertidal, interregnum
intra-	intraarterial, intrazonal, intracranial
macro-	macroeconomics, macrosphere, macromolecular
meta-	metalanguage, metagalaxy, metaethical, metastable
micro-	microminiaturized, microimage, micromethod
mid-	midocean, midtown, midgut
mini-	minibus, miniskirt, minibike
multi-	multifaceted, multistory, multiconductor

TABLE 6.1—*Continued*

PREFIX	EXAMPLES
non-	nonviolent, nonperson, nonplus, nonnative (*or* non-native)
over-	overlong, overeager, overanalyzed
post- ("after")	postdoctoral, postface, postwar, postparturition
pre-	preempt, precognition, preconference, premalignant
pro-	progovernment, procathedral, procephalic
pseudo-	pseudopregnancy, pseudoclassic, pseudoheroic
re-	reedit, reunify, redigitalize, reexamine
semi-	semiopaque, semiconductor, *but* semi-independent, semi-indirect
sub-	subjacent, subbasement, subcrustal
super-	supertanker, superhigh (frequency), superpose
supra-	supranational, suprarenal, supraliminal
trans-	transoceanic, transmembrane, transsocietal
ultra-	ultrafiche, ultramontane, ultraorganized
un-	unfunded, unchurched, uncoiffed, unneutered
under-	underused, undersea, underpowered, underreport

7 *Names and Terms*

Introduction 7.1
    Capitalization 7.2
    Italics and Quotation Marks with Names 7.5
Personal Names 7.6
    English Names with Particles 7.7
    Foreign Names 7.8
        French names 7.8
        Italian, Portuguese, German, Dutch names 7.9
        Spanish names 7.10
        Arabic names 7.11
        Chinese names 7.12
        Russian names 7.13
        Hungarian names 7.14
    Titles and Offices 7.15
        Civil titles and offices 7.18
        Military titles and offices 7.19
        Religious titles and offices 7.20
        Professional titles 7.21
        Titles of nobility 7.22
    Academic Degrees and Honors 7.26
    Honorific Titles 7.27
    Epithets 7.28
    Fictitious Names 7.29
    Kinship Names 7.30
    Personification 7.31
Nationalities, Tribes, and Other Groups of People 7.32
Place Names 7.34
    Parts of the World 7.34
        Popular names 7.36
    Political Divisions 7.37
    Topographical Names 7.38
    Structures and Public Places 7.43
Words Derived from Proper Names 7.46
Names of Organizations 7.47
    Governmental and Judicial Bodies 7.47
        Legislative and deliberative 7.48
        Administrative 7.49
        Judicial 7.50
    Political and Economic Organizations and Alliances 7.54
    Institutions and Companies 7.57
    Associations and Conferences 7.58
Historical and Cultural Terms 7.60
    Periods 7.60
    Events 7.65

Cultural Movements and Styles 7.66
Acts, Treaties, and Government Programs 7.67
Legal Cases 7.69
Awards 7.70
Calendar and Time Designations 7.71
Seasons and Days of the Week 7.71
Holidays and Holy Days 7.72
Time and Time Zones 7.73
Religious Names and Terms 7.74
God, Deities, and Revered Persons 7.75
The one God 7.76
Revered persons 7.78
Platonic ideas 7.79
Religious Bodies 7.80
Broad groups 7.80
Denominations and other groups and movements 7.81
Local groups 7.82
Councils, synods, and meetings 7.83
Religious Writings 7.84
The Bible 7.84
Other works 7.85
Adjectives 7.86
Shorter religious writings and utterances 7.87
Creeds and confessions 7.88
Events and Concepts 7.89
Religious Services 7.90
Eucharistic rite 7.90
Other services 7.91
Objects of Religious Use or Significance 7.92
Military Terms 7.93
Forces and Groups of Participants 7.93
Wars, Battles, Campaigns, and Theaters of War 7.94
Military Awards and Citations 7.95
Ships, Aircraft, and Spacecraft 7.96
Scientific Terminology 7.98
Scientific Names of Plants and Animals 7.98
Genus and species 7.99
Larger divisions 7.102
English derivatives 7.103
Vernacular Names of Plants and Animals 7.104
Geological Terms 7.108
Astronomical Terms 7.110
Medical Terms 7.115
Diseases and syndromes 7.115
Drugs 7.117
Physical and Chemical Terms 7.118
Laws, principles, etc. 7.118
Chemical symbols and names 7.119
Trademarks 7.121
Titles of Works 7.122
General Rules 7.122
Capitalization 7.123

Spelling 7.125
Punctuation 7.126
Books and Periodicals 7.129
  Articles and parts of a book 7.134
  Series and editions 7.137
Poems and Plays 7.138
Unpublished Works 7.142
Motion Pictures and Television and Radio Programs 7.143
Musical Compositions 7.144
Paintings and Sculpture 7.148
Notices 7.149
Mottoes 7.150
Computer Terms 7.151
For Further Reference 7.154

INTRODUCTION

7.1   The purpose of this chapter is to establish a pattern in the use of names and of terms associated with names: names of persons and places, of events and movements, of governmental bodies and their actions, of certain things and classifications, as well as titles of literary and artistic works. Which of these should always be capitalized and what titles are commonly set in italics are questions that must be resolved before any reasonable editorial consistency can be attained in a book or journal.

CAPITALIZATION

7.2   Modern publishers of works in the English language, American perhaps more than British, usually discourage excessive use of capital letters in text matter. Proper nouns are still conventionally capitalized,[1] but many words derived from or associated with them may be lowercased with no loss of clarity or significance. Questions and differences of opinion arise over just what is a proper noun, other than the name of a person or a place. It is with this realm of uncertainty that the following rules attempt to deal. They reflect the tendency toward the use of fewer capitals, toward what is called a *down* (lowercase) style as opposed to an *up* (uppercase, i.e., capital letter) style.

7.3   Although the pattern of capitalization for various categories illustrated in this chapter is preferred by the University of Chicago Press and is adaptable to most publications, it may require modification in some specialized works. *Experienced editors realize that no set of rules in*

1. To *capitalize* a word means to capitalize only the initial letter. A word or phrase printed all in capital letters, LIKE THIS, is said to be set in *full caps*.

the area of capitalization can be universally applicable. And particular authors may have particular and valid reasons for capitalizing certain terms normally lowercased in other works. When authors do have reason to depart from the usual patterns, however, they should so inform their publishers by providing a list of the terms involved. If an editor can find no valid reason for an author's departure from convention, there should be a consultation between editor and author, and agreement or compromise reached, before the editor undertakes to prepare the manuscript for publication.

7.4 Most authors, however, do not feel strongly about capitalization, and many are oblivious to inconsistencies in their manuscripts. The manuscript editor must therefore establish a logical, acceptable style and regularize any departures from it (see 2.90). The following categories and lists will, it is hoped, provide a helpful pattern for editors to follow. Rules for capitalizing or lowercasing specific names or terms can seldom be applied to every case. The editor, understanding the nature of the work, must use discretion, judgment, and intuition in deciding when to follow the pattern and when to depart from it.

ITALICS AND QUOTATION MARKS WITH NAMES

7.5 Some names of things and titles of works are conventionally set in italic type. Other titles, chiefly of shorter works or parts of larger works, are set in roman type and enclosed in quotation marks. Still others are capitalized but neither italicized nor quoted. Like the conventions of capitalization these may also be altered in certain situations. For example, the author of a critical study in literature or music containing many references to short stories or essays as well as book-length works or to both long and short poems or musical compositions is well advised to give *all* titles in italics.

PERSONAL NAMES

7.6 Names and initials of persons are capitalized:

C. K. Scott Moncrieff	R. W. B. Lewis
W. Theodore Watts-Dunton	C. V. Wedgwood
John F. Kennedy	LBJ

The space between initials should be the same as the space between initial and name (*not* R.W.B. Lewis). For most names, the Press uses the spelling in *Webster's Biographical Dictionary* (or the Biographical Names section of *Webster's New Collegiate Dictionary*), *Who's Who*, and *Who's Who in America*.

ENGLISH NAMES WITH PARTICLES

7.7   Many names of French, Spanish, Portuguese, Italian, German, and Dutch derivation include particles: *de, du, la, l', della, von, van, van der, ten,* etc. For names of this type borne by people in English-speaking countries, practice with regard to capitalizing the particles varies widely, and competent authority should be consulted in doubtful cases.[2] Generally the surname retains the particle when used alone:

> Eugen D'Albert; D'Albert
> Lee De Forest; De Forest
> Walter de la Mare; de la Mare
> Daphne du Maurier; du Maurier
> Eva Le Gallienne; Le Gallienne
> Abraham Ten Broeck; Ten Broeck
> Martin Van Buren; Van Buren
> Wernher Von Braun; Von Braun
> Alexander de Seversky; de Seversky
> Eamon de Valera; de Valera

FOREIGN NAMES

7.8   *French names.* In French practice, the articles *le, la,* and *les,* as well as the contractions *du* and *des,* are capitalized whether or not a first name or title precedes (in many family names, of course, they are run in—Desmoulins, Lafayette):

> François, duc de La Rochefoucauld; La Rochefoucauld
> Philippe Du Puy de Clinchamps; Du Puy de Clinchamps

The preposition *de* (or *d'*) is always lowercased and is often dropped when the surname is used alone:

> Alexis de Tocqueville; Tocqueville
> Alfred de Musset; Musset
> > *but:*
> Charles de Gaulle; de Gaulle
> Jean d'Alembert; d'Alembert
> Comte de Grasse; Admiral de Grasse; de Grasse

7.9   *Italian, Portuguese, German, Dutch names.* For other names with particles, Romance or Germanic, the particles are lowercased and are usually dropped when the surname is used alone in the original language. In English, writers have shown little consistency in their treatment of such names. The frequent older practice was to retain and capitalize the particle when the surname was used alone. Consequently, for many names the form with the particle is the only familiar one and must necessarily be used. As with French names Press style follows native practice as far as possible:

2. For alphabetizing names with particles see 18.102.

Giovanni da Verrazano; Verrazano
Luca della Robbia; *in English contexts,* della Robbia
Vasco da Gama; *in English contexts,* da Gama
Heinrich Friedrich Karl vom und zum Stein; Stein
Alexander von Humboldt; Humboldt
Maximilian von Spee; Spee
Friedrich von Steuben; *in English contexts often* von (*or* Von) Steuben
Ludwig van Beethoven; Beethoven
Vincent van Gogh; *in English usually* van Gogh
Bernard ter Haar; ter Haar
van't Hoff, Jacobus Hendricus; van't Hoff
Van Twiller, Wouter; Van Twiller

7.10   *Spanish names.* Many Spanish surnames are composed of both the father's and the mother's family names, in that order, sometimes joined by *y* (and). These names are often shortened to a single name (usually but not always the first of the two). It is never incorrect to use both names, but tradition or the person's own preference sometimes dictates the use of only one:

José Ortega y Gasset; Ortega y Gasset *or* Ortega
Pascual Ortiz Rubio; Ortiz Rubio *or* Ortiz
Federico García Lorca; Lorca

Many Spanish names are compounded with an article, a preposition, or both, as are many French names:

Tomás de Torquemada; Torquemada
Manuel de Falla; *in English contexts,* de Falla
Bartolomé de las Casas; Las Casas

(For more on Spanish names see 18.106.)

7.11   *Arabic names.* Surnames of Arabic origin often are prefixed by such elements as *Abu, Abd* (*Abdul, Abdel*), *ibn, al,* or *el.* These are part of the surname and should not be dropped when the surname is used alone (for alphabetizing Arabic names see 18.110–11):

Syed Abu Zafar Navdi; Abu Zafar Navdi
Aziz ibn-Saud; ibn-Saud

Names of rulers of older times, however, are often shortened to the first name rather than the last:

Harun al-Rashid; Harun

7.12   *Chinese names.* In Chinese practice, the family name comes before the given name, which is usually of two elements. As romanized in the Wade-Giles system, the family name and the first element of the given name are capitalized, and the given name is hyphenated: Chiang Kai-shek, Pai Ch'ung-hsi. Chinese may be referred to by family name alone: Chiang; Pai. Ancient Chinese names are often of only two elements, which may not be separated: Li Po, Tu Fu, Lao Tzu. The pinyin romanization system, generally used since the late 1970s for Chinese names in material in the English language, employs no hyphens or apostrophes and spells given names as one word (see 9.113).

7.13 *Russian names.* Russian family names, as well as middle names (patronymics), sometimes but not always take different endings for male and female members of the family. For example, Lenin's real name was Vladimir Ilyich Ulyanov; his sister was Maria Ilyinichna Ulyanova. Often in text matter only the given name and patronymic are used; in the index, of course, the name should be listed under the family name, whether this appears in the text or not.

7.14 *Hungarian names.* In Hungarian practice the family name precedes the given name—Molnár Ferenc—but (as with this playwright) the names are often inverted to normal English order when used in a non-Hungarian context: Ferenc Molnár.

TITLES AND OFFICES

7.15 Civil, military, religious, and professional titles and titles of nobility are capitalized when they immediately precede a personal name, as part of the name:

> President Buchanan
> General Eisenhower
> Cardinal Newman
> Emperor Maximilian

Note that when such titles are used in apposition to a name they are not part of the name and so are lowercased:

> the emperor Maximilian (i.e., the emperor who was Maximilian)
> French president François Mitterrand (*better:* President François Mitterrand of France)

7.16 In formal usage, such as acknowledgments and lists of contributors, titles following a personal name are usually capitalized. A title used alone, in place of a personal name, is capitalized in such contexts as toasts or formal introductions:

> The translators wish to acknowledge their indebtedness to C. R. Dodwell, Fellow and Librarian of Trinity College, Cambridge.
> Ladies and gentlemen, the President of the United States.

Titles used informally in place of names in direct address are capitalized:

> I would have done it, Captain, but the ship was sinking.
> Please, Judge, you are standing on my foot.
> Only yesterday, Professor, you said . . .

7.17   In text matter, titles following a personal name or used alone in place of a name are, with few exceptions, lowercased.[3] The following lists show various titles and words related to them as they might appear in text sentences.

7.18   *Civil titles and offices*

Abraham Lincoln, president of the United States; President Lincoln; the president of the United States; the president; the presidency; presidential; the Lincoln administration

William Henry Seward, secretary of state; Secretary (of State) Seward; the secretary of state; the secretary

Charles H. Percy, senator from Illinois; Senator Percy; the senator from Illinois; the senator

Thomas P. O'Neill, Speaker of the House of Representatives; Congressman[4] O'Neill; the Speaker[5] of the House; the congressman; the representative from Massachusetts; *informal:* Congressman "Tip" O'Neill

Jane M. Byrne, mayor of Chicago; Mayor Byrne; the mayor of Chicago; the mayor

Warren E. Burger, chief justice of the United States; Chief Justice Burger; the chief justice

John Paul Stevens, associate justice of the Supreme Court; Justice Stevens (*or* Mr. Justice Stevens); the justice

Kingman Brewster, ambassador to the Court of St. James's *or* ambassador to Great Britain; the ambassador to Great Britain; the American ambassador; the ambassador; the American embassy

James R. Thompson, governor of the state of Illinois; the governor of Illinois

Frederick Lord North, prime minister of England; Lord North; the prime minister of England; the North ministry

Geoffrey Windermere, member of Parliament (*or* M.P.); a member of Parliament

George Canning, foreign minister of Great Britain; the British foreign minister

Emperor William (*or* Wilhelm) II of Germany; William II, emperor of Germany; Kaiser Wilhelm; the kaiser

Chancellor Adolf Hitler; the chancellor; the führer

7.19   *Military titles and offices*

General Ulysses S. Grant, commander in chief of the Union army; General Grant; the commander in chief; the general

3. Named professorships and fellowships are usually capitalized wherever they appear, especially if they include a personal name: Ferdinand Schevill Distinguished Service Professor. *But:* Fulbright scholar.

4. *Congressman,* not *Representative,* is commonly used for a member of the U.S. House of Representatives.

5. Usually capitalized even when used alone, to avoid ambiguity.

Omar N. Bradley, General of the Army;[6] General Bradley, chairman of the Joint Chiefs of Staff; the general

Chester W. Nimitz, Fleet Admiral; Admiral Nimitz, commander of the Pacific Fleet; the admiral

Sergeant John Doe; a noncommissioned officer (NCO); the sergeant

General Sir Guy Carleton, British commander in New York City; Sir Guy; the general

7.20   *Religious titles and offices*

Pope John Paul II; the pope; papacy

Francis Cardinal Spellman, *or, less formally,* Cardinal Francis Spellman; Cardinal Spellman; the cardinal; the sacred college of cardinals

Archbishop Makarios III; the archbishop

Frederick Temple, archbishop of Canterbury; the archbishop of Canterbury; the archbishop

Rabbi Stephen Wise; the rabbi

the Reverend James Neal, minister of Third Presbyterian Church; Mr. (*or* Dr.) Neal; Rev. James Neal (see 14.7); the minister

the Right Reverend Gerald Francis Burrill, bishop of Chicago [Anglican]; Bishop Burrill; the bishop of Chicago; the bishop; bishopric; diocese

the Reverend George Smith, rector of Saint David's Church [Anglican]; Father Smith *or* Mr. Smith *or* the Reverend Mr. Smith (*not* Reverend Smith); the rector

the Most Reverend John A. Donovan, bishop of Toledo [Roman Catholic]; Bishop Donovan; the bishop of Toledo

the Reverend John Dunn, pastor of Saint Thomas Aquinas Church [Roman Catholic]; Father Dunn; the pastor

the Catholic bishop of New Orleans

the mother superior of the Ursuline convent

the patriarch of Constantinople; the patriarchate

7.21   *Professional titles*

Hanna H. Gray, president of the University of Chicago; Mrs. Gray; President Gray; the president; the president's office; President and Mr. Gray

Norman F. Maclean, William Rainey Harper Professor Emeritus in the College; Professor Maclean; the professor of English; a professor emeritus

Peter F. Dembowski, chairman of the Department of Romance Languages and Literatures; Professor Dembowski; the chairman of the department

Edward Smith, president of Smith Corporation; Mr. Smith; the president of the corporation

6. The formal titles *General of the Army* and *Fleet Admiral* are capitalized to avoid ambiguity.

7.22   *Titles of nobility*

> Elizabeth II, queen of England; Queen Elizabeth; the queen of England; the queen
>
> Emperor Charles V; the emperor Charles V; the emperor; *but* the Holy Roman Emperor Charles V
>
> Anthony Ashley Cooper, third earl of Shaftesbury; the earl of Shaftesbury; the earl
>
> Sir Humphrey Blimp, Bart.; Sir Humphrey; the baronet
>
> Prince Philip, duke[7] of Edinburgh; the duke
>
> Dowager Queen Mary; the dowager queen
>
> Count (*or* Graf) Helmuth von Moltke; Count von Moltke; the count
>
> François de Lorraine, duc de Guise; the second duc de Guise; the duke

7.23   For the sake of clarity, or perhaps unbreakable tradition, some British titles are capitalized when used without a personal name:

> | Prince of Wales | Princess Royal |
> |---|---|
> | Queen Mother | Dame of Sark |
>
> *but:* prince consort

British usage favors a more liberal use of capitals for titles than that recommended above.

7.24   In newspaper and magazine writing, epithets denoting roles, such as *citizen, schoolboy, housewife, defendant, historian,* are sometimes capitalized preceding a name. This practice should be avoided in book publishing; the article *the* usually precedes such an epithet:

> the historian Arthur Schlesinger, Sr. (*not* Historian Schlesinger)

7.25   Terms designating academic years are lowercased:

> | freshman | junior |
> |---|---|
> | sophomore | senior |

ACADEMIC DEGREES AND HONORS

7.26   The names of academic degrees and honors should be capitalized when following a personal name, whether abbreviated or written in full:

> Clyde M. Haverstick, Doctor of Law
> John K. Follett, M.D.
> Lee Wallek, Fellow of the Royal Academy

But when academic degrees are referred to in such general terms as *doctorate, doctor's, bachelor's, master of science,* they are not capitalized.

7. Often capitalized in this honorary title.

7.27   Honorific titles and forms of address should be capitalized in any context:

Her (His) Majesty	Your Grace	Excellency
His (Her) Royal Highness	His Eminence	Your Honor
	but:	
my lord	sir	madam

EPITHETS

7.28   A characterizing word or phrase used as part of, or a substitute for, a personal name is capitalized and not quoted:

the Great Emancipator	the Sun King
the Wizard of Menlo Park	the Young Pretender
Stonewall Jackson	the Great Commoner
the Autocrat of the Breakfast Table	the Iron Duke
Babe Ruth	the Swedish Nightingale

When an epithet is used in addition to a full name, it is usually enclosed in quotation marks:

George Herman ("Babe") Ruth
Jenny Lind, "the Swedish Nightingale"
Huey Long, "the Kingfish"

FICTITIOUS NAMES

7.29   The names of fictitious or anonymous persons and names used as personifications are capitalized—

John Doe	John Barleycorn	Johnny Reb
Jane Doe	John Bull	Uncle Sam

—except when used in such expressions as:

by george	every man jack

KINSHIP NAMES

7.30   Kinship names are lowercased when preceded by modifiers. When used before a proper name or alone, in place of the name, they are usually capitalized:

His father died at the age of ninety-three.
My brother and sister live in California.
the Grimké sisters
"Happy birthday, Uncle Ed."
I know that Mother's middle name is Marie.
Please, Dad, let's go.

PERSONIFICATION

7.31   The personification of abstractions—giving them the attributes of persons—is not a common device in today's prose writing. When it is used, the personified noun is usually capitalized:

> When Nature designed her masterpiece, she never dreamed he'd turn out thus.
> In the springtime nature is at its best.
> Then Spring—with her warm showers—arrived.
> The icy blasts of winter had departed.
> Like Milton, he bade Melancholy begone.
> He had suffered from melancholy all his life.

Where there is doubt, the word should be lowercased:

> It was a battle between head and heart; reason finally won.

NATIONALITIES, TRIBES, AND OTHER GROUPS OF PEOPLE

7.32   The names of racial, linguistic, tribal, religious, and other groupings of mankind are capitalized:

Afro-American	Latino, Latina
Aryan	Magyar
Bushman	Malay
Caucasian (caucasoid)	Mongol (mongoloid)
Chicano(s), Chicana(s)	Mormon
Frenchman	Negro (negroid)
Hispanic(s)	Nordic
Indo-European	Oriental
Kaffir	Pygmy

but: native American (i.e., American Indian)

7.33   Designations based only on color, size, or local usage are lowercased:

aborigine	colored	red man
black	highlander	redneck
bushman	pygmy	white

PLACE NAMES

PARTS OF THE WORLD

7.34   Certain nouns and some adjectives designating parts of the world or regions of a continent or a country are generally (but not always) capitalized:

> Antarctica; Antarctic Circle; the Arctic; arctic climate; subantarctic

East; Orient; Far East(ern); Near East(ern); Middle East(ern);
Eastern customs; oriental (adj.); the East (U.S.); eastern (direction or
locality)

West; Occident; Western world; occidental (adj.); the West, West
Coast, Northwest, Pacific Northwest, Far West, Middle West, Midwest
(U.S.); western, far western, middle western, midwestern(er)

Central America; central Europe, Asia, United States, etc.

the Continent (Europe); continental Europe; the European continent;
Continental customs

North Pole; North Polar ice cap; polar regions

North American continent

North Atlantic; northern Atlantic

North Africa; East (West) Africa; northern, southern, central, eastern
Africa

Northern (Southern) Hemisphere

South Pacific

the South, the Southwest (U.S.); the south of France (the Midi); southern; southwestern

South Temperate Zone

Tropic of Capricorn; Neotropic(al); the tropics; tropical; subtropical

the equator; Equatorial Current; equatorial Africa

Southeast Asia; southeastern, southern, central Asia

Upper Michigan; the Upper Peninsula; northern Michigan

7.35   In works dealing with the years following World War II it is customary
to capitalize *Western Europe* and *Eastern Europe* when referring to
the political rather than simply geographical divisions of the Continent. Similarly, *Central Europe* is capitalized when referring to the
political division of World War I. In American Civil War contexts,
Southern(er) and *Northern(er)* are capitalized.

7.36   *Popular names.* Popular and legendary names of places are usually
capitalized and not enclosed in quotation marks:

> Albion
> Back Bay (Boston)
> Badlands (South Dakota)
> Bay Area (San Francisco)
> the Badger State
> Benelux countries
> Cathay
> the Channel (English Channel)
> City of Brotherly Love
> Deep South (U.S.); Old South; antebellum South
> the Delta (region in state of Mississippi)
> Eastern Shore (of Chesapeake Bay)
> Eternal City
> Fertile Crescent
> Foggy Bottom

Lake District
Land of the Rising Sun
Left Bank (Paris)
the Levant
the Loop (Chicago)
Near North (Chicago)
New World; Old World
Old Dominion (Virginia)
Promised Land
Panhandle
the Piedmont
Skid Row
South Seas
the States (U.S.)
Sun Belt
Tenderloin (San Francisco)
Twin Cities
the Village (New York)
West Side (New York or Chicago)
Wild West
    but:
iron curtain countries

As a generic name for an idealized state *utopia* is lowercased.

POLITICAL DIVISIONS

7.37   In general, words designating political divisions of the world, a country, state, city, and so forth, are capitalized when they follow the name and form an accepted part of it: *empire, state, county, city, kingdom, colony, territory,* etc. They are usually, though not always, lowercased when they precede the name or stand alone:

Roman Empire; the empire under Augustus; the empire
Washington State; the state of Washington
New England states; Middle Atlantic states
Hennepin County; the county of Hennepin[8]
New York City; the city of New York[9]
Massachusetts Bay Colony; the colony at Massachusetts Bay
the British colonies; the thirteen colonies
the Province of Ontario; the province
the Union of Soviet Socialist Republics; the Soviet Union; the USSR
the Union of South Africa; the Union
the Union (U.S.)
Northwest Territory
Indiana Territory; the territory of Indiana
Evanston Township; the town of Evanston

8. Irish usage: county Kildare.

9. The City, meaning the financial center, the old city, of London, is always capitalized.

Eleventh Congressional District; his congressional district
Fifth Ward; the ward; ward politics
Sixth Precinct; the precinct
the Dominion of Canada; the dominion *or* the Dominion
the Republic of France; the French republic; the republic *or* the Republic; the Fifth Republic
the Republic (U.S.)

TOPOGRAPHICAL NAMES

7.38   Names of mountains, rivers, oceans, islands, and so forth are capitalized. A generic term—such as *lake, mountain, river, valley*—used as part of a name is also capitalized, whether or not it is capitalized in the gazetteer or atlas, where all doubtful spellings should be checked by author or editor:

> Bering Strait
> Black Forest
> Cape Sable
> Great Barrier Reef
> Himalaya Mountains; the Himalayas
> Iberian Peninsula; the peninsula
> Indian Ocean
> Kaskaskia River (*but* the river Elbe)
> Mozambique Channel
> Nile Delta
> Silver Lake
> the Sea of Azov
> South China Sea
> Walden Pond
> Windward Islands; the Windwards

7.39   When a generic term is used in the plural following more than one name, it is lowercased:

> between the Hudson and the Mississippi rivers
> the Adirondack and Catskill mountains

7.40   When a generic term precedes more than one name, it is usually capitalized:

> Lakes Michigan and Huron
> Mounts Everest and Rainier

7.41   When a generic term is used descriptively rather than as part of the name, or when used alone, it is lowercased:

> the valley of the Mississippi
> the Hudson River valley
> the French coast (*but* the West Coast [U.S.])
> the California desert
> the Kansas prairie

> the Indian peninsula (*but* the Malay Peninsula)
> along the Pacific coast (*but* Pacific Coast *if the region is meant*)

7.42   When a foreign term forms part of a geographic name in English, the meaning of the foreign term should be observed when citing:

> Rio Grande (*not* Rio Grande River)
> Sierra Nevada (*not* Sierra Nevada Mountains *or* the Sierras)
> Mauna Loa (*not* Mount Mauna Loa *or* Mauna Loa Mountain)
> Fujiyama (Fuji-san) *or* Mount Fuji (*not* Mount Fujiyama *or* Fujiyama Mountain)

STRUCTURES AND PUBLIC PLACES

7.43   Names of buildings, thoroughfares, monuments, and the like are capitalized:

> the White House
> the Capitol (national; distinguish between *capital*, a city, and *capitol*, a building)
> the Mall (Washington, D.C.; London)
> Statue of Liberty[10]
> the Midway (Chicago)
> the Pyramids (*but* the Egyptian pyramids)
> the Sphinx
> Leaning Tower of Pisa
> Stone of Scone

7.44   Such terms as *avenue, boulevard, bridge, building, church, fountain, hotel, park, room, square, street, theater,* are capitalized when part of a specific official or formal name. When they stand alone or are used collectively following two or more proper names, they are lowercased:

> Adler Planetarium; the planetarium
> Empire State Building; the Empire State
> the Empire State and Chrysler buildings
> Fifth Avenue (*by New Yorkers sometimes called* the Avenue)
> Fifty-seventh Street
> First Congregational Church; the church
> Golden Gate Bridge
> 4146 Grand Avenue
> Lincoln Park; the park
> the Oval Office; the president's office
> the Outer Drive; the drive
> the Persian Room (*of a hotel; but* room 16)

10. Regarded as a monument, not a piece of sculpture, and therefore not italicized. For names of statues, etc., see 7.148.

Philharmonic Hall in Lincoln Center for the Performing Arts; the hall; the center
Phoenix Theatre (*in this case not* Theater); the theater
Piccadilly Circus
U.S. Route 66
Spassky Gate
Times Square
Madison and State streets

7.45 Titles of foreign structures, streets, etc., given in the original language are not italicized (see also 9.20):

Bibliothèque Nationale
Bois de Boulogne
Champs-Elysées
Palacio Nacional
Palais Royal
Piazza delle Terme
Puente de Segovia
18, rue de Provence
Via Nazionale

WORDS DERIVED FROM PROPER NAMES

7.46 Nouns, adjectives, and verbs derived from personal or geographical names are lowercased when used with a specialized meaning:

anglicize
arabic figures
arctic boots
bohemian
brussels sprouts
china (ceramic ware)
diesel engine
dutch oven
frankfurter
french fries, dressing, windows
herculean
homeric
india ink
italicize
japan (varnish)
jeremiad
lombardy poplar

macadam road
manila envelope
mecca
morocco (leather)
paris green
pasteurize
pharisaic
philistine
plaster of paris
quixotic
roman type
roman numerals
russian dressing
scotch whisky
sienna (pigment)
venetian blinds
vulcanize

NAMES OF ORGANIZATIONS

GOVERNMENTAL AND JUDICIAL BODIES

7.47 Full names of legislative, deliberative, administrative, and judicial bodies, departments, bureaus, and offices are usually capitalized. Ad-

199

jectives derived from them are lowercased, as are paraphrastic or incomplete designations, except abbreviations.

7.48　　*Legislative and deliberative*

United Nations Security Council; the Security Council; the council

United States Congress; the Ninety-seventh Congress; Congress; congressional

Senate (U.S.); the upper house of Congress

House of Representatives; the House; the lower house of Congress

Committee on Foreign Affairs; Foreign Affairs Committee; Fulbright committee; the committee

General Assembly of Illinois; Illinois legislature; assembly; state legislature; state senate

Chicago City Council; city council; council

Parliament; parliamentary; an early parliament; both houses of Parliament

House of Commons; the Commons

the Crown (British monarchy); Crown lands

Cortes (Spain)

Curia Regis; the great council (England)

Duma (Russia)

States General *or* Estates General (France)

Reichstag (Germany)

7.49　　*Administrative*

Department of State; State Department; the department

National Labor Relations Board; the board; NLRB

Bureau of the Census; Census Bureau; the bureau; the census of 1960

Agency for International Development; AID; the agency

Peace Corps

Chicago Board of Education; the board

7.50　　*Judicial*

United States Supreme Court; the Supreme Court; the Court[11]

Arizona Supreme Court; state supreme court

United States Court of Appeals for the Second Circuit; court of appeals; circuit court; the court

Circuit Court of Cook County; county court; circuit court

Municipal Court of Chicago; municipal court

District Court for the Southern District of New York; district court

Juvenile Division of the County Department of the Circuit Court of Cook County

Court of King's Bench; the court

Star Chamber

11. The word *court* when used alone is capitalized only in references to the U.S. Supreme Court.

7.51 Generic terms designating courts are frequently used in place of a full name. They are lowercased, even when they refer to a specific court:

traffic court　　　family court　　　juvenile court

7.52 Each state has its own system for denominating its courts. Sometimes capitalization other than that suggested above is desirable for clarity. For example, in New York and Maryland the highest state court is not the supreme court but the court of appeals:

New York Court of Appeals; the Court of Appeals (capitalized to distinguish it from the U.S. court); the court

7.53 Not usually capitalized are:

administration; Eisenhower administration
brain trust
cabinet (*but* Kitchen Cabinet in the Jackson administration)
church and state
city hall (i.e., the municipal government)
court (royal)
electoral college
executive, legislative, or judicial branch
federal (government, agency, court, powers, etc.)
government
ministry
monarchy
parlement (*but* Parlement of Paris)
state (powers, laws, etc.; state's attorney)
witenagemot

POLITICAL AND ECONOMIC ORGANIZATIONS AND ALLIANCES

7.54 Names of national and international organizations, movements, and alliances and of members of political parties are capitalized, but not the words *party*,[12] *movement, platform,* and so forth (see also 7.56):

Bolshevik(i); Bolshevist(s)
Communist party; Communist(s); Communist bloc
Common Market
Entente Cordiale; the Entente
Fascist party; Fascist(s); Fascista (*pl.* Fascisti)
Federalist party; Federalist(s) (U.S. history)
Free-Soil party; Free-Soiler(s)
Hanseatic League; Hansa
Holy Alliance
Know-Nothing party; Know-Nothing(s)
Labour party; Labourites favor the interests of labor[13]

12. In certain contexts—for example, a work on the Communist party—where *party* is used in place of the full name and other parties may also be mentioned, the word *party* may be capitalized in references to the Communist party to avoid ambiguity.
13. In capitalized British names, British spelling is retained. If *Labourite* (meaning a person who votes for the Labour party) is lowercased, as it sometimes is, American spelling should be used in a work published in the United States: *laborite*.

> Loyalist(s) (American Revolution; Spanish civil war; etc.)
> Nazi party; Nazi(s)
> North Atlantic Treaty Organization; NATO
> Progressive party, movement; Progressive(s)
> Quadruple Alliance
> Republican party, platform; Republican(s)
> Tammany Hall; Tammany

7.55 Appellations of political groups other than parties are usually lower-cased:

> independent(s)
> labor bloc
> mugwump(s)
> opposition[14]
> right wing; right-winger; leftist (*but usually* the Right; the Left)

7.56 Nouns and adjectives designating political and economic systems of thought and their proponents are lowercased, unless derived from a proper noun:

> bolshevism
> communism
> democracy
> fascism
> Marxism-Leninism
> nazism
> progressivism
> socialism
> utilitarianism

INSTITUTIONS AND COMPANIES

7.57 Full titles of institutions and companies and the names of their departments and divisions are capitalized, but such words as *school* or *company*, as well as generic or descriptive terms, are lowercased when used alone:

> the University of Chicago;[15] the Law School; the Department of History; the university; the history department
>
> the Universities of Chicago and California; Harvard and Northwestern Universities
>
> Iowa Falls High School; the high school
>
> the Library of Congress (*not* Congressional Library); the Manuscripts Division; the library
>
> Smithsonian Institution (*not* Institute); the Smithsonian
>
> Hudson's Bay Company; the company
>
> General Foods Corporation; General Foods; the corporation
>
> Illinois Central Gulf Railroad; the Illinois Central; the railroad

14. Often capitalized in British contexts, meaning the party out of power.
15. The word *the* at the beginning of such titles is capitalized only when the official corporate name of the institution is called for: © 1982 by The University of Chicago.

the Board of Regents of the University of California; the board of regents; the board; the regents
New York Philharmonic
Washington National Symphony
Chicago Curled Hair Division of General Felt Industries

7.58   Full official names of associations, societies, unions, meetings, and conferences are capitalized. A *the* preceding a name is lowercased in textual matter, even when it is part of the official title. Such words as *society, union, conference,* are lowercased when used alone:

> Boy Scouts of America; a Boy Scout; a Scout
> Congress of Industrial Organizations; CIO
> Fifty-second Annual Meeting of the American Historical Association; the annual meeting of the association
> Green Bay Packers; the Packers; the team
> Independent Order of Odd Fellows; IOOF; an Odd Fellow
> Industrial Workers of the World; IWW; Wobblies
> Ku Klux Klan; KKK; the Klan
> League of Women Voters; the league
> New York Historical Society; the society
> Republican National Convention; the national convention; the convention
> Textile Workers Union of America; the union
> Union League Club; the club
> Young Men's Christian Association; YMCA

7.59   A substantive title given to a conference is enclosed in quotation marks:

> "Systematic Investigation of the African Later Tertiary and Quaternary," a symposium held at Burg Wartenstein, Austria, July–August 1965
>   *but:*
> the 1965 International Conference on Family Planning Programs

HISTORICAL AND CULTURAL TERMS

7.60   A numerical designation of a period is lowercased unless it is part of a proper name:

> eighteenth century
> the twenties
> quattrocento (fifteenth century)
> the seventeen hundreds

> Eighteenth Dynasty (*but* Sung dynasty)
> the period of the Fourth Republic

(For numerical designations in figures see 8.40.)

7.61 Some names applied to historical or cultural periods are capitalized, either by tradition or to avoid ambiguity. Such appellations are not enclosed in quotation marks:

> Christian Era
> Middle Ages; High Middle Ages; late Middle Ages
> Restoration
> Old Regime; *l'ancien régime* (*or* the ancien régime)
> Age of Louis XIV
> Era of Good Feelings
> Progressive Era
> Gilded Age
> Mauve Decade
> Roaring Twenties
> Dark Ages
> Renaissance; High Renaissance
> Reformation; Counter-Reformation
> Enlightenment
> Age of Reason
> Augustan Age

7.62 Most period designations, however, are lowercased except for proper nouns and adjectives:

> antiquity; ancient Greece; ancient Rome
> colonial period (U.S.)
> Victorian era
> baroque period
> romantic period
> fin de siècle

7.63 Names of cultural periods recognized by archaeologists and anthropologists and based upon characteristic technology are capitalized:

> Stone Age; Old Stone Age   Bronze Age
> Neolithic, Paleolithic times   Iron Age

(For geological periods see 7.108–9.)

7.64 Analogous latter-day designations, often capitalized in popular writing, are best lowercased:

> age of steam   nuclear age   space age

EVENTS

7.65 Appellations of historical, quasi-historical, political, economic, and cultural events, plans, and so forth are generally capitalized:

> Fall of Rome
> Reign of Terror

South Sea Bubble
Battle of the Books
Boston Tea Party
Industrial Revolution (often lowercased)
Reconstruction (U.S.)
Prohibition
Great Depression; the depression
New Deal
War on Poverty
Kentucky Derby
New York World's Fair
the Baltimore Museum of Art's exhibition American Prints, 1870–1950;
   the museum's exhibition of American prints
but:
gold rush; California gold rush
westward movement
panic of 1837
XYZ affair
Dreyfus affair
cold war
civil rights movement

(For wars, battles, conquests, see 7.94; for religious events, 7.89; for acts, treaties, 7.67.)

CULTURAL MOVEMENTS AND STYLES

7.66 Nouns and adjectives designating philosophical, literary, musical, and artistic movements, styles, and schools and their adherents are capitalized when they are derived from proper nouns. Others are usually lowercased unless, in certain contexts, capitalization is needed to distinguish the name of a movement or group from the same word in its general sense. This classification of names and terms is one most dependent on editorial discretion. In any given work a particular term must be consistently treated. The following list illustrates commonly acceptable style; terms lowercased here may sometimes require capitalization:

Aristotelian	Gothic
baroque	Gregorian chant; plainsong
camp	Hudson River school
Cartesian	humanism
Chicago school of architecture	idealism
classical	imagism
concrete poetry	impressionism
cubism	jazz
Cynic(ism)	miracle plays
dada(ism)	morality plays
Doric	mystic(ism)
Epicurean	naturalism
existentialism	neoclassic(ism)

Neoplatonism	romantic(ism)
New Criticism	Scholastics; Schoolmen
nominalism	Scholasticism
op art	scientific rationalism
Peripatetic	Sophist(s)
philosophe	Stoic(ism)
Physiocrat	structural(ism)
pop art	Sturm und Drang
Pre-Raphaelite	surrealism
realism	symbolism
rococo	theater of the absurd
Romanesque	transcendentalism

(For religious movements and schools of thought see 7.81.)

ACTS, TREATIES, AND GOVERNMENT PROGRAMS

7.67   Full formal or accepted titles of pacts, plans, policies, treaties, acts, laws, and similar documents or agreements, together with names of programs resulting from them, are usually capitalized and set in roman type without quotation marks. Incomplete names are usually lower-cased:

> Mayflower Compact; the compact
>
> Constitution of the United States; United States (*or* U.S.) Constitution; the Constitution (usually capitalized when referring to the U.S. Constitution)
>
> Illinois Constitution; the state constitution; the constitution
>
> Fifteenth Amendment (to the U.S. Constitution); the amendment; the Smith amendment
>
> Bill of Rights (first ten amendments to the U.S. Constitution; also England, 1689)
>
> due process clause (*sometimes* Due Process Clause)
>
> Articles of Confederation
>
> Declaration of Independence
>
> Wilmot Proviso
>
> Monroe Doctrine; the doctrine
>
> Open Door policy (*sometimes* open door policy)
>
> Peace of Utrecht
>
> Treaty of Versailles; the Versailles treaty; the treaty at Versailles
>
> Pact of Paris (*or, frequently but less correctly,*. Kellogg-Briand Pact); the pact
>
> Hawley-Smoot Tariff Act; the tariff act; the act
>
> Atomic Energy Act *or* McMahon Act; the act
>
> Federal Housing Act of 1961; the act of 1961; the 1961 act
>
> Marshall Plan; the plan
>
> Social Security (*or* social security)
>
> Medicare; Medicaid (*or* medicare; medicaid)
>
> Reform Bills; Reform Bill of 1832 (England); the 1832 bill
>
> Corn Laws (England) (*sometimes* corn laws)

New Economic Policy (USSR); NEP
Second Five-Year Plan; five-year plans

7.68 Descriptive references to pending legislation are lowercased:

The anti-injunction bill was introduced on Tuesday.
A gun-control law is being considered.

LEGAL CASES

7.69 The names of legal cases (plaintiff and defendant) are usually italicized; *v.* (versus) may be roman or italic, provided that use is consistent:

Miranda v. *Arizona*
Green v. *Department of Public Welfare*
West Coast Hotel Co. v. *Parrish*

In works dealing primarily with law, case names are not italicized when accompanied by their citations in text or notes:[16]

Thompson v. Shapiro, 270 F. Supp. 331 (D. Conn. 1967)

In a discussion a case name may be shortened:

the *Miranda* case
Miranda

Where the person rather than the case is meant, the name should of course be in roman type:

Escobedo's case, trial

AWARDS

7.70 Names of awards and prizes are capitalized:

Nobel Prize in physics; Nobel Peace Prize; Nobel Prize winners
Pulitzer Prize in fiction
Academy Award; Oscar; Emmy Award
International Music Scholarship
Heywood Broun Memorial Award
Laetare Medal
Guggenheim Fellowship (*but* Guggenheim grant)
National Merit scholarships

CALENDAR AND TIME DESIGNATIONS

SEASONS AND DAYS OF THE WEEK

7.71 Names of days of the week and months of the year are capitalized. The four seasons are lowercased (unless personified; see 7.31).

16. For more information on acceptable legal style, see *A Uniform System of Citation,* published by the Harvard Law Review Association.

| Tuesday | spring | the vernal (spring) equinox |
| November | fall | winter solstice |

(For *centuries* and *decades* see 7.60.)

HOLIDAYS AND HOLY DAYS

7.72   The names of religious holidays and seasons are capitalized:

Ash Wednesday	Maundy Thursday
Christmas Eve	Michaelmas
Easter Day (*not* Sunday)	Passover
Good Friday	Pentecost
Halloween; All Hallows' Eve	Ramadan
Hanukkah	Twelfth Night
Holy Week	Yom Kippur
Lent	Yuletide

So too are most secular holidays and other specially designated days:

All Fools' Day, April Fools' Day	New Year's Day
Arbor Day	National Book Week
Fourth of July; the Fourth;	Thanksgiving Day
Independence Day	V-E Day
Labor Day	Veterans Day
Mother's Day	*but:* D day

Mere descriptive appellations like *election day* or *inauguration day* are lowercased.

TIME AND TIME ZONES

7.73   When spelled out, designations of time and time zones are lowercased. Abbreviations are capitalized:

Greenwich mean time (GMT)	central daylight time (CDT)
daylight saving time (DST)	eastern standard time (EST)

RELIGIOUS NAMES AND TERMS

7.74   In few areas is an author more tempted to overcapitalize or an editor more loath to urge a lowercase style than in that of religion. That this is probably due to unanalyzed acceptance of the pious customs of an earlier age, to an unconscious feeling about words as in themselves numinous, or to fear of offending religious persons is suggested by the fact that overcapitalization is seldom seen in texts on the religions of antiquity or latter-day primitive religions. It is in the contexts of Christianity, Judaism, Islam, Buddhism, and Hinduism that we are tempted and fall. The editors of the University of Chicago Press urge a spare, *down* style in this field as in others: capitalize what are clearly proper nouns and adjectives, and lowercase all else except to avoid ambiguity. The following paragraphs attempt to be an empirical guide to the present state of capitalization in religious contexts. (For religious titles and offices see 7.20.)

GOD, DEITIES, AND REVERED PERSONS

7.75 Like all proper nouns the names of the one supreme God (as Allah, El, God, Jehovah, Yahweh) as well as the names of other deities (Astarte, Dagon, Diana, Pan, Shiva) are capitalized.

7.76 *The one God.* Other references to deity as the one supreme God, including references to the persons of the Christian Trinity, are capitalized:

Adonai	Most High
the Almighty	the Omnipotent
Christ	the Paraclete
the Father	Prince of Peace
the First Cause	Providence
Holy Ghost; Holy Spirit	the Savior (Jesus Christ)
the Holy One	Son of God
King of Kings	Son of man
Lamb of God	the Supreme Being
the Logos	the Supreme Shepherd
the Lord, our Lord	the Third Person (of the Trinity)
Messiah (Jesus Christ)	the Word

7.77 Pronouns referring to the foregoing are today preferably not capitalized:

God in his mercy
Jesus and his disciples

Nor are most derivatives, whether adjectives or nouns, capitalized:

(God's) fatherhood, kingship, omnipotence
(Jesus') sonship
messianic hope
godlike; godly
christological
            but:
Christology; Christlike; Christian

7.78 *Revered persons.* Appellations of revered persons such as prophets, apostles, and saints are often capitalized:

the Apostle to the Gentiles	the Fathers; church fathers
the Baptist	the Lawgiver
the Beloved Apostle	Messiah (Jewish)
the Blessed Virgin	Mother of God
Buddha	our Lady
the Divine Doctor	the Prophet (Muhammad)

209

Queen of Heaven   the Twelve
Saint Mark the Evangelist   the Virgin (Mary)

7.79   *Platonic ideas*. Words for transcendent ideas in the Platonic sense, especially when used in a religious context, are often capitalized:

> Good; Beauty; Truth; One

RELIGIOUS BODIES

7.80   *Broad groups*. Names of religions, churches, and communions and of their members, as well as derived adjectives, are capitalized:

> Anglicanism; an Anglican; the Anglican church; the Anglican communion
>
> Buddhism; a Buddhist; Buddhist ideas
>
> Catholicism; the Church Catholic; the Catholic church
>
> the Church of England, of Scotland, of Sweden, etc.
>
> Holy See
>
> Islam; Islamic; Muslim
>
> Judaism; Orthodox Judaism; Reform Judaism; an Orthodox Jew
>
> Orthodoxy; the Orthodox church; the (Greek, Russian, Serbian, etc.) Orthodox churches; Eastern church
>
> Protestantism; Protestant
>
> the Reformed Church in America; the Reformed church
>
> Roman Catholicism; a Roman Catholic; the Roman Catholic church; the Roman communion
>
> Shinto
>
> Vedanta
>
> > *but:*
>
> the mother church of the area
>
> church fathers

7.81   *Denominations and other groups and movements*. Treat similarly Christian denominations, sects, and orders; non-Christian sects; and most religious movements:[17]

> Arianism; the Arian heresy
>
> the Baptist church
>
> Christian Brothers
>
> Christian Science; a Christian Scientist
>
> Dissenter
>
> Essene; the Essenes
>
> a Gentile; gentile laws
>
> Gnosticism; a Gnostic; the Gnostic heresy, gospels
>
> High Church (*or* high church) movement, party
>
> Hussite

17. Many of these terms are used either specifically or generically and capitalized or lowercased accordingly—e.g., Puritan and puritan, Fundamentalism and fundamentalism.

Jehovah's Witnesses
Methodism; Methodist; the Methodist church
Monophysitism; Monophysite; Monophysite *or* Monophysitic churches
Mormonism; Mormon; the Mormon church; Latter-day Saints (Utah); Latter Day Saints (Missouri)
Nonconformist
Order of Preachers; the Dominican order; the order; a Dominican
Society of Jesus; a Jesuit; Jesuit teaching; jesuit, jesuitical (*derogatory*)
Sufi; Sufism
Theosophy; Theosophist
Zen; Zen Buddhism

7.82 *Local groups*. The names of smaller organized religious bodies and the buildings in which they meet are usually capitalized:

> Abbey of Mont Saint-Michel
> Bethany Evangelical Lutheran Church
> Church of the Redeemer
> Congregation Anshe Mizrach
> Grace Presbyterian Church
> Midwest Baptist Conference
> Our Lady of Sorrows Basilica
> Saint Andrew's Greek Orthodox Church
> Saint Leonard's House
> Saint Mary's Cathedral, Salisbury (*but* Salisbury cathedral)
> Sinai Temple

Note that in the foregoing examples, *church* is capitalized when it is part of the official name of an organized body of Christians or of a building (the Church of England, Saint Matthew's Church) but lowercased when merely descriptive (the Presbyterian church). When standing alone, *Church* is often capitalized when it refers to the whole body of Christians, worldwide or throughout time, but lowercased when it refers to a division of the universal Church or to a denomination. Terms like *cathedral, congregation, meeting* (Quaker), *mosque, synagogue,* and *temple* likewise are capitalized only when part of an official name.

7.83 *Councils, synods, and meetings*. The accepted names of historic councils and synods and the official names of modern counterparts are capitalized:

> Council of Chalcedon; Fourth General Council
> Council of Nicaea
> General Convention (Episcopal church)
> Second Vatican Council; Vatican II
> Synod of Whitby

RELIGIOUS WRITINGS

7.84 *The Bible*. Capitalize names—and use roman type—for the Judeo-Christian Bible and its versions and editions:

> Authorized, or King James (*not* Saint James) Version
> Bible; biblical
> Breeches Bible
> Codex Sinaiticus
> Complutensian Polyglot Bible
> Douay (Rheims-Douay) Version
> Gospels (*but* the gospel)
> Holy Bible
> Holy Writ
> Jerusalem Bible
> New English Bible
> Peshitta
> Revised Standard Version
> Scripture(s) (i.e., the Bible); scriptural
> Septuagint
> Vinegar Bible
> Vulgate

Also the books of the Bible (but note exceptions):

> Genesis
> Chronicles
> Job; Book of Job
> Psalms; Psalm 22 (*but* a psalm); Twenty-third Psalm
> Ezekiel
> 2 Maccabees
> the Rest of Esther
> John; the Gospel of John; the Fourth Gospel
> Acts; the Acts; Acts of the Apostles
> Romans; the Epistle to the Romans
> 3 John
> Revelation (*not* Revelations); the Revelation of Saint John the Divine; the Apocalypse

(For abbreviations of the books of the Bible see 14.34.)

And various divisions and sections of the Bible:

> Old Testament; New Testament
> Apocrypha
> the Law; the Prophets; the Writings
> Pentateuch
> Hagiographa
> the Gospels; the Epistles
> the synoptic Gospels
> the pastoral Epistles

7.85 *Other works*. Other sacred or highly revered works are similarly treated:

> Book of the Dead   Dead Sea Scrolls

Koran	Tripitaka
Mishnah	Upanishads
Talmud	Vedas

7.86   *Adjectives.* Adjectives derived from the names of sacred books are generally lowercased (apocryphal, biblical, scriptural, talmudic), but a few retain the initial capital (Koranic, Mishnaic, Vedic).

7.87   *Shorter religious writings and utterances.* Various scriptural selections of special importance bear names that are usually capitalized:

> the Decalogue, Ten Commandments
> the Beatitudes
> Sermon on the Mount
> the Miserere
> the Shema
> *but:*
> the parable of the unjust steward

So also many special prayers and canticles (mostly of scriptural origin) used devotionally:

Gloria Patri (*but* doxology)	the Litany of the Saints
Hail Mary, Ave Maria	the Lord's Prayer; the Our Father
Kaddish (*or* kaddish)	Nunc Dimittis
the Litany (Anglican)	Te Deum

7.88   *Creeds and confessions.* Names of particular creeds and confessions are also capitalized:

Apostles' Creed	Nicene Creed
Augsburg Confession	the Thirty-nine Articles
Luther's Ninety-five Theses	Westminster Confession

EVENTS AND CONCEPTS

7.89   Biblical and other religious events and religious concepts of major theological importance are often capitalized:

the Atonement	Hegira (Muhammad's)
the Creation	Inquisition
the Crucifixion	Original Sin
Crusades; Crusaders	Pilgrimage of Grace
the Deluge; the Flood	Redemption
Diaspora (of the Jews)	Resurrection
the Exodus (from Egypt)	the Second Coming (of Christ)
the Fall (of Man)	the Second Covenant

RELIGIOUS SERVICES

7.90   *Eucharistic rite.* In referring to the eucharistic sacrament, the expression *the Mass* is always capitalized, as are equivalent expressions:

213

the Divine Liturgy	the Liturgy of the Lord's Supper
Holy Communion	

The terms *High Mass* and *Low Mass* are sometimes capitalized when used generically. In reference to individual celebrations, however, lowercase style is used:

> There is a high mass at noon.
> Three masses are said daily.

Terms for the elements of the Holy Communion are capitalized in contexts where the doctrine of the real presence is assumed:

Body and Blood of Christ	Precious Blood
the Divine Species	the Sacrament

7.91   *Other services.* Names of other rites and services are not capitalized in run of text:

prime, terce, sext, etc.	seder
morning prayer; matins (mattins)	confirmation
evening prayer; evensong	vesper service
bar mitzvah; bas mitzvah	worship service
baptism	

OBJECTS OF RELIGIOUS USE OR SIGNIFICANCE

7.92   Objects of religious use or significance are preferably given lowercase treatment:

ark	relic of the true cross
chalice and paten	rosary
holy water	sanctuary
mezuzah	shofar
phylacteries	stations of the cross

MILITARY TERMS

FORCES AND GROUPS OF PARTICIPANTS

7.93   Full titles of armies, navies, air forces, fleets, regiments, battalions, companies, corps, and so forth are capitalized. The words *army, navy,* etc., are lowercased when standing alone or used collectively in the plural or when they are not part of an official title:

> Afrika Korps (German, World War II)
> Allied armies
> Allied Expeditionary Force; the AEF
> the Allies (World Wars I and II); Allied forces
> Army of Northern Virginia
> Army of the Potomac; the army
> Axis powers (World War II)

Central Powers (World War I)
Combined Chiefs of Staff (World War II)
Continental navy (American Revolution)
Eighth Air Force
Fifth Army; the Fifth; the army
First Battalion, 178th Infantry; the battalion; the 178th
French foreign legion
Highland Light Infantry
Joint Chiefs of Staff (U.S.)
King's Own Yorkshire Light Infantry
Luftwaffe
National Guard; the guard
Pacific Fleet (U.S.; World War II)
Red Army; Russian army
Rough Riders
Royal Air Force; British air force
Royal Army Educational Corps
Royal Artillery; the British army
Royal Horse Guards
Royal Navy; the British navy
Royal Scots Fusiliers; the fusiliers
Seventh Fleet; the fleet
Task Force Fifty-eight; the task force
Thirty-third Infantry Division; the division; the infantry
Union army (American Civil War)
United States Army; the army; the American army; the armed forces
United States Coast Guard; the Coast Guard
United States Marine Corps; the Marine Corps; the U.S. Marines; the marines
United States Signal Corps; the Signal Corps

WARS, BATTLES, CAMPAIGNS, AND THEATERS OF WAR

7.94   Full titles of wars are capitalized. The words *war* and *battle* are lowercased when used alone (*battle* is often lowercased also when used with the name of the spot where the battle took place).

American Civil War;[18] the Civil War; the war

American Revolution; American War of Independence; the Revolution; the revolutionary war; the American and French revolutions

18. ''The earlier official title, War of the Rebellion, has been dropped, out of deference to Southern wishes; and the cumbrous title 'The War Between the States' is grossly inaccurate. 'The War for Southern Independence' suggested by the historian Channing is well enough; but why change 'The American Civil War,' which it was? During the war it was generally called 'The Second American Revolution' or 'The War for Separation' in the South.'' (Samuel Eliot Morison, *The Oxford History of the American People* [New York: Oxford University Press, 1965], 614 n.)

Battle of Bunker Hill *or* battle of Bunker Hill; the battle at Bunker Hill
Battle of the Bulge
Conquest of Mexico; the conquest
Crusades; the Sixth Crusade
European theater of operations (World War II); ETO
French Revolution; the Revolution; revolutionary France
Korean War
Maginot line
Mexican border campaign
Napoleonic Wars
Norman Conquest; the conquest of England; the conquest
Operation Overlord
revolution(s) of 1848
Seven Years' War
Shays's Rebellion
Spanish-American War
Spanish civil war
Third Battle of Ypres *or* third battle of Ypres
Vicksburg campaign
Vietnam War
War of Jenkins' Ear
western front (World War I)
western theater of war (American Civil War)
Whisky Rebellion
World War I; the First World War; the Great War; the war; the two world wars

MILITARY AWARDS AND CITATIONS

7.95   Specific names of medals and awards are capitalized:

Medal of Honor; congressional medal
Distinguished Flying Cross
Distinguished Service Cross
Purple Heart
but: croix de guerre

SHIPS, AIRCRAFT, AND SPACECRAFT

7.96   Names of specific ships, submarines, airplanes, spacecraft, and artificial satellites are italicized, but not such abbreviations as *SS* or *HMS*[19] preceding them:

Bonhomme Richard	CSS *Shenandoah*
HMS *Frolic*	SS *United States*

19. Do not use *ship, schooner, frigate, aircraft carrier,* or other such designations with these abbreviations.

USS *SC-530*	*Pioneer 11*
Graf Zeppelin	*Voyager 2*
Spirit of St. Louis	*Uhuru*
Sputnik II	*IUE*
Mariner 4	*SMM*

7.97 Designations of class or make, names of trains, and names of space programs are capitalized but not italicized:

U-boat	ICBM
DC-3	Nike
Boeing 707	Project Apollo
Broadway Limited	Concorde

SCIENTIFIC TERMINOLOGY

SCIENTIFIC NAMES OF PLANTS AND ANIMALS

7.98 The rules for the naming (taxonomy) of plants and animals are complex, and the style conventions are not as immutable as they sometimes appear to laymen. The rule, cited below, on lowercasing the species name, for example, is not universally observed. (For technical assistance and bibliography of scientific references see the *Council of Biology Editors Style Manual* and the U.S. Geological Survey's *Suggestions for Authors*.) The discussion and examples in the following paragraphs should help the inexperienced copyeditor avoid the most dangerous pitfalls in this field.

7.99 *Genus and species.* Whether in lists or in run of text, the generic and specific (Latin) names of plants and animals are set in italic type. The genus name is capitalized, the species name lowercased (even though it may be a proper adjective):

> Many specific names, such as *Rosa caroliniana* and *Styrax californica*, reflect the locale of the first specimens described.
> The Pleistocene saber-toothed cats all belonged to the genus *Smilodon*.
> In Europe the pike, *Esox lucius,* is valued for food as well as sport.

After the first use the genus name may be abbreviated:

> The "quaking" of the aspen, *Populus tremuloides,* is due to the construction of the petiole. An analogous phenomenon noted in the cottonwood, *P. deltoides,* is similarly effected.

7.100 Subspecies names, when used, follow the specific name and are also set in italic type:

> *Trogon collaris puella*
> *Noctilio labialis labialis* (also written *Noctilio l. labialis*)

217

In systematic work the name of the person (or persons) who proposed a specific or subspecific name is added in roman type, the name often being abbreviated:

Molossus coibensis J. A. Allen
Diaemus youngii cypselinus Thomas
Felis leo Scop.
Quercus alba L.
Euchistenes hartii (Thomas)

Use of parentheses in the last example means that Thomas described the species *hartii* but referred it to a different genus.

7.101 Other designations following generic, specific, or subspecific names are also set in roman type:

Viola sp.   *Rosa rugosa* var.

7.102 *Larger divisions.* Divisions larger than genus—phylum, class, order, and family—are capitalized and set in roman type:

Chordata [phylum]   Monotremata [order]
Chondrichthyes [class]   Hominidae [family]

So also are intermediate groupings:

Ruminantia [a suborder]
Felinae [a subfamily]
Selachii [a term used of various groups of cartilaginous fishes]

7.103 *English derivatives.* English derivatives of scientific names are lower-cased:

amoeba, amoebas [from *Amoeba*]
mastodon [like the foregoing, identical with the generic name]
carnivores [from the order Carnivora]
felids [from the family Felidae]

VERNACULAR NAMES OF PLANTS AND ANIMALS

7.104 Common names of plants and animals are capitalized in a bewildering variety of ways, even in lists and catalogs having professional status. It is often appropriate to follow the style of an "official" list, and authors doing so should let their editors know what list they are following.

7.105 In the absence of such a list the University of Chicago Press prefers a *down* style for names of wild plants and animals, capitalizing only proper nouns and adjectives used with their original reference:

dutchman's breeches   Cooper's hawk
mayapple   Canada thistle
black-eyed susan   Virginia creeper
New England aster   jack-in-the-pulpit

Michaelmas daisy   Rocky Mountain sheep
rhesus monkey   black bass

7.106 The same principles may usually be followed for breeds of domestic animals and horticultural varieties of plants, especially the older ones:

white leghorn fowl   golden retriever
Rhode Island red   King Charles spaniel
Hereford cattle   brahma fowl (*but* Brahman
Poland China swine   or Brahma cattle)
Dandie Dinmont   boysenberry
English setter   rambler rose

7.107 Many domestic breeds and varieties, however, have been given special names, sometimes fanciful, that must be respected. This is particularly true of horticultural varieties of plants that may be patented or may possess names registered as trademarks:

Queen of the Market aster   Golden Bantam corn
Peace rose   Hale Haven peach

GEOLOGICAL TERMS

7.108 Names of geological eras, periods, epochs, series, and episodes are capitalized (but not the words *era, period,* etc.):

Cenozoic era
Tertiary period
Pliocene epoch
Lower Jurassic period
Pennsylvanian (or Upper Carboniferous) period

Modifiers such as *early, middle,* or *late,* used merely descriptively, are usually lowercased:

the early Pliocene
late Pleistocene times

7.109 The term *Ice Age* is capitalized in reference to the Recent or Pleistocene glacial epochs but lowercased when used in a general sense. Glacial and interglacial stages are lowercased:

Illinoian (*European:* Riss) stage
second interglacial stage *or* II interglacial

(For prehistoric cultural periods see 7.63.)

ASTRONOMICAL TERMS

7.110 The names of asteroids, planets and their satellites, stars, and constellations are capitalized:

Big Dipper   85 Pegasi
North Star   Scorpius
Cassiopeia's Chair   Saturn
Aldebaran   Ursa Major

α Centauri (*or* Alpha Centauri)   Phobos

(For artificial satellites see 7.96.)

7.111   Names of other unique celestial objects are capitalized except for generic words forming part of the name:

the Milky Way	the Magellanic Clouds
the Crab nebula	the Coalsack
the Galaxy (*but* a galaxy,	Halley's comet
our galaxy)	Solar System

7.112   Objects listed in well-known catalogs are designated by the catalog name, usually abbreviated, and a number:

NGC 6165   Bond 619   Lalande 5761

7.113   The names *earth, sun,* and *moon,* ordinarily lowercased, are often capitalized when used in connection with the names of other bodies of the Solar System:

The planets Venus and Earth, respectively second and third in order outward from the Sun, resemble each other closely.

7.114   Terms merely descriptive in nature applied to unique celestial objects or phenomena are not capitalized:

the gegenschein   the rings of Saturn

Nor are terms applied to meteorological phenomena:

aurora borealis   sun dog

MEDICAL TERMS

7.115   *Diseases and syndromes.* The names of diseases, syndromes, signs, symptoms, tests, and the like should be lowercased, except for proper names forming part of the term:

Hodgkin's disease	dumping syndrome
infectious granuloma	syndrome of Weber
Ménière's syndrome	finger-nose test

7.116   Names of infectious organisms are treated like other taxonomic terms (see 7.98–103), but the names of diseases or pathological conditions based upon such names are lowercased and set in roman type:

In streptococcemia, or streptococcus infection, microorganisms of the genus *Streptococcus* are present in the blood.

The disease condition trichinosis is characterized by infestation by trichinae, small parasitic nematodes. It is commonly caused by eating underdone pork containing *Trichinella spiralis*.

7.117   *Drugs.* Generic names of drugs should be used so far as possible and given lowercase treatment. Proprietary names (trade names or brands), if used at all, should be capitalized and enclosed within parentheses after the first use of the generic term:

The patient was kept tranquilized with meprobamate (Miltown).

PHYSICAL AND CHEMICAL TERMS

7.118   *Laws, principles, etc.* Only proper names attached to the names of laws, theorems, principles, etc., are capitalized:

Boyle's law
Avogadro's theorem
Planck's constant
(Einstein's) general theory of relativity
the second law of thermodynamics
Newton's first law

7.119   *Chemical symbols and names.* Names of chemical elements and compounds are lowercased when written out; the chemical symbols, however, are capitalized and set without periods (for a complete list see 14.54):

sulfuric acid; H_2SO_4	tungsten carbide; WC
sodium chloride; NaCl	ozone; O_3

The figure giving the number of atoms in a molecule is placed in the inferior position after the symbol for the element, as in the examples above.

7.120   The *mass number,* formerly placed in the superior position to the right of the element symbol, is now according to international agreement placed in the superior position to the left of the symbol: ^{238}U, ^{14}C. In work intended for a nonprofessional audience, however, the mass number is still often placed in the old position (U^{238}, C^{14}). Such locutions as

uranium 238; U-238   carbon 14; C-14

are also seen in popular writing and need not be changed.

TRADEMARKS

7.121   Dictionaries indicate registered trademark names. A reasonable effort should be made to capitalize such names:

Coca-Cola (*but* cola drink)
Gold Medal flour
Levi's
Anacin, Bufferin, Excedrin (*but* aspirin)
Frigidaire (*but* refrigerator)
Kleenex (*but* tissue)
Ping-Pong (*but* table tennis)

Pyrex dishes
Vaseline (*but* petroleum jelly)
Orlon
Dacron (*but* polyester)
Xerox (*but* photocopier)

TITLES OF WORKS

GENERAL RULES

7.122   The following rules concerning capitalization, spelling, punctuation, italics, and quotation marks apply to titles mentioned in textual matter.[20] (For various styles of capitalization in bibliographies see chapter 16; for titles in notes see chapter 17; for capitalization in foreign titles see 9.4–6.) The rules govern titles of all publications (books, journals, newspapers, magazines, pamphlets, reports, etc.); of short works (poems, stories, articles); of divisions of long works (parts, chapters, sections); of unpublished lectures, papers, documents; of plays and radio and television programs; and of musical and graphic works.

7.123   *Capitalization.* Capitalize the first and last words and all nouns, pronouns, adjectives, verbs, adverbs, and subordinate conjunctions. Lowercase articles (*the, a, an*), coordinate conjunctions (*and, or, for, nor*), and prepositions, regardless of length, unless they are the first or last words of the title or subtitle. Lowercase the *to* in infinitives. Long titles of works published in earlier centuries may retain the original capitalization, except that any word in full capitals should carry only an initial capital. No word in a quoted title should ever be set in full capitals, regardless of how it appears on the title page of the book itself. Small capitals cannot be used in italic titles because there is no such thing in most typefaces as *italic* small caps. When the abbreviations A.D. and B.C. (set in small capitals in running text) appear in italic titles, they are set as full capitals: *A.D., B.C.*

7.124   How to capitalize hyphenated compounds in titles is often a question. A rule of thumb that usually proves satisfactory is (1) always capitalize the first element and (2) capitalize the second element if it is a noun or proper adjective or if it has equal force with the first element:

Twentieth-Century Literature   Non-Christian
Tool-Maker   City-State

20. In many publishing houses there is a custom of typing book titles in full caps instead of underlining (which takes twice as long). This is a useful, time-saving device, but typists should remember that its use should be reserved for reports, interdepartmental memorandums, letters to authors or other publishers, and the like. Never should titles in copy intended for publication be so typed.

Do not capitalize the second element if (*a*) it is a participle modifying the first element or (*b*) both elements constitute a single word:

English-speaking People
Medium-sized Library
E-flat Minor
Re-establish
Self-sustaining Reaction

Note that although modern practice tends toward deleting traditional hyphens (*reestablish, tool maker*) they should be retained where they are used in the original title. Only capitalization and punctuation may be altered.

7.125   *Spelling.* Retain the spelling of the original title. But change & to *and,* and spell out names of centuries (*12th Century* becomes *Twelfth Century*) and other numbers usually spelled out in text.

7.126   *Punctuation.* Add punctuation if necessary. (Title pages are usually designed to require a minimum of punctuation; elements of a title may be set on separate lines or in different type sizes. When such titles are cited and run in one line, they must be punctuated for clarity.) Insert a colon (not a semicolon or a dash) between the main title and the subtitle (be sure it *is* a subtitle and not a part of the main title requiring only a comma before it). If there is a dash in the original title, retain it. Add commas in series, including one before the *and* preceding the final word in a series. Set off, with commas, dates not grammatically related to the rest of the title.

7.127   Old-fashioned titles connected by *or* are usually treated so:

England's Monitor; or, The History of the Separation

7.128   Some examples of titles showing modern capitalization and punctuation:

Disease, Pain, and Sacrifice: Toward a Psychology of Suffering
Melodrama Unveiled: American Theater and Culture, 1800–1850
Browning's Roman Murder Story: A Reading of "The Ring and the Book"
The Labour Party in Perspective—and Twelve Years Later
Thought and Letters in Western Europe, A.D. 500–900
Foreign Aid Re-examined
"The Take-off into Self-sustained Growth"
Sonata in B-flat Major
"Digression concerning Madness"
Learning to Look
Noble-Gas Compounds
"What to Listen For"

(For rules of capitalization governing titles in foreign languages see 9.4–6.)

BOOKS AND PERIODICALS

7.129 As in notes, titles and subtitles of published books, pamphlets, proceedings and collections, periodicals, and newspapers and sections of newspapers published separately (*New York Times Book Review*) are set in italics when they are mentioned in the text. Such titles issued in microfilm are also italicized. In works where titles are otherwise treated in references and notes (see 16.5), titles mentioned in the text are nevertheless italicized and usually capitalized according to the rule outlined above (7.123).

7.130 Obviously, a title mentioned in the text need not be complete there when it is cited in full in a note or a list of references. Also, as part of an expository sentence, it may be adjusted to fit the syntax of the sentence. Thus an initial article, *A* or *The,* following a possessive noun or pronoun is awkward and should be omitted:

> Had she read Faulkner's *Fable?* (*But:* Faulkner's novel *A Fable* was first on the list of required readings.)
>
> His *Rise of the West* won the National Book Award.

An initial article should also be omitted if an adjective or another article precedes it:

> That dreadful *Old Curiosity Shop* character, Quilp . . .
>
> An *Oxford Universal Dictionary* definition . . .

Where an initial article does not offend the syntax, it should be retained as part of the title (except in newspaper titles):

> In *The Old Curiosity Shop,* Dickens . . .

7.131 When newspapers and periodicals are mentioned in the text, an initial *The,* omitted in note citations, is set in roman type and, unless it begins a sentence, is lowercased:

> She reads the *Sun-Times* every morning.
>
> The *New York Times* and the *Christian Science Monitor* are among the most widely respected newspapers.
>
> His book is reviewed in the *American Historical Review.*

7.132 A title as the object of a preposition such as *on* or *about* is a locution avoided by many careful writers.

Questionable:

> In his well-known book on *Modern English Usage* Fowler provides an excellent article on the use and abuse of italics for emphasis.

Better:

> In his well-known book on English usage Fowler . . .
> *or:*
> In his well-known *Dictionary of Modern English Usage* . . .

7.133   A title is a singular noun and must therefore take a singular verb:

> *The Counterfeiters* is perhaps Gide's best-known work.
> *Ends and Means* marks a new turn in Aldous Huxley's thought.

7.134   *Articles and parts of a book.* Titles of articles and features in periodicals and newspapers, chapter titles and part titles, titles of short stories, essays, and individual selections in books are set in roman type and enclosed in quotation marks:

> "A Defense of Shelley's Poetry," by Kathleen Raine in the *Southern Review*
> Caldwell's "Country Full of Swedes"
> "Talk of the Town" in last week's *New Yorker*
> "Wordsworth in the Tropics," from Huxley's *Collected Essays*
> "Maternal Behavior and Attitudes," chapter 14 of *Human Development*

7.135   Such common titles as *foreword, preface, introduction, contents, appendix, glossary, bibliography, index,* are lowercased in passing references:

> In his preface to . . .
> The editor's preface gives an excellent summary.
> Allan Nevins wrote the foreword to . . .
> The table of contents lists all the subheadings.
> The bibliographical essay is incomplete.
> The book contains a glossary, a subject index, and an index of names.

These titles are usually capitalized (no quotation marks) when cross-reference is made from one part to another of the same book:

> Full citations are listed in the Bibliography.
> Further examples will be found in the Appendix (*but* in appendix A; in app. A).

7.136   The word *chapter* is lowercased and spelled out in text; it may be abbreviated in parenthetical references: (chap. 3). Chapter numbers in text references are given in arabic figures, even when the actual chapter numbers are spelled out or in roman numerals.

7.137   *Series and editions.* Titles of book series and editions are capitalized and set in roman type without quotation marks. The words *series* and *edition* are lowercased when they are not part of the title:

> Chicago History of American Civilization series

Modern Library edition
Phoenix Books

POEMS AND PLAYS

7.138   Titles of collections of poetry and of long poems published separately are italicized. Titles of short poems are in roman type and quoted:

> *Paradise Lost*
> "The Love Song of J. Alfred Prufrock," from *Prufrock and Other Observations*

In literary studies where many poems are mentioned it is better—and easier for editor and reader—to set all the titles alike, in italics.

7.139   When a poem is referred to by its first line rather than a title, capitalization should follow the poem, not the rules for capitalizing titles:

> "Shall I compare thee to a Summer's day?"

7.140   Titles of plays are italicized, regardless of the length of the play or whether it is published separately or in a collection:

> Shaw's *Arms and the Man,* in volume 2 of his *Plays: Pleasant and Unpleasant*

7.141   Words denoting parts of poems and plays are usually lowercased and set in roman type, with arabic figures:

> canto 2   act 3
> stanza 4   scene 5

UNPUBLISHED WORKS

7.142   Titles of dissertations and theses, manuscripts in collections, lectures and papers read at meetings, machine copies of typescripts (mimeograph, Xerox, etc.), are set in roman type and quoted. Names of depositories, archives, and the like, and names of manuscript collections are capitalized and set in roman type without quotation marks. Such words as *diary, journal, memorandum,* are set in roman type, not quoted, and usually lowercased in text references:

> In a master's thesis, "Charles Valentin Alkan and His Pianoforte Works"
> "A Canal Boat Journey, 1857," an anonymous manuscript in the Library of Congress Manuscripts Division
> Papers of the Continental Congress in the National Archives

MOTION PICTURES AND TELEVISION AND RADIO PROGRAMS

7.143   Titles of motion pictures are italicized. Titles of television and radio programs are in roman type and quoted.

the movie *Chinatown*
A Man for All Seasons
PBS's "Sesame Street"
Harry Bouras's "Critic's Choice" on WFMT

MUSICAL COMPOSITIONS

7.144   Titles of operas, oratorios, motets, tone poems, and other long musical compositions are italicized. Titles of songs and short compositions are usually set in roman type and quoted:

Harold in Italy	"Jesu Joy of Man's Desiring"
Don Giovanni	"Wohin" from *Die schöne Müllerin*
Death and Transfiguration	"Ode to Billie Joe"

As with other such arbitrary distinctions (e.g., poems), where many titles of musical compositions are mentioned in a critical study, all may be italicized regardless of individual length.

7.145   Many musical compositions, because of the nature of the art, do not have descriptive titles but are identified by the name of a musical form in which they are written plus a number or a key or both. When used as the title of a work the name of the form and the key are usually capitalized:

Fantasy in C Minor   Sonata in E-flat

(For lowercase letters indicating minor keys see 6.76.)

7.146   The abbreviations op. (opus; *pl.* opp. *or* opera) and no. (number; *pl.* nos.) are usually lowercased, but both are sometimes capitalized; either style is acceptable if consistency is observed. An abbreviation designating a catalog of a particular composer's works is always capitalized (e.g., BWV [Bach-Werke-Verzeichnis] for Bach; D. [Deutsch] for Schubert; K. [Köchel] for Mozart). When a number, or an opus or catalog number, is used restrictively—i.e., identifies the work—no comma precedes it:

Sonata op. 31, no. 3; Sonata in E-flat, op. 31, no. 3
Hungarian Rhapsody no. 12; Brahms's twelfth Hungarian Rhapsody
Fantasy in C Minor, K. 475
Symphony no. [*or* No.] 5 in C Minor; Beethoven's Fifth Symphony

7.147   A descriptive title given to a work, either by the composer or by a later critic or performer, is italicized if the work is long, quoted if it is short:

Air with Variations ("The Harmonious Blacksmith") from Handel's Suite no. 5 in E

Bach's Prelude and Fugue in E-flat ("St. Anne")

Messiah or the *Messiah* (not *The Messiah*)

Piano Sonata no. 2 (*Concord, Mass., 1840–60*); the *Concord* Sonata, by Charles Ives

227

Piano Concerto no. 5 (*Emperor*); the *Emperor* Concerto, by Beethoven
String Quartet in D Minor (*Death and the Maiden*); *Death and the Maiden* Quartet (but the song: "Death and the Maiden")
Symphony no. 41 (*Jupiter*); the *Jupiter* Symphony
William Tell Overture

PAINTINGS AND SCULPTURE

7.148 Titles of paintings, drawings, statues, and other works of art are italicized:

Grant Wood's *American Gothic*
El Greco's *View of Toledo*
Hogarth's series of drawings *The Rake's Progress*
Rembrandt's etching *Christ Presented to the People*
Rodin's *The Thinker*

Traditional or descriptive titles of works of art are given in roman:

Victory of Samothrace
Apollo Belvedere
Mona Lisa

NOTICES

7.149 Specific wording of short signs or notices run in textual matter should be capitalized like titles but neither italicized nor quoted:

He has a No Smoking sign in his car.
The door was marked Authorized Personnel Only.

MOTTOES

7.150 Mottoes and inscriptions may well be treated the same way:

The flag bore the motto Dont Tread on Me.

COMPUTER TERMS

7.151 Many computer terms are familiar English words or word combinations with specific new meanings: a few common ones are

access (v.)
data base (*often* database)
data file
debug
format; formatting; formatter
hard copy; hard code; hardwired
input (v.)
log on (v.); logging on (n.)
on line; off line (*sometimes* online; offline)
program; programming; programmer
realtime (*or* real time)

7.152 Names of hardware (machines), assigned by the manufacturers, are often given in full capitals as acronyms; sometimes with initial capital only, as a person's name:

DEC-20   Amdahl

7.153 Software (languages, programs, systems, packages, routines, subroutines, statements, commands) terms indicating specific units are generally in full capitals, with a few exceptions given with initial capitals only:

LANGUAGES

APL	SCRIPT
BASIC	SAIL
COBOL	Assembler
FORTRAN	Pascal

PROGRAMS, PACKAGES, SYSTEMS

SPSS (initial caps if spelled out: Statistical Package for the Social Sciences)

TREATISE   SYSTEM 1022   PENTA

ROUTINES, SUBROUTINES, COMMANDS

SIN   COS   GOTO 400

FOR FURTHER REFERENCE

7.154 The most readily available and generally accurate sources for the spelling and capitalization of personal names are *Webster's Biographical Dictionary, Who's Who, Who's Who in America, Dictionary of American Biography, Dictionary of Canadian Biography,* and *Dictionary of National Biography* (British). For geographical names: *Webster's Geographical Dictionary* and *The Columbia Gazetteer of the World.*

8 *Numbers*

General Principles 8.2
    Figures or Words? 8.3
    Ordinals 8.4
    Round Numbers 8.5
    Consistency 8.8
    First Word in Sentence 8.9
Special Cases 8.11
    Physical Quantities 8.11
      Scientific usage 8.11
      Nonscientific usage 8.12
      Abbreviations 8.15
      Symbols 8.16
    Percentages and Decimal Fractions 8.17
      Percentages 8.18
      Decimal fractions 8.19
    Money 8.23
      United States currency 8.23
      British currency 8.26
      Other currencies 8.29
    Parts of a Book 8.32
    Dates 8.33
      The year alone 8.34
      The year abbreviated 8.35
      The day of the month 8.36
      Month and year 8.39
      Centuries and decades 8.40
      Eras 8.41
      All-figure dates and other brief forms 8.43
    Time of Day 8.47
    Names 8.50
      Monarchs, etc. 8.50
      Vehicles, etc. 8.51
      Family names 8.52
    Governmental Designations 8.55
      Governments 8.55
      Political divisions 8.56
      Military units 8.57
    Organizations 8.58
      Churches, etc. 8.58
      Unions and lodges 8.59
    Addresses and Thoroughfares 8.60
      Highways 8.60
      Numbered streets 8.61
      Building numbers 8.62
Forms and Uses of Numbers 8.63

Plurals of Numbers 8.63
Use of the Comma 8.64
    Nonscientific copy 8.64
    Scientific copy 8.66
Inclusive Numbers 8.67
Roman Numerals 8.71
Enumerations 8.72
    Outline style 8.73
For Further Reference 8.76

8.1   It is difficult if not impossible to be entirely consistent in the use of numbers in textual matter. As soon as one thinks one has arrived at a simple rule for handling some category of numbers, exceptions begin to appear and one realizes that the rule has to be made more complicated than one had originally thought. This chapter summarizes some of the conventions observed by the University of Chicago Press in handling numbers, especially in making the choice of spelling them out or using figures. Following a short explanation of the general rules appear brief discussions of various special categories of number use, many of them involving exceptions to the general rules. Detailed discussions of some of these categories, as well as of others not treated here, appear elsewhere in this volume; for these consult the index.

GENERAL PRINCIPLES

8.2   Several factors work together to govern the choice of spelling out or using figures for any particular number. Among them are whether the number is large or small, whether it is an approximation or an exact quantity, what kind of entity it stands for, and what kind of text it appears in—scientific or technological on the one hand, humanistic on the other.

FIGURES OR WORDS?

8.3   According to Press style the following are spelled out in ordinary text (for scientific or technical style see 8.11–22, 8.66):

Whole numbers from one through ninety-nine
Any of these followed by *hundred, thousand, million,* etc.

For all other numbers figures are used.[1]

> Thirty leading Republicans from eleven states urged the governor to declare his candidacy.

1. It should be noted, perhaps, that newspaper style, as well as that of some general publishers and scholarly journals, decrees that only the numbers from one through nine and such multiples as *one hundred* or *nine thousand* are to be spelled out.

The property is held on a ninety-nine-year lease.

His son is twenty-four years old.

The first edition ran to 2,670 pages in three volumes, with 160 copper-plate engravings.

The entire length of 4,066 feet is divided into twelve spans of paired parabolic ribs.

The three new parking lots will provide space for 540 more cars.

If a number between one thousand and ten thousand can be expressed in terms of hundreds, that style is preferred to figures:

In response to the question he wrote an essay of fifteen hundred words.

When spelled-out numbers would cluster thickly in a sentence or paragraph, however, it is often better to use figures:

The ages of the eight members of the city council are 69, 64, 58, 54 (two members), 47, 45, and 35.

Only six communities in the county number one thousand or more in population: Allegan, 4,500; southern part of Holland, 4,500; Otsego, 4,000; Plainwell, 3,200; Wayland, 2,100; and Saugatuck, 1,000.

ORDINALS

8.4   Note that the general rule applies to ordinal as well as cardinal numbers:

He found himself in 125th position on a scale of 360.

Roberts singled in the top half of the eighth inning.

Note also that the preferred figure form of the ordinals *second* and *third* is with *d* alone, not *nd* and *rd:*

The 122d and 123d days of the strike were marked by renewed violence.

ROUND NUMBERS

8.5   Round numbers—that is, approximations used in place of exact numbers—generally fit the category of numbers that are spelled out according to the general rule:

Her essay summarizes two thousand years of Christian history.

Local officials announced that some forty thousand persons had attended the Allegan County Fair.

8.6   In addition to these, round numbers that are even hundred thousands are usually spelled out:

The population of Grand Rapids, Michigan, is about two hundred thousand.

8.7   Very large numbers may be expressed in figures followed by *million, billion,* etc.:

> By the end of the fourteenth century the population of Britain had probably reached 2.3 million.
>
> A figure of 4.5 billion years is often given as the age of the Solar System.

CONSISTENCY

8.8 Numbers applicable to the same category should be treated alike within the same context, whether paragraph or series of paragraphs; do not use figures for some and spell out others. If according to rule you must use figures for one of the numbers in a given category, then for consistency's sake use figures for all the numbers in that category:

> There are 25 graduate students in the philosophy department, 56 in the classics department, and 117 in the romance languages department, making a total of 198 students in the three departments.
>
> In the past ten years fifteen new buildings have been erected. In one block a 103-story office building rises between two old apartment houses only 3 and 4 stories high.
>
> The population of Gary, Indiana, grew from 10,000 to 175,000 in only thirty years.

FIRST WORD IN SENTENCE

8.9 At the beginning of a sentence any number that would ordinarily be set in figures is spelled out, regardless of any inconsistency this may create:

> One hundred ten men and 103 women will receive advanced degrees this quarter.
>
> Twenty-seven percent of the cost was guaranteed.
>
> Nineteen seventy-six was the year of the nation's bicentennial celebration.

8.10 If this is impracticable or cumbersome, the sentence should be recast so that it does not begin with a number:

> The nation celebrated its bicentennial in 1976.
>
> The year 1976 was marked by the nation's bicentennial celebration.

SPECIAL CASES

PHYSICAL QUANTITIES

8.11 *Scientific usage.* In mathematical, statistical, technical, or scientific text, physical quantities, such as distances, lengths, areas, volumes, pressures, and so on, are expressed in figures, whether whole numbers or fractions:

45 miles	240 volts
3 cubic feet	45 pounds

21 hectares   6 meters
10 picas   30 cubic centimeters
10°C, 10.5°C   an 8-point table with 6-point heads
10° (of arc), 10°.5 *or* 10°30′

8.12 *Nonscientific usage.* In ordinary text matter such quantities should be treated according to the rules governing the spelling out of numbers:

> The temperature dropped twenty degrees in less than an hour.
> The train approached at a speed of seventy-five miles an hour.
> Some students live more than fifteen kilometers from the school.
> Type the entries on three-by-five-inch index cards.

8.13 Included under the rule are common fractions:

> More than two-thirds of the registered voters stayed away from the polls on election day.

8.14 Quantities consisting of both whole numbers and fractions, however, are often cumbersome to write out and should then be expressed in figures:

> All manuscripts are to be typed on 8½-by-11-inch paper.

8.15 *Abbreviations.* If an abbreviation is used for the unit of measure, the quantity should always be expressed by a figure:

> 3 mi   12 V   50 lb   35-mm film
> 55 MPH 7 hr   13 g   137 km

8.16 *Symbols.* If a symbol is used instead of an abbreviation, the quantity is expressed by a figure:

> 3½″   36°30′ N 9′

And for two or more quantities, the symbol should usually be repeated:

> 3″ × 5″   30°–50°

PERCENTAGES AND DECIMAL FRACTIONS

8.17 Percentages and decimal fractions (including academic grades) are set in figures in humanistic as well as scientific copy:

> For these purposes pi will be considered equal to 3.14.
> Grades of 3.8 and 95 are identical.

8.18 *Percentages.* In scientific and statistical copy use the symbol "%" for a percentage, in humanistic copy, the word *percent:*

> Of the cultures tested, fewer than 23% yielded positive results.
> The five-year credit will carry interest of 3 percent.

8.19   *Decimal fractions.* In scientific contexts decimal fractions of less than 1.00 are set with an initial zero if the quantity expressed is capable of equaling or exceeding 1.00:

a mean of 0.73   the ratio 0.85

8.20   If the quantity never equals 1.00, as in probabilities, levels of significance, correlation coefficients, factor loadings, etc., no zero is used:

$p < .05$ $R = .10$

8.21   When decimal fractions appear in humanistic contexts, the foregoing distinction is seldom observed:

> The average number of children born to college graduates dropped from 2.3 to .95 per couple.
>
> Last season Mendoza batted .327.
>
> On retirement Boyer traded his .38 police special for a .22-caliber single-shot rifle.

8.22   Note that in older British practice the decimal point was a raised dot (3·14159); that style is sometimes still used by conservative writers. In Continental practice the decimal point is a comma (3,14159).

MONEY

8.23   *United States currency.* Isolated references to amounts of money in United States currency are spelled out or expressed in figures in accord with the general rules (8.2–10). If the number is spelled out, so is the unit of currency, and if figures are used, the symbol "$" precedes them:

> The fare has been raised to twenty-five cents.
> The committee raised a total of $325.
> Hundreds of collectors paid five dollars each to attend the annual event.

8.24   Fractional amounts over one dollar are set in figures like other decimal fractions. Whole-dollar amounts are set with ciphers after the decimal point when they appear in the same context with fractional amounts— and only then:

> In a very short time the price of gold rose from the controlled $35 an ounce to $375.
> Articles bought for $6.00 were sold for $6.75.
> The agent received $5.50, $33.75, and $175.00 for the three sales.

8.25   Like other very large round numbers, sums of money that would be cumbersome to express in figures or to spell out in full may be expressed in units of millions or billions, accompanied by figures and a dollar sign:

> A price of $3 million was agreed upon by both firms.

Teen-age consumers account for an annual market of some $15 billion.
The military establishment was slated to receive an additional $7.3 billion over the previous year's appropriation.

8.26 *British currency.* Sums of money in pounds and pence are handled similarly to those in dollars and cents:

To anyone used to paying fifty pence, three pounds seemed a steep price.
The freehold on the house is offered for £35,375.
Receipts for the three days' sales were £175.64, £225.36, and £207.00.
The eventual cost of the program is estimated to be £7.8 million.

The term *billion* should be avoided, since in British usage a billion is equal to a million million, not a thousand million as in American usage.

8.27 Before decimalization of the currency in 1971 three monetary units were in use: the pound, the shilling (one-twentieth of a pound), and the penny (one-twelfth of a shilling):

four pence	nineteen shillings	twenty pounds
£123	£52 million	£1,346 million

In fractional sums the abbreviation for shillings (*s.*) and for pence (*d.*) followed the figures they applied to:

£14 19*s.* 6*d.* (*but sometimes simply* £14.19.6)

8.28 For some purposes, mainly professional fees and prices of luxury items, sums of money were expressed in terms of guineas (a unit of value equal to twenty-one shillings, or in modern currency, £1.05):

thirty guineas   342 guineas (gns.)

8.29 *Other currencies.* Sums of money in other currencies are generally handled similarly to those in United States or decimalized British currency. Note, however, that if an abbreviation rather than a symbol is used for the monetary unit (as Fr for francs and DM for deutsche marks), space is left between the abbreviation and the figure:

Fr 342.46   DM 45 million

8.30 If a distinction has to be made between sums of money in two currencies employing the same symbol for the monetary unit, a prefix or suffix is used:

In Canada the current quotation was $2.69 (U.S. $2.47) a pound.

8.31 An author or editor having to deal with names and abbreviations of monetary units in currencies other than American or British may find it helpful to consult the table "Foreign Money" in the United States Government Printing Office *Style Manual.*

PARTS OF A BOOK

8.32   Numbers referring to parts of a book, periodical, or manuscript—
chapters and other divisions, pages, plates and text figures, tables,
and so on—are invariably set as figures. Except for the preliminary
pages of a book, which are still traditionally set in lowercase roman
numerals, the University of Chicago Press prefers that all such numbers be set in arabic figures:

> See *Modern Philology* 52 (1954): 100–109.
> Plate 7 and figures 23–29 appear in chapter 6.
> The preface of the book will be found on pages vii–xiv and the intro-
> duction on pages 3–46.
> (pp. 426–29)   (see vol. 3, introd.)   (fol. 8r)

DATES

8.33   The numbers used for dates—the day of the month and the year itself—constitute an important group of exceptions to the general rule
on spelling out exact numbers.

8.34   *The year alone.* Year numbers are invariably expressed in figures,
whatever their magnitude (but see 8.9, above):

> Octavian was born in 63 B.C., became emperor in 27 B.C., and died in
> A.D. 14.

8.35   *The year abbreviated.* In informal contexts the full number of a particular year is sometimes abbreviated:

> the class of '84   the spirit of '76
> He told them he was born in '07.

8.36   *The day of the month.* The University of Chicago Press prefers that in
all text, including notes and bibliographies, exact dates be written in
the sequence day-month-year, without internal punctuation:

> *Newsweek,* 27 April 1981, 27.
> On 4 February 1945 Roosevelt, Stalin, and Churchill met at the Black
> Sea resort town of Yalta.

Note that if the alternative sequence month-day-year is employed (in
spite of Press preferences), the year is set off by commas before and
after it:

> The events of April 18, 1775, have long been celebrated in song and
> story.

8.37   After an exact date has been used, an elliptical reference to another
date in the same month is spelled out:

> On 5 November the national elections took place. By the morning of
> the sixth, returns for all but a few precincts were in.

8.38   Although the day of the month is actually an ordinal (and so pronounced in speaking), the American practice is invariably to write it as a cardinal number: 18 April or April 18, *not* 18th April (the British preference) or April 18th.

8.39   *Month and year.* When a period of time is identified by the month and year, no internal punctuation is necessary or appropriate:

> The events of August 1945 were decisive to the outcome of the war.

8.40   *Centuries and decades.* Spell out (in lowercase letters) references to particular centuries and decades:

> the twentieth century   during the sixties and seventies

If decades are identified by their century, figures are used:

> the 1880s and 1890s (*never* the 1880s and '90s)

8.41   *Eras.* Figures are used for year numbers followed or preceded by era designations, and words are used for centuries. The abbreviations for eras are conventionally set in small caps. Among the most frequently used era designations are A.D. (*anno Domini*, "in the year of the Lord"); A.H. (*anno Hegirae*, "in the year of [Muhammad's] Hegira," or *anno Hebraico*, "in the Hebrew year"); A.U.C. (*ab urbe condita*, "from the founding of the city" [i.e., Rome, in 753 B.C.]); B.C. ("before Christ"); C.E. and B.C.E. ("of the common era" and "before the common era"—equivalent to A.D. and B.C.); and B.P. ("before the present"). Note that the abbreviations A.D. and A.H. properly precede the year number, whereas others follow it.

> Greek philosophy reached its highest development in the fourth century B.C.
> Britain was invaded successfully in 55 B.C. and A.D. 1066
> Mubarak published his survey at Cairo in A.H. 1306 (A.D. 1888).
> After 621 B.C.E. worship was permitted only at Jerusalem.
> Radiocarbon dating indicates that the campsite was in use by about 13,500 B.P.

In the last example note the use of the comma in a year number of more than four digits (see 8.64).

8.42   Because of the literal meaning of A.D., conservative usage formerly rejected such an expression as "the second century A.D." in favor of "the second century of the Christian Era" or "the second century after Christ." Recognizing, however, that A.D. has taken on a purely conventional significance, most scholars and scholarly editors have long since withdrawn their objections to the locution.

8.43   *All-figure dates and other brief forms.* Although the all-figure style of writing dates—5/10/82 or 5-10-82—finds no place in formal writing, it sometimes falls to the lot of scholars to interpret dates so written. Accordingly, perhaps, something should be said about them here. The trouble is that Americans on the one hand and the British (as well as many Canadians) on the other use two different conventions of abbreviation, and this results in dates that often look alike but mean quite different things on either side of the Atlantic. For example, 5/10/82 to an American stands for the tenth day of May in the year 1982, but to an Englishman it means the fifth day of October. The lesson, of course, is to be sure you know which convention a writer is using when you decipher a date that could be interpreted either way.

8.44 One way of getting around the ambiguity of all-figure dates is to use a lowercase roman numeral for the month, as many Continentals do. Thus 10 May 1982 is written 10.v.82 (the periods not only separate the figures but, in the Continental convention, make ordinals of the figures they follow: i.e., *tenth* and *fifth*). This style commends itself to many scholars and editors for dating memorandums and informal communications.

8.45 Another system, less elegant but equally unambiguous, is one employed by the military. In this the order day-month-year is preserved, but the name of the month is abbreviated to three letters where necessary, without a period. Thus 31 December 1981 appears as 31 Dec 81 (army style) or 31 DEC 81 (navy style).

8.46 Still another system of all-figure dating is the one used by people involved with computers, which are usually programmed to read and accept dates only in this form. Here ten keystrokes are always used, and the year comes first, then the month, and finally the day. Thus 10 May 1982 appears as 1982-05-10.

TIME OF DAY

8.47 Times of day in even, half, and quarter hours are usually spelled out in text matter:

> The directors expected the meeting to continue until half past three.
> Freshmen must be in their rooms by midnight on weekdays.
> He left the office at a quarter of four.
> The family always ate dinner at seven o'clock.

But figures are used (with ciphers for even hours) when the exact moment of time is to be emphasized:

> The program is televised at 2:30 in the afternoon.
> If we don't eat dinner, we can catch the 6:20 train.
> The county will return to standard time tomorrow morning at 2:00.

(In Britain a period rather than a colon is used between hour and minutes—2.30.)

8.48   Figures are used in designations of time with A.M. or P.M. Never use A.M. with *morning* or P.M. with *evening,* and never use *o'clock* with either A.M. or P.M. or figures:

at 4:00 P.M.   12:00 M. (noon)
at 10:45 in the morning   12:00 P.M. (midnight)
11:30 A.M.   eight o'clock

Note that the abbreviations A.M. and P.M. (*ante* and *post meridiem*) are set in small caps with no space between them. This is a common American style and the preference of the University of Chicago Press. British practice is to use lowercase—a.m. and p.m.—an alternative that is acceptable here also.

8.49   In the twenty-four-hour system of expressing time, no punctuation is used between the hours and minutes:

General quarters sounded at 0415.
Visiting hours are from 0930 to 1100 and from 1800 to 2030.

NAMES

8.50   *Monarchs, etc.* Sovereigns, emperors, and popes with the same names are differentiated by numerals, traditionally roman:

Elizabeth II   John XXIII

In Continental practice the numeral is sometimes followed by a period or a superscript abbreviation, indicating that the number is an ordinal (Wilhelm II., François Ier). These should be edited out in an English context.

8.51   *Vehicles, etc.* Sometimes similarly treated are yachts and racing automobiles:

America IV   *Bluebird III*

Earlier spacecraft generally carried roman numerals, but current custom is to use arabic (see 7.96).

8.52   *Family names.* Roman numerals are also used to differentiate male members of the same family with identical names. Two different conventions govern the use of such numbers. According to the older custom the system works as follows. If Robert Allen Smith's son or grandson is given the same name, the latter adds "Jr." to the name (a nephew or grandnephew would use "II"). If later a third member of the family is given the name, he adds "III." On the death of the eldest of the name, Robert Allen Smith, Jr., drops the "Jr.," and Robert Allen Smith III (if a grandson) becomes Robert Allen Smith, Jr. Exceptionally, within this system, if the original or some subsequent bearer of the name is a famous person, a younger namesake often keeps the suffix:

Douglas Fairbanks, Jr.   Adlai E. Stevenson III

8.53   Perhaps under the influence of these exceptions, a newer custom has grown up in some American families given to using the same names in successive generations. In these families same-name males sometimes keep their suffixes throughout life and go to the grave, like emperors and popes, with III or IV or V still attached to their names.

8.54   Editors should note that whereas ''Jr.'' is set off by commas, a numeral suffix bears no punctuation.

GOVERNMENTAL DESIGNATIONS

8.55   *Governments*. Particular dynasties, governments, and governing bodies in a succession are usually designated by an ordinal number, spelled out if one hundred or less, preceding the noun:

Eighteenth Dynasty   Third Reich
Fifth Republic   Second International
Second Continental Congress   Ninety-seventh Congress
The 107th Congress will be elected in the year 2000.

8.56   *Political divisions*. Spell out in ordinal form numerals of one hundred or less designating political divisions:

Fifth Ward   Fourteenth Precinct
Court of Appeals for the Tenth Second Congressional District
  Circuit   Ninth Naval District

8.57   *Military units*. Similarly, spell out in ordinal form numerals of one hundred or less designating military subdivisions:

Fifth Army   Seventy-seventh Regiment
Second Infantry Division   323d Fighter Wing
Third Battalion, 122d Artillery

ORGANIZATIONS

8.58   *Churches, etc*. Numerals designating a religious organization or house of worship are generally spelled out in ordinal form before the name:

First Baptist Church   Seventh-day Adventists
Twenty-first Church of Christ, Scientist

8.59   *Unions and lodges*. Numerals designating local branches of labor unions and of fraternal lodges are usually expressed in arabic figures after the name:

Typographical Union No. 16

American Legion, Department of Illinois, Crispus Attucks Post No. 1268

Amalgamated Meat Cutters and Butcher Workmen of North America, Local No. 15

ADDRESSES AND THOROUGHFARES

8.60   *Highways.* State, federal, and interstate highways are designated by arabic numerals:

U.S. Route 41 (U.S. 41)   Interstate 90 (I-90)   Illinois 12

8.61   *Numbered streets.* It is preferable, except where space is at a premium, to spell out the names of numbered streets of one hundred or less:

Fifth Avenue   Twenty-third Street

The address "1212 Fifth Street" is easier to read than "1212—5th Street," a device sometimes employed in typing addresses.

8.62   *Building numbers.* Address numbers are written in arabic numerals before the name of the street in both British and American addresses (the older British practice of using a comma after the building number has been generally abandoned there):

5801 Ellis Avenue, Chicago, Illinois 60637
126 Buckingham Palace Road, London SW1W 9SD

When a building's name is its address, the number is often spelled out:

One Thousand Lake Shore Drive   One Park Avenue

FORMS AND USES OF NUMBERS

PLURALS OF NUMBERS

8.63   The plurals of spelled-out numbers are formed like the plurals of other nouns:

The contestants were in their twenties and thirties.
The family was at sixes and sevens.

The plurals of figures are formed by the addition of *s* alone:

Among the scores were two 240s and three 238s.
The bonds offered were convertible 4½s.
Jazz forms developed in the 1920s became popular in the 1930s.

USE OF THE COMMA

8.64   *Nonscientific copy.* In most figures of one thousand or more, commas should be used between groups of three digits, counting from the right:

243

32,987   1,512   1,000,000

Exceptions to this rule are page numbers, addresses, numbers of chapters of fraternal organizations and the like, decimal fractions of less than one (but see 8.66), and year numbers of four digits, which are written in figures without commas. (Year numbers of five or more digits use the comma—for an example see 8.41.)

8.65 British practice is similar to American in marking off groups of three digits with commas. In Continental practice, however, periods or spaces are often used: 93.000.000; 93 000 000. Except in quoted matter or in scientific work (see below) numbers like these should be edited to conform to American standards.

8.66 *Scientific copy.* In scientific copy long numerals are commonly avoided by the use of special units of measure and by the use of multipliers and powers of ten. When such figures do occur, however, the digits are usually marked off in groups of three by spaces, starting from the decimal point and going both to the left and (unlike the common usage) to the right:

3 426 869   0.000 007

INCLUSIVE NUMBERS

8.67 Inclusive numbers (continued numbers) are separated by an en dash. The University of Chicago Press abbreviates inclusive numbers according to the following principles (examples are page numbers):

FIRST NUMBER	SECOND NUMBER	EXAMPLES
Less than 100	Use all digits	3–10; 71–72
100 or multiple of 100	Use all digits	100–104; 600–613; 1100–1123
101 through 109 (in multiples of 100)	Use changed part only, omitting unneeded zeros	107–8; 505–17; 1002–6
110 through 199 (in multiples of 100)	Use two digits, or more as needed	321–25; 415–532; 1536–38; 11564–68; 13792–803
	But if numbers are four digits long and three digits change, use all digits	1496–1504; 2787–2816

8.68 Note the following instances of continued numbers other than pages:

the war of 1914–18   the years 1597–1601
the winter of 1900–1901   fiscal year 1975–76 (*or* 1975/76)
A.D. 325–27   A.D. 300–325   *but:* 327–325 B.C.

8.69 When inclusive dates occur in titles, it is usual to repeat all the digits:

An English Mission to Muscovy, 1589–1591

8.70 The University of Chicago Press is sometimes taken to task by authors or by editors at other publishing houses for its espousal of the system described here. It is unnecessarily complicated, say some. In reply Press editors would point out that the system is only complicated enough to produce graphic displays that are consistently easy to grasp at a glance and usually reflect the way we *say* continued numbers in speaking. The "cures" most frequently recommended are two: (1) for the second number use only the changed part of the first, or (2) use all digits of the second number. Yet neither of these systems works without complicating exceptions: "See pp. 200–4" is confusing in the extreme, and "pp. 1378–1379" is monstrous, we feel. So until someone invents a simpler system offering the same advantages as our venerable one (it appeared in the first edition of this manual), we expect to stick with it.

ROMAN NUMERALS

8.71   Table 8.1 shows the formation of roman numerals with their arabic equivalents. The general principle is that a smaller letter before a larger one subtracts from its value, and a small letter after a larger one adds to it; a bar over a letter multiplies its value by one thousand. Roman numerals may also be written in lowercase letters (i, ii, iii, iv, etc.), and in older practice a final *i* was often made like a *j* (vij, viij). Also, in early printed works, IƆ is sometimes seen for D, CIƆ for M, and IIII for IV. The University of Chicago Press now uses arabic numerals in many situations where roman numerals formerly were common, as in references to volume numbers of books and journals and in references to chapters of books (8.32).

TABLE 8.1: ROMAN AND ARABIC NUMERALS

Arabic	Roman	Arabic	Roman	Arabic	Roman
1	I	16	XVI	90	XC
2	II	17	XVII	100	C
3	III	18	XVIII	200	CC
4	IV	19	XIX	300	CCC
5	V	20	XX	400	CD
6	VI	21	XXI	500	D
7	VII	22	XXII	600	DC
8	VIII	23	XXIII	700	DCC
9	IX	24	XXIV	800	DCCC
10	X	30	XXX	900	CM
11	XI	40	XL	1,000	M
12	XII	50	L	2,000	MM
13	XIII	60	LX	3,000	MMM
14	XIV	70	LXX	4,000	M$\overline{\text{V}}$
15	XV	80	LXXX	5,000	$\overline{\text{V}}$ (*or* ℨ)

ENUMERATIONS

8.72   Enumerations that are run into the text may be indicated by figures or italic letters between parentheses. In a simple series with little or no punctuation within each item, separation by commas is sufficient. Otherwise, semicolons are used:

> This was determined by a chi-square test using as observed frequencies *(a)* the occurrence of one class and *(b)* the total occurrence of all classes among the neighbors of the subject classes.

> Data are available on three different groups of counsel: (1) the Public Defender of Cook County, (2) the member attorneys of the Chicago Bar Association's Defense of Prisoners Committee, and (3) all other attorneys.

> Specifically, the committee set down fundamental principles, which in its opinion were so well established that they were no longer open to controversy: (1) the commerce power was complete, except as constitutionally limited; (2) the power included the authority absolutely to prohibit specified persons and things from interstate transit; (3) the only limitation upon this authority, as far as the Keating-Owen bill was concerned, was the Fifth Amendment, which protected against arbitrary interference with private rights; and (4) this authority might be exercised in the interest of the public welfare as well as in the direct interest of commerce.

8.73   *Outline style.* For long enumerations it is preferable to begin each item on a line by itself. The numerals are aligned on the periods that follow them, and are either set flush with the text or indented. In either case runover lines are best aligned with the first word following the numeral (University of Chicago Press preference, where this is known as *outline* style):

> The inadequacy of the methods proposed for the solution of both histological and mounting problems is emphasized by the number and variety of the published procedures, which fall into the following groups:
>
> 1. Slightly modified classical histological techniques with fluid fixation, wax embedding, and aqueous mounting of the section or the emulsion
> 2. Sandwich technique with separate processing of tissue and photographic film after exposure
> 3. Protective coating of tissue to prevent leaching during application of stripping film or liquid emulsion
> 4. Freeze substitution of tissue with or without embedding followed by film application
> 5. Vacuum freeze-drying of tissue blocks followed by embedding
> 6. Mounting of frozen sections on emulsion, using heat or adhesive liquids

If such an enumeration is syntactically part of the sentence preceding it (as in the earlier, run-in examples), items are set lowercase and carry appropriate end punctuation. Whenever possible, however, it is better to avoid this style.

8.74   When referring to an item in an enumeration by letter or number only, enclose the letter or numeral in parentheses, whatever the style of the enumeration itself; if a category name is used, however, open style is preferable:

> From (*a*), (*b*), and (*d*) it is apparent . . .
> Methods 4, 5, and 6 all require special laboratory equipment.

8.75 For an enumeration in which items are subdivided, a more elaborate form of outline style is called for. The following example illustrates the form favored by the University of Chicago Press. Note that the divisional numerals or letters for the top three levels are set off by periods and those for the lower levels by single or double parentheses:

> I. Historical introduction
> II. Dentition in various groups of vertebrates
>   A. Reptilia
>   1. Histology and development of reptile teeth
>   2. Survey of forms
>   B. Mammalia
>   1. Histology and development of mammalian teeth
>   2. Survey of forms
>   *a*) Primates
>   (1) Lemuroidea
>   (2) Anthropoidea
>   (*a*) Platyrrhini
>   (*b*) Catarrhini
>   i) Circopithecidae
>   ii) Pongidae
>   *b*) Carnivora
>   (1) Creodonta
>   (2) Fissipedia
>   (*a*) Aeluroidea
>   (*b*) Arctoidea
>   (3) Pinnipedia
>   *c*) Etc. . . .

In the foregoing example, note that roman numerals, since they vary in width, are aligned on the following period or parenthesis. Any run-over lines would be aligned as in the preceding example.

FOR FURTHER REFERENCE

8.76 For special uses of numbers not covered in this chapter, the reader is referred to the United States Government Printing Office *Style Manual.*

9 *Foreign Languages in Type*

Languages Using the Latin Alphabet 9.3
  General Principles 9.4
    Capitalization 9.4
    Punctuation 9.7
    Word division 9.9
    Special characters 9.10
  Czech 9.12
    Capitalization 9.12
    Special characters 9.13
  Danish 9.14
    Capitalization 9.14
    Special characters 9.15
  Dutch 9.16
    Capitalization 9.16
    Special characters 9.17
  Finnish 9.18
    Capitalization 9.18
    Special characters 9.19
  French 9.20
    Capitalization 9.20
    Punctuation 9.21
    Word division 9.27
    Special characters 9.32
  German 9.33
    Capitalization 9.33
    Punctuation 9.34
    Word division 9.36
    Special characters 9.42
  Hungarian 9.43
    Capitalization 9.43
    Special characters 9.44
  Italian 9.45
    Capitalization 9.45
    Punctuation 9.46
    Word division 9.49
    Special characters 9.54
  Latin 9.55
    Capitalization 9.55
    Word division 9.56
    Special characters 9.60
  Norwegian 9.61
    Capitalization 9.61
    Special characters 9.62
  Polish 9.63
    Capitalization 9.63

Special characters 9.64
Word division 9.65
Portuguese 9.66
Capitalization 9.66
Special characters 9.67
Spanish 9.68
Capitalization 9.68
Punctuation 9.69
Word division 9.72
Special characters 9.79
Swedish 9.80
Capitalization 9.80
Special characters 9.81
Turkish 9.82
Capitalization 9.82
Special characters 9.83
African Languages 9.84
Transliterated and Romanized Languages 9.85
Russian 9.86
Capitalization 9.87
Punctuation 9.90
Word division 9.93
Arabic 9.102
Transliteration 9.103
Special characters 9.104
Spelling 9.105
Capitalization 9.107
Personal names 9.109
South Asian Languages 9.110
Chinese and Japanese 9.111
Romanization 9.111
Capitalization and italics 9.116
Editing and Composing Classical Greek 9.119
Transliteration 9.121
Breathings 9.122
Accents 9.125
Punctuation 9.128
Numbers 9.129
Word Division 9.130
Old English and Middle English 9.136
For Further Reference 9.138

9.1   This chapter is intended as an aid to authors and editors in solving some of the problems that arise in preparing foreign language copy for setting in type. Some of the suggestions are addressed primarily to authors (such as the recommendations on choice of transliteration systems), others primarily to manuscript editors (such as the hints on what kinds of capitalization one is likely to encounter in various languages). It should be emphasized that the chapter does not pretend to constitute a style manual for any of the languages treated. Nor does it pretend to be comprehensive: only the languages that editors are likely to meet in the course of general bookwork are covered at all, and of these some are covered more completely than others, depending partly upon the relative importance of the languages in scholarly work and partly upon the complexity of the problems they raise.

9.2   The kinds of problems one encounters with foreign language copy differ according to whether the copy was originally written with the same alphabet as English, whether it has been transliterated or romanized, or whether it is to be set in the alphabet of the original (Greek being the only common example of the last). The organization of the chapter reflects these three categories.

LANGUAGES USING THE LATIN ALPHABET

9.3   With languages using an alphabet basically similar to that of English (the *Latin* alphabet), editorial questions arise mainly from differing systems of capitalization, punctuation, and syllabication (word division). But since some of these languages supplement the basic Latin alphabet with additional letters or use a variety of accents and diacritics on the familiar letters, there is the mechanical problem of making sure that the typesetter can reproduce these special characters.

GENERAL PRINCIPLES

9.4   *Capitalization.* The chief problem concerning capitalization is what to do with titles of books and articles in bibliographies, notes, and run of text. Here the University of Chicago Press recommends following a simple rule: In any language but English capitalize only the words that would be capitalized in normal prose. For all the languages in question this means capitalizing the first word of the title and any proper nouns that occur in it.[1] For German it means capitalizing common nouns also. For Dutch it means capitalizing proper adjectives also, but not common nouns. (This rule is followed for all languages, including English, in some bibliographic styles [see 16.5–6].) The rule can easily be extended to the names of foreign journals and even of learned socie-

---

1. The rule for French titles followed by the *French Review, PMLA,* and *Romanic Review,* and recommended by the University of Chicago Department of Romance Languages and Literatures, is as follows. Always capitalize the first word and any proper nouns in the title; if the first word is an article, capitalize the substantive and any intervening adjective(s); if the first word is neither an article nor an adjective, lowercase all following words. Thus: *Le Rouge et le noir; L'Illusion comique; Les Fausses Vérités; A la recherche du temps perdu; Dans le labyrinthe.* The Press accepts this rule for studies in French literature but for general use (especially when works in several languages are cited) prefers the simpler rule stated in the text.

ties, although in practice these are often capitalized in the same way as their English counterparts. See examples of foreign language titles in 16.38–40, 16.121–23, and 17.42–43, 17.54.

9.5 In English, capitalization is applied to more classes of words than in any other European language. Consequently, it is always surprising to English-speaking persons learning their first foreign language—say, French—to discover that the equivalents of *I* and *American* and *Tuesday* are spelled with no capitals. The remarks under "Capitalization" in the sections that follow are an attempt to mitigate some of the manuscript editor's surprises—to suggest some of the more obvious ways in which various languages differ from English in their use of capitals.

9.6 Except where it is stated to the contrary, the language in question is assumed to use lowercase type for all adjectives (except adjectives used as proper nouns), all pronouns, the names of the months, and the days of the week. In addition, it can be assumed that capitals are used much more sparingly than in English for names of offices, institutions, places, organizations, and so on. (For the capitalization of foreign personal names see 7.6–14.)

9.7 *Punctuation.* Continental punctuation is in some ways even more "foreign" to the English-speaking editor than Continental capitalization. The remarks under "Punctuation" in the sections below are an attempt to point out some of the more obvious departures from what is familiar to us. Further information on foreign punctuation can be found in chapter 6.

9.8 Note too that the remarks apply to foreign punctuation in a foreign language context, that is, in an article or book in that language. A bit of foreign language dialogue or a longer passage quoted in a foreign language introduced into an English context would be punctuated in English fashion, especially with regard to quotation marks:

> "L'état," said the Sun King modestly, "c'est moi."

9.9 *Word division.* Anyone who has ever read a book in English that was composed and printed in a non-English-speaking country knows how easy it is to err in word division when working with a language not one's own. Condensed rules for dividing words in the Latin-alphabet foreign languages most frequently met in book and journal work are given below.

9.10 *Special characters.* English is one of very few languages that can be set without accents, diacritics, or special alphabetic characters for native words. Whenever passages in a foreign language occur in a book, or foreign titles in reference lists or notes, the manuscript editor should scan them carefully for special characters, especially unusual ones. The ordinary umlauted (as in German) and accented (as in French and Spanish) lowercase vowels are readily available in most type fonts, but anything more unusual, including accented capital letters, should be listed or circled on a copy of table 9.1, for the information of the typesetter (see 2.154).

9.11 Names of diacritical marks most commonly used in European and Asian languages written in the Latin alphabet are acute accent (é), grave accent (è), diaeresis or umlaut (ü), circumflex (ê), tilde (ñ), cedilla (ç), macron (ē), and breve (ĕ).

CZECH

9.12 *Capitalization*. See 9.4–6.

9.13 *Special characters*. Czech, a Slavonic language, is written in the Latin alphabet but uses many diacritical marks to indicate sounds not represented by this alphabet:

Á á, Č č, Ď ď, É é, Ě ě, Í í, Ň ň, Ó ó, Ř ř, Š š, Ť ť, Ů ů, Ú ú, Ý ý, Ž ž

DANISH

9.14 *Capitalization*. See 9.4–6. The polite personal pronouns *De, Dem, Deres,* and the familiar *I* are capitalized in Danish. Formerly, common nouns were capitalized as in German.

9.15 *Special characters*. Danish has three additional alphabetic letters, and special characters are required for these:

Å å, Æ æ, Ø ø

DUTCH

9.16 *Capitalization*. See 9.4–6. The pronouns *U, Uw,* and *Gij* when they appear in personal correspondence are capitalized. Proper adjectives are capitalized as in English. When a word beginning with the diphthong *ij* is capitalized, both letters are capitals: *IJsland*. When a single letter begins a sentence, it is set lowercase, but the next word is capitalized: *'k Heb niet. . . .* (For the capitalization of particles with personal names see 7.9.)

9.17 *Special characters*. Dutch requires no special characters outside the ordinary Latin alphabet.

FINNISH

9.18 *Capitalization*. See 9.4–6.

TABLE 9.1: Special Characters in the Latin Alphabet

Á	á	Ğ	ğ	Ǫ	ǫ
À	à	Ḥ	ḥ	Œ	œ
Ä	ä	Í	í	Ṛ	ṛ
Â	â	Ì	ì	Ṝ	ṝ
Ā	ā	Ï	ï	Ř	ř
Ā	ā	Î	î	Ś	ś
Ă	ă	Ī	ī	Ṣ	ṣ
Å	å	Ĭ	ĭ	Š	š
Ą	ą	İ	i	Ş	ş
Æ	æ	Ḱ	ḱ		ß
Ǣ	ǣ	Ł	ł	Ṭ	ṭ
Б ʻВ	ƃ	Ḷ	ḷ	Ť	t'
Ć	ć	Ḹ	ḹ	Ţ	ţ
Ç	ç	Ṃ	ṃ	þ	þ
Č	č	Ń	ń	Ù	ù
Ḍ	ḍ	Ñ	ñ	Ü	ü
Ď	d'	Ň	ň	Ű	ű
Đ ʻD	ḍ ɗ	Ṇ	ṇ	Û	û
Đ	ð	Ṅ	ṅ	Ū	ū
É	é	Ŋ	ŋ	Ŭ	ŭ
È	è	Ó	ó	Ú	ú
Ë	ë	Ò	ò	Ụ	ụ
Ê	ê	Ö	ö	Ů	ů
Ē	ē	Ő	ő	Ý	ý
Ĕ	ĕ	Ô	ô	Ź	ź
Ě	ě	Ō	ō	Ż	ż
Ė	ė	Õ	õ	Ž	ž
Ę	ę	Ŏ	ŏ	Ʒ	ʒ
Ğ	ğ	Ø	ø		

9.19   *Special characters.* Finnish requires two umlauted vowels:

Ä ä, Ö ö

FRENCH

9.20   *Capitalization.* See 9.4–6. Names denoting roadways, squares, etc., are lowercased, whether part of an address or used alone:

le boulevard Saint-Germain   13, rue des Beaux-Arts
la place de l'Opéra   le carrefour de Buci

In names of political, military, religious, or other institutions, the first substantive only is capitalized:

l'Académie française   le Conservatoire de musique
l'Assemblée nationale   la Légion d'honneur
l'Eglise catholique (*but* l'église de Saint-Eustache)

If such names are hyphenated (and French makes frequent use of hyphens), both elements are capitalized:

la Comédie-Française

Names of buildings are generally capitalized:

l'Hôtel des Invalides   le Palais du Louvre

Names of members of religious groups are lowercased:

un chrétien   des juifs   une carmélite   un protestant

In most geographical names, the substantive is lowercased and the modifying word capitalized:

la mer Rouge   le pic du Midi   le massif Central

9.21   *Punctuation.* Small angle marks called *guillemets* (« ») are used for quotation marks and are placed on the lower part of the type body (but see 9.8). A small amount of space is added between the guillemets and the quoted material:

A vrai dire, Abélard n'avoue pas un tel rationalisme: «je ne veux pas être si philosophe, écrit-il, que je résiste à Paul, ni si aristotélicien que je me sépare du Christ», ou encore: «Vois combien il est présomptueux de discuter par la raison ce qui dépasse l'homme et de ne pas s'arrêter avant d'avoir éclairé toutes ses paroles par le sens ou la raison humaine.»[2]

9.22   Punctuation belonging to the quoted matter is placed inside the closing guillemets:

«Va-t'en!» m'a-t-il dit.

2. Emile Bréhier, *Histoire de la philosophie,* vol. 1, fasc. 3 (Paris: Presses universitaires de France, 1931), 517.

255

Punctuation belonging to the including sentence is placed outside, and a period belonging to the quotation is dropped:

D'où vient l'expression «sur le tapis»?
Est-ce Louis XV qui a dit: «Après moi, le déluge»?

When the end punctuation of the simultaneously terminating quotation and including sentence is identical, the mark outside the closing guillemets is dropped:

Qui a dit: «Où sont les neiges d'antan?»

9.23 If a quotation in text (that is, not a block quotation) is more than one paragraph long, guillemets are placed at the beginning of each additional paragraph and closing guillemets at the end of the last.

9.24 Guillemets are also used for quotations within quotations. When the second quotation runs over to additional lines, each runover line begins with opening guillemets. If the two quotations end simultaneously, however, only one pair of terminating guillemets is used:

Raoul suggéra à sa sœur: «Tu connais sans doute la parole «De «l'abondance du cœur la bouche parle.»

9.25 In quoted conversation, the guillemets are frequently replaced by dashes. The dash is used before each successive speech but is not repeated at the end of the speech. A space is added after the dash:

— Vous viendrez aussitôt que possible? a-t-il demandé.
— Tout de suite.
— Bien. Bonne chance!

If a quotation is used in dialogue, guillemets are employed to set off the quotation.

9.26 Three closely spaced periods, suspension points, are frequently used to indicate interruptions or sudden breaks in thought. A space is used after, but not before, such points:

«Ce n'est pas que je n'aime plus l'Algérie... mon Dieu! un ciel! des arbres!... et le reste!... Toutefois, sept ans de discipline.... »

9.27 *Word division.* The fundamental principle of French word division is to divide as far as possible on a vowel, avoiding consonantal ending of syllables except where *n* nasalizes a preceding vowel:

a-che-ter   ba-lan-cer (*not* bal-anc-er)
in-di-vi-si-bi-li-té   ta-bleau (*not* tab-leau)

9.28 Two adjacent and different consonants of which the second is *l* or *r* (but not the combinations *rl* and *lr*) are both carried over to the following syllable. Otherwise, different consonants are divided:

é-cri-vain   par-ler   plas-tic

qua-tre   Mal-raux   ob-jet

9.29   In groups of three adjacent consonants the first goes with the preceding syllable; the others are carried over:

es-prit   res-plendir

9.30   There are as many syllables as there are vowels or diphthongs, even if some vowels are not sounded:

fui-te   guer-re   sor-tent

A mute *e* following a vowel, however, does not form a syllable:

é-taient   re-çue

9.31   When preceding other vowels and sounded as consonants, *i, y, o, ou,* and *u* do not form syllables:

bien   é-tions   loin
é-cuel-le   fouet-ter   yeux

Nor should division be made after an apostrophe:

jus-qu'à demain

9.32   *Special characters.* French as sometimes set employs the following special characters:

À à, Â â, Ç ç, É é, È è, Ê ê, Ë ë, Î î, Ï ï, Ô ô, Œ œ, Ù ù, Û û, Ü ü

Note, however, that French may be set without accents on capital letters (University of Chicago Press preference),[3] and if necessary the ligature Œ *œ* may be set as separate characters (*OE oe*). This leaves as the essential minimum the *C c* with cedilla and the lowercase accented vowels, characters that are found in many English and American fonts.

GERMAN

9.33   *Capitalization.* See 9.4–6. The most striking feature of German capitalization is that all nouns and words used as nouns are capitalized:

ein Haus   Weltanschauung   das Sein

Although proper adjectives are generally lowercased, those derived from personal names, and used with their original signification, are capitalized:

die deutsche Literatur   die Platonischen Dialoge

3. French printers vary in practice, some retaining accents on all capitals (except the preposition *à*, which never carries the accent when capitalized), some retaining accents only on *E*, some omitting them altogether. English and American publishers reflect all these practices.

The pronouns *Sie, Ihr,* and *Ihnen,* as polite second-person forms, are capitalized. As third-person pronouns they are lowercased. Also, in correspondence such forms as *Du, Dein, Ihr, Euch,* etc., are capitalized.

9.34   *Punctuation.* The apostrophe is used to note the colloquial omission of *e:*

wie geht's   was gibt's   hab' ich

The apostrophe is also used to note the omission of the genitive ending, *s,* after proper names ending in *s, ß, x, z:*

Jaspers' Philosophie   Leibniz' Meinung

9.35   In German, quotations take pairs of primes („"), double, inverted quotation marks (,, "), or (sometimes inverted) guillemets (but see 9.8):

Adam Smith hat sehr wohl gesehen, daß in ,,Wirklichkeit die Verschiedenheit der natürlichen Anlagen zwischen den Individuen weit geringer ist als wir glauben."

Punctuation is placed inside or outside closing quotation marks according to whether it belongs to the quotation or the including sentence.

9.36   *Word division.* The fundamental principle of German word division is to divide on a vowel as far as possible:

Fa-brik   hü-ten   Bu-ße

9.37   If two or more consonants stand between vowels, usually only the last is carried over:

Karp-fen   Klir-ren   Ver-wand-te
Klemp-ner   Rit-ter   Was-ser

9.38   The consonantal groups *ch, sch, ph, st,* and *th* are separated only when the letters belong to different syllables:

Hä-scher   Philoso-phie   Morgen-stern
(*but* Häus-chen)   (*but* Klapp-hut)   (*but* Reichs-tag)

9.39   If *ck* must be divided, it is separated into *k-k:*

Deckel—Dek-kel

9.40   In non-German words combinations of *b, d, g, k, p,* and *t* with *l* or *r* are carried over:

Hy-drant   Me-trum   Pu-bli-kum

9.41   Compound words are separated first into their component elements, and within each element the foregoing rules apply:

Für-sten-schloß   In-ter-esse   Tür-an-gel

9.42   *Special characters.* German is almost never set in the old *Fraktur* type nowadays. For setting in roman type, one special character (ß) is needed, plus the umlauted vowels:

Ä ä, Ö ö, Ü ü

It is acceptable to set ß as *ss* and umlauted capitals as *Ae, Oe,* and *Ue,* but seldom should lowercase umlauted letters be so set.

HUNGARIAN

9.43   *Capitalization.* See 9.4–6.

9.44   *Special characters.* Hungarian requires several varieties of accented vowels:

Á á, É é, Í í, Ó ó, Ö ö, Ő ő, Ú ú, Ü ü, Ű ű

ITALIAN

9.45   *Capitalization.* See 9.4–6. In Italian, titles preceding a proper name are normally lowercased:

il commendatore Ugo Emiliano   la signora Rossi

The formal second-person pronouns *Ella, Lei, Loro* are capitalized.

9.46   *Punctuation.* A series of closely spaced dots is used to indicate a sudden break in thought or an interruption in faltering speech. If other punctuation precedes the series, three periods are used; otherwise, four periods are used:

«Piano!... Ho sentito muovere di là.... C'è qualcuno.... Dev'essere la.... cosa dell'ingegnere....»

9.47   The apostrophe is used to indicate the omission of a letter. Space should be added after an apostrophe that follows a vowel. No space is used after an apostrophe that follows a consonant:

po' duro   de' malevoli   l'onda   all'aura

9.48   Quotation marks in Italian are the same as French guillemets (but see 9.8):

Anche il primo incontro di Henry James con l'Italia, nel 1869, riflette il tradizionale atteggiamento americano del tempo. Le lettere che scrive a casa mentre dal Gottardo, attraverso Milano, Verona, Padova, Venezia, Mantova, Firenze, scende a Roma, parlano con insistenza della «meraviglia profonda», dell' «estasi e della passione» che lo invadono via ch'egli viene a contatto con «l'atmosfera italiana», «la melodiosa lingua d'Italia», lo «Spirito del Sud», finché la sera della sua prima giornata romana, trascorsa «vagando come ubriaco per le strade, in

preda a una gioia delirante», scrive al fratello William: «Finalmente —
per la prima volta — io vivo!»[4]

In dialogue, however, dashes are used instead of guillemets. Each
successive speech is introduced by a dash, and if other matter follows
the speech in the same paragraph, another dash is used at the end of
the speech.

—Avremo la neve— annunziò la vecchia.

9.49   *Word division.* The fundamental principle of Italian word division is to
divide after the vowel, letting each syllable begin with a consonant as
far as possible. Where there is only one consonant in intervocalic
position, place it with the following vowel:

a-cro-po-li   mi-se-ra-bi-le   ta-vo-li-no

9.50   Certain consonantal groups must also be placed with the following
vowel. These are *ch, gh, qu, gli, sc,* and *r* or *l* preceded by any consonant other than themselves:

a-qua-rio	na-sce	rau-che
fi-glio	pa-dre	ri-flet-te-re
la-ghi	pe-sta	u-sci-re

9.51   Consonants, however, must be divided when (1) double, (2) in the
group *cqu,* and (3) in a group beginning with *l, m, n,* or *r:*

ac-qua	cam-po	par-te
af-fre-schi	com-pra	poz-zo
cal-do	den-tro	sen-to

9.52   Vowel combinations are not divided:

miei   pia-ga   pie-no   tuo

9.53   No division occurs immediately after an apostrophe:

dal-l'accusa	quel-l'uomo
del-l'or-ga-no	un'ar-te

9.54   *Special characters.* In Italian, the grave accent on uppercase vowels
is usually optional, but in stressed final syllables it must be retained to
avoid confusion.

CANTÒ (he sang)   CANTO (I sing)

LATIN

9.55   *Capitalization.* The tendency of editors around the world is to capitalize Latin according to the principles of their own languages. In English-speaking countries, however, titles of ancient and medieval

4. Franca Piazza, trans., *Città e paesaggi di Toscana visti da Henry James* (Florence:
G. Barbèra, 1961), 7–8.

books and shorter pieces are capitalized not as English titles but as English prose; that is, only the first word, proper nouns, and proper adjectives are capitalized:

De bello Gallico   *De viris illustribus*
Cur Deus homo?   but: *Sic et Non*

Modern works with Latin titles are usually capitalized in the English fashion:

Novum Organum   *Religio Medici*

9.56   *Word division.* A Latin word has as many syllables as it has vowels or diphthongs (*ae, au, ei, eu, oe, ui*):

o-pe-re   gra-ti-a   na-tu-ra

9.57   When a single consonant occurs between two vowels, divide before the consonant:

Cae-sar   me-ri-di-es

9.58   In the case of two or more consonants, divide before the last consonant except in the combinations: mute (*p, ph, b, t, th, d, c, ch, g*)+ liquid (*l, r*), and *qu* or *gu:*

cunc-tus   scrip-tus
om-nis   (*but* pa-tris, e-quus, lin-gua, ex-em-pla)

9.59   Compound words are separated first into their component elements; within each element the foregoing rules apply:

ab-rum-po   ad-est   red-e-o   trans-i-go

9.60   *Special characters.* Latin requires no special characters for setting ordinary copy. Elementary texts, however, usually mark the long vowels, and so all five vowels with the macron would be needed for setting such works. Also, authors occasionally like to mark short quantities, and so vowels with the breve may be useful as well. The entire series for elementary Latin thus is:

Ā ā, Ă ă, Ē ē, Ĕ ĕ, Ī ī, Ĭ ĭ, Ō ō, Ŏ ŏ, Ū ū, Ŭ ŭ

NORWEGIAN

9.61   *Capitalization.* See 9.4–6. As in Danish, the polite personal pronouns *De, Dem,* and *Deres* are capitalized. Formerly, common nouns were capitalized as in German.

9.62   *Special characters.* Norwegian requires the same special characters as Danish:

Å å, Æ æ, Ø ø

POLISH

9.63   *Capitalization.* See 9.4–6.

9.64   *Special characters.* Polish requires the following special characters:

Ą ą, Ć ć, Ę ę, Ł ł, Ń ń, Ó ó, Ś ś, Ź ź, Ż ż

Since Ł and ł are likely to confuse the typesetter, the editor should note in the margin "canceled el" or "slashed el" or some such description.

9.65   *Word division.* Division of Polish words is similar to that of transliterated Russian (see 9.93–101).

PORTUGUESE

9.66   *Capitalization.* See 9.4–6.

9.67   *Special characters.* Portuguese employs three special characters:

Ã ã, Ç ç, Õ õ

In addition, however, Portuguese makes extensive use of accents: all five vowels with both the acute and the grave are needed, plus *a, e,* and *o* with the circumflex. The vowels *i* and *u* sometimes appear with the diaeresis (*ï, ü*), but the same letters with the grave may be substituted for them. If display lines are to be set in full or small capitals, accented characters must be available, but for text work they may be dispensed with.

SPANISH

9.68   *Capitalization.* See 9.4–6. Titles preceding names are lowercased in Spanish: *el señor Jaime López.* When a question or an exclamation occurs within a sentence, its first word is lowercased (see example in 9.71).

9.69   *Punctuation.* Guillemets are used for quotation marks, and in a quotation enclosed by guillemets, dashes may be used to set off words identifying the speaker (but see 9.8):

> El demonio, el activo demonio cuyo poder había quebrantado Hernán Cortés con espada y con lanza, gozaba utilizando al hijo como instrumento de sus infernales designios. «Vino el negocio a tanto —comenta Suárez—, que ya andaban muchos tomados por el diablo». Los frailes, desde los púlpitos, lanzaban catilinarias y aconsejaban a los padres sobre la forma en que debían salvaguardar el honor de sus familiares.[5]

> 5. Fernando Benítez, *Los primeros Mexicanos: La vida criolla en el siglo XVI,* 3d ed. (Mexico, F.D.: Ediciones ERA, 1962), 181.

In dialogue, dashes are used to introduce each successive speech. If other matter follows the quoted speech in the same paragraph, a dash should be added at the end of the speech.

—Esto es el arca de Noé— afirmó el estanciero.

9.70 A series of three periods is used to indicate a sudden break in thought or an interruption in faltering speech:

Hemos comenzado la vida juntos... quizá la terminaremos juntos también...

9.71 In Spanish, the question mark and the exclamation point precede, in inverted form, the beginning of a question or an exclamation:

¿Qué pasa, amigo?
Por favor, señor ¿dónde está la biblioteca municipal?
Alguien viene. ¡Vámonos!

9.72 *Word division.* The fundamental principle of Spanish word division is to divide on a vowel or group of vowels. Two or more adjacent vowels may not be divided:

au-tor	fue-go	re-cla-mo
bue-no	mu-jer	se-ño-ri-ta
cam-biáis	ne-ga-ti-va	tie-ne
ca-ra-co-les	pre-fe-rir	viu-da

9.73 A single vowel may not stand alone at the end of a line:

acei-te (*not* a-ceite)	ene-ro (*not* e-nero)
áti-co (*not* á-tico)	uni-dad (*not* u-nidad)

9.74 Some two- and three-syllable words may be divided, while others may not:

aho-ra	cie-go	leer
ao-jo	creer	lí-nea
aún	ellos	oa-sis
au-to	eo-lio	oí-do
baúl	ideas	oír

9.75 A single intervocalic consonant goes with the following vowel, except that compound words are usually divided according to derivation:

ave-ri-güéis	mal-es-tar	semi-es-fe-ra
des-igual	nos-otros	sub-or-di-nar
fle-xi-bi-li-dad	re-ba-ño	(*but* bien-aven-tu-ra-do)
in-útil	re-unión	

9.76 Spanish *ch, ll,* and *rr* are considered single characters:

ci-ga-rri-llo	mu-cha-cho

9.77   Two adjacent consonants may usually be separated:

ac-cio-nis-ta	al-cal-de	efec-to
ad-ver-ten-cia	an-cho	is-la

The following pairs, however, containing *l* or *r*, except rarely in compounds, are inseparable: *bl, cl, fl, gl, pl,* and *br, cr, dr, fr, gr, pr, tr:*

ci-fra	ma-dre	re-gla
co-pla	ne-gro	se-cre-to
im-po-si-ble	no-ble	te-cla
le-pra	pa-tria	(*but* sub-lu-nar, sub-ra-yar)
li-bro	re-fle-jo	

9.78   Groups of three consonants not ending with one of the inseparable pairs listed always have an *s* in the middle. They are divided after the second consonant, since an *s* is always disjoined from a following consonant:

cons-pi-rar	ins-tan-te	obs-cu-ro
cons-ta	in-ters-ti-cio	obs-tan-te

9.79   *Special characters.* Spanish employs one special character:

Ñ ñ

In addition, however, all five vowels with the acute accent are needed, plus *u* with the diaeresis (*ü*). As with Portuguese, accented capitals can probably be safely dispensed with for ordinary text work.

SWEDISH

9.80   *Capitalization.* See 9.4–6. In Swedish the second-person pronouns *Ni, Eder,* and *Er* are capitalized in correspondence.

9.81   *Special characters.* Swedish requires the following special characters:

Å å, Ä ä, Ö ö

TURKISH

9.82   *Capitalization.* See 9.4–6. In Turkish the names of months and days of the week are capitalized.

9.83   *Special characters.* Turkish requires the following special characters:

Â â, Ç ç, Ğ ğ (*or* Ğ ğ), İ ı, Ö ö, Ş ş, Û û, Ü ü

Note that there are dotted and undotted varieties of both the capital and the lowercase *i*. A dotted lowercase *i* retains its dot when capitalized.

AFRICAN LANGUAGES

9.84   African languages, other than the Arabic of the northern African countries, use the Latin alphabet and follow the English style of capitalization and punctuation. Of the two most widely spoken languages, Swahili uses no additional letters or diacritics. Hausa adds a symbol for the nasal *n* (Ŋ ŋ) and other special characters: Ɓ 'Ɓ ɓ, Ɗ 'D ɖ ɗ, Ƙ ƙ, Ọ ọ. Hausa, spoken by about 15,000,000 people, and the language used in trade in Western Africa, provides the phonetic base for transcribing other languages, e.g., Kriol.

TRANSLITERATED AND ROMANIZED LANGUAGES

9.85   In general work it is usual to *transliterate* Russian and Arabic from their original alphabets to the Latin alphabet and to transcribe the spoken forms of Chinese and Japanese into Latin characters, that is, to *romanize* these languages.

RUSSIAN

9.86   There are many systems for transliterating Russian, the most important of which are summarized in table 9.2. Journals of Slavic studies generally prefer a "linguistic" system making free use of diacritics, since such a system more nearly reflects the one-symbol-to-one-sound nature of the Cyrillic alphabet. But for a book or article reaching a more general audience, a system without diacritics or ligatures is desirable. The preference of the University of Chicago Press, for general use, is the system of the United States Board on Geographic Names. Regardless of the system of transliteration, however, well-known Russian names should be given in the form in which they have become familiar to English-speaking readers: that is, the spellings of *Webster's Biographical Dictionary* and the *Columbia Lippincott Gazetteer* or *Webster's Geographical Dictionary* should prevail:

Tchaikovsky	Moscow
Chekhov	Nizhni Novgorod (Gorki)
Catherine the Great	Dnieper

9.87   *Capitalization.* Conventions of capitalization in the Cyrillic original are about the same as those of French and should be preserved in transliteration. Pronouns, days of the week, months, and most proper adjectives are lowercased. Geographical designations are capitalized when they apply to formal political units or formal institutions but otherwise are lowercased:

Tverskaya guberniya	Moskovskiy universitet
tverskoe zemstvo	russkiy kompozitor

TABLE 9.2: TRANSLITERATION OF RUSSIAN

CYRILLIC ALPHABET		U.S. BOARD ON GEO- GRAPHIC NAMES	LIBRARY OF CONGRESS	"LINGUISTIC" SYSTEM
Upright	Cursive			
А а	*А а*	a		
Б б	*Б б*	b		
В в	*В в*	v		
Г г	*Г г*	g		
Д д	*Д д*	d		
Е е	*Е е*	ye,[1] e	e	e
Ё ё[2]	*Ё ё*	yĕ,[1] ё	ё	e, ё
Ж ж	*Ж ж*	zh		ž
З з	*З з*	z		
И и	*И и*	i		
Й й	*Й й*	y	ĭ	j
К к	*К к*	k		
Л л	*Л л*	l		
М м	*М м*	m		
Н н	*Н н*	n		
О о	*О о*	o		
П п	*П п*	p		
Р р	*Р р*	r		
С с	*С с*	s		
Т т	*Т т*	t		
У у	*У у*	u		
Ф ф	*Ф ф*	f		
Х х	*Х х*	kh		x, ch
Ц ц	*Ц ц*	ts	t͡s	c
Ч ч	*Ч ч*	ch		č
Ш ш	*Ш ш*	sh		š
Щ щ	*Щ щ*	shch		šč
Ъ ъ[3]	*Ъ ъ*	"	″	″
Ы ы[3]	*Ы ы*	y		
Ь ь[3]	*Ь ь*	'	′	′
Э э	*Э э*	e	ė	è
Ю ю	*Ю ю*	yu	i͡u	ju
Я я	*Я я*	ya	i͡a	ja

NOTE: The Library of Congress and "linguistic" systems employ the same characters as the U.S. Board system except where noted.
1. Initially and after a vowel or ъ or ь.
2. Not considered a separate letter.
3. Does not occur initially.

9.88 Titles of books and articles and the names of periodicals are lower-cased except for the first word and proper nouns:

N. A. Kuryakin. *Lenin i Trotskiy.*

O. I. Skorokhodova. *Kak ya vosprinimayu i predstavlyayu okruzha-yushchiy mir* [How I perceive and imagine the external world]. Moscow: Izd. Akad. Pedag. Nauk, 1954.

9.89 In the Cyrillic originals of these citations the author's name and the title are both set in ordinary type (called in Russian *pryamoy,* "upright''); the author's name, however, is letterspaced. The Cyrillic *kursiv* is more sparingly used than our italic—never for book titles.

9.90 *Punctuation.* Russian resembles French in its use of guillemets for quotations and of dashes for dialogue:

> «Bozhe, bozhe, bozhe!» govorit Boris.
> — S kem ya rabotayu?
> — S tovarishchem.
> — Kak my rabotaem?
> — S interesom.

Quotation marks of the German type (see 9.35) are sometimes used instead (but see 9.8).

9.91 Suspension points are also used in Russian as in French:

> Ya... vy... my tol'ko chto priyekhali.

An exclamation mark or question mark, however, in Russian takes the place of one dot:

> Mitya!.. Gde vy byli?..

9.92 A dash is sometimes used between subject and complement when the equivalent of *is* or *are* is omitted:

> Moskva—stolitsa Rossii.

A dash is also used in place of a verb omitted because it would be identical to the preceding verb:

> Ivan i Sonya poyedut v Moskvu poyezdom, Lëv i Lyuba — avtobusom.

9.93 *Word division.* Transliterated Russian should be divided according to the rules governing word division in the Cyrillic original. In the rules and examples that follow, the transliteration system of the United States Board on Geographic Names is the one used.

9.94 Combinations representing single Cyrillic letters should never be divided:

> ye, yë, zh, kh, ts, ch, sh, shch, yu, ya

9.95 Combinations of a vowel plus short *i* (transliterated *y*) should never be divided:

> ay, ey, yey, *etc.*

9.96 The following consonantal combinations may not be broken:

b *or* p		bl, pl	br, pr
g *or* k } *plus* l *or* r, *namely:* {		gl, kl	gr, kr
f *or* v		fl, vl	fr, vr

also:

dv, dr	tv, tr	sk, skv, skr	st, stv, str	zhd	ml

267

9.97   Words may be divided after prefixes, but generally the prefixes themselves should not be divided:

bes-poryadok   za-dat'   na-zhat'   obo-gnat'
pere-vod   pred-lozhit'   pro-vesti

9.98   Words may be divided after a vowel or diphthong before a single (Cyrillic) consonant:

Si-bir'   voy-na   Khru-shchëv   da-zhe

or before a consonantal combination (see 9.96):

puteshe-stvennik   khi-trit'   pro-stak   ru-brika

9.99   Division may be made between single consonants or between consonants and consonantal combinations:

ubor-ku   mol-cha   mor-skoy
chudes-nym   sred-stvo

9.100   Division may be made between single vowels or between a single vowel and a diphthong:

ma-yak   nochna-ya   oke-an
ori-entirovat'   svo-yëm

9.101   Compound words are preferably divided between parts:

radio-priyëmnik   gor-sovet   kino-teatr

ARABIC

9.102   In transcribing from Arabic—or Aramaic, Hebrew, Persian, Ottoman Turkish, Urdu, etc.—the author should use a system employing as few diacritics as possible, except in linguistic or highly specialized studies. If the *hamza* (ʾ) and the ʿayn (ʿ) are used, they may be represented in typescript by an apostrophe and a raised *c*.

9.103   *Transliteration.* There is no universally accepted form for the transliteration of Arabic. The most widely used system is the one followed by the Library of Congress, described in Bulletins 91 (Arabic) and 92 (Persian) published (September 1970) by the Processing Department of the Cataloging Service of the library.

9.104   *Special characters.* For Arabic materials to be set in type, sorts for the hamza and ʿayn should be obtained in the appropriate sizes. If necessary, a Greek smooth breathing (ʾ) may be used for the hamza and a rough breathing (ʿ) for the ʿayn. Sometimes an apostrophe (ʾ) and a turned comma (ʿ) are used for these two signs.

9.105   *Spelling.* Having selected a system of transliteration, the author should stick to it with as few exceptions as possible. Of course, isolated references in text to well-known persons or places should employ the forms familiar to English-speaking readers: *Avicenna,* not *ibn-Sina; Mecca,* not *Makka; Faiyum,* not *Madinat al-Fayyum* or some other variant.

9.106 In particular, the definite article, *al,* should always be joined to the noun with a hyphen: *al-Islam.* And although the sounds *t, d, r, z, s, sh,* and *n* are elided with the article in speech, the preferred scholarly usage is to write the article-noun combination without indication of the elision:

> al-Nafud (*not* an-Nafud)   Bahr al-Safi (*not* Bahr as-Safi)

Preferably, also, the *h* so often appended to Arabic words ending in *a* should be omitted:

> Adiwaya (*not* Adiwayah)   al-mudda (*not* al-muddah)

9.107 *Capitalization.* Problems of Arabic capitalization occur only in transliterations, since the Arabic alphabet does not distinguish between capital and lowercase letter forms, as the Latin and Cyrillic alphabets do. Hence practice in capitalizing transliterated Arabic varies widely. For transliterated titles of books and articles in Arabic the preference of the University of Chicago Press is to capitalize only the first word and proper nouns:[6]

> ʿAbd al-Rahman al-Jabarti, ʿAjaʾib al-athar fi al-tarajim wa al-akhbar (The marvelous remains in biography and history) (Cairo, A.H. 1297 [A.D. 1879]).

9.108 The same system may appropriately be used for the names of journals and organizations. Note that the article in Arabic is never capitalized except at the beginning of a sentence or at the beginning of a book or article title.

9.109 *Personal names.* In alphabetizing Arabic personal names the article is ignored and the person is listed under the capital letter of his last name. Thus, an Ishaq al-Husayni is listed as al-Husayni, Ishaq, and alphabetized with the H's. (For other Press preferences in citing Arabic names see 7.11.)

SOUTH ASIAN LANGUAGES

9.110 Transliteration of the principal South Asian languages requires some or all of the following special characters:

> Ā ā, Æ æ, Ǣ ǣ, Ē ē, Ī ī, Ō ō, Ū ū, Ḍ ḍ, Ḥ ḥ, Ḷ ḷ,
> Ḹ ḹ, Ṃ ṃ, Ṇ ṇ, Ṅ ṅ, Ñ ñ, Ṛ ṛ, Ṝ ṝ, Ṣ ṣ, Ś ś

---

6. The Library of Congress preference, it should be stated, is to capitalize *all* nouns.

CHINESE AND JAPANESE

9.111   *Romanization.* The romanization system called *pinyin,* introduced by
the Chinese in the 1950s, has now largely supplanted the older Wade-
Giles romanization system and the place-name spellings of the *Postal
Atlas of China.* Many individual scholars, however, long familiar with
Wade-Giles or other older systems, have not switched to pinyin in
their books, and some use pinyin only sporadically (resulting in index
problems). To encourage consistent spelling throughout a book one
sensible practice for scholarly publications is to use Wade-Giles in
books about the pre-1949 period and pinyin in those about the period
after 1949.

9.112   Even where pinyin is adopted as the primary romanization system,
exceptions and modifications are possible. Place names long familiar
in the Western world, e.g., names listed in *Webster's Dictionary of
Geographical Names,* generally retain their old spelling. A modification recommended by some writers is to use the old spelling for the
names of persons no longer living and pinyin for the names of those
still alive. Another is to spell names in pinyin followed by the old
spellings in parentheses. Whatever system or modification is followed, names must be spelled consistently throughout a book. Copyeditors must be wary of altering spellings without the advice of an
expert; the complexities of the Chinese language, with its dialects and
nuances, preclude any simple formula for its romanization. Table 9.3
is included as an aid for those familiar enough with the Wade-Giles
system to find a conversion table useful, not as a tool for the novice.[7]

9.113   In an attempt to reproduce sounds more accurately, pinyin spellings
often differ markedly from the older ones, and personal names are
usually spelled without apostrophes or hyphens; an apostrophe is
sometimes used, however, to avoid ambiguity when syllables are run
together (as in Chang'an to distinguish it from Chan'gan.

9.114   Some names frequently encountered:

DYNASTIES

Wade-Giles	*pinyin*	*Wade-Giles*	*pinyin*
Chou	Zhou	Sung	Song
Ch'in	Qin	Yüan	Yuan
T'ang	Tang	Ch'ing	Qing

7. A useful and comprehensive reference book on the conversion to pinyin is *Reform
of the Chinese Written Language* (Peking: Foreign Languages Press, 1958). For the
older, modified Wade-Giles system, see the "List of Syllabic Headings," pp.
xviii–xxi, in the revised American edition of R. H. Mathews's *Chinese-English Dictionary,* published for Harvard-Yenching Institute, 1943.

PERSONAL NAMES

Wade-Giles	*pinyin*	*Wade-Giles*	*pinyin*
Mao Tse-tung	Mao Zedong	Hua Kuo-feng	Hua Guofeng
Chou En-lai	Zhou Enlai	Lin Piao	Lin Biao

But: Mao Tse-tung, Chou En-lai, Sun Yat-sen, Chiang Kai-shek are usually written in Wade-Giles.

GEOGRAPHICAL NAMES

Wade-Giles	*pinyin*	*Postal Atlas*
Kuang-tung	Guangdong	Kwangtung
Su-chou	Suzhou	Soochow
Ta-lien	Dalian	Dairen
Pei-ching (Pei-p'ing)	Beijing	Peking (Peiping)
Shang-hai	Shanghai	Shanghai

9.115 Japanese is usually romanized following the system used in Kenkyu-sha's *New Japanese-English Dictionary.* This system places an apostrophe after *n* at the end of a syllable when followed by a vowel or *y: Gen'e, San'yo.* A macron is used over a long vowel in all Japanese words except well-known place names (Kyoto, Tokyo, Hokkaido) and words that have entered the English language and are thus not italicized (shogun, daimyo). Hyphens should be used sparingly: *Meiji jidai shi no shinkenkyū.*

9.116 *Capitalization and italics.* Since there are neither capital letters nor italic type in Chinese and Japanese, writers in these languages show little concern about what English-speaking editors do with their words when they are romanized. Rules applicable to other languages are therefore generally used for romanized oriental languages. Proper nouns (personal and place names) are capitalized (see 7.12) and set in roman type. Common nouns and other words used as words in an English sentence are lowercased and set in italics as foreign words (see 6.54). Names of institutions, schools of thought, religions, and so forth are usually in roman type if they are capitalized, in italics if they are lowercased (the Wade-Giles romanization system is used for the Chinese in the following examples):

> Tung-lin Academy; Tung-lin movement
>
> Buddhism, Taoism, *feng-shui* and other forms of magic . . .
>
> Under the Ming dynasty the postal service was administered by the Board of War (*ping-pu*) through a central office in Peking (*hui-t'ung kuan*).
>
> The heirs of the Seiyūkai and Minseitō are the Liberal and Progressive parties of Japan.
>
> It was Genrō Saionji (the *genrō* were the elder statesmen of Japan) who said . . . [note that *genrō* is both singular and plural]

9.117 Titles of books and periodicals are set in italics, and titles of articles are set in roman and enclosed in quotation marks:

Wade-Giles to Pinyin

Wade-Giles	Pinyin	Wade-Giles	Pinyin	Wade-Giles	Pinyin	Wade-Giles	Pinyin	Wade-Giles	Pinyin	Wade-Giles	Pinyin
a	a	ch'ün	qun	ka	ga	mao	mao	po	bo	tou	dou
ai	ai	chung	zhong	k'a	ka	mei	mei	p'o	po	t'ou	tou
an	an	ch'ung	chong	kai	gai	men	men	pou	bou	tsa	za
ang	ang			k'ai	kai	meng	meng	p'ou	pou	ts'a	ca
ao	ao	en	en	kan	gan	mi	mi	pu	bu	tsai	zai
		erh	er	k'an	kan	miao	miao	p'u	pu	ts'ai	cai
cha	zha			kang	gang	mieh	mie			tsan	zan
ch'a	cha	fa	fa	k'ang	kang	mien	mian	sa	sa	ts'an	can
chai	zhai	fan	fan	kao	gao	min	min	sai	sai	tsang	zang
ch'ai	chai	fang	fang	k'ao	kao	ming	ming	san	san	ts'ang	cang
chan	zhan	fei	fei	kei	gei	miu	miu	sang	sang	tsao	zao
ch'an	chan	fen	fen	k'ei	kei	mo	mo	sao	sao	ts'ao	cao
chang	zhang	feng	feng	ken	gen	mou	mou	se	se	tse	ze
ch'ang	chang	fo	fo	k'en	ken	mu	mu	sen	sen	ts'e	ce
chao	zhao	fou	fou	keng	geng			seng	seng	tsei	zei
ch'ao	chao	fu	fu	k'eng	keng	na	na	sha	sha	tsen	zen
che	zhe			ko	ge	nai	nai	shai	shai	ts'en	cen
ch'e	che	ha	ha	k'o	ke	nan	nan	shan	shan	tseng	zeng
chen	zhen	hai	hai	kou	gou	nang	nang	shang	shang	ts'eng	ceng
ch'en	chen	han	han	k'ou	kou	nao	nao	shao	shao	tso	zuo
cheng	zheng	hang	hang	ku	gu	nei	nei	she	she	ts'o	cuo
ch'eng	cheng	hao	hao	k'u	ku	nen	nen	shen	shen	tsou	zou
chi	ji	hei	hei	kua	gua	neng	neng	sheng	sheng	ts'ou	cou
ch'i	qi	hen	hen	k'ua	kua	ni	ni	shih	shi	tsu	zu
chia	jia	heng	heng	kuai	guai	niang	niang	shou	shou	ts'u	cu
ch'ia	qia	ho	he	k'uai	kuai	niao	niao	shu	shu	tsuan	zuan
chiang	jiang	hou	hou	kuan	guan	nieh	nie	shua	shua	ts'uan	cuan
ch'iang	qiang	hsi	xi	k'uan	kuan	nien	nian	shuai	shuai	tsui	zui
chiao	jiao	hsia	xia	kuang	guang	nin	nin	shuan	shuan	ts'ui	cui
ch'iao	qiao	hsiang	xiang	k'uang	kuang	ning	ning	shuang	shuang	tsun	zun
chieh	jie	hsiao	xiao	kuei	gui	niu	niu	shui	shui	ts'un	cun
ch'ieh	qie	hsieh	xie	k'uei	kui	no	nuo	shun	shun	tsung	zong
chien	jian	hsien	xian	kun	gun	nou	nou	shuo	shuo	ts'ung	cong
ch'ien	qian	hsin	xin	k'un	kun	nu	nu	so	suo	tu	du
chih	zhi	hsing	xing	kung	gong	nü	nü	sou	sou	t'u	tu
ch'ih	chi	hsiu	xiu	k'ung	kong	nuan	nuan	ssu	si	tuan	duan
chin	jin	hsiung	xiong	kuo	guo	nüeh	nüe	su	su	t'uan	tuan
ch'in	qin	hsü	xu	k'uo	kuo	nung	nong	suan	suan	tui	dui
ching	jing	hsüan	xuan					sui	sui	t'ui	tui
ch'ing	qing	hsüeh	xue	la	la	o	e	sun	sun	tun	dun
chiu	jiu	hsün	xun	lai	lai	ou	ou	sung	song	t'un	tun
ch'iu	qiu	hu	hu	lan	lan					tung	dong
chiung	jiong	hua	hua	lang	lang	pa	ba			t'ung	tong
ch'iung	qiong	huai	huai	lao	lao	p'a	pa	ta	da	tzu	zi
cho	zhuo	huan	huan	le	le	pai	bai	t'a	ta	tz'u	ci
ch'o	chuo	huang	huang	lei	lei	p'ai	pai	tai	dai		
chou	zhou	hui	hui	leng	leng	pan	ban	t'ai	tai	wa	wa
ch'ou	chou	hun	hun	li	li	p'an	pan	tan	dan	wai	wai
chu	zhu	hung	hong	lia	lia	pang	bang	t'an	tan	wan	wan
ch'u	chu	huo	huo	liang	liang	p'ang	pang	tang	dang	wang	wang
chü	ju			liao	liao	pao	bao	t'ang	tang	wei	wei
ch'ü	qu	i	yi	lieh	lie	p'ao	pao	tao	dao	wen	wen
chua	zhua			lien	lian	pei	bei	t'ao	tao	weng	weng
ch'ua	chua	jan	ran	lin	lin	p'ei	pei	te	de	wo	wo
chuai	zhuai	jang	rang	ling	ling	pen	ben	t'e	te	wu	wu
ch'uai	chuai	jao	rao	liu	liu	p'en	pen	teng	deng		
chuan	zhuan	je	re	lo	luo	peng	beng	t'eng	teng	ya	ya
ch'uan	chuan	jen	ren	lou	lou	p'eng	peng	ti	di	yai	yai
chüan	juan	jeng	reng	lu	lu	pi	bi	t'i	ti	yang	yang
ch'üan	quan	jih	ri	lü	lü	p'i	pi	tiao	diao	yao	yao
chuang	zhuang	jo	ruo	luan	luan	piao	biao	t'iao	tiao	yeh	ye
ch'uang	chuang	jou	rou	lüan	lüan	p'iao	piao	tieh	die	yen	yan
chüeh	jue	ju	ru	lüeh	lüe	pieh	bie	t'ieh	tie	yin	yin
ch'üeh	que	juan	ruan	lun	lun	p'ieh	pie	tien	dian	ying	ying
chui	zhui	jui	rui	lung	long	pien	bian	t'ien	tian	yu	you
ch'ui	chui	jun	run			p'ien	pian	ting	ding	yü	yu
chun	zhun	jung	rong	ma	ma	pin	bin	t'ing	ting	yüan	yuan
ch'un	chun			mai	mai	p'in	pin	tiu	diu	yüeh	yue
chün	jun			man	man	ping	bing	to	duo	yün	yun
				mang	mang	p'ing	ping	t'o	tuo	yung	yong

Pinyin to Wade-Giles

Pinyin	Wade-Giles
a	a
ai	ai
an	an
ang	ang
ao	ao
ba	pa
bai	pai
ban	pan
bang	pang
bao	pao
bei	pei
ben	pen
beng	peng
bi	pi
bian	pien
biao	piao
bie	pieh
bin	pin
bing	ping
bo	po
bou	pou
bu	pu
ca	ts'a
cai	ts'ai
can	ts'an
cang	ts'ang
cao	ts'ao
ce	ts'e
cen	ts'en
ceng	ts'eng
cha	ch'a
chai	ch'ai
chan	ch'an
chang	ch'ang
chao	ch'ao
che	ch'e
chen	ch'en
cheng	ch'eng
chi	ch'ih
chong	ch'ung
chou	ch'ou
chu	ch'u
chua	ch'ua
chuai	ch'uai
chuan	ch'uan
chuang	ch'uang
chui	ch'ui
chun	ch'un
chuo	ch'o
ci	tz'u
cong	ts'ung
cou	ts'ou
cu	ts'u
cuan	ts'uan
cui	ts'ui
cun	ts'un
cuo	ts'o
da	ta
dai	tai
dan	tan
dang	tang
dao	tao
de	te
deng	teng
di	ti
dian	tien
diao	tiao
die	tieh
ding	ting
diu	tiu
dong	tung
dou	tou
du	tu
duan	tuan
dui	tui
dun	tun
duo	to
e	o
en	en
er	erh
fa	fa
fan	fan
fang	fang
fei	fei
fen	fen
feng	feng
fo	fo
fou	fou
fu	fu
ga	ka
gai	kai
gan	kan
gang	kang
gao	kao
ge	ko
gei	kei
gen	ken
geng	keng
gong	kung
gou	kou
gu	ku
gua	kua
guai	kuai
guan	kuan
guang	kuang
gui	kuei
gun	kun
guo	kuo
ha	ha
hai	hai
han	han
hang	hang
hao	hao
he	ho
hei	hei
hen	hen
heng	heng
hong	hung
hou	hou
hu	hu
hua	hua
huai	huai
huan	huan
huang	huang
hui	hui
hun	hun
huo	huo
ji	chi
jia	chia
jian	chien
jiang	chiang
jiao	chiao
jie	chieh
jin	chin
jing	ching
jiong	chiung
jiu	chiu
ju	chü
juan	chüan
jue	chüeh
jun	chün
ka	k'a
kai	k'ai
kan	k'an
kang	k'ang
kao	k'ao
ke	k'o
kei	k'ei
ken	k'en
keng	k'eng
kong	k'ung
kou	k'ou
ku	k'u
kua	k'ua
kuai	k'uai
kuan	k'uan
kuang	k'uang
kui	k'uei
kun	k'un
kuo	k'uo
la	la
lai	lai
lan	lan
lang	lang
lao	lao
le	le
lei	lei
leng	leng
li	li
lia	lia
lian	lien
liang	liang
liao	liao
lie	lieh
lin	lin
ling	ling
liu	liu
long	lung
lou	lou
lu	lu
lü	lü
luan	luan
lüan	lüan
lüe	lüeh
lun	lun
luo	lo
ma	ma
mai	mai
man	man
mang	mang
mao	mao
mei	mei
men	men
meng	meng
mi	mi
mian	mien
miao	miao
mie	mieh
min	min
ming	ming
miu	miu
mo	mo
mou	mou
mu	mu
na	na
nai	nai
nan	nan
nang	nang
nao	nao
nei	nei
nen	nen
neng	neng
ni	ni
nian	nien
niang	niang
niao	niao
nie	nieh
nin	nin
ning	ning
niu	niu
nong	nung
nou	nou
nu	nu
nü	nü
nuan	nuan
nüe	nüeh
nuo	no
ou	ou
pa	p'a
pai	p'ai
pan	p'an
pang	p'ang
pao	p'ao
pei	p'ei
pen	p'en
peng	p'eng
pi	p'i
pian	p'ien
piao	p'iao
pie	p'ieh
pin	p'in
ping	p'ing
po	p'o
pou	p'ou
pu	p'u
qi	ch'i
qia	ch'ia
qian	ch'ien
qiang	ch'iang
qiao	ch'iao
qie	ch'ieh
qin	ch'in
qing	ch'ing
qiong	ch'iung
qiu	ch'iu
qu	ch'ü
quan	ch'üan
que	ch'üeh
qun	ch'ün
ran	jan
rang	jang
rao	jao
re	je
ren	jen
reng	jeng
ri	jih
rong	jung
rou	jou
ru	ju
ruan	juan
rui	jui
run	jun
ruo	jo
sa	sa
sai	sai
san	san
sang	sang
sao	sao
se	se
sen	sen
seng	seng
sha	sha
shai	shai
shan	shan
shang	shang
shao	shao
she	she
shen	shen
sheng	sheng
shi	shih
shou	shou
shu	shu
shua	shua
shuai	shuai
shuan	shuan
shuang	shuang
shui	shui
shun	shun
shuo	shuo
si	ssu
song	sung
sou	sou
su	su
suan	suan
sui	sui
sun	sun
suo	so
ta	t'a
tai	t'ai
tan	t'an
tang	t'ang
tao	t'ao
te	t'e
teng	t'eng
ti	t'i
tian	t'ien
tiao	t'iao
tie	t'ieh
ting	t'ing
tong	t'ung
tou	t'ou
tu	t'u
tuan	t'uan
tui	t'ui
tun	t'un
tuo	t'o
wa	wa
wai	wai
wan	wan
wang	wang
wei	wei
wen	wen
weng	weng
wo	wo
wu	wu
xi	hsi
xia	hsia
xian	hsien
xiang	hsiang
xiao	hsiao
xie	hsieh
xin	hsin
xing	hsing
xiong	hsiung
xiu	hsiu
xu	hsü
xuan	hsüan
xue	hsüeh
xun	hsün
ya	ya
yai	yai
yan	yen
yang	yang
yao	yao
ye	yeh
yi	i
yin	yin
ying	ying
yong	yung
you	yu
yu	yü
yuan	yüan
yue	yüeh
yun	yün
za	tsa
zai	tsai
zan	tsan
zang	tsang
zao	tsao
ze	tse
zei	tsei
zen	tsen
zeng	tseng
zha	cha
zhai	chai
zhan	chan
zhang	chang
zhao	chao
zhe	che
zhen	chen
zheng	cheng
zhi	chih
zhong	chung
zhou	chou
zhu	chu
zhua	chua
zhuai	chuai
zhuan	chuan
zhuang	chuang
zhui	chui
zhun	chun
zhuo	cho
zi	tzu
zong	tsung
zou	tsou
zu	tsu
zuan	tsuan
zui	tsui
zun	tsun
zuo	tso

Source: *People's Republic of China: Administrative Atlas* (Washington, D.C.: Central Intelligence Agency, 1975), 46–47.

Ch'en Shih-ch'i, *Ming-tai kuan shou-kung-yeh ti yen-chiu* (Studies on government-operated handicrafts during the Ming dynasty)

Fang Hao, "Liu-lo yü hsi p'u ti chung-kuo wen-hsien" (The lost Chinese historical literature in Spain and Portugal), *Hsüeh-shu chi-k'an* (Academy Review Quarterly)

Okamoto Yoshitomo, *Jūrokuseiki Nichi-Ō kōtsūchi no kenkyū* (Study of the intercourse between Japan and Europe during the sixteenth century)

Akiyama Kenzō, "Goresu wa Ryūkyūjin de aru" (The Gores are the Ryukyuans), *Shigaku-Zasshi* 39 (1928): 268–85.

The first word of a romanized title is always capitalized, and proper names (especially in Japanese) often are.

9.118 Chinese and Japanese characters, while difficult for the printer, are necessary in references to works that can be found, even in Western libraries, only if the characters for the author's name and the title of the work are known. In general, their use should be confined to bibliographies and glossaries; in running text they disrupt the type line and should be avoided. When characters are used in a bibliography, they follow the romanized version of the item they represent (asterisks here show where the characters should be placed):

Fang Hao * *. "Liu-lo yü hsi p'u ti chung-kuo wen-hsien" * * * * * * * * * (The lost Chinese historical literature in Spain and Portugal), *Hsüeh-shu chi-k'an* * * * * (Academy Review Quarterly) 1 (1953): 161–79.

Characters must be either typeset in East Asia, generally Tokyo, or photographed for offset reproduction from expert hand-done calligraphy, the latter being more economical and practical in the United States.

EDITING AND COMPOSING CLASSICAL GREEK

9.119 The following information is intended to aid editors who do not read Greek, as well as proofreaders and typesetters, in handling terms and quotations in classical Greek that appear in English works. This information may even be sufficient for the prospective editor of an entire book in Greek, but for one who does not know Greek such work is so time-consuming and the chances for error are so numerous that if possible it should be turned over to a specialist.

9.120 The first thing necessary for setting Greek is a font of Greek type. If a book contains any Greek at all, the publisher should make certain well ahead of copy deadline that the typesetter can set the Greek words in the required sizes, with accents and breathing marks. If this turns out to be impossible, (1) the publisher or typesetter will have to have the passages set elsewhere and inserted in the English pages, (2) the Greek copy will have to be killed or translated into English, or (3) it will have to be transliterated into the Latin alphabet—something that should be done only if the Greek consists of isolated words and phrases or of short passages.

TRANSLITERATION

9.121   Table 9.4 shows the usual way to transliterate Greek letters. Omit all Greek accents. Use the macron (ˉ) to distinguish long vowels eta and omega (*ē* and *ō*) from short vowels epsilon and omicron (*e* and *o*). Transliterate the iota subscript by an *i* on the line, following the vowel with which it is associated (ἀνθρώπῳ, *anthrōpōi*). The rough breathing is transliterated by *h,* which precedes a vowel or diphthong and follows the letter rho (as in the English word *rhythm*). The smooth breathing is ignored, since it represents merely the absence of the *h*-sound. Transliterated Greek words or phrases are usually italicized, unless the same words occur frequently.

BREATHINGS

9.122   When Greek is written or set in Greek characters, every initial vowel or diphthong and the letter rho standing at the beginning of a Greek word must be marked either with the "rough" breathing (‛), to indicate the sound *h,* or with the "smooth" breathing (’), to indicate absence of the sound *h.* (Thus ἕν, meaning "one," is pronounced *hen,* while ἐν, meaning "in," is pronounced *en.*) Initial rho and upsilon always receive the rough breathing.

9.123   The breathing mark is placed directly over the initial lowercase vowel (over the second vowel of a diphthong); it is placed to the left of capital letters.

αὖτε, ἕτερες, Ἕλλην, ἥβη, Ἶρις, ὑπέχω, ὠκύς, ῥᾴδιος

9.124   Typesetters sometimes become confused and set a single quotation mark in place of a breathing mark before a capital letter; the single quotation mark cannot function as a breathing because it is of the wrong size and does not sit close enough to the letter.

ACCENTS

9.125   There are three Greek accent marks: acute (´), circumflex (^), and grave (`). Use of the circumflex is restricted to the two final syllables of a word. The grave accent can occur only on the last syllable, and it is used then only in this circumstance: an acute accent standing on the final syllable is changed to grave when it directly precedes another

275

TABLE 9.4: GREEK ALPHABET AND TRANSLITERATION

Name of Letter	Greek Alphabet		Transliteration
Alpha	A	α	a
Beta	B	β	b
Gamma	Γ	γ	g
Delta	Δ	$\delta\ \partial^1$	d
Epsilon	E	ϵ	e
Zeta	Z	ζ	z
Eta	H	η	ē
Theta	Θ	$\theta\ \vartheta^1$	th
Iota	I	ι	i
Kappa	K	κ	k
Lambda	Λ	λ	l
Mu	M	μ	m
Nu	N	ν	n
Xi	Ξ	ξ	x
Omicron	O	o	o
Pi	Π	π	p
Rho	P	ρ	r; *initially,* rh
Sigma	Σ	$\sigma\ s^2$	s
Tau	T	τ	t
Upsilon	Υ	υ	u; *exc. after* a, e, ē, i, *often* y
Phi	Φ	$\phi\ \varphi^1$	ph
Chi	X	χ	kh
Psi	Ψ	ψ	ps
Omega	Ω	ω	ō

1. Old-style character. Usually used in mathematical formulas; should not be combined with other fonts.
2. Final letter.

accented word in the same clause. Like the breathings, the accents are placed over the lowercase vowels, over the second vowel of a diphthong, and to the left of capital vowels.

9.126   With two exceptions, *all* Greek words are marked by accents, usually by one, very occasionally by two (see below). The two exceptions to this rule are: (1) a group of monosyllabic words called proclitics, which are closely connected with the word following them (the proclitics are the forms of the article ὁ, ἡ, οἱ, αἱ; the prepositions εἰς, ἐν, ἐκ [ἐξ]; the conjunctions εἰ, ὡς; and the adverb οὐ [οὐκ, οὐξ]); and (2) enclitics—short words pronounced as if part of the word preceding them; they usually lose their accents altogether ('Αρταξερξής τε) and in certain circumstances the word preceding them actually gains a second accent (φοιβεῖταί τις). The diaeresis is used in Greek, as in French (*naïve*), to indicate that two successive vowels do not form a diphthong but are to be voiced separately.

9.127   Vowels complete with breathing marks and accents, in all combinations, are an integral part of every Greek font. Each font should, for example, be able to provide, not only lowercase eta—η, ή, ῆ, ἠ—but ἡ, ἤ, ἥ, ἦ, ἧ, ἣ, ἢ, ᾖ, ᾗ, and, for uppercase eta, Ἡ, Ἧ, Ἥ, Ἤ, Ἦ, Ἣ, Ἢ, Ἡ.

PUNCTUATION

9.128   In Greek, the period and comma are the same as in English; the colon and semicolon are both represented by a raised period (·); the Greek interrogation point is the same as the English semicolon (;). The English apostrophe (') is used as an elision mark when the final vowel of one word is elided before a second word beginning with a vowel. In English texts, quotations set in Greek, of whatever length, should not be enclosed in quotation marks.

NUMBERS

9.129   Numbers, when not written out, are represented in ordinary Greek text by the letters of the alphabet, supplemented by three obsolete Greek letters, ϛ' = 6, ϟ' = 90, and ϡ' = 900. The diacritical mark resembling an acute accent distinguishes the letters as numerals, and is added to a sign standing alone or to the last sign in a series, 111 = ρια'. For thousands, the foregoing signs are used with a different diacritical mark: ͵α = 1,000, ͵αρια' = 1,111, ͵βσκβ' = 2,222. The entire series of Greek numerals is shown in table 9.5.

WORD DIVISION

9.130   In Greek, word division follows rules that are straightforward and fairly easy to apply.

9.131   When a single consonant occurs between two vowels, divide before the consonant:

ἔ-χω   ἐ-γώ   ἐ-σπέ-ρα

277

TABLE 9.5: GREEK NUMERALS

1	α'	24	κδ'
2	β'	30	λ'
3	γ'	40	μ'
4	δ'	50	ν'
5	ε'	60	ξ'
6	ς'	70	ο'
7	ζ'	80	π'
8	η'	90	ϙ'
9	θ'	100	ρ'
10	ι'	200	σ'
11	ια'	300	τ'
12	ιβ'	400	υ'
13	ιγ'	500	φ'
14	ιδ'	600	χ'
15	ιε'	700	ψ'
16	ις'	800	ω'
17	ιζ'	900	ϡ'
18	ιη'	1,000	,α
19	ιθ'	2,000	,β
20	κ'	3,000	,γ
21	κα'	4,000	,δ
22	κβ'	5,000	,ε
23	κγ'		

9.132 If a consonant is doubled, or if a mute is followed by its corresponding aspirate, divide after the first consonant:

Ἐλ-λάς   ὦμ-μαι   ἀῖσ-σω   ὀρ-ρωδία
ἀπ-φύς   ᾿Ατ-θίς   Βακ-χίς   ἔγ-χος

9.133 If the combination of two or more consonants begins with a liquid (λ, ρ) or a nasal (μ, ν), divide after the liquid or nasal:

ἄλ-σος   ἀρ-γός   ἄμ-φω   ἄν-θος
(But before μν: μέ-μνημαι)

9.134 The division comes before all other combinations of two or more consonants:

πρᾶ-γμα   ἀ-κμή   ἄ-φνω   ἔ-τνος   ἄ-στρον

9.135 Compound words are divided into their original parts; within each part the foregoing rules apply. The most common type of compound word begins with a preposition:

ἀμφ-   ἀν-   ἀπ-   ὑπ-   ἐξ-έβαλον
ἀφ-   ἐφ-   ὑφ-   κατ-   καθ-ίστημι

OLD ENGLISH AND MIDDLE ENGLISH

9.136   Several letters once but no longer used in the English language are considered "special characters" by typesetters. These occur in both lowercase and capital letters:

ð   Ð   Called "eth" and pronounced as *th* in *them*.

þ   þ   Called "thorn" and pronounced as *th* in *three*.

3   3   Called "yogh"; occurs in ME sometimes for a *y* as in *year*, sometimes for *gh* as in *light*.

æ   Æ   Ligature; should not be printed as two letters in OE names and text (Ælfric).

Since a typesetter may easily mistake a thorn for a *p* and a yogh for a *g* or even a *3*, the copyeditor should flag each occurrence either by writing the names of the characters in the margin when there are few or by color-coding (underlining or circling with a colored pencil) when there are many.

9.137   Two characters occasionally found in OE texts are 7 for *and* (ampersand) and þ (wyn) for *w*, but the modern ampersand and *w* may be substituted for these.

FOR FURTHER REFERENCE

9.138   The United States Government Printing Office *Style Manual* answers a good many questions about setting foreign language copy not considered in this manual. Hart's *Rules* is also useful. (See the Bibliography.)

10 *Quotations*

Introduction 10.1
    What Not to Quote 10.3
Accuracy 10.4
    Permissible Changes 10.6
Relation to Text 10.8
    Run In or Set Off 10.9
    Syntax 10.11
    Initial Capital or Lowercase 10.12
    Introductory Phrases and Punctuation 10.16
    Paragraphing Block Quotations 10.19
    Block Quotations Beginning in Text 10.20
    Poetry 10.21
Quotation Marks 10.24
    Double and Single 10.24
    With More Than One Paragraph 10.25
    In Block Quotations 10.29
    With Speech 10.30
        Direct discourse 10.30
        Indirect discourse 10.32
        Yes and no 10.33
        Plays and discussions 10.34
    With Display Type 10.35
Ellipses 10.36
    Within a Sentence 10.40
    Between Sentences 10.42
    Full Lines or Paragraphs Omitted 10.45
    When Not to Use Ellipsis Points 10.47
    Capitalization Following Ellipses 10.49
Interpolations and Alterations 10.50
    Sic 10.51
    Italics Added 10.52
Citing Sources in Text 10.54
    In Running Text 10.61
    Following Block Quotations 10.66
Foreign Language Quotations 10.69
    Translating Quotations 10.70

INTRODUCTION

10.1   Almost every serious study depends in part on works that have preceded it. The temptation to use apt quotations gathered during research may lead, in extreme cases, to self-effacement of the author and irritation of the reader. Ideally, authors of works of original scholarship present their arguments in their own words, illustrating and amplifying the text by judicious choice of quotations from the works of others. In selecting quotations, authors are well advised to consider future readers. Is direct quotation desirable, or would a paraphrase be more effective? Will the reader who, for lack of time or inclination, chooses to skip over long or frequent direct quotations miss any significant point? This is not to denigrate the use of quotations, however, but only to caution against their overuse or misuse. "Quoting other writers and citing the places where their words are to be found are by now such common practices that it is pardonable to look upon the habit as natural, not to say instinctive. It is of course nothing of the kind, but a very sophisticated act, peculiar to a civilization that uses printed books, believes in evidence, and makes a point of assigning credit or blame in a detailed, verifiable way."[1]

10.2   Whether authors paraphrase or quote from sources directly, they should give credit to words and ideas taken from others. In most instances a note[2] or a parenthetical reference in the text to the bibliography or list of sources is sufficient acknowledgment. If an author quotes at length, or uses many short passages, from a copyrighted work or from certain manuscript materials, written permission must be obtained from the holder of the copyright or of the literary rights (see chap. 4).

WHAT NOT TO QUOTE

10.3   Commonly known facts, available in numerous sources, should not be enclosed in quotation marks or given a source citation unless the wording is taken directly from another. Also not to be treated as quotations are proverbial, biblical, and well-known literary expressions used as part of the author's text:

> On 14 April 1865, a few days after Lee's surrender, Lincoln was assassinated. [No note necessary.]
>
> No one can convince the young that practice makes perfect.
>
> If reading maketh a full man, Henry is half empty.

1. Jacques Barzun and Henry F. Graff, *The Modern Researcher,* 3d ed. (New York: Harcourt Brace Jovanovich, 1977), 262. The present chapter takes up rules and suggestions for incorporating quoted matter in text. The use of quotation marks for purposes other than direct quotation is described in chapters 5 and 6. Rules for citing, in footnotes, the sources of quotations are to be found in chapter 17. Chapter 2 explains how to type block quotations in preparing a manuscript for publication (2.20) and describes the manuscript editor's responsibilities regarding quoted material (2.96).

2. The word *note* throughout this chapter refers to a note at the foot of the page or at the back of a book, at the end of an article or in parentheses in the text—wherever such documentation appears in a printed work (see chap. 15).

ACCURACY

10.4   It is impossible to overemphasize the importance of meticulous accuracy in quoting from the works of others. Authors should check every direct quotation against the original if possible or against a first, careful transcription of the passage. (Authors who take notes carelessly are in for trouble later if they no longer have access to the sources.)

10.5   Checking quotations is an operation to be performed on the *final typescript,* not left until type has been set (see 2.125[2]). Resetting type to rectify an author's sins of transcription is an extremely costly process, and is chargeable to the author. Thus, rigorous attention to accuracy *in the typescript* (or final tape) saves time at the proof stage, avoids excessive alteration costs, and lessens the chance of further errors being introduced in proofs.

PERMISSIBLE CHANGES

10.6   Direct quotations must reproduce *exactly* not only the wording but the spelling, capitalization, and internal punctuation of the original, except that single quotation marks may be changed to double quotation marks (see 10.29). A few other changes are permissible to make the passage fit smoothly into the syntax and typography of the work in which it is quoted:

1. The initial letter may be changed to a capital or a lowercase letter (see 10.49).
2. The final punctuation mark may be changed, and punctuation marks may be omitted where ellipsis points are used (see 10.42).
3. Original note reference marks in a short quotation from a scholarly work should usually be omitted. And authors may insert note references of their own within quotations.
4. In a passage quoted from a modern book, journal, or newspaper an obvious typographical error may be silently corrected, but in a passage from an older work or from a manuscript source any idiosyncrasy of spelling should be preserved.
5. In quoting from older works authors may consider it desirable to modernize spelling and punctuation for the sake of clarity. The reader should be informed of any such alterations, either in a note or, in a book containing many such quotations, by an explanation in the preface or elsewhere.

10.7   Typographical style, particularly of display type, may be changed to agree with the style of the work in which the quotation occurs. In a quotation from a play, for example, the names of speakers might be changed from the small caps of the original to italic and moved from a centered position to flush left, or vice versa; stage directions might be changed from roman to italic. A word or words in full caps in the text of the original may be set in small caps, if these are available, to maintain the effect; if small caps are not available, the full caps should be reproduced in the quotation. In other words those elements of typography which are not an author's doing but the publisher's or the printer's need not, and often should not, be reproduced exactly. (For changing typography when citing titles of works see 7.123, 16.31; for typography and other design considerations of plays see 19.64–68.)

RELATION TO TEXT

10.8 Quotations may be incorporated in the text in two ways: (1) run in, that is, in the same type size as the text and enclosed in quotation marks (see example in 10.11); or (2) set off from the text, without quotation marks. Quotations of the latter sort may be set in smaller type, or with all lines indented from the left, or with unjustified lines (if text lines are justified), or with less space between lines than the text—or some combination of these typographical devices may be specified by the book designer (see one example in 10.13). Quotations set off from the text are called *block quotations, extracts,* or *excerpts.*

RUN IN OR SET OFF

10.9 Whether to run in or set off a quotation is commonly determined by its length. In general, quoted matter that runs to eight or ten typed lines is set off from the text; shorter quotations are run into the text. Before arbitrarily following this rule, however, author (and editor) should consider the nature of the material, the number of quotations, and the appearance of the printed page. Many quotations of varying lengths—some over ten typed lines—skillfully integrated with the text in which they appear are less distracting to the reader if they are all run in, regardless of length. On the other hand, in material where the quotations are being compared or otherwise used as entities in themselves it is best to set them all off from the text, even quotations of one or two lines. In other words, comparable quotations in the text should be typographically comparable.

10.10 Quotations of two or more lines of poetry are usually set off from the text (see 10.21). If more than one line is run into the text, the end of a line of poetry is marked by a solidus (/), with equal space on either side:

Andrew Marvell's praise of John Milton, "Thou hast not missed one thought that could be fit, / And all that was improper dost omit" ("On *Paradise Lost*"), might well serve as our motto.

It is permissible to omit the solidus where each line begins with a capital and there are no other capitals in the quotation. Consistency in the matter should be maintained throughout an article or a book.

SYNTAX

10.11 The skill with which fragmentary quotations are incorporated into a text reflects an author's awareness of syntax, verb tenses, personal pronouns, and so forth. Only as much of the source as necessary should be quoted and the sentence should be phrased in such a way that the quoted words fit logically, as grammatical parts of it. Master of the felicitous quotation, Ronald S. Crane provides many illustrations in his two-volume *The Idea of the Humanities* (Chicago: University of Chicago Press, 1967). Among them:

> In short, there has been "almost a continual improvement" in all branches of human knowledge; and since this improvement has taken place not merely in the speculative sciences but likewise in those other forms of learning, such as politics, morality, and religion, "which apparently have a more immediate influence upon the welfare of civil life, and man's comfortable subsistence in it," it seems to follow, "as a corollary, plainly deducible from a proposition already demonstrated," that human happiness has also increased. (1:281)

INITIAL CAPITAL OR LOWERCASE

10.12 When a quotation is used as a syntactical part of a sentence, it begins with a lowercase letter, even though the original is a complete sentence beginning with a capital:[3]

> Benjamin Franklin admonishes us to "plough deep while sluggards sleep."
>
> With another aphorism, he reminded his readers that "experience keeps a dear school, but fools will learn in no other"—an observation as true today as then.

But when the quotation is not syntactically dependent on the rest of the sentence, the initial letter is capitalized. Note also the punctuation in the following:

> As Franklin advised, "Plough deep while sluggards sleep."
>
> With another aphorism, "Experience keeps a dear school, but fools will learn in no other," he puts his finger on a common weakness of mankind.
>
> His aphorism "Experience keeps a dear school, but fools will learn in no other" is a cogent warning to men of all ages.

3. For altering capitalization other than the initial letter of a quotation see 10.49.

10.13   The initial letter of a block quotation may also be lowercased if the syntax demands it. In the following example, the quotation from Aristotle in the Jowett translation (Modern Library) begins with a capital letter and a paragraph indention:

> In discussing the reasons for political disturbances Aristotle observes that
>
>> revolutions also break out when opposite parties, e.g. the rich and the people, are equally balanced, and there is little or no middle class; for, if either party were manifestly superior, the other would not risk an attack upon them. And, for this reason, those who are eminent in virtue usually do not stir up insurrections, always a minority. Such are the beginnings and causes of the disturbances and revolutions to which every form of government is liable. (*Politics* 5.4)

10.14   Similarly, if a quotation that is only part of a sentence in the original forms a complete sentence as quoted, a lowercase letter may be changed to a capital where the structure of the text suggests it. To use the second sentence in the preceding quotation from Aristotle:

> As Aristotle remarked, "Those who are eminent in virtue usually do not stir up insurrections, always a minority."
>
> *but:*
>
> Aristotle's observation that "those who are eminent in virtue usually do not stir up insurrections, always a minority" might serve as a subject for debate.

10.15   In legal works any such change in capitalization is indicated by brackets:

> [r]evolutions . . .
> [T]hose . . .

INTRODUCTORY PHRASES AND PUNCTUATION

10.16   A formal introductory phrase, such as *thus* or *the following,* is usually followed by a colon:

> The role of the author has been variously described. Henry Fielding, at the beginning of his *History of Tom Jones,* defines it thus: "An author ought to consider himself, not as a gentleman who gives a private or eleemosynary treat, but rather as one who keeps a public ordinary, at which all persons are welcome for their money."
>
> Of the Ten Commandments he had already broken the following:
>
>> Thou shalt not take the name of the Lord thy God in vain.
>> Honor thy father and thy mother.
>> Thou shalt not bear false witness against thy neighbor.

10.17   Such introductory phrases as

> Professor Jones writes:
> She said (stated, observed, etc.),

are often awkward and redundant. A sensitive writer will avoid them.

10.18 A quotation consisting of more than one complete sentence is usually introduced by a colon if the text preceding the quotation is not a complete sentence but a phrase like

> As the president of the council suggested:
> And again:

If the quotation is only one sentence, a comma follows such a phrase instead of a colon. A colon is usually not used if the introductory text is a complete sentence.

> The president of the council suggested an alternative.
> What, you might ask, is the alternative?

(See also 5.63–64.)

PARAGRAPHING BLOCK QUOTATIONS

10.19 When a block quotation begins with a complete sentence, it may begin either with a paragraph indention or flush, no paragraph. The usual practice is to follow the original; if the quoted matter does not begin a paragraph in the source from which it is taken, the block quotation begins flush, with no ellipsis points (see 10.47). If ellipsis points *are* used to indicate the omission of the first part of a paragraph, the ellipsis points begin after a paragraph indention. It may sometimes be desirable, however, to paragraph quotations as if they were part of the text, taking into account the sense of the discussion. In quotations of more than one paragraph, internal paragraphing should be retained. Note that only the first paragraph of a continuous prose quotation set off from the text may begin with no paragraph indention. When several paragraphs, or items with runover lines, begin flush left, with no indention, extra space (leading) should be inserted between them.

BLOCK QUOTATIONS BEGINNING IN TEXT

10.20 A long quotation may begin with a few words, or a sentence, run into the text and the rest of the quotation set off. This device should be used only if a few words of text intervene between the quoted matter in the text and its continuation:

> "There is no safe trusting to dictionaries and definitions," in Charles Lamb's opinion.
>
> > We should more willingly fall in with this popular language, if we did not find *brutality* sometimes awkwardly coupled with *valour* in the same vocabulary. The comic writers . . . have contributed not a little to mislead us upon this point. To see a hectoring fellow

exposed and beaten upon the stage, has something in it wonder-
fully diverting. ("Popular Fallacies," *Essays of Elia*)

"In short," says Crane, summarizing Gordon's philosophy,
there has been "almost a continual improvement" in all branches
of human knowledge; . . .

Less felicitous, but permissible in most instances, is to set off the
entire quotation, putting the intervening words of text in brackets as
an interpolation:

In short [says Crane, summarizing Gordon's philosophy], there
has been . . .

POETRY

10.21 Quotations from poetry are usually centered on the page and set line
for line.[4] Alignment of the original should be reproduced as closely as
possible:

> Sure there was wine
> Before my sighs did drie it: there was corn
> Before my tears did drown it.
> Is the yeare onely lost to me?
> Have I no bayes to crown it?
> No flowers, no garlands gay? all blasted?
> All wasted?
> (George Herbert, "The Collar")

If the quotation does not begin with a full line, placement should approximate that of the original:

> there was corn
> Before my tears did drown it.

10.22 In a work containing quotations from poems with lines too long to be
centered on the page, such as Walt Whitman's "Song of Myself," all
poetic quotations may be set with a uniform indention—for example,
two or three picas from the left, any runover lines being further indented:

> My tongue, every atom of my blood, form'd from this soil, this air,
> Born here of parents born here from parents the same, and their
>   parents the same,
> I, now thirty-seven years old in perfect health begin,
> Hoping to cease not till death.

Uniform indention is usually specified too where all or most quotations in a work consist of blank verse (as in studies of Shakespeare).

10.23 Quotation marks at the beginning of a line of poetry are aligned with
the first letter of the line above:

4. For lines of poetry run into the text see 10.10. For examples of typography and
other design considerations see 19.61–63.

> He holds him with his skinny hand,
> "There was a ship," quoth he.
> "Hold off! unhand me, grey-beard loon!"
> Eftsoons his hand dropt he.
>
> (Coleridge, *The Ancient Mariner*)

In older practice, sometimes followed today, such quotation marks were *cleared,* that is, placed outside the alignment of the poem:

> He holds him with his skinny hand,
> "There was a ship," quoth he.

QUOTATION MARKS

DOUBLE AND SINGLE

10.24 Quoted words, phrases, and sentences run into the text are enclosed in double quotation marks. (Note that in the fields of linguistics and philosophy single marks are used in certain contexts to enclose individual words or letters; see 6.56, 6.63.) Single quotation marks enclose quotations within quotations; double marks, quotations within these; and so on:

> "Don't be absurd!" said Henry. "To say that 'I mean what I say' is the same as 'I say what I mean' is to be as confused as Alice at the Mad Hatter's tea party. You remember what the Hatter said to her: 'Not the same thing a bit! Why you might just as well say that "I see what I eat" is the same thing as "I eat what I see"!' "

British practice is often, though not always, the reverse: single marks are used first, then double, and so on.

WITH MORE THAN ONE PARAGRAPH

10.25 If a passage of more than one paragraph from the same source is quoted and is not to be set as an excerpt, quotation marks are used at the beginning of each paragraph and at the end of the last paragraph. That is, quotation marks are not used at the *end* of any paragraph in the quotation except the last one.

10.26 Poetry quotations, when not treated as excerpts, take quotation marks at the beginning of the quotation, at the beginning of each stanza, and at the end of the quotation.

10.27 A quotation of a letter carries quotation marks before the first line (usually the salutation) and after the last line (usually the signature), as well as at the beginning of each new paragraph within the letter.

10.28 Note that the usual practice of setting these kinds of material as block quotations obviates the use of quotation marks.

10.29   Material set off from the text as a block quotation is not enclosed in quotation marks. Any quoted matter within a block quotation should be enclosed in double quotation marks, even if the source quoted uses single marks. Therefore, when a quotation run into the text in the typescript is converted into a block quotation by author or editor, the initial and final quotation marks must be deleted and the internal marks changed. If, for example, the Mad Hatter's retort to Alice quoted in the example (10.24) became a block quotation, the quotation marks would be changed:

> "Not the same thing a bit! Why you might just as well say that 'I see what I eat' is the same thing as 'I eat what I see'!"

Similarly, if a quotation set off from the text in the typescript is run into the text by the author or the editor, initial and final quotation marks must be added and any internal quotation marks changed accordingly.

10.30   *Direct discourse.* Direct discourse or dialogue, whether run into or set off from the text, should always be enclosed in quotation marks. A change in speaker is usually indicated by a new paragraph. If one speech occupies more than a paragraph, the rule for repeating quotation marks with more than one paragraph applies (see 10.25).

> "Ransomed? What's that?"
> "I don't know. But that's what they do. I've seen it in books; and so of course that's what we've got to do."
> "But how can we do it if we don't know what it is?"
> "Why, blame it all, we've *got* to do it. Don't I tell you it's in the books? Do you want to go to doing different from what's in the books, and get things all muddled up?"
> (Mark Twain, *The Adventures of Huckleberry Finn*)

10.31   When a tale is told largely through direct discourse, the paragraphing should depend on the narrative rather than on a change of speaker. The speeches of various speakers are then run along, with clear indications given of who is speaking:

> Hearing this, Po-ch'in reflected a while. He then said, "Elder, for generations this humble family has never kept a vegetarian diet. We could, I suppose, find some bamboo shoots and wood ears and prepare some dried vegetables and bean cakes, but they would all be cooked with the fat of deer or tigers. Even our pots and pans are grease-soaked! What am I to do? I must ask the elder's pardon." "Don't fret," said Tripitaka. "Enjoy the food yourself. Even if I were not to eat for three or four days, I could bear the hunger. But I dare not break the dietary commandment." "Suppose you starve to death," said Po-ch'in, "what

then?'" "I am indebted to the Heavenly kindness of the Guardian," said Tripitaka, "for saving me from the packs of tigers and wolves. Starving to death is better than being food for a tiger." (Yu, trans., *Journey to the West* 1:292)

10.32   *Indirect discourse.* No quotation marks are used with indirect discourse or with rhetorical, unspoken, or imaginary questions:

> Tom told Huck they had to do it that way because the books said so.
> What am I doing here? she wondered.
> Very well, you say, but is there no choice?
> He thought suddenly, I have been here before.
> The question is, What do we do now?

(See also 5.17–19, 5.66.)

10.33   *Yes and no.* The words *yes* and *no* and other such words should not be quoted except in direct discourse:

> Ezra always answered yes; he could never say no to a friend.
> Please stop asking why.
> > *but:*
> "Yes," he replied weakly.
> Again she repeated, "Why?"

10.34   *Plays and discussions.* Where the name of the speaker introduces the speech, as in a play or a discussion, no quotation marks are used:

> *R. Roister Doister.* Except I have her to my wife, I shall run mad.
> *M. Merygreeke.* Nay, "unwise" perhaps, but I warrant you for "mad."
> *R. Roister.* I am utterly dead unless I have my desire.
> *M. Mery.* Where be the bellows that blew this sudden fire?

> DR. LEVENE: Mr. Chairman, we have heard the revolutionary notion today, first of all, that the smooth muscle cell can behave like the fibroblast to synthesize collagen, and, second, that it does the job of a macrophage: it takes up fat. . . .

> DR. TAYLOR: I wish to inquire as to how those proposing the smooth muscle theory reconcile their thoughts with the concept that was given considerable support by the late Dr. Lyman Guff and also by Dr. McMillan; . . .

WITH DISPLAY TYPE

10.35   Quotation marks are not used with display quotations (quotations used as ornaments to the text rather than as part of the text itself) or before a display initial letter beginning a chapter or section:

> *Oh, what a tangled web we weave,*
> *When first we practice to deceive!*
> > —Sir Walter Scott

> It is a truth universally acknowledged, that a single man in possession of a good fortune must be in want of a wife.
> > —Jane Austen, *Pride and Prejudice*

O F THE MAKING OF MANY BOOKS there is no end," declared an ancient Hebrew sage, who had himself magnificently aggravated the situation he was decrying.

(For the stylistic treatment of epigraphs see 1.29–30; for typographic treatment, 19.50.)

ELLIPSES

10.36 Any omission of a word or phrase, line or paragraph, from *within* a quoted passage must be indicated by ellipsis points (dots), also called suspension points, never by asterisks (stars).[5] The ellipsis points are printed on the line like periods, not above it like multiplication dots in mathematics. They are usually separated from each other and from the text and any contiguous punctuation by 3-to-em spaces (see Glossary under "spacing"). The number of dots and the spacing between them and the preceding and following words should be checked carefully by the manuscript editor for consistency.

10.37 Two commonly used methods of using ellipsis points are described here. The University of Chicago Press prefers the second one, but will allow the first if the author of a book-length manuscript has used it consistently.

10.38 The first method is, briefly, to use three dots for any omission, regardless of whether it comes in the middle of a sentence or between sentences:

> For instance, consider the rule about ellipses in broken quotations—that when a quoted sentence ends with a period, this period should be printed close up, followed by three dots to show ellipsis . . . In my opinion those publishers and journals who have decided to forget about this nicety and now invariably use three dots . . . must be congratulated on their common sense. (Eleanor Harman, "A Reconsideration of Manuscript Editing," *Scholarly Publishing* 7 [January 1976]: 151)

10.39 The second method distinguishes between omissions within a sentence and omissions between sentences. This method is described in the following paragraphs.

WITHIN A SENTENCE

10.40 Three dots indicate an omission within a sentence or between the first and last words of a quoted fragment of a sentence. Thus an omission in the sentence

5. Letters, words, or phrases missing or illegible in a fragmentary original are sometimes indicated by ellipsis points (see 10.48).

> The glottal stop, which is common in this family of languages, is marked by an apostrophe

could be shortened as

> The glottal stop . . . is marked by an apostrophe.

10.41   Other punctuation may be used on either side of the three ellipsis dots if it helps the sense or better shows what has been omitted. Consider the following passage (Dan. 3:4–6) in original and cut versions:

> Then an herald cried aloud, To you it is commanded, O people, nations, and languages, that at what time ye hear the sound of the cornet, flute, harp, sackbut, psaltery, dulcimer, and all kinds of musick, ye fall down and worship the golden image that Nebuchadnezzar the king hath set up: and whoso falleth not down and worshippeth shall the same hour be cast into the midst of a burning fiery furnace.

> To you it is commanded . . . that at what time ye hear the sound of the cornet, flute, . . . and all kinds of musick, ye fall down and worship the golden image . . . : and whoso falleth not down and worshippeth shall . . . be cast into . . . a burning fiery furnace.

Here the comma after "flute" and the colon after "image . . ." are optional rather than required.

BETWEEN SENTENCES

10.42   Four dots—a period, followed by three spaced dots—indicate the omission of (1) the last part of the quoted sentence, (2) the first part of the next sentence, (3) a whole sentence or more, or (4) a whole paragraph or more. When a sentence ends with a question mark or an exclamation point in the original, this mark is retained and three dots used for the ellipsis:

> Let such Imps of Ill-nature . . . rail on. . . . But to my gentle Readers of another Cast, I would willingly apologize, and endeavour to rescue my Heroine from sharing too much of their Censure. . . . Pray imagine yourselves in her Situation.

> Why is it that they array themselves against me? . . . Where were they during the rebellion?

10.43   When four dots indicate the omission of the *end of a sentence,* the first dot is the period—that is, there is no space between it and the preceding word. What precedes an ellipsis indicated by four dots should be a grammatically complete sentence, either as it is quoted or in combination with the text preceding it. Similarly, what follows four dots should also be a sentence. In other words, every succession of words preceding or following *four* ellipsis points should be functionally a sentence. A complete passage from Emerson's essay "Politics" reads:

293

> The spirit of our American radicalism is destructive and aimless: it is not loving, it has no ulterior and divine ends; but is destructive only out of hatred and selfishness. On the other side, the conservative party, composed of the most moderate, able, and cultivated part of the population, is timid, and merely defensive of property. It vindicates no right, it aspires to no real good, it brands no crime, it proposes no generous policy, it does not build, nor write, nor cherish the arts, nor foster religion, nor establish schools, nor encourage science, nor emancipate the slave, nor befriend the poor, or the Indian, or the immigrant. From neither party, when in power, has the world any benefit to expect in science, art, or humanity, at all commensurate with the resources of the nation.

The passage might be shortened as follows:

> The spirit of our American radicalism is destructive and aimless. . . . the conservative party . . . is timid, and merely defensive of property. It vindicates no right, it aspires to no real good. . . . From neither party . . . has the world any benefit to expect in science, art, or humanity, at all commensurate with the resources of the nation.

10.44 Three dots—no period—are used at the end of a quoted sentence that is deliberately and grammatically incomplete:

> Everyone knows that the Declaration of Independence begins with the sentence "When, in the course of human events . . ." But how many people can recite more than the first few lines of the document?

> Please look at the example beginning "The spirit of our American radicalism . . ." and tell me how you would shorten it.

(For the use of the dash for interrupted speech see 5.83; for when to use no ellipsis points see 10.47.)

FULL LINES OR PARAGRAPHS OMITTED

10.45 The omission of one full line or several consecutive lines of verse is indicated by one line of em-spaced dots approximately the length of the line above it (or of the missing line, if that is determinable).

> I will arise and go now, and go to Innisfree,
>
> . . . .
> And live alone in the bee-loud glade.
> > (W. B. Yeats, "The Lake Isle of Innisfree")

> Heard melodies are sweet, but those unheard
> Are sweeter; therefore, ye soft pipes, play on;
>
> . . . .
> Pipe to the spirit ditties of no tone.
> > (John Keats, "Ode on a Grecian Urn")

10.46 A full line of dots may be used to indicate omission of a number of paragraphs or pages in a prose quotation consisting of widely scattered bits from the original. Usually, however, in a quotation of several paragraphs, the omission of an intervening paragraph or paragraphs is adequately indicated by a period and three ellipsis points at the end of the paragraph preceding the omitted part. And if a paragraph in the quotation, other than the first paragraph, begins with a sentence that does not open a paragraph in the original, it should be preceded by three dots following the usual paragraph indention. It is thus possible on occasion to use ellipsis points at the end of one paragraph *and* at the beginning of the next in a block quotation:

> In summarizing the action of a drama, the writer should use the present tense. In summarizing a poem, story, or novel, he should also use the present, though he may use the past if it seems more natural to do so. . . .
>   . . . whichever tense the writer chooses he should use throughout. Shifting from one tense to another gives the appearance of uncertainty and irresolution. (Strunk and White, *The Elements of Style,* 3d ed., 31)

WHEN NOT TO USE ELLIPSIS POINTS

10.47   In general, no ellipsis points should be used (1) before or after an obviously incomplete sentence, (2) before or after a run-in quotation of a complete sentence, (3) before a block quotation beginning with a complete sentence or an incomplete sentence that completes a sentence in the text, (4) after a block quotation ending with a complete sentence. If ellipsis points are considered necessary before or after a quoted passage—and sometimes it is desirable to include them—three should precede and four, including the period, should follow the quoted matter if it ends with a complete sentence or if it ends the sentence in the text. But ellipsis points are seldom used at the beginning or end of a quoted passage. After all, unless it is the opening or closing sentence in a work that is being quoted, something precedes and follows the passage, and it is not necessary to emphasize the fact. For examples of points (1) and (2) see 10.11, 10.12, for points (3) and (4) see 10.19.

10.48   To indicate words missing or illegible in the original a 1- or 2-em space, with or without brackets, is customary, rather than ellipsis dots. In some cases a line of dots may be used to indicate missing or illegible lines in a manuscript or inscription. (For interpolations of missing letters or words see 10.50.)

> Although the Genl.'s victory in the Supreme has sa[ved him] from the mortification of being ejected by our late   it has not from the vexation of being pursued by   [He] is now trying the skill of his lawyer in framing a new a[ppeal] and means to carry the Genl. over the whole ground [again.] (Madison to Joseph Jones, 24 Oct. 1780, *The Papers of James Madison,* 2:147)
>
> I have great marvel that ye will so soon incline to every man his device and [counsel and   ] specially in matters of small impor[tance   ] yea, and as [it is] reported [unto me   ] causes as meseemeth

> th[at   ] nothing to [   ] ne gentlewomen. (Thomas Cromwell to Lord Lisle, 1 Sept. 1533, *The Lisle Letters,* ed. Byrne, 1:552–53)

CAPITALIZATION FOLLOWING ELLIPSES

10.49   The first word of a sentence following four dots, in a quotation from a modern work, may be capitalized even though it is not the first word of the sentence in the original. For example, the second sentence in the extract from Emerson's "Politics" (see 10.43) may be changed as follows:

> The spirit of our American radicalism is destructive. . . . The conservative party . . .

But in scholarly works usually and in legal works always, an original lowercase letter following the four dots should not be capitalized, so that the reader attempting to locate the quotation in its source will not be misled. If a change *is* made, brackets may be used to indicate it (see 10.15).

> . . . destructive. . . . [T]he conservative party . . .

In a quotation from an older work where many words are capitalized, it is also best to make no such changes:

> Let such Imps of Ill-nature . . . rail on. . . . to my gentle Readers of another Cast, I would willingly apologize.

In some cases, instead of introducing a capital it may be desirable to add a connective in brackets:

> The spirit of our American radicalism is destructive and aimless . . . [and] the conservative party . . . is timid, and merely defensive of property.

(For capitalizing the *first* word of a quotation see 10.12–15.)

INTERPOLATIONS AND ALTERATIONS

10.50   Insertions may be made in quoted material (1) to clarify an ambiguity, (2) to provide a missing word or letters, (3) to give the original foreign word or phrase where an English translation does not convey the exact sense. Any such interpolations are enclosed in brackets (not parentheses). When an interpolated word takes the place of a word in the original, ellipsis points are omitted:

> In disbelief he, like Horatio, asked scornfully, "What, has this thing [the ghost of Hamlet's father] appear'd again tonight?"
>
> "Well," said she, "if Mr. L[owel]l won't go, then neither will I."
>
> James "preferred to subvert the religion and laws of his people" rather than to "follow the character and reasons of his state [*indolis rationesque sui Regni*]."

Even in its romantic origins, Jebb tells us, satire "is the only [form] which has a continuous development extending from the vigorous age of the Commonwealth into the second century of the Empire."

Contempt, scorn, or doubt may sometimes be expressed by [!] or [?], although such interpolations are usually best left unmade.

"SIC"

10.51 *Sic* ("so," "thus," "in this manner") may be inserted in brackets, following a word misspelled or wrongly used in the original. (Note that *sic* is a complete word, not an abbreviation, and therefore takes no period.) Overuse of this device, however, is to be discouraged. In most books it is wholly unnecessary to call attention to every variant spelling, every oddity of expression, in quoted material. An exclamation point should never be used after *sic;* the insertion of *sic* alone is enough to call attention to the error in the source. While not really necessary, it would be permissible to use *sic* in the following sentence from Thoreau's *Walden:*

> Or on a Sunday afternoon, if I chanced to be at home, I heard the cronching [*sic*] of the snow made by the step of a long-headed farmer, who from far through the woods sought my house, to have a social "crack."

ITALICS ADDED

10.52 When it is desirable to call attention to a certain word or words in material being quoted, these may be underlined so that they will be printed in italics. The reader should be told when this has been done, either in the note giving the source of the quotation, in parentheses directly following the quotation, or in brackets following the italicized passage in the quotation; one or the other system should be used throughout a book. "Italics mine," "italics added," "emphasis added," are all acceptable phrases, but, again, choose one and stick with it.[6]

10.53 Occasionally it may be desirable to point out that italics in a quotation were *not* the present author's doing but were indeed in the original. Here, the usual phrase is "italics in original" or, better, the name of the quoted author, "Tocqueville's italics."

6. Note that an explanation such as "Underlined words do not appear in the second edition" makes sense in the manuscript but not in print, where the words in question are set in italics, not underlined. Hence in a manuscript intended for publication the explanation should read, "Words in italics do not appear in the second edition."

CITING SOURCES IN TEXT

10.54   In a scholarly work the source of a direct quotation is often given in a note, but in many cases it may be given in the text, in whole or in part and enclosed in parentheses. Such text references present some editorial problems in placement and punctuation.

10.55   In a work containing no notes or bibliography and only a few quoted passages a source may be given, in full, in parentheses following the quotation, or it may be worked into the text:

> The programs of today reflect the demands of a musically more sophisticated audience. "The age is fortunately nearly past when eighteenth-century composers were subject in concert programs to a kind of 'type-casting' in which a few Scarlatti pieces, or a little Couperin on the part of the more adventurous, a Mozart sonata or a Bach organ fugue were served up as well-styled appetizers to be unregretted by late-comers and to act as finger warmers and curtain raisers to the 'really expressive' music of the nineteenth century" (Ralph Kirkpatrick, *Domenico Scarlatti* [Princeton: Princeton University Press, 1953], 280).

> At the beginning of the introduction to her well-known book *Mythology* (Boston: Little, Brown & Co., 1942) Edith Hamilton observes that "the real interest of the myths is that they lead us back to a time when the world was young and people had a connection with the earth, with trees and seas and flowers and hills, unlike anything we ourselves can feel."

10.56   If another passage is quoted from the same source in the next page or two of text, and there is no intervening quotation from a different source, "ibid." may be used in the parenthetical reference: (ibid., 282). If a different source has been cited or more than two or three pages have elapsed, a short title should be given: (Kirkpatrick, *Scarlatti*, 282).

10.57   In works, particularly literary studies, using frequent quotations from a single source, each needing its own identification, it is usually preferable to give such identifying page or line numbers, act and scene, book, part, or the like in parentheses following each quotation instead of in the notes (see 15.66 [3–4]).

10.58   The full citation to the source may be given in a note the first time it is mentioned with, if relevant, the explanation that all subsequent quotations from the source are to the edition cited. (If there is a reason to use more than one edition of a work, this fact must of course be mentioned and the edition specified each time.)

10.59   If part designations are explained in the note, it is unnecessary to include their abbreviations in the text references. For example, if the note says

> References are to act, scene, and line

the text reference following a passage may read simply

> 1.2.14–15 (meaning act 1, scene 2, lines 14–15)[7]

or, similarly, following appropriate explanation in a note,

> 3:22–23 (meaning volume 3, pages 22–23)
> 12.45–50, *or* 12:45–50 (meaning book 12, lines 45–50)
> 2.8.14 (meaning book 2, canto 8, stanza 14)

"Ibid." should not be used for subsequent text references to act, scene, etc., because to repeat the part numbers generally takes less space.

10.60 Where a number of sources are used this way, it is well to devise an abbreviation for each and, instead of giving full citations and explanations in the notes, to compile a list of abbreviations to be placed at the front or back of the book (or article) (see 1.45, 15.67). In a study of Shakespeare's comedies, for example, one might refer to a passage from *A Midsummer Night's Dream* and abbreviate the identification in the text: (*MND* 2.2.1–8).

IN RUNNING TEXT

10.61 If the quotation comes in the middle of the text sentence, the source is given after the closing quotation mark and the rest of the text sentence follows:

> With his "Nothing will come of nothing; speak again" (1.1.92) Lear, exasperated, tries to draw from his youngest daughter a verbal expression of filial devotion.

10.62 When the quoted passage falls at the end of a sentence and is not itself a question or an exclamation, the source follows the final quotation mark, and the period or other terminal punctuation is given outside the final parenthesis:

> Lear, trying to draw from his youngest daughter an expression of filial devotion, says with some exasperation, "Nothing will come of nothing; speak again" (1.1.92).

This rule holds even when the quotation is more than one sentence:

> It has been three-quarters of a century since Henry Adams said: "Fifty years ago, science took for granted that the rate of acceleration could not last. The world forgets quickly, but even today the habit remains of founding statistics on the faith that consumption will continue nearly stationary" (*Education*, 493).

10.63 When a quotation comes at the end of a sentence and is itself a question or an exclamation, demanding its own final punctuation, that

7. If roman numerals are preferred for act numbers, the citation would read: (I, 2, 14–15). Or, roman numerals for both act and scene: (I, ii, 14–15) or (I.ii.14–15).

punctuation is retained, as part of the quotation, and a period is added after the parenthesis:

> And finally, in the frenzy of grief that kills him, Lear rails, "Why should a dog, a horse, a rat, have life, / And thou no breath at all?" (5.3.306).

10.64 A less desirable method of punctuating quotations and their sources at the ends of sentences is to put the punctuation mark concluding the whole sentence inside the final quotation mark and to use no punctuation following the source citation:

> Lear says with some exasperation, "Nothing will come of nothing; speak again." (1.1.92)

A rather old-fashioned and fussy variant of this is: ". . . again." (1.1.92.)

10.65 One or the other of the two methods (10.62–63, 10.64) must be used consistently throughout a book, or an issue of a journal. The University of Chicago Press prefers the method given in 10.62–63.

FOLLOWING BLOCK QUOTATIONS

10.66 The source of a set-off or block quotation is usually given in parentheses at the end of the quotation and in the same type size as the set-off quotation. It is best put after the final punctuation mark so that it will not be read as part of the quotation. If the reference begins with a word or abbreviation, the first letter is usually capitalized: (Vol. 3). No punctuation is used following the source.

10.67 A citation following a prose quotation is placed right after the final punctuation mark.

From Joseph Addison in *The Spectator:*

> I shall endeavour to enliven morality with wit, and to temper wit with morality. . . . The mind that lies fallow but a single day sprouts up in follies that are only to be killed by a constant and assiduous culture. (No. 10, 12 March 1710/11)

From W[illiam] D[ean] Howells, *Literary Friends and Acquaintance* (New York: Harper & Bros., 1900):

> Then and always he [Walt Whitman] gave me the sense of a sweet and true soul. . . . The apostle of the rough, the uncouth, was the gentlest person; his barbaric yawp, translated into the terms of social encounter, was an address of singular quiet, delivered in a voice of winning and endearing friendliness. (P. 75)

10.68 Citations following poetry quotations should be dropped to the line below the last line of the quotation and centered on the last letter of the longest line of the quotation, or set flush right, or indented uniformly from the right margin (placement is often specified by the designer). Citations in the following examples are all set flush right:

From Milton's *Paradise Lost;* reference is to book and lines:

> So glistered the dire Snake, and into fraud
> Led Eve, our credulous mother, to the Tree
> Of Prohibition, root of all our woe.
>
> (9.643–45)

From Alexander Pope, *The Rape of the Lock;* reference is to canto and lines:

> The meeting points the sacred hair dissever
> From the fair head, forever, and forever!
>
> (3.153–54)

From Shakespeare's *Love's Labour's Lost;* reference is to act, scene, and lines:

> For wisdom's sake, a word that all men love;
> Or for love's sake, a word that loves all men.
>
> (4.3.354–55)

From Edmund Spenser, *The Faerie Queene;* reference is to book, canto, and stanza:

> Who will not mercie unto others shew,
> How can he mercy ever hope to have?
>
> (6.1.42)

FOREIGN LANGUAGE QUOTATIONS

10.69   Quotations in a foreign language that are incorporated into an English text are treated like quotations in English. They are not italicized. Quotation marks and ellipsis points follow English style. Foreign styles of punctuating quoted matter vary widely and are used only when an entire work is in a foreign language (see chap. 9).

TRANSLATING QUOTATIONS

10.70   Whether an author should provide translations of quoted passages or not depends upon the linguistic abilities of the possible readers. As a general rule, in a literary study of, say, Racine, quotations from Racine's plays should be given in the original French only. Similarly, in a work to be read by classicists, Latin or Greek sources[8] may be quoted freely in the original. In a scholarly work where there is a

---

8. Most typesetters make extra charges for setting Greek, Cyrillic, or other non-Latin alphabets. Authors who quote from works in languages using these alphabets and who do not wish to transliterate the passages should so advise their publishers.

possibility that not all readers will be able to grasp the original, both the original and a translation may be given. In this case the translation is usually put in a note, but there are often compelling reasons to put the translation in the text and the original in the note, or even both in the text. In works where quotations are used for their content alone, not for their style, only the English translation need appear, with of course the proper attribution.

10.71   Passages in a foreign language may be translated by the person quoting them if no acceptable English translation of the source has been published; in this case "my translation" should be added either in parentheses following the translation or in the note identifying the source. Where a published translation is used, the title of the translation, the translator's name, and the bibliographical details should be given in a note or in the bibliography, and the relevant page number of the translation should be used in identifying the quotation. Finally, never *re*-translate from a foreign language a passage from a book originally published in English! Find the original and use it.

11 *Illustrations, Captions, and Legends*

Illustrations 11.1
    Definitions 11.1
        Line and continuous-tone copy 11.2
        Text figures and plates 11.4
        Offset and letterpress 11.5
    Artwork for Offset Reproduction 11.6
        Placement and numbering 11.7
        Physical handling 11.10
        Markup 11.12
        Cropping 11.15
        Scaling 11.17
    Artwork for Letterpress Reproduction 11.21
    Corrections on Art Copy 11.23
Captions and Legends 11.25
    Editorial Conventions and Typography 11.27
        Punctuation 11.28
        Numeration 11.29
        Abbreviating "figure" and "plate" 11.31
        Identifying parts of an illustration 11.32
    Credit Lines 11.34
        Permissions 11.35
        Placement 11.36
        Form 11.37
        Previously published material 11.38
        Original material 11.40
The List of Illustrations 11.44
    Preparing the list 11.45
    Editing captions 11.46
Checking Illustrations in Proofs 11.47
For Further Reference 11.50

ILLUSTRATIONS

DEFINITIONS

11.1 The term *illustration* refers to a variety of materials such as line draw-ings, paintings, photographs, charts, graphs, and maps. Tables, since they are set in type rather than reproduced from artwork, are not considered illustrations. In a book in which tables occur they are sep-arately listed in the preliminary pages and separately numbered—and in this manual they are discussed separately in a chapter of their own.

Although each type of illustration requires slightly different treatment, peculiar to its own kind, some general remarks can be made about the preparation of all these materials for reproduction. At this point, however, a few definitions and distinctions are in order.

11.2 *Line and continuous-tone copy.* First, artwork containing only blacks and whites, with no shading—a pen-and-ink drawing, for instance, or a bar chart—is known as *line copy.* Artwork that does contain shading—such as a painting, a wash drawing, or a photograph—is known as *continuous-tone copy* or, less accurately, *halftone copy.* Mechanically the two kinds of copy are handled differently for reproduction, and authors and editors should keep the distinction in mind.

11.3 Both kinds of copy must be photographed by the publisher's supplier before they can be reproduced. Line copy, however, is shot directly, whereas continuous-tone copy—say, a photograph—is shot through a *screen* that breaks the image up into hundreds of tiny dots of varying size. The resulting *halftone* is actually a printed reproduction of these dots (quite visible under a magnifying glass) which the naked eye sees as various tones of gray shading into one another.

11.4 *Text figures and plates.* Second, illustrations in a book may print along with the text, in which case they are called *text figures,* or they may print separately, grouped in one or more sections containing nothing but illustrations, in which case they are called *plates.* If all the illustrations for a book, whether text figures or plates, are gathered into a single section, this is often called a *gallery.* Plate sections are not counted in the page-numbering sequence of the book. A section of text figures may sometimes be numbered with the text, provided that the illustration program for the book has been fully settled upon before paging begins—but even then it is not uncommon to exclude these pages from the text sequence.

11.5 *Offset and letterpress.* Third, the printing method used nowadays for nearly all scholarly books containing only text, or a combination of text and text figures, is the *offset* process. If book illustrations appear only in special plate sections, those sections may be printed by the *letterpress* process and joined with the rest of a book printed by offset. (Or they may indeed also be printed by offset and gathered in plate sections simply because that is an old, familiar, and sometimes convenient way of handling illustrations.) In any case, methods of handling art copy for offset and letterpress reproduction differ to some degree, and they will be separately described in what follows. (For more on offset and letterpress, see chapter 20, where those processes are more fully described. Not treated there in any detail, and not discussed here at all, is a third process—*gravure*—used chiefly for art books and for illustrated work printed in very long press runs, such as mail-order catalogs.)

11.6   Because in offset reproduction halftones and line work normally print together, editorial preparation of the copy is simpler and will be described first.

11.7   *Placement and numbering.* An illustration should be placed as close as possible to the first text reference to it, or after that point—but not before it. To show placement the author or editor writes (for example) "fig. 1 here" or simply "fig. 1" in the margin of the manuscript at the best place for the illustration, encircling the words so they will not be set by mistake. The editor must later see that these directions are transferred to the text proofs, as a guide to the printer in making up the pages.

11.8   If there are many illustrations, they should be numbered, and text references to them should be by the numbers: "figure 1 shows . . . ," "see figure 2," "(fig. 3)." *Never* should a figure be referred to as "the figure opposite" or "the photograph reproduced on this page." The exigencies of page makeup may well be such as to rule out that placement—and then the reference will have to be rewritten in proof. The examples given illustrate some of the conventions observed at the University of Chicago Press: "figure" (or "plate"—see the later discussion) is set in roman lowercase type and the number is an arabic numeral. The word "figure" is spelled out unless the reference is a simple parenthetical one.

11.9   In a book in which line and halftone illustrations are mixed and distributed through the text, they should be numbered continuously throughout, beginning with figure 1. There are exceptions, of course. Maps, unless they are used to illustrate specific points, are usually separately numbered (map 1, map 2, etc.) or not numbered at all. (Tables, we have seen, are always numbered separately, not being considered illustrations.) Also, in a book in which the chapters are by different authors—a book of conference papers or a symposium—numeration of figures customarily starts over with each chapter. This is true also of a book (such as this style manual) employing *double numeration* throughout. Here a figure is given a number consisting of the number of the chapter in which it appears plus the number of the figure within that chapter. For example, figure 9.3 is the third figure in chapter 9.

11.10   *Physical handling.* For a book containing a large number of illustrations, just physically handling the art copy and photographs after they come to the publisher's office—sorting, identifying, and marking them—is often a job of some magnitude, and one that frequently falls to the lot of the manuscript editor in charge of the project. Some cautions must be observed in handling copy for illustrations:

> Never use staples to attach anything to a photograph or piece of artwork.
>
> Never use paperclips either, unless they are padded with several thicknesses of paper to prevent scratching or indentation.
>
> Except for crop marks make no marks of any kind on the front of the copy: use a tissue overlay or write on the back.
>
> When writing on the back of a photograph or piece of artwork, use nothing harder than the softest of lead pencils—grease pencil is best. *Never* use a ballpoint pen.

11.11   When a large package of illustrations arrives, a number of editorial tasks should be done immediately. Before opening the package, or at least before spreading out the contents, the editor's desk should be cleared or (preferably) a large table found that can be totally cleared of all papers. There is nothing more frustrating to an editor than to mislay a small bit of illustration copy by letting it slip unobserved among other papers on the editorial desk. The chief things to do then are the following:

> Inventory everything received, first arranging items in sequence and then checking them off individually on a list provided by the author. If the author provided no such list, you will have to make one. It is important at this point to note any items missing: later no one will believe you didn't lose them yourself.
>
> Turn each illustration over to make sure it is completely identified on the back. The minimum is author, short title, and chapter and figure numbers. For a volume of conference papers the name of the author of the particular chapter, rather than the chapter number, should be used.
>
> If any of the necessary identifying information is missing, supply it by writing *lightly* on the back of the piece.
>
> If legend copy has not been supplied by the author, transcribe legends pasted to the backs of photographs, etc., or if legends appear on flaps pasted to the bottom edges of the illustrations, tear these off and paste them up in numerical order for later editing. The typesetter cannot set from anything attached to illustrations.
>
> If legend copy has to be removed from an illustration, as just mentioned, it is a good idea to make some brief record, on the back of

the piece, of its subject, in addition to the purely formal identification data there.

It is very easy for the printer to get some kinds of illustrations wrong side up if they are not marked—tissue sections and photomicrographs of all kinds are notorious in this regard. The editor should consequently mark *TOP* on the back of any illustration subject to this kind of mistake.

11.12 *Markup.* In a large publishing house editors seldom have occasion to mark illustration copy for reproduction, but in a house too small to boast a production department, art and photo markup is a normal editorial task. What follows is only a sketch of what is typically involved in simple markup, not a set of directions. Unless one is thoroughly conversant with art and photo markup for the particular process and materials being used, one should seek advice from a trained production person or from a supplier before doing any markup.

11.13 For black-and-white copy (and this is all we are considering in this chapter) the chief things to tell the offset cameraman are (1) whether or not the negative is to be screened (for halftone reproduction) and if so what grade of screen is to be used, and (2) what the dimensions of the finished reproduction should be.

11.14 For (1) the editor might write "Make halftone, 133-line screen, crop as shown" or "Make line neg, size as shown." Such directions are best written in the margin of any piece of illustration copy, but for a photograph they may be written on the back, where there is more room.

11.15 *Cropping.* For (2) the editor must decide how much of the illustration is to be used (photographs, particularly, are commonly *cropped* in reproduction—that is, only part of the image appears on the printed page). A pair of L-shaped pieces of cardboard can be used to frame the area of interest and to help the editor see what the picture will look like as cropped (see fig. 11.l). The person doing the cropping should make sure that any verticals in the picture—the corner of a building, for instance, or the trunks of forest trees—appear to be vertical as the photograph is cropped. Photographs shot by nonprofessionals are often faulty in this regard. If there is a horizon in the picture it should be horizontal, but other horizontals, like stairs or building cornices often, quite correctly, appear slanted because of the effect of perspective. When correcting verticals, pick a vertical near the center of the image to judge by, not one near the edge, since parallax in the camera often makes these diverge.

Fig. 11.1. Two L-shaped pieces of cardboard are a useful aid in cropping a photograph.

11.16   When the area to be used has been decided upon, small *crop marks* are placed in the margin to show just what area the cameraman is to include—all of the photograph or only part of it. Ordinary soft pencil is best for marking on artwork, black grease pencil on photographs. Then one of the dimensions of the finished reproduction, usually the width, is written between the appropriate crop marks. (This is recommended for the nonprofessional in preference to the direction "reduce 2 : 1" or "reduce 50%" or whatever, as often used by professionals.)

11.17   *Scaling.* When a photograph or piece of artwork is to be reduced to fit a particular space, it must be *scaled;* that is, finished dimensions must be computed from original dimensions. There are many ways of doing this, all of them based on the fact that when a piece of artwork is reduced in the engraving process, all dimensions shrink in the same proportion. That is, when the long side of an eight-by-ten-inch photograph is reduced to five inches, the short side automatically reduces to four inches. We will describe two common methods of scaling, one mechanical (or better, visual), the other arithmetical.

11.18 First method (see fig. 11.2): When the photograph has been cropped, lay a piece of tracing paper over it and draw—lightly!—a rectangle the size of the usable area of the photograph (*A*). Next (*B*), mark on the top line the width you want the reproduction to be, and draw a diagonal line across the rectangle. Then (*C*) drop a vertical line from the mark you made to the diagonal line, using a draftsman's triangle or a rectangular piece of cardboard, such as a tablet back. Finally (*D*), run another line, parallel to the top and bottom of the rectangle, from the point where your vertical line hits the diagonal to the left side of the rectangle. You now have a small rectangle inside the large one, and this represents the actual size of the finished halftone.

11.19 Second method: Measure between crop marks the height and width of the image *in picas* to the nearest half pica. (Why picas? The type area of a printed page is always measured in picas, and since picas are so much smaller than inches, fractions give less trouble in computation.) Substitute these two figures ("original width" and "original height") in the following equation:

$$\text{reduced height} = \frac{\text{original height} \times \text{reduced width}}{\text{original width}} .$$

Now determine from the page specifications how wide the finished halftone must be and substitute this figure in the equation ("reduced width"). Finally, perform the computation (a pocket calculator is a great help) to obtain the height of the finished product.

11.20 For example: The usable area of the original photograph measures 35.5 picas wide by 55 picas high, and the halftone is to drop into a type column that is 15 picas wide. Substituting these figures in the equation, we obtain

$$\text{reduced height} = \frac{55 \times 15}{35.5} = 23.239 .$$

So if we count on a height of 23½ picas for the finished halftone, we will be close enough. To this we would add a little white space, say half a line above and half a line below (if the illustration is to go in the middle of the column), plus enough space for the caption and legend, to figure how big a "hole" to leave in the column for the illustration.

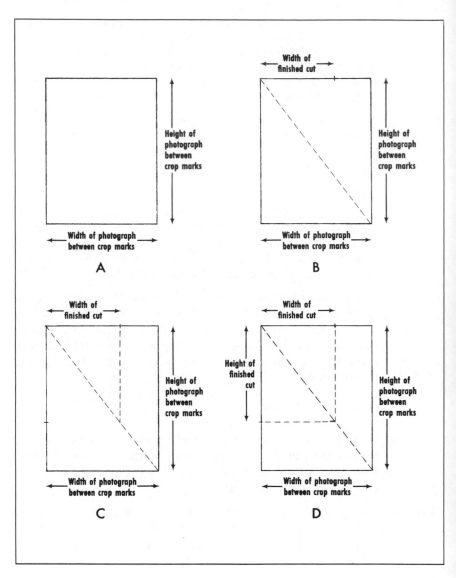

Fig. 11.2. Scaling a photograph by means of an overlay and diagonal

ARTWORK FOR LETTERPRESS REPRODUCTION

11.21 Preparing copy for reproduction by letterpress is very similar to what has been described for offset. The chief differences exist when a distinction must be made in the book between text figures, printed with the text, and plates, printed from halftone *engravings* on special paper.

11.22 The two types of art copy should be kept separate and appropriately marked: "figure 1," "figure 2," etc., and "plate 1," "plate 2," etc. Both are scaled according to the editor's favorite method, and for the plates the engraver will be told to "make halftone on copper" with such-and-such—perhaps 133-line—screen.

CORRECTIONS ON ART COPY

11.23 Unless drawings have been made especially for reproduction after consultation between author, editor, and production controller, they often require changes, major or minor, before they can be reproduced. Changes are of two sorts: (1) those necessary to ready the artwork physically for reproduction—strengthening weak lines, redrawing fuzzy line copy, whiting out unwanted marks in the background, and so on, and (2) editorial changes—bringing spelling and capitalization of labels into conformity with other drawings and with the text, attaining consistency in the use of symbols and wording, improving clarity, and so on. All names on a map that is to be redrawn and any words appearing in other kinds of illustrations must be typed as a separate list for typesetting. In a publishing house with a production department, a production controller is responsible for seeing that artwork corrections are made, an editor for editorial changes. In a small house, the editor is responsible for all.

11.24 Corrections on artwork, unless they are so gross and simple that an editor's unskilled and shaky hand is not likely to spoil the drawing, should be left to an artist. The directions to the artist are not written on the drawing or photograph itself, but on a flap of tracing paper (*overlay*) taped to the back of the piece and folded down over the face. On this the editor marks what is to be done, writing with the least possible pressure. Then when the corrections have been made, the editor removes the overlay before sending the copy to the engraver or platemaker.

CAPTIONS AND LEGENDS

11.25   Most text figures and plates require some sort of explanatory material to make them understandable to the reader. This is supplied by the *caption* and *legend*—two terms often confused or considered synonymous, but at the University of Chicago Press distinguished elegantly the one from the other. A caption is a title or headline, especially one placed in the traditional location, above the illustration. A legend is an explanation, sometimes (like a caption) in title form but more commonly in the form of a statement and consisting of one or more sentences. (On a map, of course, the legend is the key to the symbols used—something quite different from what we are describing here.) The following is an example of a traditional caption and legend—for a halftone plate, as are the two following examples:

> COLINTON PARISH CHURCH AS IT APPEARED IN WALKER'S TIME
>
> This photograph shows the church as it appeared before 1908, when it was extensively enlarged and reconstructed. It had changed little from the time of Walker's ministry until then. The coffin-shaped object in the foreground is an eighteenth-century mortsafe, a block of cast iron placed over a newly made grave to discourage "resurrectionists" from digging up the body for sale to anatomists. (Courtesy of the Reverend W. B. Johnston, B.D., minister of Colinton.)

Less traditionally, caption and legend may be run on. Note the period after the caption:

> PLATE 1
>
> A GROUP OF ARTIFACTS FROM SITE 3. In all these objects the high degree of finish and the aesthetic appeal are notable. *A, C, E,* flint points, and *B,* obsidian bird point, all approximately natural size; *D,* grain-storage jar of grayish clay decorated in black (× 1/20); *F,* votive figure of red clay, undecorated (× 1/5).

When the identifying copy for a plate is a mere tag, and especially if real captions and legends are used for other plates in the book, it should be set as a caption:

> PLATE 2. WALL DRAWING OF HUNTSMEN

11.26   Text figures nowadays frequently carry legends only, captions being omitted, especially in scientific writing, where such figures are used in profusion:

> Fig. 1. Clearly visible here are the giant transparent vacuole *V* and its septa *S* wrapped around the end of the resorbing bone.

An identifying tag, functionally a caption, is often used but set as if it were part of the legend:

Fig. 2. Photomicrographs of mouse-radius rudiments. *A*, left radius cultivated for 3 days in PTE; *B*, right radius similarly cultivated; *C*, left radius cultivated for 2 days in PTE.

Fig. 3. Idealized random distribution curve

EDITORIAL CONVENTIONS AND TYPOGRAPHY

11.27 The University of Chicago Press has long since abandoned its insistence upon particular type specifications for the captions and legends in its books and lets designers do pretty much what they wish with these elements. There are a few editorial conventions that it prefers to see observed, and these are discussed in the paragraphs that follow.

11.28 *Punctuation.* A period is not used after a caption set on a line by itself but is used if the caption and legend are run together. Similarly, the · period is not used after a one-line legend that is a mere title (see examples above).

11.29 *Numeration.* Press preference is for the use of arabic numerals with plates as well as text figures. Further, if halftone illustrations print with the text, preference is to number them with the text figures, not separately as if they were plates. In a book containing numbered figures, each figure should bear its own number. Even though figures are printed side by side and are to be compared, it is preferred that they be numbered separately—figures 37 and 38, for example, not figures 37a and 37b. Especially painful to a careful editor is a figure stuck in at the last moment and given a designation such as figure 43A. If the figure *must* be included and no other nearby figure can be killed, and if it is too late or too expensive to renumber the rest of the figures, of course this must be done. And if it is done, the example given illustrates the typographical preference of the Press in handling the makeshift (the sequence would then be 43, 43A, 44, etc.).

11.30 If a book is illustrated wholly with photographs, reproduced either as plates or as text illustrations, the author and editor might consider whether they need to be numbered at all. The criterion is text reference. If the illustrations are not referred to in the text or are referred to in such a way that they can easily be identified without numbers, numbers are useless and should be eliminated. In such a case, however, illustrations and legends must still be assigned temporary numbers (not to be used in the printed book) to identify them and to make sure they will be matched up properly in printing. The number should be written on the back of the art copy (and—for letterpress illustrations—transferred to the engraver's proof when it comes in). The same number should be written on the typed legend copy (encircled so that it will not be set) and transferred to the type proof when it comes in.

11.31 *Abbreviating "figure" and "plate."* The label "Fig. 1" (for example) is commonly so abbreviated when a caption or legend follows. If no captions or legends are used with the figures in a book, the editor may appropriately decide to spell out the label—"Figure 1"—especially when there are only a few figures. "Plate" is usually spelled out, but could be abbreviated—"Pl. 1, Pl. 2," etc.—if there are many small plates close together.

11.32 *Identifying parts of an illustration.* Such words as *top, bottom, left, right, above, below, left to right, clockwise from left,* and the like, are frequently used in legends to identify individual subjects in an illustration or parts of a composite. These are set in italics, and Press preference is that they precede rather than follow the phrase identifying the object or person:

> Fig. 4. *Above left,* William Livingston; *right,* Henry Brockholst Livingston; *below left,* John Jay; *right,* Sarah Livingston Jay.

If a list follows the introductory tag, a colon rather than a comma is preferred:

> *Left to right:* Dean Acheson, Harry Hopkins, President Roosevelt, Harold Ickes.

11.33 Letters of the Latin alphabet, abbreviations, and symbols are all used as keys for identifying parts of a figure. When such a key is referred to in a legend, the form used in the legend should reflect as closely as possible the form used in the figure itself. If capital letters are used in the figure, capitals should be used in the legend, and so on. The typeface used in the legend for the key should, however, always be italic, whatever is employed in the figure.

> Fig. 5. Four types of Hawaiian fishhooks: *a,* barbed hook of tortoise shell; *b,* trolling hook with pearl shell lure and point of human bone; *c,* octopus lure with cowrie shell, stone sinker, and large bone hook; *d,* barbed hook of human thigh bone.

> Fig. 6. Facial traits of (*A*) *Propithecus verreauxi verreauxi* and (*B*) *Lemur catta,* which vary from one individual to the next; *ea,* ear; *ca,* cap; *cpl,* capline; *br,* brow.

When symbols are used in a figure, use of the same symbols in the legend requires the least effort of the reader:

> Fig. 7. Dependence of half-life on atomic weight for elements in the radium-uranium region: $\bigcirc$ = even α-emitters; $\bullet$ = odd α-emitters; $\square$ = isotopes capable of K-capture or β-decay.

If the symbols are not available in type or in the appropriate size of type, they must then be described:

Fig. 8. Dependence of half-life on atomic weight for elements in the radium-uranium region: *open circles,* even alpha-emitters; *solid circles,* odd alpha-emitters; *open squares,* isotopes capable of *K*-capture or beta-decay.

In the last example, note also that in a scientific context the names of the Greek letters may usually be substituted for the letters themselves.

CREDIT LINES

11.34   In connection with most illustrative matter used in a book or a journal article a *credit line*—a brief statement of the source of the illustration—is either necessary or appropriate. The only significant exception is an illustration (chart, graph, drawing, photograph, etc.) of the author's own creation.

11.35   *Permissions.* Illustrative material in copyright, whether published or unpublished, requires permission of the copyright owner before it can be reproduced. It is the author's responsibility, not the publisher's, to make sure what is in copyright and to obtain permission to reproduce it. An author working with a publisher, however, should always consult the publisher about the form in which to request permission (see 4.48–52).

11.36   *Placement.* The credit line may appear in any one of several locations and in various forms. Set in very small type, a short credit line may run parallel to the lower edge of the illustration or even to one of the vertical edges, especially if the illustration is a photograph. It may run at the end of the legend, usually in parentheses and sometimes in a different style of type, or the pertinent facts may be worked into the legend copy. Again, if most or all of the illustrations are from a single source, that fact may be stated in the preface or acknowledgments or on the copyright page. Finally, in a heavily illustrated book, especially one in which it is desirable to keep the illustrated pages uncluttered, what are called *box credits* may be resorted to. This is a lumping together of all the picture credits for a volume on one page or a series of pages in the front or the back of the book. Picture agencies, incidentally, may demand a higher fee for the use of an illustration if box credits are employed.

11.37   *Form.* The form of the credit line itself varies according to its placement and according to the type and copyright status of the illustration. For material in copyright, the copyright holder may demand a certain form of credit line, but, apart from this contingency, credit lines of a given type (say, those for charts reproduced from published works) should follow a consistent pattern. If the credit appears on a line by itself, end punctuation is omitted. In the discussion and examples that

315

follow, we attempt to suggest some simple and workable patterns for credit lines of various types. In all, the assumption is that the credit line will run under the illustration or at the end of the legend.

11.38   *Previously published material.* An illustration reproduced from a source protected by copyright always requires formal permission from the copyright holder. There is no fixed style for such credit lines, but they should be consistent and for a work of book length should include a page number, figure number, or the like. A short form is appropriate if the work from which the illustration has been taken is listed in the bibliography. The person who grants permission to reproduce the illustration may, however, specify a certain form of credit line including the full facts of publication and even a copyright notice.

> [*a kinship diagram*] Reprinted, by permission, from Wagner, *Curse of Souw,* 82.
>
> [*a portrait engraving*] From a drawing by J. Webber for Cook's *Voyage to the Pacific Ocean, 1776–1780,* reprinted, by permission of the author, from Edwin H. Bryan, Jr., *Ancient Hawaiian Life* (Honolulu, 1938), 10.
>
> [*a photograph of a lemur*] Reprinted, by permission, from Alison Jolly, *Lemur Behavior,* pl. 6. Photograph by C. H. Fraser Rowell. © 1966 by The University of Chicago.

11.39   Illustrations may be reproduced from published works without seeking permission if the work is in the public domain. A work is in the public domain if it was never in copyright (as is true of most publications of the United States government) or if the copyright has run full term and lapsed. Even though permission is not required, it is good policy to use a credit line, however—out of deference to the reader if not the creator of the material.

> Illustration by Joseph Pennell for Henry James, *English Hours* (Boston, 1905), facing p. 82.
>
> Reprinted from John D. Shortridge, *Italian Harpsichord Building in the Sixteenth and Seventeenth Centuries,* U.S. National Museum Bulletin 225 (Washington, n.d.).

11.40   *Original material.* It was mentioned above that any illustrations that are the author's own do not need credit lines. This is not to say that credit lines should *not* be used, however, if there is some reason for the inclusion. And there are often reasons apart from vanity for appending a credit line to an illustration of the author's own creation. If, for example, all but a few of the illustrations in a book are from one source and this source is acknowledged in the preliminaries, it would be appropriate to place under a photograph taken by the author a line reading:

> Photograph by the author, *or,* Photo by author

Somewhat different is the case of material commissioned by the author for a book, usually maps, photographs, or drawings. Ordinarily such material is produced under a "work made for hire" contract (see 4.10), and so no credit is legally owed the supplier. But professional courtesy dictates mention of the creator of the material either in the preliminaries or below each piece, where the credit line might read:

> Map by Gerald F. Pyle
> Photograph by James L. Ballard
> Drawing by Joseph E. Alderfer

If a map or drawing is signed and the signature is reproduced, nothing further is needed, of course.

11.41 For material that the author has obtained free of charge and without restrictions on its use, a credit line is again seldom legally required but usually appended nonetheless. In such credit lines it is appropriate to use the word *courtesy:*

> Photograph courtesy of Ford Motor Company
> *or:* Courtesy Ford Motor Co.

If the name of the photographer is well known or if the supplier of the print requests it, the photographer's name may be given also:

> Photograph by Henri Cartier-Bresson, courtesy of the Museum of Modern Art.

11.42 Agency material—photographs and reproductions of prints, drawings, paintings, and the like, obtained from a commercial agency—usually requires a credit line. The contract or bill of sale will specify what is expected. Typical credits might be

> Woodcut from Historical Pictures Service, Chicago
> Photograph from Wide World Photos

11.43 Sometimes an author does not directly pick up and reproduce another's material but nonetheless is indebted to that person. The author may, for example, use data from a table in another book to construct a chart, or revise another's graph with fresh data, or redraw a figure with or without significant changes. In such situations, although the author's material is technically original, a credit line is in order. Again there is no set form. Thus for a chart based on a table in another book the credit line might read:

> Data from John F. Witte, *Democracy, Authority, and Alienation in Work* (Chicago: University of Chicago Press, 1980), table 10.

If the book is fully listed elsewhere, the citation could be

> Data from Witte, *Democracy, Authority, and Alienation in Work,* table 10.
> *or:* Data from Witte 1980, table 10.

Other typical credit lines are

[*a graph*] Adapted from Pauly 1980, fig. 4.1.
[*a map*] Redrawn from Day, *Guide to Fossil Man,* fig. 32.

THE LIST OF ILLUSTRATIONS

11.44   A task often falling to the manuscript editor (but more properly done by the author) is preparing the list of illustrations. Not every illustrated book requires such a list, of course. The criterion is, Are the illustrations of interest apart from the text they illustrate? For a scientific monograph on interstellar particles, illustrated largely by graphs, the answer is obviously no. For a book on Roman architecture, illustrated by photographs of ancient buildings, the answer is obviously yes. For some other illustrated books, the answer may not be so easy to give, and the author and editor must decide whether the list of illustrations is worth the space it will take.

11.45   *Preparing the list.* The list of illustrations follows the table of contents, normally on a new recto page, and is headed simply Illustrations. (The list of tables, if there is one, follows on another recto page.) *Headline style* (important words capitalized) is usually employed for the identifying titles. If illustrations are of more than one type, they are listed by category, as Plates, Figures, Maps, etc., and by number if numbers are used in the text (see 11.30, also fig. 11.3). For figures and maps that print with the text (and hence have folios assigned to them, whether or not the folios are actually expressed on the page) page numbers are given (*000* in the copy as first prepared). For plates and for maps printed separately, another type of location is given. If plates are to be inserted in groups of four or more pages at one location, each group is listed under the tag *Following page 000* when copy is prepared. If they are to be inserted in the text two pages at a time (each page of plates accordingly lying opposite a text page), the location is given as *facing page 000.* Needless to say, each *000* is changed to a real number once page proofs are out and page numbers are known.

11.46   *Editing captions.* It should be remembered that the list of illustrations is a *list,* not a reprinting of the captions and legends. If the captions are short and adequately identify the subjects of the pictures, they may do double duty in the list of illustrations. Long captions, however, should be shortened, and discursive legends should never be used here. Remember too that readers do not have the illustrations in front of them as they scan the list, so a cryptic, "cute," or allusive caption is of no use to them in identifying the subject of an illustration. Such captions should be rewritten for use in the list of illustrations.

CHECKING ILLUSTRATIONS IN PROOFS

11.47 Among the various tasks often performed after a book is in proof is the preparation of the list of illustrations, just discussed. For that reason the editor should make an extra copy of the captions and legends before they are sent out for typesetting. Proofs for captions and legends often do not come back with the proofs of the text, and thus the editor may be without anything from which to prepare the list.

11.48 Captions, legends, illustrations, and text all conjoin at some particular stage in the production of a letterpress book, usually in page proofs. At this stage the author and editor should make sure that the illustrations are (1) in correct sequence, (2) in appropriate places, (3) not upside down or sideways (sometimes hard to detect in a photomicrograph), (4) not "flopped" (that is, not a mirror image of what should appear), (5) accompanied by the correct captions and legends, and (6) correctly listed in the preliminaries.

11.49 For an offset book, checking these things is trickier: since engravings are not made, we never see proof (in the normal sense) of the illustra-

---

ILLUSTRATIONS

Plates

Hermetic Silence, from Achilles Bocchius's *Symbolicarum quaestionum* . . . (1555)	*frontispiece*
The Wisdom of Thomas Aquinas, fresco by Andrea da Firenze	*facing page* 50
Justice and Peace, fresco by Ambrogio Lorenzetti (detail)	81
The Zodiac, from Robert Fludd's *Ars memoriae*	336
The De Witt Sketch of the Swan Theater	337

Figures

1. The Human Image on a Memory *Locus*	*page* 111
2. The Ladder of Ascent and Descent, from Ramon Lull's *Liber de ascensu et descensu intellectus* (Valencia, 1512)	180
3. Memory Theater, or Repository, from J. Willis's *Mnemonica* (1618)	209
4. Suggested Plan of the Globe Theater	358

Fig. 11.3. A somewhat complicated list of illustrations for a scholarly book (see also figs. 1.10, 1.11).

tions. Page proofs of an offset book include only type matter, blank spaces being left where illustrations are to go. It is then up to the offset platemaker, guided by adequate instructions from the author and editor, to drop the illustrations in the right holes, and the next stage the editor sees is printed sheets or even bound books. For many editors this requires too arduous an act of faith, and so they demand a further stage of "proof"—photographic prints made from the negatives from which plates will be made—for all pages or for those with illustrations. Various kinds of prints are made—among them, *blueprints* ("blues"), *silver prints,* and *vandykes*—but all have the same function. At the University of Chicago Press such prints are mandatory for any illustrated book printed by the offset process (see also 3.51).

FOR FURTHER REFERENCE

11.50 The reader who wants to know more about the mechanical processes involved in the reproduction of illustrations may consult the lucidly written and beautifully illustrated book *Bookmaking,* by Marshall Lee. Frances W. Zweifel's *Handbook of Biological Illustration* discusses preparation of various kinds of illustrative materials, not only biological. Both books are fully listed in the Bibliography.

12 *Tables*

Planning and Constructing Statistical Tables 12.3
Arrangement of the Elements 12.12
    Table Number 12.15
    Title 12.21
    Column Headings 12.26
    The Stub 12.32
    The Body 12.39
    Footnotes 12.46
Estimating Size and Correcting Odd Shapes 12.53
Special Types of Tables 12.57
    Matrix 12.58
    Table in Words 12.59
    Genealogical Table 12.60
    Genetic Table 12.61
Editing Tables 12.62
    Titles and Headings 12.64
    The Stub and the Body 12.68
    Footnotes 12.72
    Ruling 12.74
    Copyfitting Large Tables 12.75
        Wide tables 12.76
        Long tables 12.79
Examples of Table Style 12.85

12.1   Tables offer a useful means of presenting large amounts of detailed information in small space. A simple table can give information that would require several paragraphs to present textually and can do so with greater clarity. Tabular presentation is often not simply the best but the only way that large numbers of individual, similar facts can be arranged. Whenever bulk of information to be conveyed threatens to bog down a textual presentation, an author should give serious consideration to use of a table.

12.2   This chapter, like most others in this manual, is addressed to both authors and editors. The first section, "Planning and Constructing Statistical Tables," is intended primarily for authors who have never compiled a table from raw data and are uncertain how to begin; other readers may wish to skip this section and go on to the next. The final two sections of the chapter, beginning with "Editing Tables" (12.62), will probably be found of more interest to editors than to authors.

PLANNING AND CONSTRUCTING STATISTICAL TABLES

12.3   Although other kinds of tables exist (see 12.57–61), most tables are constructed to present information in numerical form—percentages, tallies of occurrences, amounts of money, and the like—and are known as statistical tables. As a simple example, say that a scholar has completed a survey on smoking among American adults, a survey incorporating information on the respondents' date of birth, sex, income, social background, etc., and wishes to present some of the data in tabular form. The survey has produced responses from 7,308 individuals—3,362 males and 3,946 females, all eighteen or over.

12.4   In any one table a single category of responses is always at the center of attention. The table is constructed to illustrate the variations in that category of responses (the dependent variable) with respect to some other set or sets of data (independent variables). Here the dependent variable would be whether or not the respondent smoked, and the independent variable could be any of several other categories of facts concerning the respondent, say the person's sex. Classifying responses according to these two variables might then result in the simple array shown in table 12.1. (Our survey, needless to say, is imaginary, and all the data derived from it are entirely hypothetical.)

12.5   An array of raw data like this is relatively useless, however: for purposes of comparison the data must be presented in terms of percentages. This has been done in table 12.2. In any statistical table employing percentages (or other proportional figures) the compiler should always give the finite number—the *data base*, or *N*—from which the percentages are derived. Here *N* is given in a separate column, but other arrangements are appropriate.

12.6   Table 12.2 represents an extremely simple statistical situation: both the independent variable (sex) and the dependent variable (smoke / don't smoke) are *dichotomies*—entities that divide into two mutually exclusive categories. When either variable consists of more than two categories, tabular presentation necessarily becomes more complex.

Table 12.1

Smokers and Nonsmokers, by Sex

	Smoke	Don't Smoke	Total
Males	1,258	2,104	3,362
Females	1,194	2,752	3,946
Total	2,452	4,856	7,308

Table 12.2

Smokers and Nonsmokers, by Sex

	N	Smoke	Don't Smoke
Males	3,362	37.4%	62.6%
Females	3,946	30.3%	69.7%
Total	7,308	33.6%	66.4%

12.7   Say the researcher wishes to present the data in terms of age rather than sex. For this purpose birth dates would be grouped by years or spans of years to represent respondents' ages at the time of the survey, and these groups would be divided according to the smoke/don't smoke dichotomy. The results could be presented as in table 12.3. Here age is broken down into four categories, the first three of which consist of fifteen-year spans, but smaller groupings could be used.

Table 12.3

Smoking among American Adults, by Age

Age	N	Smoke (%)	Don't Smoke (%)
18-32	1,722	30.5	69.4
33-47	2,012	37.1	62.9
48-62	1,928	35.2	64.8
63+	1,646	30.5	69.5
Total N	7,308		

12.8   If the author wishes to present the data by both age and sex, the responses would be subdivided once more. The data might then be presented as in table 12.4.

12.9   Actually, let us say, respondents were asked other questions about smoking—whether they had quit smoking or ever tried to quit and (if they smoked at all) whether or not they smoked cigarettes. Presenting these data in meaningful ways would involve expanding the tabular display and making it more complicated.

12.10   Take the data on quitting smoking. If these statistics are to be presented in connection with age and sex as the independent variables, they might be arranged as in table 12.5. Here each half of the basic

Table 12.4

Smoking among American Adults, by Age and Sex

Age and Sex	N	Smoke (%)	Don't Smoke (%)
Males			
18-32	792	30.0	70.0
33-47	926	44.9	55.1
48-62	886	34.5	65.5
63+	758	39.3	60.7
Total (males)	3,362		
Females			
18-32	930	31.0	69.0
33-47	1,086	30.4	69.6
48-62	1,042	35.7	64.3
63+	888	23.0	77.0
Total (females)	3,946		
Total (both)	7,308		

smoke/don't smoke dichotomy has been further split according to whether the respondent has quit smoking or tried to quit. N for each age group also must be split between smokers and nonsmokers. Note that each column of Ns applies to the two columns immediately to the right of it.

12.11 Finally, let us say, our author wants to present the data on cigarette smoking in connection with an element of social background— whether the respondent came from a rural, small-town, or big-city environment—as well as age and sex. (The question eliciting this response would of course have to be a definite one, like "Which of these categories comes closest to the type of place you were living in when you were sixteen years old?"—followed by a listing of various kinds of locales.) Responses are first sorted by age and sex, as for table 12.4, and then by background of the respondent—with "Don't know" answers omitted. The twenty-four groups created by dividing the responses in this manner constitute the data bases for the final dichotomy into those who smoke cigarettes and everybody else (table 12.6). As before, the total in each category is expressed as a percentage of N. Here it is impractical to show Ns in columns of their own, and so another device has been adopted: the N for each category is

Table 12.5

Smoking History of American Adults, by Age and Sex

		Smoke			Don't Smoke	
	N	Have Tried to Quit (%)	Never Tried to Quit (%)	N	Never Smoked Regularly (%)	Quit Success- fully (%)
Males						
18-32	238	15.1	84.9	554	93.9	6.1
33-47	416	28.8	71.2	510	72.2	27.8
48-62	306	60.1	39.9	580	46.6	53.4
63+	298	88.6	11.4	460	38.7	61.3
Total (males)	1,258	48.0	52.0	2,104	63.5	36.5
Females						
18-32	288	18.8	81.2	642	40.3	9.7
33-47	330	28.5	71.5	756	68.5	31.5
48-62	372	62.4	37.6	670	50.4	49.6
63+	204	89.2	10.8	684	41.8	58.2
Total (females)	1,194	47.1	52.9	2,752	62.6	37.4
Total (both)	2,452	47.6	52.4	4,856	45.2	54.8

shown in parentheses below and slightly to the right of the percentage figure. Other arrangements are possible, but this is the one preferred by most people who work with statistics.

ARRANGEMENT OF THE ELEMENTS

12.12 The conventions governing the arrangement of the various elements of a statistical table, though not immutable, are pretty well agreed upon by those who make frequent use of them. Consequently, authors and editors are well advised to follow existing fashion rather than try to set new ones when it comes to the basics of tabular presentation.

12.13 One style that has changed since the last edition of this manual was published is the use of vertical rules in tabular matter. In line with a nearly universal trend among scholarly and commercial publishers, the University of Chicago Press has given up vertical rules as a standard feature of tables in the books and journals that it publishes. The handwork necessitated by including vertical rules is costly no matter what mode of composition is used, and in the Press's view the expense of it can no longer be justified by the additional refinement it brings.

12.14 Anyone preparing a set of tables for publication in a particular journal should inquire about the journal's preferences (or requirements) regarding spacing, centering or flushing of elements, ruling, etc., before

Table 12.6

Smoking among Adult Americans, by Type of

Background, Urban or Rural

	Country (%)	Town, Small City (%)	Big City & Suburbs (%)
Males			
18-32	26.5 (98)	29.6 (294)	29.9 (398)
33-47	34.6 (153)	41.2 (306)	43.0 (460)
48-62	28.6 (220)	31.4 (385)	34.1 (270)
63+	34.8 (273)	35.1 (279)	36.5 (189)
Total (males)	31.8 (744)	34.2 (1,264)	36.3 (1,317)
Females			
18-32	28.4 (116)	31.0 (348)	31.5 (463)
33-47	27.9 (179)	30.6 (359)	31.1 (540)
48-62	27.7 (260)	35.8 (450)	42.3 (319)
63+	21.5 (329)	23.1 (325)	25.8 (213)
Total (females)	25.6 (884)	30.6 (1,482)	32.8 (1,535)
Total (both)	28.4 (1,628)	32.2 (2,746)	34.4 (2,852)

Note: Figures in parentheses are base $\underline{N}$s for the adjacent percentages. Total $\underline{N}$ = 7,226 (3,325 males, 3901 females). Respondents (82) who did not know where they were living at age 16 have been excluded from the data base.

typing final copy. The typing suggestions included in the discussion that follows will result in a simple, flush-left style for most elements of a table (for an alternative and equally acceptable mode see the typing suggestions in 2.23–26). Copy prepared along these lines is acceptable to most publishers of scholarly books—but not necessarily to all journal publishers. Like all copy intended for publication in typeset form, tables should of course be double-spaced in typing; single spacing, however, is permissible for column headings and, in a table consisting of all words, for the tabular items, so long as double space is left between items.

TABLE NUMBER

12.15 Every table should be given a number and should be cited in the text by that number, either directly or parenthetically:

> The wide-ranging nature of the committee's discussions can be judged from the topics enumerated in table 14.
>
> Topics covered by the worker-management committee in three years of deliberations fell into five general categories (table 14).

12.16 References of the type "Table 14 shows . . ." or, worse, "Table 14 proves . . ." are best avoided. Tables show or prove nothing: authors do, with the aid of the statistics or other information included in tables. Even worse, perhaps, are references of the type "Table 14 is a list of . . . ," when this is obvious from a glance at the body or title of the table. References to tables, like discussions of them, should do more than simply describe the table or repeat the facts presented in it. If actual discussion is not necessary, then a simple cross-reference may suffice: "See table 14."

12.17 Tables are numbered in the order in which they are to appear in the text—which should also be the order in which they are first mentioned. Arabic numerals are used, and each table is given a number, even though there may be only a few tables in the work. Tables intended to be compared should be given separate numbers (14, 15, 16, *not* 14a, 14b, 14c).

12.18 Numeration of tables normally continues straight through the text. One exception is a book consisting of individual contributions by different authors. There numeration starts over with each chapter or paper. Another exception is a book, often a textbook or a reference work like this manual, in which text sections, figures, and tables are given double numbers reflecting their locations in the book (see 1.63).

12.19   Tables in an appendix to a book are usually numbered separately from the text (A-1, A-2, A-3, etc.), and if there is more than one appendix, numeration starts over in each (A-1, A-2, . . . , B-1, B-2, . . . , C-1, C-2, . . . , etc.).

12.20   In typing, the table number ("Table 14," for example) should be placed flush left, on a line by itself. (It may be best to finish typing all or part of the table itself before adding the table number and title.)

TITLE

12.21   The title, or caption, set above the body of the table, should identify the table briefly. It should not furnish background information or describe the results illustrated by the table. For example,

```
Effect of DMSO on Arthritic Rats and Nonarthritic

Rats after 20, 60, and 90 Days of Treatment
```

should be pared down to something like

```
Effect of DMSO on Rats
```

The column headings 20, 60, and 90 days and the cross rows for arthritic and nonarthritic rats will give the results. Also, the kind of editorial comment implied by a title like

```
High Degree of Recidivism among Reform School Parolees
```

should be eliminated.

```
Recidivism among Reform School Parolees
```

is sufficient. A table should merely give facts—discussion and comment being reserved for the text.

12.22   Grammatically, the title should be substantival in form. Relative clauses should be avoided in favor of participles. Not

```
Number of Families That Subscribe to Weekly News Magazines
```

but rather,

```
Families Subscribing to Weekly News Magazines
```

12.23   A minor point of usage: in conservative practice, *percent* is still not considered a noun, although colloquially it is commonly so used. Accordingly, a title reading

```
Percent of Cases Diagnosed Correctly
```

should preferably be made to read

```
Percentage [or Proportion] of Cases Diagnosed Correctly
```

12.24   The table title may carry a subheading, usually enclosed in parentheses:

> Investment in Automotive Vehicles since 1900
>
> (In Thousands of Dollars)
>
>
> Effect of Age on Accumulation of PAH by Kidney Slices of
>
> Female Rats
>
> ($\underline{M}$ = 200 μg PAH/cc; $\underline{t}$ = 15 min)

Indication of the number of individuals in a group under consideration (for example, $N = 253$) may be treated as a subheading if it applies to the whole table.

12.25   The table title and subheading (if any) are typed on separate lines, flush left, below the table number. Capitalization may be headline style (as in the foregoing examples) or sentence style (first word and proper names only). Never type a title in full caps.

COLUMN HEADINGS

12.26   A table must have at least two columns and usually has more. The columns carry *headings* (or *heads*—the terms are synonymous) at the top, brief indications of the material in the columns. These were formerly called *boxheadings* or *boxheads,* from the fact that in a fully ruled table they were enclosed in rectangles of rules, or *boxes*. The term is occasionally still heard.

12.27   Like the table title the column headings are substantival in form, and the same grammatical strictures apply to them. If the first column of a table (the *stub,* discussed below) carries a heading, it should be singular in number. The other headings may be singular or plural according to sense.

12.28   Column heads may carry subheadings when they are needed, usually to indicate the unit of measurement employed in the column below. Subheadings are normally enclosed in parentheses, and abbreviations, if used consistently throughout a series of tables, are acceptable: ($), (lb), (%), (mi), ($\times$ 100 km), (millions), and so on. If the columns of a table must be numbered for purposes of text reference, arabic numerals are set in parentheses as subheads.

12.29   The nature of tabular matter sometimes demands two or more levels of headings, and then *decked heads* must be used. A decked head consists of a *spanner head* and the two or more column heads to which it applies. A horizontal rule is set between spanner and column heads to show what columns the spanner applies to (see tables 12.5 and 12.7). Decked heads should seldom exceed two levels, as larger ones are hard to follow down the columns of an unruled table.

12.30   Excessive decking of the heads can sometimes be avoided by using a *cut-in head*—a head that cuts across the statistical columns of the table and applies to all the tabular matter lying below it. For an example of cut-in heads, see table 12.7.

12.31   In typing column heads leave at least two spaces between the widest words in adjacent headings. The width of the column headings generally determines the total width of a table, so they should be kept as brief as possible. Use either headline- or sentence-style capitalization,

Table 12.7

Elections in Gotefrith Province, 1900-1910

Party	1900		1906		1910	
	% of Vote	Seats Won	% of Vote	Seats Won	% of Vote	Seats Won
Provincial Assembly						
Conservative	35.6	47	26.0	37	30.9	52
Socialist	12.4	18	27.1	44	24.8	39
Christian Democrat	49.2	85	41.2	68	39.2	59
Other	2.8	0	5.7	1[a]	5.1	0
Total	100.0	150	100.0	150	100.0	150
National Assembly						
Conservative	32.6	4	23.8	3	28.3	3
Socialist	13.5	1	27.3	3	24.1	2
Christian Democrat	52.1	7	42.8	6	46.4	8
Other	1.8	0	6.1	0	1.2	0
Total	100.0	12	100.0	12	100.0	13[b]

Source: Erewhon National Yearbooks for the years cited.

[a] This one seat was won by a Radical Socialist, who became a member of the Conservative coalition.

[b] Reapportionment in 1910 gave Gotefrith an additional seat in the National Assembly.

and type successive lines flush left. Spanner and cut-in heads, however, must be centered above the columns they pertain to. The column head with the most lines defines the vertical space available for all the heads. In typing, it is simplest to align the last lines of all the other heads horizontally with the last line of the longest one. Any subheads are typed on the line below this one. Rules running the full width of the table are customarily typed or drawn above and below the column heads and any spanners used. The rule below a spanner head is exactly as wide as the column headings spanned, and the rules above and below a cut-in head are exactly as wide as the column heads they apply to (usually just the statistical columns but sometimes the first column as well).

THE STUB

12.32 The left-hand column of a table is known as the *stub*. It is a vertical listing of categories or individuals about which information is given in the columns of the table. It may carry a heading if one is needed, but often the table title makes clear what is in the stub. There is no hard and fast rule about placing one type of variable (dependent or independent) in the stub and the other in the column headings, but once the choice is made, it should be applied consistently to all the tables in the same series.

12.33 Consistency within the stub is also important. Items that are logically similar should be treated similarly: Authors, Publishers, Printers, *not* Authors, Publishing concerns, Operates printshop. In a series of tables, the same item should always bear the same name in the stub: the Union of Soviet Socialist Republics, for instance, should not appear as USSR in one table and Soviet Union in another.

12.34 Items in the stub may form a straight sequential list (as all the states of the Union listed alphabetically) or a classified one (as the states listed by geographic sections). In the latter instance the categories are given as subheadings within the stub. Subheadings may be typed flush left and the items that follow indented two spaces (as in table 12.4). If there are two or more levels of subheads, successive levels are indented successively (see fig. 12.1).

12.35 Stub items are not numbered unless they need to be referred to in the text by number, and ditto marks must never be used. Runover lines are indented two spaces more than the maximum regular indention.

12.36 If the word *Total* appears at the foot of the column, it is indented two spaces more than the greatest indention above it. And if there are subtotals and a grand total, the grand total is given a further indention.

12.37 Leaders (spaced periods following a stub item) should *not* be used; if they are needed in a complicated table to connect stub items and the rows they apply to, they will be supplied by the publisher.

12.38 Capitalization of items in the stub of a table is invariably sentence style, and no periods are used at the ends of items.

```
Amphibians
    Frogs and toads
    Caudates
        Newts
        Salamanders
    Caecilians
Reptiles
    Crocodilians
```

Fig. 12.1. Part of a stub in which successive levels of subheadings are indented successively.

THE BODY

12.39 By the *body* of a table is meant the vertical columns, typically consisting of figures, to the right of the stub and below the column headings. These columns comprise the real substance of the table, the array of information which the rest of the table merely supports and clarifies. They should accordingly be arranged in as clear and orderly a fashion as can be achieved.

12.40 Whenever possible avoid mixing different kinds of information in one column. For instance, place amounts of money in one column, percentages in another, and information expressed in words in another. If a column heading does not apply to one of the items in the stub, that *cell* (as the intersection is called) should be left blank: it is unnecessary to insert *N.A.,* for "not applicable." If there are no data for a particular cell, a dash (two hyphens on the typewriter) or three or more leaders are inserted there. If the quantity in a cell is zero, however, *0* should be typed.

12.41 Attention should be given to the horizontal and vertical alignment of the information in the columns. Horizontally, each cell aligns with the item in the stub to which it applies. If the stub item occupies more than one line and the column entry one line, align on the last line of the stub item. If both contain more than one line, align first lines.

12.42 Vertically, align a column of figures on the decimal points and commas (figures of 1,000 or more should have commas). Dollar signs and percentage signs are aligned, and in a column containing all the same kinds of figures they are used only at the top of the column and after any horizontal rule cutting across it. Or if the table title or column head shows what the figures are, the signs are omitted. Mathematical operating signs ($+$, $-$, $<$, $=$, etc.) are aligned if they precede quantities in a column of figures. If all figures in a column begin with a zero to the left of the decimal point, all the zeros (in conservative practice, all but the first and last) may be omitted. When practicable, all decimal fractions in a column ought to be carried to the same number of places.

12.43   In a column consisting of information expressed in words, appearance governs vertical alignment. If all the items are short, they could be centered in the column. Longer items generally look best if they are flush left.

12.44   When a table includes totals at the feet of some or all of the columns, either a horizontal rule or a blank line is placed above the totals. If a rule is used, it cuts across the body columns but not the stub. Subtotals, averages, and means are similarly treated, and if the table continues below these figures, another rule or blank line separates them from the continuation.

12.45   Totals at the feet of columns of percentages present special problems. They may be included or not, according to how useful they are to the presentation. When the percentages in the column are based on different Ns, a final percentage based on the total N may be elucidating, and if so it should be included (see table 12.2 and others in that series). When the percentages in a column are all based on the same N (as in table 12.7), the total may also be given, to show that nothing has been left out, or the total may be omitted as unnecessary. If the total is given, the actual total (which may be 99.9% or 100.2% or some other figure) should be given, not a pro forma 100.0%. Discrepancies due to rounding often cause such a total to be slightly more or slightly less than 100.0%. If totals are off for this reason, a note explaining why should be appended to the table in which the discrepancy first occurs. It need not be repeated in other tables of a series.

FOOTNOTES

12.46   Footnotes to a table are of four general kinds and should appear in this order: (1) source notes, (2) other general notes, (3) notes on specific parts of the table, and (4) notes on level of probability. If data for a table are not the author's own but are taken from another source, the author will wish to include a source note, introduced by the word *Source(s):*

Source: Michael H. Day, Guide to Fossil Man, 3d ed.
(Chicago: University of Chicago Press, 1977), 291-304.

12.47 Other unnumbered notes, applying to the table as a whole, follow and are introduced by the word *Note(s)*. These might include remarks on reliability of the data presented or how they were gathered or handled; when practical, such notes should be gathered into one paragraph. If the entire table is reproduced without change from another source, credit is best given in a general note such as that illustrated in the second of the following examples:

Notes: Since data were not available for all items on all individuals, there is some disparity in the totals. This table may be compared with table 14, which presents similar data for Cincinnati, Ohio.

Note: Reprinted, by permission of the publisher, from Ana-Maria Rizzuto, "Freud, God, the Devil, and the Theory of Object Representation," International Review of Psycho-Analysis 31 (1976): 165.

12.48 For notes on specific parts of a table, superior letters, beginning again in each table with *a*, are usually employed as reference marks. They may be used on the column headings, the stub items, and the body of the table, but not on the table number or title. Any note applying to the number or title would be a general note and should be so treated. The reference marks are placed on the table in whatever order the reader will find easiest to follow, normally beginning at the upper left and extending across the table and downward, row by row. The same mark may be used on two or more elements if the corresponding note applies to them.

12.49 For a table consisting only of words superior numbers could be used as reference marks (though even here letters are quite usual), and for a table that includes mathematical or chemical equations a series of arbitrary symbols may be used, because of the danger of mistaking letters or figures for exponents. The series is as follows:

* (asterisk or star), † (dagger), ‡ (double dagger), § (section mark), ‖ (parallels), # (number sign)

When more symbols are needed, these may be doubled and tripled in the same sequence:

, ††, ‡‡, §§, ‖ ‖, ##, *, †††, ‡‡‡, §§§, ‖ ‖ ‖, ###

12.50 In notes to tables the reference marks—letters, numbers, or symbols—are conventionally placed in superior position, not on the line as numbers generally are in textual notes. The reason for this may be not simple conservatism but a desire to avoid the appearance of an enumeration when lettered or numbered notes follow a general note.

12.51 If a table contains values for which levels of probability are given, a fourth type of note is used, following the other specific notes. By convention asterisks are used for these notes, both on the value in the body of the table and before the note at the foot. A single asterisk is used for the lowest level of probability, two for the next higher, and so on, with the specific levels being given in the notes below:

*$p < .05$.   **$p < .01$.   ***$p < .001$.

12.52 Footnotes are typed below the body of the table, double spaced and flush left. An extra blank line should be left between notes.

ESTIMATING SIZE AND CORRECTING ODD SHAPES

12.53 In planning a table an author should give attention to its physical dimensions, making sure that it does not exceed the limits imposed by the printed page. If a table is intended for journal publication, the editor can give an author the maximum dimensions of tables for that journal. These will be expressed in terms of typewriter characters for width and a certain number of lines for depth.

12.54 For book publication a maximum width of about 85 characters and a maximum depth of about 60 lines are safe limits for vertical 8-point tables in a book measuring 6 inches by 9 inches. In other words, if a table is typed the ordinary way, in elite type, double-spaced, on 8½-by-11-inch paper, with one-inch margins, a full-page table in typescript will make a half-page table when set the ordinary way. In counting characters for width, one must allow at least two characters for space between column headings, with no overlapping, and indentions in the stub must be at least two characters. In counting lines for the depth of the table, one must include the table number and title and all blank lines in the count; any horizontal rules count as one line each. For a *broadside* table (one that runs the long way of the page) safe maximums are 135 characters in width and 45 lines in depth. Both vertical and broadside tables can continue on another page, of course:

335

depth alone—the number of lines in the table—is seldom a serious problem in fitting a table onto the printed page.

12.55   The significant factor is the width of the table, and this is controlled by the number of columns and the width of the material in them. If a table is too wide to run vertically, the editor or designer may elect to run it broadside (some journals, however, will not accept broadside tables). If it is still too wide, they may decide to run it vertically across two pages or set it in smaller type—perhaps 7- or 6-point instead of 8-point—or both. But this is the limit. There are no further remedies for a table that is too wide except to print it separately on a large sheet of paper and bind it in the book as a foldout insert. This is an extremely expensive operation, and something no publisher is likely to do except for a very important table in a very important book.

12.56   The shape of a table, as well as its overall size, is something else an author should keep in mind while working on tables in the draft stage. No publisher is happy to see a long, narrow table, two or three columns wide and half a page deep, or a shallow, wide one that must be printed broadside. Both waste a great deal of expensive white space on the printed page. The remedy for a long skinny table is to double it up—run the table in two halves side by side, with the column heads repeated over the second half (see table 12.8). For a wide, shallow table the remedy is applied the other way round—divide column heads and the material under them in two, and run one half over the other, with the stub items repeated for the lower half. This works best when column heads are repeated (as in tables 12.6 or 12.7) but can be made to work even if they are not. Another possible solution is to turn the table around, making column heads of the stub items and stub items

Table 12.8

Relative Contents of Odd Isotopes for Heavy Elements

Element	z	γ	Element	z	γ
Sm	62	1.48	W	74	0.505
Gd	64	0.691	Os	76	0.811
Dy	66	0.930	Pt	78	1.160
Eb	68	0.759	Hg	80	0.500
Yb	70	0.601	Pb	82	0.550
Hf	72	0.440			

of the column heads; if the table turns out to be too long and narrow that way, it can then be doubled up.

SPECIAL TYPES OF TABLES

12.57   Statistical tables and enumerations are the commonest types of tabular matter employed in scholarly work, but there are many other kinds as well. Some of these are illustrated below.

MATRIX

12.58   A matrix is designed to show mutual or reciprocal relationships within a group of individuals, which may be made up of human beings, animals (as in table 12.9), or even concepts. In a matrix the column headings and the stub items are identical, and there may or may not be totals for the vertical columns and horizontal rows. A matrix works best with an absolute minimum of ruling.

TABLE 12.9

Observations of Mutual Grooming by
Age and Sex Classes

	ANIMALS GROOMED					
ANIMALS GROOMING	Silver-backed male	Black-backed male	Female	Juvenile	Infant	TOTAL
Silver-backed male	0	0	0	0	3	3
Black-backed male	0	0	0	0	0	0
Female	0	1	5	13	76	95
Juvenile	1	1	9	10	12	33
Infant	0	0	2	0	1	3
TOTAL	1	2	16	23	92	134

TABLE IN WORDS

12.59   A very complex discussion in the text of an article or book can often be lucidly illustrated and simplified by use of a "visual aid" such as table 12.10. Alignment of the items in such a table is discussed in 12.42 and 12.44.

TABLE 12.10

Role-Style Differentiae in the Lewin, Lippitt, and
White "Group Atmosphere" Studies

Authoritarian	Democratic	Laissez-faire
All determination of policy by leader	All policies a matter of group discussion and decision, encouraged and assisted by the leader	Complete freedom for group or individual decision, with a minimum of leader participation
Techniques and activity steps dictated by the authority, one at a time, so that future steps were uncertain to a large degree	Activity perspective gained during discussion period. General steps to group goal sketched, and when technical advice was needed the leader suggested two or more alternative procedures from which choice could be made	Various materials supplied by leader, who made it clear that he would supply information when asked. He took no other part in work discussion
Leader usually dictated the task and companion of each member	Members were free to work with whomever they chose, and division of tasks was left to the group	Complete nonparticipation of the leader
Leader tended to be "personal" in his praise and criticism of each member's work; remained aloof from active group participation except when demonstrating	Leader was "objective" in his praise and criticism, and tried to be a regular group member in spirit without doing too much work	Leader did not comment on member activities unless questioned, did not attempt to appraise or regulate the course of events

GENEALOGICAL TABLE

12.60   A pedigree (not illustrated here) is a simple table showing the ancestry of one individual—human being or purebred animal—in a branching array of names. No attempt is made to avoid repetitions: if the same individual appears twice among the eight great-grandparents or sixteen great-great-grandparents, the name is simply repeated. A genealogical table like table 12.11 is considerably more complex. Such a table attempts to show important relationships within a family or several families by means of branching and connecting lines. If possible, names are not repeated. Equals signs show marriages or liaisons, and usually all children are listed or noted. A good genealogical table takes careful planning so that it shows the intended relationships without crossing lines and stays within a reproducible shape and size.

GENETIC TABLE

12.61   Somewhat analogous to pedigrees and genealogical tables are the genetic tables designed to show the results of cross-breeding in plants or animals according to Mendelian principles (see table 12.12). Here

TABLE 12.11

THE FAMILY OF GALLA PLACIDIA AUGUSTA

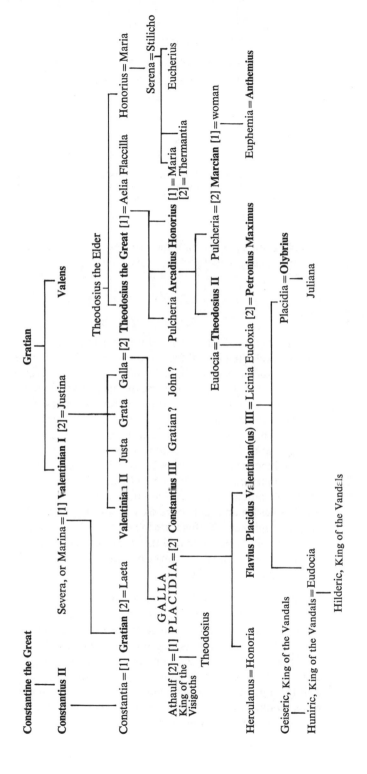

NOTE: Stemma are simplified. Emperors are shown in boldface type.

TABLE 12.12

MENDELIAN CROSS: COCKER SPANIEL AND BASENJI

CS ♀, Cocker Spaniel × BA ♂, Basenji   CS ♂, Cocker Spaniel, × BA ♀, Basenji

⌐× —BCSF₁ ♂ × BCSF₁ ♀   CSB ♀ × CSB ♂ — ×⌐
         ↓   ↓   ↓
BCS × CS   BCSF₂   CSBF₂   CSB × BA

BACKCROSS TO COCKER   BACKCROSS TO BASENJI

BCS CROSS   *CSB CROSS*

NOTE: The basic plan was to repeat each of the two crosses with four matings and obtain two litters from each mating. Because of deaths among the cocker spaniel females, replication was completed only three times in the BCS cross.

multiplication signs indicate the crosses and symbols and abbreviations the genetic makeup of the individual.

EDITING TABLES

12.62 Editing a series of tables should be little more than a simple job of markup, and often it is. If the author is unfamiliar with the principles of good tabular presentation, however, the manuscript editor may have to pitch in and help, showing the author how to recast a table or even doing it for the author. The commonest errors are probably inconsistency—as, for example, when a given variable is listed in the column headings in one table and in the stub in another—and constructing sprawling or misshapen tables that are difficult or impossible to reproduce in type. Often a table that is technically acceptable may still be improved in appearance and made to occupy less space with no loss of content or impact. The editor may wish to review the entire set of tables for an article or book with this in mind before turning to the job of markup. At this time the editor will also want to check all tables for their relevance and freedom from duplication. Tables are expensive to set, and if any can be eliminated or combined, this should be suggested to the author.

12.63 It is mainly in bookwork that an editor or designer has any latitude concerning the type dress of a set of tables. Every journal that accepts tables (not all do) has its own style for tables, as for other editorial elements, and this style is seldom if ever departed from. In books, tables are usually set in the same typeface as the body of the book—and in a book containing a great many tables a typeface that works well for tabular setting (like Times Roman) is often chosen for the whole book. Most tables are set in 8-point type, with footnotes (and sometimes column headings) in 7-point.

12.64　　The table number and the title are set in the same point size as the body of the table, normally 8-point. If there is a subheading it may be set in a smaller size or different style (such as italic with a roman title). All headings—column heads, spanners, and cut-in heads—are treated alike as to type size and style, usually 8-point roman, but 7-point can be used if space must be conserved. Apart from these conventions, there are a good many options open to the designer or editor in the treatment of these elements (the same treatment is usually given to both the title and the table headings).

12.65　　In alignment, the choice is between flush style (normally flush left) and centered style. If flush-left style is adopted, the table number and the title are aligned with the left edge of the table, and each column heading is aligned within the space allotted to it. (As noted earlier, spanner heads and cut-in heads must be centered over the columns they apply to, even when flush style is used for the column heads.) If centered style is used, the table number and title are centered, one over the other, above the whole table, and column heads are each centered within the available space. With centered style, column heads of different lengths usually "float" within the vertical space given them, whereas with flush style their last lines ordinarily align across the page, but there is no set rule for this.

12.66　　In type style, roman is usual, and there are two main options for titles and column headings: caps and small caps or caps and lowercase. Both work well. Caps and small caps are more formal, caps and lowercase more informal and (some think) more modern. The word TABLE may be set in full caps, but titles and headings should never be: full caps take up too much room and are hard to read. For some kinds of tables italic or boldface may work for titles; but both are hard to read in large doses and difficult to handle aesthetically, so it is better not to use them for column heads. The expression N, which appears frequently in headings, must always be set either as an italic cap or (roman) small cap (N or N).

12.67　　In capitalizing titles and headings, one can choose between the traditional headline style (The Anatomy of Dissent) and the more "contemporary" sentence style (The anatomy of dissent). The former works with any type style, but the latter looks best with caps and lowercase.

THE STUB AND THE BODY

12.68　　Fewer options are open in the design of the stub and body of a table. Both are set in the same size and style of type, normally 8-point roman caps and lowercase. Capitalization is sentence style in both.

12.69 In the stub, subheads are sometimes set in italic and may be centered in the column or set flush left. The style in which the manuscript is typed need not be followed if an alternate is preferable. In flush-left style, stub items are usually indented one em under the subhead. Runovers in stub items are indented one em from where they begin; subtotals and totals are each indented one further em.

12.70 With two or more levels of subheads in the stub, it is often better not to rely solely on indention for distinguishing levels, or the stub may grow disproportionately wide. The top level may be centered and the second level flush left, or different type may be used (small caps, italic, roman) and everything kept flush left. Another solution is to use cut-in heads for the top-level subheads (in this case the rules above and below the cut-in heads extend across the stub as well as the body of the table). When stub items are long, space can often be saved by *not* indenting the runovers; extra space must then be left between items.

12.71 One of the things to watch for in editing a table is the alignment of stub items with the rows they govern and the vertical alignment of the elements within the columns. These considerations are discussed (from the author's point of view) in earlier sections of this chapter (12.42–44). If leaders seem necessary to make alignment clear, they may be used after stub items. Leaders may also be used in empty cells, but centered em dashes are more usual nowadays.

FOOTNOTES

12.72 Footnotes are normally set one size smaller than the body of a table (i.e., 7-point with an 8-point table). Long notes run the full width of the table, but short notes may be set two or more to the line. Notes may be set paragraph style or flush left, and in the latter case a point or two of leading should be used between notes. The words *Source(s)* and *Note(s)* are traditionally distinguished typographically from the note that follows, either by caps and small caps or italic caps and lowercase (SOURCE; *Source*).

12.73 As noted earlier, reference marks on specific notes are conventionally set in superior position, and the series starts over for each table. (Occasionally an inexperienced author will integrate table notes and textual notes. If this happens, the editor has simply got to dis-integrate them.)

RULING

12.74 Some of the ruling in a table is functional, but much of it is aesthetic and can be so handled. The rule below a spanner head is functional: it makes clear just which columns of the table are governed by the head. It is also possible to make this clear by using additional space to the right and left of the columns affected, but it is much easier to accomplish the same thing with the rule. A rule above a row of totals is traditional, but a blank line works just as well if that is preferred—so, too, below the totals if the table continues. The full-width rules at the top and bottom of a table are also traditional, but aesthetically they are harder to dispense with than internal rules. Individual tables in a series often vary greatly in size, shape, and configuration, and the only thing tying them together visually is the pair of rules at top and bottom. The rules in a conventional table are usually half-point rules, but rules of any size consistent with the design of a book can be used, especially for those that are nonfunctional.

COPYFITTING LARGE TABLES

12.75   An important part of an editor's job in handling a series of tables is to foresee production problems and solve them before the tables get as far as the typesetting stage. The commonest problem is size—the table that is too big for the space available for it. Tables are generally set to fit within the *type page* area (see 20.39) of the publication. If the outer (fore-edge) margin is fairly wide, a pica or two is often stolen from it to accommodate a wide vertical table, but the inner (back) margin is usually too narrow to permit encroachment. For a full-page table the area occupied by the running head at the top of the page may be utilized (running heads are not set on pages with full-page tables), and when necessary, part of the deep bottom (tail) margin may be encroached upon. Some of the ways of handling extrawide tables have been discussed in connection with compiling tables (12.54–55), as have techniques for dealing with tables that are oddly shaped (12.56).

12.76   *Wide tables.* If you have a table that looks too wide, the first thing to do is to measure the width of the table in terms of typewriter characters. Count every character in the widest stub item and in the columns or column headings, whichever is wider, and allow two characters for space between columns. If the total is 100 and your type page allows 85 characters for a table, some squeezing is in order. (If you do not know the allowable width in characters, you can multiply the width of the type page in picas by three for the equivalent in typewriter characters: most 8-point faces set about three characters per pica.)

12.77   You may be able to save the requisite number of characters by running over some of the stub items, by dividing words in the column headings, or by introducing abbreviations. A few characters of excess width may be accommodated by setting column heads one size smaller. Consider, also, whether the stub can be narrowed by any of the devices discussed above in connection with editing stub items (12.70). In an emergency you can have the type in the column headings set on edge, so they read up the page rather than across, but this is undesirable if any other solution is available, because vertical heads are hard to read.

12.78   If the number of characters across a table greatly exceeds the available width of the type page, the table will have to run broadside, or vertically on facing pages, as described earlier. Measuring for this kind of placement can be done the same way, only with different limits on the allowable space. Remember that in a broadside table the headings must read *up* the page, not down.

12.79   *Long tables.* An extralong table of normal width is not so much of a problem to deal with, because it can be continued on successive pages. There are some conventions for setting continued tables, however, that have to be observed.

12.80   Continued lines are used as needed, the one at the foot of a page reading, perhaps,

> *Continued on next page*

and the one at the top of a page reading (for example),

> Table 14—*Continued*

12.81   For a vertical table the column heads are repeated on each page, but the title is not. For a broadside table the column headings are repeated only on the verso page, and the columns of the table jump over the back margins of the pages to continue on the recto. *Continued* lines are then placed only where they are needed.

12.82   In a continued table containing columns of figures representing money, with totals at the end, it is usual to strike subtotals at the foot of any page except the last. These subtotals appear below a rule or a blank line opposite a stub entry *Carried forward*. At the head of the next page they are repeated opposite a stub entry *Brought forward*.

12.83   Footnotes in a continued table must be divided up according to what they refer to. Source notes and other general notes are placed at the foot of the first page or two-page spread. Specific notes are preferably placed on the pages to which they apply, or if need be, they can be gathered at the end of the whole table.

12.84   In marking up a long table for typesetting the editor should circle the repeated column headings on all manuscript pages but the first (meaning ''do not set''), as the page breaks will probably not come at these points. A note to the typesetter should explain what headings and continued lines are wanted on the runover parts of the table.

EXAMPLES OF TABLE STYLE

12.85   There was a time when all tables tended to look pretty much alike, but that is no longer true. In the examples that follow the same table has been set in several different styles to show what can be done within the rather strict confines of tabular presentation. Specifications are given for each example.

Table 12.13

Typeface:	Times Roman
Table number:	8/9 bold caps and lowercase
Title:	8/9 bold caps and lowercase (indented 6 picas and set in two lines, flush left)
Column heads:	8/9
Body and stub:	8/9
Notes:	8/9 flush left with 2 points of leading between entries
Ruling:	Hairline rules, horizontal only

Table 12.13   **Wages by Skill Level and Nationality, 1971 (Thousand CFA Francs per Month)**

Skill Category	Median Wage[a]				Minimum Wage[b]
	Ivor	MA	NA	Average	
Management					
Direction	104.5	61.8	191.2	174.6	—
Cadre	105.3	114.9	185.5	165.3	61.4–144.5
Skilled labor					
Supervisory	57.5	60.1	143.6	73.0	38.8–64.2
White-collar	34.8	34.8	90.1	38.8	22.8–38.9
Blue-collar	26.6	26.0	71.9	26.5	18.0–39.7
Unskilled labor[c]					
Semiskilled white-collar	19.2	15.3	—	17.0	10.1–17.5
Semiskilled blue-collar	17.8	15.9	—	17.1	12.6–15.8
Unskilled	12.8	8.7	—	9.7	10.1–11.5

Sources: RCI Ministère du Plan (1973), vol. 2, various tables; RCI Ministère du Plan (1972).

[a] Ivor = Ivorians; MA = migrant Africans; NA = non-Africans.

[b] The range given is for the various skill categories within each occupational level for a person with less than three years' experience. For *cadres*, the work week is forty-eight hours. There is no minimum wage for the direction category in the private sector.

[c] Data for apprentices were not available.

346

Table 12.14

Typeface:	Baskerville
Table number:	9/10 caps, centered
Title:	9/10 caps and lowercase italic, centered
Column heads:	Top level, 8/9 caps and small caps; lower level, 8/9 caps and lowercase
Body and stub:	8/9
Notes:	7/9 flush left with 2 points of leading between entries
Ruling:	Hairline rules, horizontal only

TABLE 12.14

Wages by Skill Level and Nationality, 1971 (Thousand CFA Francs per Month)

	MEDIAN WAGE[a]				
SKILL CATEGORY	Ivor	MA	NA	Average	MINIMUM WAGE[b]
Management					
Direction	104.5	61.8	191.2	174.6	—
Cadre	105.3	114.9	185.5	165.3	61.4–144.5
Skilled labor					
Supervisory	57.5	60.1	143.6	73.0	38.8–64.2
White-collar	34.8	34.8	90.1	38.8	22.8–38.9
Blue-collar	26.6	26.0	71.9	26.5	18.0–39.7
Unskilled labor[c]					
Semiskilled white-collar	19.2	15.3	—	17.0	10.1–17.5
Semiskilled blue-collar	17.8	15.9	—	17.1	12.6–15.8
Unskilled	12.8	8.7	—	9.7	10.1–11.5

Sources: RCI Ministère du Plan (1973), vol. 2, various tables; RCI Ministère du Plan (1972).

[a]Ivor = Ivorians; MA = migrant Africans; NA = non-Africans.

[b]The range given is for the various skill categories within each occupational level for a person with less than three years' experience. For *cadres*, the work week is forty-eight hours. There is no minimum wage for the direction category in the private sector.

[c]Data for apprentices were not available.

347

Table 12.15

Typeface:	Garamond
Table number:	9/10 caps, flush left
Title:	9/10 caps and small caps, flush left
Column heads:	Top level, 8/9 caps and small caps; lower level, 8/9 caps and lowercase
Body and stub:	9/10
Notes:	8/9 with paragraph indents
Ruling:	Hairline rules, horizontal only
	Note: Garamond appears slightly *smaller* than other typefaces of the same point size.

TABLE 12.15

WAGES BY SKILL LEVEL AND NATIONALITY, 1971
(THOUSAND CFA FRANCS PER MONTH)

	MEDIAN WAGE[a]				
SKILL CATEGORY	Ivor	MA	NA	Average	MINIMUM WAGE[b]
Management					
Direction	104.5	61.8	191.2	174.6	—
Cadre	105.3	114.9	185.5	165.3	61.4–144.5
Skilled labor					
Supervisory	57.5	60.1	143.6	73.0	38.8–64.2
White-collar	34.8	34.8	90.1	38.8	22.8–38.9
Blue-collar	26.6	26.0	71.9	26.5	18.0–39.7
Unskilled labor[c]					
Semiskilled white-collar	19.2	15.3	—	17.0	10.1–17.5
Semiskilled blue-collar	17.8	15.9	—	17.1	12.6–15.8
Unskilled	12.8	8.7	—	9.7	10.1–11.5

SOURCES: RCI Ministère du Plan (1973), vol. 2, various tables; RCI Ministère du Plan (1972).
[a]Ivor = Ivorians; MA = migrant Africans; NA = non-Africans.
[b]The range given is for the various skill categories within each occupational level for a person with less than three years' experience. For *cadres,* the work week is forty-eight hours. There is no minimum wage for the direction category in the private sector.
[c]Data for apprentices were not available.

Table 12.16

Typeface:	Helvetica
Table number:	8/9 bold caps, flush left
Title:	8/9 bold caps and lowercase, flush left
Column heads:	Top level, 7/8 caps; lower level, 7/8 caps and lowercase
Body and stub:	8/9, flush stub entries bold caps and lowercase; indented stub entries caps and lowercase
Notes:	7/8 with paragraph indentions
Ruling:	Hairline rules, horizontal only
	Note: Helvetica appears slightly *larger* than other typefaces of the same point size

TABLE 12.16

Wages by Skill Level and Nationality, 1971 (Thousand CFA Francs per Month)

	MEDIAN WAGE[a]				
SKILL CATEGORY	Ivor	MA	NA	Average	MINIMUM WAGE[b]
Management					
Direction	104.5	61.8	191.2	174.6	—
Cadre	105.3	114.9	185.5	165.3	61.4–144.5
Skilled labor					
Supervisory	57.5	60.1	143.6	73.0	38.8–64.2
White-collar	34.8	34.8	90.1	38.8	22.8–38.9
Blue-collar	26.6	26.0	71.9	26.5	18.0–39.7
Unskilled labor[c]					
Semiskilled white-collar	19.2	15.3	—	17.0	10.1–17.5
Semiskilled blue-collar	17.8	15.9	—	17.1	12.6–15.8
Unskilled	12.8	8.7	—	9.7	10.1–11.5

Sources: RCI Ministère du Plan (1973), vol. 2, various tables; RCI Ministère du Plan (1972).

[a]Ivor = Ivorians; MA = migrant Africans; NA = non-Africans.

[b]The range given is for the various skill categories within each occupational level for a person with less than three years' experience. For *cadres,* the work week is forty-eight hours. There is no minimum wage for the direction category in the private sector.

[c]Data for apprentices were not available.

Table 12.17

Typefaces: IBM typewriter, 10-pitch Delegate and 12-pitch Light Italic, both typed at 12 pitch (i.e., 12 characters to the inch) on a Selectric I machine. Copy was typed to a width of 79 characters (39½ picas, approximately) and reduced photographically one-third.

Rules are Delegate underlining, raised half a line to center the lines, as are the "em dashes" in columns 4 and 6. The "en dashes" used with the continued numbers in column 6 are hyphens from the Light Italic font, slightly wider than the Delegate hyphens.

Vertical spacing is all straight single-line or double-line spacing, except between the three principal categories listed in the stub, where a half-line space was used.

TABLE 12.17   Wages by Skill Level and Nationality, 1971
(Thousand CFA Francs per Month)

Skill Category	Median Wage[a]				Minimum Wage[b]
	Ivor	MA	NA	Average	
Management					
Direction	104.5	61.8	191.2	174.6	—
Cadre	105.3	114.9	185.5	165.3	61.4–144.5
Skilled labor					
Supervisory	57.5	60.1	143.6	73.0	38.8–64.2
White-collar	34.8	34.8	90.1	38.8	22.8–38.9
Blue-collar	26.6	26.0	71.9	26.5	18.0–39.7
Unskilled labor[c]					
Semiskilled white-collar	19.2	15.3	—	17.0	10.1–17.5
Semiskilled blue-collar	17.8	15.9	—	17.1	12.6–15.8
Unskilled	12.8	8.7	—	9.7	10.1–11.5

Sources: RCI Ministère du Plan (1973), vol. 2, various tables; RCI Ministère du Plan (1972).

[a]Ivor = Ivorians; MA = migrant Africans; NA = non-Africans.

[b]The range given is for the various skill categories within each occupational level for a person with less than three years' experience. For *cadres*, the work week is forty-eight hours. There is no minimum wage for the direction category in the private sector.

[c]Data for apprentices were not available.

13 *Mathematics in Type*

Composition 13.3
Signs and Symbols, the First Problem 13.10
    The List of Symbols and Special Characters 13.11
    Substitutions for Easier Composition 13.14
    Unusual Type Sizes 13.16
Manuscript Preparation 13.17
    Style and General Usage 13.20
        Punctuation 13.23
        Numeration 13.25
        Signs of aggregation 13.27
    Difficult Expressions 13.29
        Fractions 13.30
        Vectors 13.32
        Overbars 13.33
        Exponents 13.34
    Breaking Displayed Equations 13.35
    Illustrations 13.39
Marking Mathematical Copy 13.41
    Italic Type 13.41
    Letters in Nonitalic Type 13.42
        Abbreviations 13.42
        Single letters 13.43
        Using correct terminology 13.44
    Definitions, Theorems, Proofs, etc. 13.45
    Marking for Clarity 13.47
        Mistaken identity 13.51
For Further Reference 13.53

13.1   Mathematics is known in the printing trade as *difficult,* or *penalty, copy* because it is slower, more difficult, and more expensive to set in type than any other kind of copy normally occurring in books and journals. The uninformed author, by exercising poor judgment in selecting notation and by ignoring precepts of good manuscript preparation, can add enormously to the cost of setting mathematical material in type. Book and journal editors are continually faced with this problem and may even in a borderline case have to reject a manuscript for such nonmathematical considerations.

13.2   This chapter will attempt to explain some of the common problems that arise in setting technical material and to suggest ways in which these problems can be solved or circumvented. The chapter is intended for authors, who are often unfamiliar with techniques of type-setting, and for copyeditors, who seldom are blessed with a mathematical background. For more on typesetting and printing in general see chapter 20.

COMPOSITION

13.3   The advent of sophisticated phototypesetting systems has revolution-ized the setting of mathematical copy in recent years. Many expres-sions and arrangements of expressions that formerly were impossible or very difficult to set are now relatively easy to achieve. Not every manuscript involving mathematical expressions is necessarily set with such a system, however, and authors and editors should have some idea of what they can expect of the particular typesetting system em-ployed for the manuscript in hand.

13.4   Typesetting systems can be thought of on four levels of sophistication so far as their mathematical capabilities are concerned. Least sophis-ticated are the systems designed for setting straight matter. These in-clude hot-metal systems such as Linotype and Intertype and phototypesetting systems such as Compuwriter I or II, equipped only with "reader" fonts—fonts intended for ordinary book and job work. Also included at this level of sophistication is the ordinary office type-writer. Mathematical copy of an elementary sort *can* be set with such a system if it is to be printed by offset (as almost everything is nowa-days), but only with a good deal of handwork on the reproduction proofs or the typescript. In typewriter work of this sort superior and inferior expressions necessarily appear in the same size of type as the expressions to which they are attached.

13.5   On the second level of sophistication is the "math" typewriter. This is usually an IBM Selectric machine equipped with an assortment of "golf ball" heads capable of typing many of the symbols and alphabets used in mathematics, as well as a head for typing straight matter. A mathematics head makes available almost all the most commonly used symbols, but oversize characters, like large summation and in-tegral signs, as well as any esoteric characters, must be drawn in on the typescript. Typewriter composition is not as "efficient" as type-setting—a book page of math printed from copy prepared on the type-writer will contain scarcely more than half as much material as a similar typeset page—but it offers an attractive alternative to the more sophisticated (and expensive) methods described below when costs must be kept down.

13.6   On the third level is the classic hot-metal Four-Line Mathematics system of the Monotype Corporation. This system produces elegant work using a very wide range of symbols and alphabets. A good deal of the makeup can be done by the operator at the keyboard, but most displayed equations must be set twice to get the spacing right. Rules and extralarge (more than 14-point) braces, brackets, summation signs, integrals, etc., must be inserted by hand. Corrections are relatively easy to make in the metal type because the Monotype system produces individual pieces of type that can be picked out by hand "on the stone" and replaced by the correct characters. The chief disadvantages of Monotype are first, that fewer and fewer typesetting houses offer it, and second, that producing new, unlisted characters is extremely expensive and time-consuming.

13.7   Phototypesetting systems have largely taken over mathematical setting at this level of sophistication. These systems use film negatives of type characters to produce a positive photographic image on paper of the composition. This is used as a "repro proof" for printing by the offset method. Phototypesetting generally requires that mathematical copy be set twice to get alignment and spacing correct. Corrections are made by resetting all or part of an equation and pasting the correct version over the incorrect one. Film negatives of new characters are fairly easy to produce, though there may be a delay of a few weeks before they are available.

13.8   On the fourth level of sophistication are the electronic typesetting machines that generate type characters, from information stored digitally in a computer, on the face of a cathode-ray tube, from which they are transferred photographically to a paper print. Systems employing electronic typesetters are only as sophisticated as the computer programs used to drive them, but some of these are very sophisticated indeed. For example, the PENTA mathematics program, used for setting this chapter, is capable of making a wide variety of decisions regarding spacing and alignment and can handle characters of any size. Equations need be keyboarded only once. New characters, provided suitable copy is available, can be converted to digital form and added to the type font with little trouble.

13.9   *All* mathematics composition, it should be emphasized, is expensive. Older systems were expensive, and the advent of electronic setting has made little difference in the cost of setting a page of complicated mathematics. Math composition requires time—operators' time, which is expensive, and computer time, which is even more so—and math setting uses more of both than almost any other kind of composition. The moral here is, of course, to make the setting of our mathematical copy as easy and as un-time-consuming as it can be made.

SIGNS AND SYMBOLS, THE FIRST PROBLEM

13.10 Whatever the mode of composition employed, setting high-level mathematics is bound to present some problems with signs and symbols, problems that the author and editor should face as early as possible. Typesetters who specialize in mathematics have fonts containing all the traditional characters needed for this kind of work, and many of the more specialized ones, but no fonts contain all the possible variants. The number of special signs and symbols is almost limitless, and new ones are constantly being introduced. Typesetters are understandably reluctant to make available every new character, as many of them will be used only rarely, and generating a totally new character always requires additional time and expense—in Monotype a great deal of both.

THE LIST OF SYMBOLS AND SPECIAL CHARACTERS

13.11 Before editing begins, either the author or the copyeditor, preferably the former, should prepare a list of all mathematical symbols and special characters in the manuscript. For any unusual or new characters the first and last pages on which they occur should be given, along with an estimate of how many times they are used.

13.12 A copy of the list should then be given to the production controller, who will check with the typesetter to make sure the necessary sorts are available. If some are not, the author may be asked to try to employ some more accessible forms, or if that is impossible, the typesetter must be asked to obtain or generate the sorts that are needed.

13.13 Waiting until the manuscript is edited and ready for composition before inquiring about needed symbols may result in frustrating production delays, especially if hot-metal composition is being used. The typesetter may then need three months or more to obtain the needed characters.

SUBSTITUTIONS FOR EASIER COMPOSITION

13.14 It may also be advisable for the editor to suggest to the author other substitutions that can facilitate composition. A number of "embellished," or accented, characters are readily available, including, for example, $\dot{a}$, $\ddot{a}$, $\bar{a}$, $\bar{\bar{a}}$, $\tilde{a}$, and $\hat{a}$. Embellishments under an ordinary italic letter may be troublesome to set—$\underline{a}$, $a̠$, $a̡$, for example—as may embellished characters from other alphabets, such as roman or Greek. Frequently, some easily set character can be substituted, such as a character with the embellishment at one side or the other: $a\uparrow$, $a\downarrow$, a', a'', $'a$, $''a$, $a*$, $a\dagger$, $a\#$, etc. It is important to confer with the typesetter before making final choices.

13.15   Mathematicians often employ notation in handwriting to make distinctions between characters that are otherwise distinguished in type. One of these devices is "blackboard bold," in which part of the letter is doubled when it stands for what would be boldface in type, as ℝ for **R**. An author should not ask for letters of this kind in type, but specify boldface, sans serif, or something else. Blackboard bold should be confined to the classroom.

UNUSUAL TYPE SIZES

13.16   Most mathematics work is set in 10-point type, the size in which the greatest number of mathematical symbols are available. If a book is planned for a type size other than 10 point, or if it includes reduced matter (such as extracts or footnotes) containing mathematical expressions, the editor should check early on the availability of the special characters and symbols involved. Although odd sizes of type present no problem in filmset or electronic composition, they frequently do in hot metal, and they should ordinarily be avoided. What would be a footnote can be incorporated in the text, either parenthetically or as a "Remark." The latter device is now widely accepted by mathematicians and warmly appreciated by editors. Bibliographic footnotes can be eliminated by citing the author and date of the work (see 15.4–33) and including a reference list at the end of the book or article.

MANUSCRIPT PREPARATION

13.17   The author who is preparing a manuscript for a specific publisher should obtain from the publisher either a style sheet or, perhaps, another book that can be followed generally for style. The more care and attention given to manuscript preparation, the fewer problems there will be in processing the manuscript—and the more likely it is that the manuscript will be accepted for publication. No manuscript has ever been accepted simply because it was clean and well prepared, but some have been rejected because they were sloppy and ill prepared.

13.18   In general, the more of the manuscript that can be done on the typewriter the better. It may not be possible, however, for the author to type all the copy, even on a "math" typewriter.[1] Some signs and symbols, especially the Greek, German, script, and sans serif characters, and newer or more esoteric symbols, may have to be drawn by hand. Neatness is very important here, for a poorly prepared manuscript with special characters drawn in an illegible hand can become, after the addition of editorial changes and typographical instructions, a nightmare for compositor, proofreader, and editor; and, in checking proofs, the author will be faced with a great many errors to correct—and heavy alterations charges to be shared with the publisher.

13.19 Manuscript for mathematical papers and books should be typed double space on 8½-by-11-inch white paper, with 1¼-inch margins for text and 2-inch margins for display work. If handwritten equations or symbols are to be inserted in the typescript, generous space should be allowed for them. Since marginal notes to the typesetter nearly always have to be added by the editor, ample margins are particularly important in mathematics.

STYLE AND GENERAL USAGE

13.20 Obviously the author and editor will give careful attention to matters of style, usage, sense, meaning, clarity, accuracy, and consistency. For example, 0.2×10^5 should not be used in one place and 0.02×10^6 in another unless there is a reason. Decimal fractions in text should be preceded by a zero—0.25, not .25—except for quantities (like probabilities) that never exceed unity.

13.21 All copy, including the equations, should be in good sentence form and should "read" as clearly and grammatically as any other kind of copy. The signs are substitutes for words: $A + B < C$ reads "A plus B is less than C."

13.22 Qualifying expressions should be couched in a consistent style. That preferred by the University of Chicago Press is as illustrated:

Therefore $a + b = c$, where $a = 2$.

(When the equation is displayed, of course, "Therefore" and the qualifying clause are in the text, not the display.)

13.23 *Punctuation.* Without punctuation in mathematical copy it may be difficult to tell where one sentence ends and another begins, especially

1. Anyone using a Selectric typewriter for manuscript that will be submitted to a publisher and eventually set in type should avoid using the miniature characters now available as subscripts and superscripts. If a Xerox or other machine copy has to be made of the manuscript, as it often does, these small characters often become unreadable. They are intended for use in direct-reproduction copy (see 13.5), and for this purpose they serve very well.

where there is a heavy use of signs and symbols. This press prefers to see mathematical copy punctuated, but it accepts copy without punctuation, so long as the author writes so as to avoid ambiguity.

13.24 In elisions, if commas or operational signs are required, they should come after each term and after the three ellipsis dots if a final term follows them. For example:

$$x_1, x_2, \ldots, x_n \qquad \text{NOT} \qquad x_1, x_2, \ldots x_n$$

$$x_1 + x_2 + \cdots + x_n \qquad \text{NOT} \qquad x_1 + x_2 + \cdots x_n$$

$$y = 0, 1, 2, \ldots \qquad \text{NOT} \qquad y = 0, 1, 2 \ldots$$

In the second example above note that centered ellipsis dots have been used between operational signs, for appearance' sake. Centered dots may also be used in an expression like

$$a_1 a_2 \cdots a_n$$

for the same reason. It is never incorrect to use on-the-line ellipsis dots, however, and they are always used in ordinary text.

13.25 *Numeration.* Sections, theorems, and equations may be numbered, and, if the numeration system is not too cumbersome, this offers a convenient and space-saving method of cross-referring. The system preferred by most mathematicians is double numeration; that is, chapter number is followed by equation number, starting with number 1 in each chapter.

13.26 There is little point in numbering all displayed equations. Usually only those that are referred to elsewhere should be numbered. All numbered equations should be displayed. For example:

Wrong:

Hence it is apparent that $abc = xyz$. (1.1)

Right:

Hence it is apparent that

$$abc = xyz. \tag{1.1}$$

The displayed equation is either centered on the line or given a standard indention from the left margin (as in this chapter). The equation number is usually placed flush right, but it is not uncommon for it to be placed flush left.

13.27 *Signs of aggregation.* The preferred order for enclosures is as follows:

$$\left\{ \left[\left({\scriptstyle \{[(\quad)]\}} \right) \right] \right\}$$

These signs of aggregation, or "fences," may be supplemented with double brackets when needed:

$$\left[\!\left[\left\{\left[\left(\left[\!\left[\left\{\left[\left(\qquad\right)\right]\right\}\right]\!\right]\right)\right]\right\}\right]\!\right]$$

Angle brackets, bars, and double bars often carry special mathematical significance as fences and should not be used to supplement the usual series shown above.

13.28　Note that when using fences in mathematics one starts with parentheses and works "from the inside out":

$$[(x+y)^2 z],$$

just the opposite of the practice in ordinary text, where one works "from the outside in":

(e.g., see eq. [4]).

DIFFICULT EXPRESSIONS

13.29　"Difficult" terms and equations may occur both in displayed work and in text ("in line"). Such expressions in line require the lines of type to be spread apart to accommodate them. This makes for an unsightly column and, when the setting is in metal, an expensive one, because of the handwork involved. Some mathematical journals do not allow any in-line difficult expressions and a few go so far as to disallow any equations whatever in line. As examples of difficult expressions, the terms $\sum\limits_{n=0}^{\infty}$ and $\prod\limits_{n=0}^{\infty}$ require leading above and below line, but $\Sigma_{n=0}^{\infty}$ and $\Pi_{n=0}^{\infty}$ can be substituted without any change of meaning.

13.30　*Fractions.* If an equation like $\dfrac{x}{a} + \dfrac{y}{b} = 1$ occurs in line rather than displayed, it is advisable to set it with a solidus, or shilling mark (/): $x/a + y/b = 1$. The use of the solidus can make it much easier for the compositor to set some fractions: for subscripts and superscripts, solidus fractions should always be used.

FOR	USE
$\dfrac{x}{a} + \dfrac{y}{\dfrac{4}{a}}$	$\dfrac{x}{a} + \dfrac{y}{4/a}$　OR　$x/a + ay/4$

FOR   USE

$$\frac{\dfrac{A}{B}}{\sqrt{A - \dfrac{B}{C}}} \qquad \frac{A/B}{(A - B/C)^{1/2}} \quad \text{OR} \quad (A/B)/(A - B/C)^{1/2}$$

$$(x^2 + y^2)^{\frac{a^2 + b^2}{2ab}} \qquad (x^2 + y^2)^{(a^2 + b^2)/2ab}$$

$$\int_0^{\frac{a}{b}} \qquad\qquad \int_0^{a/b}$$

$$\prod_{\frac{a}{b}}^{\infty} \qquad\qquad \prod_{a/b}^{\infty}$$

Note that parentheses must often be used to preserve meaning when converting fractions to the solidus form.

13.31   Some difficult equations involving fractions should always be displayed, as, for example:

$$a = \frac{\displaystyle\sum_{k=1}^{n} x_k m_k}{\displaystyle\sum_{k=1}^{n} x_m} .$$

But here again the form of the same equation employing the solidus instead of the horizontal fraction rule may well be used because of the saving in white space on the page:

$$a = \sum_{k=1}^{n} x_k m_k \Big/ \sum_{k=1}^{n} x_m .$$

13.32   *Vectors.* In mathematical copy vectors are often indicated by the use of an arrow over an expression, but boldface letters carry the same meaning and are preferable typographically. That is,

FOR   USE

$$\vec{a} \quad \overrightarrow{AB} \qquad\qquad \mathbf{a} \quad \mathbf{AB}$$

Since boldface type is also used for tensors, some authors and editors use boldface italic (***AB***) for vectors and boldface roman (**AB**) for tensors. The distinction between vectors and tensors is usually apparent from context, however.

13.33   *Overbars.* In hot-metal composition bars over groups of letters, such as those used with the radical sign and with averages, should be avoided whenever possible because they usually involve costly handwork. With film or electronic composition these cause no trouble in display work, but they should be avoided in line because they frequently interfere with characters in the line above. For example:

FOR	USE		
$\sqrt{xy}$	$\sqrt{(xy)}$	OR	$(xy)^{1/2}$
$\dfrac{1}{\sqrt{xy}}$	$1/\sqrt{(xy)}$	OR	$(xy)^{-1/2}$
$\sqrt{x+y}$	$\sqrt{(x+y)}$	OR	$(x+y)^{1/2}$
$\sqrt{\dfrac{x}{y}}$	$\sqrt{(x/y)}$	OR	$(x/y)^{1/2}$
$\sqrt{\dfrac{x+y-z}{a-b+c}}$	$\sqrt{[(x+y-z)/(a-b+c)]}$ OR $[(x+y-z)/(a-b+c)]^{1/2}$		
$\overline{mv}$	$\langle mv \rangle_{av}$		

13.34   *Exponents.* If an exponential expression, particularly in text, is very complex, it may be worthwhile to rewrite it in a simpler form. An exponential function such as

$$e^{\frac{2\pi i\, \Sigma n_j}{\sqrt{(x^2+y^2)}}}$$

can be set in line as exp $[2\pi i\Sigma n_j/\sqrt{(x^2+y^2)}]$. For other expressions with complicated exponents, make a simple substitution. For example,

$$A^{\frac{2\pi i\Sigma n_j}{\sqrt{(x^2+y^2)}}}$$

can be set in line as "A^α, where $\alpha = 2\pi i\Sigma n_j/\sqrt{(x^2+y^2)}$." The same device may be used for complicated limits to integrals.

BREAKING DISPLAYED EQUATIONS

13.35   When long equations occur in line they should always be changed to the displayed form because of the probability that they will break badly at the end of a line. Even in displayed form, however, some long equations may not fit on one line. An equation that runs over one line to make two lines should, if possible, be broken before an operational sign. The second line may be set either flush right, a standard indention from the right margin (to allow space for an equation number), or aligned on operational signs.

$$\|T_a f - f\| = \sup_s \|T_s^{s+a} f(s + a) - f(s)\|$$
$$- \sup_{s \leq A} \|T_s^{s+a} f(s + a) - f(s)\| + 2 \sup_{s \geq A} \|f(s)\| \, .$$

13.36   If the equation takes more than two lines, it is common practice to align runover lines on operational or descriptive signs:

$$X, Y(s, t) = \int_{-\infty}^{\infty} \cdots \int_{-\infty}^{\infty} e^{i(sx + ty)} \, dF_{x,y}(x, y)$$
$$= \int_{-\infty}^{\infty} e^{ity} \left[\int_{-\infty}^{\infty} e^{isx} \, dF_{x|y}(x) \right] dF_y(y)$$
$$= \int_{-\infty}^{\infty} e^{ity} x \, | \, y(s|y) \, dF_y(y) \, .$$

13.37   Fractions and expressions in parentheses ( ), in brackets [ ], in braces { }, and following radical signs should not be broken unless it is absolutely necessary.

13.38   A determinant or matrix that occupies several lines in the text and that the author feels cannot be cut (one part appearing at the bottom of one page and the second part at the top of the next) without its readability being destroyed should be labeled as a figure and referred to in the text by the figure number. The compositor can then move it to a nearby location to avoid breaking it. Column matrices such as

$$\begin{bmatrix} a \\ b \\ c \end{bmatrix}$$

may be set in line as {*a, b, c*} or col. (*a, b, c*).

ILLUSTRATIONS

13.39   Most of the illustrations used in mathematics are line drawings (rather than halftones), usually charts and graphs. These should be numbered sequentially (preferably, in a book, by double numeration, like equations). If the illustrations include letters, signs, or symbols corresponding to those in the text, the lettering in the illustration should approximate that in the text. It can be confusing, for example, if points *A, B,* and *C* appear in the text in italic type and in an illustration in roman.

13.40   Some mathematical material is too difficult, if not downright impossible, to set wholly in type and may have to be produced by a combination of type and artwork:

To produce the configuration above, type was set and space left between the two parts of the expression. Then on the final reproduction copy an artist drew in the broken line before the copy was photographed for offset reproduction.

MARKING MATHEMATICAL COPY

ITALIC TYPE

13.41   The editor may either underline all copy to be set in italic or give general instructions to the compositor to set all letters used as mathematical terms in italic unless they are marked otherwise. Since compositors experienced in setting mathematics understand that mathematical terms, such as $A + B = C$, are set in italic type, it is not usually necessary to mark such expressions, although the editor should prepare general instructions covering even such obvious matters as this. The general instructions to the compositor should also specify italic type for letters used in subscripts and superscripts.

LETTERS IN NONITALIC TYPE

13.42   *Abbreviations.* Abbreviations such as log (logarithm), max (maximum), exp (exponential function), tan (tangent), cos (cosine), cosh (hyperbolic cosine), lim (limit), arg (argument), cov (covariance), diag (diagonal), ln (natural logarithm), and var (variance) are set in roman:

$$\sin x \qquad \log_a x \qquad \langle mv \rangle_{av} \qquad y_{min}$$

These need not be marked for an experienced compositor. Abbreviations for units of measurement and for chemical elements, which are also set in roman type, are marked only where ambiguity could occur.

13.43   *Single letters.* Special marking must be used, however, when single letters are to be set in any face other than italic. Although it is rather uncommon, a mathematics book may require the use of some letters in roman, usually to indicate properties different from those expressed by the same letters in italic. Underlining is the standard method of indicating italic, but it can be used instead, with covering instruction to the compositor, to indicate letters that are to be in a roman face. If, however, the editor does not use general instructions but underlines all letters to be set italic, then another method—circling, overscoring, or color coding—may be used to show roman letters. Double underlining is used to indicate small capitals. Wavy underlining is used to indicate boldface type, normally used for vectors, matrices, and tensors. (The author should clearly identify all vectors, to distinguish them from their components, which are set in lightface italic. The editor will find it difficult to make the distinction.) Color codes are often used to indicate other typefaces. For example, red underlining or circling can be used to indicate German, blue to indicate script, green to indicate sans serif, and so forth. The covering instructions to the compositor must explain clearly the marking and coding system used. If a Xerox or other machine copy must be made of the edited manuscript for estimating by the typesetter or for querying the author, however, color coding should be avoided.

13.44 *Using correct terminology.* The copyeditor and typesetter are often misled by authors who confuse German with script, specifying the latter when they mean the former. Boldface and sans serif are also frequently mislabeled. Examples of each are shown below:

GERMAN	SCRIPT	BOLDFACE	SANS SERIF
𝔄𝔅ℭ𝔇	𝒜ℬ𝒞𝒟	**ABCD**	ABCD

It should be noted that to a typesetter the term *gothic* means a somewhat heavy sans serif face, like that illustrated above, *not* German or Old English. Standard terminology for typefaces used in mathematical setting is given in table 13.3, at the end of the chapter.

DEFINITIONS, THEOREMS, PROOFS, ETC.

13.45 For definitions, theorems, propositions, corollaries, and lemmas, it is common practice to set the head in caps and small caps and the text—including all mathematical expressions—in italic, and this material should be underlined properly by the editor.

> DEFINITION 1.1. *The graph of an equation consists of all the points whose coordinates satisfy the given equation.*
>
> THEOREM 2.2. *Two nonvertical lines are parallel if and only if their slopes are equal.*
>
> LEMMA 3.3. *K is unbounded if and only if A = B.*
>
> ASSUMPTION. *Time t is finite and always greater than 0.*
>
> RULE 4.4. *The length of a vertical segment joining two points is the ordinate of the upper point minus the ordinate of the lower.*

In the Assumption above note that the expression t is preceded by an identifying word so as to avoid beginning the sentence with a lower-case letter. Some mathematicians and editors would also object to beginning Lemma 3.3 with the expression K, even though it is a capital letter, preferring to write *"The quantity K. . . ."*

13.46   The texts of proofs, examples, remarks, demonstrations, and solutions are usually set in roman, with only the word "proof," for example, set in italic.

> *Proof.* Let $A = B$. Hence $C = D$.
> *Solution.* If $y = 0$, then $x = 5$.

MARKING FOR CLARITY

13.47   What may be perfectly clear to the author can be utterly bewildering to anyone who is not a mathematician. The author must take particular care to clarify ambiguous expressions.

13.48   It is not advisable, however, for either the author or the editor to mark the copy excessively. Provided that inferior and superior characters have been marked in a few places by the symbols $\vee$ and $\wedge$ (see example below), and new characters or symbols identified when they first appear, a trained compositor will have no difficulty with well-prepared copy. If the spatial relationship of terms is *not* clearly shown in typed or handwritten expressions, they should be marked so that there can be no doubt in the mind of the compositor. For example, in the expression

$$x^k_{t1}$$

it may not be clear in the manuscript whether this means

$$X^k_{t1} \quad \text{OR} \quad X^k_{t^1} \quad \text{OR} \quad X^k_{t_1} ;$$

it should be marked in one of the following ways for complete clarity:

$$x^{\cancel{k}}_{\cancel{t1}} \quad \text{OR} \quad x^{\cancel{k}}_{\cancel{t1}}, \quad \text{OR} \quad x^{\cancel{k}}_{\cancel{t1}} .$$

13.49   The examples above show the subscripts and superscripts aligned, the setting generally preferred by authors for elegance and clarity. In filmset or electronic composition this can generally be achieved without extra work or expense, but in metal the aligning may require considerable handwork, particularly if subscripts and superscripts occur together frequently throughout a book. If that is the case, it may be advisable to instruct the typesetter to stagger them for ease and economy in setting. (There should be previous agreement between the editor and the author on this point, however, as on any other departure from the form in the typescript.) If they are staggered, the general rule is to set the subscript before the superscript:

$$X_1{}^2 \qquad Y_m{}^n$$

If the subscript or the superscript is lengthy, however, the two should be set aligned or parentheses should be added for clarity:

$$X_{2v_{n-1}}^3 \quad \text{OR} \quad (X_{2v_{n-1}})^3 \quad \text{NOT} \quad X_{2v_{n-1}}{}^3$$

NOTE: A prime (′) is always set adjacent to a letter or symbol:

$$X'_{x,y} \quad \text{NOT} \quad X_{x,y}{}'$$

13.50 Figure 13.1 shows a page of manuscript as marked initially by the author and then by the editor before being sent to the typesetter. Figure 13.2 shows the same page set in type. The author's marks merely identify ambiguous symbols. The editor's marking was done for a compositor experienced in mathematical setting; for an inexperienced compositor the marking must be more elaborate.

13.51 *Mistaken identity.* In the manuscript certain letters, numbers, and symbols can be easily misread, especially when Greek, German, script, and sans serif letters are handwritten rather than typed. Some of the handwritten and typed characters that cause the most difficulty are shown in table 13.1.

13.52 These and other signs and symbols that can be misread by the compositor should be clearly identified, either by marginal notations or otherwise. (For lists of symbols and special characters commonly used in mathematics see tables 13.2 and 13.3.) Illegible handwriting and unidentifiable signs and symbols can reduce composition speed and result in time-consuming and costly corrections. In the folklore of publishing, the story is told of an author who drowned himself when, on reading proof of his thousand-page manuscript, he found that χ had been set as x throughout. It may be inconceivable to an author that a compositor, even though working on the third shift in a plant a thousand miles a way, or in another country, could make such a misinterpretation. Unfortunately, authors are seldom available at the time of composition to answer questions, and decisions or interpretations have to be made. Although experienced typesetters become very skillful at deciphering, they do make mistakes.

FOR FURTHER REFERENCE

13.53 Readers who need or wish to explore more fully the problems of mathematical typesetting are referred to *Mathematics into Type,* by Ellen Swanson (1979).

Opr.: Letter symbols in ital. unless marked

Therefore $F_x^n \subset G \cap B_n$ and $F_x^n \cap B_m = \emptyset$ for $n \neq m$ since $b \in G$.

null set   *"element of"*

The temperature function is

$$u(x, t) = \frac{2}{L} \sum_1^\infty \exp\left(-\frac{u^2\pi^2 kt}{L^2}\right) \sin\frac{n\pi x}{L} \int_0^L f(x') \sin\frac{n\pi x'}{L} dx'. \quad (3.1)$$

An $m \times n$ matrix $\underset{\sim}{A}$ over a field F is a rectangular array of mn elements a_j^i in F, arranged in m rows and n columns:

$$\underset{\sim}{A} = \begin{bmatrix} a_1^1 & a_2^1 & \cdots & a_n^1 \\ a_1^2 & a_2^2 & \cdots & a_n^2 \\ \cdot & \cdot & \cdots & \cdot \\ a_1^m & a_2^m & \cdots & a_n^m \end{bmatrix}.$$

The modulus of the correlation coefficient of X_1 and X_2 is

"greater than"

$$\rho = |\langle x_1, x_2\rangle| / \|x_1\| \, \|x_2\| \quad \text{for} \quad \|x_1\| > 0, \quad 1 = 1, 2.$$

angle brackets   *all*   *all*

Hence

$$\frac{\partial F}{\partial x} = \lim_{\Delta x \to 0} \frac{\Delta F}{\Delta x} = \lim_{\Delta x \to 0} \frac{1}{\Delta x}\left\{\int_{a,b}^{x+\Delta x, y} P\,dx + Q\,dy - \int_{a,b}^{x,y} P\,dx + Q\,dy\right\} + P + Q.$$

From equation (2.4), where $M = [(a + b - 1)/(k + 1)]$, we obtain

$$\alpha_\nu(a + b) = (-1)^\nu \sum{}' \frac{(i_1 + \cdots + i_M)!}{i_1! \cdots i_M!} \prod_{h=1}^M (-1)^{i_h}\binom{a + b - kh - 1}{h}^{i_h},$$

lc Gr. nu

the sum being extended over all sets $(i_1, \cdots, i_M)$.

To summarize our findings:

lc Gr. eta

$$v^*(z, t_n) \geqslant H_{6_1}[v(x) + o(1)] - 2\eta \geqslant v(z) + o(1) + \eta^{1/2}o(1).$$

lc ital   *lc ital*   *cap ital*

Fig. 13.1. An example of a well-prepared page of mathematical copy with suggested marking for clarity. This page is not intended to make mathematical sense, but merely to illustrate good preparation of mathematical copy.

366

Therefore $F_z{}^n \subseteq G \cap B_n$ and $F_z{}^n \cap B_m = \emptyset$ for $n \neq m$ since $b \in G$. The temperature function is

$$u(x, t) = \frac{2}{L} \sum_1^\infty \exp\left(-\frac{u^2\pi^2 kt}{L^2}\right) \sin \frac{n\pi x}{L}$$

$$\times \int_0^L f(x') \sin \frac{n\pi x'}{L} dx' . \qquad (3.1)$$

An $m \times n$ matrix $\mathbf{A}$ over a field F is a rectangular array of mn elements $a_j{}^i$ in F, arranged in m rows and n columns:

$$\mathbf{A} = \begin{bmatrix} a_1{}^1 & a_2{}^1 & \ldots & a_n{}^1 \\ a_1{}^2 & a_2{}^2 & \ldots & a_n{}^2 \\ . & . & \ldots & . \\ a_1{}^m & a_2{}^m & \ldots & a_n{}^m \end{bmatrix} .$$

The modulus of the correlation coefficient of X_1 and X_2 is

$$\rho = |\langle X_1, X_2 \rangle| / \|X_1\| \, \|X_2\| \quad \text{for} \quad \|X_l\| > 0 , \quad l = 1, 2 .$$

Hence

$$\frac{\partial F}{\partial x} = \lim_{\Delta x \to 0} \frac{\Delta F}{\Delta x} = \lim_{\Delta x \to 0} \frac{1}{\Delta x} \left\{ \int_{a,b}^{x+\Delta x, y} P \, dx + Q \, dy \right.$$

$$\left. - \int_{a,b}^{x,y} P \, dx + Q \, dy \right\} + P + Q .$$

From equation (2.4), where $M = [(a + b - 1)/(k + 1)]$, we obtain

$$a_\nu(a + b) = (-1)^\nu \sum{}' \frac{(i_1 + \ldots + i_M)!}{i_1! \ldots i_M!}$$

$$\times \prod_{h=1}^M (-1)^{i_h} \binom{a + b - kh - 1}{h}^{i_h} ,$$

the sum being extended over all sets $(i_1, \ldots, i_M)$.

To summarize our findings:

$$v^*(z, t_n) \geq H_{\delta_1}[v(x) + o(1)] - 2\eta \geq v(z) + o(1) + \eta^{1/2} O(1)$$

Fig. 13.2. The page of manuscript shown in figure 13.1 set in type

TABLE 13.1

Ambiguous Mathematical Symbols

Hand-written Symbols and Letters[a]	Symbols Set in Type[b]	Marginal Notation to Operator[c]	Remarks and Suggestions for Manuscript Preparation
a	a	lc "aye"	In typescript, leave single space before
α	a	lc Gr. alpha	and after $\propto$ and all other descrip-
$\propto$	$\propto$	variation	tive signs ($=$, $\leq$, $\in$, $\cap$, $\subset$, etc.)
∞	∞	infinity	
B	B	cap "bee"	
β	β	lc Gr. beta	
χ	χ	lc Gr. chi	Carelessly written χ also easily misread
X	X	cap "ex"	as numeral 4
x	x	lc "ex"	
$\times$	$\times$	"times" or "mult"	Leave single space before and after $\times$ and all other operational signs ($+$, $-$, $\div$, etc.)
δ, ∂	δ	lc Gr. delta	
∂	∂	partial differential	Simpler to use printer's term "round dee"
d	d	lc "dee"	
ϵ	ϵ	lc Gr. epsilon	
$\in$	$\in$	"element of"	
η	η	lc Gr. eta	
n	n	lc "en"	
γ	γ	lc Gr. gamma	
τ	τ	lc Gr. tau	
r	r	lc "are"	
t	t	lc "tee"	
ι	ι	lc Gr. iota	Author should avoid using ι and i to-
i	i	lc "eye"	gether because of similarity in print
κ	κ	lc Gr. kappa	
k	k	lc "kay"	
K	K	cap Gr. kappa	
K	K	cap "kay"	
l	l	lc "ell"	Typed l and 1 identical; note "ell" but
1	1	numeral 1	leave numeral unmarked[d]
ν	ν	lc Gr. nu	Avoid using ν and v together because
v	v	lc "vee"	of similarity in print

[a] Symbols and letters commonly mistaken for each other are arranged in groups.

[b] Letters in mathematical expressions will automatically be set in italics unless marked otherwise.

[c] Only if symbols, letters, or numbers are badly written is it necessary to identify them for the compositor.

[d] Some math typewriters now have a special symbol for "ell."

TABLE 13.1—*Continued*

Handwritten Symbols and Letters	Symbols Set in Type	Marginal Notation to Operator	Remarks and Suggestions for Manuscript Preparation
O	O	cap "oh"	Zero usually unmarked; degree sign (if
o	o	lc "oh"	typed as lc "oh") and Greek letters
o	0	zero	identified in margin
O	O	cap Gr. omicron	
o	o	lc Gr. omicron	
$\circ$	$\circ$	degree sign	
Λ	Λ	cap Gr. lambda	
$\wedge$	$\wedge$	matrix symbol	
ϕ φ	ϕ, φ	lc Gr. phi	Preference for form φ should be speci
$\emptyset$	$\emptyset$	empty set or null set	fied by author; ϕ more commonly used
$\prod$	Π	product	
π	Π	cap Gr. pi	
π	π	lc Gr. pi	
ρ	ρ	lc Gr. rho	
p	p	lc "pee"	
θ ϑ	θ, ϑ	lc Gr. theta	Preference for form ϑ should be speci
Θ	Θ	cap Gr. theta	fied by author; θ more commonly used
U	U	cap "you"	
U $\cup$	$U, \cup$	union symbol	
υ	υ	lc Gr. upsilon	
μ	μ	lc Gr. mu	
u	u	lc "you"	
ω	ω	lc Gr. omega	
w	w	lc "doubleyou"	
Z	Z	cap "zee"	
z	z	lc "zee"	
2	2	numeral 2	
$'$	$'$	prime	Type apostrophe for prime; raise su
1	^{1}	superscript 1	perscript one-half space above line
$)$	$,$	comma	In handwritten formulas, take care to
1	$_1$	subscript 1	distinguish comma from subscript 1 and prime from superscript 1
—	—	em dash	Type two hyphens for em dash; no space on either side
—	—	minus sign	To indicate subtraction, leave single space on each side of sign; omit space after sign if negative quantity is represented
•	·	multiplication dot	Type period one-half space above line for multiplication dot, allowing single space on each side; do *not* show space around a center dot in a chemical formula ($CO_3 \cdot H_2$)

TABLE 13.2

Standard Signs and Symbols

N.B. It should be remembered that operating signs are abbreviations for inflected verbs: that is, for example, the sign > stands for *is* or *are greater than*, not simply *greater than*. The necessary verbs are not always indicated in the table below.

+	Plus	∼	Difference
−	Minus	∽	Difference
×	Multiplied by	⧣	Equal and parallel
÷	Divided by	≑	Approaches a limit
=	Equal to	≞	Is measured by
±	Plus or minus	⊥	Perpendicular to
∓	Minus or plus	⊥s	Perpendiculars
⩲	Plus or equal	∥	Parallel
++	Double plus	∥s	Parallels
≏	Difference between	∦	Not parallels
-:	Difference excess	∠	Angle
≡	Identical with, congruent	∡	Angle
≢	Not identical with	∢	Angle
≠	Not equal to	⦜	Angles
≈	Nearly equal to	∟	Right angle
≅	Equals approximately	≚	Equal angles
≊	Equals approximately	△	Triangle
≧	Equal to or greater than	▲	Triangles
≦	Equal to or less than	/	Rising diagonal
<	Less than	\	Falling diagonal
⌐	Less than	//	Parallel rising diagonal
>	Greater than	\\	Parallel falling diagonal
⌐	Greater than	///	Rising parallels
≷	Greater than or less than	\\\	Falling parallels
≮	Not less than	‖‖	Triple vertical
≯	Not greater than	⦀	Quadruple parallels
≤	Less than or equal to	⌢	Arc
≤	Less than or equal to	⌣	Arc
≦	Less than or equal to	⌔	Sector
≤	Less than or equal to	⌓	Segment
≶	Less than or greater than	○	Circle
≥	Greater than or equal to	Ⓢ	Circles
≥	Greater than or equal to	0	Ellipse
≥	Greater than or equal to	⌀	Diameter
≥	Greater than or equal to	□	Square
≍	Equivalent to	Ⓢ	Squares
≭	Not equivalent	▭	Rectangle
≢	Not equivalent	Ⓢ	Rectangles
⊂	Included in	⊞	Cube
⊃	Excluded from	▱	Rhomboid

TABLE 13.2—*Continued*

⑤	Rhomboids	⌐⟍	Horizontal integral
⬠	Pentagon	˘	Mathmodifier
⬡	Hexagon	ˏ	Mathmodifier
∴	Hence, therefore	∿	Cycle sine
∵	Because	Ⅹ	Quantic
·	Multiplied by	∕	Single bond
:	Ratio	∣	Single bond
::	Proportion	∖	Single bond
÷	Geometrical proportion	∣	Single bond
′	Minute	∣	Single bond (punched to right)
″	Second		
°	Degree	⟍⟍	Double bond
⋰	Dotted minute	‖	Double bond
⋰	Dotted second	∕∕	Double bond
⋰	Dotted degree	‖	Double bond
⋰	Canceled second	⋮	Triple bond
‴	Triple prime	↔	Reaction goes both right and left
√	Square root		
∛	Cube root	↕	Reaction goes both up and down
∜	Fourth root		
ⁿ√	*n*th root	⇋	Equilibrium reaction beginning at right
⟋	Horizontal radical		
Σ	Summation of	⇌	Equilibrium reaction beginning at left
Π	Product sign		
π	Pi (3.1416)	⇌	Reversible reaction beginning at left
∪	Union sign		
∩	Intersection sign	⇆	Reaction begins at right and is completed to left
!	Factorial sign		
∅	Empty set; null set	⇉	Reaction begins at right and is completed to right
∈	Is an element of		
∉	Is not an element of	⇄	Reaction begins at left and is completed to right
e	Base (2.718) of natural logarithms		
		⇄	Reaction begins at left and is completed to left
e	Charge of the electron		
Δ	Delta	⇆	Reversible reaction beginning at right
∇	Nabla; del		
∝	Variation	↕	Reversible
∞	Infinity	⇑	Elimination
㎳	Mills	⇓	Absorption
⊢	Assertion sign	⇕	Exchange
h	Planck's constant	↯	Electrolysis
ℏ	*h*/2π	⊃	Ring opening
k	Boltzmann's constant	↻	Repositioning
c̄	Mean value of *c*	○	Ring cycle
∂	Partial differential	⤢	Reversible reaction
∂	Partial differential	⤡	Reversible reaction
∫	Integral		
∮	Contour integral		

TABLE 13.3

REPRESENTATIVE SAMPLES OF TEN-POINT MONOTYPE
TYPEFACES COMMONLY USED FOR MATHEMATICS

ROMAN LOWERCASE. a b c . . . z æ œ ff fi fl ffi ffl

ROMAN SMALL CAPS. A B C . . . Z Æ Œ &

ROMAN CAPS. A B C . . . Z Æ Œ &

ROMAN FIGURES AND FRACTIONS. 1 2 3 4 5 6 7 8 9 0
$\frac{1}{2}$ $\frac{1}{3}$ $\frac{2}{3}$ $\frac{1}{4}$ $\frac{3}{4}$ $\frac{1}{6}$ $\frac{1}{8}$ $\frac{3}{8}$ $\frac{5}{8}$ $\frac{7}{8}$

ROMAN PUNCTUATION. . , ; : - ' ! ? ([

ITALIC LOWERCASE, FIGURES, AND ACCENTS. Identical with the corresponding roman type.

ITALIC CAPS. *A B C . . . Z Æ Œ &*

ITALIC FIGURES. *1 2 3 4 5 6 7 8 9 0*

GERMAN. 𝕬𝕭𝕮𝕯𝕰𝕱𝕲𝕳𝕵𝕶𝕷𝕸𝕹𝕺𝕻𝕼𝕽𝕾𝕿𝖀 𝖁𝖂𝖃𝖄𝖅
abcdefghijklmnopqrſstuvwxyz

GERMAN BOLD. 𝕬𝕭𝕮𝕯𝕰𝕱𝕲𝕳𝕵𝕶𝕷𝕸𝕹𝕺𝕻𝕼𝕽𝕾𝕿 𝖀𝖁𝖂𝖃𝖄𝖅
abcdefghijklmnopqrſstuvwxyz

GREEK. Α Β Γ Δ Ε Ζ Η Θ Ι Κ Λ Μ Ν Ξ Ο Π Σ Τ Υ Φ Χ Ψ Ω
α β γ δ ε ζ η θ ι κ λ μ ν ξ ο π ρ σ τ υ φ χ ψ ω ϝ ∂ ϑ ς

GREEK BOLD. **Α Β Γ Δ Ε Ζ Η Θ Ι Κ Λ Μ Ν Ξ Ο Π Ρ Σ Τ Υ Φ Χ Ψ Ω**
α β γ δ ε ζ η θ ι κ λ μ ν ξ ο π ρ σ τ υ φ χ ψ ω ϱ

SUPERIOR AND INFERIOR GREEK LOWERCASE. $\mathrm{H}^{\alpha\beta\gamma\delta\epsilon\zeta\eta\theta\iota\kappa\lambda\mu\nu\xi o\pi\rho\sigma\tau\upsilon\phi\chi\psi\omega\ \digamma\varphi\varsigma}$

$\mathrm{H}_{\alpha\beta\gamma\delta\epsilon\zeta\eta\theta\iota\kappa\lambda\mu\nu\xi o\pi\rho\sigma\tau\upsilon\phi\chi\psi\omega\ \digamma\partial\varphi\varsigma}$

HEBREW. תשרקצפעסנמלכיטחזוהדגבא

TABLE 13.3—*Continued*

RUSSIAN.	А Б В Г Д Е Ж З И Й К Л М Н О П Р С Т У Ф Х Ц Ч Ш Щ Ъ Ы Ь Ѣ Э Ю Я Ѵ
CUSHING.	A B C D E F G H I J K L M N O P Q R S T U V W X Y Z a b c d e f g h i j k l m n o p q r s t u v w x y z
CUSHING ITALIC.	*A B C D E F G H I J K L M N O P Q R S T U V W X Y Z* *a b c d e f g h i j k l m n o p q r s t u v w x y z*
GOTHIC (SANS SERIF).	A B C D E F G H I J K L M N O P Q R S T U V W X Y Z
SCRIPT.	𝒶 𝒷 𝒸 𝒹 𝑒 𝒻 𝑔 𝒽 𝒾 𝒿 𝒦 𝓁 𝓂 𝓃 𝑜 𝓅 𝓆 𝓇 𝓈 𝓉 𝓊 𝓋 𝓌 𝓍 𝓎 𝓏

SUPERIOR LETTERS. A^{ABC} A^{abc} $A^{\alpha\beta\gamma}$ A^{123}

INFERIOR LETTERS. A stock similar to the superior letters. Examples are: B_{DEF} B_{def} $B_{\delta\epsilon\zeta}$ B_{456}

SYMBOLS. $+ \; - \; \times \; \div \; = \; \pm \; \mp \; / \; \| \; < \; > \; \leq \; \geq \; \equiv \; \neq \; \not\equiv \; \doteqdot \; \sim$
$\simeq \rightarrow \surd \; () \; \{\} \; [] \; \infty \; \propto \; {}^\circ \; ' \; ''$

$\| \; () \; \{\} \; [] \; / \; \sqrt{} \; \int \; \oint \; [\![\;]\!] \; \langle \rangle$

SUPERIOR SYMBOLS. $A^{+\,-\,=\,\times\,\div\,\pm\,<\,>\,\leqq\,\geqq\,\surd\,\odot\,\infty\,/\,()\,\{\}\,[]\,1/2\,1/4\,\S\,,\,.}$
$A'^{\,\| \, | \, \perp}$

INFERIOR SYMBOLS. $B_{+\,-\,=\,\times\,\div\,\pm\,<\,>\,\leqq\,\geqq\,\surd\,\odot\,\infty\,/\,()\,\{\}\,[]\,1/2\,1/4\,\S\,\|}$
$B_{.\,,\,;\,:\,'\,\|\,\perp}$

SPLIT FRACTIONS. $\dfrac{1\;2\;3\;4\;5\;6\;7\;8\;9\;0}{1\;2\;3\;4\;5\;6\;7\;8\;9\;0}$

MISCELLANEOUS. ϖ ♉ ! ? ″ % @ ¶ ℱ ⊃ ⚠ ∠ ⊙ ◎ ⊕ Ⓢ ⊖ ⊝
⊛ ⊃ ⊥ ⊿ ※ ∘ *(6 pt.) †(6 pt.) * † ‡ § $ # ᵈ ʰ ˢ
ᵐᵍ ᴹ ≩ ≢ ⌗ ≮ ⪅ ⪆ ↔ ⇆ ⇄ ⇌ ♂ ☿ ♀ ⫣

14 *Abbreviations*

Introduction 14.1
Names and Titles 14.4
    Personal Names 14.4
      Titles before names 14.5
      Titles, degrees, affiliations, etc., after names 14.8
    Company Names 14.12
    Agencies and Organizations 14.15
    Names with *Saint* 14.16
Geographical Terms 14.17
    States 14.17
    Names with *Fort, Saint,* etc. 14.18
    Names of Countries 14.19
    Addresses 14.21
    Points of the Compass 14.23
    Latitude and Longitude 14.24
Time 14.26
    Years 14.27
    Months 14.28
    Days of the Week 14.29
    Time of Day 14.30
Scholarship 14.31
Bible 14.33
    Books 14.33
    Versions and Sections 14.35
Measure 14.36
    English Measure 14.37
      Length, area, and volume 14.38
      Weight and capacity 14.39
      Time 14.40
    International Measure 14.41
      Base units 14.42
      Derived units 14.44
      Use of figures with SI units 14.48
Science and Technology 14.50
    Astronomy 14.51
      Celestial coordinates 14.52
      Other units and abbreviations 14.53
    Chemical Elements 14.54
Commercial Copy 14.55
Constitutions and Bylaws 14.56
For Further Reference 14.57

INTRODUCTION

14.1   For several centuries the use of abbreviations and symbols in formal, general writing has become less and less frequent, whereas during the past few decades the use of both has been on the increase in technical writing of all kinds. In the main this chapter is concerned with abbreviations and symbols in general writing—authors and editors of technical material in a fast-changing field usually know and can follow the fashions of that field—but the chapter does offer some guidance in technical work, especially to the generalist editor confronted with special-interest copy to prepare for typesetting. Outside the area of science and technology, abbreviations and symbols appear most frequently in tabular matter, notes, bibliographies, and lists of various kinds.

14.2   It is often an open question whether or not periods should be used with particular abbreviations.[1] The trend now is strongly away from the use of periods with all kinds of abbreviations that have carried them in the past. In our view this is to the good: anything that reduces the fussiness of typography makes for easier reading. In the examples that follow, however, the periods have been left wherever they have traditionally appeared, to make clear which abbreviations in conservative practice have been free of periods. It is simple enough for users of this manual to omit periods if that is the style they wish to adopt. One caution: If periods are omitted after abbreviations that spell words (for example, *in., a., no.*), these may be confusing in some contexts. Another caution, if periods are used: In an abbreviation with internal periods (A.M., *N.Y., Litt.D., N.Dak.,* U.S.), there should be no space after the internal periods. (Initials of personal names, however, are followed by regular word spaces: E. F. Benson.)

14.3   Despite the long-continued trend in general writing to get along without abbreviations, some few words are almost never spelled out. Among these are *Mr., Mrs., Messrs.,* and *Dr.* (and, of course, *Ms.,* which has no spelled-out form) before a name, abbreviations for affiliations or scholarly degrees after a name (*Litt.D., M.P., Ph.D.*), and abbreviations such as A.M. and P.M., A.D. and B.C. On the other hand, a symbol or figure beginning a sentence is nearly always spelled out, or if it cannot be, the sentence is recast:

> Alpha particles are . . . (*not* α particles are . . .)
> Eighteen forty-five was . . . (*not* 1845 was . . .)

For other advice on the use of figures in run of text see chapter 8.

1. In British practice, a distinction is made between a true abbreviation, in which the end of the word is lopped off (*vol., Inc., diam.*), and a suspension, in which the interior of the word is removed (*Mr., dept., acct.*). It is usual in Britain to spell the latter class without periods. This logical practice shows few signs of catching on in America, however.

NAMES AND TITLES

PERSONAL NAMES

14.4 Normally, abbreviations should not be used for given names:

> Benjamin (*not* Benj.) Harrison William (*not* Wm.) Warfield

A signature, however, should be transcribed as the person wrote it:

> Benj. Franklin Geo. D. Fuller Ch. Virolleaud

Some names contain a middle initial that does not stand for a name, and some given names consist only of initials. A purist would omit the period after these initials. For convenience and consistency it is recommended that all initials given with a name be followed by a period:

> Charles C. Thomas Harry S. Truman
> P. J. Carter

When persons are referred to by initials only, such as some American presidents or the subject of a biography, no periods are used:

> JFK (John Fitzgerald Kennedy) SM (Stanley Morison)
> FDR (Franklin Delano Roosevelt)

14.5 *Titles before names.* When a civil or military title is used with the surname alone, the title must be spelled out:

> General Washington Senator Borah
> Lieutenant Colonel Smith Alderman Farley

With full names, most such titles are abbreviated:

> Brig. Gen. Thomas Tilney Sen. Robert A. Taft

(Within the armed services briefer forms of abbreviation are commonly used, but these have little currency in the civilian world.)

CIVIL AND MILITARY TITLES

Adj. Gen.	Fr., Father	Pfc, private, first
Adm.	1st Lt.	class
Ald.	1st Sgt.	PO, petty officer
Alc., airman, first	Gen.	Pres.
class	Gov.	Prof.
Asst. Prof.	Insp. Gen.	Pvt.
Assoc. Prof.	Judge Adv. Gen.	Q.M. Gen.
Brig. Gen.	Lt.	Q.M. Sgt.
Bvt., brevet	Lt. Col.	Rear Adm.
Capt.	Lt. Comdr.	Rep., Representative
Col.	Lt. Gen.	S1c., seaman, first
Comdr.	Lt. Gov.	class
Cpl.	Lt. (jg)	2d Lt.
CWO, chief warrant	Maj.	Sen.
officer	Maj. Gen.	Sfc., sergeant, first
Ens.	M. Sgt.	class

Sgt.	S. Sgt.	T. Sgt.
Sp3c., specialist,	Supt.	Vice Adm.
third class	T2g., technician,	WO, warrant officer
Sr., Sister	second grade	

14.6   Always abbreviated, whether with the full name or surname, are the social titles:

Mr.   Mrs.   Messrs.   Ms.   M.   MM.   Mme   Mlle   Dr.

14.7   The titles *Reverend* and *Honorable* are spelled out if preceded by *the:*

the Reverend Henry L. Brown; the Reverend Mr. (*or* Dr.) Brown (*never* Reverend Brown *or* the Reverend Brown)

the Very Reverend Robert C. Wilson; the Right Reverend David O. Carlson; the Right Reverend Monsignor Thomas L. Bennett

the Honorable Frank R. Hawkins

In other instances with the full name the title is abbreviated :

Rev. Henry L. Brown; Very Rev. Robert C. Wilson; Rt. Rev. David O. Carlson; Rt. Rev. Msgr. Thomas L. Bennett; Hon. Frank R. Hawkins

14.8   *Titles, degrees, affiliations, etc., after names.* The abbreviations *Jr., Sr., II, III* (or *2d, 3d*), etc., after a person's name are part of that name and so are used in connection with any titles or honorifics. *Jr.* and *Sr.* are set off by commas; the others are not:

Mrs. James Jefferson, Sr., widow of the governor
Dexter Harrison III, LL.D.   Rev. Oliver C. Jones, Jr.

Note that these abbreviations are used only with the full name—never, for example, Mr. Kelly, Jr. (See also 8.52–54.)

14.9   The abbreviation *Esq.* is never used when any other title is given, either before or after the name:

Anthony Wright, Esq. (*not* Mr. Anthony Wright, Esq. *or* Anthony Wright, Esq., M.A.)

14.10   *Mr., Mrs.,* and *Dr.* are also dropped if another title is used:

Leroy S. Wells, Ph.D.

14.11   The following list includes many frequently used abbreviations:

SCHOLARLY DEGREES AND TITLES OF RESPECT

A.B., Artium Baccalaureus (Bachelor of Arts)

A.M., Artium Magister (Master of Arts)

B.A., Bachelor of Arts

B.D., Bachelor of Divinity

B.S., Bachelor of Science

D.B., Divinitatis Baccalaureus (Bachelor of Divinity)

D.D., Divinitatis Doctor (Doctor of Divinity)

D.D.S., Doctor of Dental Surgery

D.O., Doctor of Osteopathy

D.V.M., Doctor of Veterinary
  Medicine
Esq., Esquire
F.R.S., Fellow of the Royal
  Society
J.D., Juris Doctor (Doctor of
  Law)
J.P., justice of the peace
L.H.D., Litterarum Humaniorum
  Doctor (Doctor of Humanities)
Litt.D., Litterarum Doctor
  (Doctor of Letters)
LL.B., Legum Baccalaureus
  (Bachelor of Laws)
LL.D., Legum Doctor (Doctor of
  Laws)

M.A., Master of Arts
M.D., Medicinae Doctor (Doctor
  of Medicine)
M.P., Member of Parliament
M.S., Master of Science
Ph.B., Philosophiae Baccalaureus
  (Bachelor of Philosophy)
Ph.D., Philosophiae Doctor
  (Doctor of Philosophy)
Ph.G., Graduate in Pharmacy
S.B., Bachelor of Science
S.M., Master of Science
S.T.B., Sacrae Theologiae Bacca-
  laureus (Bachelor of Sacred
  Theology)

COMPANY NAMES

14.12   The following abbreviations are frequently used as parts of firm names:

> Bro., Bros., Co., Corp., Inc., Ltd., &

In straight text it is best to give a firm name in its full form, but *Inc.* or *Ltd.* is usually dropped:

> A. G. Becker and Company   Aldine Publishing Company

14.13   In notes, bibliographies, lists, etc., the abbreviations listed above may be freely (but consistently) used:

> Macmillan Co.   Chicago & North Western Railroad
> Ginn & Co.   Great Lakes Dredge & Dock Co.

(For the further abbreviation of publishers' names in bibliographies and notes, see 16.76.)

14.14   In closely set tabular matter further abbreviation is often used (*RR, Ry, Assoc., Mfg.,* etc.).

AGENCIES AND ORGANIZATIONS

14.15   Both in run of text (preferably after one spelled-out use) and in tabular matter, notes, etc., the names of government agencies, network broadcasting companies, associations, fraternal and service organizations, unions, and other groups are often abbreviated. Such abbreviations are usually set in full caps with no periods:

AAAS	HOLC	NEH	TVA
AFL-CIO	IOOF	NFL	UN
AMA	NAACP	NIMH	UNESCO
AT & T	NATO	NSF	VA
FTC	NBC	OPEC	YMCA

NAMES WITH "SAINT"

14.16   *Saint* is often abbreviated (*St.*, pl. *SS.*) when it stands before the name of a Christian saint, but many prefer to spell the word out in text, abbreviating only where space is at a premium:

> Saint Ignatius Loyola wrote . . .
> Saint Michael the Archangel
> the Church of Saints Constantine and Helena
> Saint Paul's Cathedral

Saint is usually omitted before the names of apostles, evangelists, and church fathers:

> Matthew, Mark, Luke, Paul, Peter, Bartholomew, Augustine, Ambrose, Jerome, etc.

When *Saint* forms part of a personal name, the bearer's usage is followed:

> Augustus Saint-Gaudens   Ruth St. Denis
> Muriel St. Clare Byrne

GEOGRAPHICAL TERMS

STATES

14.17   The names of states, territories, and possessions of the United States should always be spelled in full when standing alone. When they follow the name of a city or any other geographical term, it is preferable to spell them out except in lists, tabular matter, notes, bibliographies, and indexes. In such instances the first of the two forms illustrated is preferred; the two-letter form is specified by the U.S. government for use with zip-code addresses and is often useful in other contexts:

Ala.	AL	Kans.	KS	Ohio	OH
Alaska	AK	Ky.	KY	Okla.	OK
Amer. Samoa	AS	La.	LA	Oreg.	OR
Ariz.	AZ	Maine	ME	Pa.	PA
Ark.	AR	Md.	MD	P.R.	PR
Calif.	CA	Mass.	MA	R.I.	RI
C.Z.	CZ	Mich.	MI	S.C.	SC
Colo.	CO	Minn.	MN	S.Dak.	SD
Conn.	CT	Miss.	MS	Tenn.	TN
Del.	DE	Mo.	MO	Tex.	TX
D.C.	DC	Mont.	MT	Utah	UT
Fla.	FL	Nebr.	NE	Vt.	VT
Ga.	GA	Nev.	NV	Va.	VA
Guam	GU	N.H.	NH	V.I.	VI
Hawaii	HI	N.J.	NJ	Wash.	WA
Idaho	ID	N.Mex.	NM	W.Va.	WV
Ill.	IL	N.Y.	NY	Wis.	WI
Ind.	IN	N.C.	NC	Wyo.	WY
Iowa	IA	N.Dak.	ND		

NAMES WITH "FORT," "SAINT," ETC.

14.18   Prefixes of most geographic names should not be abbreviated in text:

Fort Wayne	Mount Airy	South Orange
Saint Cloud	San Diego	Port Arthur

Many editors make an exception of names beginning with *Saint* (St. Louis, St. Lawrence), and where space must be saved, any such prefixes (except *San, Santa,* etc.) may be abbreviated (*Ft., Pt., Mt., S.* [*South*], etc.).

NAMES OF COUNTRIES

14.19   The names of countries, except for the Soviet Union, which is often abbreviated *USSR,* are spelled out in text. In tabular and other tight matter they may be abbreviated as necessary:

U.S.   U.K. (*or* G.B.)   Fr.   W.Ger.   Swed.   It.

14.20   As an adjective, *U.S.* has gained currency in serious prose, although it is still not used in the most formal writing:

U.S. courts	U.S. dollars	U.S. involvement in Asia

ADDRESSES

14.21   In text (or in letter writing, which this manual does not deal with) addresses should be spelled out, including the following words:

Avenue, Boulevard, Building, Court, Drive, Lane, Parkway, Place, Road, Square, Street, Terrace; North, South, East, West

Exceptions are the abbreviations

NW, NE, SE, and SW,

used in some city addresses after the street name. State names are spelled out in addresses. (For the use of figures in addresses see 8.61–62.)

14.22   Again, addresses may be abbreviated in close-set matter, especially state names and the words mentioned above as spelled out in text:

Ave., Blvd., Bldg., Ct., Dr., La. *or* Ln., Pkwy., Pl., Rd., Sq., St., Terr.; N., S., E., W. (*before street name*)

POINTS OF THE COMPASS

14.23   When abbreviation of the points of the compass is called for (seldom in formal text), the following system may be used:

Cardinal: N, E, S, W; *intercardinal:* NE, SE, SW, NW
Others: NNE, ENE, ESE, etc.; N by E, NE by N, NE by E, etc.

381

LATITUDE AND LONGITUDE

14.24   When standing alone, and in running text, the words *latitude* and *longitude* are never abbreviated:

> the polar latitudes
> the zone from ten to forty degrees north latitude
> from 10°30′ north latitude to 10°30′ south latitude
> longitude 90° west

14.25   In technical work and in tabulations of coordinates, one of the following systems is used:

lat. 42°15′30″ N	long. 89°17′45″ W
lat. 42-15-30 N	long. 89-17-45 W
lat. 42°15.5′ N	long. 89°17.75′ W
lat. 42°15.̣5 N	long. 89°17.̣75 W

In any of these systems periods may be omitted after *lat.* and *long.*, or the designations may be dropped altogether, since *E, W, N,* or *S* identifies the coordinate:

> The chart showed shoal water at 19°29.65′ N, 107°45.36′ W.

TIME

14.26   Note that *units* of time are treated in a later section of this chapter (see 14.40).

YEARS

14.27   Accepted abbreviations for various systems of chronology are used in text or other matter, normally in small caps. The first four abbreviations listed below usually precede the year number; the others follow it. (For further explanation and examples see 8.41–42.)

> A.D., *anno Domini* (in the year of [our] Lord)
>
> A.H., *anno Hegirae* (in the year of the Hegira); *anno Hebraico* (in the Hebrew year)
>
> A.M., *anno mundi* (in the year of the world)
>
> A.S., *anno salutis* (in the year of salvation)
>
> A.U.C., *ab urbe condita* (from the founding of the city—i.e., Rome, in 753 B.C.)
>
> B.C., before Christ
>
> B.C.E., before the common era
>
> B.P., before the present
>
> C.E., common era
>
> M.Y.B.P., million years before the present

MONTHS

14.28   Names of the months are always spelled out in text, whether alone or in dates. In chronologies, notes, tabular matter, etc., they may be abbreviated according to one of the following systems, preferably the first. The second is used mainly in indexes of periodical literature.

> Jan.   Feb.   Mar.   Apr.   May   June   July   Aug.   Sept.
> Oct.   Nov.   Dec.
> Ja   F   Mr   Ap   My   Je   Jl   Ag   S   O   N   D

DAYS OF THE WEEK

14.29   Like the months, the names of the days of the week should be spelled out in text but may be abbreviated in other situations according to one of the following systems. The second is used only in very closely set catalogs and the like.

> Sun.   Mon.   Tues.   Wed.   Thurs.   Fri.   Sat.
> Su   M   Tu   W   Th   F   Sa

TIME OF DAY

14.30   The abbreviations indicating which half of the day clock time applies to are used in regular text as well as tabular and other such matter:

> A.M., *ante meridiem* (before noon)
> M., *meridies* (noon)
> P.M., *post meridiem* (after noon)

These abbreviations are usually set in small caps, as in the example, but lowercase italic (usual in Britain) may be used:

> *a.m.*   *m.*   *p.m.*

(For the use of figures with these abbreviations, see 8.47–48.)

SCHOLARSHIP

14.31   Abbreviations have a very long history of use in the realm of scholarship, and general principles concerning their use are widely agreed upon:

> To the greatest extent possible, abbreviations should be kept out of running text, except in technical matter.
>
> General abbreviations such as *etc., e.g.,* and *i.e.* are preferably confined to parenthetical references.
>
> The purely scholarly abbreviations such as *ibid., cf.,* and *s.v.* are preferably used only in notes and other forms of scholarly apparatus.

14.32   The following is a list of abbreviations frequently encountered in editing general scholarly text:

ab init., *ab initio,* from the beginning
abbr., abbreviated, -ion
abl., ablative
abr., abridged; abridgment
acc., accusative
act., active
ad inf., *ad infinitum,* to infinity
ad init., *ad initium,* at the beginning
ad int., *ad interim,* in the meantime
adj., adjective
ad lib., *ad libitum,* at will
ad loc., *ad locum,* at the place
adv., adverb
aet., *aetatis,* aged
AFr., Anglo-French
AN, Anglo-Norman
anon., anonymous
app., appendix
art., article
AS, Anglo-Saxon
b., born; brother
bibl., *bibliotheca,* library
bibliog., bibliography, -er, -ical
biog., biography, -er, -ical
biol., biology, -ical, -ist
bk., block; book
c., chapter (in law citations); *circa*
ca., *circa,* about, approximately
Cantab., *Cantabrigiensis,* of Cambridge
cf., *confer,* compare
chap., chapter
Cia, *Compañia,* Company (no period)
Cie, *Compagnie,* Company (no period)
col., column
colloq., colloquial, -ly, -ism
comp., compiler (*pl.* comps.); compiled by
compar., comparative
con., *contra,* against
conj., conjunction; conjugation
cons., consonant
constr., construction
cont., continued
contr., contraction
copr. or ©, copyright
cp., compare
d., daughter; died
dat., dative
def., definite, definition
dept., department

deriv., derivative
d.h., *das heißt*, namely
d.i., *das ist*, that is
dial., dialect
dict., dictionary
dim., diminutive
dist., district
div., division; divorced
do., ditto (the same)
doz., dozen
dram. pers., *dramatis personae*
Dr. u. Vrl., *Druck und Verlag*, printer and publisher
D.V., *Deo volente*, God willing
ea., each
ed., editor (*pl.* eds.); edition; edited by
EE, Early English
e.g., *exempli gratia*, for example
encyc., encyclopedia
Eng., English
engg., engineering
engr., engineer
eq., equation (*pl.* eqq. *or* eqs.)
esp., especially
et al., *et alii*, and others
etc., *et cetera*, and so forth
et seq., *et sequentes*, and the following
ex., example (*pl.* exx.)
f. *or* fem., feminine; female
f., and following (*pl.* ff.)
fasc., fascicle
fig., figure
fl., *floruit*, flourished
fol., folio
Fr., French
fr., from
fut., future
f.v., *folio verso*, on the back of the page
G. *or* Ger., German
Gael., Gaelic
gen., genitive; genus
geog., geography, -er, -ical
geol., geology, -ical, -ist
geom., geometry, -ical
ger., gerund
Gk., Greek
hdqrs., headquarters (*also* HQ)
hist., history, -ical, -ian
ibid., *ibidem*, in the same place
id., *idem*, the same
IE, Indo-European
i.e., *id est*, that is
imper., imperative

385

incl., inclusive; including; includes
indef., indefinite
indic., indicative
inf., *infra,* below
infin., infinitive
infra dig., *infra dignitatem,* undignified
in pr., *in principio,* in the beginning
inst., instant, this month; institute; institution
instr., instrumental
interj., interjection
intrans., intransitive
introd. *or* intro., introduction
I.Q. *or* IQ, intelligence quotient
irreg., irregular
It., Italian
L., left (in stage directions); Latin
l., line (*pl.* ll.) (*best not abbreviated*)
lang., language
Lat., Latin
lit., literally
loc., locative
loc. cit., *loco citato,* in the place cited
loq., *loquitur,* he/she speaks
m., married; male; measure (*pl.* mm.)
m. *or* masc., masculine
marg., margin, -al
math., mathematics, -ical
ME, Middle English
med., median; medical; medieval; medium
memo, memorandum
mgr., manager
MHG, Middle High German
misc., miscellaneous
MM, Maelzel's metronome (*tempo indication*)
m.m., *mutatis mutandis,* necessary changes being made
Mod. E., Modern English
MS (*pl.* MSS), *manuscriptum(-a),* manuscript(s)
mus., museum; music, -al
n., *natus,* born; note, footnote (*pl.* nn.); noun
nat., national; natural
N.B., *nota bene,* take careful note
n.d., no date
neg., negative
neut., neuter
no., number
nom., nominative
non obs., *non obstante,* notwithstanding
non seq., *non sequitur,* it does not follow
n.p., no place; no publisher
N.S., New Style (dates)
n.s., new series
ob., *obiit,* died

obs., obsolete
OE, Old English
OFr, Old French
OHG, Old High German
ON, Old Norse
op. cit., *opere citato*, in the work cited
O.S., Old Style (dates)
o.s., old series
Oxon., *Oxoniensis*, of Oxford
p., page (*pl.* pp.); past
par., paragraph
part., participle
pass., *passim*, throughout; passive
path., pathology, -ist, -ical
perf., perfect; perforated
perh., perhaps
pers., person, personal
pl., plate; plural
p.p., past participle
PPS, *post postscriptum*, a later postscript
prep., preposition
pres., present
pron., pronoun
pro tem., *pro tempore*, for the time being
prox., *proximo*, next month
PS, *postscriptum*, postscript
pt., part
pub., publication, publisher; published by
Q.E.D., *quod erat demonstrandum*, which was to be demonstrated
quart., quarterly
q.v., *quod vide*, which see
R., *rex*, king; *regina*, queen; right (in stage directions)
r., reigned; recto
refl., reflexive
repr., reprint, reprinted
rev., review; revised, revision
R.I.P., *requiescat in pace*, may he/she rest in peace
s., son; substantive
S.A., Société Anonyme
s.a., *sine anno*, without year; *sub anno*, under the year
sc., scene; *scilicet*, namely; *sculpsit*, carved by
s.d., *sine die*, without setting a day for reconvening
sec., section; *secundum*, according to
ser., series
sg. *or* sing., singular
s.l., *sine loco*, without place
sociol., sociology
Sp., Spanish
st., stanza
subj., subject, subjective
subst., substantive, -al
sup., *supra*, above

superl., superlative
supp. *or* suppl., supplement
s.v., *sub verbo, sub voce,* under the word (*pl.* s.vv.)
syn., synonym, -ous
theol., theology, -ian, -ical
trans., transitive; translated, -or
treas., treasurer
ult., *ultimo,* last month
univ., university
usw., *und so weiter,* and so forth
ut sup., *ut supra,* as above
v., verse (*pl.* vv.); verso; *vide,* see
v. *or* vb., verb
v.i., verb intransitive
viz., *videlicet,* namely
voc., vocative
vol., volume
vs. *or* v., *versus,* against
v.t., verb transitive
yr., your; year

BIBLE

BOOKS

14.33   In text, references to whole books of the Bible or whole chapters are spelled out:

> The opening chapters of Ephesians constitute Paul's most compelling sermon on love.
>
> Jeremiah, chapters 42–44, records the flight of the Jews to Egypt when Jerusalem fell in 586 B.C.
>
> As Falstaff lay dying, he apparently sought comfort in reciting the Twenty-third Psalm.

14.34   Exact references to scriptural passages, whether used in text, in parenthetical citations, or in notes, employ abbreviations for the names of most books of the Bible (see 17.63 for the form of such citations). The following list gives the books of the Bible as they appear in the Authorized (King James) Version, along with the usual abbreviations. Protestant and Anglican scholars generally use these names and abbreviations in citing Scripture in later English-language versions also.

OLD TESTAMENT

Genesis	Gen.	Joshua	Josh.
Exodus	Exod.	Judges	Judg.
Leviticus	Lev.	Ruth	Ruth
Numbers	Num.	1 Samuel	1 Sam.
Deuteronomy	Deut.	2 Samuel	2 Sam.

1 Kings	1 Kings	Ezekiel	Ezek.
2 Kings	2 Kings	Daniel	Dan.
1 Chronicles	1 Chron.	Hosea	Hos.
2 Chronicles	2 Chron.	Joel	Joel
Ezra	Ezra	Amos	Amos
Nehemiah	Neh.	Obadiah	Obad.
Esther	Esther	Jonah	Jon.
Job	Job	Micah	Mic.
Psalms	Ps. (*pl.* Pss.)	Nahum	Nah.
Proverbs	Prov.	Habakkuk	Hab.
Ecclesiastes	Eccles.	Zephaniah	Zeph.
Song of Solomon	Song of Sol.	Haggai	Hag.
Isaiah	Isa.	Zechariah	Zech.
Jeremiah	Jer.	Malachi	Mal.
Lamentations	Lam.		

APOCRYPHA

1 Esdras	1 Esd.
2 Esdras	2 Esd.
Tobit	Tob.
Judith	Jth.
The Rest of Esther	Rest of Esther
The Wisdom of Solomon	Wisd. of Sol.
Ecclesiasticus	Ecclus.
Baruch	Bar.
The Song of the Three Holy Children	Song of Three Children
Susanna	Sus.
Bel and the Dragon	Bel and Dragon
Prayer of Manasses (*or* Manasseh)	Pr. of Man.
1 Maccabees	1 Macc.
2 Maccabees	2 Macc.

NEW TESTAMENT

Matthew	Matt.	1 Timothy	1 Tim.
Mark	Mark	2 Timothy	2 Tim.
Luke	Luke	Titus	Titus
John	John	Philemon	Philem.
Acts of the Apostles	Acts	Hebrews	Heb.
Romans	Rom.	James	James
1 Corinthians	1 Cor.	1 Peter	1 Pet.
2 Corinthians	2 Cor.	2 Peter	2 Pet.
Galatians	Gal.	1 John	1 John
Ephesians	Eph.	2 John	2 John
Philippians	Phil.	3 John	3 John
Colossians	Col.	Jude	Jude
1 Thessalonians	1 Thess.	Revelation	Rev.
2 Thessalonians	2 Thess.		

Roman Catholic versions of the Bible include the Apocrypha within the canon of the Old Testament, and so the sequence of books is somewhat different. The following is a list of the books as they appear in the New American Bible, along with the abbreviations used by the scholars who prepared that version. The very brief forms should be useful in any scriptural studies.

OLD TESTAMENT

Genesis	Gn	Proverbs	Prv
Exodus	Ex	Ecclesiastes	Eccl
Leviticus	Lv	Song of Songs	Sg (Song)
Numbers	Nm	Wisdom	Wis
Deuteronomy	Dt	Sirach	Sir
Joshua	Jos	Isaiah	Is
Judges	Jgs	Jeremiah	Jer
Ruth	Ru	Lamentations	Lam
1 Samuel	1 Sm	Baruch	Bar
2 Samuel	2 Sm	Ezekiel	Ez
1 Kings	1 Kgs	Daniel	Dn
2 Kings	2 Kgs	Hosea	Hos
1 Chronicles	1 Chr	Joel	Jl
2 Chronicles	2 Chr	Amos	Am
Ezra	Ezr	Obadiah	Ob
Nehemiah	Neh	Jonah	Jon
Tobit	Tb	Micah	Mi
Judith	Jdt	Nahum	Na
Esther	Est	Habakkuk	Hb
1 Maccabees	1 Mc	Zephaniah	Zep
2 Maccabees	2 Mc	Haggai	Hg
Job	Jb	Zechariah	Zec
Psalms	Ps(s)	Malachi	Mal

NEW TESTAMENT

Matthew	Mt	1 Timothy	1 Tm
Mark	Mk	2 Timothy	2 Tm
Luke	Lk	Titus	Ti
John	Jn	Philemon	Phlm
Acts of the Apostles	Acts	Hebrews	Heb
Romans	Rom	James	Jas
1 Corinthians	1 Cor	1 Peter	1 Pt
2 Corinthians	2 Cor	2 Peter	2 Pt
Galatians	Gal	1 John	1 Jn
Ephesians	Eph	2 John	2 Jn
Philippians	Phil	3 John	3 Jn
Colossians	Col	Jude	Jude
1 Thessalonians	1 Thes	Revelation	Rv
2 Thessalonians	2 Thes		

VERSIONS AND SECTIONS

14.35   In the field of biblical scholarship, it is customary to refer to various versions and sections of the Bible by abbreviations:

Syr.	Syriac
MT	Masoretic text
LXX	Septuagint

Vulg.	Vulgate
AV	Authorized (King James) Version
DV	Douay Version
RV	Revised Version
RV m	Revised Version, margin
ERV	English Revised Version
ERV m	English Revised Version, margin
ARV	American Revised Version
ARV m	American Revised Version, margin
RSV	Revised Standard Version
EV	English version(s)
AT	American Translation
NAB	New American Bible
NEB	New English Bible
JB	Jerusalem Bible
OT	Old Testament
Apoc.	Apocrypha
NT	New Testament

MEASURE

14.36 Abbreviations of units of measure are identical in the singular and plural.

ENGLISH MEASURE

14.37 Abbreviations for the English units of measure find very little use in straight text except for technical work. On the rare occasions in which they are used in scientific copy they are usually set without periods. Like other abbreviations these are most useful in tabular work. (For the use of figures with abbreviations, see 8.15–16.)

14.38 *Length, area, and volume*

LENGTH	AREA	VOLUME
in. *or* ", inch	sq. in., square inch	cu. in., cubic inch
ft. *or* ', foot	sq. ft., square foot	cu. ft., cubic foot
yd., yard	sq. yd., square yard	cu. yd., cubic yard
rd., rod	sq. rd:, square rod	
mi., mile	sq. mi., square mile	
	a., acre	

Sometimes exponents are used with the common abbreviations to designate areas or volumes:

The area of the floor to be covered is 425 ft.^{2}.
The volume of the tank was estimated to be 638 ft.^{3}.

14.39 *Weight and capacity.* The complicated English system of measures is further complicated in the case of weight by having three systems to deal with: *avoirdupois* (the common system), *troy* (used mainly by jewelers), and *apothecaries'* measure. There is little chance of confusion between systems, however, and the abbreviations are similar. If need be, an abbreviation can be referred to the appropriate system in this way: *lb. av., lb. t., lb. ap.* Also, the systems of capacity measure used in the United States and in parts of the British Commonwealth differ, but the names of the units are the same, and abbreviations seldom have to be distinguished.

WEIGHT	DRY MEASURE	LIQUID MEASURE
gr., grain	pt., pint	min. *or* ♍, minim
s. *or* ℈, scruple	qt., quart	fl. dr. or f. ʒ, fluid dram
dr. *or* ʒ, dram	pk., peck	fl. oz. *or* f. ℥, fluid ounce
dwt., pennyweight	bu., bushel	gi., gill
oz. *or* ℥, ounce		pt., pint
lb. *or* # (*avdp. only*),		qt., quart
pound		gal., gallon
cwt., hundredweight		bbl., barrel
tn. *or* ton		

14.40 *Time*. English abbreviations for the standard units of time are given here. (For other abbreviations concerned with time, see 14.26–30.)

sec., second	h., hr., hour	mo., month
min., minute	d. *or* day	yr., year

INTERNATIONAL MEASURE

14.41 The International System of Units (*Système international d'unités,* abbreviated "SI") is used generally by scientists around the world. It is roughly equivalent to what is popularly called the metric system.

14.42 *Base units*. As the system is currently used, there are seven fundamental SI units, termed "base units":

	UNIT	ABBREVIATION
length	meter	m
mass	kilogram	kg
time	second	s
electric current	ampere	A
thermodynamic temperature	kelvin	K
amount of substance	mole	mol
luminous intensity	candela	cd

14.43 SI units are all written in lowercase style; abbreviations are also lowercase except for those derived from proper names. No periods are used with any of the abbreviations in the international system.

14.44 *Derived units*. In addition to the base units of the system, a host of derived units, which stem from the base units, are employed. One class of these is formed by adding a prefix, representing a power of ten, to the base unit. For example, a *kilometer* is equal to 1,000 meters, and a *millisecond* is 0.001 (that is, 1/1,000) second. The prefixes in current use are as follows:

SI PREFIXES

Factor	Prefix	Symbol		Factor	Prefix	Symbol
10^{18}	exa	E		10^{-1}	deci	d
10^{15}	peta	P		10^{-2}	centi	c
10^{12}	tera	T		10^{-3}	milli	m
10^{9}	giga	G		10^{-6}	micro	μ
10^{6}	mega	M		10^{-9}	nano	n
10^{3}	kilo	k		10^{-12}	pico	p
10^{2}	hecto	h		10^{-15}	femto	f
10^{1}	deka	da		10^{-18}	atto	a

14.45   Although, for historical reasons, the kilogram rather than the gram was chosen as the base unit, prefixes are applied to the term *gram* instead of to the official base unit: megagram (Mg), milligram (mg), nanogram (ng), etc.

14.46   Another class of derived units consists of powers of base units and of base units in algebraic relationships. Some of the more familiar of these are the following:

	UNIT	SYMBOL
area	square meter	m^2
volume	cubic meter	m^3
velocity	meter per second	m/s
acceleration	meter per second squared	m/s^2
density	kilogram per cubic meter	kg/m^3
luminescence	candela per square meter	cd/m^2

14.47   Many derived SI units have names of their own:

	UNIT	SYMBOL	EQUIVALENT
frequency	hertz	Hz	cycles per second
force	newton	N	kilogram-meters per second squared
pressure	pascal	Pa	newtons per square meter
energy	joule	J	kilogram-meter
power	watt	W	joules per second
quantity of electricity	coulomb	C	ampere-second
electric potential	volt	V	watts per ampere
capacitance	farad	F	coulombs per volt
electrical resistance	ohm	Ω	volts per ampere

14.48   *Use of figures with SI units.* In the international system it is considered preferable to use only numbers between 0.1 and 1,000 in expressing the quantity of any SI unit. Thus the quantity 12,000 meters is expressed as 12 km, not 12,000 m. So too, 0.003 cubic centimeter is preferably written 3 mm³, not 0.003 cm³.

14.49   For the decimal point, the international system permits either a dot (the British and American practice) or a comma (the French practice). Note that the comma is *not* used in international work to mark off groups of three digits in large numbers: if such figures cannot be avoided, spaces are left between the groups of three—to the right of the decimal point as well as to the left:

    31 000 000   0.000 000 31

SCIENCE AND TECHNOLOGY

14.50   The international system has by no means displaced older units and modes of expression in all places and in all branches of science. A number of disciplines accept the SI units and usages only insofar as they retain the elements of older scientific vocabulary, and others accept the system but supplement it with units and practices of their own. What follows is a list of units of measure and their abbreviations, as well as other common abbreviations, used in various branches of the physical and biological sciences, or by engineers and technicians. A few of these units are identical with units of the *Système international,* many are compatible with the system, some are altogether unrelated to it.

Å *or* A, angstrom (unit of wavelength: 10^{-10} m)
AC, alternating current
AF, audiofrequency
AH, ampere-hour
AM, amplitude modulation
amp, ampere
atm, standard atmosphere (unit of pressure)
at wt, atomic weight
av *or* avdp, avoirdupois
bar, barometer, barometric
° Bé, degrees Baumé
BHP, brake horsepower
BP, boiling point
Bq, becquerel
Btu, British thermal unit
° C, degrees Celsius ("centigrade")
Cal, large, or kilogram, calorie
cal, small, or gram, calorie
cc, cubic centimeter
CP, candlepower
CPS, cycles per second
cu, cubic

db, decibel
DC, direct current
df *or* DOF, degrees of freedom
dyn, dyne (10^{-5} N)
EMF, electromotive force
erg, erg (10^{-7} J)
eV, electron volt
° F, degrees Fahrenheit
FM, frequency modulation
ft lb, foot-pound
GeV, billion (10^9) electron volts
ha, hectare (10^4 m²)
HP, horsepower
kbar, kilobar
kc, kilocycle
kn, knot (wind velocity: nautical mile per hour)
KPH, kilometers per hour
kw, kilowatt
kwh, kilowatt-hour
l, liter
mc, millicurie, megacycle
MeV, million electron volts
ml, milliliter
MP, melting point
MPG, miles per gallon
MPH, miles per hour
$\mu\mu$farad, micro-microfarad
MS, mean square
N or ɴ, number (data base)
neg, negative
NM *or* naut mi, nautical mile (1,852 m)
NS *or* n.s., not significant
p, probability
pH, measure of acidity or alkalinity
pos, positive
R, roentgen (X-ray exposure)
° R, degrees Réaumur
RF, radio frequency
rms, root mean square
RPM, revolutions per minute
SD *or* s.d., standard deviation
SE *or* s.e., standard error
sp gr, specific gravity
sq, square
SS, sum of squares
std, standard
STP, standard temperature and pressure
STPA, standard temperature and pressure, absolute
STPG, standard temperature and pressure, gauge
T *or* t, metric ton (10^3 kg)
temp, temperature

ASTRONOMY

14.51   Astronomers and astrophysicists employ the international system of measure but supplement it with special terminology and abbreviations. Some of these are detailed in the paragraphs that follow.

14.52   *Celestial coordinates. Right ascension,* abbreviated α, is given in hours, minutes, and seconds of sidereal time, and *declination,* abbreviated δ, is given in degrees, minutes, and seconds of arc north (marked $+$ or left unmarked) or south (marked $-$) of the celestial equator:

$$14^h6^m7^s \qquad -49°8'22''$$

If decimal fractions of the basic units are employed, they are indicated as shown:

$$14^h6^m7\overset{s}{.}2 \qquad +34\overset{°}{.}26$$

14.53   *Other units and abbreviations.* Some other units and abbreviations used in astronomy are the following:

AU, astronomical unit (mean earth-sun distance)
lt-yr, light-year (distance light travels in a year: 9.46×10^{12} km)
pc, parsec (*pa*rallax *sec*ond: 3.084×10^{13} km), kpc (1,000 pc), Mpc (10^6 pc)
UT *or* UTC, universal time

CHEMICAL ELEMENTS

14.54   The symbols for the chemical elements are one- or two-letter abbreviations of the official names of the elements (e.g., lead = *plumbum*). They are used in text as well as in equations, formulas, and tabular matter. These abbreviations are never set with periods. (For the use of mass and molecular numbers with names of the elements, see 7.120.)

actinium	Ac	carbon	C
aluminum	Al	cerium	Ce
americium	Am	cesium	Cs
antimony	Sb	chlorine	Cl
argon	Ar	chromium	Cr
arsenic	As	cobalt	Co
astatine	At	columbium	Cb
barium	Ba	copper	Cu
berkelium	Bk	curium	Cm
beryllium	Be	[deuterium	D]
bismuth	Bi	dysprosium	Dy
boron	B	einsteinium	Es
bromine	Br	erbium	Er
cadmium	Cd	europium	Eu
calcium	Ca	fermium	Fm
californium	Cf	fluorine	F

francium	Fr	polonium	Po
gadolinium	Gd	potassium	K
gallium	Ga	praseodymium	Pr
germanium	Ge	promethium	Pm
gold	Au	protactinium	Pa
hafnium	Hf	radium	Ra
helium	He	radon	Rn
holmium	Ho	rhenium	Re
hydrogen	H	rhodium	Rh
indium	In	rubidium	Rb
iodine	I	ruthenium	Ru
iridium	Ir	samarium	Sm
iron	Fe	scandium	Sc
krypton	Kr	selenium	Se
lanthanum	La	silicon	Si
lawrencium	Lr	silver	Ag
lead	Pb	sodium	Na
lithium	Li	strontium	Sr
lutetium	Lu	sulfur	S
magnesium	Mg	tantalum	Ta
manganese	Mn	technetium	Tc
mendelevium	Md	tellurium	Te
mercury	Hg	terbium	Tb
molybdenum	Mo	thallium	Tl
neodymium	Nd	thorium	Th
neon	Ne	thulium	Tm
neptunium	Np	tin	Sn
nickel	Ni	titanium	Ti
niobium	Nb	[tritium	T]
nitrogen	N	tungsten	W
nobelium	No	uranium	U
osmium	Os	vanadium	V
oxygen	O	xenon	Xe
palladium	Pd	ytterbium	Yb
phosphorus	P	yttrium	Y
platinum	Pt	zinc	Z
plutonium	Pu	zirconium	Zr

COMMERCIAL COPY

14.55 Copy concerned with commerce, especially tabular matter, makes frequent use of many of the abbreviations and symbols given here.

GENERAL ABBREVIATIONS

acct., account	COD, cash on delivery
agt., agent	cr., credit, -or
a/v, ad valorem	cwt., hundredweight
bal., balance	doz., dozen
bbl., barrel	dr., debit, debtor
bdl., bundle	ea., each
bu., bushel	f.o.b., free on board
c.l., carload	gro., gross

397

mdse., merchandise	pk., peck
mfg., manufacturing	std., standard
mfr., manufacturer	ult., *ultimo* (last)
pd., paid	

SYMBOLS

℔ *or* /, per	©, copyright
#, number; pound	Mex.$, Mexican peso
%, percent	Can$, Canadian dollar
℅, in care of	£, pound
@, at	p., penny
$ *or* dol., dollar	I £, Israeli pound
c., ct., *or* ¢, cent	

CONSTITUTIONS AND BYLAWS

14.56 In quoting from constitutions, bylaws, and the like, the words *section* and *article* are spelled out the first time they are used and abbreviated thereafter. Caps and small caps are traditionally employed for these words:

> SECTION 1. The name of the association . . .
> SEC. 2. The object of the association . . .
> ARTICLE 234. It shall be the duty of . . .
> ART. 235. It shall be the duty of . . .

FOR FURTHER REFERENCE

14.57 *Webster's New Collegiate Dictionary* includes a great many abbreviations from all fields in the body of the work—in strict, letter-by-letter alphabetical order.

15 Documentation: References, Notes, and Bibliographies

Introduction 15.1
Author-Date System 15.4
    Text References 15.7
        Form 15.7
        Placement 15.31
        Agreement of citation and reference 15.33
    Author-Date System with Notes 15.34
Notes 15.36
    Numbering 15.38
    Note Contents 15.46
        Citations 15.46
        Order of items 15.48
        Quotations 15.51
        "See also" and "Cf." 15.53
    Endnotes 15.54
        Placement 15.54
        Arrangement 15.55
        Running heads 15.56
    Footnotes 15.58
        Page makeup 15.58
        Reducing length and number 15.61
    Endnotes versus Footnotes 15.65
    Abbreviations in Notes 15.67
    Dual System of Notes 15.68
        Endnotes plus footnotes 15.68
        Editor's or translator's plus author's notes 15.69
    Unnumbered Notes 15.70
Reference Lists and Bibliographies 15.74
    Reference-List Style 15.78
        Cross-references 15.81
    Bibliography Style 15.82
        One list 15.82
        Divided into sections 15.83
        Annotated 15.84
        Bibliographical essay 15.85
    Arrangement of Entries 15.87
        Alphabetizing 15.88
        Three-em dash for repeated name 15.94

INTRODUCTION

15.1   Almost every work that is neither fiction nor an account based on personal experience relies in part on secondary sources (other publications on the same or related subjects) or on primary sources (manuscript collections, archives, contemporary accounts, diaries, books, personal interviews, and so on). Ethics, as well as the laws of copyright, requires authors to identify their sources, particularly when quoting directly from them. Conventions and practices for thus documenting a text have long varied from discipline to discipline, from publisher to publisher, and from journal to journal. Increasingly, however, the old distinctions are becoming blurred as scholars cross disciplinary lines, and publishers, more than ever concerned about the balance sheet, urge conciseness and practicality over scholarly indulgence in documentation.

15.2   This chapter discusses and illustrates four methods used to document texts: (1) Author-date (name and year) references in the text with full citations in a reference list at the end of the book or article, a method long used by the biological and physical scientists and now rapidly gaining adherents in the social sciences and the humanities (15.4–35). (2) Endnotes (backnotes), like footnotes but placed all together at the end of the book or article (15.54–57). (3) Footnotes, still beloved by traditionalists, especially those in the humanities (15.58–64). (4) Unnumbered notes, and notes keyed to line or page numbers and placed either at the foot of the page or at the back of the book (15.70–73). Also discussed in this chapter are various kinds of bibliographies and their relation to text references and notes (15.74–86). Authors and editors should be aware of the advantages and limitations of each system, as well as how to prepare copy expeditiously and accurately.

15.3   Specific rules for and examples of individual bibliography entries are given in chapter 16. Specific examples of note forms, both endnotes and footnotes, appear in chapter 17. For citing sources in the text rather than in notes see 10.54–68.

AUTHOR-DATE SYSTEM

15.4   The system of documentation generally most economical in space, in time (for author, editor, and typesetter), and in cost (to publisher and public)—in short, the most practical—is the *author-date* system. Authors' names and dates of publication are given in the text, usually in parentheses, and keyed to a list of works cited, which is placed at the end of the book or article. This list is arranged alphabetically and may bear the title "Reference List," "Works Cited," "Literature Cited,"

"Bibliography," or some variation of these, depending on what seems most appropriate.

15.5 The University of Chicago Press strongly recommends the author-date system of documentation for all its books in the natural sciences and most of those in the social sciences. Authors in other fields who are willing to adjust their documentation to this system are encouraged to do so.

15.6 A related, but in our opinion less satisfactory, method of text reference gives only a number in the text: (9) or [9] or, in some medical publications, [9]. This number refers not to a note but to a numbered list of works cited, at the end of the text, which is arranged either alphabetically by authors' names or in order of the first appearance of each source in the text. The chief disadvantage of this system is that additions or deletions cannot be made after the manuscript is typed without changing numbers in both text references and list. The author-date system, on the other hand, permits additions or deletions up to the moment the manuscript is set in type and has the added advantage that readers familiar with the sources will not have to turn to the list of works cited each time a reference is given in the text.

TEXT REFERENCES

15.7 *Form.* The basic reference in the author-date system consists of the last name of an author and the year of publication of the work, with no punctuation between them:

(Smith 1978)

15.8 A specific page, section, equation, or other division of the cited work follows the date, preceded by a comma:

(Piaget 1980, 74)	(Johnson 1979, sec. 24.5)
(Pratt 1975, 121–25)	(Fowler and Hoyle 1965, eq. [87])

15.9 A colon instead of a comma is sometimes used between date and page number: (Piaget 1980:74). The University of Chicago Press prefers the comma.

15.10 Unless confusion would result, "p." or "pp." is omitted with page numbers.

15.11 When the reference is to both volume and page of the author's work, a colon will distinguish between the two:

(Barnes 1981, 3:125)
(García 1982, 2:26, 35; 3:50–53)

15.12   A reference to a volume only, no page number, usually requires "vol." for clarity:

> (García 1982, vol. 2)

15.13   "Author" as used in these paragraphs means the name under which the work is alphabetized in the list of works cited and may thus refer to an editor or compiler or organization as well as an individual author or group of authors. Note that "ed." or "comp." is not given in the text reference.

15.14   For works of multiple authorship use names for *two* or *three* authors:

> (Meredith and Lewis 1979)
> (Wynken, Blynkin, and Nodd 1988)

15.15   Although "and" is generally preferred, an ampersand (&) may be used between names in parenthetical references, but not in the text itself:

> (Wynken, Blynkin & Nodd 1988)
> *but:*
> Wynken, Blynkin, and Nodd (1988) believe that . . .

Note that no comma is used before an ampersand.

15.16   In a reference to a work by two family members with the same last name, the name is repeated:

> (Weinberg and Weinberg 1980)

The plural of the name may be used in the text when the reference is to the persons rather than the work:

> The Weinbergs (1980) maintain that Darrow . . .

15.17   For more than three authors use the name of the first followed by "et al." or "and others": Thus, for a work by Zipursky, Hull, White, and Israels:

> (Zipursky et al. 1959)

15.18   If, as sometimes happens, there is another work *of the same date* that would also abbreviate to "Zipursky et al."—say, a paper by Zipursky, Smith, Jones, and Brown—one must give either the group of names in full or a short title identifying the work cited:

> (Zipursky, Smith, Jones, and Brown 1958)
> *or:*
> (Zipursky et al., *Brief notes,* 1958)

15.19   Another way sometimes, but rarely, used to distinguish such works is to cite the first *two* names followed by et al.:

> (Zipursky, Hull, et al. 1958)
> (Zipursky, Smith, et al. 1958)

15.20   When a book or pamphlet carries no individual author's name, or group of authors' names, on the title page and is published or sponsored by a corporation, government agency, association, or other named group, the name of that group usually serves as author's name in text references and in the reference list. Most of these present no problem and may be used in full:

>   (International Rice Research Institute 1977)
>   (Federal Reserve Bank of Boston 1976)

15.21   Some group names, being lengthy or composed of several parts, are awkward in text references, particularly when they recur throughout a work. Abbreviations or shortened forms are desirable for these, but care must be exercised to make the entry in the reference list begin with the element used in the text reference (see 16.143). If, for example, a text reference reads "(Center for Human Resource Research 1977)," but the work appears in the reference list under "Ohio State University, College of Administrative Science," how is an interested reader going to find it? Since the full reference, "(Ohio State University, College of Administrative Science, Center for Human Resource Research 1977)," is clearly a bit too long for more than, at the most, one text reference, it would be advisable to use either "(Ohio State University 1977)" or "(Center for Human Resource Research 1977)" with a cross-reference in the reference list:

>   Center for Human Resource Research. *See* Ohio State University.

15.22   A few such cross-references in the list are useful, but when there are many abbreviations, especially when initials or acronyms are used in text references, a separate list of abbreviations in addition to the reference list is advisable (see 1.45, and fig. 15.3). Such a list should precede the reference list.

15.23   Government agencies as authors present frequent problems in citations because of the length of their names. No body of rules could be drawn up to solve all such problems; citation forms must often be devised by author, or editor, on an ad hoc basis, using common sense and a regard for the reader's convenience. The same form, once decided upon, must of course be used for all references to a particular work throughout a book or article.

15.24   Two or more references given together are separated by semicolons:

>   (Light 1972; Light and Wong 1975; Kingston 1976)

15.25   Several works by the same author are cited by date only and separated by commas; when page numbers are given, the references are separated by semicolons and the name is repeated:

> (Kelley 1896a, 1896b, 1907)
> (Kelley 1896a, 10; Kelley 1896b; Kelley 1907, 3)

15.26   Note that the order in which multiple references are given is determined by the author who cites them. Editorial rearranging in alphabetical or chronological order without consultation with the author is not recommended.

15.27   Citation of a new edition of an older work should include the original date as well as the date of the edition used (see 16.57).

> (Piaget [1924] 1969, 75)

Note that the date of the modern edition is essential if a page reference to it is given.

15.28   Citation of a source not in the reference list, such as a personal letter or interview, should give the full name of the letter writer or the person interviewed (unless it appears in the text) and the description and date of the communication:

> Spieth has indicated that some men they studied who had hypertensive drugs were indeed faster in psychomotor speed than nontreated hypertensives (Walter Spieth, letter to the author, June 1962).
>
> Zebadiah Zulch (telephone interview, 1 April 1978) has maintained that he never agreed with Zipursky in the matter.

15.29   Citations to collections of unpublished manuscripts or archives may usually be handled by mentioning the specific item and its date, if any, in the text itself and listing the collection and its depository in the references:

> Mary E. Carpenter, a farmer's wife who lived near Rochester in 1871, listed what she did in one day at harvesting time. "My hand is so tired perhaps you'll excuse penciling," she began a letter to her cousin Laura on 18 August.

One might add "(Carpenter Papers)" at the end of the above, but it is unnecessary here because the name mentioned in the text is the same as the name of the collection listed in the references and there could be no confusion with another collection. The reference listing would read:

> Carpenter, Mary E. Lovell, and Family Papers. Minnesota Historical Society. St. Paul.

15.30   For more examples of unpublished materials in bibliographies see 16.134–40.

15.31   *Placement.* If possible, a reference should be placed just before a mark of punctuation:

Before proceeding with a more detailed discussion of our methods of analysis, we will describe the system of scaling quantitative scores (Guilford 1950).

If this placement is impractical, the reference should be inserted at a logical place in the sentence:

Various investigators (Jones and Carter 1980) have reported findings at variance with the foregoing.

15.32   When all or part of the citation is incorporated in the sentence, it is not enclosed in parentheses:

Jones and Carter (1980) report findings at variance with the foregoing.

All I can do is present the daughter-dependency equivalent of the transformational analysis which I advocate in Hudson 1976b. In this paper I argue for an analysis very similar in spirit to the one in Stockwell, Schachter, and Partee 1973, in which the result . . .

15.33   *Agreement of citation and reference.* It goes without saying that author-date citations in the text must agree exactly with the list of references. Any discrepancies in the spelling of names or the dates of publication must be rectified by the author or the editor before the manuscript is sent to the typesetter.

AUTHOR-DATE SYSTEM WITH NOTES

15.34   When more documentation than simple source citations is called for, endnotes at the back of the book or at the end of an article (see 15.54) may solve the problem. Here both notes and text use author-date citations referring to the reference list, which follows the note section:

1. This notion seems to have something in common with Piaget's (1977) concept of nonbalance and equilibrium in the area of knowledge.

15.35   A few footnotes—notes at the bottom of the page—may sometimes be combined with the author-date references, but they usually should concern only such matters as identification of an author or permission to quote copyright material. Footnotes, as opposed to endnotes, add to the cost of a publication, and some publishers may not permit them.

NOTES

15.36   Notes documenting the text, and corresponding to reference numbers in the text, are properly called *footnotes* when they are printed at the foot of the page and *notes* or *endnotes* (sometimes *backnotes*) when they are printed at the back of the book, at the end of a chapter, or at the end of an article in a journal. In practice, however, a note documenting or adding to the text is often called a footnote regardless of where it appears.

15.37   In book manuscripts employing the note system of documentation, the University of Chicago Press, generally for economic reasons, prefers that authors use endnotes rather than footnotes. This manual is one of the exceptions. (For typing notes see 2.21–22. For specific note forms see chap. 17.)

NUMBERING

15.38   Notes should be numbered consecutively, beginning with 1, throughout a chapter of a book or an article in a journal. Although in scholarly books this sometimes results in three-digit numbers (undesirable, particularly from a book designer's point of view), it is far more practical than the old-fashioned system of numbering footnotes beginning with 1 on each page, which required numbers to be reset in proof.

15.39   Note numbers in the text *follow* any punctuation marks (except a dash), and are placed outside a closing parenthesis:

> "This," George Templeton Strong wrote approvingly, "is what our tailors can do."[1]
> (In an earlier book he had said quite the opposite.)[2]
> This was obvious in the Shotwell series[3]—and it must be remembered that Shotwell was a student of Robinson.

15.40   Wherever possible a note number should come at the end of a sentence, or at least at the end of a clause. Numbers set between subject and verb or between other related words in a sentence are distracting to the reader.

15.41   Preferably, the note number *follows* a quotation, whether the quotation is short and run into the text or long and set off from the text. Occasionally it may be inserted after an author's name or after matter preceding the quotation.

15.42   Placing note numbers at the end of, or within, a line of display type is discouraged. A note applicable to an entire chapter, or article, should be unnumbered (see 15.70). A reference number that appears at the end of a subhead should be moved to an appropriate spot in the text.

15.43   The same reference number should not be repeated in the text (in tables with footnotes this is permissible, often desirable; see 12.48). Where a subsequent reference is made to a source cited earlier, the new note contains either the shortened form of the citation or, if the citation is exactly the same, a reference to the earlier note:

> 3. See note 1 above.

15.44   If a note is added, or deleted, in the typescript, the following numbers throughout the chapter must be changed and any cross-references to notes adjusted. Such evidence of negligence as a note numbered 4a is unprofessional. If the book has been typeset, any material to be added should be inserted in the proofs at the end of an existing note, or in parentheses in the text. In page proofs, nothing should be added that would alter the length of the type page.

15.45   Notes to tables, charts, graphs, or other illustrative material are not numbered with the text notes. Symbols or letters, sometimes numbers, indicate notes to such material (see 12.49), and the notes are printed below the table or illustration, not at the foot of the text page or at the end of the book or article.

NOTE CONTENTS

15.46   *Citations*. In a work with no bibliography or with only a discursive bibliographical essay or other nonalphabetical arrangement of sources, a note—either endnote or footnote—documenting the first reference to a source should include full bibliographical details (see 17.2). Subsequent citations to the same source may use a short form (l7.6). In a work with many references cited in footnotes, repetition of the full citation at first appearance in each chapter is often helpful, but not essential. With endnotes a full citation of the same source in each chapter is usually unnecessary and even undesirable because the note section, besides being keyed to the text, becomes a section of the book in itself wherein the reader may find all references to a given work much more readily than if they were scattered throughout as footnotes.

15.47   When endnotes or footnotes are extensive or when references to a particular source are far apart, a cross-reference to the note giving the full citation will aid the reader:

> 95. Miller, *Quest* (see chap. 1, n. 4), 81.

15.48   *Order of items*. Wherever possible, all items in a note should be run together in a single paragraph. A long endnote may sometimes consist of several paragraphs, but a footnote of more than one paragraph may present a problem in page makeup.

15.49   When a note contains not only the source of a quotation in the text but other related material as well, the source of the quotation comes first. The following material may start a new sentence or may be separated from the first item by a semicolon, depending on the nature of the material.

15.50   Several references documenting a single fact in the text should be separated by semicolons, the last one followed by a period (see example in 15.62).

15.51   *Quotations.* When a note includes a quotation, or other matter to be documented, the source is given in parentheses, after the quotation and before the final period.

> 4. One estimate of the size of the reading public at this time was that of Sydney Smith: "Readers are fourfold in number compared with what they were before the beginning of the French war. . . . There are four or five hundred thousand readers more than there were thirty years ago, among the lower orders" (*Letters*, ed. Nowell C. Smith [New York: Oxford University Press, 1953], 1:341, 343).

An acceptable alternative is to give the source following the quotation without parentheses; the quotation then carries terminal punctuation, and the source citation ends with a period:

> ". . . among the lower orders." *Letters,* ed. Nowell C. Smith (New York: Oxford University Press, 1953), 1:341, 343.

Consistency in this matter should be observed throughout a book.

15.52   A long quotation in an endnote may be treated in the same way as a block quotation (extract) in the text (see 10.13), such as by indenting it from the left.

"SEE ALSO" AND "CF."

15.53   Authors should keep in mind the distinction between *see* or *see also* and *cf.* (*confer,* "compare"). Cf. is not italicized (except in legal style) and is capitalized only when it begins a sentence (as here) or a note.

ENDNOTES

15.54   *Placement.* Endnotes are best placed at the back of a book, in a section entitled "Notes," after any appendix material and before a bibliography. Notes may be placed at the end of a chapter in a volume where each chapter has a different author, such as collections of essays, symposium papers, or reports. (Notes *must* be printed with their respective papers when offprints are to be supplied.) Most readers, however, consider notes at the end of a chapter harder to find and therefore more of a nuisance than notes printed all together at the end of a book, with running heads by which to locate them.

15.55   *Arrangement.* Endnotes are arranged by chapter in the note section. The chapter number or title or both must be given—usually as an *A*-level subhead (see 1.71). Book designers' specifications will differ, of course, but one way to print notes is given in figure 15.1.

15.56   *Running heads.* To enable the reader to locate specific notes with a minimum of difficulty, each page of the note section, except the opening page, should carry a running head giving the inclusive text pages on which the references to the notes on that page appear (see fig. 15.1).

40. Moore, *A Voyage to Georgia*, 45. Moore is actually citing a companion who went with Oglethorpe to Darien.

41. Oglethorpe to [the Trustees], 27 February 1736, "Oglethorpe Letters," 15.

42. Moore, *A Voyage to Georgia*, 47–49, 51–52.

43. Oglethorpe to the Trustees, 28 April 1741, "Oglethorpe Letters," 113.

44. Oglethorpe to the Trustees, 24 January 1740, ibid., 104. See also Oglethorpe to the Trustees, 29 June 1741, ibid., 117.

45. Oglethorpe to the Trustees, 28 April 1741, ibid., 113.

46. See Richard S. Dunn, "The Trustees of Georgia and the House of Commons, 1732–1752," *William and Mary Quarterly*, 3d ser., 11 (October 1954): 551–65.

47. Oglethorpe to Field Marshal James Keith, 3 May 1756, Historical Manuscripts Commission, *Manuscripts of Lord Elphinstone*, 9, Part 2 (1883): 229.

48. *CRG*, 2:513–14.

Chapter 3. CORRESPONDENCE AND FINANCES

1. David Bettelson, *The Lazy South* (New York: Oxford University Press, 1967), 90. For an excellent account of the Georgia promotional literature, see Verner W. Crane, "The Promotion Literature of Georgia," in *Bibliographical Essays: A Tribute to Wilberforce Eames* (Cambridge: Harvard University Press, 1925), 281–98.

2. Oglethorpe to the Trustees, 10 February 1733, Egmont Papers, 14200:34.

3. Oglethorpe to Sir Hans Sloane, 19 September 1733, Sloane MSS, 4053, fol. 53, British Library.

4. *Journal of Peter Gordon*, 63.

5. Egmont, *Diary*, 2:41. Vernon also complained at the same time about certain "young members" on the board who paid too little heed to religion. Their leader was reputed to be the secretary of the Trust, Benjamin Martyn.

6. Ibid., 55. Such a person was to be assured proper payment.

7. Oglethorpe to Verelst, 3 December 1735. "Oglethorpe Letters," 6–7.

8. See a series of letters by Oglethorpe to Jean Vat, John Wesley, Boltzius, Baron Philipp von Reck, all dated 16 March 1736, ibid., 22–25. For a fuller understanding of this complex affair consult *Detailed Reports*, vol. 3, and "The Secret Diary of . . . Boltzius," 78–110.

9. Oglethorpe to [the Trustees], 28 March 1736, "Oglethorpe Letters," 27–28.

10. Oglethorpe to the Trustees, 11 May 1736, ibid., 33.

11. Oglethorpe to [the Trustees], June 1736, Egmont Papers, 14201:517–22, 523–24.

Fig. 15.1. A page of endnotes, showing how notes are divided by chapter and how the running head gives the location of the references to the notes on this page.

Page numbers in these running heads must be inserted, after all pages have been made up, by either the author or the editor; they must never be left to the typesetter or the printer.

15.57   To determine the text page numbers to be used in the running head for a particular page of the note section, take the number of the first note beginning on that page of the note section (discounting any runovers of a note from a previous page) and the number of the last note beginning on the page, and find the text pages where the references to these two notes occur; these will define the inclusive pages to be used in the running head for that particular page of the note section. Reference numbers in the text will be easy to find if the proofreader puts a mark in the margin next to each one.

FOOTNOTES

15.58   *Page makeup.* Computer elements, both hardware and software, can now be programmed to cope adequately and expeditiously and economically with the scholar's predilection for notes at bottoms of pages, but until such technology, today available to a few, has become widely available to all publishers, the footnote method of documentation must be considered a difficult luxury. Many of the photocomposition processes that have taken the place of the old typesetting methods produce continuous reproduction proofs, which are cut into lengths resembling galley proofs. Text and notes are set on separate proofs. Pages are made up by cutting apart these proofs, by hand, and pasting the pieces to fit the desired size of a page. The complicated adjusting of notes to text and the meticulous pasting of tiny strips of footnotes are skills not always available in the typesetting establishment. Even where they are available, or where the older method—moving blocks of metal type from galley to page forms—is still in use, the time involved is significant, and costly.

15.59   When the publisher and the author, aware of the costs and the technical hazards, have agreed on the use of footnotes, the author can minimize the problems that will arise in page makeup by limiting both the number of footnotes per page and the length of individual notes. Good bookmaking still requires that the type pages, including the footnotes, all be the same length and that each footnote appear on the same page as the reference to it, although the final note on a page may run over to the next page. Thus, a manuscript peppered with footnote references, two or more of which might fall in the last line of text on the printed page, may well be a typesetter's nightmare. Similarly, several long footnotes, the references to which fall close together toward the end of a page, present a sometimes insoluble problem in any kind of page makeup.

15.60 In addition to the typesetter's problems involved in reproducing heavy documentation as footnotes, there is the matter of appearance. A page of type containing more footnote material than text not only is unpleasant to the eye but may discourage all but the most determined reader. In those few scholarly works where footnotes necessarily outweigh the text, publisher and typesetter must understand and cope with the difficulties. In most instances, however, authors, by careful planning, can avoid the pitfalls of excessive documentation without sacrificing their obligations to scholarship.

15.61 *Reducing length and number.* The author may reconsider a lengthy discursive note amplifying the text. Is *all* of it essential? May some or all of it be included in the text rather than in a note?

15.62 The *number* of footnote references in the text may be cut down by grouping several citations in one note instead of giving each in a separate note. For example, a sentence such as the following requires only one footnote, not five:

> Only when we gather the work of several men—Walter Sutton's explications of some of Whitman's shorter poems; Paul Fussell's careful study of structure in "Cradle"; S. K. Coffman's close readings of "Crossing Brooklyn Ferry" and "Passage to India"; and the attempts of Thomas I. Rountree and John Lovell, dealing with "Song of Myself" and "Passage to India," respectively, to elucidate the strategy in "indirection"—do we begin to get a sense of both the extent and specificity of Whitman's forms.[1]

> 1. Sutton, "The Analysis of Free Verse Form, Illustrated by a Reading of Whitman," *Journal of Aesthetics and Art Criticism* 18 (December 1959): 241–54; Fussell, "Whitman's Curious Warble: Reminiscence and Reconciliation," in *The Presence of Whitman,* ed. R. W. B. Lewis, 28–51; Coffman, " 'Crossing Brooklyn Ferry': Note on the Catalog Technique in Whitman's Poetry," *Modern Philology* 51 (May 1954): 225–32, and "Form and Meaning in Whitman's 'Passage to India,' " *PMLA* 70 (June 1955): 337–49; Rountree, "Whitman's Indirect Expression and Its Application to 'Song of Myself,' " *PMLA* 73 (December 1958): 549–55; and Lovell, "Appreciating Whitman: 'Passage to India,' " *Modern Language Quarterly* 21 (June 1960): 131–41.

15.63 A paragraph containing several short quotations may carry one footnote reference at the end of the paragraph or following the last of the quotations. The corresponding note must, of course, list the citations in order of their appearance in the paragraph. Here, in deference to the reader, the author must be judicious. One footnote listing four references when there are, say, six unidentified quotations in the paragraph is unclear. One footnote reference should never apply to material in *more* than one paragraph (except, of course, to a single quotation of more than one paragraph).

15.64 Complicated tabular material, lists, and other entities that are not part of the text should be put in an appendix at the back of the book, not included in footnotes. The footnote may read simply:

> 2. For a list of institutions involved see Appendix A.

Remember that if endnotes instead of footnotes are used, simple tables, lists, etc., may be included in the notes rather than set up as separate appendixes.

ENDNOTES VERSUS FOOTNOTES

15.65 An advantage of endnotes over footnotes is that the length of each note is not a problem, as notes and text do not have to be juggled about to make them fit on the same printed page. The author may therefore include discursive adjuncts to the text, lists, poems, and so on in the notes. It is desirable, however, that the note section not overbalance the text.

15.66 When preparing endnotes, the author accustomed to footnotes on the page will need to keep certain differences in mind. In endnotes:

1. Put in the text any material necessary for understanding the argument, instead of in a note, where the incurious might miss it.

2. Include the name of the author and the title of the work in the first note citation to it, even though one or both have been mentioned in the text. Such repetition from text to note is unnecessary in a footnote.

3. Avoid exasperating readers with endnotes consisting of nothing but a page number—or just "Ibid." When a number of references are made to a single work, page or line numbers may be given in the text, enclosed in parentheses (see 10.54–68). The note accompanying the first appearance of the work should give the full citation. For example, an endnote may read:

> 1. Unless otherwise stated, the poetry of Wallace Stevens is quoted from *The Collected Poems* (New York: Alfred A. Knopf, 1954), that of Marianne Moore from *The Complete Poems* (New York: Viking Press, 1967), and that of Robert Frost from *The Poetry of Robert Frost,* ed. Edward Connery Lathem (New York: Holt, Rinehart, and Winston, 1969).

Page numbers for all quotations from Stevens, Moore, and Frost may then be given in the text rather than in the notes. For example:

> Frost found the indefinite pronoun a useful device:
> Something there is that doesn't love a wall.
> (p. 33)

4. Similarly, cite frequently mentioned works of the same author by abbreviations in the text, with full titles in a note at first appearance. For example:

Text:

> . . . he wrote to his close friend Gorham Munson: "The more I think about my *Bridge* poem the more thrilling its symbolical possibilities become, and since my reading of you and [Waldo] Frank (I recently bought *City Block*) I begin to feel myself directly connected with Whitman. I feel myself in currents that are positively awesome in their extent and possibilities" (*L*, 128).[1] This confession that *The Bridge* and Whitman were, from the outset, inextricably mixed . . .

Endnote:

> 1. Quotations from Hart Crane's works are cited in the text using the following abbreviations; when lines are sufficiently located, by title of short poems or sections of poems, no citation appears:
>
> L: *The Letters of Hart Crane, 1916–1932,* ed. Brom Weber (Berkeley and Los Angeles: University of California Press, 1965)
>
> CP: *The Complete Poems and Selected Letters and Prose,* ed. Brom Weber (Garden City: Doubleday & Co., Anchor Books, 1966)

Subsequent text appearance:

> Crane himself explained, in "General Aims and Theories" (written some time in 1924–26): "When I started writing 'Faust & Helen' it was my intention to embody in modern terms . . . a contemporary approximation to an ancient human culture. . . . And in so doing I found that I was really building a bridge between so-called classic experience and many divergent realities of our seething, confused cosmos of today, which has no formulated mythology yet for classic reference or for religious exploitation" (*CP,* 217).

For the use of many such abbreviations in text and notes see the following paragraph.

ABBREVIATIONS IN NOTES

15.67   Where many abbreviations of titles, manuscript collections, personal names, or other entities—say, ten or more—are used throughout a book, or just throughout the notes, they are best listed alphabetically in a separate section preceding the note section. If the list occupies less than about half a page, the abbreviations may be placed between the heading "Notes" and the beginning of the notes themselves (fig. 15. 2). A longer list is usually given the heading "Abbreviations"—set in a style parallel to "Notes"—and placed on a page, or pages, preceding the note section (fig. 15.3). Where abbreviations are used in footnotes rather than endnotes, the list of abbreviations may be printed at the end of the preliminary pages or at the end of the text.

Notes

In citing works in the notes, short titles have generally been used. Works frequently cited have been identified by the following abbreviations:

Ac. Sc.	Archives de l'Académie des sciences.
A.P.	*Archives parlementaires de 1787 à 1860, première série (1787 à 1799)*. Edited by M. J. Mavidal and M. E. Laurent. 2d ed. 82 vols. Paris, 1879–1913.
Best.	Theodore Besterman, ed. *Voltaire's Correspondence*. 107 vols. Geneva, 1953–65.
B. Inst.	Bibliothèque de l'Institut de France.
B.N., nouv. acqu.	Bibliothèque Nationale. Fonds français, nouvelles acquisitions.
Corresp. inéd.	Charles Henry, ed. *Correspondance inédite de Condorcet et de Turgot (1770–1779)*. Paris, 1883.
HMAS	*Histoire de l'Académie royale des sciences. Avec les mémoires de mathématique et de physique . . . tirés des registres de cette académie (1699–1790)*. 92 vols. Paris, 1702–97. Each volume comprises two separately paginated parts, referred to as *Hist.* and *Mém.*, respectively.
Inéd. Lespinasse	Charles Henry, ed. *Lettres inédites de Mlle de Lespinasse*. Paris, 1887.
O.C.	A. Condorcet-O'Connor and F. Arago, eds. *Oeuvres de Condorcet*. 12 vols. Paris, 1847–49.

Preface

1. Peter Gay, *The Enlightenment: An Interpretation*, 2 vols. (New York, 1966–69), 2:319. I have suggested some criticisms of Gay's treatment of this theme in a review of the second volume of his work, *American Historical Review* 85 (1970): 1410–14.

2. Georges Gusdorf, *Introduction aux sciences humaines: Essai critique sur leurs origines et leur développement* (Strasbourg and Paris, 1960), 105–331.

Fig. 15.2. A short list of abbreviations preceding endnotes

DUAL SYSTEM OF NOTES

15.68   *Endnotes plus footnotes.* In a heavily documented work it is sometimes helpful to separate substantive notes from those largely devoted to citing sources. In such a system the citation notes should be numbered and set as endnotes. The substantive notes, indicated by symbols beginning with an asterisk for the first note on each printed page (sequence of symbols: *†‡§; see also 12.49), are set as footnotes. Before electing a dual system such as both foot- and endnotes, an author should consider the less cumbersome and more economic combina-

Abbreviations

ALHUA	Archives of Labor History and Urban Affairs, Wayne State University, Detroit, Michigan
DFP	*Detroit Free Press*
DLN	*Detroit Labor News*
DN	*Detroit News*
DT	*Detroit Times*
EG	Eugene Gressman
EG Papers	Eugene Gressman Papers, Michigan Historical Collections, Ann Arbor, Michigan
EGK	Edward G. Kemp
EGK Papers	Edward G. Kemp Papers, Michigan Historical Collections
EGK-BHC	Edward G. Kemp Papers, Burton Historical Collection, Detroit, Michigan
EMB	Eleanor M. Bumgardner
EMB Papers	Eleanor M. Bumgardner Papers, Michigan Historical Collections
FDR	Franklin D. Roosevelt
FDRL	Franklin D. Roosevelt Library, Hyde Park, New York
FM	Frank Murphy
FM Papers	Frank Murphy Papers, Michigan Historical Collections
GM	George Murphy
GM Papers	George Murphy Papers, Michigan Historical Collections
HM	Harold Murphy
HM Papers	Harold Murphy Papers, Michigan Historical Collections
HSB	Norman H. Hill Scrapbooks, Michigan Historical Collections
IM	Irene Murphy
IM Papers	Irene Murphy Papers, Michigan Historical Collections
JAF	James A. Farley
JRH	Joseph Ralston Hayden

Fig. 15.3. First page of a list of abbreviations including personal names as well as manuscript collections and newspaper titles, all of which are used extensively in the note section that follows. Note that abbreviations of publications are italicized; other abbreviations are roman.

tion of author-date references for all source citations with endnotes to accommodate further documentary requirements (see 15.34).

15.69 *Editor's or translator's plus author's notes.* Notes supplied by an editor, translator, or compiler in a work including original notes by the author must be differentiated from the original notes. Two acceptable ways to do this are: (1) "—ED." or "—TRANS." following the period ending the note, or (2) square brackets enclosing the entire note, except for the note number. The same method must be used throughout a work. Such notes may be numbered in sequence with the author's notes or, where there are only a few of them, treated as footnotes and indicated with symbols, whereas the author's notes are numbered and treated as endnotes.

UNNUMBERED NOTES

15.70 In anthologies, books of readings, and other collections of previously published material, the source of each chapter, or other division, may be put in an unnumbered note and inserted, before any numbered notes, either on the first page of that chapter or preceding the endnotes for the chapter. For material still in copyright from a previous publication the note should include mention of permission from the copyright holder to reprint; it may also include a copyright notice (and must do so when the copyright holder asks for one). A note containing a copyright notice is usually best treated as a footnote on the first page of the chapter or article, even when the rest of the notes are endnotes.

Source notes:

> Reprinted with permission of The Macmillan Company and Geoffrey Bles, Ltd., from *A Guide to Communist Jargon*, by R. N. Carew Hunt. Copyright 1957 by R. N. Carew Hunt.
>
> From Ali al-Giritli, *Tarikh al-sinaʿa fi Misr* (The history of industry in Egypt) (Cairo, [1952]), 40–51, 97–104, 141–50; reproduced by kind permission of the author.
>
> From Maxim Gorky, *Days with Lenin* (New York, 1932), 3–7, 11–57, by permission of International Publishers Co., Inc.
>
> Reprinted, with changes, from *The Metropolis in Modern Life*, ed. Robert Moore Fisher (New York: Doubleday & Co., 1955), 125–48, by permission of the author and the publisher. Copyright 1955 by The Trustees of Columbia University in the City of New York.
>
> Reprinted from *Geographic Reports*, Series GEO, no. 1, August 1951, 1–3. Washington, D.C.: U.S. Department of Commerce, Bureau of the Census.

(For source notes with tables see 12.46.)

15.71 In symposia and other multiauthor works the authors of the chapters may be identified in unnumbered notes similarly placed. Such identifying notes are unnecessary in books containing a "List of Contributors'' in which the authors' affiliations are given (see 1.47). Special acknowledgments may also be given in an unnumbered note.

Notes identifying authors and acknowledging aid:

> Philip B. Kurland is professor of law, University of Chicago.
>
> Ramiro Delgado García, M.D., is president, Interdisciplinary Committee, Division of Population Studies, Colombian Association of Medical Schools; vice-president, Colombian Association for the Scientific Study of Population; and executive secretary, University Committee for Population Research, Universidad del Valle, Colombia. This paper represents the personal opinions of the author and has not been officially endorsed by the institutions of which he is a member.
>
> This paper was supported in part by Grant AM-04855, National Institutes of Health, and in part by Grant 5-M01-FR-0047-04, United States Public Health Service.
>
> The author gratefully acknowledges the assistance of Dr. Oscar J. Blunk of the National Cyanide Laboratory in the preparation of this paper.

15.72 Where there are endnotes, unnumbered identification or acknowledgment notes in multiauthor works (like source notes) may be inserted before note 1 in their respective chapters. Where the author-date system is used instead of endnotes, each such note becomes a footnote on the opening page of the chapter.

15.73 In some works—translations and editions of the classics, for example—it is desirable to omit note numbers in the text. Any notes—variants, definitions or identifications, or other editorial explanations—must then be keyed to the text by line or page number, usually followed by the word being explained in the note. In a scholarly edition such notes usually appear at the foot of the page; in a work designed for a wider readership they are often placed in the back of the book so that the reader need not be distracted by scholarly apparatus on the text pages. In figures 15.4 and 15.5, the notes are keyed to lines and set at the foot of the page; the first consists of variants, the second of editorial explanation. Figure 15.6 shows one way to set notes in the back of the book, keyed to the text by page numbers, because the text lines are not numbered.

O sweete soule Phillis w'haue liu'd and lou'd for a great while,   45
(If that a man may keepe any mortal ioy for a great while)
Like louing Turtles and Turtledoues for a great while:
One loue, one liking, one sence, one soule for a great while,
Therfore one deaths wound, one graue, one funeral only
Should haue ioyned in one both loue and louer Amintas.   50
　　O good God what a griefe is this that death to remember?
For such grace, gesture, face, feature, beautie, behauiour,
Neuer afore was seene, is neuer againe to be lookt for.
O frowning fortune, ô death and desteny dismal:
Thus be the poplar trees that spred their tops to the heauens,   55
Of their flouring leaues despoil'd in an houre, in a moment:
Thus be the sweete violets that gaue such grace to the garden,
Of their purpled roabe despoyld in an houre, in a moment.
　　O how oft did I roare and crie with an horrible howling,
When for want of breath Phillis lay feintily gasping?   60
O how oft did I wish that Phœbus would fro my Phillis
Driue this feuer away: or send his sonne from Olympus,
Who, when lady Venus by a chaunce was prickt with a
　　bramble,
Healed her hand with his oyles, and fine knacks kept for a
　　purpose.
Or that I could perceiue Podalyrius order in healing,   65
Or that I could obtaine Medæas exquisite ointments,
And baths most precious, which old men freshly renewed.
Or that I were as wise, as was that craftie Prometheus,
Who made pictures liue with fire that he stole from Olympus.
Thus did I cal and crie, but no body came to Amintas,   70
Then did I raile and raue, but nought did I get by my railing,   [C₄ᵛ]
Whilst that I cald and cry'd, and rag'd, and rau'd as a mad
　　man,

45 for] *omit* C E
49 Therfore] Thefore A
58 roabe] roabes B C D E
59 roare and crie] cry, and
roare D

62 this] that D
64 his] *omit* E　　purpose.] purpose:
　　C E; purpose? D
70 Amintas,] Amintas. C E;
　　Amintas: D

Fig. 15.4. Footnotes showing textual variants and keyed to line numbers

Florimell. What's that?   115

Celadon. Such an Ovall face, clear skin, hazle eyes, thick brown Eye-browes, and Hair as you have for all the world.

Flavia. But I can assure you she has nothing of all this.

Celadon. Hold thy peace Envy; nay I can be constant an' I set on't.   120

Florimell. 'Tis true she tells you.

Celadon. I, I, you may slander your self as you please; then you have, ——— let me see.

Florimell. I'll swear you shan'not see. ———   125

Celadon. A turn'd up Nose: that gives an air to your face: Oh, I find I am more and more in love with you! a full neather-lip, an out-mouth, that makes mine water at it: the bottom of your cheeks a little blub, and two dimples when you smile: for your stature 'tis well, and for   130 your wit 'twas given you by one that knew it had been thrown away upon an ill face; come you are handsome, there's no denying it.

Florimell. Can you settle your spirits to see an ugly face, and not be frighted, I could find in my heart   135 to lift up my Masque and disabuse you.

Celadon. I defie your Masque, would you would try the experiment.

Florimell. No, I won'not; for your ignorance is the Mother of your devotion to me.   140

Celadon. Since you will not take the pains to convert me I'll make bold to keep my faith: a miserable man I am sure you have made me.

Flavia. This is pleasant.

Celadon. It may be so to you but it is not to me; for   145 ought I see, I am going to be the most constant *Maudlin. lin.* ———

116 *Ovall face*] probably a description of Nell Gwyn. See the illustration facing p. 31; one incongruous detail, the turned-up nose, may have been included as a joke, like the ironic description of King George in the person of the Emperor of Lilliput (*Gulliver's Travels,* I, ii).

128 *out-mouth*] i.e., having full lips.

129 *blub*] swelling.   134 *Can*] if you can.

Fig. 15.5. Footnotes annotating text and keyed to line numbers

P. 43   OUR BIRD-WATCHER CAROLS ... : Horace's three and a half lines in the Latin text constitute a clever paraphrase of a six-line epigram by Callimachus (*Anthologia Palatina,* xii. 102).

P. 44   TO DISTINGUISH BETWEEN ... : Horace says, "to distinguish between the solid and the void" (*inane abscindere soldo*), with reference to Epicurean physics, where the atoms or matter (*solidum*) move in the void or empty space (*inane*).

ILIA: The mother of Romulus.

EGERIA: Tutelary nymph and consort of Numa.

P. 46   TIGELLIUS: The Sardinian singer.

Fig. 15.6. Endnotes keyed to page numbers

REFERENCE LISTS AND BIBLIOGRAPHIES

15.74   A list of books and other references used by an author in preparing a scholarly work may be titled Bibliography or Select Bibliography or, if it includes only works referred to in the text, Works Cited, Literature Cited, or References; other appropriate titles are not ruled out.

15.75   A bibliographical list is best placed at the end of the book, before the index. Lists are sometimes placed at the ends of the chapters to which they apply, particularly in textbooks and in multiauthor books when there are to be offprints.

15.76   A bibliography appended to a scholarly work rarely includes all works available in the field. Where it is desirable, in the author's opinion, to mention the principle of selection, a note may precede the list (see fig. 15.11). Similarly, a list of abbreviations used in text and bibliography may precede the entries, just as an abbreviation list may accompany a note section (see figs. 15.2, 15.3). It is not necessary to list standard abbreviations of journal titles.

15.77   The form a bibliography takes depends largely on which documentation system is used in the work. The author-date system requires a reference list including all works cited in the text, but rarely any works not cited. Note systems of documentation do not in themselves require bibliographies because full bibliographical details can be given in a note accompanying the first reference to a work. But, in a work containing many citations in notes, a bibliography in addition to the notes is a most useful device for the reader and an economical one for the author and publisher: the reader not only can locate each source readily but can also see at a glance the sources the author has relied on or has selected as most germane to the subject. When the book does include many citations in notes, full particulars for each source need appear only in the bibliography; citations in the notes may thus be considerably shortened or abbreviated. Various forms such a bibliography may take are (1) a straight alphabetical list; (2) a list divided into sections according to kinds of material, subject matter, or other appropriate categories; (3) an annotated bibliography; (4) a bibliographical essay. Author's preference, nature of the material, and convenience to the reader dictate the form to be used.

REFERENCE-LIST STYLE

15.78   When the author-date system of text reference is used, the reader is best served by references arranged in one alphabetical list (see fig. 15.7); there is rarely need to divide the list into sections.

15.79   Also for the reader's convenience, the dates of publication should be placed immediately after authors' names, rather than at the end of listings as in other kinds of bibliographies. Where many works by the same author(s) are cited, authors' names may stand alone, their works listed by date below (fig. 15.8).

15.80   Some reference lists follow a severely abbreviated style in which article titles are omitted and journal titles abbreviated (fig. 15.9). This style, and variations of it, is found principally in reference lists accompanying articles in scientific journals. It is not recommended for a list in a book written for a wider audience. (For discussion and examples of individual entries in a reference list see chapter 16.)

15.81   *Cross-references.* When an author-date citation in the text does not correspond exactly to the alphabetical listing of the source, a cross-reference may be necessary in the reference list (see 15.21). Cross-references may also be used to shorten repeated listings of the same book, such as a multiauthor book from which several authors' contributions are cited:

> Hay, Douglas. 1975. "Poaching and the Game Laws on Canning Chase." In *Albion's Fatal Tree: Crime and Society in Eighteenth-Century England,* by Douglas Hay, Peter Linebaugh, John G. Rule, E. P. Thompson, and Cal Winslow. New York: Pantheon.
> Linebaugh, Peter. 1975. "The Tyburn Riot against the Surgeons." In *Albion's Fatal Tree. See* Hay 1975.

REFERENCES

Allen, C. E. 1930. Gametophytic inheritance in Sphaerocarpos. IV. Further studies of tuftedness and polyclady. *Genetics* 15:150–88.

Allison, A. C. 1955. Aspects of polymorphism in man. *Cold Spring Harbor Symp. Quant. Biol.* 20:239–55.

Alpatov. W. W., and A. M. Boschko-Stepanenko. 1928. Variation and correlation in serially situated organs in insects, fishes and birds. *Amer. Nat.* 62:409–24.

Anderson, Edgar. 1928. The problem of species in the northern blue flags. *Iris versicolor* L. and *Iris virginica* L. *Ann. Missouri Bot. Garden* 15:241–332.

———. 1949. *Introgressive hybridization.* New York: John Wiley & Sons.

Anderson, E. G. 1923. Maternal inheritance of chlorophyll in maize. *Bot. Gaz.* 76:411–18.

Andersson-Kottö, I. 1923. The genetics of variegation in a fern. *Jour. Genet.* 13:1–12.

———. 1930. Variegation in three species of ferns (*Polystichum angulare, Lastraea atrata,* and *Scolopendrium vulgare*). *Zeit. ind. Abst. Vererb.* 56:115–201.

Auerbach, C. 1949. Chemical mutagenesis. *Biol. Rev.* 24:355–91.

Avery, O. T., C. M. MacLeod, and M. McCarty. 1944. Studies on the chemical nature of the substance inducing transformation of Pneumococcal types. Induction of transformation by a desoxyribonucleic acid fraction isolated from Pneumococcus type III. *J. Exp. Med.* 76:137–58.

Baltzer, F. 1925. Untersuchungen über die Entwicklung und Geschlechtsbestimmung der Bonellia. *Publ. Staz. Zool. Napoli* 6:223–85.

Bateson, W. 1909. *Mendel's principles of heredity.* Cambridge: At the University Press, 1930.

Bateson, W., and H. H. Brindley. 1892. On some cases of variation in secondary sexual characters statistically examined. *Proc. Zool. Soc.* 1892:585–94.

Bateson, W., and R. C. Punnett. 1905. Experimental studies in the physiology of heredity. *Rept. to the Evolution Com. of Roy. Soc. II.*

Baur, E. 1909. Das Wesen und die Erblichkeitsverhältnisse der "Variatates albomarginatae hort." von Pelargonium zonale. *Zeit. ind. Abst. Vererb.* 1:330–51.

Beadle, G. W., and B. Ephrussi. 1936. The differentiation of eye pigments in Drosophila as studied by transplantation. *Genetics* 21:225–47.

Beadle, G. W., and E. L. Tatum. 1941. Genetic control of biochemical reactions in Neurospora. *Proc. Nat. Acad. Sci.* 27:499–506.

Fig. 15.7. First page of a reference list showing alphabetical arrangement, placement of dates of publication, and full citation of titles.

15.82 *One list.* The bibliography arranged in a single alphabetical list is the most common and usually the best form for a work with, or without, notes to the text. All sources to be included—books, articles, pa-

---

Clark, T. N.
1968   Emile Durkheim and the institutionalization of sociology in the French university system. *Eur. J. Soc.* 9:37–71.
Coser, L. A.
1971   *Masters of sociological thought: Ideas in historical and social context.* New York: Harcourt Brace Jovanovich.
Dahlgren, K. G.
1945   *On suicide and attempted suicide: A psychiatrical and statistical investigation.* Lund, Sweden: Lindstedts.
Deshaies, G.
1947   *Psychologie du suicide.* Paris: Presses Universitaires de France.
Douglas, J. D.
1967   *The social meanings of suicide.* Princeton: Princeton University Press.
Durkheim, E.
1888   Suicide et natalité: Etude de statistique morale. *Revue philosophique de la France et de l'étranger* 26:446–63.
1930   *Le suicide: Etude de sociologie.* 2d ed. Paris: Librairie Felix Alcan.
1950   *The rules of sociological method.* Translated by S. A. Solovay and J. H. Mueller. New York: Free Press.
1951   *Suicide: A study in sociology.* Translated by J. A. Spaulding and G. Simpson. Glencoe: Free Press.
1953   *Sociology and philosophy.* Translated by D. F. Pocock. Glencoe: Free Press.
1960   *The division of labor in society.* Translated by G. Simpson. Glencoe: Free Press.
1964   The dualism of human nature and its social conditions. In *Essays on sociology and philosophy,* edited by K. H. Wolff, 325–40. New York: Harper Torchbooks.
1965a   *The elementary forms of the religious life.* Translated by J. W. Swain. New York: Free Press.
1965b   *Montesquieu and Rousseau: Forerunners of sociology.* Translated by R. Manheim. Ann Arbor: University of Michigan Press.
1973   Individualism and the intellectuals. Translated by M. Traugott. In *Emile Durkheim on morality and society,* ed. R. N. Bellah, 43–57. Chicago: University of Chicago Press.

Fig. 15.8. A page of a reference list illustrating form used when many works by one author are cited.

References

Algire, G. H., and F. T. Legallais. 1948. Biology of melanomas, ed. R. W. Miner, 159–70. New York: New York Academy of Sciences.

Anderson, N. G. 1956. Quart. Rev. Biol. 31:169.

Andres, G. 1955. J. Exper. Zoöl. 130:221.

Beale, G. H. 1952. Genetics 37:62.

Beams, H. W., and R. L. King. 1942. Anat. Rec. 83:2.

Beatty, A. V., and J. W. Beatty. 1954. Am. J. Bot. 41:242.

Bélǎr, K. 1926. Ergebn. Zool. 6:235.

Bergquist, H., and B. Kallen. 1954. J. Comp. Neurol. 100:627.

Bizzozero, G. 1894. Arch. sci. med. 18:245.

Borghese, E. 1954. Arch. ital. anat. embriol. 58:388.

———. 1955. Monit. zool. ital. 63 (Suppl.): 50.

Boveri, T. 1907. Die Entwicklung dispermer Seeigleier: Ein Beitrag zur Befruchtungslehre und zur Theorie des Kerns. Jena: G. Fischer.

Boyd, J. S. K. 1951. Nature 167:1061.

Brachet, A. 1922. Arch. biol. (Liège) 32:205.

Bridges, C. B. 1921. Proc. Nat. Acad. Sc. 7:186.

Briggs, R., and T. J. King. 1955. Biological specificity and growth, chap. 11. Princeton: Princeton University Press.

Brues, A. M. 1952. Am. J. Path. 28:547.

Brues, A. M., and B. B. Marble. 1937. J. Exper. Med. 65:15.

Brues, A. M., and L. Rietz. 1951. Cancer Res. 11:240.

Bucher, O. 1947. Acta anat. 4:60.

———. 1952. Verhandl. anat. Gesellsch. 50:41.

———. 1955. Ztschr. Anat. 118:531.

———. 1956. Histologie und mikroskopische Anatomie des Menschen. 2d ed. Bern: Verlag Huber.

Bucher, O., and J. Deleze. 1955. Anat. Anz. 102:1.

Bullough, W. S. 1950. Exper. Cell Res. 1:410.

Burr, H. S. 1916. J. Comp. Neurol. 26:203.

———. 1934. Determinants of organization in the cerebral hemispheres. In: Localization of function in the cerebral cortex, 39–48. Baltimore: Williams & Wilkins.

Carlson, J. G. 1952. Chromosoma 5:199.

———. 1956. Science 124:203.

Carlson, J. G., and A. Hollaender. 1948. J. Cell. & Comp. Physiol. 31:149.

Chalkley, D. T. 1954. J. Morphol. 94:21.

Chalkley, H. W. 1942. J. Nat. Cancer Inst. 2:425.

Chambers, R. 1929. In: General cytology, ed. E. V. Cowdry, 293. Chicago: University of Chicago Press.

Fig. 15.9. Part of a list of references in shortened form, omitting article titles and abbreviating journal titles.

pers—are alphabetically arranged, by the last names of the authors, in a single list.

15.83 *Divided into sections.* A long bibliography may be broken into sections if division into categories would really make it more useful to the reader (sometimes division merely makes finding a given item more difficult). For example, in a work using manuscript sources as well as printed works the two kinds of sources may be put in separate sections, the manuscripts arranged either by depository or by name of collection. In a work with many references to newspapers, the newspapers may be separated from the rest of the bibliography and listed together, each with its run of relevant dates. In a lengthy bibliography listing many printed sources, books are sometimes separated from articles (see fig. 15.10). Some bibliographies may be classified by subject if the distinctions are clear (see fig. 15.11). In a study of the work of one person, it is usually best to list works *by* that person separately from works *about* him or her (see fig. 15.12). Note that a list of works by one person is usually arranged in chronological order (i.e., by date of publication) rather than alphabetical order. In a book about one person, such a list sometimes constitutes the entire bibliography. Division of references according to the chapter or part in which they are cited may be feasible, particularly if each chapter or part cites references not used in the other chapters or parts. Whatever the arrangement of a bibliography, it is recommended that no source be listed more than once; if the need for more than one listing for the same work arises, the arrangement is probably faulty. When a bibliography is divided into sections, a headnote sometimes states the fact and indicates the titles of the sections.

15.84 *Annotated.* When a bibliography is intended to direct the reader to other works for further reading and study, an annotated bibliography is useful. This is a list of books (sometimes articles as well) in alphabetical order with comments appended to some or all of the entries. The comments may be run in (see fig. 15.13) or set on separate lines (see the bibliography at the end of this volume). A long annotated bibliography is sometimes divided into series of lists with subject headings (see 15.83).

15.85 *Bibliographical essay.* An informal way to provide information for further reading is a bibliographical essay, in which the author treats the literature of the field discursively, giving the facts of publication in parentheses following each title. The material may be arranged in one continuous essay or it may be divided by chapter or by subject category, with, or without, subheads marking the divisions (see fig. 15.14). Often called Suggested Reading, this kind of bibliography is best

Select Bibliography

Books

Abelard, Peter. *Peter Abelard's Ethics*. Edited and translated by D. E. Luscombe. Oxford: Clarendon Press, 1971.

Adkins, Arthur W. H. *Merit and Responsibility: A Study in Greek Values*. Oxford: Clarendon Press, 1960.

Anscombe, G. E. M. *Intention*. 2d ed. Oxford: Blackwell, 1963.

Atkinson, Ronald. *Sexual Morality*. London: Hutchinson, 1965.

Austin, J. L. *Philosophical Papers*. Oxford: Clarendon Press, 1961.

The Babylonian Talmud. Translated into English . . . under the editorship of Rabbi Dr. I. Epstein. London: Soncino Press, 1948–52.

Baier, Kurt. *The Moral Point of View: A Rational Basis of Ethics*. Ithaca: Cornell University Press, 1958.

Baxter, Richard. *A Christian Directory, or a Sum of Practical Theology and Cases of Conscience. The Practical Works of Richard Baxter*. Edited by W. Orme. 23 vols. London: Duncan, 1830. References are to part, chapter, and (where appropriate) direction and question, to which a reference to the volume and page of the *Practical Works (P.W.)* is added.

Beck, Lewis White. *A Commentary on Kant's Critique of Practical Reason*. Chicago: University of Chicago Press, 1960.

———. *Early German Philosophy*. Cambridge: Harvard University Press, Belknap Press, 1969.

———. *Studies in the Philosophy of Kant*. Indianapolis: Bobbs-Merrill, 1965.

. . . .

Articles

Anscombe, G. E. M. "Modern Moral Philosophy." *Philosophy* 33 (1958): 1–19.

———. "Thought and Action in Aristotle." In *New Essays on Plato and Aristotle,* edited by Renford Bambrough, 143–58. London: Routledge and Kegan Paul, 1965.

———. "Contraception and Chastity." *Human World,* no. 7 (May 1972): 9–30.

Fig. 15.10. Part of a bibliography of printed sources divided into books and articles.

SELECT BIBLIOGRAPHY

I list here only the writings that have been of use in the making of this book. This bibliography is by no means a complete record of all the works and sources I have consulted. It indicates the substance and range of reading upon which I have formed my ideas, and I intend it to serve as a convenience for those who wish to pursue the study of humor, comic literature, the history of comic processes, the British novel, and the particular writers and fictions that are the subjects of this inquiry. (Unless there is a standard edition or only one widely available edition of the complete works of the novelists I study, I have not listed their complete works.)

1. THE THEORY, PSYCHOLOGY, AND HISTORY OF THE COMIC

Auden, W. H. "Notes on the Comic." In *Comedy: Meaning and Form*, edited by Robert Corrigan, 61–72. San Francisco: Chandler, 1965.

Bakhtin, Mikhail. *Rabelais and His World*. Translated from the Russian by Helene Iswolsky. Cambridge, Mass.: M.I.T. Press, 1968.

.   .   .   .

2. JANE AUSTEN AND *EMMA*

Austen, Jane. *The Novels of Jane Austen*. Edited by R. W. Chapman. 5 vols. 3d ed. London: Oxford University Press, 1932–34.

———. *Jane Austen's Letters to Her Sister Cassandra and Others*. Edited by R. W. Chapman. 2d ed. London: Oxford University Press, 1952.

———. *Minor Works*. Edited by R. W. Chapman. Vol. 6 of *The Novels of Jane Austen*. London: Oxford University Press, 1954.

———. *"Emma": An Authoritative Text, Backgrounds, Reviews, and Criticism*. Edited by Stephen M. Parrish. Includes commentary and criticism by Sir Walter Scott, George Henry Lewes, Richard Simpson, Henry James, A. C. Bradley, Reginald Ferrar, Virginia Woolf, E. M. Forster, Mary Lascelles, Arnold Kettle, Wayne Booth, G. Armour Craig, A. Walton Litz, W. A. Craik, and W. J. Harvey. New York: W. W. Norton, 1972.

Fig. 15.11. Bibliography divided into sections according to subjects reflecting the organization of the text. Example shows part of the first two of ten sections and the author's note explaining the principle of selection.

suited to books intended for the general reader, books with few or no text references to specific sources and no notes dependent on an alphabetical list. It may, however, be used in addition to a reference list and should precede such a list; here the works discussed in the essay may be cited by author and date if they are in the list, just as they are cited in the text itself. An essay may also be used in a book with footnotes or endnotes, but it must be remembered that essay and notes

---

Publications by Joseph J. Schwab

"A Further Study of the Effect of Temperature on Crossing-over." *American Naturalist* 69 (1935): 187–92.

With Edna Bailey and Anita D. E. Laton. *Suggestions for Teaching Selected Material from the Field of Genetics.* Bureau of Educational Research in Science, Monograph 1. New York: Columbia University, Teachers College, 1939.

"A Study of the Effects of a Random Group of Genes on Shape of Spermatheca in *Drosophila melanogaster.*" *Genetics* 25 (1940): 157–77.

"Deriving the Objectives and Content of the College Curriculum." In *New Frontiers in Collegiate Education: Proceedings of the Institute for Administrative Officers of Higher Education,* vol. 13, edited by John Dale Russell, 35–52. Chicago: University of Chicago Press, 1941.

"The Role of Biology in General Education: The Problem of Value." *Bios* 12 (1941): 87–97.

"The Fight for Education." *Atlantic Monthly* 169 (1942): 727–31.

"The Science Programs in the College of the University of Chicago." In *Science and General Education,* edited by Earl McGrath, 38–58. Dubuque, Iowa: William C. Brown Co., 1947.

.   .   .   .

"On Reviving Liberal Education." In *The Philosophy of the Curriculum,* edited by Sidney Hook et al., 37–48. Buffalo, N.Y.: Prometheus Books, 1975.

"Education and the State: Learning Community." In *The Great Ideas Today, 1976,* 234–71. Chicago: Encyclopaedia Britannica, 1976.

"Freedom and the Scope of Liberal Education." In *The President as Educational Leader,* 610–88. Washington, D.C.: Association of American Colleges, 1976.

"Teaching and Learning." *The Center Magazine* 9, no. 6 (November–December 1976): 36–45.

Fig. 15.12. The beginning and end of a list of one author's works, arranged in chronological order by date of publication. Such a list may be entitled "Works by ———" and include unpublished as well as published material.

Bibliography

. . . .

Sorokin, Boris. "Lev Tolstoj in Pre-Revolutionary Russian Criticism." Doctoral dissertation, University of Chicago, 1973. Survey of major prerevolutionary criticism and extensive bibliography.

Zhilina, E. N. *Lev Nikolaevich Tolstoi, 1828–1910.* Leningrad, 1960. A bibliographical aid; includes selective secondary literature on individual works.

II. *Reminiscences and Biographies*

Alexandre, Aimée. *Le mythe de Tolstoi.* Paris, 1960.

Asquith, Cynthia. *Married to Tolstoy.* London, 1960. A defense of Tolstoy's wife in her difficulties with Tolstoy.

Biryukov, P. *Lev Nikolaevich Tolstoy.* 4 vols. Moscow, 1911–23. Still perhaps the best biography of Tolstoy.

Brodsky, N. A., et al., eds. *L. N. Tolstoi v vospominaniyakh sovremennikov.* 2 vols. Moscow, 1955. There is also a 1960 edition, ed. S. N. Golubov et al., with some additional material. These are very important volumes. The English edition is considerably abbreviated and awkwardly translated by the Moscow Foreign Publishing House. The 1960 Soviet volume adds some items and drops others, especially of recently published separate books of reminiscences, such as Bulgakov's and Goldenweizer's.

Bulgakov, Valentin. *The Last Year of Leo Tolstoy.* Translated by Ann Dunnigan. Introduction by George Steiner. New York, 1971. Fascinating account (by Tolstoy's male secretary) of Tolstoy's last year and his torturous relations with his wife.

———. *O Tolstom, vospominaniya i rasskazy.* Tula, 1964. Supplementary to his *Poslednii god,* but written after the events, the account does not have the sharply vivid sense of the diary. Often a record of objects in the room and other inconsequential matters.

Bunin, Ivan. *Osvobozhdenie Tolstogo.* Paris, 1937. Draws upon personal recollections, as well as the diary, letters, and reminiscences of others. Beautifully written.

Dole, Nathan Haskell. *The Life of Count Lyof N. Tolstoi.* New York, 1911.

Fig. 15.13 Excerpts from an annotated bibliography. Note that not every entry bears an annotation.

Suggested Readings

The most thorough bibliography of American religion is Nelson R. Burr, *A Critical Bibliography of Religion in America*, 2 vols. (Princeton, 1961). More recent and more selective is the same author's contribution to the Goldentree Bibliographies in American History, called *Religion in American Life* (New York, 1971). Specialized lists of writings on Catholicism are John Paul Cadden, *The Historiography of the American Catholic Church, 1745–1943* (Washington, 1944); . . . On books on American Judaism, see Moses Rischin, *An Inventory of American Jewish History* (Cambridge, 1954). The old standby in this general field, still useful, is Peter G. Mode, *Source Book and Bibliographical Guide for American Church History* (Menasha, Wis., 1921).

The sections in all the above works listing books and articles and theses that deal historically with religious thought and theology are instructive, partly by reason of their brevity. . . .

For a study of religion with neatly balanced attention to Catholicism and Judaism as well as Protestantism, Winthrop S. Hudson, *Religion in America*, rev. ed. (New York, 1973), serves well and provides useful bibliographical guides. The most encyclopedic work by a single author is Sydney E. Ahlstrom's mammoth and remarkably detailed book, *A Religious History of the American People* (New Haven, 1972).

. . . .

The more strictly theological heritage of Edwards, down to the last Edwardian, is surveyed in Frank Hugh Foster, *A Genetic History of the New England Theology* (Chicago, 1907). The rival theology of Unitarianism, of course, had its own tradition going back in America to Edwards's own day, as is shown by Conrad Wright, *The Beginnings of Unitarianism in America* (Boston, 1955), covering 1735–1805.

FROM EMERSON TO JAMES

The more theologically inclined thinkers who are treated in this second "Interlude" have been studied in great detail, but the full range and variety of religious thought during Emerson's lifetime and down to the beginnings of pragmatism have yet to be surveyed in a reliable volume. The theology of Emerson and the Transcendentalists, of the Princeton and Mercersburg theologians, and of Bushnell is woven into the history of Continental and British theological movements by Claude Welch, *Protestant Thought in the Nineteenth Century*, vol. 1 (New Haven, 1972), which also reckons with other Americans such as Lyman Beecher, Brownson, Channing, Dwight, Edwards, Finney, Hopkins, James, Parker, Schmucker, and, at some length, Taylor.

Fig. 15.14. Excerpts from a bibliographical essay addressed to the general reader.

are not interdependent: a work cited in a note and discussed in the essay must be given full bibliographical details in both places.

15.86 A discursive essay, an annotated list, or a combination of both is often used to explain the contents, relevance, or value of specific bodies of material, such as manuscript collections (see figs. 15.15, 15.16).

ARRANGEMENT OF ENTRIES

15.87 The most practical and useful way to arrange entries in a reference list or a bibliography is in alphabetical order, by authors, either running through the whole list or in each section of it. There is rarely any reason to number the items (see 15.6). Authors who wish to list sources in order of their importance to the work at hand rather than alphabetically should consider whether the reader will need to find a specific source quickly; if so, an alphabetically arranged, annotated bibliography would serve both purposes.

15.88 *Alphabetizing.* Rules for alphabetizing an index (chap. 18) obtain also in a bibliographical list. Special problems may be solved by observing the following principles.

15.89 A single-author entry comes before a multiauthor entry beginning with the same name.

15.90 In a reference list, with author-date text references to it, all works attributed to one person, whether original or edited (or translated or compiled), should be listed together and arranged chronologically by date of publication. This arrangement makes for easy reference from the citation in the text:

> Xerxes, Amos, ed. 1984. *The name of the game: Essays in honor of C. Q. Plunkett.* Hometown, Ill.: Small Univ. Press.
> ———. 1985. Fossils of the Moose River Basin. *Three Rivers Archeological Journal* 47:25–40.

15.91 Also in a reference list, two or more works by the same author(s) and published *in the same year* are distinguished by letters after the date:

> Langston, W., Jr., 1965a. Fossil crocodilians from Colombia and the Cenozoic history of the Crocodilia in South America. *Univ. Calif. Publ. Geol. Sci.* 52:1–157.
> ———. 1965b. *Oedaleops campi* (Reptilia: Pelycosauria): A new genus and species from the Lower Permian of New Mexico, and the family Eothyrididae. *Bull. Tex. Mem. Mus.* 9:1–47.

Note that works published in the same year are alphabetized by title.

15.92 In bibliographies, as opposed to reference lists, original works usually precede edited works by the same author. Works by the same author

Bibliography

. . . .

MANUSCRIPT SOURCES

1. Private Papers
France
Larras MSS. Archives. Ministère de la Guerre. Section d'Afrique, Paris. The papers of General Larras, who served with the French military mission in Morocco from 1898 to 1905. He was responsible for preparing many of the maps of Morocco later utilized during the first stages of pacification. The papers relate principally to the period of his service in Morocco.
Mangin MSS. Archives Nationales, Paris. The papers and reports of General Charles Mangin, the hero of the battle of Sidi Bou Outhman and deliverer of Marrakech. In its essentials, it duplicates the holdings of the Ministère de la Guerre, Section d'Afrique, although there are additional papers. Only a portion deals with Mangin's Moroccan career.

. . . .

Great Britain
Satow Papers. Public Record Office, London. PRO 30/33. Includes the correspondence of Sir Ernest Satow from his mission to Morocco in 1893 and his correspondence with Sir James Macleod, H.M. Consul at Fez, 1893–1916. Of subsidiary interest only.
Nicolson Papers. Public Record Office, London. F.O. 800/336–381. Miscellaneous papers of Sir Arthur Nicolson, H.M. Minister at Tangier from 1894 to 1904. Of little interest.

. . . .

2. Official Papers
France
Archives de l'Alliance Israélite Universelle, Paris. Valuable chiefly for the annual reports of the official inspectors sent to survey the works of the Alliance in Morocco.
Archives de l'Ancien Gouvernement Général de l'Algérie, Aix-en-Provence. Série H. Affaires Musulmans et Sahariennes. Little of value on central Morocco. Of great importance for French penetration into eastern Morocco.

Fig. 15.15. Excerpts from a long bibliography, showing entries for manuscript collections with annotations explaining their relevance to the author's subject.

British Archives

The shift from a fifty- to a thirty-year rule has opened extensive British records to scholars, though it must be noted that many documents and whole files are being kept closed until 1990, 2015, and even later. Most important for this project have been the voluminous papers of the Foreign Office at the Public Record Office; also used have been cabinet papers, prime minister's papers, the records of such cabinet committees as the Committee on Imperial Defence and the Committee on Foreign Policy, and the papers of Lord Halifax, Sir Nevile Henderson, Sir John Simon, Sir Alexander Cadogan, Sir Archibald Clark Kerr, and Viscount Runciman in the FO 800 series.

At Cambridge University I have used the Baldwin and Templewood papers; at the Beaverbrook Library the Lloyd George papers; at the London School of Economics the Dalton papers; at King's College the Ismay papers; and at the Scottish Record Office the Lothian muniments.

Other Archives

The Soviet archives are closed. Some French archives have been made available to certain scholars, but there has been as yet no general opening similar to the American or British. Publications of documents from Soviet and French, as well as other, archives are listed in the bibliography.

No effort has been made to make this bibliography exhaustive. Only works actually cited in this book are included, together with a *small* selection of other works whose general ideas, organizing concepts, or supplementary details were of real significance in shaping the account. The bibliographies listed in section I and many of the secondary works in section IV provide additional listings.

I. Bibliographies, Guides, Archives Inventories, and Other Reference Works

American Historical Association, Committee for the Study of War Documents, and National Archives and Records Service. *Guides to German Records Microfilmed at Alexandria, Va.* Washington: National Archives, 1958–.

Bauer, Yehuda, ed. *Guide to Unpublished Materials of the Holocaust Period.* Vol. 3. Jerusalem: Hebrew University, 1975.

Fig. 15.16. A small segment of a scholarly bibliography with discursive accounts of archival material preceding a list of printed works arranged by category.

may be arranged either *chronologically* by date of publication or *alphabetically* by title (discounting an initial article).

Chronological order:

> McKeon, Richard. *The Philosophy of Spinoza: The Unity of His Thought*. New York: Longmans, Green, 1928.
> ———. "Aristotle's Conception of the Development and the Nature of Scientific Method." *Journal of the History of Ideas* 8 (1947): 3–44.
> ———. "Rhetoric and Poetic in the Philosophy of Aristotle." In *Aristotle's "Poetics" and English Literature,* edited by Elder Olson, 201–36. Chicago: University of Chicago Press, 1965.
> ———. "The Hellenistic and Roman Foundations of the Tradition of Aristotle in the West." *Review of Metaphysics* 32 (1979): 677–715.
> ———, ed. *The Basic Works of Aristotle.* New York: Random House, 1941.

Alphabetical order:

> McKeon, Richard. "Aristotle's Conception of the Development and the Nature of Scientific Method." *Journal of the History of Ideas* 8 (1947): 3–44.
> ———. "The Hellenistic and Roman Foundations of the Tradition of Aristotle in the West." *Review of Metaphysics* 32 (1979): 677–715.
> ———. *The Philosophy of Spinoza: The Unity of His Thought.* New York: Longmans, Green, 1928.
> ———. "Rhetoric and Poetic in the Philosophy of Aristotle." In *Aristotle's "Poetics" and English Literature,* edited by Elder Olson, 201–36. Chicago: University of Chicago Press, 1965.
> ———, ed. *The Basic Works of Aristotle.* New York: Random House, 1941.

The last entry in both lists illustrates placement of edited work *after* original works in a bibliography. In most bibliographies this particular work would appear under the author's name:

> Aristotle. *The Basic Works of Aristotle.* Edited by Richard McKeon. New York: Random House, 1941.

15.93 Works by one author are sometimes further divided by listing books first, articles second.

15.94 *Three-em dash for repeated name.* As may be observed in the preceding examples, for successive works by the same author a 3-em dash is used in place of the author's name after the first appearance. When a reference list has a preponderance of dashes, however, one might consider the alternative arrangement illustrated in figure 15.8.

15.95 The dash should not be used when a coauthor is added. Repeat the name:

> Sorokin, Pitirim A. *Social and Cultural Dynamics.* Vol. 4. *Basic Problems, Principles, and Methods.* New York: Bedminster Press, 1941.
> ———. *Sociocultural Causality, Space, Time.* Durham, N.C.: Duke University Press, 1943.

Sorokin, Pitirim A., and Robert K. Merton. "Social Time: A Methodological and Functional Analysis." *American Journal of Sociology* 42 (1937): 615–29.

15.96   One dash may signify several authors (avoid using more than one dash per entry):

West, Donald J., and D. P. Farrington. *Who Becomes Delinquent?* London: Heinemann, 1973.
———. *The Delinquent Way of Life*. London: Heinemann, 1977.

15.97   A dash may also be used for institutional or corporate authors. It takes the place of as much of the name as is the same:

U.S. Senate. Committee on Foreign Relations. *Investigation of Mexican Affairs*. 2 vols. 66th Cong., 2d sess., 1919–20.
———. Committee on Public Lands. *Leasing of Oil Lands*. 65th Cong., 1st sess., 1917.
[Dash stands for U.S. Senate.]
———. *Leases upon Naval Oil Reserves*. 68th Cong., 1st sess., 1924.
[Dash stands for U.S. Senate. Committee on Public Lands.]

16   Bibliographic Forms

The Individual Entry 16.2
    Facts to Be Included 16.2
    Two Basic Styles 16.5
Books 16.11
    Name of the Author 16.11
        One author 16.14
        Two or more authors 16.15
        Pseudonyms 16.18
        Anonymous works 16.21
        Editor, compiler, or translator 16.24
        Organization, association, or corporation 16.29
    Titles 16.31
        Titles within titles 16.33
        Older titles 16.37
        Foreign titles 16.38
    Volumes 16.41
    Series 16.44
    Chapters or Parts of a Book 16.49
    Edition 16.54
    Modern Editions of Classics 16.55
    Reprint Editions 16.57
    Microform Editions 16.59
    Facts of Publication 16.61
        Alternatives 16.64
        Place 16.68
        Publisher 16.76
        Date of publication 16.88
Journal Articles 16.98
    Basic Styles 16.98
        Article title omitted 16.115
        Article published in more than one issue 16.116
        Article published in two places 16.117
        Place of publication 16.118
        No volume number 16.119
    Foreign Language Journals 16.121
    Popular Magazines 16.124
    Book Reviews 16.126
    Newspapers 16.127
Unpublished Material 16.128
    Theses, Lectures, and Other Unpublished Works 16.128
        Dissertation or thesis 16.129
        Paper read at a meeting 16.130
        Unpublished duplicated material 16.131
        Interviews 16.132
        Personal communications 16.133

Manuscript Collections 16.134

Public Documents 16.141

United States 16.146
  Congress 16.147
    House and Senate Journals 16.149
    Debates 16.150
    Reports and Documents 16.153
  Executive Departments 16.155
  Statutes and Judicial Documents 16.156
  Unpublished Documents 16.158
  State and Local Governments 16.160

United Kingdom 16.161
  Parliament 16.165
    Debates 16.166
    Parliamentary Papers 16.167
    Statutes 16.169
    Unpublished Documents 16.171
    Published Records 16.173

Canada 16.174

International Bodies 16.175

Nonbook Materials 16.176
  Printed Musical Scores 16.176
  Sound Recordings 16.177
  Videorecordings 16.179
    Slides and films 16.180
    Text from a film 16.181
  Computer Programs 16.182

16.1 Examination of the kinds of bibliographies illustrated in chapter 15 reveals variation also in the style of individual items in the lists. These styles are the subject of this chapter.

THE INDIVIDUAL ENTRY

FACTS TO BE INCLUDED

16.2 In the main, individual entries in all scholarly reference lists and bibliographies include similar information about a published work. For a book, these facts are

> Name of the author or authors, the editors, or the institution responsible for the writing of the book
> Full title of the book, including the subtitle, if any
> Title of series, if any, and volume or number in the series
> Volume number or total number of volumes of a multivolume work
> Edition, if not the original
> City of publication
> Publisher's name (sometimes omitted)
> Date of publication

16.3   For an article in a periodical, the facts given are

> Name of the author
> Title of the article
> Name of the periodical
> Volume number (sometimes issue number)
> Date
> Pages occupied by the article

16.4   Note that the physical facts about a work—dimensions, number of pages, number of illustrations, and so on—are not given. Such facts are listed on library catalog cards and on booksellers' lists but are generally omitted from scholarly bibliographies.

TWO BASIC STYLES

16.5   Tradition in the world of scholarship in all fields has produced two basic styles for a bibliography entry. One, favored by writers in literature, history, and the arts, we will here call *A* for purposes of illustration. The other, favored by writers in both the natural and the social sciences, we will call *B*. The order does not indicate a preference for *A* over *B*. Either one, and sometimes a variation using elements of each, is acceptable when followed consistently throughout a bibliography. The principal differences can readily be observed in the following examples of entries for a book and a journal article:

> *A*   Smith, John Q. *Urban Turmoil: The Politics of Hope.* New City: Polis Publishing Co., 1986.
>
> Wise, Penelope. "Money Today: Two Cents for a Dollar." *No Profit Review* 2 (1987): 123–42.
>
> *B*   Smith, J. Q. 1986. *Urban turmoil: The politics of hope.* New City: Polis.
> *or:*
> Smith, J. Q. 1986. *Urban turmoil.* New City: Polis.
>
> Wise, P. 1987. Money today: Two cents for a dollar. *No Profit Rev.* 2:123–42.
> *or:*
> Wise, P. 1987. Money today. *No Profit Rev.* 2:123–42.
> *or:*
> Wise, P. 1987. *No Profit Rev.* 2:123–42.

16.6   Thus the basic differences between the two styles are

1. *A* spells out the author's given name; *B* often uses only initials. (This is not a rigid distinction: *B* often spells out names; *A* may use only initials.)

2. *A* puts the date of publication after the publisher of a book, and after the volume number of a journal; *B,* because this style is most commonly used with the author-date system of text references (see 15.4), puts the date right after the author's name, for easier reference.

3. *A* uses title capitalization (see 7.123) for all titles; *B* uses a down style—capitalizing only the first letter of the main title, the subtitle, and any proper nouns—for the titles of books and articles, but capitalizes journal titles as in style *A*.

4. *A* uses the full title of a book or article; *B* often omits the subtitle and sometimes the whole article title.

5. *A* uses quotation marks around article titles; *B* does not.

6. *B* is more likely to abbreviate the names of publishers and the names of journals, although *A* frequently does likewise.

16.7   Both styles use a period after each main segment of an entry:

Author's name. Title. Publication data.

16.8   There are many acceptable alternatives to and combinations of these basic styles. Which form of documentation is adopted in a work—author-date or notes—will dictate the placement of the date of publication, for example. And where space is at a premium the shortest possible forms, as in *B,* may be adopted, even when the rest of the style follows *A*. A consistent style must of course be followed throughout a bibliography, not just because the publisher says so but because inconsistency in bibliographical details confuses readers and suggests careless research methods.

16.9   In setting forth the various kinds of published material commonly found in bibliographies, we have attempted to provide examples illustrating both *A* and *B* styles where applicable.

16.10   The forms suggested are designed for clarity and economy. Thus, arabic numerals are used throughout for volume numbers of printed material: vol. 3 or 138, *not* III or CXXXVIII. A minimum of punctuation is used. Only two styles of type appear: roman and italic.[1] From these sample entries, together with a grasp of the principles dictating them, authors and editors should, it is hoped, be able to fashion logical listings of their own devising to meet almost any contingency.

BOOKS

NAME OF THE AUTHOR

16.11   Authors' names should be spelled in a bibliography as they appear on the title pages of their books, except that first names may be given in full in place of initials. Degrees or affiliations following names should

---

1. Other typefaces sometimes used in bibliographies and reference lists—for example, caps and small caps for authors' names or boldface for volume numbers of journals—raise costs without increasing clarity.

normally be omitted (except "M.D." for an author of a medical work). Several references to the same author in one bibliography should follow the same style. For example, an author listed as "Jones, Mary L." should not in another entry (as coauthor or editor) appear as "M. L. Jones." Use one or the other for both. Note that initials are spaced (see 7.6).

16.12   When the first name of the author is supplied, the part of the name not on the title page *may* be enclosed in square brackets: Cranfield, G[eoffrey] A. Names should *not* be supplied for authors who always use only initials: T. S. Eliot, J. B. S. Haldane, O. Henry [pseud.], e. e. cummings, F. R. Leavis, C. S. Lewis, G. E. Moore, J. D. Salinger, C. P. Snow, J. M. Synge, A. J. P. Taylor, C. V. Wedgwood, H. G. Wells.

> Eliot, T. S. *Four Quartets.* London: Faber and Faber, 1944.
>
> Crane, Ronald S. *The Idea of the Humanities and Other Essays Critical and Historical.* 2 vols. Chicago: University of Chicago Press, 1967.

In the latter entry, the author's name could be given as Crane, R[onald] S., since "R. S." appears on the title page, but for most scholarly purposes this is a needless refinement.

16.13   Conversely, especially in style *B,* initials may be used for all given names, regardless of how they appear on a title page or at the head of an article.

16.14   *One author.* A personal name that governs the placement of an entry in a bibliography, as in any alphabetically arranged list, must be given in inverse order, last name first:

> *A*   Woodthrush, John R. *Songs My Father Taught Me.* New Haven: Birdwatchers Press, 1985.
>
> *B*   Barbour, Ian. 1974. *Myths, models, and paradigms: A comparative study in science and religion.* New York: Harper & Row.

16.15   *Two or more authors.* Where there is more than one author, the name of the first is reversed and the following names are either (1) *not* reversed, and separated by commas, or (2) all reversed and, when more than two, separated by semicolons. The University of Chicago Press prefers (1)[2] but will accept (2) when it is used consistently. The following examples illustrate both forms in style *A:*

> (1)   Unwin, L. P., and Joseph Galloway. *Peace in Ireland.* Boston: No Such Press, 1984.
>   [*Note to copyeditor:* Be sure that a comma *follows* as well as precedes the given name or initials of the first author.]

2. This style is a reversal of the preference expressed in the twelfth edition of this manual, where reversal of all names was recommended.

> Merk, Jane S., Ida J. Fogg, and C. Q. Snowe. *Meteorologists' Handbook*. Chicago: Alwether and Clere, 1983.
>
> Brett, P. D., S. W. Johnson, Jr., C. P. E. Bach, and Charles L. Samuels. *Mastering String Quartets* . San Francisco: Amati Press, 1986.

(2)   Unwin, L. P., and Galloway, Joseph. *Peace in Ireland*. Boston: No Such Press, 1984.

> Merk, Jane S.; Fogg, Ida J.; and Snowe, C. Q. *Meteorologists' Handbook*. Chicago: Alwether and Clere, 1983.
>
> Brett, P. D.; Johnson, S. W., Jr.; Bach, C. P. E.; and Samuels, Charles L. *Mastering String Quartets*. San Francisco: Amati Press, 1986. [Note comma before "Jr."]

In style *B:*

(1)   Stockwell, R. P., P. Schachter, and B. H. Partee. 1973. *The major syntactic structures of English*. New York: Holt, Rinehart & Winston.

16.16   A listing for a multiauthor book normally includes all the authors in the order given on the title page. References in the text or notes to works by more than three authors use only the first name followed by "et al." or "and others" (see 15.17).

16.17   Where two authors have the same last name, the name is usually repeated:

> Weinberg, Arthur, and Lila Weinberg. *Clarence Darrow: A Sentimental Rebel*. New York: Putnam's, 1980.

Sometimes the name is given only once:

> Weinberg, Arthur and Lila. . . .

But see 15.16.

16.18   *Pseudonyms.* A book published under a pseudonym should be listed under the pseudonym if that is the name by which the author is primarily known. The author's real name, if it is known, may be given in brackets; if the author's real name is not known, "pseud." may be given in brackets. With well-known pseudonyms, however, it is quite unnecessary to identify the author further; library catalogs provide ample cross-references.

> Stendhal [Marie Henri Beyle]. *The Charterhouse of Parma*. Translated by C. K. Scott-Moncrieff. New York: Boni and Liveright, 1925.
> *or*:
> Stendhal. *The Charterhouse of Parma*. . . .
>
> Centinel [pseud.]. Letters. In *The Complete Anti-Federalist,* edited by Herbert J. Storing, vol. 2. Chicago: University of Chicago Press, 1981.

16.19   Works published under a pseudonym by authors better known by their own names should generally be listed by the author's real name:

Brontë, Charlotte [Currer Bell, pseud.]. *Jane Eyre*. London, 1847.
or:
Brontë, Charlotte. *Jane Eyre*. By Currer Bell. London, 1847.

16.20   If a bibliography should happen to include a number of works published by one author under various pseudonyms, all may be listed under the real name followed by the appropriate pseudonym in brackets or each may be listed under its pseudonym with the real name in brackets and a cross-reference at the real name to each pseudonym listed:

Creasey, John [Gordon Ashe, pseud.]. *A Blast of Trumpets*. New York: Holt, Rinehart, and Winston, 1976.

———— [Anthony Morton, pseud.]. *Hide the Baron*. New York: Walker, 1978.

———— [Jeremy York, pseud.]. *Death to My Killer*. New York: Macmillan Co., 1966.
or:
Ashe, Gordon [John Creasey]. *A Blast of Trumpets*. New York: Holt, Rinehart, and Winston, 1976.

Creasey, John. *See* Ashe, Gordon; Morton, Anthony; York, Jeremy

16.21   *Anonymous works.* If the authorship of a work is known but not revealed on the title page, the name is given in brackets:

[Horsley, Samuel.] *On the Prosodies of the Greek and Latin Languages*. 1796.

16.22   If a work is assumed to be by a specific author, but the fact of authorship cannot be reliably established, the name, followed immediately by a question mark, may be given in brackets:

[Haine, William?] *Certain Epistles of Tully Verbally Translated*. 1611.
[Cook, Ebenezer?] *Sotweed Redivivus; or, The Planter's Looking-Glass*. By "E. C., Gent." Annapolis, 1730.

16.23   If there is no ascertainable "author" (editor, compiler, or other), the reference begins with the title of the work. The use of "Anonymous" or "Anon." is to be avoided.

A True and Sincere Declaration of the Purpose and Ends of the Plantation Begun in Virginia, of the Degrees Which It Hath Received: and Meanes by Which It Hath Been Advanced: . . . 1610.

Discount the initial article; alphabetize under the following word (see 15.92).

16.24   *Editor, compiler, or translator.* A work is listed by its editor, compiler, or translator when no author's name appears on the title page. These are abbreviated "ed." or "comp." (plural "eds." or "comps.") or "trans." and follow the name, preceded by a comma:

A   Wiley, Bell I., ed. *Slaves No More: Letters from Liberia, 1833–1869*. Lexington: University Press of Kentucky, 1980.

Kamrany, Nake M., and Richard H. Day, eds. *Economic Issues of the Eighties*. Baltimore: Johns Hopkins University Press, 1980.

Lenz, Carolyn Ruth Swift, Gayle Greene, and Carol Thomas Neely, eds. *The Woman's Part: Feminist Criticism of Shakespeare*. Champaign: University of Illinois Press, 1980.

Gage, John, ed. and trans. *Goethe on Art*. Berkeley and Los Angeles: University of California Press, 1980.

McBurney, William Harlin, comp. *A Check List of English Prose Fiction, 1700–1739*. Cambridge: Harvard University Press, 1960.

Wang, Jen Yu, and Gerald L. Berger, eds. and comps. *Bibliography of Agricultural Meteorology*. Madison: University of Wisconsin Press, 1962.

Zeydel, Edwin H., trans. *Ecbasis cuiusdam captivi per tropologiam— Escape of a Certain Captive Told in a Figurative Manner: An Eleventh-Century Latin Beast Epic*. Studies in Germanic Languages and Literatures, no. 46. Chapel Hill: University of North Carolina Press, 1964.

Adams, Eleanor B., and Fray Angelico Chavez, eds. and trans. *The Missions of New Mexico, 1776: A Description by Fray Francisco Atanasio Domínguez, with Other Contemporary Documents*. Albuquerque: University of New Mexico Press, 1975.

B   Greenberger, Martin, Julius Aronofsky, James L. McKenney, and William F. Massy, eds. 1974. *Networks for research and education: Sharing of computer and information resources nationwide*. Cambridge: MIT Press.

Harris, James E., and Edward F. Wente, eds. 1980. *An X-ray atlas of the royal mummies*. Chicago: Univ. of Chicago Press.

Mellars, Paul, ed. 1979. *The early postglacial settlement of northern Europe: An ecological perspective*. Pittsburgh: Univ. of Pittsburgh Press.

16.25   The edited work of one author is normally listed by that author's name, rather than the name of the editor or translator. The editor's or translator's name follows the title and is preceded by "Edited by" or "Translated by" (sometimes abbreviated, especially in style *B*):

A   Cartwright, Peter. *Autobiography of Peter Cartwright, the Backwoods Preacher*. Edited by W. P. Strickland. Cincinnati: L. Swormstedt and A. Poe, 1856.

Dryden, John. *The Works of John Dryden*. Edited by H. T. Swedenberg. 8 vols. Berkeley and Los Angeles: University of California Press, 1956–62.

Ariès, Philippe. *Centuries of Childhood: A Social History of Family Life*. Translated by Robert Baldick. New York: Alfred A. Knopf, 1962.

Baudelaire, Charles. *One Hundred Poems from "Les fleurs du mal."* Translated by C. F. MacIntyre. Berkeley and Los Angeles: University of California Press, 1947.
[Note the use of quotation marks for a title within a title; see 16.33.]

Unseld, Siegfried. *The Author and His Publisher.* Translated by Hunter Hannum and Hildegarde Hannum. Chicago: University of Chicago Press, 1980.
[Note repetition of last name, preferable to "Hunter and Hildegarde Hannum"; see 16.17.]

Bamberger, Ludwig. *Bismarcks grosses Spiel: Die geheimen Tagebücher Ludwig Bambergers.* Edited by Ernst Feder. Frankfurt, 1932.

Burke, Edmund. *The Correspondence of Edmund Burke.* Edited by Thomas W. Copeland. Vol. 3, *July 1774–June 1778.* Edited by George H. Guttridge. Cambridge: Cambridge University Press; Chicago: University of Chicago Press, 1961.

The last is an example of a multivolume work with a general editor—Professor Copeland—and individual editors for each volume. The editor's name follows that part of the work for which he is responsible.

B   Newton, Isaac. 1976. *The mathematical papers of Isaac Newton.* Ed. D. T. Whiteside and M. A. Hoskins. Vol. 7, *1691–1695.* Cambridge: Cambridge Univ. Press.

Naumov, N. P. 1972. *The ecology of animals.* Translated from the Russian by Frederick K. Plous, Jr., and edited by Norman D. Levine. Champaign: Univ. of Illinois Press.

Or, to shorten this entry:

. . . Trans. F. K. Plous, Jr.; ed. N. D. Levine. . . .

16.26   In a work where the editor or the translator is more important to the discussion than the original author, the editor's (translator's) name is given first. For example, in a work on Eliot:

Eliot, T. S., ed. *Literary Essays,* by Ezra Pound. New York: New Directions, 1953.

16.27   Amplifications of the editor's or translator's role indicated by such phrases as "Edited and with an Introduction (Notes) by" or "Translated and with a Foreword by" are usually simplified to "ed." or "Edited by," "trans." or "Translated by." For example, for a book whose title page reads:

The Red Notebook of Charles Darwin
Edited with an Introduction and Notes
by Sandra Herbert

the listing should be rendered:

Herbert, Sandra, ed. *The Red Notebook of Charles Darwin.* Ithaca, N.Y.: Cornell University Press, 1980.
or:
Darwin, Charles. *The Red Notebook of Charles Darwin.* Edited by Sandra Herbert. Ithaca, N.Y.: Cornell University Press, 1980.

16.28   Authors of forewords or introductions to books by other authors, often listed on title pages, should be omitted from a bibliography entry unless the foreword or introduction is of special importance to the work in which the bibliography appears:

> Harris, Mark. Introduction to *With the Procession,* by Henry B. Fuller. Chicago: University of Chicago Press, 1965.
>
> Luce, Clare Boothe. Foreword to *MacArthur and Wainwright: Sacrifice of the Philippines,* by John Jacob Beck. Albuquerque: University of New Mexico Press, 1974.

16.29   *Organization, association, or corporation.* If a publication issued by an organization bears no personal author's name on the title page, it should be listed by the organization, even if the name is repeated in the title or in the series title or as the publisher:

> A   International Monetary Fund. *Surveys of African Economies.* Vol. 7, *Algeria, Mali, Morocco, and Tunisia.* Washington, D.C.: International Monetary Fund, 1977.
> [The facts of publication here could be simply: Washington, D.C., 1977. *or:* Washington, D.C.: IMF, 1977.]
>
> Modern Language Association of America. *1973 MLA International Bibliography of Books and Articles on the Modern Languages and Literatures.* 3 vols. New York: Modern Language Association of America, 1975.
> [*or:* New York: MLA, 1975. *or:* New York, 1975.]
>
> International Statistics Institute. *Proceedings of the 34th Session, International Statistics Institute, Ottawa, 1963.* 2 vols. Toronto: University of Toronto Press, 1964.
>
> B   Ohio State University College of Administrative Science. Center for Human Resource Research. 1977. *The national longitudinal surveys handbook.* Rev. ed. Columbus.
>
> Washington University and the Federal Reserve Bank of St. Louis. Center for the Study of American Business. 1977. *Financing economic growth: The problem of capital formation.* CSAB Working Paper no. 19. St. Louis.
>
> *or:*
>
> Center for the Study of American Business (CSAB). Washington University and the Federal Reserve Bank of St. Louis. . . .
>
> Brunswick Public Welfare Department. Pest Control Division. Rodent Activities Termination Section (RATS). 1985. *The piper and the rats: A musical experiment.* Report no. 1984. Hamelin.

16.30   Where a bibliography includes a number of works published or sponsored by the same organization, some with individual authors and some without, it is helpful to list all alike, either under the name of the organization or by individual author or title.

> Better Books Association. *The Art of Bookbinding,* by Clarence Stamp. Centerville, Mass., 1988.
>
> ———. *How to Prepare a Bibliography in Seven Steps.* Centerville, Mass ., 1987.

> *or:*
> *How to Prepare a Bibliography in Seven Steps.* Centerville, Mass.: Better Books Association, 1987.
>
> Stamp, Clarence. *The Art of Bookbinding.* Centerville, Mass.: Better Books Association, 1988.

(For more publications issued by agencies and departments of federal and local governments see 16.141–75.)

TITLES

16.31   Compiling a bibliography raises questions of how much editing may be done to the title of a printed work in applying rules of style. Because capitalization, punctuation, and the use of italics on a title page are generally matters determined by the publisher rather than the author, scholars agree that these may be changed within limits but that the author's spelling must not be altered. Thus the title page of a book may read:

THOMAS MANN'S
Doctor Faustus
The Sources and Structure of the Novel

Transcribed and reduced to bibliographical form, this will read, in *A* style: *Thomas Mann's "Doctor Faustus": The Sources and Structure of the Novel;* in *B* style: *Thomas Mann's "Doctor Faustus": The sources and structure of the novel.* That is, the entire title has been put in italics, the title within the title has been enclosed in quotation marks, and a colon has been introduced between title and subtitle.

16.32   In other words, the rules governing capitalization, spelling, punctuation, italics, and quotation marks for titles in bibliographies, particularly for style *A* (16.2), are much the same as those set forth in chapter 7 (7.122–45) for titles mentioned in the text. The following examples illustrate those rules as applied to bibliography listings, with some possible alternatives.

16.33   *Titles within titles.* Titles of long or short works appearing within an italicized title are usually set off by quotation marks:

> Forte, Allen. *The Harmonic Organization of "The Rite of Spring."* New Haven: Yale University Press, 1978.
>
> McHugh, Roland. *Annotations to "Finnegans Wake."* Baltimore: Johns Hopkins University Press, 1980.

16.34   An alternative method sometimes used for the title of a long, or book-length, work included in another is to set it in roman type without quotation marks:

> McHugh, Roland. *Annotations to* Finnegans Wake. Baltimore: Johns Hopkins University Press, 1980.

16.35   Some titles within titles are clear enough without being set off:

> Kottler, Barnet, and Alan M. Markman. *A Concordance to Five Middle English Poems: Cleanness, St. Erkenwald, Sir Gawain and the Green Knight, Patience, and Pearl.* Pittsburgh: University of Pittsburgh Press, 1966.
>
> Zall, P. M., ed. *A Nest of Ninnies and Other English Jestbooks of the Seventeenth Century.* Lincoln: University of Nebraska Press, 1970.

16.36   Some names of works are not titles in the usual sense (see 7.145) and so never take quotation marks:

> Romano, Horace W. *Another Analysis of Mozart's Symphony in C Major.* Waco, Tex.: St. Cecilia Press, 1988.
> *but:*
> . . . *Another Analysis of Mozart's "Jupiter" Symphony.* . . .

16.37   *Older titles.* Titles of works published in earlier centuries may retain their original punctuation and capitalization (except whole words in capital letters, which should be given an initial capital only). These titles may be shortened, omissions being indicated by three ellipsis dots within a title and four, including the period, at the end:

> Ray, John. *Observations Topographical, Moral, and Physiological: Made in a Journey Through part of the Low-Countries, Germany, Italy, and France: with A Catalogue of Plants not Native of England . . . Whereunto is added A brief Account of Francis Willughby, Esq., his Voyage through a great part of Spain.* [London], 1673.
>
> [Beverley, Robert.] *The History and Present State of Virginia . . . by a Native of the Place.* London, 1705.
>
> Escalante, Bernardino. *A Discourse of the Navigation which the Portugales doe make to the Realmes and Provinces of the East Partes of the Worlde.* . . . Translated by John Frampton. London, 1579.

16.38   *Foreign titles.* Titles of works in foreign languages are treated the same as titles in English except that capitalization follows the conventions of the language of the work (see chap. 9, and 16.121–23).

> A   Vail, Eugène A. *De la littérature et des hommes de lettres des Etats-Unis d'Amérique.* Paris, 1841.
>
> Cesbron, Henry. *Histoire critique de l'hystérie.* Paris: Asselin & Houzeau, 1909.
>
> Gundert, Wilhelm. *Japanische Religionsgeschichte: Die Religionen der Japaner und Koreaner in geschichtlichem Abriss dargestellt.* Stuttgart: Gundert Verlag, 1943.
>
> Hersche, Peter. *Der Spätjansenismus in Österreich.* Veröffentlichungen der Kommission für Geschichte Österreichs, vol. 7. Schriften des DDr. Franz Josef Mayer-Gunthof-Fonds, no. 11. Vienna: Verlag der Österreichischen Akademie der Wissenschaften, 1977.
>
> B   Guérin, G. 1928. *La vie des chouettes: Régime et croissance de l'effraye commune Tyto alba alba (L.) en Vendée.* Paris: P. Lechevalier.

16.39   When it is desirable to provide readers with a translation of a title, the translation follows the title and is enclosed in parentheses (sometimes in square brackets). It is set in roman type, without quotation marks, and only the first word (of title and subtitle) and proper nouns and adjectives are capitalized. When a summary in another language is provided, that fact is also included in parentheses:

> Pirumova, N. M. *Zemskoe liberal'noe dvizhenie: Sotsial'nye korni i evoliutsiia do nachala XX veka* (The zemstvo liberal movement: Its social roots and evolution to the beginning of the twentieth century). Moscow: Izdatel'stvo "Nauka," 1977.
>
> Wereszycki, Henryk. *Koniec sojuszu trzech cesarzy* (The end of the three emperors' league; summary in German). Warsaw: PWN, 1977.

16.40   If a title is given only in translation (more often done with a journal article than with a book; see 16.123), the original language must be specified:

> Pirumova, N. M. *The Zemstvo Liberal Movement: Its Social Roots and Evolution to the Beginning of the Twentieth Century* (in Russian). Moscow: Izdatel'stvo "Nauka," 1977.

VOLUMES

16.41   When a work is published in more than one volume, the number of volumes is given after the general title if no individual volume title is given:

> *A*   Byrne, Muriel St. Clare, ed. *The Lisle Letters.* 6 vols. Chicago: University of Chicago Press, 1981.
>
> *B*   Wright, Sewall. 1968–78. *Evolution and the genetics of populations.* 4 vols. Chicago: Univ. of Chicago Press.

16.42   When only one of several volumes is listed, the general title may be given first, followed by the volume number and the title of the particular volume; or the title of the volume may be given first, followed by its volume number and the general title:

> *A*   Pelikan, Jaroslav. *The Christian Tradition: A History of the Development of Doctrine.* Vol. 3, *The Growth of Medieval Theology (600–1300).* Chicago: University of Chicago Press, 1978.
>   *or:*
>   Pelikan, Jaroslav. *The Growth of Medieval Theology (600–1300).* Vol. 3 of *The Christian Tradition: A History of the Development of Doctrine.* Chicago: University of Chicago Press, 1978.
>
> *B*   Wright, Sewall. 1978. *Evolution and the genetics of populations.* Vol. 4, *Variability within and among natural populations.* Chicago: Univ. of Chicago Press.
>   *or:*
>   Wright, Sewall. 1978. *Variability within and among natural populations.* Vol. 4 of *Evolution and the genetics of populations.* Chicago: Univ. of Chicago Press.

16.43   Volume numbers for books, as for journals (16.103), are always given in arabic figures even when they appear as roman numerals in the book itself.

16.44   A series title may indicate the publishing agency (Smithsonian Miscellaneous Collections), the general subject of the series (Nature of Human Society), or both (Chicago History of American Civilization; Logan Museum Publications in Anthropology). Its name is capitalized as a title, set in roman type, and not enclosed in quotation marks or parentheses. Many series do not number their volumes; others use both volume numbers and subsidiary numbers. Any such number should follow the series title in the reference, separated from it by a comma if the title is complete without the number (Middle American Research Records, vol. 1, no. 14), no comma if the number is part of the title (Bureau of American Ethnology Bulletin no. 143). The name of the series editor may be included but is usually omitted. If the publisher's name appears in the series title, or as the author, it need not be repeated in the facts of publication. Ambiguous series titles should be avoided (Current Report no. 4; Bulletin no. 143; Research Records, no. 5); the responsible agency should appear somewhere in the listing:

A   Caldwell, Helen. *The Brazilian Othello of Machado de Assis: A Study of "Dom Casmurro."* Perspectives in Criticism, vol. 6. Berkeley and Los Angeles: University of California Press, 1960.

Wolf, Theta Holmes. *The Effects of Praise and Competition on the Persisting Behavior of Kindergarten Children.* Child Welfare Monograph Series, no. 15. Minneapolis: University of Minnesota Press, 1938.

Freed, John B. *The Friars and German Society in the Thirteenth Century.* Medieval Academy of America Publications, no. 86. Cambridge, Mass.: The Academy, 1977.

Biays, Pierre. *Les marges de l'œkoumène dans l'est du Canada: Partie orientale du Bouclier canadien et île de Terre-Neuve.* Travaux et documents du Centre d'études nordiques. Quebec: Les Presses de l'université Laval, 1964.

Türk, Egbert. *"Nugae Curialium": Le règne d'Henri II Plantagenêt (1145–1189) et l'éthique politique.* Centre de recherches d'histoire et de philologie, Hautes études médiévales et modernes, no. 28. Geneva: Librairie Droz, 1977.

B   Kendeigh, S. C. 1952. *Parental care and its evolution in birds.* Illinois Biological Monographs, vol. 22, nos. 1–3. Champaign: Univ. of Illinois Press.

Chapman, Jefferson. 1975. *The Icehouse Bottom Site—40MR23.* University of Tennessee Department of Anthropology Publication no. 23. Knoxville: Univ. of Tennessee Press.

Hershkovitz, P. 1962. *Evolution of Neotropical cricetine rodents (Muridae) with special reference to the phyllotine group.* Fieldiana: Zoology, vol. 46. Chicago: Field Museum of Natural History.

16.45   When the series editor's name is included, it follows the series title:

Issawi, Charles. *The Economic History of Turkey, 1800–1914.* Publications of the Center for Middle Eastern Studies, edited by Richard L. Chambers, no. 13. Chicago: University of Chicago Press, 1980.

16.46   If a book within a series is itself a multivolume work, the number of volumes or (if the reference is to a particular volume) the volume number follows the book title and is set off by periods:

Ferrer Benimeli, José Antonio. *Masoneria, iglesia e illustración.* Vol. 1, *Las bases de un conflicto (1700–1739).* Vol. 2, *Inquisición: Procesos históricos (1739–1750).* Publicaciones de la Fundación Universitaria Española, Monografías, no. 17. Madrid, 1976.

16.47   Some series have been going so long that, like some journals, they have begun numbering their volumes over again in a new series (n.s.; old series: o.s.), sometimes designated by number (2d ser., 3d ser.).

Boxer, Charles R., ed. *South China in the Sixteenth Century.* Hakluyt Society Publications, 2d ser., vol. 106. London, 1953.

Palmatary, Helen C. *The Pottery of Marajó Island, Brazil.* Transactions of the American Philosophical Society, n.s. 39, pt. 3. Philadelphia, 1950.

16.48   Names of reprint series (Midway Reprints), paperback series (Phoenix Books), microfiche or text-fiche series (Chicago Visual Library), and others indicating publishing or production methods are properly part of the facts of publication (see 16.58, 16.59), not series titles reflecting subject categories.

CHAPTERS OR PARTS OF A BOOK

16.49   Titles of chapters or parts of a book, such as a symposium, are given in quotation marks and followed by "In" in roman and the title of the whole book in italics. The name of the editor(s) follows the title, preceded by a comma:

Kaiser, Ernest. "The Literature of Harlem." In *Harlem: A Community in Transition,* edited by J. H. Clarke. New York: Citadel Press, 1964.

16.50   Inclusive page numbers may be given if desired and should follow the reference to the book and its editor:

Ogilvy, David. "The Creative Chef." In *The Creative Organization,* edited by Gary A. Steiner, 199–213. Chicago: University of Chicago Press, 1965.

16.51   Part (of) or chapter (in) may be specified:

> McNeill, William H. "The Era of Middle Eastern Dominance to 500 B.C." Part 1 of *The Rise of the West*. Chicago: University of Chicago Press, 1963.
>
> Thomson, Virgil. "Cage and the Collage of Noises." Chap. 8 in *American Music since 1910*. New York: Holt, Rinehart, and Winston, 1971.

16.52   If the part is an entity in itself—such as a play or a long poem—both titles are italicized:

> Gordon, Robert. *The Tunes of Chicken Little*. In *Playwrights for Tomorrow: A Collection of Plays*, edited by Arthur H. Ballet, vol. 13. Minneapolis: University of Minnesota Press, 1975.
> [One of four plays included in vol. 13.]
>
> Milton, John. *Paradise Lost*. In *The Complete Poetical Works of John Milton*, edited by William Vaughn Moody. Student's Cambridge Edition. Boston: Houghton Mifflin, 1924.

16.53   Because much scientific research is published in collections of papers such as the proceedings of professional meetings, this form appears often in style *B*. Titles of papers are treated like titles of journal articles, without quotation marks, and "edited by" is usually shortened to "ed.":

> Chomsky, N. 1973. Conditions on transformations. In *A festschrift for Morris Halle*, ed. S. R. Anderson and P. Kiparsky. New York: Holt, Rinehart & Winston.
>
> Dorsey, J. Owen, and Paul Radin. 1912. Winnebago. In *Handbook of American Indians north of Mexico*, ed. F. W. Hodge, 958–61. Bureau of American Ethnology Bulletin no. 30, pt. 2. Washington, D.C.
>
> Chave, K. E. 1964. Skeletal durability and preservation. In *Approaches to paleoecology*, ed. J. Imbrie and N. Newel, 377–87. New York: Wiley.
>
> Dawson, M. R. 1967. Lagomorph history and the stratigraphic record. In *Essays in paleontology and stratigraphy: Raymond C. Moore commemorative volume*, 227–316. University of Kansas, Department of Geology Special Publication no. 2. Lawrence.

(For the use of cross-references when a bibliography contains many references to the same volume see 15.81.)

EDITION

16.54   When an edition other than the first is used, the number or description of the edition follows the title in the listing. The number of an edition and its date of publication may be found in the copyright notice of the book (see 16.89). A new edition may be called "Revised Edition" (no number), "Second Edition, Revised and Enlarged," or other variants. In bibliography entries or notes these are commonly abbreviated:

"rev. ed.," "2d ed., rev. and enl." (or just "2d ed."), "2 vols. in 1," etc. Such terms and their abbreviations should be given in English even though the book is in a foreign language.

> A Bober, M. M. *Karl Marx's Interpretation of History.* 2d ed. Harvard Economic Studies. Cambridge: Harvard University Press, 1948.
> B Smart, Ninian. 1976. *The religious experience of mankind.* 2d ed. New York: Scribner.
>
> Le Gros Clark, W. E. 1978. *The fossil evidence for human evolution.* 3d ed., ed. B. Campbell. Chicago: Univ. of Chicago Press.
>
> Weber, M., H. M. de Burlet, and O. Abel. 1928. *Die Säugetiere.* 2d ed. 2 vols. Jena: Gustav Fischer.

(For reprint and paperback editions see 16.57–58.)

MODERN EDITIONS OF CLASSICS

16.55 When classics are referred to by page number, the edition used must be specified either in a note or in the bibliography or both. For well-known editions only the name of the edition and the date of the volume are necessary:

> Horace. *Satires, Epistles, and Ars poetica.* Loeb Classical Library. 1932.
> Dryden, John. *Dramatic Essays.* Everyman's Library. 1906.

16.56 Editor, place of publication, and publisher should be added for less well known editions:

> Maimonides. *The Code of Maimonides. Book 5: The Book of Holiness.* Translated and edited by Louis I. Rabinowitz and Philip Grossman. Yale Judaica Series. New Haven: Yale University Press, 1965.
> Wharton, Edith. *The House of Mirth.* Edited by R. W. B. Lewis. The Gotham Library. New York: New York University Press, 1977.

REPRINT EDITIONS

16.57 A reprint, or reprint edition, is either a book that is reissued by its original publisher in a new form, paperback or hardbound, or one that is issued as a photo-offset reproduction by a second publisher who has bought rights to it from the original publisher or a similar reproduction of a book no longer in copyright.[3] For older works, sometimes only the date of the original publication is given in addition to the facts of publication for the reprint, and sometimes full publication data for both editions. There are many ways to cite reprints; an editor may have to devise an ad hoc style to handle particular problems.

3. A book bound in paper is not necessarily a reprint; original paperbacks are no longer unusual. Also, a *reprint edition* is not the same as a *new impression,* or new printing, issued by a publisher to keep a book in print after an earlier printing has been sold out (see 16.89).

16.58 When citing a paperback reprint, authors of scholarly works should try to give original publication data in a bibliography entry as well as the reprint data. Where an author has failed to provide both, the editor should see that either the word "reprint" or the name of a reprint series (Anchor Books, Phoenix Books) appears in the listing:

A   Myrdal, Gunnar. *Population: A Problem for Democracy.* 1940. Reprint. Gloucester, Mass.: Peter Smith, 1956.

Audsley, George Ashdown. *The Art of Organ Building.* 2 vols. 1905. Reprint (2 vols. in 1). New York: Dover Publications, 1964.

Sinclair, Angus. *Development of the Locomotive Engine.* New York: Angus Sinclair Publishing Co., 1907. Reprint. Cambridge: MIT Press, 1970.

Shelley, Mary Wollstonecraft. *Frankenstein; or, The Modern Prometheus (The 1818 Text).* Edited by James Rieger. Indianapolis: Bobbs-Merrill, 1974; Chicago: University of Chicago Press, Phoenix Books, 1982.

Litwack, Leon F. *North of Slavery: The Negro in the Free States, 1790–1860.* Chicago: University of Chicago Press, 1961; Phoenix Books, 1965.

B   Small, Robert. [1804] 1963. *An account of the astronomical discoveries of Kepler.* Reprint, with foreword by William D. Stahlman. Madison: Univ. of Wisconsin Press.

Wallace, A. F. C. 1970. *The death and rebirth of the Seneca.* New York: Random House, Vintage Books.

MICROFORM EDITIONS

16.59 Works issued commercially in microfilm, microfiche, or text-fiche (printed text and microfiche illustrations issued together) are treated much like books, except that the form of publication is given at the end of the entry (if it is not given in the name of the publisher) and a sponsoring organization may be listed as well as the publisher:

Tauber, Abraham. *Spelling Reform in the United States.* Ann Arbor, Mich.: University Microfilms, 1958.

Peale, Charles Willson. *The Collected Papers of Charles Willson Peale and His Family.* Edited by Lillian B. Miller. National Portrait Gallery, Smithsonian Institution, Washington, D.C. Millwood, N.Y.: Kraus-Thomson Organization, 1980. Microfiche.

Joachim, Harold. *French Drawings and Sketchbooks of the Nineteenth Century.* Art Institute of Chicago. 2 vols. Chicago: University of Chicago Press, 1978–79. Text-fiche.
or:
Art Institute of Chicago. *French Drawings and Sketchbooks of the Nineteenth Century,* by Harold Joachim. 2 vols. Chicago: University of Chicago Press, 1978–79. Text-fiche.

U.S. Congress. House of Representatives. *Hearings and Reports of the House Committee on Un-American Activities, 1945–54.* Washington, D.C.: Brookhaven Press, 1977. Microfilm.

16.60 Microfilm or other photographic processes used only to preserve printed material, such as newspaper files, in a library are usually not mentioned as such in a citation. The source is treated as it would be in its original published version.

FACTS OF PUBLICATION

16.61 The facts of publication of a book traditionally include the place (city), the publisher, and the date (year). All are usually included in bibliography listings or full note references for books and pamphlets printed or in microform, and for material issued in machine copies.

16.62 In style *A* all three items are placed at the end of the entry. A colon follows the place name (regular word space after the colon); a comma follows the publisher's name, and a period follows the date:

> Massie, Robert K. *Peter the Great: His Life and World.* New York: Alfred A. Knopf, 1980.

16.63 In style *B,* to accommodate the author-date system of reference (see 15.79), the date follows the author's name and is set off by periods:

> Riegert, P. W. 1980. *From arsenic to DDT.* Toronto: Univ. of Toronto Press.

16.64 *Alternatives.* Although the use of full bibliographic details is preferred in bibliography listings of modern works, alternatives are acceptable in certain cases. One is place and date (no publisher's name), the other date alone (no place or publisher's name). The first, place and date, is the practice of many academic journals and of authors who follow a particular journal style in their book manuscripts. The University of Chicago Press accepts this practice in bibliographies in a book manuscript where an author has consistently employed it. When only place and date are used, a comma (not a colon) is usual following the place, in style *A* (though the need for a comma here is debatable):

> Akers, Charles. *Abigail Adams: An American Woman.* Boston, 1980.
> Kennedy, George A. *Classical Rhetoric and Its Christian and Secular Tradition from Ancient to Modern Times.* Chapel Hill, N.C., 1980.

In style *B* the place stands alone:

> Machado, M. A., Jr. 1980. *The North Mexican cattle industry, 1910–1975: Ideology, conflict, and change.* College Station, Tex.

16.65 The second alternative, the date of publication alone, is both economical in that it saves space and realistic in that the date is usually the fact of publication most important to the scholar; the publisher of the book cited may be discovered by the interested reader in a library catalog or the current *Books in Print,* available for consultation in most bookstores. The University of Chicago Press will accept this practice in books where it is consistently used and seems appropriate to the subject:

Vonnegut, Kurt. *Jailbird*. 1979.
Morgan, Edmund S. *The Birth of the Republic, 1763–89*. 1956. Rev. ed. 1977.

(For a discussion of how to determine the date of publication of a book see 16.88.)

16.66 For works published in earlier centuries whose publishers have long ceased to exist or cannot be determined, either place and date or date alone is entirely acceptable even when mixed in a list containing modern works accompanied by full facts of publication:

Baldwin, William. *A Treatise of morall philosophy Contaynynge the sayings of the wyse*. London, 1579.
Bunyan, John. *A Few Sighs from Hell, or the Groans of a damned Soul*. 1658.

16.67 The inclusion of the publisher's name is, of course, essential in references to quoted material for which permission to reprint has been granted by the publisher as holder of the copyright (see chap. 4).

16.68 *Place*. The name of the city where the publisher's main editorial offices are located is usually sufficient:

New York: Macmillan Co., 1980.

16.69 If the title page of the book cited lists two cities with the publisher's name, the city listed first is the one to use; it is permissible, but not necessary, to use both:

Chicago and London: University of Chicago Press, 1981.

(If "London" does not appear on the title page of the book being cited, it must not be given in the reference.) The University of California Press prefers the use of "Berkeley and Los Angeles" in references to its publications.

16.70 If the place of publication is not widely known, the abbreviation of the state name should follow it:

Menasha, Wis.: Banta Publishing Co., 1965.
Englewood Cliffs, N.J.: Prentice-Hall, 1975.

16.71 The distinction between Cambridge, England, and Cambridge, Massachusetts, should be made. In the absence of contrary indications—such as inclusion of the state name or mention of Harvard University or MIT—it will be assumed that the English city is meant.

16.72 Thus the following are all acceptable:

Cambridge: Cambridge University Press, 1979.

Cambridge, 1979.

Cambridge: Harvard University Press, 1979.

Cambridge: MIT Press, 1979.

Cambridge, Mass., 1979.

16.73 For foreign cities the English name, where there is one, should usually be substituted in the facts of publication: Vienna (Wien), Cologne (Köln), Turin (Torino), Rome (Roma), Milan (Milano), Munich (München), Brunswick (Braunschweig), Prague (Praha), The Hague ('s Gravenhage); *but* Frankfurt am Main (*not* Frankfort on the Main).

16.74 Where neither place of publication nor publisher's name appears on the title page, "N.p." may take the place of both:

N.p. 1840.

In such cases, however, it is less pedantic to use the date alone.

16.75 When no facts of publication are to be found, "N.p., n.d." (no place, no date) may be used, indicating that neither is available.

16.76 *Publisher.* The publisher's name may be given either in full, as printed on the title page of the book, or in an acceptable abbreviated form. American publishers' names and the usual abbreviations for them are listed in *Books in Print,* published annually by R. R. Bowker Co., and British publishers' names may be found in *British Books in Print,* published by J. Whitaker & Sons and R. R. Bowker Co. An initial "The" as well as "Inc.," Ltd.," or "S.A." following the name is generally omitted, even when the full name is given. The use of either long or short forms of publishers' names must be consistent throughout a bibliography.

16.77 The word *University* in names of university presses may be shortened to Univ., particularly when style *B* is followed. A place name that is part of a publisher's name, however, should always be spelled out: Univ. of South Carolina Press. The word *Press* should not be omitted from the name of a university press because the university itself may issue publications independently of its press. Where there is no ambiguity, the word may be omitted, for example, Pergamon as a short form of Pergamon Press.

16.78 Punctuation and spelling of publishers' names should be carefully observed. For example, there is now no comma in Houghton Mifflin Co.; there is a comma in both Little, Brown & Co. and the former Harcourt, Brace & Co., now Harcourt Brace Jovanovich without any comma whatever. There is no capital "M" in the middle of Macmillan; the London firm is Macmillan & Co., and the New York firm is Macmillan Co.; both are abbreviated "Macmillan."

16.79 Either "and" or "&" may be used in a publisher's name, regardless of how it is rendered on the title page, provided consistency is observed throughout a bibliography:

> Harper and Row   *or*   Harper & Row
> Duncker und Humblot   *or*   Duncker & Humblot

16.80 No part of a foreign publisher's name should be translated, even though the place of publication has been anglicized:

> Paris: Presses universitaires de France, 1982.
> Mexico City: Fondo de Cultura Económica, 1981.
> Munich: Carl Hanser Verlag, 1980.

16.81 If the name of the publisher has changed since the book was published, the name on the title page is the one to use, not the present name, e.g., Henry Holt & Co., not Holt, Rinehart & Winston. Such recent additions to title pages as "A Division of ——— Corporation" should not be added to the publisher's name in a scholarly bibliography.

16.82 For copublished books—books published simultaneously by two different publishers, e.g., one in the United States and one in another country—it is permissible, but not necessary, to give both in the facts of publication:

> Bloch, Marc. *Feudal Society.* Translated by L. A. Manyon. Chicago: University of Chicago Press; London: Routledge & Kegan Paul, 1961.

16.83 A bibliography entry or a full note reference in a book published in the United States and addressed principally to American readers should give the American edition of a copublished book, or both—not just the British edition.

16.84 When a book is published under one publisher's name and distributed under another's, use the name on the title page of the book; add the distributor's name only if this fact would be useful to the reader:

> Woods, Shirley E., Jr. *The Squirrels of Canada.* Ottawa: National Museums of Canada, 1980; distributed in U.S. by University of Chicago Press.

16.85 When a publishing arrangement specified on the title page tells something about the nature of the book, it should be included:

> Sophocles. *Oedipus the King.* Translated and adapted by Anthony Burgess. Minnesota Drama Editions, edited by Michael Langham, no. 8. Minneapolis: University of Minnesota Press in association with the Guthrie Theater Company, 1972.

16.86 Some publishers issue certain categories of books through a special publishing division or under a special imprint. In such instances the imprint may be given after the publisher's name:

> Cooper, James Fenimore. *The Letters and Journals of James Fenimore Cooper.* Edited by J. F. Beard. 2 vols. Cambridge: Harvard University Press, Belknap Press, 1960.

The same style is used for paperback reprints (see 16.58).

16.87 The publisher of a foreign language work does not appear in the facts of publication of the English translation unless the foreign language title is also given:

> Derrida, Jacques. *Writing and Difference.* Translated by Alan Bass. Chicago: University of Chicago Press, 1978. Originally published as *L'écriture et la différence* (Paris: Editions du Seuil, 1967).
>
> *or:*
>
> Derrida, Jacques. *L'écriture et la différence.* Paris: Editions du Seuil, 1967. Translated by Alan Bass, under the title *Writing and Difference.* Chicago: University of Chicago Press, 1978.

16.88 *Date of publication.* The date of publication of a book means the *year* of publication—not the month or day. Sometimes the date of publication may be found on the title page of a book. More often it appears only on the copyright page and is the same as the date of copyright.

16.89 If an edition other than the first is used, both date and number of the edition must be given (see 16.54). Copyright pages often list successive *printings* or *impressions,* with the dates of each. These are not new *editions* of the book and therefore should be ignored in determining the date of publication. See figure 1.1, showing a third edition published in 1976, a sixth impression of which was issued in 1978—1976 is the date to be used in a reference to the "3d ed." of this volume:

> Turabian, Kate L. *Student's Guide for Writing College Papers.* 3d ed. Chicago: University of Chicago Press, 1976.

16.90 A reference to a work of several volumes published in different years should give inclusive dates:

> Tillich, Paul. *Systematic Theology.* 3 vols. Chicago: University of Chicago Press, 1951–63.

16.91 If the work has not yet been completed, the date of the first volume is followed by an en dash (an em dash if an en is not available):

> Pelikan, Jaroslav. *The Christian Tradition: A History of the Development of Doctrine.* 3 vols. to date. Chicago: University of Chicago Press, 1971–.

16.92 When only one of several volumes is mentioned, only the year of publication of the particular volume is given:

> Freeman, Douglas Southall. *George Washington.* Vol. 3, *Planter and Patriot.* New York: Charles Scribner's Sons, 1951.

(See also 16.41–42.)

16.93 When there is no ascertainable date of publication in a printed book, "n.d." (no date) takes the place of the date in the facts of publication. When the date is ascertainable, but not printed in the book, it is enclosed in brackets.

A   Phillips, Marjorie S. *Book-Trading as a Business.* Excelsior, Minn.: Self-Help Publishing Co., n.d.

Moonbeam, Sir Oliver. *Memoirs of an Inveterate Procrastinator.* Waiting-upon-Tyme, Wessex: Privately printed, [1846].
or: . . . Wessex, [1846].

B   Gross, P. D. n.d. *Reading and comprehension at the third-grade level.* Beaver Dam, Mont.: Educational Press.

Hunter, R. M. [1902]. *Agates of the central states.* Indianapolis: Minerals Press.

16.94 When a book will be published but the date has not been determined at the time it is listed in a bibliography, either "Forthcoming" or "In press" (if true) takes the place of the facts of publication:

A   Putnam, Jane S. *Trees in Paintings of the Early Twentieth Century.* In press.

Mitchell, D. C. *The Historian as Prophet.* Forthcoming.

B   Abrams, S. E. In press. *The life of science.*

But see 16.97.

16.95 In the author-date system of references, where a date of publication is often of paramount importance in identifying the source, it is permissible to use either an announced publication date or "n.d." in place of the date. While not strictly accurate, "n.d." is better than "Forthcoming" or "In press" in reference lists because it takes the same amount of space as a date, which may be available in time to be inserted in the proofs. If either "n.d." or an announced future date is used this way, either "Forthcoming" or "In press" should be added at the end of the reference list entry so that the reader will know that the work has not yet been published:

Abrams, S. E. 1983. *The life of science.* Forthcoming.

Brain, C. K. n.d. Some aspects of the South African australopithecine sites and their bone accumulations. In *African Hominidae of the Plio-Pleistocene,* ed. C. Jolly. Forthcoming.

Partridge, T. C., and A. S. Talma. N.d. *Carbon and oxygen isotope measurements at Makapansgat and Sterkfontein, and their palaeoenvironmental significance.* In press.

16.96 The publisher, if known, may be included:

A Manual of Style. 13th ed. Chicago: University of Chicago Press, forthcoming.

16.97   A manuscript not yet assured of publication is considered unpublished (see 16.128).

JOURNAL ARTICLES

BASIC STYLES

16.98   The basic styles for listing journal articles in a bibliography are illustrated in 16.2. For the differences between styles *A* and *B* see 16.5. Amplifications of these styles are given in the following paragraphs. Compilers of bibliographies may use combinations or modifications of these styles to meet particular needs.

16.99   The names of authors of journal articles are treated the same as names of book authors (16.11–30); that is, in style *A* one or more of an author's given names are spelled out, in style *B* initials are used for all given names, but users of one style may prefer the practice of the other or may mix them (some names, some initials) when following authors' preferences.

16.100   Titles of articles are given title capitalization (7.123) and enclosed in quotation marks in style *A*. Style *B* uses sentence capitalization, no quotation marks, and may omit the subtitle, or the whole title, leaving the reader to find the article in the given issue of the journal.

16.101   The titles of journals themselves are italicized and capitalized as titles, in both styles. They may be abbreviated, provided the abbreviations are clear to readers and are used consistently. Abbreviations of journal titles are most widely used in the various scientific fields, probably because such a large proportion of the research in these fields is published in the form of journal articles, and authors therefore make fre quent reference to this literature. Readers in these fields will readily understand the accepted abbreviations. Lists of recommended abbreviations are printed by *Chemical Abstracts* and *Index Medicus*. Titles of foreign and less well known journals are generally best spelled out, and it is never incorrect to spell out all journal titles in a reference list. The editor can more easily abbreviate spelled-out titles than spell out abbreviated ones.

16.102   In literature, history, and the arts, abbreviations should be used with caution. With the exception of *PMLA, ELH,* and other abbreviations that are themselves titles of journals, it is usually best to spell out journal names in bibliographies. When abbreviation seems desirable, a list of abbreviations may precede the note section or the bibliography (see figs. 15.2, 15.3). Of limited use as guides to abbreviations are lists published in the annual *MLA International Bibliography* (the average

461

reader without handy access to this list will not recognize these abbreviations) and in the American Historical Association's *Recently Published Articles* (individual words commonly used in titles are abbreviated, not the titles themselves).

16.103   The volume number follows the journal title with no punctuation separating them. Arabic figures are used for volume numbers even when a journal itself uses roman numerals.

16.104   The date (year) of the issue is given in parentheses following the volume number in style *A;* in style *B* it follows the author's name (16.6 [2]).

16.105   The month or season or number of the issue may also be given, if consistency is observed in all citations to the same journal; identification of the issue is required only when each issue is paginated separately—most scholarly journals are paginated consecutively throughout a volume—but identification is often helpful, particularly of recently published issues not yet bound into volumes.

16.106   Inclusive (first and last) page numbers are usually provided for journal articles in bibliography entries; they not only help the reader find the article but indicate the length of it.

16.107   A colon between volume number and pages precludes the necessity of "vol." or "pp." to distinguish them (see 16.10 and n.1). If the volume number is followed by a date or other facts in parentheses, a word space follows the colon: 14 (1969): 139–60. If volume and page numbers come together, no space follows the colon: 14:139–60.

16.108   Inclusive page numbers should follow University of Chicago Press style (8.67), as illustrated in the following sequences:

> 3–17, 23–26, 100–103, 104–7, 124–28, 1115–20

16.109   A typical bibliography entry in style *A* illustrating all or some of the above elements:

> Robertson, Noel. "The Dorian Migration and Corinthian Ritual." *Classical Philology* 75 (1980): 1–22.

16.110   Alternative forms for issue, date, and pages, acceptable if followed consistently:

> *Classical Philology* 75 (January 1980): 1–22.
> *Classical Philology* 75, no. 1 (1980): 1–22.
> *Classical Philology* 75 (1): 1–22 (January 1980).
> *Classical Philology* 75 (1): 1–22 (1980).

16.111   A typical entry in style *B:*

> Cormack, A. M. 1980. Early two-dimensional reconstruction and recent topics stemming from it. *Science* 209:1482–86.

16.112   If desirable, the date or the number of the issue might be added after the volume number (see 16.105):

> *Science* 209 (26 Sept.): 1482–86.
> *Science* 209 (no. 4464): 1482–86.

16.113   References to journals that are paginated by issue rather than by volume *must* identify the issue:

> Eisenberg, J. F. 1970. A splendid predator does its own thing untroubled by man. *Smithsonian* 1 (June): 48–53.

16.114   The following examples illustrate various kinds of journal entries likely to be found in bibliographies and reference lists. (For explanation of the styles see 16.98 ff.) Note punctuation and capitalization:

A   Gilman, Ernest B. "Words and Image in Quarles' *Emblemes.*" *Critical Inquiry* 6 (Spring 1980): 385–410.

Baum, Dale. " 'Noisy but Not Numerous': The Revolt of the Massachusetts Mugwumps." *Historian* 41 (February 1979): 241–56.

Loomis, C. C., Jr. "Structure and Sympathy in Joyce's 'The Dead.' " *PMLA* 75 (1960): 149–51.

Bundy, William P. "Who Lost Patagonia? Foreign Policy in the 1980 Campaign." *Foreign Affairs* 58 (Fall 1979): 1–27.

Ash, James L., Jr. " 'Oh, No, It Is Not the Scriptures!' The Bible and the Spirit in George Fox." *Quaker History* 63 (1974): 94–107.

Cooper, Patricia A. "What Ever Happened to Adolph Strasser?" *Labor History* 20 (Summer 1979): 17–30.

Martin, Albro. "Uneasy Partners: Government-Business Relations in Twentieth-Century American History." *Prologue* 11 (Summer 1979): 91–105.

Tuerk, Richard. "Jacob Riis and the Jews." *New-York Historical Society Quarterly* 42 (July 1979): 179–201.

Holmes, Jack D. L. "Up the Tombigbee with the Spaniards: Juan de la Villebeuvre and the Treaty of Boucfouca (1793)." *Alabama Historical Quarterly* 40 (Spring–Summer 1978): 51–61.

Joyce, William L. "The Manuscript Collections of the American Antiquarian Society." *Proceedings of the American Antiquarian Society* 89, pt. 1 (1979): 123–52.

Armstrong, Paul B. "E. M. Forster's *Howards End:* The Existential Crisis of the Liberal Imagination." *Mosaic* 8, no. 1 (1974): 183–99.

B   Jackson, Richard. 1979. Running down the up-escalator: Regional inequality in Papua New Guinea. *Australian Geographer* 14 (May): 175–84.

Meltzer, Françoise. 1979 . On Rimbaud's "Voyelles." *Modern Philology* 76:344–54.

463

Bennett, John W. 1946. The interpretation of Pueblo culture: A question of values. *Southwestern Journal of Anthropology* 2:361–74.

Brain, C. K., and V. Brain. 1977. Microfaunal remains from Mirabib: Some evidence of palaeoecological changes in the Namib. *Madoqua* 10 (4): 285–93.

Sommerstein, A. R. 1972. On the so-called definite article in English. *Linguistic Inquiry* 3:197–209.

Orshansky, Mollie, 1965. Counting the poor: Another look at the poverty profile. *Social Security Bulletin* 28 (January): 3–29.

Broom, R., and J. T. Robinson. 1950. Man contemporaneous with the Swartkrans ape-man. *Am. J. Phys. Anthrop.*, n.s. 8:151–56. [n.s. = new series; see 16.47.]

Gibson, E. P. 1954. Ancient mounds near Grand Rapids in the lower Grand River Valley and in southwestern Michigan. *Michigan Archaeological Society News* (Ann Arbor) 1, no. 3:3–10.

16.115   *Article title omitted*

Elliot, O., and J. P. Scott. 1961. *J. Genet. Psychol.* 99:3–22.

(See 16.6 [4].)

16.116   *Article published in more than one issue*

A   Patrick, Elizabeth Nelson. "The Black Experience in Southern Nevada." Parts 1, 2. *Nevada Historical Society Quarterly* 22 (Summer, Fall 1979): 128–40, 209–20.

B   Patch, C. Ross. 1985–86. The next to last angry man. Parts 1–3. *World's End Review* 8:315–30; 9:27–52, 125–42.

Rowe, E. G. 1947. The breeding biology of *Aquila verreauxi* Lesson. Parts 1, 2. *Ibis* 89:387–410, 576–606.

Dougherty, R. C. 1970. A grammar of coordinate conjoined structures, I. *Language* 46:850–98.

16.117   *Article published in two places.* When it is desirable to list more than one place in which an article has appeared, the main listing should be the one referred to in the text; the other is given in parentheses following the listing:

McKeon, Richard. "Dialogue and Controversy in Philosophy." *Philosophy and Phenomenological Research* 17 (1955): 143–63. (First published in *Entretiens philosophiques d'Athènes*, 161–78. Athens: Institut international de philosophie, 1955.)

16.118   *Place of publication.* If a journal might be confused with another with the same or a similar title or if it is not well known to the users of the bibliography, the name of the place or institution where it is published may be given in parentheses after the title:

A   Garrett, Marvin P. "Language and Design in *Pippa Passes.*" *Victorian Poetry* (West Virginia University) 13, no. 1 (1975): 47–60.

Stearns, Peter N. "Sequence in History Teaching: Some Opportunities." *History Teacher* (Long Beach, Calif.) 12 (August 1979): 471–80.

B   Hughes, A . R., and P. V. Tobias. 1977. A fossil skull probably of the genus *Homo* from Sterkfontein, Transvaal. *Nature* (London) 265:310–12.

16.119   *No volume number.* Some journals carry only the issue number (no volume number). If the issues are numbered consecutively from the beginning of publication, the number is followed by the date, in parentheses. Here a comma is appropriate after the journal title, the abbreviation "no." precedes the issue number, and a colon precedes the page numbers:

> Meyerovitch, Eva. "The Gnostic Manuscripts of Upper Egypt." *Diogenes*, no . 25 (1959): 84–117.

16.120   If issue numbers begin with 1 each year, the year serves as a volume number and is not enclosed in parentheses; the issue number follows it:

> Rozner, I. G. "The War of Liberation of the Ukrainian People in 1648–1654 and Russia" (in Russian). *Voprosy Istorii,* 1979, no. 4:51–64.

FOREIGN LANGUAGE JOURNALS

16.121   Titles of foreign language articles are capitalized, like book titles, according to the conventions of their respective languages (see chap. 9 and 16.38). Journal names also follow the foreign language convention, as a rule, but may be capitalized as English titles are (9.4) if an author prefers this system and follows it consistently. Dates and such abbreviations as "no.," "pt.," "ser." are given in English (but see 17.22).

> Bouchard, Gérard. "Un essai d'anthropologie régionale: L'histoire sociale du Saguenay aux XIXe et XXe siècles." *Annales: Economies, sociétés, civilisations* 34 (January 1979): 106–25.
>
> Saulnier, Verdun L. "Dix années d'études sur Rabelais." *Bibliothèque d'humanisme et renaissance* 11 (1949): 105–28.
>
> Broszat, Martin. " 'Holocaust' und die Geschichtswissenschaft." *Vierteljahrshefte Zeitgeschichte* 27 (April 1979): 285–98.
>
> Kern, W. "Waar verzamelde Pigafetta zijn Maleise woorden?" *Tijdschrift voor Indische taal-, land- en volkenkunde* 78 (1938): 271–73.

16.122   A translation of an article title may be given:

> Kern, W. "Waar verzamelde Pigafetta zijn Maleise woorden?" (Where did Pigafetta collect his Malaysian words?) *Tijdschrift voor Indische taal-, land- en volkenkunde* 78 (1938): 271–73.
>
> Bouchard, Gérard. "Un essai d'anthropologie régionale: L'histoire sociale du Saguenay aux XIXe et XXe siècles" (A study in regional anthropology: The social history of the Saguenay in the nineteenth and twentieth centuries). *Annales: Economies, sociétés, civilisations* 34 (January 1979): 106–25.

16.123   If the title of the article is given only in translation, the original language is specified in parentheses:

> Hori, Sunao. "Some Problems regarding Ch'ing Rule over Southern Sinkiang" (in Japanese). *Shigaku Zasshi* 88 (March 1979): 1–36.
>
> Krasuski, J. "On the Sixtieth Anniversary of Poland's Independence" (in Polish). *Przegląd Zachodni*, 1978, no. 5/6:190–211.
>
> Kosman, M. "Evolution of Paganism in the Baltic States" (in Russian; English summary). *Voprosy Istorii*, 1979, no. 5:30–44.

POPULAR MAGAZINES

16.124   Popular weekly or monthly magazines are usually (but not always) cited only by date; page numbers may be omitted, but when they are included, a comma, not a colon, separates them from the date of the issue:

> *A*   Miller, Lillian B. "The Peale Family." *Smithsonian*, April 1979, 66–77.
> *or: . . . Smithsonian* 10 (April 1979): 66–77.
>
> Spencer, Scott. "Childhood's End." *Harper's*, May 1979, 16–19.
>
> *B*   Prufer, Olaf. 1964. The Hopewell Cult. *Scientific American*, Dec., 90–102.

16.125   If the magazine quoted is one in which an article begins in the front and jumps to the back, inclusive pages are meaningless and should be omitted:

> Schickel, Richard. "Far beyond Reality: The New Technology of Hollywood's Special Effects." *New York Times Magazine*, 18 May 1980.

BOOK REVIEWS

16.126   *A*   Kastan, David Scott. Review of *Jonson's Gypsies Unmasked: Background and Theme of "The Gypsies Metamorphos'd,"* by Dale B. J. Randall. *Modern Philology* 76 (May 1979): 391–94.

> Lardner, Susan. "Third Eye Open." Review of *The Salt Eaters*, by Toni Cade Bambara. *New Yorker*, 5 May 1980, 169.
>
> *B*   Wolfe, Alan. 1980. Review of *Free to Choose*, by Milton Friedman and Rose Friedman. *Saturday Review*, 2 February, 35.
>
> Daynard, Richard A. 1979. Review of *Watergate and the Constitution*, by Philip B. Kurland. *American Journal of Legal History* 23:368–70.

NEWSPAPERS

16.127   News items from daily papers are rarely listed separately in a bibliography. Rather, the name of the paper and the relevant run of dates may be given either in the general alphabetical list or in a separate section devoted to newspapers. Articles from Sunday supplements or other special sections are treated like listings from popular magazines (see 16.125). In a work containing both a bibliography and notes, ci-

tations to specific items may be given in the notes or in the text and
not listed in the bibliography.

UNPUBLISHED MATERIAL

THESES, LECTURES, AND OTHER UNPUBLISHED WORKS

16.128   The title of an unpublished paper (manuscript, typescript, machine
copy) is treated like the title of a journal article: in roman type and
with quotation marks in style *A*, without quotation marks in style *B*.
The word *unpublished* is unnecessary. Location or sponsoring body
or both should appear as well, and a date if possible.

16.129   *Dissertation or thesis*

A   King, Andrew J. "Law and Land Use in Chicago: A Pre-history of
Modern Zoning." Ph.D. diss., University of Wisconsin, 1976.

Ross, Dorothy. "The Irish-Catholic Immigrant, 1880–1900: A Study in
Social Mobility." Master's thesis, Columbia University, n.d.

B   Mann, A. E. 1968. The palaeodemography of *Australopithecus*. Ph.D.
diss., University of California, Berkeley.

Maguire, J. 1976. A taxonomic and ecological study of the living and
fossil Hystricidae with particular reference to southern Africa. Ph.D.
diss., Department of Geology, University of the Witwatersrand, Jo-
hannesburg.

A dissertation issued on microfilm is treated as a published book (see
16.59).

16.130   *Paper read at a meeting*

A   Zerubavel, Eviatar. "The Benedictine Ethic and the Spirit of Schedul-
ing." Paper presented at the annual meeting of the International Society for the Comparative Study of Civilizations, Milwaukee, April
1978.

B   Speth, J. D., and D. D. Davis. 1975. Seasonal variability in early hom-
inid predation. Paper presented at symposium, Archeology in Anthropology: Broadening Subject Matter. Seventy-fourth annual
meeting of the American Anthropological Association.

Royce, John C. 1988. Finches of Du Page County. Paper read at 22d
Annual Conference on Practical Bird Watching, 24–26 May, at Mid-
land University, Flat Prairie, Illinois.

Papers printed in published proceedings of meetings are treated as
chapters in a book (see 16.49).

16.131   *Unpublished duplicated material*

A   Alarcón, Salvador Florencio de. "Compendio de las noticias corres-
pondientes a el real y minas de San Francisco de Aziz de Río Chico
. . . de 20 de octubre [1777]." Department of Geography, University
of California, Berkeley. Photocopy.

> *B*   Downes, W. J. 1974. Systemic grammar and structural sentence relatedness. London School of Economics. Mimeo.
>
> Cooke, H. B. S. N.d. South African Pleistocene mammals in the University of California collections. Typescript.

16.132   *Interviews.* The rare appearance of an interview in a bibliography should include the names of both the person who was interviewed and the interviewer ("author" is used for the name of the author of the book or article in which the interview is listed), the place and date of the interview, and, if possible, where a transcript may be found:

> Roemer, Mrs. Merle A. Interview with author. Millington, Maryland, 26 July 1973.
>
> Bowers, Claude G. " The Reminiscences of Claude Bowers." 1957. Oral History Research Office, Columbia University.
>
> Hunt, Horace [pseud.]. Interview by Ronald Schatz, 16 May 1976. Tape recording, Pennsylvania Historical and Museum Commission, Harrisburg.

16.133   *Personal communications.* Letters to the author and other forms of personal communication are best cited in the text—e.g., "J. Hoodwink (pers. com. 1982) has challenged the validity . . ." When they are listed in a bibliography, the entry begins with the name of the letter writer or the caller:

> Ewing, Nancy J. Letter to author, 24 January 1985.
>
> Ewing, Paul Q. Telephone conversation with author, 2 February 1985.

MANUSCRIPT COLLECTIONS

16.134   The following suggestion on what to include in citing unpublished documents is useful in determining the content of a bibliography entry as well as a note. It is applicable to both private and public documents:

> The most convenient citation for archives is one similar to that used for personal papers and other historical manuscripts. Full identification of most unpublished material usually requires giving the title and date of the item, series title (if applicable), name of the collection, and the name of the depository. Except for placing the cited item first [in a note], there is no general agreement on the sequence of the remaining elements in the citation. . . . Whatever sequence is adopted, however, should be used consistently throughout the same work.[4]

16.135   There are two principal sequences one might follow in listing manuscript collections in a bibliography. One begins with the particular— the name of the author of the manuscripts or the title of the item being

---

4. *Guide to the National Archives of the United States* (Washington, D.C.: National Archives and Record Service, General Services Administration, 1974), 761.

cited—and ends with the depository and, where desirable, its location. This sequence is the most feasible for all collections of correspondence and other personal papers named for an individual or a group.

> Butler, Nicholas Murray. Papers. Columbia University Library, New York.
>
> Women's Organization for National Prohibition Reform Papers. Alice Belin du Pont files, Pierre S. du Pont Papers. Eleutherian Mills Historical Library, Wilmington, Delaware.
>
> Roosevelt, Franklin D. General Political Correspondence, 1921–28. Franklin D. Roosevelt Library, Hyde Park, New York.

Thus when a letter or telegram or diary entry or other specific reference is cited in the text or in a note, the reader will easily locate the collection from which it came in the bibliography or reference list.

16.136 The second possible sequence begins with the depository (or its location) and ends with the collection or item being cited. This sequence is useful when a number of collections from the same depository are cited and it is desirable to list them together in the bibliography or when a text reference is more easily or economically made to a depository than to an individual item in it, e.g., "NA, RG 119," which would be quite clear to a reader familiar with the National Archives material. A bibliography entry would read:

> National Archives. Records of the National Youth Administration. Record Group 119. Administrative Reports Received from N.Y.A. State Officers, 1935–38.

(See also 16.158.)

16.137 Individual items cited from a collection, such as specific letters or diary entries, are mentioned in the text (see 15.29) or in a note (see 17.77). If only one item from a collection has been cited, it may be listed under its own author or title in the bibliography:

> Dinkel, Joseph. Description of Louis Agassiz written at the request of Elizabeth Cary Agassiz. Agassiz Papers. Houghton Library, Harvard University, Cambridge, Mass.

16.138 Quotation marks may be used, in style *A,* to indicate the title of a specific manuscript:

> Purcell, Joseph. "A Map of the Southern Indian District of North America, [ca. 1772]." MS. 228, Ayer Collection. Newberry Library, Chicago.

16.139 Titles of collections and descriptive designations such as Diary or Correspondence or Records are usually capitalized in a bibliography listing but not given in quotation marks:

House, Edward M. Diary. Edward M. House Papers. Yale University Library, New Haven, Conn.

16.140   It is impossible to formulate specific rules applicable to all bibliography listings of manuscript materials because methods of arranging and cataloging differ from one depository to another, and kinds of material differ as well. Librarians and archivists are usually willing and able to explain to an author what is required in citations to the documents in their charge. A publisher's editor may add or delete or rearrange items in listings only with the consent of the author.

PUBLIC DOCUMENTS

16.141   References to printed public documents, like other references, should include elements needed to find them in a library catalog. In general these elements are

Country, state, city, county, or other government division issuing the document
Legislative body, executive department, court, bureau, board, commission, or committee
Subsidiary divisions, regional offices, etc.
Title, if any, of the document or collection
Individual author (editor, compiler) if given
Report number or any other identification necessary or useful in finding the specific document
Publisher, if different from the issuing body
Date

16.142   All the above elements may not be essential in a bibliography entry. For example, a work in the field of American history or politics with many references to government publications may omit "U.S." in its citations, and further abbreviation is often desirable.

16.143   The order in which elements of the citation appear may differ from work to work, according to preference of authors and relevance to subjects. When the same reference is given in a shortened form in a note and in full in the bibliography, it is well to begin both with the same element to avoid confusing the reader. Similarly, in author-date text references keyed to reference lists, the listing should begin with the element most suitable or convenient for use in the text reference (see 15.20–21). For example:

Text reference:

(U.S. Department of Justice 1970)   *or:*   (LEAA 1970)

Reference list:

> U.S. Department of Justice. Law Enforcement Assistance Administration. 1970. *Criminal Justice Agencies in Pennsylvania*. Washington, D.C.: Government Printing Office.
> *or:*
> Law Enforcement Assistance Administration (LEAA), Department of Justice. 1970. *Criminal Justice Agencies in Pennsylvania*. Washington: GPO.

16.144 In short, citations to public documents may take various forms, from the formal, full listing beginning, like a library catalog card, with the name of the country, state, or other geographical division, to an abbreviated form where the context dictates it. Discretion and common sense are useful in deciding in any given case how much information is necessary for the reader to locate the material.

16.145 The number and variety of government publications preclude all-inclusive representation in this manual. The classifications illustrated below are those most commonly encountered in bibliographies and notes.[5] For documents that do not fit these patterns, the author or editor should be able to devise a logical form of citation.

UNITED STATES

16.146 Publications are issued by both houses of the Congress (Senate and House of Representatives) and by the executive departments (State, Justice, Labor, etc.) and agencies (Federal Trade Commission, General Services Administration, etc.). Most government publications are printed and distributed by the Government Printing Office (GPO) in Washington, D.C.; bibliographies, references, and notes may use, consistently, one of the following:

> Washington, D.C.: U.S. Government Printing Office, 1980
> Washington, D.C.: Government Printing Office, 1980.
> Washington, D.C.: GPO, 1980.
> Washington, 1980.

These facts of publication are often omitted when other identifying data are given, such as those for congressional documents.

CONGRESS

16.147 Congressional publications include the journals of the House and Senate; debates; reports, hearings, and documents of committees; and statutes. Bibliographical references to these documents usually begin with "U.S. Congress" and include: name of house, committee and subcommittee if any, title of document, number of the Congress and

5. Detailed instructions for citing legislative sources in law publications can be found in *A Uniform System of Citation*.

session number, date of publication (sometimes omitted when the congressional session is identified), and number and description of the document (e.g., H. Doc. 487), if available.

16.148   The House of Representatives is abbreviated "House" in citations and names of committees, "H.R." in references to numbered bills (H.R. 7107), and "H." in references to specific reports and the like (H. Rept. 1638). The Senate is abbreviated "S." in references to numbered bills or reports (S. 1278, S. Rept. 917). Congress and session are identified thus:

> 87th Cong. 2d sess.   *or:*   87 Cong. 2 sess.

16.149   *House and Senate Journals.* The *Journals* contain motions, actions taken, votes on roll calls, etc., and are published at the end of each session.

> U.S. Congress. Senate. *Journal.* 16th Cong., 1st sess., 7 December 1819.

16.150   *Debates.* Since 1873 congressional debates have been printed by the government in the *Congressional Record:*

> *Congressional Record.* 71st Cong., 2d sess., 1930. Vol. 72, pt. 10.

The *Congressional Record* may also be cited in full, or with the run of dates consulted:

> *Congressional Record.* Washington, D.C., 1873–.
> *Congressional Record.* 1940–45. Washington, D.C.

16.151   Before 1874 congressional debates were privately printed in *Annals of Congress* (1789–1824), *Congressional Debates* (1824–37), and *Congressional Globe* (1833–73). In a bibliography these are usually given in full, with specific dates and page numbers appearing only in text or note references (see 17.85):

> *Annals of the Congress of the United States, 1789–1824.* 42 vols. Washington, D.C., 1834–56.
> *Congressional Globe.* 46 vols. Washington, D.C., 1834–73.

16.152   The bibliography listing for any of these collections of debates may begin with "U.S. Congress" when it is desirable to list them with other congressional publications.

16.153   *Reports and Documents.* The House and Senate Documents and House and Senate Reports are each numbered serially through one session (one year) or through one Congress (two years). Therefore any reference to them should include the Congress and session numbers, and the series number if possible. Since 1817, with the Fifteenth Congress, all these publications have been bound together serially in volumes numbered consecutively and called the *serial set.* (These volumes are now being issued in microfiche by the Congressional Information Service, which also publishes an index to the contents of the serial set.) The serial numbers, which appear only on the spines of the volumes, are sometimes given in references to these documents. Another form of congressional publication is the Committee Print, generally a research report, not part of the four series mentioned above.

> U.S. Congress. Senate. Committee on Foreign Relations. *The Mutual Security Act of 1956*. 84th Cong., 2d sess., 1956. S. Rept. 2273.
>
> U.S. Congress. House. *Report of Activities of the National Advisory Council on International Monetary and Financial Problems to March 31, 1947*. 80th Cong., 1st sess., 1947. H. Doc. 365.
>
> U.S. Congress. House. Committee on Banking and Currency. *Bretton Woods Agreements Act: Hearings on H.R. 3314*. 79th Cong., 1st sess., 1945.
>
> ————. *Participation of the United States in the International Monetary Fund and the International Bank for Reconstruction and Development: Report to Accompany H.R. 3314*. 79th Cong., 1st sess., 1945. S. Rept. 452, pts. 1 and 2.
> [For use of dash see 15.94.]
>
> U.S. Congress. House. Committee on Ways and Means. *Hearings on Extension of the Reciprocal Trade Agreements Act*. 76th Cong., 1st sess., 1940. Vol. 1.
>
> U.S. Congress. House. Committee on Interior and Insular Affairs. Subcommittee on Energy and the Environment. *International Proliferation of Nuclear Technology*. Report prepared by Warren H. Donnelly and Barbara Rather. 94th Cong., 2d sess., 1976. Committee Print 15.
>
> > *or:*
>
> Donnelly, Warren H., and Barbara Rather. *International Proliferation of Nuclear Technology*. Report prepared for the Subcommittee on Energy and the Environment of the House Committee on Interior and Insular Affairs. 94th Cong., 2d sess., 1976. Committee Print 15.
>
> U.S. Congress. House. Committee on Foreign Affairs. *Background Material on Mutual Defense and Development Programs: Fiscal Year 1965*. 88th Cong., 2d sess., 1964. Committee Print.
> [Number of the Committee Print not available but the date will locate it.]
>
> U.S. Congress. *Declarations of a State of War with Japan, Germany, and Italy*. 77th Cong., 1st sess., 1941. S. Doc. 148. Serial 10575.
>
> U.S. Congress. Senate. *History of the Washington Monument*. 57th Cong., 2d sess. S. Doc. 224. Serial 4436.
> [Date not essential when congressional session specified.]

16.154   Documents printed privately for the early Congresses are collected in the *American State Papers*, 38 volumes (1789–1838); both legislative and executive documents, these papers are organized in ten classes—for example, I. *Foreign Relations;* III. *Finance;* VIII. *Public Lands—* each class having several volumes.

> *American State Papers:* V. *Military Affairs.* VI. *Naval Affairs.*

Or, if specific volumes are cited in a bibliography, the number of the class may be omitted:

> *American State Papers: Naval Affairs.* Vol. 4.

There are various edited collections of early papers, among them:

> *Journals of the Continental Congress, 1774–1789.* Edited by Worthington C. Ford et al. 34 vols. Washington, D.C., 1904–37.

EXECUTIVE DEPARTMENTS

16.155   Bibliographic references to publications of executive departments and agencies usually begin with the issuing body but may sometimes be listed by author or title. Publisher (GPO) and date of publication are sometimes omitted when identifying data such as serial numbers are given.

> *A*   U.S. Treasury Department. Bureau of Prohibition. *Digest of Supreme Court Decisions Interpreting the National Prohibition Act and Willis-Campbell Act.* Washington: Government Printing Office, 1929.
>
> U.S. Department of State. *Postwar Policy Preparation, 1939–1945.* General Policy Series, no. 15.
> [Date of publication unnecessary, but could be added.]
>
> President's Commission on Law Enforcement and Administration of Justice. *Task Force Report: Juvenile Delinquency and Youth Crime.* Washington: GPO, 1967.
>
> *Public Papers of the Presidents of the United States: Herbert Hoover, 1929–33.* 4 vols. Washington: GPO, 1974–77.
> *or:*
> Hoover, Herbert. *Public Papers of the Presidents of the United States: Herbert Hoover, 1929–33.* 4 vols. Washington: GPO, 1974–77.
>
> Straus, Ralph I. *Expanding Private Investment for Free World Economic Growth.* A special report prepared at the request of the Department of State. April 1959.
> *or:*
> U.S. Department of State. *Expanding Private Investment for Free World Economic Growth.* Special report prepared by Ralph I. Straus. April 1959.
>
> U.S. Department of Commerce. Market Research and Service Division. *Shellfish: Market Review and Outlook.* Washington, D.C.: GPO, 1973.
>
> U.S. Bureau of the Census. *Median Gross Rent by Counties of the United States, 1970.* Prepared by the Geography Division in cooperation with the Housing Division, Bureau of the Census. Washington, D.C., 1975.
> [Census Bureau publications may be listed under "U.S. Department of Commerce. Bureau of the Census" but this is unnecessary—and the *National Union Catalog* lists them all as above, with a cross-reference under Department of Commerce.]

B   U.S. Atomic Energy Commission. 1974. *General environmental statement on mixed oxides (GESMO)* (draft). WASH-1327. Washington: GPO, August.

U.S. Nuclear Regulatory Commission. 1976. *Final generic environmental impact statement on the use of recycled plutonium in mixed oxide fuel in light water-cooled reactors.* NUREG-0002. Washington: Office of Nuclear Safety and Safeguards, August.

U.S. Bureau of the Census. 1967. Negro population: March, 1966. *Current population reports,* ser. P-20, no. 168. Washington, D.C., 22 December.

National Institute of Mental Health. Center for Studies of Crime and Delinquency. 1971. *Community-based correctional programs.* Public Health Service Publication no. 2130.

President's Commission on Income Maintenance Programs. 1969. *Poverty amid plenty: The American paradox.* Washington, D.C.: U.S. Government Printing Office.

————. 1970. *Background papers.* Washington, D.C.: U.S. Government Printing Office.

President's National Advisory Commission on Civil Disorders. 1968. *Report of the National Advisory Commission on Civil Disorders.* Washington, D.C.: U.S. Government Printing Office.

STATUTES AND JUDICIAL DOCUMENTS

16.156   Statutory material and court decisions are usually cited in the text or in notes, not listed separately in a bibliography. United States laws are published in the volumes of the *United States Code (U.S.C.),* revised every six years, and in

Statutes at Large of the United States of America, 1789–1873. 17 vols. Washington, D.C., 1850–73.

United States Statutes at Large. 1874–.

16.157   Decisions of the United States Supreme Court until 1875 were compiled and printed under the names of the various official court reporters, for example:

Cranch, William. *Reports of Cases Argued and Adjudged in the Supreme Court of the United States, 1801–1815.* 9 vols. Washington, 1804–17.

Since 1875 the decisions have been published officially in *U.S. Reports.*

UNPUBLISHED DOCUMENTS

16.158   Most United States unpublished documents are housed in the National Archives (NA) in Washington, D.C., or one of its branches. All the materials, including manuscript and typescript records, films, still photographs, and sound recordings, are cited by record group (RG) number. They may be further identified by title and by subsection and file number. Names of specific documents are given in quotation marks. The order of items in a bibliography entry is not fixed but should be consistent within one bibliography (see 16.134–36); either of the following may be adopted:

> National Archives. Files of the Senate Committee on the Judiciary. Record Group 46. "Lobbying." File 71A-F15.
>
> Washington National Records Center, Suitland, Md. Records of the National Commission on Law Observance and Enforcement. Record Group 10.
>
> *or:*
>
> United States. Congress. Senate. Committee on the Judiciary. "Lobbying." File 71A-F15. Files of the Committee. Record Group 46. National Archives.
>
> United States. National Commission on Law Observance and Enforcement. Records of the Commission. Record Group 10. Washington National Records Center, Suitland, Md.

16.159 For a list of the record groups and their numbers see *Guide to the National Archives of the United States.*

STATE AND LOCAL GOVERNMENTS

16.160 Bibliography and note citations parallel the forms for federal documents:

> A Illinois. General Assembly. House of Representatives. Labor and Commerce Committee. Subcommittee on Shortened Workweek: *Transcript of the . . . 80th General Assembly, Chicago, Sept. 15, 1977, Rock Island, Sept. 19, 1977, Springfield, Sept. 20, 1977.* Springfield, Ill., 1977.
>
> Illinois. General Assembly. Law Revision Commission. *Report to the 80th General Assembly of the State of Illinois.* Chicago: The Commission, 1977.
>
> B Illinois Institute for Environmental Quality (IIEQ). 1977. *Review and synopsis of public participation regarding sulfur dioxide and particulate emissions.* By Sidney M. Marder. IIEQ Document no. 77/21. Chicago.

UNITED KINGDOM

16.161 The British have been keeping records at least since the Norman conquest in 1066. Among the numerous guides to this vast amount of material for the scholar (and editor) are *Guide to the Contents of the Public Record Office; A Guide to British Government Publications* by Frank Rodgers; and *British Official Publications* by John E. Pemberton—all listed in the Bibliography. The following paragraphs attempt only a general description, noting some common abbreviations and some pitfalls to be avoided by copyeditors.

16.162   Like U.S. government publications, British publications fall into two main categories, parliamentary and nonparliamentary (i.e., departmental). The nonparliamentary publications "have an immense subject coverage . . . from the highly technical report on the pressure drag of aerofoils at supersonic speeds to the practical leaflet on how to deal with ants indoors" (Pemberton, *British Official Publications*, 196). These are usually cited like privately published books and pamphlets: author or issuing body, title (shortened if necessary), series if any, place of publication, publisher, and date.

16.163   The publisher of most government material is Her (His) Majesty's Stationery Office (HMSO) in London.

16.164   British government publications are listed under United Kingdom (U.K.) or Great Britain; the former is recommended by the most recent edition of *Anglo-American Cataloguing Rules*.

PARLIAMENT

16.165   Parliamentary publications include all materials issued by both houses of Parliament, the House of Commons (H.C.) and the House of Lords (H.L.): journals of both houses (sometimes abbreviated *C.J.* and *L.J.*); votes and proceedings; debates; bills, reports, papers; Acts of Parliament.

16.166   *Debates.* Until 1908 House of Lords and House of Commons debates were published together; since 1908 they have been published in separate series:

> *Hansard Parliamentary Debates*, 1st series (1803–20)
> *Hansard Parliamentary Debates*, 2d series (1820–30)
> *Hansard Parliamentary Debates*, 3d series (1830–91)
> *Parliamentary Debates*, 4th series (1892–1908)
> *Parliamentary Debates*, Commons, 5th series (1909–)
> *Parliamentary Debates*, House of Lords, 5th series (1909–)

Although no longer the official name of the parliamentary debates, *Hansard* (sometimes *Hansard's*) is still frequently used in citations to all series of debates. The debates are cited by series and volume number, to which dates may be added; references in notes are to column or page (see 17.88 and n.3):

> United Kingdom. [*or:* U.K.] *Hansard Parliamentary Debates*, 3d ser., vol. 249 (1879).
> ———. *Parliamentary Debates* (Commons), 5th ser., vol. 26 (1911).
> *or:*
> U.K. Parliament. *Debates*, 3d ser., vol. 249 (1879).
> ———. *H.C. Debates*, 5th ser., vol. 26 (1911).

16.167   *Parliamentary Papers*. The bills, reports, and papers issued separately by Parliament are bound together at the end of each session into volumes referred to as Parliamentary Papers or Sessional Papers. References to these volumes include the date of the session and the volume number. References may be only to the individual paper, by title, date, and number, without reference to the volume.

16.168   Many of the documents in these series are "command papers," so-called because they originated outside Parliament and were ostensibly presented to it "By command of Her Majesty." There have been five series of command papers to date:

1833–69	No. 1 to No. 4222
1870–99	C. 1 to C. 9550
1900–1918	Cd. 1 to Cd. 9239
1919–56	Cmd. 1 to Cmd. 9889
1956–	Cmnd. 1–

Note that the form of the abbreviation for "command" indicates the series and so must not be altered by the copyeditor. (Do not add "s" for plural: Cmnd. 3834, 3835.) An individual paper may be a pamphlet or several volumes and may bear a month date or just the year date.

> United Kingdom. Parliament. *The Basle Facility and the Sterling Area.* Cmnd. 3787. October 1968.
>
> United Kingdom. Parliament. *First Interim Report of the Committee on Currency and Foreign Exchanges after the War.* Cd. 9182. 1918.
>
> United Kingdom. Parliament. *Report of the Royal Commission on Indian Currency and Finance.* Vol. 2, Appendices. Cmd. 2687. 1926.
>
> United Kingdom. Parliament. Committee on the Working of the Monetary System [Radcliffe Committee] *Principal Memoranda of Evidence.* Vol. 1. London, 1960.

16.169   *Statutes*. More often cited in notes or text than in bibliographies, the Acts of Parliament are identified by title (roman type), date (regnal year before 1962, calendar year after 1962), and chapter (c. or cap.) number (arabic for national, roman for local). Monarchs' names in regnal year citations are abbreviated: Car. (Charles), Edw., Eliz., Geo., Hen., Jac. (James), Phil. & M., Rich., Vict., Will., W. & M. The number(s) of the year precedes the name, the monarch's ordinal, if any, follows it (15 Geo. 6); both are arabic. The ampersand may be used between regnal years and between the names of dual monarchs (1 & 2 W. & M.).

> Act of Settlement, 12 & 13 Will. 3, c. 2.
> Consolidated Fund Act, 1963, c. 1.
> Manchester Corporation Act, 1967, c. xl.

16.170   Chief compilations of statutory material are

> *Statutes*. Statutes of the period 1235–1948, with the exception of the years 1642–60.
>
> *Acts and Ordinances of the Interregnum*, ed. C. H. Firth and R. S. Rait, 3 vols. (London, 1911). Includes statutes not listed in the preceding.
>
> *Public General Acts and Measures*, published annually since 1831 by HMSO.

UNPUBLISHED DOCUMENTS

16.171   Unpublished government documents are kept in the Public Record Office (PRO, sometimes RO) in London; in the British Library (BL), before 1973 a part of the British Museum (BM); and in local and private libraries. Documents in the Public Record Office are classified by government departments. References to them usually include the abbreviation of the name of the department or collection, the collection number, volume number, and, in notes, the folio (sometimes called page) number(s). Among classifications frequently cited are Admiralty (Adm.), Chancery (C.), Colonial Office (C.O.), Exchequer (E.), Foreign Office (F.O.), State Papers (S.P.); these abbreviations often appear without periods, e.g., CO, FO, SP.

> London. Public Record Office. Lisle Papers. S.P.3. 18 vols.
>
> ———. Patent Rolls, Philip and Mary. C.66/870.

16.172   Collections in the British Library frequently cited are the Cotton Manuscripts with subdivisions named after Roman emperors (e.g., Cotton MSS., Caligula [Calig.] D.VII), the Harleian Manuscripts, the Sloane Manuscripts, and the Additional Manuscripts (Addit. or Add.). For references to specific manuscripts in these collections see 17.94.

PUBLISHED RECORDS

16.173   There are many compilations of British historical records, some of which are transcriptions or calendars of the documents preserved in the Public Record Office. Sample bibliography entries for a few of these, followed by abbreviations (in brackets) commonly used only in note citations, are as follows:

> *Rotuli parliamentorum* . . . (1278–1504). 6 vols. N.p., n.d. [*Rot. parl.*]
>
> *Statutes of the Realm*. Edited by A. Luders et al. 11 vols. London, 1810–28. [*Statutes*]
>
> *Acts of the Privy Council of England*. Edited by J. R. Dasent. 32 vols. London, 1890–1907. [*Acts* or *A.P.C.*]
>
> *Calendar of Patent Rolls, Henry VII, 1485–1509*. 2 vols. London, 1914–16. [*Cal. Pat. Rolls* or *Patent Rolls*]

> *Calendar of State Papers, Domestic* [cited by reign and date]. [*Cal. S.P. Dom.*]
>
> *Calendar of State Papers, Foreign* [cited by reign and date]. [*Cal. S.P. For.*]
>
> *Calendar of State Papers, Spanish, 1485–1558.* 13 vols. and 2 supplements. London, 1862–1954. [*Span. Cal.*]
>
> *Calendar of State Papers, Venetian, 1202–1603.* 9 vols. London, 1864–98. [*Ven. Cal.*]

CANADA

16.174   Canadian government documents are issued by both houses of the Canadian Parliament (Senate and House of Commons) and by the various executive departments. Statutes are published in the *Statutes of Canada* and identified by both calendar and regnal year and by chapter (c.) number. Unpublished records are housed in the Public Archives of Canada (PAC) and identified by the name of the record group, series, and volume.

> Canada. Senate. *Debates,* 8 October 1970.
>
> Canada. House of Commons. *Order Paper and Notices,* 16 February 1972.
>
> Canada. Senate. Special Committee on the Mass Media. *Report.* 3 vols. Ottawa, 1970.
>
> Canada. House of Commons. Standing Committee on External Affairs. *Minutes of Proceedings and Evidence,* no. 4, 24 April 1956.
>
> Canada. Department of External Affairs. *Statements and Speeches,* 53/30, 11 June 1953.
>
> Canada. *Sessional Papers,* 1917, no. 20g, "Report of the Royal Commission to Inquire into Railways and Transportation in Canada."
>
> *Statutes of Canada,* 1919, 10 Geo. 5, c. 17.
>
> Public Archives of Canada. Privy Council Office Records. Series 1, vol. 1477.

INTERNATIONAL BODIES

16.175   Citations to publications of intergovernmental agencies should include series and publication numbers if possible (retain roman numerals in publication numbers).

> League of Nations. *Position of Women of Russian Origin in the Far East.* Ser. L.o.N.P. 1935. IV.3.
>
> League of Nations. *Monetary and Economic Conference: Draft Annotated Agenda Submitted by the Preparatory Commission of Experts.* II. Economic and Financial. 1933. II.Spec.I.
>
> League of Nations. *International Currency Experience: Lessons of the Inter-war Period.* Geneva, 1944. II.A.4.

United Nations [*or* U.N.]. Secretariat. Department of Economic Affairs. *Methods of Financing Economic Development in Underdeveloped Countries.* 1951. II.B.2.

U.N. General Assembly. Ninth Session. Official Records, Supplement 19. *Special United Nations Fund for Economic Development: Final Report.* Prepared by Raymond Scheyven in pursuance of U.N. General Assembly Resolution 724B (VIII), A/2728. 1954.

UNESCO. *The Development of Higher Education in Africa.* Paris, 1963.

General Agreement on Tariffs and Trade (GATT) . *Agreement on Implementation of Article VI (Anti-dumping Code).* Geneva, 1969.

NONBOOK MATERIALS

PRINTED MUSICAL SCORES

16.176   Bibliography entries for musical scores follow rules similar to those for books:

> Verdi, Giuseppe. *Rigoletto.* Melodrama in three acts by Francesco Maria Piave. Edited by Martin Chusid. *The Works of Giuseppe Verdi.* Series 1: *Operas.* Chicago and London: University of Chicago Press; Milan: G. Ricordi, 1982.
>
> Mozart, Wolfgang Amadeus. *Sonatas and Fantasies for the Piano.* Prepared from the autographs and earliest printed sources by Nathan Broder. Rev. ed. Bryn Mawr, Pa.: Theodore Presser, 1960.
>
> Schubert, Franz. "Das Wandern (Wandering)," *Die schöne Müllerin* (*The Maid of the Mill*). In *First Vocal Album* (for high voice). New York: G. Schirmer, 1895.
> [Words and titles printed in both German and English.]

SOUND RECORDINGS

16.177   Records, tapes, and other forms of recorded sound are generally listed under the name of the composer, writer, or other person(s) responsible for the content. Collections or anonymous works are listed by title. The title of a record or album is italicized. If included, the name of the performer follows the title. The recording company and the number of the record are usually sufficient to identify it. Facts added when desirable are date of copyright, kind of recording (stereo, quadraphonic, four-track cassette, etc.), the number of records in an album, and so on. This information may be found on the label of a recording or on its container (sleeve, box, etc.) or in printed material accompanying it.

16.178   If the fact that it is a recording is not implicit in the designation from the label, a description may be added to the listing: "sound recording" or "sound disk," "sound cassette," etc. It is well to remember that

481

disks, cassettes, and tapes may be used to record not only sound but pictures and computer programming, including text to be printed.

> Bach, Johann Sebastian [*or* J. S.]. *The Brandenburg Concertos.* Paillard Chamber Orchestra. RCA CRL2-5801.
>
> Howell, Peg Leg. "Blood Red River." *The Legendary Peg Leg Howell.* Testament T-2204.
>
> Green, Archie. Introduction to brochure notes for Glenn Ohrlin, *The Hell-Bound Train.* University of Illinois Campus Folksong Club CFC 301. Reissued as Puritan 5009.
>
> Carter, Elliott. "Eight Etudes for Woodwind Quintet." On record 1 of *The Chamber Music Society of Lincoln Center.* Classics Record Library SQM 80-5731.
>
> *Genesis of a Novel: A Documentary on the Writing Regimen of Georges Simenon.* Tucson, Ariz.: Motivational Programming Corp., 1969. Sound cassette.
>
> Senn, M. J. E. *Masters and Pupils.* Audiotapes of lectures by Lawrence S. Kubie, Jane Loevinger, and M. J. E. Senn, presented at meeting of the Society for Research in Child Development, Philadelphia, March 1973. Chicago: University of Chicago Press, 1974.

VIDEORECORDINGS

16.179 The many varieties of visual (and audiovisual) materials now available render futile any attempt at universal rulemaking. The nature of the material, its use to the researcher listing it, and the facts necessary to find (retrieve) it should govern the substance of any bibliographic citation to it.

16.180 *Slides and films*

> Mihalyi, Louis J. *Landscapes of Zambia, Central Africa.* Santa Barbara, Calif.: Visual Education, 1975. Slides.
>
> *The Greek and Roman World.* Chicago: Society for Visual Education, 1977. Filmstrip.
>
> *China: An End to Isolation?* 16mm, 25 min. 1970. Distributed by ACI Films, New York.
>
> Wolff, L. (producer). *Rock-a-bye Baby.* New York: Time-Life Films, 1971.

16.181 *Text from a film*

> Sartre, Jean-Paul. *Sartre.* Full text from a film produced by Alexandre Astruc and Michel Contat with the participation of Simone de Beauvoir, Jacques-Laurent Bost, André Gortz, and Jean Pouillon. Paris: Gallimard, 1977.

COMPUTER PROGRAMS

16.182 A bibliographic reference to a computer program, package, language, system, etc., all collectively known as software, should include, in general:

The fully spelled-out title, except for the common ones such as BASIC, FORTRAN, COBOL.

The identifying detail, such as version, level, or release number, or the date.

In parentheses, the short name or acronym where applicable and any other information necessary for specific identification.

The city and name of the person, company, or organization having the proprietary rights to the software.

The following examples suggest how to make the names of computer programs into printed bibliography entries:

FORTRAN H-extended Version [*or* Ver.] 2.3. White Plains, N.Y.: IBM.

Houston Automatic Spooling Priority II Ver. 4.0 (HASP II 4.0). White Plains, N.Y.: IBM.

International Mathematical Subroutine Library Edition 8 (IMSL 8). Houston, Tex.: International Mathematical Subroutine Library, Inc.

Operating System/Virtual Storage Rel. 1.7 (OS/VS 1.7). White Plains, N.Y.: IBM.

Statistical Package for the Social Sciences Level M Ver. 8.1 (SPSS Lev. M 8.1). Chicago: SPSS.

17 Note Forms

General Rules 17.2
    Full References 17.2
    Shortened References 17.6
        Last name of the author 17.10
        Short title 17.11
        Op. cit. and *loc. cit.* 17.12
        Ibid. 17.13
        Idem 17.14
        Abbreviations 17.15
    Reference Numbers 17.16
Specific Rules 17.26
    Name of the Author 17.27
        One author 17.28
        Two authors 17.29
        Three authors 17.30
        More than three authors 17.31
        Author's name in title 17.32
        Pseudonym 17.33
        Anonymous 17.34
        Editor, compiler, or translator 17.35
    Titles 17.38
        Titles within titles 17.39
        Older titles 17.40
        Foreign titles 17.42
    Multivolume Works and Series 17.44
    Part of a Book 17.46
    Edition 17.47
    Reprint Editions 17.48
    Microform Editions 17.49
    Facts of Publication 17.50
    Journal Articles 17.51
        Basic style 17.51
        Series number 17.52
        Year as volume number 17.53
        Foreign language journals 17.54
        Popular magazines 17.55
        Book reviews 17.56
        Newspapers 17.57
    Unpublished Papers 17.59
    Interviews and Personal Communications 17.61
Special Types of References 17.62
    Reference Books 17.62
    Bible 17.63
    Plays and Poems 17.64
    Classical References 17.65

>>>>> Legal References 17.76
>>>>> Collections of Letters and Papers 17.77
>>>>>>> Printed collections 17.81
>>>>>>> Manuscript collections 17.82
>>>>> Public Documents 17.85
>>>>>>> Government publications 17.85
>>>>>>> Archives 17.93
>>> Nonbook Materials 17.97

17.1 Documentation of scholarly works using notes at the end of the book or the foot of the page is discussed in chapter 15. This chapter deals with the style used for individual notes of various kinds. Unless otherwise specified, all suggestions apply to endnotes and footnotes alike.

GENERAL RULES

FULL REFERENCES

17.2 A source should be given a full reference the first time it is cited in a book or article, unless it appears in an alphabetical bibliography at the end of the work (see 15.82). Items to be included in a full reference are listed below in the order in which they are normally given.

BOOK

Author's full name
Complete title of the book
Editor, compiler, or translator, if any
Series, if any, and volume or number in the series
Edition, if not the original
Number of volumes
Facts of publication—city where published, publisher (sometimes omitted), date of publication
Volume number, if any
Page number(s) of the particular citation

ARTICLE IN A PERIODICAL

Author's full name
Title of the article
Name of the periodical
Volume (and number) of the periodical
Date of the volume or of the issue
Page number(s) of the particular citation

UNPUBLISHED MATERIAL

Title of document, if any, and date
Folio number or other identifying number
Name of collection
Depository, and city where it is located

486

17.3   Most of the recommendations concerning the bibliography entry
(style *A*) in chapter 16 apply also to a full citation in a note. The chief
differences between a bibliography entry and a note are that in a note
the author's name is not reversed as it is in an alphabetically arranged
bibliography, and punctuation between author's name, title of the
work, and facts of publication consists of commas and parentheses
rather than periods. Also a note usually carries the page number(s) or
other specific references to the source cited. The following examples
show the basic differences between notes and bibliography in book
and journal references:

NOTES

1. David Stafford, *Britain and European Resistance, 1940–1945* (Toronto:
University of Toronto Press, 1980), 90.

2. James F. Powers, "Frontier Municipal Baths and Social Interaction in Thirteenth-Century Spain," *American Historical Review* 84 (June 1979): 655.

BIBLIOGRAPHY

Stafford, David. *Britain and European Resistance, 1940–1945*. Toronto: University of Toronto Press, 1980.

Powers, James F. "Frontier Municipal Baths and Social Interaction in
Thirteenth-Century Spain." *American Historical Review* 84 (June
1979): 649–67.

17.4   In sum, the full reference in a note, as in a bibliography entry, must
include enough information to enable the interested reader to find it in
a library, though the form of the note need not correspond precisely
to that of the library catalog card.

17.5   Although it is hoped that authors who use a note system of documentation for their books will follow the style outlined in this chapter,
logical variations are permissible provided consistency is maintained
and the publisher is informed of the author's preferences before the
manuscript is edited for publication.

SHORTENED REFERENCES

17.6   After the first, full reference in a note, subsequent references to a
particular source are shortened; a reference may also be shortened
even at first appearance when the source is given in full in an alphabetical bibliography (see 15.46). There are two acceptable ways to
shorten references to books and articles. The first is to use the short-
title form described in the following paragraphs. The second, commonly used in scholarly journals, is to omit the title of the work and
give only the last name of the author followed by a comma and the
page number of the reference; when more than one work by the same
author has been cited, a short title is necessary, in addition to the
author's last name.

17.7 A shortened reference to a *book* includes only the last name of the author and the short title of the book, in italics, followed by the page number of the reference.

17.8 A shortened reference to an article in a periodical includes only the last name of the author and the short title of the article, in quotation marks, and the page number of the reference.

17.9 A shortened reference to a manuscript collection omits the name of the depository, unless more than one collection with the same name has been cited; where this is true, the depository must be given.

17.10 *Last name of the author.* Only the last name of the author, or of the editor if given first in the full reference, is needed. First names or initials are included only where two or more authors with the same last name have been cited. "Ed.," "trans.," and "comp." following a name in the first reference may be omitted from subsequent references. If a work has two or three authors, the last name of each should be given; for more than three authors, the last name of the first author followed by "et al." or "and others."

17.11 *Short title.* The short title contains the key word or words from the main title of the work (book or article). Abbreviations or words from the subtitle are not included unless this fact is noted in the first reference (see 17.15). The order of words in the title should not be changed; for example, *Politics in the Twentieth Century* should not be shortened to *Twentieth-Century Politics*. In foreign language titles one must be careful not to omit a word that governs the case ending of a word included in the shortened title. In general, titles of from two to five words should not be shortened:

> *Deep South*
> *North of Slavery*
> *Elizabethan and Metaphysical Imagery*

For many titles the omission of the initial "The" or "A" is sufficient:

> *Rise of the West*

Examples of shortened titles:

FULL MAIN TITLE	SHORT TITLE
Health Progress in the United States, 1900–1960	*Health Progress*
The Culture of Ancient Egypt	*Ancient Egypt*
A Compilation of the Messages and Papers of the Presidents, 1789–1897.	*Papers of the Presidents*
Kriegstagebuch des Oberkommandos der Wehrmacht, 1940–1945	*Kriegstagebuch*
"A Brief Account of the Reconstruction of Aristotle's *Protrepticus*"	"Aristotle's *Protrepticus*"

17.12   *"Op. cit." and "loc. cit."* Op. cit. *(opere citato,* "in the work cited") and loc. cit. *(loco citato,* "in the place cited") have long served as space savers in scholarly footnotes. Both, used with the author's last name, stand in place of the title of a work cited earlier in the chapter or article. But consider, for example, the frustration of the reader on meeting "Wells, op. cit., p. 10" in note 95 and finding the title of the work by Wells back in note 2, or, in a carelessly edited book, finding *two* works by Wells cited earlier, or none at all. To save the reader's nerves, not to mention the editor's, and for greater clarity, the University of Chicago Press does not use either op. cit. or loc. cit. but the short-title form described above .

17.13   *"Ibid."* Ibid. *(ibidem,* "in the same place") refers to a single work cited in the note immediately preceding. It should not be used if more than one work is given in the preceding note. Ibid. takes the place of the author's name, the title of the work, and as much of the succeeding material as is identical. The author's name is never used with ibid., nor is a title. Ibid. may also be used in place of the name of a journal or book of essays in successive references to the same journal or book within one note.

Examples of full and shortened references:

3. John P. Roche, *The Quest for the Dream: The Development of Civil Rights and Human Relations in Modern America* (New York: Macmillan Co., 1963), 204–6.

4. J. H. Hexter, "The Loom of Language and the Fabric of Imperatives: The Case of *Il Principe* and *Utopia*," *American Historical Review* 69 (1964): 945–68.

5. Stevens to Sumner, 26 August 1865, Charles Sumner Papers, Harvard College Library, Cambridge, Mass.

6. James Losh, *The Diaries and Correspondence of James Losh,* ed. Edward Hughes, 2 vols., Publication of the Surtees Society, vols. 171, 172 (Durham, England: Andrews & Co. for the Society, 1962–63), 2:200–212.

7. Roche, *Quest for the Dream,* 175.

8. Hexter, "Loom of Language," 949.

9. Stearns to Sumner, 28 August 1865, Sumner Papers.

10. Losh, *Diaries and Correspondence* 1:150.

11. Ibid. 2:175.

12. Ibid., 176. [The same volume number as in the preceding note.]

13. Ibid. [The same page as in the preceding note.]

It should be noted here that both ibid. and idem (see below) are used much less frequently than they once were, and both may soon be as obsolete as op. cit. and loc. cit.

17.14   *"Idem."* Idem ("the same," sometimes abbreviated as id.) may be used in place of an author's name in successive references within one note to several works by the same person. It is not used for titles, except in legal references.

14. Arthur I. Gates, "Vocabulary Control in Basal Reading Material," *Reading Teacher* 15 (November 1961): 81–85; idem, "The Word Recognition Ability and the Reading Vocabulary of Second- and Third-Grade Children," ibid. 15 (May 1962): 443–48.

17.15 *Abbreviations.* If a work is cited frequently throughout a chapter or a book, its title may be abbreviated after its first appearance. The full title should be given the first time it is cited, followed by an indication in parentheses of the abbreviation to be used for it thereafter. An abbreviated title differs from a shortened title in that words may be abbreviated and the order changed.

15. Nathaniel B. Shurtleff, ed., *Records of the Governor and Company of the Massachusetts Bay in New England (1628–86),* 5 vols. (Boston, 1853–54), 1:126 (hereafter cited as *Mass. Records).*

The parenthetical note giving the abbreviation may be placed directly after the title of the work, but it is easier to find if it comes at the end of the reference. (For listing abbreviations used in notes see 15.67.)

REFERENCE NUMBERS

17.16 In source citations in notes, the designations volume, part, number, book, chapter, page(s), note(s), appendix, folio, plate, figure are abbreviated and lowercased as vol., pt., no., bk., chap., p. (pp.), n. (nn.), app., fol., pl., fig. Plurals add "s" for all but p. and n. The abbreviation l. (ll.) for line(s) should be avoided, except in works containing many such references. (The letter *l* on some typewriters is used also for the arabic figure 1 and may thus confuse the compositor. If the abbreviation is used, it is helpful to write "el" or "ell" and circle it, above the letter or in the margin, at least the first time it appears in a typescript.)

17.17 An abbreviation that begins a note (or a sentence) is capitalized:

16. P. 104.
17. Pp. 15–20.
18. Fol. 5v.

17.18 The abbreviation p. (pp.) should be omitted from page references in source citations unless the number would be ambiguous without it,[1] such as a note reference consisting only of a page number (no author or title; see 17.17):

19. Derrida, *Positions,* 75, 81.

If an author consistently uses p. (pp.), however, the editor should not delete it:

19. Derrida, *Positions,* pp. 75, 81.

1. This is a change from the previous edition of this manual, which recommended the use of p. (pp.) for all page numbers not accompanied by a volume number.

The University of Chicago Press accepts either practice in book manuscripts. When writing for a specific journal, authors should follow the journal's style in this and other particulars.

17.19 References to early printed books which carry pagination only on the recto side, sheet by sheet, add the letters *r* (recto) or *v* (verso) to the page number: e.g., 176r, 292v. The same designations are used for manuscript folios (see 17.79).

17.20 When volume and page numbers come together, the abbreviation vol. is omitted as well as p., and a colon separates the numbers (for spacing see 16.107):

> 20. Freeman, *Washington* 3:50.
> 21. *Critical Inquiry* 7 (1981): 697.

The abbreviation vol. is used when the volume number stands alone or when it is separated from the page number by, for example, the title of the volume:

> 22. Freeman, *Washington*, vol. 3.
> 23. Douglas Southall Freeman, *George Washington*, vol. 3, *Planter and Patriot* (New York: Charles Scribner's Sons, 1951), 50.

Note that when a volume number immediately follows an italic title, as in notes 20 and 21, no comma is used between them; the comma is used, however, when the abbreviation "vol."—or anything else—intervenes.

17.21 The abbreviation n. (nn.) in a source citation is usually preceded by the number of the page on which the note appears. The note number may also be given:

> 24. Hans Baron, *From Petrarch to Leonardo Bruni* (Chicago: University of Chicago Press, 1968), 58 n. 21, 60 nn. 26, 27.

When n. (nn.) is used without the note number, the period is omitted and there is either no space following the page number (5n, 6nn) or a hair space (5n, 6nn; see Glossary).

17.22 Foreign language designations for volume, part, number, page, edition, and so on may be translated into their English equivalents in notes (and bibliographies).[2] Editors without a reasonably good knowledge of the foreign language should, however, not attempt to translate even single words but should keep the author's original. (An editor with a guidebook grasp of terminology might triumphantly translate "zweite Auflage" into "2d ed." only to discover, in another note, a phrase such as "Herausgegeben von Heribert Jussen, im Auftrag und

---

2. A list of French and German bibliographic terms and abbreviations, with translations, is given in Judith Butcher's *Copy-Editing;* partial lists of foreign bibliographic terms and of abbreviations (without translations) are given in the U.S. Geological Survey's *Suggestions to Authors.*

mit Förderung des Deutschen Instituts für wissenschaftliche Päda-
gogik."

17.23 Arabic numerals are used for volume numbers (even when a title page
carries a roman numeral) and for all other designations mentioned in
the preceding paragraphs, except that lowercase roman numerals are
used in references to pages so numbered in the source being cited.

17.24 References to a passage extending over several pages should give the
first and last page numbers (see 16.108). The use of f. (and the following page) or ff. (and the following pages) after a page number is discouraged, but when one or the other *is* used either no space or a hair
space should separate it from the preceding page number: 22f. or
22f., 76ff. or 76ff.

17.25 *Passim* ("here and there") should be used sparingly, and only after
inclusive page numbers indicating a reasonable stretch of text or after
a reference to a whole section such as a chapter or a part. Passim,
being a complete word, is not followed by a period unless it falls at the
end of a citation.

SPECIFIC RULES

17.26 The following rules have much in common with those for bibliographic
forms. Cross-references to the relevant paragraphs in chapter 16 are
given here to avoid repetition.

NAME OF THE AUTHOR

See 16.11–30.

17.27 Rules pertaining to authors' names in bibliographies apply also to authors' names in notes, except that no name is inverted in a note, and
whereas more than three authors may be given in a bibliography, usually only the first one, followed by "et al.," is used in a note reference
to a work by more than three authors.

17.28 *One author*

> 25. Charles R. Simpson, *SoHo: The Artist in the City* (Chicago: University of
> Chicago Press, 1981), 217–18.

17.29 *Two authors*

> 26. Melvin Gurtov and Byong-Moo Hwang, *China under Threat: The Politics
> of Strategy and Diplomacy* (Baltimore: Johns Hopkins University Press,
> 1981), 100.
> 27. Arthur Weinberg and Lila Weinberg, *Clarence Darrow: A Sentimental
> Rebel* (New York: G. P. Putnam's Sons, 1980), 25–26.

17.30   *Three authors*

> 28. Richard K. Beardsley, John W. Hall, and Robert E. Ward, *Village Japan* (Chicago: University of Chicago Press, 1959), 303–4.

17.31   *More than three authors*

> 29. Jaroslav Pelikan et al., *Religion and the University,* York University Invitation Lecture Series (Toronto: University of Toronto Press, 1964), 109.

17.32   *Author's name in title.* When an author's name appears in the title of the work cited, such as a collection of letters, an autobiography, or an edition of the complete works, a note begins with the title (or the editor's name), whereas a bibliography entry usually begins with the author's name even if it is also in the title (see 16.25):

> 30. *The Education of Henry Adams: An Autobiography* (Boston: Houghton Mifflin, 1918), 163–65.
>
> 31. *The Letters of George Meredith,* ed. C. L. Cline, 3 vols. (Oxford: Clarendon Press, 1970), 1:125.
>
> 32. *Vanity Fair* in *The Complete Works of William Makepeace Thackeray* (Boston, 1889), 2:271.

17.33   *Pseudonym.* A pseudonym is generally treated in a note as if it were the author's name, unless the sense of the text demands the real name (and see 16.18–20). It is rarely necessary to include "[pseud.]" in a note:

> 33. Lewis Carroll, *Through the Looking-Glass,* in *The Annotated Alice,* with introduction and notes by Martin Gardner (New York: Clarkson N. Potter, 1960), 174.

17.34   *Anonymous* (see 16.21–23)

> 34. [Antonio de Espejo], *New Mexico: otherwise the voiage of Anthony of Espeio . . . translated out of the Spanish copie printed first at Madreel* [Madrid], *1586, and afterward at Paris, in the same yeare* (London, 1587).
>
> 35. *What the South Is Fighting For,* Tracts on Slavery in America, no. 1 (London, 1862).
>
> 36. A Cotton Manufacturer, *An Inquiry into the Causes of the Present Long-continued Depression in the Cotton Trade, with Suggestions for Its Improvement* (Bury, 1869).

17.35   *Editor, compiler, or translator* (see 16.24–28)

> 37. H. H. Rowley, ed., *The Old Testament and Modern Study* (Oxford: Clarendon Press, 1951), 50.
>
> 38. Urban T. Holmes and Kenneth R. Scholberg, eds., *French and Provençal Lexicography* (Columbus: Ohio State University Press, 1964), 138.
>
> 39. Alexander Dallin et al., eds., *Diversity in International Communism: A Documentary Record, 1961–63* (New York: Columbia University Press, 1963), 24–26.
>
> 40. William Harlin McBurney, comp., *A Check List of English Prose Fiction, 1700–1739* (Cambridge: Harvard University Press, 1960), 76.
>
> 41. Maynard A. Amerine and Louise B. Wheeler, comps., *A Check List of Books and Pamphlets on Grapes and Wine and Related Subjects, 1938–1948* (Berkeley and Los Angeles: University of California Press, 1951), 121.

42. Jen Yu Wang and Gerald L. Berger, eds. and comps., *Bibliography of Agricultural Meteorology* (Madison: University of Wisconsin Press, 1962), 520–30.

43. Boleslaw Szczesniak, ed. and trans., *The Russian Revolution and Religion, 1917–1925* (Notre Dame, Ind.: University of Notre Dame Press, 1959), 175–79.

44. Mark Graubard, trans., and John Parker, ed., *Tidings out of Brazil* (Minneapolis: University of Minnesota Press, 1957), 13.

17.36　When the editor's (translator's, compiler's) name comes after the title, the function is usually abbreviated: ed. (here meaning "edited by" and thus never "eds."), trans. ("translated by"), comp. ("compiled by"; never "comps."):

45. John Stuart Mill, *Autobiography and Literary Essays*, ed. John M. Robson and Jack Stillinger (Toronto: University of Toronto Press, 1980), 15.

46. G. W. F. Hegel, "The Philosophy of Fine Art," trans. F. P. B. Osmaston, in *Theories of Comedy*, ed. Paul Lauter (Garden City, N.Y.: Doubleday, 1964), 351.

17.37　When matters are more complicated, these functions may need to be spelled out:

47. *Chaucer Life-Records*, edited by Martin M. Crow and Clair C. Olson from materials compiled by John M. Manly and Edith Rickert, with the assistance of Lilian J. Redstone and others (London: Oxford University Press, 1966), 372–74.

TITLES

See 16.31–40.

17.38　Titles of works cited in full in a note are treated in the same way as in a bibliography (usually following style *A;* see 16.5). For capitalization see 7.122–48. For shortening titles in notes see 17.11. The following examples show various kinds of titles appearing in full notes:

48. Georges Duby, *The Age of the Cathedrals: Art and Society, 980–1420*, trans. Eleanor Levieux and Barbara Thompson (Chicago: University of Chicago Press, 1981), 15–16.
[Dates set off with commas.]

49. James M. Vardaman, *Call Collect, Ask for Birdman: The Record-breaking Attempt to Sight 700 Species of American Birds within One Year* (New York: St. Martin's Press, 1980), 175.
[Figures in titles may be spelled out or retained, as here.]

50. Walter La Feber, " 'Ah, If We Had Studied It More Carefully': The Fortunes of American Diplomatic History," *Prologue* 11 (Summer 1979): 125.
[Quotation in a quoted title.]

51. G. M. Kirkwood, ed., *Poetry and Poetics from Ancient Greece to the Renaissance: Studies in Honor of James Hutton*, Cornell Studies in Classical Philology, no. 38 (Ithaca, N.Y.: Cornell University Press, 1975), 125.
[Titles of festschrifts include the name of the person honored.]

52. Jane Doe, "Eureka! The Goose Has Laid a Golden Egg!" in *Myths or Fantasies?* ed. John Roe (East Bend: Archimedes Press, 1990), 65, fig. 2.
[When a title ends with an exclamation point or a question mark, regular note punctuation—colon or comma—is omitted.]

17.39   *Titles within titles* (see 16.33–36)

> 53. A. Rey, *Skelton's Satirical Poems in Their Relation to Lydgate's "Order of Fools," "Cock Lorell's Bote," and Barclay's "Ship of Fools"* (Bern: K. J. Wyss, 1899), 23–30.
>
> 54. John Gardner, *The Alliterative Morte Arthure, The Owl and the Nightingale, and Five Other Middle English Poems in a Modernized Version with Comments on Poems and Notes* (Carbondale, Ill.: Southern Illinois University Press, 1971).
>
> 55. Barbara Nolan and David Farley-Hills, "The Authorship of *Pearl:* Two Notes," *Review of English Studies* 22 (1971): 298.
>
> 56. D. J. Conacher, *Aeschylus' "Prometheus Bound"* (Toronto: University of Toronto Press, 1980).

17.40   *Older titles* (see 16.37)

> 57. "Ut Pictura Poesis, by Mr. Nourse, late of All-Souls College, Oxon., 1741," in *A Collection of Poems . . . by Several Hands* (London, 1758), 95.

17.41   An elegant variation found in some older titles and occasionally used today is the use of a semicolon instead of a colon between the title and a subtitle introduced by "or." The "or" is lowercased and followed by a comma, and the subtitle (really an alternative title) begins with a capital letter:

> 58. A. W. Brunner, ed., *Cottages; or, Hints on Economical Building* (New York: W. T. Comstock, 1884).
>
> 59. John Gardner, "The Case against the 'Bradshaw Shift'; or, The Mystery of the Manuscript in the Trunk," *Papers on Language and Literature* 3 (1967): 80–106.

This punctuation style is not mandatory.

17.42   *Foreign titles* (see 16.38–40)

> 60. Henri Xavier Arquillière, *L'augustinisme politique: Essai sur la formation des théories politiques du moyen-âge,* 2d ed. (Paris, 1955).
>
> 61. Emile Amann, "L'adoptionisme espagnol du VIIIe siècle," *Revue des sciences religieuses* 16 (1936): 281–317.
>
> 62. F. Brisset, "Guillaume le Grand et l'église," *Bulletin de la Société des antiquaires de l'Ouest,* 4th ser., 11 (1972): 441–60.
>
> 63. George Huppert, "Naissance de l'histoire en France: Les 'Recherches' d'Estienne Pasquier," *Annales: Economies, sociétés, civilisations* 30 (1968): 69–105.
>
> 64. G. Martellotti et al., *La letteratura italiana: Storia e testi,* vol. 7 (Milan: Riccardo Ricciardi, 1955), 26.
>
> 65. Isidro Fabela, ed., *Documentos históricos de la Revolución Mexicana,* 12 vols. (Mexico City: Fondo de Cultura Económica, 1960–68), 10:52–53.
>
> 66. A. Teixeira da Mota, "A evolução da ciência nautica durante os séculos XV–XVI na cartografia portuguesa da época," *Memórias de Academia das ciências de Lisboa, Classe de letras* 7 (1962): 247–66.
>
> 67. F. Eulen, *Vom Gewerbefleiss zur Industrie: Ein Beitrag zur Wirtschaftsgeschichte des 18. Jahrhunderts* (Berlin, 1967), 180 ff.
>
> 68. Veit Valentin, *Frankfurt-am-Main und die Revolution von 1848/49* (Stuttgart and Berlin, 1908), 2.

17.43 With translation of title:

69. Krijn Strijd, *Structuur en Inhoud van Anselmus' "Cur Deus Homo"* (The structure and content of Anselm's *Cur Deus Homo)* (Assen, 1957).

70. N. Ia. Ivanov, *Kornilovshchina i ee razgrom: Iz istorii bor'by s kontrrevoliutsiei v 1917 g.* (The Kornilov affair and its liquidation: The history of the struggle by the counterrevolutionaries in 1917) (Leningrad: Izdatel'stvo Leningradskogo universiteta, 1965).

71. Natan Gross, Itamar Yaoz-Kest, and Rinah Klinov, eds., *Ha-Shoah be-Shirah ha-Ivrit: Mivhar* (The Holocaust in Hebrew poetry: An anthology) (Ha-Kibbutz ha-Me'uhad, 1974).

MULTIVOLUME WORKS AND SERIES

17.44 The style of citations of multivolume works is more flexible in notes than in bibliography entries (see 16.42). The following variations are all acceptable:

72. William Makepeace Thackeray, *The English Humorists of the Eighteenth Century,* vol. 13 of *The Complete Works* (Boston, 1889), 111–330.

72. *The English Humorists of the Eighteenth Century,* vol. 13 of *The Complete Works of William Makepeace Thackeray* (Boston, 1889), 111–330.

72. William Makepeace Thackeray, *The Complete Works* (Boston, 1889), vol. 13, *The English Humorists of the Eighteenth Century,* 111–330.

72. *The Complete Works of William Makepeace Thackeray* (Boston, 1889), 13:111–330.

Possible shortened versions:

73. Thackeray, *Complete Works* 13:111–330.

73. Thackeray, *English Humorists,* 111–330.

17.45 A series title is treated much the same as in a bibliography (see 16.44). To save space, however, the series title is often omitted in a note reference if the work could be located without it.

74. Julian H. Steward, ed., *Handbook of South American Indians,* Smithsonian Institution, Bureau of American Ethnology Bulletin no. 143 (Washington, D.C., 1949), 10.

75. Wendell C. Bennett, ed., *A Reappraisal of Peruvian Archaeology,* Society for American Archaeology Memoir no. 4 (Menasha, Wis., 1948), 10.

76. *Directorio de librerías y casas editoriales en America latina,* 4th ed., Pan American Union, Bibliographic Series, no. 2, pt. 3 (Washington, D.C., 1958).

77. Robert Wauchope, *A Tentative Sequence of Pre-Classic Ceramics in Middle America,* Middle American Research Records, vol. 1, no. 14 (New Orleans: Tulane University, 1950), 10.

78. Arthur H. R. Fairchild, *Shakespeare and the Arts of Design,* University of Missouri Studies, vol. 12 (Columbia, 1937), 104, 109.

79. C. N. Stavron, *Whitman and Nietzsche: A Comparative Study of Their Thought,* University of North Carolina Studies in the Germanic Languages and Literature, no. 48 (Chapel Hill, 1964), 139.

80. Kenneth M. Setton, *The Papacy and the Levant (1204–1571),* vol. 1, *The Thirteenth and Fourteenth Centuries,* Memoirs of the American Philosophical Society, no. 114 (Philadelphia: The Society, 1976), 398–400.

81. Joachim Hopp, *Untersuchungen zur Geschichte der letzten Attaliden,* Vestigia, Beiträge zur alten Geschichte, no. 25 (Munich: C. H. Back'sche Verlag, 1977), 115–20.

PART OF A BOOK

17.46   See 16.49–53.

82. "O Youth and Beauty!" in *The Stories of John Cheever* (New York: Alfred A. Knopf, 1978), 210–18.

83. Dorothy Van Ghent, "The Dickens World: A View from Todgers's," in *The Dickens Critics,* ed. George H. Ford and Lauriat Lane, Jr. (Ithaca, N.Y.: Cornell University Press, 1961), 213–32.

Possible, though less desirable, alternative:

83. Dorothy Van Ghent, "The Dickens World: A View from Todgers's," in George H. Ford and Lauriat Lane, Jr., eds., *The Dickens Critics* (Ithaca, N.Y.: Cornell University Press, 1961), 213–32.

(For "ed." and "eds." see 17.35–36.)

EDITION

17.47   See 16.54.

84. John N. Hazard, *The Soviet System of Government,* 5th ed. (Chicago: University of Chicago Press, 1980), 25.

85. Halsey Stevens, *The Life and Music of Béla Bartók,* rev. ed. (New York: Oxford University Press, 1964), 128–29.

86. Charles Dickens, *The Life and Adventures of Martin Chuzzlewit,* New Oxford Illustrated Dickens (London: Oxford University Press, 1951), 733; all subsequent citations are to this edition.

REPRINT EDITIONS

17.48   See 16.57–58.

87. Albert Schweitzer, *J. S. Bach,* trans. Ernest Newman (1911; reprint, New York: Dover Publications, 1966), 1:265–94.

88. Neil Harris, *The Artist in American Society: The Formative Years, 1790–1860* (New York: George Braziller, 1966; Chicago: University of Chicago Press, Phoenix Books, 1982), 43–44.

MICROFORM EDITIONS

17.49   See 16.59.

89. William Voelke, ed., *Masterpieces of Medieval Painting: The Art of Illumination* (Pierpont Morgan Library; Chicago: University of Chicago Press, 1980, text-fiche), p. 56, 4F6–4F10.

Here the page reference is to the printed text ("p." is used to avoid confusion with fiche numbers); the reference to the microfiche part of this publication gives the *fiche* number, the letter indicating the *row,* and the *frame* number: 4F6. Even when they are the same, fiche and row are repeated when giving inclusive frame numbers.

FACTS OF PUBLICATION

See 16.61–97.

17.50   Place, publisher, and date of publication of a book are enclosed in parentheses in a note but not in a bibliography entry. Otherwise rules and alternatives are the same:

> 90. Kathryn L. Morgan, *Children of Strangers: The Stories of a Black Family* (Philadelphia: Temple University Press, 1980), 51–52.
>
> 91. Alan Feduccia, *The Age of Birds* (Cambridge, Mass., 1980).
>
> 92. Iris Murdoch, *Nuns and Soldiers* (1981).
>
> 93. John Burton, *A Deadline to Remember* (n.p., n.d.), i–iii.
>
> 94. Jeremy Treglown, ed., *The Letters of John Wilmot, Earl of Rochester* (Chicago: University of Chicago Press; Oxford: Basil Blackwell, 1980), 13–16.
>
> 95. Keith Branigan, *The Roman Villa in South-West England* (Bradford-on-Avon: Moonraker Press; distributed by Humanities Press, Atlantic Highlands, N.J., 1976), 95.
>
> 96. Paul Tillich, *Systematic Theology,* 3 vols. (Chicago: University of Chicago Press, 1951–63), 3:45.

JOURNAL ARTICLES

See 16.98–127.

17.51   *Basic style.* For the basic style of a note reference to a publication appearing at regular intervals see 17.3. Only the page number (or numbers) of the citation is given in a note, rather than inclusive pages as in a bibliography entry:

> 97. Marshall Brown, "Mozart and After: The Revolution in Musical Consciousness," *Critical Inquiry* 7 (Summer 1981): 694.

17.52   *Series number* (see 16.47)

> 98. "Letters of Jonathan Sewall," *Proceedings of the Massachusetts Historical Society,* 2d ser., 10 (January 1896): 414.
>
> 99. G. M. Moraes, "St. Francis Xavier, Apostolic Nuncio, 1542–52," *Journal of the Bombay Branch of the Royal Asiatic Society,* n.s., 26 (1950): 279–313.
>
> 100. Jean Filliozat, "Les premières étapes de l'Indianisme," *Bulletin de l'Association Guillaume Budé,* 3d ser., no. 3 (1953): 83–96.

17.53   *Year as volume number* (see 16.120)

> 101. M. E. Sergeenko, "Kolumbarii Statiliev Tavrov," *Vestnik drevnei istorii,* 1964, no. 4:399.

17.54   *Foreign language journals* (see 16.121–23)

> 102. Jean Bernard, "La langue française et la médecine dans le monde," *Revue des deux mondes,* July 1979:46–47.
>
> 103. Marcel Garaud, "Recherches sur les défrichements dans la Gâtine poitevine aux XIe et XIIe siècles," *Bulletin de la Société des antiquaires de l'Ouest,* 4th ser., 9 (1967): 11–27.

[The first word of the name of an organization in a journal name is usually capitalized.]

(See also 17.42 nn. 61–63.)

17.55   *Popular magazines.* Titles of articles are treated as in a bibliography (see 16.124). Names of regular departments or features of a magazine are capitalized like titles but not in italics or quotation marks. Names of months may be consistently either abbreviated or spelled out.

> 104. E. W. Caspari and R. E. Marshak, "The Rise and Fall of Lyscnko," *Science,* 16 July 1965, 275–78.
> 105. Currents in the News, *U.S. News & World Report,* 11 Feb. 1980, 5.

17.56   *Book reviews* (see 16.126)

> 106. David Scott Kastan, review of *Jonson's Gypsies Unmasked,* by Dale B. J. Randall, *Modern Philology* 76 (May 1979): 393.

17.57   *Newspapers* (see 16.127). In references to daily newspapers the day, month (usually abbreviated), and year are essential; page numbers are usually omitted. For a news item in a large city paper that prints several editions a day, the name of the edition is useful (first edition, city edition, late edition, etc.) because the item might not appear in all editions. (Do not confuse *edition* with *issue,* which means any edition published on a specific day. Thus, a newspaper's issue of 22 February 1980 might consist of several editions.) The name of the edition is not included in references to editorials or features or other material that appears in all editions of the day. If page and column numbers are included, use "p." and " col." to avoid ambiguity—e.g., p. 3, col. 4.

> 107. Editorial, *Chicago Sun-Times,* 29 July 1981.
> 108. "Robert Moses, Master Builder, Is Dead at 92," *New York Times,* 30 July 1981, Midwest edition.

17.58   References to papers published in sections—almost all Sunday newspapers and large daily newspapers such as the *New York Times* and the *Chicago Tribune*—usually include the name or number of the section.

> 109 William Robbins, "Big Wheels: The Rotary Club at 75," *New York Times,* Sunday, 17 Feb. 1980, sec. 3.
> *or:*
> 109. *New York Times,* 17 Feb. 1980, Business and Finance section.
> [Note that "section" is spelled out when not followed by a number.]

UNPUBLISHED PAPERS

17.59   See 16.128–31.

> 110. Richard Simon, "Comedy, Suffering, and Human Existence" (Ph.D. diss., Stanford University, 1977), 100–102.

111. Pedro Carrasco, "Kinship and Territorial Groups in Pre-Spanish Guatemala" (Paper delivered at the Fifty-seventh Annual Meeting of the American Anthropological Association, Washington, D.C., 20 November 1958), 10.

112. United States Educational Foundation for Egypt, "Annual Program Proposal, 1952–53" (U.S. Department of State, Washington, D.C., 1951, Mimeographed), 28.

17.60   For manuscript collections see 17.77.

INTERVIEWS AND PERSONAL COMMUNICATIONS

See 16.132–33.

17.61   References to interviews, conversations, in person or by telephone, and letters to the author are usually best included in the text or in an informal note:

113. Senator Flood informed me by telephone in January 1980 that he would vote against any . . .

114. When I interviewed her on 26 July 1973 in Millington, Maryland, Mrs. Roemer was certain that . . .

But, if more suitable, a formal reference may be given in a note:

113. Sen. Q. T. Flood (R., Minn.), telephone conversation with author, 10 January 1980.

114. Mrs. Merle A. Roemer, interview with author, Millington, Md., 26 July 1973.

115. Benjamin Spock, interview by Milton J. E. Senn, 20 Nov. 1974, interview 67A, transcript, Senn Oral History Collection, National Library of Medicine, Bethesda, Md.

SPECIAL TYPES OF REFERENCES

REFERENCE BOOKS

17.62   In citing well-known reference books the facts of publication (place of publication, publisher, and date) are usually omitted, but the edition if not the first must be specified. References to an encyclopedia, dictionary, or other alphabetically arranged work give the item (not the volume or page number) preceded by "s.v." (*sub verbo,* "under the word").

116. *Encyclopaedia Britannica,* 11th ed., s.v. "original package."

117. *Webster's New International Dictionary,* 2d ed., s.v. "epistrophe."

118. *Columbia Encyclopedia,* 4th ed., s.v. "cold war."

119. *Dictionary of American Biography,* s.v. "Wadsworth, Jeremiah."

BIBLE

17.63   References to the Bible should include book, in roman type and abbreviated (see 14.34), chapter, and verse—never, of course, a page number. Traditionally, a colon is used between chapter and verse, as in the first three examples, but a period, as in the next two examples, serves equally well and is frequently seen in current biblical work:

> 120. Heb. 13:8.
> 121. 1 Thess. 4:11.
> 122. Ruth 3:1–18.
> 123. Gen. 25.19–37.1.
> 124. 2 Kings 11.12.
> 125. 1 Sam. 10.

PLAYS AND POEMS

17.64 References to plays and poems carrying section and line or stanza numbers may omit edition and facts of publication. (These should not be omitted, of course, where they are essential to a discussion of texts.)

> 126. *The Winter's Tale,* act 5, sc. 1, lines 13–16.
> 127. *The Faerie Queene,* bk. 2, canto 8, stanza 14.

In works of literary criticism including many such references, the form of citation may be shortened:

> 128. *WT* 5.1.13–16.
> 129. *FQ* 2.8.14.

Such shortened references are usually best put into the text in parentheses (see 15.66).

CLASSICAL REFERENCES

17.65 Abbreviations are used extensively in classical references for the author's name; for the title of the work; for collections of inscriptions, papyri, ostraca, etc.; for titles of well-known periodicals and reference tools. The most widely accepted standard for abbreviations is the comprehensive list in the front of the *Oxford Classical Dictionary.*

17.66 The numbers identifying the various parts of classical works (e.g., books, sections, lines) remain the same in *all* editions, whether in the original language or in translation. (Exceptions occur in collections of fragments of classical authors; see 17.74.) References to these parts therefore should not include page numbers. References to information supplied by a modern editor, however (in an introduction, commentary, note, appendix), must give page numbers.

17.67 The edition used should be specified the first time it is cited in a work; if several editions of the same source have been cited, the edition must be given in each citation. Credit for a translation should be given in a note accompanying its first use. In a work addressed to classicists, the name of an editor or translator alone will identify the edition referred to (see nn. 139, 149–55 below). In a work addressed to a wider audience, the full title and facts of publication should be given the first time an edition is used.

17.68 Titles of individual works, collections, and periodicals are in italics, whether given in full or abbreviated form. Titles of unpublished collections are in roman, without quotation marks. In Latin and Greek titles given in the Latin alphabet, only the first word and proper nouns and adjectives derived from proper nouns are capitalized.

17.69 In references to individual works there is no punctuation between the author's name and the title of the work or between the title and numerical references to divisions of the work. (In works of a general nature where classical references are mixed with other references it is quite acceptable to put a comma after the author's name.) The names of these divisions are omitted unless they are needed for clarity. If "ibid." is used in succeeding references, it is followed by a comma, but the preferred classical form is the use of the abbreviated title.

17.70 Different levels of division of a work (book, section, line, etc.) are separated by periods; commas are used between several references to the same level; the en dash is used between continuing numbers. If explanatory abbreviations are necessary before the numerical references for clarity (bk. 1, sec. 3), commas rather than periods are used to separate the different elements. Arabic numerals are used for all subdivisions of individual works:

> 130. Homer *Odyssey* 9.266–71.
> *or:*
> 130. Hom. *Od.* 9.266–71.
> 131. Plato *Republic* 360E–361B.
> 132. Lucan *Bellum civile* 3.682.
> 133. Cicero *De officiis* 1.133, 140.
> 134. Ovid *Amores* 1.7.27.
> 135. Thucydides *History of the Peloponnesian War* 2.40.2–3.
> *or:*
> 135. Thucydides 2.40.2–3.
> *or:*
> 135. Thuc. 2.40.2–3.
> 136. Pindar *Isthmian Odes* 7.43–45.
> *or:*
> 136. Pind. *Isthm.* 7.43–45.
> 137. Aristophanes *Frogs* 1019–30.
> 138. Sappho *Invocation to Aphrodite,* st. 2, ll. 1–6.
> 139. Solon (Edmond's numbering) 36.20–27.

17.71 In references to volumes in collections of inscriptions, arabic numerals are now generally used for a volume in a collection (where roman numerals were specified in the twelfth edition of this manual). Periods follow the volume number and the inscription number, and further subdivisions are treated as in other classical references. Although it is not necessary, a comma may follow the title (or the abbreviation of the title) provided the usage is consistently followed in similar references:

> 140. *IG* 2².3274.
> [= *Inscriptiones Graecae,* vol. 2, 2d ed., inscription no. 3274.]
> 141. *IG Rom.* 3.739.9.10, 17.
> [*"IG Rom."* = *Inscriptiones Graecae ad res Romanas pertinentes.*]
> 142. *POxy.* 1485.
> [= *Oxyrhynchus Papyri,* document no. 1485.]

17.72 Some collections are cited only by the name of the editor, in roman.

> 143. Dessau, 6964.23–29.
> ["Dessau" = H. Dessau, ed., *Inscriptiones Latinae selectae.*]

17.73 Superior figures or letters are used in several ways in classical references. When a superior number is used immediately after the title of a work or after the volume number of a collection and before the following punctuation, it indicates the number of the edition:

> 144. Stolz-Schmalz *Lat. Gram.*⁵ (rev. Leumann-Hofmann; Munich, 1928), 390–91.
> 145. *Ausgewählte Komödien des T. M. Plautus*², vol. 2 (1883).

When a superior number or a letter is placed after a number referring to a division of a work, it indicates a part, section, column, or other subdivision. An acceptable, indeed preferable, alternative to using superior letters is to put them on the line, in the text type size. Such letters, when set on the line, may be capital or lowercase according to how they appear in the source being cited. (When in doubt, make them lowercase.)

> 146. Aristotle *Metaphysics* 3.2.996ᵇ5–8.
> *or, better:*
> 146. Aristotle *Metaphysics* 3.2.996b5–8.
> 147. Aristotle *Nicomachean Ethics* 1177b31.
> 148. Roscher *Lex.* 2.2223A.15 ff.

17.74 Fragments of classical texts (some only recently discovered) are not uniformly numbered. They are published in collections, and the numbering of the fragments is usually unique to a particular edition. It is therefore necessary, in citing fragments, to include the editor's name.

> 149. Empedocles frag. 115 Diels-Kranz.
> 150. Anacreon frag. 2.10 Diehl [fragment 2, line 10].
> 151. Hesiod frag. 239.1 Merkelbach and West.

In subsequent references, the editor's name is usually abbreviated:

> 152. Anacreon frag. 5.2 D.
> 153. Hesiod frag. 220 M.-W.

Sometimes a reference includes citations to two or more editions in which the fragments are numbered differently:

154. Solon frag. 4 West (= frag. 3 Diehl).
155. Pindar frag. 133 Bergk = 127 Bowra.

17.75 The form for the classical references may properly be applied to medieval works. It may also be adapted for citations to modern sources occurring in a work where most of the references are classical.

156. Augustine *De civitate Dei* 20.2.

157. Augustine *City of God* (trans. Healey-Tasker) 20.2.

158. *Beowulf* 11.2401–7.

159. *Sir Gawain and the Green Knight* (trans. John Gardner), pt. 2, st. 1, lines 21–24.

160. Abelard *Epistle 17 to Heloïse* (Migne *PL* 180.375c–378a).

LEGAL REFERENCES

17.76 Notes in a predominantly legal work may follow the style set forth in detail in *A Uniform System of Citation,* published by the Harvard Law Review Association. In general, this style differs from nonlegal reference style as follows:

Only the surname of an author is given (unless more than one author with the same name is cited).

Authors of books and titles of books are given in caps and small caps.

Authors of articles are given in roman caps and lowercase; titles of articles are given in italics; names of periodicals are abbreviated and given in caps and small caps, preceded by the volume number.

Names of cases are given in roman, as are acts, bills, names of courts, etc.

161. HOGAN, ELECTION AND REPRESENTATION 160 (1945).

162. Smith, *Liability in the Admiralty for Injuries to Seamen,* 19 HARV. L. REV. 418 (1906).

163. Bridges v. California, 314 U.S. 252 (1941).

164. United States v. Dennis, 183 F.2d 201 (2d Cir. 1950).

This style may be modified in legal works as follows:

Names of authors of both books and articles include a full first name or two initials.

All titles—of books, of articles, and of journals—are set in roman. No italics and no small capitals are used in references.

The University of Chicago Press accepts either style in legal works. In a general or nonlegal work legal books and articles cited should be treated like the nonlegal references in the work.

COLLECTIONS OF LETTERS AND PAPERS

17.77 Citations to collections of personal letters, diaries, and other papers, printed or in manuscript, begin with the particular item in the collection. A citation to a letter gives the names (often only the last names) of the sender and the recipient, followed by the date of the letter and sometimes the place at which it was written. The word *Letter* is usually unnecessary, but other forms of communication are specified. Numbered letters in printed collections are sometimes referred to by number (no.) rather than page. Some manuscript collections have identifying numbers such as series and file which may be included in the citation, but usually the item and date, with the name of the collection and the depository, are sufficient. A citation to a diary gives the name of the diarist and the date of the entry. A title of a manuscript in a collection is given in quotation marks (e.g., "Canoeing through Northern Minnesota") but not descriptive designations such as Records or Report; when in doubt, omit the quotation marks.

17.78 In titles of manuscript collections the terms *Papers* and *Manuscripts* are synonymous, and either is acceptable, as is the abbreviation *MSS* when brevity is desirable. Some scholars differentiate between manuscript (MS) and typescript (TS). The abbreviation *MS* takes a period when an identification number for a single manuscript follows it: MS. 158.

17.79 Older manuscripts are usually numbered by folios (fol., fols.)—sheet by sheet—rather than by page. When both sides of a folio have been used, references specify which side, recto (r) or verso (v), thus: fols. 25r–27v. Note that the letters *r* and *v* are set on the line, in roman type, and without periods unless they come at the end of a sentence. Typescripts and modern manuscripts usually carry page numbers, which are of course used in a reference; it is often wise to use p. (pp.) in such references to avoid ambiguity.

17.80 Names of the months in dates may be spelled out, as in the following examples, or abbreviated consistently.

17.81 *Printed collections*

> 165. Adams to Charles Milnes Gaskell, London, 30 March 1868, *Letters of Henry Adams (1858–1891)*, ed. Worthington Chauncey Ford (Boston: Houghton Mifflin, 1930), 141.
>
> 166. EBW to Harold Ross, interoffice memo, 2 May 1946, *Letters of E. B. White*, ed. Dorothy Lobrano Guth (New York: Harper and Row, 1976), 273.
>
> 167. Paulina Jackson to John Pepys Junior, 3 October 1676, *The Letters of Samuel Pepys and His Family Circle*, ed. Helen Truesdell Heath (Oxford: Clarendon Press, 1955), no. 42.
> [Here the letter number in the collection is used rather than the page number, which could have been used instead.]

168. Secretary of State to the Special Commissioners, 27 May 1914, *Papers Relating to the Foreign Relations of the United States, 1914* (Washington, D.C., 1928), 509–10.

169. Memorandum, Minister of Foreign Relations of Mexico to the American Ambassador, 27 November 1925, Ministerio de Relaciones Exteriores, *Correspondencia oficial cambiada entre los gobiernos de México y los Estados Unidos con motivo de las dos leyes reglamentarias de la fracción primera del Artículo 27 de la Constitución Mexicana* (Mexico City, 1926).

170. Harriman to Roosevelt, Moscow, 12 October 1944, *Foreign Relations of the United States: Diplomatic Papers, 1944* 4:1013–14.

17.82   *Manuscript collections.* Locations of well-known depositories such as university libraries have been omitted from the following examples, but locations may always be included if an author so desires.

Full references:

171. George Creel to Colonel House, 25 September 1918, Edward H. House Papers, Yale University Library.

172. James Oglethorpe to the Trustees, 13 January 1733, Phillipps Collection of Egmont Manuscripts, 14200:13, University of Georgia Library (hereafter cited as Egmont MSS).

Subsequent references:

173. House diary, 6, 12 November, 10 December 1918; R. S. Baker to House, 1 November 1919, House Papers.

174. House diary, 16 December 1918.

175. Thomas Causton to his wife, 12 March 1733, Egmont MSS, 14200:53.

Full references (subsequent references are formed as in the above examples):

176. Embree to Swift, 19 March 1929, copy in Dodd Papers, with covering letter, Embree to Dodd of same date, William E. Dodd Papers, Manuscripts Division, Library of Congress.

177. Telegram, Burton to Merriam, 26 January 1923, Charles E. Merriam Papers, University of Chicago Library.
[*or:* Burton to Merriam, telegram, 26 January . . .]

178. Hiram Johnson to John Callan O'Laughlin, 13, 16 July, 28 November 1916, O'Laughlin Papers, Roosevelt Memorial Collection, Harvard College Library.

179. Memorandum by Alvin Johnson, 1937, file 36, Horace Kallen Papers, YIVO Institute, New York.

180. Minutes of the Committee for Improving the Condition of Free Blacks, Pennsylvania Abolition Society, 1790–1803, Papers of the Pennsylvania Society for the Abolition of Slavery, Historical Society of Pennsylvania, Philadelphia.

181. Louis Agassiz, Report to the Committee of Overseers . . . [28 December 1859], Overseers Reports, Professional Series, vol. 2, Harvard University Archives, Cambridge, Mass.

182. Undated correspondence between French Strother and Edward Lowry, container 1-G/961 600, Herbert Hoover Presidential Library, West Branch, Iowa.

183. Memorandum, 7 July 1917, Samuel Gompers Papers, State Historical Society of Wisconsin, Madison.

184. Memorandum, "Concerning a Court of Arbitration," n.d., Philander C. Knox Papers, Manuscripts Division, Library of Congress.

17.83   For citations to material in government archives see 17.93.

17.84   Citation to a microfilm, in a different library, rather than the original manuscript:

185. John Brownfield to the Trustees, 6 March 1736, John Brownfield's Copy Book, 1735–40, Archives of the Moravian Church, Bethlehem, Pa. (microfilm, University of Georgia Library).

PUBLIC DOCUMENTS

See 16.141–75.

17.85   *Government publications.* Unlike bibliographical entries, note references to public documents need not begin with the name of the country because this is usually obvious from the text. One *could* spell everything out (see 17.86), but short forms are nearly always clear and are certainly more economical:

186. *Senate Journal,* 14th Cong., 1st sess., 7 December [*or* Dec.] 1819, 9–19.

187. House Committee on Interior and Insular Affairs, *Fire Island National Seashore, N.Y.: Report to Accompany H.R. 7107,* 88th Cong., 2d sess., 1964, H. Rept. 1638, 5.

188. *Annals of Congress,* 2d Cong., Appendix, 1414–15.

189. *Annals of Congress,* 18th Cong., 1st sess., 358, 361.

190. *Congressional Record* [often abbreviated *Cong. Rec.*], 71st Cong., 2d sess., 1930, 72, pt. 10:10828–30.

191. 16 August 1949, *Congressional Record,* 81st Cong., 1st sess., 11584.

192. *Congressional Globe,* 39th Cong., 2d sess., 1867, 39, pt. 9:9505.

193. *American State Papers: Military Affairs* 2:558.
            or:
193. *American State Papers,* V. *Military Affairs* 2:558.

194. Mifflin to Washington, 18 July 1791, *Am. St. P.: Misc.* 1:39.
[Note abbreviated title and series.]

195. *Journals of the Continental Congress, 1774–1789* (Washington, 1904–37), 15:1341.

196. *Journals of the Continental Congress* 25 (1783): 863.

197. 17 July 1788, *Journals of the Continental Congress* [often abbreviated *JCC.*] 34:332–34.

198. Macomb to Calhoun, 2 November 1818, *Report of the Secretary of War Relative to Roads and Canals* (7 Jan. 1819), 15th Cong., 2d sess., H. Doc. 87, 13.

199. Senate Committee on Foreign Relations, *The Mutual Security Act of 1956,* 84th Cong., 2d sess., 1956, S. Rept. 2273, 5.

200. House Committee on Foreign Affairs, *Background Material on Mutual Defense and Development Programs: Fiscal Year 1965,* 88th Cong., 2d sess., 1964, Committee Print, 24.

201. Joint Session of Congress, *Declaration of a State of War with Japan, Germany, and Italy,* 77th Cong., 1st sess., 1941, S. Doc. 148 (Serial 10575).

202. Senate Special Committee on Aging, *Future Directions in Social Security,* pt. 5, 93d Cong., 1st sess., 26 July 1973, 5.

17.86   When country and issuing body are not clear from the text, fuller references may be needed in the notes:

> 203. U.S. Congress, Senate Committee on the Judiciary, *Modification or Repeal of National Prohibition: Hearings before a Subcommittee on Bills and Joint Resolutions Relative to the Prohibition Act*, 72d Cong., 1st sess., 1932, 20.
>
> 204. U.S. Congress, House Committee on Education and Labor, *White House Conference on Aging: Report to Accompany S.J. Res. 117*, 90th Cong., 2d sess., 1 May 1968, 5.
>
> 205. U.S. Congress, House Committee on Foreign Affairs, *Aid to Korea: H. Rept. 962 on H.R. 5330*, 2 pts., 81st Cong., 1st sess., 1 July 1949.
>
> 206. U.S. Department of State, *Igbo: Basic Course*, prepared for the Foreign Service Institute by L. B. Swift, A. Ahaghotu, and E. Ugorji (Washington, D.C.: Government Printing Office, 1962), 400.
>
> *or:*
>
> 206. L. B. Swift et al., *Igbo: Basic Course*, prepared for the Foreign Service Institute of the Department of State (Washington: GPO, 1962), 400.
>
> 207. Bureau of the Census, *Statistical Abstract of the United States, 1975* (Washington, 1975), 346–47.
>
> *or* (see 16.155):
>
> 207. U.S. Department of Commerce, Bureau of the Census . . .

17.87   References to British government publications may begin with U.K. (or United Kingdom or G.B. or Great Britain; see 16.164), but this is usually omitted from notes because it is obvious from the text or from the rest of the note.

17.88   For *Parliamentary Debates* series see 16.166.[3]

> 208. *Hansard Parliamentary Debates*, 3d ser., vol. 249 (1879), cols. 611–27.

Short form, date in text:

> 209. *Hansard*, 3d ser., 176:859.
>
> 210. *Parliamentary Debates*, 4th ser., vol. 13 (1893), col. 1273.
>
> 211. *Parliamentary Debates* (Lords), 5th ser., vol. 58 (1924), cols. 111–15.
>
> 212. *Parliamentary Debates* (Commons), 5th ser., vol. 26 (1911), cols. 226–27.

Short forms, which may be further shortened by omitting dates:

> 210. *Parl. Deb.*, 4th ser., 13 (1893): 1273.
>
> 211. *Parl. Deb.* (Lords), 5th ser., 58 (1924): 111–15.
>
> 212. *Parl. Deb.* (Commons [*or* H.C.]), 5th ser., 26 (1911): 226–27.

Specific item in *Debates:*

> 213. Churchill, Speech to the House of Commons, 18 January 1945, *Parliamentary Debates* (Commons), 5th ser., vol. 407 (1944–45), cols. 425–46.

17.89   For the successive series of "command papers" see 16.168.

> 214. *Report of the Royal Commission on Indian Currency and Finance*, vol. 2, Appendices, Cmd. 2687 (1926).

---

3. Official British style for citation of *Debates* in notes:
   188 *Parl. Deb.* 4s., cols. 1356–1406.
   393 *H.C. Deb.* 5s., col. 403.

215. *The Basle Facility and the Sterling Area,* Cmnd. 3787 (October 1968), 15–16.

17.90   For the Acts of Parliament of Great Britain see 16.169.

216. King's General Pardon, 1540, *Statutes of the Realm,* 32 Hen. 8, c. 49.
217. *Statutes,* 31 Vict. c. xiv, 2 April 1868.

17.91   For titles, and their abbreviations, of some published collections of British records see 16.173.

17.92   References to Canadian government publications (see 16.174) include the name of the country unless it is clear from the text or note:

218. Canada, House of Commons, *Debates,* 2 Oct. 1951, 335–37.
219. Canada, Senate, Special Committee on the Mass Media, *Report,* 3 vols. (Ottawa, 1970), 2:25.
220. "Report of the Royal Commission to Inquire into Railways and Transportation in Canada," *Sessional Papers,* 1917, no. 20g, p. xiii.

17.93   *Archives* (see 16.134–36, 16.158, 16.171). An archival reference in a note gives the cited item first, with its date if available. The order of the other parts of the reference is not fixed but should be consistent for the same and similar source references throughout a book or article.

Full reference:

221. Guy Stevens (Association of Oil Producers) to Secretary Hughes, 24 August 1923, Department of State General Records, Record Group 59, 812.6363/1438, National Archives, Washington, D.C.

Shortened reference (RG = Record Group; SD = State Department):

222. Stevens to Hughes, 24 August 1923, RG 59, 812.6363/1438.
[*or:* . . . 1923, SD 812.6363/1438.]

Full references:

223. Leven C. Allen to Joint Chiefs of Staff, 26 May 1950, and memorandum for the Secretary of Defense, n.d., CCS 383.21 Korea (3-19-45), sec. 21, Records of the United States Joint Chiefs of Staff, Record Group 218, National Archives.
224. Alice K. Leopold to the Undersecretary (James T. O'Connell), 15 April 1957, "Women," box 5, Papers of Millard Cass, Records of the Office of the Secretary of Labor, Record Group 174, National Archives.
225. H. M. Johnson to John W. Alvord, 15 April 1869, Bureau of Refugees, Freedmen, and Abandoned Lands Records, Education Division, Letters Received, September 1866–May 1869, Navy and Old Army Records Division, Record Group 105, National Archives.
226. "Lobbying," Files of the Senate Committee on the Judiciary, Record Group 46, File 71A-F15, National Archives, p. 32.

17.94   For archival documents in Great Britain see 16.171.

227. Clarendon to Lumley, 16 January 1869, PRO, FO Belgium/133, no. 6.
228. Hodgson to Halifax, 22 Feb. 1752, PRO, CO 137:48.
229. [Henry Elsynge], "The moderne forme of the Parliaments of England," BL, Add. MSS 26645.

> 230. Minutes of the General Court, 17 Apr. 1733, 3:21, BL, Add. MSS 25545.
>
> 231. Letter of a Bristol Man, BL, Add. MSS 33029:152–55.
>
> 232. PRO, Chatham Papers, G.D.8, Bundle 74, fol. 511.

17.95 Abbreviations in the above notes are usually spelled out at first appearance unless a list of abbreviations is included (Public Record Office, Foreign Office, Colonial Office; British Library, Additional Manuscripts). Where there are many references to the same collection(s), the name of the depository need not be repeated in each note. And in works whose readers will be familiar with the collections cited the depository need not be named:

> 233. Patent Rolls, 3 Rich. 2, pt. 1, m.12d (*Calendar of Patent Rolls, 1377–81*, 470).
>
> [A reference to a manuscript (in the PRO) followed by a reference, in parentheses, to its place in the printed *Calendar*.]

17.96 Other archival references:

> 234. Public Archives of Canada [*or* PAC], Privy Council Office Records, ser. 1, vol. 1477, PC 3458, 24 Dec. 1917.
>
> 235. Chevalier de la Luzerne, "Liste des membres du Congrès depuis 1779 jusqu'en 1784," Archives des Affaires Etrangères, Mémoires et Documents, Etats-Unis, vol. 1, fols. 253–87.
>
> 236. Francis to Baron Thugut, 24 November 1794, Vienna, Haus-, Hof- und Staatsarchiv, Kabinetts-Archiv, Protokoll der Allerhöchsten Hand-Billets, 1794, no. 549.
>
> 237. Archivio di Stato di Firenze, Provvisioni Registri 114, fols. 143r–144v.

NONBOOK MATERIALS

17.97 See 16.176–82, 17.49.

18 *Indexes*

Definitions 18.2
    Kinds of Indexes 18.2
    The Entry 18.3
    Subentries 18.4
    Headings and Subheadings 18.5
    Page References 18.9
    Cross-References 18.10
    Run-in and Indented Typographical Styles 18.18
The Indexer 18.19
    The Author as Indexer 18.20
    The Professional Indexer 18.21
The Mechanics of Indexing 18.24
    What Parts of the Book to Index 18.25
    Workspace and Equipment 18.28
    The Process in Brief 18.30
    First Step: Marking the Page Proofs 18.32
    Second Step: Making the Cards 18.37
    Third Step: Alphabetizing the Cards 18.40
    Fourth Step: Editing the Cards 18.45
      When to furnish subentries 18.48
      Arrangement of subentries 18.51
      The problem of sub-subentries 18.52
      Punctuation 18.54
      Cross-referencing 18.57
    Fifth Step: Typing the Index 18.58
    Gauging the Length of an Index As You Go 18.61
    What to Do about Typos You Find 18.63
General Principles of Indexing 18.64
    Choosing Terms for Entries 18.66
    When Not to Index Proper Names 18.68
    Making Choices between Variants 18.70
      Familiar forms of personal names 18.71
      Pseudonyms 18.72
      Persons with the same name 18.73
      Married women's names 18.74
      Monarchs and popes 18.76
      Titles of nobility 18.77
      Clerical titles 18.80
      Academic titles and degrees 18.81
      "Jr.," "III," etc. 18.82
      Saints 18.83
      Obscure persons 18.84
      Full form of name 18.85
      Confusing names 18.86

Acronyms and abbreviations of organization names 18.87
Daily newspapers 18.88
Periodicals 18.89
Titles of artistic works 18.90
Principles of Alphabetizing 18.92
The Two Systems 18.92
General Rules 18.95
Personal Names 18.102
Names with particles 18.102
Names with "Saint" 18.103
Compound names 18.104
Names with "Mac," etc. 18.105
Spanish names 18.106
Hungarian names 18.109
Arabic names 18.110
Chinese names 18.112
Japanese names 18.115
Vietnamese names 18.116
Indian names 18.118
Burmese names 18.119
Javanese and other Indonesian names 18.120
Thai names 18.121
Other Asian names 18.122
Place Names 18.123
Geographic names 18.123
Names beginning with articles 18.124
Names with "Saint" 18.125
Editing an Index Compiled by Someone Else 18.126
Copyediting Tasks 18.128
Markup 18.129
Typographical Considerations 18.130
General Principles 18.130
Type size and column 18.130
Justification 18.131
Indention 18.132
Bad breaks 18.133
Special typography 18.134
Examples 18.135–39

18.1 Every serious book of nonfiction should have an index if it is to achieve its maximum usefulness. A good index records every pertinent statement made within the body of the text. The key word here is *pertinent*. The subject matter and purpose of the book determine which statements are pertinent and which peripheral. An index should be considerably more than an expanded table of contents and considerably less than a concordance of words and phrases.

DEFINITIONS

KINDS OF INDEXES

18.2   Because an index should enable a reader to find every pertinent statement made in a book, it usually includes both proper-name and subject
entries. Occasionally, if the material is complex and there is a large
cast of characters, two indexes are prepared: one of persons only and
the other of subjects and proper names other than those of persons.
This division may be particularly helpful to the reader of a large historical work, for instance. A still finer division may be useful in a
history of literature, art, or music, in which a separate listing of the
works of the creators may be provided. For example, an anthology of
poetry in several parts with discursive introductions may require a
subject index, an author-and-title index, and an index of first lines.
For some kinds of scholarly work it is usual to make a listing of all
scholarly authors cited in the text (titled Author Index) and a separate
general index (titled Subject Index) of everything else, including
names of other persons. Perhaps the rarest is the index that is of subject matter only, as might be called for in a discourse on philosophy,
theology, or mathematics. Needless to say, the last-named is the most
difficult to prepare, and usually requires a specialist in the particular
field.

THE ENTRY

18.3   The *entry* is the principal subdivision of an index. A simple entry
consists of a *heading* and what is technically called a *locator*. The
locator is what tells the reader where to find material pertaining to the
subject of the heading. It can be a section number, chapter and paragraph number (as in the index of this volume), or any of several other
types of place identification; in most indexes, however, it is a *page
number* or sequence of page numbers, and that is what we shall be
calling it in the discussion that follows.

SUBENTRIES

18.4   An entry consisting of a heading and a large number of page references
is always, in good index practice, broken up into *subentries*. These
consist of subheadings, each representing some aspect of the main
heading, and page numbers. Choice of good subheadings, both logical
and useful to the reader, is one of the marks of a superior index.

HEADINGS AND SUBHEADINGS

18.5   The main heading of an index entry is normally a noun or noun phrase—the name of a person, place, object, abstraction, etc. A sequence of headings in one book on American Indians reads: Tents, skin—Teosinte—Tepary beans—Termination—Teton Dakota—Teton Sioux—Tewa organization—Textiles, cedar-bark—Theology, Navaho—Throwing stick—*Thuja plicata*—etc. Each of these headings is a substantive of some sort, and where the key word—the word a reader is most likely to look under—was not the first word in the phrase, the indexer has inverted the heading. This is an important consideration in the choice of good headings for an index.

18.6   Obviously, every subheading must bear a logical relationship to the heading. Often there is a close grammatical relationship as well; that is, it is possible to join heading and subheading in normal order and have the combined phrase make sense grammatically as well as semantically:

> Statistical material, 16, 17, 89; marking of, for printers, 176; months in, 65; proofreading, 183; states, territories, and possessions in, 65–66; time of day in, 64; units of measure in, 63

In the foregoing entry note how the heading and the first subheading unite grammatically to read "marking of statistical material for printers."

18.7   At other times, however, it is more appropriate to use subheadings that are subdivisions or units within a larger category, expressed in the principal heading:

> Sacred books: Bible, 77; Koran, 34–37; Talmud, 128–30; Upanishads, 92–96; Vedas, 143–51
>
> Indian tribes: Ahualucos, 140–41; Aztecs, 81–84; Chichimecs, 67–68; Huastecs, 154; Mixe, 178; Olmecs, 90–102; Toltecs, 128–36; Zapotecs, 168–72

In such instances, the relationship between entry and subentry is logical rather than grammatical and need not be expressed in grammatical terms.

18.8   A *complete entry* consists of the principal heading and page references, all subheadings and page references, and all cross-references.

PAGE REFERENCES

18.9   When in the book being indexed discussion of a subject continues for more than a page, the sequence of pages is given: 34–36, 192–96, etc. (University of Chicago Press style for typeset, printed indexes calls for en dashes, rather than hyphens, with continued numbers; the number of digits to use is discussed in 8.67–68.) Never in any circumstances use the abbreviations *f., ff.,* or *et seq.* in an index: use only the actual sequence of pages. A distinction is made between continued discussion of a subject (indexed, for example, 34–36) and individual references to the subject on a series of pages (34, 35, 36). If passing references to the subject over a long sequence of pages are actually important enough to index, *passim* may be used (for example, 78–89 passim), but this is a locution discouraged by this press and seldom used by professional indexers. Trivial passing references are best gathered under a subheading "mentioned" and placed at the end of the whole entry—or simply ignored in indexing.

CROSS-REFERENCES

18.10 Cross-references are devices inserted at appropriate places in the index to guide the reader to related information in the book. Properly used, they are extremely useful adjuncts to an index, but they should never be employed unless they actually lead to additional information, not just the same information indexed under other headings. Cross-references are of two general kinds, *see* references and *see also* references.

18.11 *See* references are used in the following situations:

1. When the indexer has chosen one among several key words or phrases and the reader might look under another:

Roman Catholic Church. *See* Catholicism

Adolescence. *See* Youth

2. When the subject has been treated as a subentry to a principal entry:

Book of Common Prayer. *See* Church of England: and Book of Common Prayer

Iroquois Indians. *See* Indian tribes: Iroquois

For this type of cross-reference some indexers use the expression *see under,* followed by the principal heading only. The Press does not object to this locution, provided it is clear which subentry the reader is directed to.

3. When an entry has been alphabetized under another letter of the alphabet:

The Hague. *See* Hague, The

Van Gogh, Vincent. *See* Gogh, Vincent van

4. When a personal name has been alphabetized under the real surname rather than pseudonym, name in religion, earlier name, or married name:

515

Bell, Currer. *See* Brontë, Charlotte
Louis, Father. *See* Merton, Thomas
Lunt, Mrs. Alfred. *See* Fontanne,
Lynn

Thibault, Jacques Anatole. *See*
France, Anatole

5. When reference is from a popular or shortened form of a term to the "official," scientific, or full form:

Mormon Church. *See* Latter-day
Saints, Church of Jesus Christ of
Baking soda. *See* Sodium bicar-
bonate

African violet. *See* Saintpaulia
Gray's "Elegy." *See* "Elegy Written
in a Country Churchyard" (Gray)

An entry composed merely of a heading and a *see* reference is termed a *blind entry*.

18.12   *See also* references are used when *additional* information can be found in another entry or subentry:

Elizabethan Settlement, 11–15, 17,
43; and Hooker, 13–14. *See
also* Catholicism; Church of
England; Protestantism

Maya: art of, 236–43; cities of, 178
(*see also* Chichén Itzá; Uxmal);
human sacrifice among, 184–87;
present-day, 267. *See also* Quiché
Maya; Yucatán, Indians of

Again, when the cross-reference is to a subentry, some indexers use *see also under,* followed by the principal heading.

18.13   In cross-references, headings and subheadings should usually be cited in full, with inversion and punctuation exactly as given in the entry referred to. Exceptions are sometimes made, however, for very long headings. A cross-reference to "AAAS (American Association for the Advancement of Science)" could be shortened to "*See* AAAS" without ambiguity. When more than one principal heading is cited, these should be separated by semicolons; if reference is to a subheading, its principal heading should be given first, followed by a colon or a comma and the subheading. Multiple cross-references are arranged in alphabetical order.

18.14   *See also* cross-references pertaining to a whole entry may be placed immediately after the heading (in parentheses) or at the end of the entire entry:

Location A	Location B
Calumet People (*see also* Lakes People; Prairie People): animal totem, 123, 146; clothing, 126–27; Dream Dance, 182–86; migration, 112, 136; population, 139; reservations, †37, 139	Calumet People: animal totem, 123, 146; clothing, 126–27; Dream Dance, 182–86; migration, 112, 136; population, 139; reservations, 137, 139. *See also* Lakes People; Prairie People

Location A is preferred by many indexers on the ground that it gives the user all the probable headings under which to look for material at the outset. Location B, the older and more traditional way of inserting *see also* references, is preferred by others on the ground that such references usually lead only to peripheral material and should not clutter the opening of the entry. The University of Chicago Press accepts either style, so long as it is consistently used in an index.

18.15 The foregoing remarks apply to indexes set as a whole in *run-in,* not *indented,* typographical style (for definitions see 18.18). In indented-style indexes *see also* references always follow the principal heading, as in Example *C* (18.137) and in the index of this volume.

18.16 In either style of setting, *see* or *see also* references that apply to a particular subheading or subentry are placed immediately after it.

18.17 For any kind of cross-reference the words *see* and *see also* are normally set in italic type. If what follows, however, is in italics (a book title, for example), *see* or *see also* may be set in roman to distinguish it from the rest of the cross-reference.

RUN-IN AND INDENTED TYPOGRAPHICAL STYLES

18.18 All indexes are set in what is called *flush-and-hang* style. This means that the first line is set flush and the rest of the entry is indented below it. When there are subentries, a further choice must be made, between *run-in* and *indented* styles. In run-in style the subentries follow one another with no breaks between. All the examples above of entries that include subentries are set this way. In indented style each subentry begins a new line, indented one em; subentry runovers are indented two ems, and if the main heading runs over, it should also be indented two ems:

> Iraq, the (lower Tigris-Euphrates Val-
> ley), 48, 125, 138, 245. *See also*
> Sawad
> under Abbasids, 275, 487
> agricultural investment by Sasani-
> ans in, 144, 201–3
> Arab conquest of, 301–7

Run-in style is by far the commoner way to set an index, and is used for most general books. Indented style is used mainly in reference works and in large scholarly books of a highly detailed nature. Indented style makes a very complex index easier for the eye to follow and also allows for the use of sub-subentries. Throughout this chapter, however, it is assumed that an index will be set in run-in style except where indented style is specified.

THE INDEXER

18.19   The ideal indexer sees the book as a whole—both in scope and in arbitrary limitations—understands the emphasis of the various parts and their relationships to the whole, and—perhaps most important of all—clearly pictures potential readers and anticipates their special needs. An indexer must make certain that every pertinent statement in the book has been recorded in the index in such a way that the reader will be able to find without difficulty the information sought. A good indexer must also have sufficient knowledge of both publishing and typesetting practices to be able to present the data assembled according to editorial amenities and within the mechanical limitations of typography.

THE AUTHOR AS INDEXER

18.20   The author most nearly approaches the ideal as indexer. Certainly, the author knows better than anyone else both the scope and the limitations of the work, and the audience to which it is addressed. At the same time, authors are sometimes so subjective about their own work that they are tempted to include in an index even references to milieu-establishing, peripheral statements and, as a result, prepare a concordance rather than an efficient index. Invariably, the best scholarly indexes are made by authors who have the ability to be objective about their work, who understand what a good index is, and who have mastered the mechanics of the indexing craft.

THE PROFESSIONAL INDEXER

18.21   Professionals have the advantages of objectivity and experience in many fields of interest and scholarship. Their acquaintance is seldom as deep as that of an author in any particular field, and so they may miss some subtleties, but for the author who cannot prepare an index, or does not wish to, the professional indexer is the logical choice for the task. In much of what follows in this chapter it is assumed, for purposes of fuller explanation, that the author and the indexer are not the same person.

18.22   Whoever the indexer is, he or she should be intelligent, widely read, and well acquainted with publishing practices—also level-headed, patient, scrupulous in handling detail, and analytically minded. This rare bird must—while being intelligent, level-headed, patient, accurate, and analytical—work at top speed to meet an almost impossible deadline. Less time is available for the preparation of the index than for almost any other step in the bookmaking process. For obvious reasons, most indexes cannot be completed until page proofs are available. Typesetters are anxious for those few final pages of copy; printers want to get the job on the press; binders are waiting; salesmen are clamoring for finished books—*surely* you can get that index done over the weekend?

18.23 Of course you cannot. No adequate index for a full-length book of any complexity can be—or should be—completed over a weekend, unless the weekend includes several extra days at either end. In addition to requiring intense intellectual concentration, especially if the book is not one's own, good indexing requires reflection, and reflection demands time. Not reflection of the staring-into-the-firelight kind, but reflection of the kind wherein one stops frequently, reviews a bit of the job just completed, trying to put oneself in the place of the author on one side and the reader on the other, and decides whether both have been served by the decisions one has made.

THE MECHANICS OF INDEXING

18.24 Although we speak of the sequence of tasks we perform when indexing—some of them physical, some mental—as the *mechanics* of the job, the process is far from mechanical in any literal sense. There are, of course, indexes that are mechanically—or better, electronically—produced. One is called a KWIC (for "key word in context") index. A computer is given a list of key words and terms and ordered to search a data file (such as a whole book on magnetic tape) for each instance of them, record every occurrence in a context of a few words on either side of the term, note its location (such as page and line number), record the terms in alphabetic order (and, for multiple occurrences, in order of occurrence), and print out the whole listing. A KWIC index is thus a kind of concordance of preselected terms—names, words, sequences of words, anything the computer is programmed to search for. KWIC indexes have many uses, but there is no way they can substitute for a real index compiled by a real human being of the sort described above. Indexing requires decision making of a far higher order than computers are yet capable of.

WHAT PARTS OF THE BOOK TO INDEX

18.25 The first decision to be made, what to index and what not to index in the book, is relatively straightforward. Much of the preliminary matter—title page, dedication, epigraphs, lists of illustrations and tables, and acknowledgments—should not be indexed. A preface, even a foreword by someone else, may be indexable if it concerns the subject of the book itself and not simply how the book came to be written. A true introduction to the work, which occasionally finds its way into the prelims, is of course fully indexable. Most of the back matter should not be indexed: glossary, bibliography, and so on. Appendixes should be indexed if they contain important pertinent material omitted from the main body of the text, but not if they merely reproduce documents (the text of a treaty, for example, or a questionnaire) that are discussed in the text.

18.26 Notes, whether at the foot of the page or at the back of the book, may be indexed if they continue or amplify discussion in the text (textual, or reading, notes); those that merely document statements in the text (reference notes) should not be indexed. Index references to footnotes should normally be by page number alone; for example, 134n (hair space between numeral and *n*, no period after *n*). If there are several notes on a page, the note number may be given (in this instance with a period): 134n.14, 172nn. 17, 19. If there is indexable material in a text passage and in a note on the same page which is not tied to that passage, separate references may be given: 63, 63n. When notes are printed at the back of the book (endnotes), an index reference must include the number of the note as well as the page on which it is printed.

18.27 Matter in tables, charts, graphs, maps, drawings, photographs, and other illustrative material is occasionally listed in the index when it is of particular importance to the discussion. Then too, index references to illustrations may be of great assistance to the reader who wishes to refer to a reproduction of a painting discussed in an art book. References to illustrative material can be by both page number and illustration (pl., fig., chart) or table number.

WORKSPACE AND EQUIPMENT

18.28 A word about what an indexer needs in the way of working space and equipment. Abundant desk or table space is essential—the dining-room table is a useful adjunct for indexers who work at home, especially when they come to alphabetizing the index cards, and one cannot have too much desk space for handling proofs.

18.29 Three-by-five-inch index cards are needed (professionals often use slips of paper instead, because they are less bulky), as are alphabetic tab dividers for the cards, and a file box to put them in. You will also need a typewriter and copy paper. For a scholarly book of average length and complexity you will need at least a thousand index cards, so don't skimp: they come in packages of a hundred and boxes of a thousand. Preferably, cards for an index should be typed, not handwritten, to obviate later errors arising from misinterpretation of handwritten words or numbers. A special typewriter platen for index cards speeds typing, but is not really necessary, and the long strips of perforated card stock which tear apart into three-by-five cards are another, alternate, luxury.

THE PROCESS IN BRIEF

18.30   Indexes are usually prepared from page proofs. If galley proofs are available, a good deal of work can be done with them, particularly if the book is of great length and complexity. Working on the face and in the margins of the galleys, the indexer can make decisions about headings and subheadings, and even start to prepare index cards accordingly. Entries cannot be completed until page proofs are available, however (we are speaking of an index in which locators are page numbers, not paragraph or section numbers), and so except in special circumstances it is usual to wait for page proofs before beginning work on the cards.

18.31   From the page proofs individual cards are prepared, one item to a card, and alphabetized. When all entries and subentries have been amalgamated and suitable cross-references have been made, the cards are edited into final form. Then the entire index is retyped, double space, on 8½-by-11-inch copy paper in a form that can be marked by the editor and set in type for printing. Sometimes, supposedly in the interest of speed, a publisher is willing to accept index copy on cards, but savings are largely illusory: an index costs more to set from cards, and copyediting and proofreading are much slower.

FIRST STEP: MARKING THE PAGE PROOFS

18.32   The indexing method advocated in this chapter involves doing a good deal of the actual indexing on the page proofs, before any cards are prepared. This method will not commend itself to professional indexers, since much of the work is done twice, but anyone compiling a full-length index for the first time, whether author or editor, will probably find it more reassuring and less troublesome than other, more sophisticated methods. It also makes changing one's mind and correcting mistakes easier to accomplish. In any case, anyone who does not want to do the initial marking of proofs as recommended can skip this stage and go on to the next.

18.33   All the page proofs may be marked up at once before cards are made (if galley proofs are used for this first stage of indexing, they would have to be), or the indexer may mark up one chapter, make the cards for that chapter, and go back to the proofs of the next. The latter procedure is more agreeable to many people, and as time goes on, the indexer becomes more skilled and self-assured in marking the proofs so that less underlining and fewer marginal notes suffice to dictate what goes on the cards. Marking should not become so skimpy and cryptic, however, that it is impossible to reconstruct from the proofs just what has been indexed and under what headings. That capability is one of the great advantages of this particular method.

18.34 To visualize the method advocated here, suppose you are indexing one of the earlier sections in this book, a discussion in chapter 11 of how to draw up a list of illustrations (see fig. 18.1). You have read through the chapter once and have now gone back to select headings and subheadings for indexing this particular section. You decide that the whole section (11.44–46) will have to be indexed under "List of illustrations, preparing," and so you mark the section head as shown. (For the purpose of marking the proofs, a colon follows a proposed principal heading and precedes a proposed subheading.) Then you decide that since preparing the list of illustrations is one of the tasks of manuscript editing, this section had better be indexed under "Copy-editing" and "Manuscript editor" also, so you add these headings in the top margin, with "list of illustrations" as the subheading proposed for each. Going down the page, you pass over *interstellar particles, Roman architecture,* and *photographs of ancient buildings* without making a mark (though you may be tempted): these are nonindexable examples only. But you decide to include one more subheading under the main heading "List of illustrations"; this is "when to include" (11.44 only). Note that there is no point in making an elaborate breakdown of the main heading, with many specific subheadings, when the subheadings all lead to the same few paragraphs—the reader is already there, so to speak. Continuing down the page, you underline *headline style, Plates, Figures,* and several other terms as proposed main headings, with "in" (or "for") "list of illustrations" as subheads. Note how *page numbers* is marked to be inverted (Numbers, page) for use as a main heading.

18.35 In every instance when you choose a heading, you also supply a *modification,* a word or phrase that narrows the application of the heading. Some of these will become subheadings in the index as finally edited. Some will not. But it is important to have them on hand at later stages in making the index, because if you do not, you may end up with nothing but unmodified headings followed by long strings of page numbers. These make an index all but useless.

18.36 If a text discussion extends over more than one page (in this instance, more than one paragraph), as it often does, beginning and ending references have to be given—as with the main entry above. Sometimes

Copyediting : list of illustrations
MS ed. : and list of illus.

THE LIST OF ILLUSTRATIONS : *preparing*

11.44 A task often falling to the manuscript editor (but more properly done by the author) is preparing the list of illustrations. Not every illustrated book requires such a list, of course. The criterion is: Are the illustrations of interest apart from the text they illustrate? For a scientific monograph on interstellar particles, illustrated largely by graphs, the answer is obviously no. For a book on Roman architecture, illustrated by photographs of ancient buildings, the answer is obviously yes. For some other illustrated books, the answer may not be so easy to give, and the author and editor must decide whether the list of illustrations *: when to include* is worth the space it will take.

11.45 *Preparing the list.* The list of illustrations follows the table of contents, normally on a new recto page, and is headed simply Illustrations. (The list of tables, if there is one, follows on another recto page.) _Headline style_ (important words capitalized) is usually employed for the identifying titles. If illustrations are of more than one type, they are listed by category, as Plates, Figures, Maps, etc., and by number if numbers are used in the text (see 11.30, also fig. 11.3). For figures and maps that print with the text (and hence have folios assigned to them, whether or not the folios are actually expressed on the page) page numbers are given (000 in the copy as first prepared). For plates and for maps printed separately, another type of location is given. If plates are to be inserted in groups of four or more pages at one location, each group is listed under the tag *Following page 000* when copy is prepared. If they are to be inserted in the text two pages at a time (each page of plates accordingly lying opposite a text page), the location is given as *facing page 000*. Needless to say, each *000* is changed to a real number once page proofs are out and page numbers are known.

: in list of illus.

: in list of illus.

: in list of illus.

11.46 *Editing captions.* It should be remembered that the list of illustrations *∧ Picture :* is a *list,* not a reprinting of the captions and legends. If the captions are short and adequately identify the subjects of the pictures, they may do double duty in the list of illustrations. Long captions, however, should be shortened, and discursive legends should never be used here. Remember too that readers do not have the illustrations in front of them as they scan the list, so a cryptic, "cute," or allusive caption is of no use to them in identifying the subject of an illustration. Such captions should be rewritten for use in the list of illustrations.

editing for list of illus.

∧ picture: in list of illus.

Fig. 18.1. Type proof of three paragraphs from an earlier chapter in this manual, marked for indexing (for explanation of marking see text, 18.34–36).

you can look ahead and add the closing reference immediately. At other times it is more practical to leave the closing reference open and add the figure later.

SECOND STEP: MAKING THE CARDS

18.37 When you have completed your work on the page proofs, part or all of them, the next step is making entry cards. The cards made from your markings on the page proof (fig. 18.2) essentially confirm the indexing decisions you made then, although here and there wording is

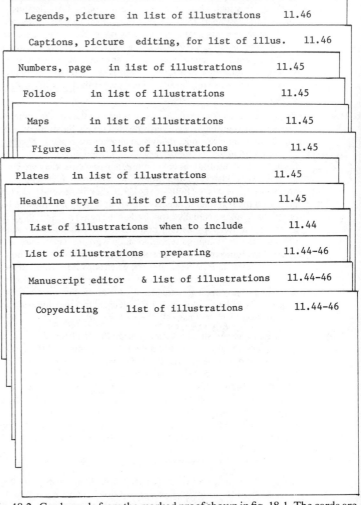

```
Legends, picture  in list of illustrations    11.46

  Captions, picture  editing, for list of illus.   11.46

Numbers, page   in list of illustrations    11.45

  Folios      in list of illustrations      11.45

  Maps       in list of illustrations      11.45

  Figures    in list of illustrations       11.45

Plates     in list of illustrations      11.45

Headline style  in list of illustrations    11.45

  List of illustrations  when to include    11.44

List of illustrations    preparing     11.44-46

  Manuscript editor   & list of illustrations   11.44-46

  Copyediting      list of illustrations    11.44-46
```

Fig. 18.2. Cards made from the marked proof shown in fig. 18.1. The cards are shown in the order in which they would be filed, and so should be read from the bottom to the top of the illustration.

changed as you have thought more about the matter. Note that every card has three elements typed on it: a heading, a modification, and a locator. Here the last is a chapter and paragraph number, rather than the page number typical of most indexes.

18.38 Every time you make a card, after pulling it from the typewriter, re-read what you have written and *verify the page number* (or other locator). Once cards have been put in alphabetical order, it will be difficult or impossible to correct miscopied page numbers, and such entries often have to be dropped from the index. If the closing reference for a long discussion has been left open, it must be added at this point. Keep the cards in the order in which you make them until you have finished making cards for the entire book. This means that you will not be able to add new page numbers to cards you have already made; but the added work is justified, especially for an amateur indexer, by the advantage of being able to check all cards against the pages they refer to before they are reshuffled in alphabetizing.

18.39 When you have completed all the cards, you should go through the whole file once more, with the page proofs at your side, and do two things. (1) Check each card to make sure that what is on its face is exactly what you intended. (2) Go through the page proofs once more to check for omissions in the indexing. You may find that unmarked items, which seemed only peripheral at first, have proved to be index-able in the light of themes developed in later chapters of the book. You may, too, have inadvertently failed to make cards for important material. In either case, make cards now and add them to the file before going on to the task of alphabetizing the cards.

THIRD STEP: ALPHABETIZING THE CARDS

18.40 To alphabetize the index cards for a full-length book you will need space—a large table or a good-sized area of the floor if you can work comfortably that way. To begin, organize the space into twenty-four divisions according to letters of the alphabet:

A	B	C	D	E	F
G	H	I	J	K	L
M	N	O	P	Q	R
S	T	U	V	W	XYZ

(Instead of the organization depicted, you could divide the alphabet into three rows of eight each, if that suits your space better.) Place a card with a large letter drawn on it in each division.

18.41 Now, with a comfortable stack of cards in one hand, start dealing them one by one on the divisions marked with their initial letters. At first you will have to keep pulling the marker cards from under the piles as they get covered up, but after a while you will know just where each alphabetic pile is located without looking. When you have completed this stage of alphabetizing, pick up the piles of cards and put them back in the file box with alphabetic dividers between them.

18.42 That done, pull out the *A*'s and do the same thing all over again, this time using the *second* letter of the heading as your guide. This will produce a much smaller number of piles, and you can probably finish alphabetizing each of these in your hand, but if any of them are large enough to merit the treatment, they can be distributed in piles by the third letter of the heading, or perhaps by individual headings. Actually, *A* is not a very popular letter for beginning English words. When you come to the *P*'s and *S*'s, there will be lots more of them.

18.43 If you use the letter-by-letter method of alphabetizing (more on this later—see 18.92), you will alphabetize each heading up to the first mark of punctuation, whether the heading consists of one word or more than one. That is, a heading like *Labor unions* or *Machine copies* or *Double-numeration system* (hyphens don't count as punctuation) is treated as one word in alphabetizing by this method. But with a heading like *Institutions, names of,* or *Line numbers, placement of,* you stop at the comma in alphabetizing with respect to headings that precede and follow.

18.44 When you have gone through all the alphabetic sections of the cards and returned them to the file box, you are ready for the next, and very important, stage of the work. (At this point, you may be tempted to think you are nearly finished with your index. You are, perhaps, barely halfway through now, in terms of both time and expenditure of intellectual effort.)

FOURTH STEP: EDITING THE CARDS

18.45 It is at this crucial stage that the index really takes shape. Editing the cards, grouping headings, determining subheadings, and furnishing an adequate but not excessive number of cross-references—all these together make the difference between an index that is an efficient, truly complete key to the material within a book and one that is merely a collection of words and page numbers. (For a simple example of a sequence of edited cards see fig. 18.3.)

18.46 From the headings and modifications on the cards you now have to make final decisions about principal headings and subheadings—main entries and subentries. You now have to make a final choice among synonymous or closely related terms—monarch, king, or ruler? agriculture, farming, or crop raising? clothing, costume, or dress? life,

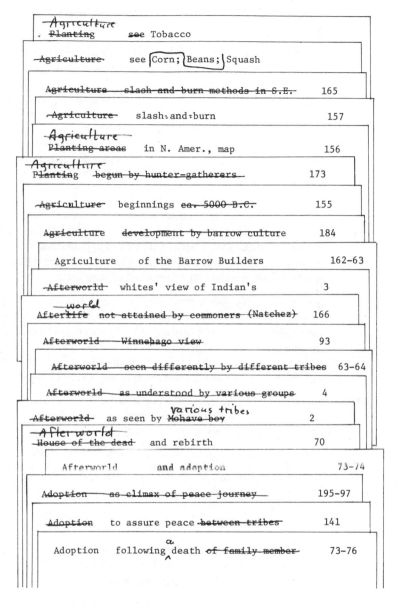

Fig. 18.3. Cards for the first three entries of an index for a book on American Indian religion. The completed cards have been alphabetized and edited, ready for typing (the beginning of the file is at the bottom of the illustration). For the typed version of these entries see fig. 18.4.

existence, or being?—and prepare suitable cross-references to reflect those choices.

18.47   You also have to decide whether certain entities will be treated as main entries or as subentries under a comprehensive principal heading—

Hopi, 00		
Iroquois, 00	*or:*	Indian tribes: Hopi, 00; Iroquois, 00;
Kwakiutl, 00		Kwakiutl, 00; Mohawk, 00
Mohawk, 00		

Painting, 00		Handicrafts: painting, 00; pottery
Pottery making, 00		making, 00; weaving, 00; wood
Weaving, 00	*or:*	carving, 00
Wood carving, 00		

—again with cross-references if needed in the context. One's main concern here, as everywhere in the preparation of an index, should be to make sure that every pertinent piece of information within the book is recorded, either as principal entry or as subentry, and that the reader will be able to find it with a minimum of searching.

18.48   *When to furnish subentries.* Main entries unmodified by subentries should not be followed by long rows of page numbers. Such an entry forces the reader to run through many pages before finding the exact information needed. A general rule of thumb—if such exists about any aspect of indexing—is to try to furnish at least one subentry if there are more than five or six references to any single heading.

18.49   If, for example, the index of a book on medical care included an entry like the one below (left), it should certainly be broken up into a number of subentries, perhaps as at the right:

Hospitals, 17, 22, 23, 24, 25, 28, 29– 31, 33, 35, 36, 38, 42, 91–92, 94, 95, 96, 98, 101, 111–14, 197	Hospitals: administration of, 22, 96; and demand for patient services, 23, 91–92; efficiency of, 17, 29–31, 33, 111–14; finances of, 28, 33, 36, 38, 42, 95, 112; and length of patient stay, 35, 94, 98, 101, 197; quality control in, 22–25, 31

The original entry would defeat any but the most patient user, whereas the second, though longer, leads the reader to the information sought with a minimum of leafing through pages.

18.50   Subentries can be overdone, of course. A main entry consisting of nothing but subheadings, each with one page number, is as undesirable as a long, unanalyzed entry. In the following example, note how the long sequence of subentries at the left can be combined meaningfully by using broader categories (indented style is used here only for easier comparison):

House renovation
  balancing heating system, 65
  building permit required, 7
  called "rehabbing," 8
  correcting overloaded electrical
    circuits, 136
  how wallboard is finished, 140–44
  installing readymade fireplace,
    191–205
  painting outside of house adds
    value, 11
  plumbing permit required, 7
  removing paint from doors and
    woodwork, 156–58
  repairing dripping faucets, 99–100
  replacing clogged water pipes,
    125–28
  replacing old wiring, 129–34
  separate chimney required for
    fireplace, 192
  straightening sagging joists, 40–42
  termite damage to sills a problem,
    25
  three ways to deal with broken
    plaster, 160–62
  violations of electrical code cor-
    rected, 135
  what is involved in, 5

House renovation, 5, 8
  electrical work, 129–34, 136
  heating and plumbing work, 65,
    99–100, 125–28, 191–205
  legal requirements, 7, 135, 192
  painting and decorating, 11,
    156–58
  structural problems, 25, 40–42
  wall and ceiling work, 140–44,
    160–62

18.51   *Arrangement of subentries.* Subentries should be arranged alphabetically according to the first important word or chronologically according to the order of appearance of the material within the book. The
University of Chicago Press prefers the former arrangement, but the
latter also is widely used, especially for historical studies and others
in which the text itself is structured on a chronological basis (see
18.101).

18.52   *The problem of sub-subentries.* Sub-subentries are difficult or impossible to use in run-in indexes but can often be avoided by repeating a
word or phrase in the subentry:

> Eskimos: language, 18; pottery,
> 432–37; tradition of, in Alaska,
> 123; tradition of, in California, 127

18.53   Another solution to the problem is illustrated in example *D* (18.138),
where 1-em dashes stand in for the principal heading in a series of
subentries with sub-subentries. This can be done in a few isolated
instances within an index, but if it looks as though an index is going to
require a great many sub-subentries, the indexer should check with

the manuscript editor before proceeding. Almost never should sub-sub-subentries be used.

18.54   *Punctuation.* An inverted phrase for the title of the main entry is of course punctuated to show the inversion:

> Balance of payments
> *or:*
> Payments, balance of

If the title is followed immediately by page references, a comma should appear between the title and the first numeral and between subsequent numerals:

> Payments, balance of, 16, 19

If the title is followed immediately by subentries, a colon precedes the first subheading:

> Payments, balance of: definition
> of, 16

All subsequent complete subentries are followed by semicolons:

> Payments, balance of: definition
> of, 16; importance of, 19

Note that there is no punctuation at the end of any complete entry. Discussion of a single point may begin, be interrupted, and then continue on subsequent, widely scattered pages. These facts must be indicated by appropriate punctuation within both main entries and subentries:

> Education, higher, 16, 36–38, 64–67,
> 119–20; at Cambridge, 37–38, 119;
> at Harvard, 16, 64–65

18.55   A *see* or *see also* cross-reference at the end of an entry is preceded by a period, and two or more cross-references are separated by semicolons:

> Learning capacity, 332, 352–53. *See*
> *also* Performance; Training

18.56   For punctuation in indented-style indexes, see examples in 18.18 and 18.137.

18.57   *Cross-referencing.* Most cross-references are added at this point in the indexing process, after the final form of entries and subentries has been determined and after the principal headings and subheadings have been edited. Cross-references that you inserted earlier, during the preparation of the cards, should be carefully examined to make certain that they agree with the final form of headings and subheadings. Blind entries should be added if for good reason information has been indexed under a heading that would not easily come to a reader's mind. But to add many entries on the pattern of

> Psychology, depth. *See* Depth psy-
> chology

or

> Magazines. *See* Periodicals

is to be overkind to the reader to the point of cluttering the index with useless headings. You should also consider whether it is not easier to duplicate references under a second heading than to make a cross-reference to an entry with only two or three references. That is, not

> Youth movements. *See* "Jeunesse"
> organizations
> "Jeunesse" organizations, 45, 67–68

but simply

> Youth movements, 45, 67–68
> "Jeunesse" organizations, 45, 67–68

FIFTH STEP: TYPING THE INDEX

·18.58 After you have completed editing the cards and have added the last cross-reference, you are ready for typing. Type the entire index in final form, double-spaced, on 8½-by-11-inch copy paper, in one column, with ample margins, so that it can be marked up by the editor and easily followed by the typesetter (see fig. 18.4). Capitalize each principal heading, unless you have been asked to use lowercase (as in some scientific indexes). Leave extra space between alphabetic sections (between the *A*'s and *B*'s, for example). Number all pages, beginning with 1.

18.59 When you have finished typing, proofread the typescript against the cards, check the alphabetic order of all entries, and make sure that all cross-references still lead somewhere and are in correct form.

18.60 Only the final index typed on copy paper should be delivered to the publisher. Keep a copy for yourself, for safety's sake and in case of telephone queries from your editor. Hold on to the cards and page proofs, too, until you know that the index has been typeset, proofread, and printed. You will not, incidentally, have a chance to proofread the index yourself, as this is ordinarily done in the publishing office to save time, and you will probably not see the final, copyedited form of your index before it appears in the printed book.

Index

Adoption: following a death, 73–76; to assure peace, 141, 195–97

Afterworld: and adoption, 73–74; and rebirth, 70; as seen by various
tribes, 2, 4, 63–64, 93, 166; whites' view of Indian's, 3

Agriculture: of the Barrow Builders, 162–63, 184; beginnings, 155, 173;
in North America, map, 156; slash-and-burn, 157, 165. See also
Beans; Corn; Squash; Tobacco

Alcoholic beverages, 3, 256, 261; in ceremony, 251. See also Liquor

Altar, 40, 146, 210–12, 266

Amulets, 12. See also Tokens

Angalok, 88. See also Shaman

Animals: attitude toward, 40–45; and Owner, 42–44, 98, 120–21; sacrifice
of, 65, 74, 187, 201; spirits of, 41–46, 83, 100, 118–19; in visions,
98, 99, 132. See also Owner; Spirits

Apache: ceremony, clowns in, 114; and fasting, 239; maiden, 57–58; and
ordeal, 239; and peyote, 266; and purification, 140; visions among,
239; and war, 137, 139; war god, 239, 251

Apology, to nature persons (animals), 12, 117, 121, 122

Avoidance: of ceremonies by men, 59; of danger from power, 19; of the
dead, 13, 66–67, 80, 243; of men's gear by women, 42, 51–52, 53; of
menstruating women, 12–13, 54; of names of the dead, 66, 69; of the
sun, 54, 55, 58, 155. See also Seclusion; Taboos; Women

Aztecs, 110, 157–59, 207, 216–17

Ball game, sacred: Aztec, 155–57, 159; Iroquois, 173–74; Natchez, 167

Barrow Builders, 78, 162–64, 184–85, 201. See also Hopewell; Mounds

Basin Indians, 54, 56, 91

Fig. 18.4. First page of the typed copy for an index. Note especially the punctuation of entries. (Cards for the first three entries appear in fig. 18.3.)

GAUGING THE LENGTH OF AN INDEX AS YOU GO

18.61   If you are an inexperienced indexer, you may want some guidance on the approximate size of the index you have undertaken to compile. The most appropriate length for the index will vary according to the relative complexity of the book: scholarly books generally need longer indexes than popular ones. For a typical scholarly book this might be (in pages) from one-fiftieth to one-twentieth the length of the text, if we assume that the index is set in two-column, run-in style, in a typeface two points smaller than the body face—all usual specifications for such an index. That is, a book of, say, three hundred pages might need an index of from six to fifteen pages, depending upon how closely written the book is (one page of a two-column index generally accommodates about a hundred lines).

18.62   What does this mean in terms of index cards? Again, much depends upon variables such as the typeface chosen for the index and the width of the column in which it is set. But as an extremely rough working figure, the indexer may assume that an average of five references per text page will yield a short index (one-fiftieth the length of the text) whereas fifteen or more references per text page will yield a fairly long index (perhaps one-twentieth the length of the text). As a running check, then, the indexer can examine the page proofs or count references on the accumulating cards from time to time and from that figure estimate the relative size of the finished product.

WHAT TO DO ABOUT TYPOS YOU FIND

18.63   The indexer must not attempt to edit the book in page proofs; at the same time, obvious typographic or other errors should be corrected on the proofs, and indexing should reflect the corrections. (The page proofs given an indexer are usually not the corrected master set, of course, but an unmarked duplicate set.) Having finished work on the page proofs, the indexer may (sometimes by prearrangement) telephone the manuscript editor with a list of corrections before undertaking later tasks in preparing the index. It is sometimes possible to make corrections even at this late stage in the manufacture of a book if they are important enough.

GENERAL PRINCIPLES OF INDEXING

18.64   An index is a working tool for one particular book, and the indexer should hold this fact in mind at all times. By page-proof time, decisions have long since been reached between author and editor concerning style and usage. If British spelling has been used consistently throughout the text, so should it be in the index. Shakspere in the text would call for Shakspere in the index. Hernando Cortez should not be indexed as Cortés, Hernán, Cortes, Hernando, or any other variant; Virgil as Vergil; Sir Walter Raleigh as Ralegh, Sir Walter. Similarly, the spelling of place names should agree with the text; if the author used the language of origin ('s Gravenhage, Köln), the name should not be changed in the index to the better-known English form (Hague, The; Cologne). Nor should geographic terms be altered to their present form (Saint Petersburg, Petrograd, Leningrad; Siam, Thailand; Byzantium, Constantinople, Istanbul). The use of accents and other diacritical marks should also be observed (Yucatán, Yucatan; Schönberg, Schoenberg). Only in the rare instance in which confusion might arise in the reader's mind should any cross-reference or parenthetical word or phrase be inserted giving "correct" or more widely used forms. In spelling, capitalization, use of italics, etc., the index should scrupulously reflect the author's usage (but see 18.85).

18.65   Before commencing the actual indexing, an indexer should gain some familiarity with the work as a whole, and the best way to do this is to run quickly through the entire set of page proofs from beginning to end. One need not, cannot, read every word in such a perusal, but one can learn a great deal about the scope of the work, chronological or otherwise, about the author's approach and self-imposed limitations— historical, philosophical, political, clinical, or whatever—and a good deal too about the terminology employed. The knowledge thus gained about the work is well worth the hour or so of time required, in terms of mistakes and false starts avoided.

CHOOSING TERMS FOR ENTRIES

18.66   In indexing a work we should as nearly as possible imagine ourselves the eventual reader and try to anticipate needs and expectations. Under what headings will a reader be most likely to look for information? How full should these headings be? Should they be expanded, modified, or broken down? What should be included? What omitted?

18.67   The wording for all entries should be clear, concise, logical, and consistent throughout. Terms should be chosen according to the author's usage as far as possible. If, for example, the author of a philosophical work uses the term *essence* to mean *being, essence* should be in the index, possibly with a cross-reference. If the author uses the same terms interchangeably, only one should be chosen for use in the index, and in this instance a cross-reference is essential:

> Essence (being), 97, 109, 119, 246,
> 359–62, 371–80
> Being. *See* Essence

Choosing the most useful key words is important. Sometimes an author's terminology cannot be reduced to a brief form for use as a heading, and some other term must be substituted. Here it is essential to put ourselves in the reader's place and choose words that will most probably come to the user's mind. Common sense is the best guide.

WHEN NOT TO INDEX PROPER NAMES

18.68   Proper names are an important element in most indexes, but there are times when they should be ignored. In a book on the history of the automobile in America, for example, an author might write, "After World War II small sports cars like the British MG, often owned by returning veterans, began to make their appearance in college towns like North Adams, Massachusetts, and Ann Arbor, Michigan." Seeing these two place names in the paragraph, an indexer might be tempted to underline them and make cards for inclusion in the index. The temptation must be resisted. The identity of the two towns mentioned has nothing to do with the theme of the book, and the names should find no place in the index. The MG sports car, on the other hand, probably should, given the subject of the work.

18.69   Scene-setting statements, employed by the author to establish historical milieu, particularly in opening sequences, should be carefully considered before they are indexed. For example, the first paragraph of John M. Rosenfield's introduction to his *Dynastic Arts of the Kushans* (Berkeley and Los Angeles: University of California Press, 1967) reads: "In the first three centuries of the Christian era, a great inland empire stretched from the Ganges River valley into the oases of Central Asia. This empire was created by a nation of former nomads whose ruling princes gave themselves the dynastic name Kushan. Opulent and powerful men, cast in much the same mold of Iranian princely ideals as Darius the Great, Timur, or Akbar, they governed a land which lay at the junction of three culture spheres—the Indian subcontinent, Iran and the Hellenized Orient, and the steppes of Central Asia." Fine scene setting, impressive cast of characters—but the indexer should simply pass it by without making a single entry.

MAKING CHOICES BETWEEN VARIANTS

18.70   Despite their importance in an index, or perhaps because of it, names probably cause more trouble for inexperienced indexers than any other aspect of the indexing craft. Particularly troublesome are names that appear within the work in more than one form, or in incomplete form. The paragraphs that follow survey some of the problems that arise frequently and recommend solutions for them.

18.71   *Familiar forms of personal names*. Personal names should be indexed as they have become widely and professionally known:

> Lawrence, D. H. [*not* Lawrence, David Herbert]
> Poe, Edgar Allan [*not* Poe, E. A., *or* Poe, Edgar A.]
> Bizet, Georges [*not* Bizet, Alexandre César Léopold]
> Cervantes, Miguel de [*not* Cervantes Saavedra, Miguel de]

(Note, however, that in a biography or critical study of Lawrence, Bizet, or Cervantes, the full name should appear in the index.)

18.72   *Pseudonyms*. Persons who have used pseudonyms professionally should be listed under their real names, with suitable cross-references:

> Ouida. *See* Ramée, Marie Louise
>   de la
> Ramée, Marie Louise de la [pseud. Ouida]
>
> Æ. *See* Russell, George William
> Russell, George William [pseud. Æ]

18.73   *Persons with the same name*. Persons with identical names should be distinguished one from the other:

> Field, David Dudley (clergyman)
> Field, David Dudley (lawyer)
>
> Pitt, William (the elder)
> Pitt, William (the younger)

If many persons with the same surname appear in the same book, particularly if they are members of the same immediate family, suitable parenthetical identifications should be furnished in the index. For example, the index to *O'Neill* by Arthur and Barbara Gelb (New York: Harper & Bros., 1962) contains the following entries:

> O'Neill, Edmund Burke (brother)
> O'Neill, Edward (grandfather)
> O'Neill, Mrs. Edward (Mary) (grandmother)
> O'Neill, Mrs. Eugene (Agnes Boulton O'Neill Kaufman)
> O'Neill, Mrs. Eugene (Carlotta Monterey O'Neill)
> O'Neill, Mrs. Eugene (Kathleen Jenkins O'Neill Pitt-Smith)
> O'Neill, Eugene Gladstone
> O'Neill, Eugene, Jr.
> O'Neill, Mrs. Eugene, Jr. (Elizabeth Green)
>
> O'Neill, Eugene, III (son of Shane)
> O'Neill, James (father)
> O'Neill, Mrs. James (mother) (Mary Ellen "Ella" Quinlan)
> O'Neill, James, Jr. ("Jamie") (brother)
> O'Neill, John (godfather)
> O'Neill, Oona (daughter by Agnes) (Mrs. Charles Chaplin)
> O'Neill, Shane Rudraighe (son by Agnes)
> O'Neill, Mrs. Shane (Catherine Givens)

18.74   *Married women's names*. Many married women are widely known by their maiden names and should usually be indexed accordingly. References to married names can, if necessary in the context, be supplied in parentheses or by means of suitable cross-references:

Sutherland, Joan (Mrs. Richard Bonynge)
Bonynge, Mrs. Richard. *See* Sutherland, Joan

Marinoff, Fania (Mrs. Carl Van Vechten)
Van Vechten, Mrs. Carl. *See* Marinoff, Fania

Others, better known by their married names, should be indexed under their married names, with references to their maiden names, husbands' full names, familiar names, and the like supplied within parentheses or by cross-references if needed:

Besant, Annie (née Wood)
Wood, Annie. *See* Besant, Annie
Browning, Elizabeth Barrett

Roosevelt, Eleanor (Mrs. Franklin D.)
Truman, Mrs. Harry S. (Bess)

18.75   Occasionally, a woman may play two roles of importance within the confines of a single book—as an unmarried person and later as a wife. For example, in a study of the Barrett family, the following index entries might be needed for one person:

Barrett, Elizabeth (later Elizabeth Barrett Browning), 12, 18–36, 79–82. *See also* Browning, Elizabeth Barrett

Browning, Elizabeth Barrett, 128, 143–45, 162–67. *See also* Barrett, Elizabeth

18.76   *Monarchs and popes.* Monarchs and popes should be listed according to their "official," not personal, names:

Charles I (king of England)   Gregory VII

If the monarch or pope is referred to in the work by other than the monarchical or papal name (as, for example, both Gregory VII and Hildebrand), a cross-reference from the alternate name should be included. And in a book on English history where only the English Charleses appear, the identifying tag shown in the example may be omitted.

18.77   *Titles of nobility.* Immediate members of royal families, like monarchs, are generally indexed under their given names:

Charles, Prince of Wales   Fabiola, Queen (of Belgium)
Margaret Rose, Princess

Other persons bearing titles of nobility are generally indexed under the title:

Shaftesbury, first earl of   Guise, third duc de
Dunmore, fourth earl of

18.78   Such rules, however, should be tempered by common sense. In a book in which the Villiers family figured prominently, for example, it would be foolish to index the seventeenth-century dukes of Buckingham under Buckingham and other members of the family under Villiers.

18.79   Titles such as Sir, Dame, Lady, or (sometimes) Baron, when used before a name, are usually retained when the name is inverted for indexing.

18.80   *Clerical titles.* Clerical titles like Reverend, Monsignor, Pastor, or (sometimes) Bishop, when used before a name, are usually retained when the name is inverted for indexing:

>   Jaki, Rev. Stanley S.   Southwick, Bp. James E.
>   Mannierre, Msgr. Charles L.

Anglican and Roman Catholic bishops are generally identified by the titles of their sees or provinces:

>   Ussher, James (archbishop of Armagh)
>   Lessard, Raymond W. (bishop of Savannah)
>   Cranmer, Thomas (archbishop of Canterbury)

18.81   *Academic titles and degrees.* Academic titles like Professor and Doctor, used before a name, are not retained in indexing, nor are abbreviations of degrees following a name, like Ph.D., M.D., or LL.D.

18.82   *"Jr.," "III," etc.* When a name includes a suffix like "Jr.," it is retained when the name is inverted for indexing but is placed after the given name:

>   Roosevelt, Theodore, Jr.   Moffett, Mrs. James, Sr.
>   Stevenson, Adlai E., III

(See also 18.73.)

18.83   *Saints.* Saints are usually indexed under their given, or Christian, names, with identifying tags to differentiate them, when necessary, from others bearing the same name:

>   Thomas, Saint   Thomas Becket, Saint
>   *or:*   Thomas Aquinas, Saint
>   Thomas, Saint (the apostle)   John Chrysostom, Saint

18.84   *Obscure persons.* Persons referred to in the book by surname or given name only should be further identified:

>   Thaxter (family physician)   John (Smith's shipmate on
>   *Stella*)

18.85   *Full form of name.* Proper names should be indexed in full, even though the author may use shortened forms in the text:

	TEXT	INDEX
"the lake"		Michigan, Lake
"the bay"		San Francisco Bay
"Shasta"		Shasta, Mount
"the Village"		Greenwich Village
"Roosevelt," "the president,"		
"TR," *or* "Teddy"		Roosevelt, Theodore

18.86   *Confusing names.* Proper names about which there might be some confusion should be clearly identified within parentheses:

New York (city)   Mississippi (state)
New York (state)   Mississippi (river)

18.87   *Acronyms and abbreviations of organization names.* Governmental, international, and other organizations that have become widely known under their abbreviated names, usually consisting of capital letters, should be indexed according to the abbreviations, particularly if the full names are cumbersome and little known:

AFL-CIO   OAS   UNESCO
NATO   OPEC   UNICEF

Abbreviations of organization names not widely known by abbreviations may appear in parentheses following the full name in the index, especially if the author has used the abbreviations anywhere in the text.

18.88   *Daily newspapers.* Most daily newspapers in English should be indexed under the name of the city of publication regardless of how the name appears on the masthead:

Chicago Sun-Times
New York Daily News [not *Daily News* or *Daily News, New York*]
          but:
Christian Science Monitor
PM
Times (London) [in Britain indexed *Times, The*]
Wall Street Journal

A foreign language newspaper should be alphabetized according to the first word following an article in its title; the place of publication may be included in parentheses:

L'aurore [or: *Aurore, L'*] (Paris)
Dziennik Zwiazkowy Zgoda (Chicago)
Jewish Daily Forward (Chicago)
La Prensa [or: *Prensa, La*] (Buenos Aires)

18.89   *Periodicals.* Periodicals are indexed according to the full title, omitting any article that may appear at the beginning:

Nation
Observer
Saturday Review [present American periodical]
Saturday Review [British periodical]
Saturday Review of Literature [American before 1952]

18.90   *Titles of artistic works.* A reference to a work by an author (or composer or painter) is usually indexed both as a main entry under its title and as a subentry under the main entry for the author. Historical and critical studies often cite the works of many authors, so the author's name should be included, in parentheses, in the main entry for the individual work; if, however, the work is by the principal subject of a biographical or critical study, such identification is not needed:

Look Homeward, Angel (Wolfe), 34–37
Wolfe, Thomas: childhood of, 6–8;
  early literary influences on, 7–10;

literary reputation of, in 1939, 44;
  Look Homeward, Angel, 34–37;
  and Maxwell Perkins, 30–41

It has been assumed that the two entries above are from the index to a book of essays about American novelists of the 1930s and 1940s; hence the "(Wolfe)" after *Look Homeward, Angel.* If these had been from the index to a biography of Thomas Wolfe, the identification within parentheses would have been unnecessary.

18.91 If there are citations to many works by the same author, the titles of these works as subentries to the main entry for the author can be grouped, for easy reference, at the end of the other subentries:

Shelley, Percy Bysshe, 167–68, 193–
  96; and atheism, 195–96; and
  Blake, 196; and Coleridge, 193–
  94, 196; and Keats, 194–95; and
  Platonism, 167, 194–95; and

religion, 167. Works: *Adonais,*
  194–95, 200; *Defence of Poetry,*
  194–96; *Mont Blanc,* 193–94;
  Prometheus Unbound, 196;
  Queen Mab, 193

Works and authors that are discussed in the text should be indexed as shown above; those that are cited in notes only as documentation should not usually be indexed in any form.

PRINCIPLES OF ALPHABETIZING

THE TWO SYSTEMS

18.92 There are two principal modes of alphabetizing, the *letter-by-letter* system and the *word-by-word* system. All alphabetizing is letter by letter in one sense: in arranging a series of words in alphabetical order, one considers first the initial letter of the word, then the second letter, the third letter, and so on:

        aardvark
        aardwolf
        Aaron
        Ab
        aba
        abaca

The need to choose between the two modes arises when one is alphabetizing not a set of single words but a set of headings, some of which consist of more than one word. How far does one carry the letter-by-letter principle? In the letter-by-letter mode one alphabetizes up to the first mark of punctuation; that is, one ignores word spaces and alphabetizes up to the comma, colon, or period at the end of the heading, or to the comma after the first part of an inverted heading. In the word-by-word mode one applies the principle through the end of the first word and then stops, using second and subsequent words only when two or more headings begin with the same word(s). In the letter-by-letter mode a compound proper name (New York, Lloyd George) is treated as a single word, and in both modes a hyphenated compound (self-pity) is so treated:

LETTER BY LETTER	WORD BY WORD
newborn	New Deal
newcomer	new economics
New Deal	New England
new economics	New Latin
newel	new math
New England	New Testament
new-fashioned	new town
New Latin	New World
newlywed	New Year's Day
new math	newborn
newsboy	newcomer
news conference	newel
newsletter	new-fashioned
newspaper	newlywed
newsprint	news conference
news release	news release
newt	newsboy
New Testament	newsletter
new town	newspaper
New World	newsprint
New Year's Day	newt

18.93   Each system has its advocates and its detractors. Strong adherents of the word-by-word approach say that the letter-by-letter system is easy on the indexer and hard on the reader. One points out that medical readers and editors would find ludicrous a sequence like

> Adrenal cortex
> Adrenalectomy
> Adrenal tumors

Perhaps so. But some on the other side would find if not ludicrous at least confusing a sequence like

> Type font
> Type metal
> Typeface
> Typeset

and would point out that everyone who ever uses a dictionary or en-cyclopedia is fully familiar with letter-by-letter alphabetization and should have no difficulty with it in a book index. Actually, for many indexes the differences are hardly detectable, because sequences of closely linked terms do not occur very often. The sequence in 18.92 was deliberately chosen to illustrate the systems and to exaggerate their differences.

18.94   In any case, the University of Chicago Press, while preferring the letter-by-letter approach for most books, is perfectly willing to accept indexes compiled on the word-by-word principle if that is the prefer-ence of the author or the custom of the discipline.

GENERAL RULES

18.95   When a person, a place, and a thing have the same name, they are indexed in that order, regardless of the demands of alphabetization (i.e., London, Jack, before London, England; Hoe, Robert, before Hoe, garden).

18.96   In personal names, an initial or initials used in place of a given name come before any name beginning with the same letter:

Coates, A. J.   Coates, E. M.
Coates, Christopher   Coates, Edward Liston

18.97   Acronyms, arbitrary combinations of letters, and most abbreviations, when used as headings, are alphabetized letter by letter (but see 18.103, 18.105). Identification may be added in parentheses:

ACTH (adrenocorticotrophic hormone)
ASCAP (American Society of Composers, Authors, and Publishers)
UNESCO (United Nations Educational, Scientific, and Cultural Or-ganization)
WFMT (Chicago radio station)
XYZ affair

For some acronyms and abbreviations it may be appropriate to supply a cross-reference from the fully spelled-out name.

18.98   Numerals are alphabetized as though spelled out:

10 Downing Street (*alphabetized as* Ten)
125th Street (*alphabetized as* One hundred twenty-fifth)
1066 (the year) (*alphabetized as* Ten sixty-six)

18.99   Accented vowels and consonants are usually to be alphabetized along with the unaccented letter in a sequence. The Press does not recommend treating *ü, ö, ä,* as *ue, oe, ae,* or *ş* as *sh,* and so on. In an index containing a great many headings beginning with such accented letters it might be best to put them in separate sections following the unaccented letters, as would be done in a dictionary of the language from which they are taken. But a note at the head of the index should signal that this has been done.

18.100   In alphabetizing subheadings, introductory articles, prepositions, and conjunctions are disregarded:

Marinoff, Fania (Mrs. Carl Van Vechten): caricatured by Covarrubias, 128; childhood of, in Boston, 45; marriage of, 83; in *Spring's* Awakening, 133; at Stage Door Canteen, 145; as Trina in *Life's Whirlpool,* 137

(This Press rule of long standing is based on the assumption that a reader scanning a long list of subheadings is looking for key terms and will find them most readily if they are in alphabetical order. If subheadings are alphabetized according to *and, in, of,* and the like, the reader has to outguess the indexer, so to speak, while searching for terms: the choice of one such introductory word over another is often pretty arbitrary.)

18.101   Occasionally, subheadings are arranged according to chronological, mathematical, or other sense, rather than alphabetical (see also 18.51):

Dynasties, Egyptian: First, 10; Second, 12, 141; Third, 45; Fourth, 47–49
Holmes, Oliver Wendell (1841–1935): childhood and youth, 20–26, 40, 125–26; Civil War years, 70–84, 92; at Harvard, 101–7, 246; as writer, lecturer, and barrister, 132–34, 148–56, 160, 170–73; as Massachusetts jurist, 7, 165, 182–193; as U.S. Supreme Court justice, 8–11, 108, 138–40, 196–205
Flora, alpine: at 1,000-meter level, 46, 130–35; at 1,500-meter level, 146–54; at 2,000-meter level, 49, 163–74

PERSONAL NAMES

18.102   *Names with particles.* Family names containing particles often present a perplexing problem to the indexer. Both the spelling and the alphabetizing of these names should follow the personal preference of, or accumulated tradition concerning, the individual, as best exemplified in *Webster's Biographical Dictionary.* Note the wide variations in the following list of actual names arranged as they should appear in an index:

Becket, Thomas à (*or* Thomas Becket, Saint)
Braun, Wernher von
D'Annunzio, Gabriele
de Gaulle, Charles
de Kooning, Willem
De La Rey, Jacobus Hercules
De Mille, Agnes G.
De Valera, Eamon
Deventer, Jacob Louis van

de Vere, Aubrey Thomas
De Vries, Hugo
DiMaggio, Joseph Paul
Gogh, Vincent van
Guardia, Ricardo Adolfo de la
Hindenburg, Paul von
Lafontaine, Henri
La Fontaine, Jean de

La Guardia, Fiorello H.
Linde, Otto zur
Ramée, Marie Louise de la
Robbia, Luca della
Thomas a Kempis
Van Devanter, Willis
Van Rensselaer, Stephen

18.103 *Names with "Saint."* A personal name in the form of a saint's name should be spelled and alphabetized according to the preference of the person bearing the name. Again, if the person is well known, *Webster's Biographical Dictionary* should help. If spelled with the abbreviation, such names are nevertheless alphabetized as if spelled out:

St. Denis, Ruth
Sainte-Beuve, Charles Augustin
Saint-Gaudens, Augustus

St. Laurent, Louis Stephen
Saint-Saëns, Camille

In alphabetizing the names of Christian saints, the word Saint never precedes the personal name (see 18.83).

18.104 *Compound names.* Alphabetize compound surnames, with or without hyphens, according to preferences of individuals or established usage:

Ap Ellis, Augustine
Campbell-Bannerman, Henry
Castelnuovo-Tedesco, Mario
Fénelon, François de Salignac
de La Mothe-
Gatti-Casazza, Giulio
Ippolitov-Ivanov, Mikhail
Larevellière-Lépeaux, Louis
Marie

Lloyd George, David
Mendes, Frederic de Sola
Mendès-France, Pierre
Merle d'Aubigne, Jean Henri
Merry del Val, Rafael
Pinto, Fernám Mendes
Teilhard de Chardin, Pierre
Vaughan Williams, Ralph

18.105 *Names with "Mac," etc.* Personal names beginning with "Mc," or "M'," the abbreviated forms of "Mac," should be indexed under "Mac," as though the full form were used:

Mabie, Hamilton W.
McAdoo, William G.
Macalister, Donald
McAllister, Alister
MacArthur, Douglas

Macaulay, Rose
McAuley, Catharine
MacMillan, Donald B.
Macmillan, Harold

18.106 *Spanish names.* Almost without exception Spanish names should be alphabetized according to the father's name. The custom in Spain and Latin America is to use a double surname, the first element of which is the father's family name and the second the mother's maiden name (that is, *her* father's family name). A boy named Juan, whose father's name is Jorge Sánchez Mendoza and whose mother's maiden name was María Esquivel López, is named Juan Sánchez Esquivel. His sister, Juana, is Juana Sánchez Esquivel. A woman keeps her maiden name after marriage but drops her mother's family name and replaces it with *de* plus her husband's family name. Thus the mother of the two children just mentioned is called María Esquivel de Sánchez. In this example, then, the father, mother, son, and daughter would be indexed, respectively, as

> Sánchez Mendoza, Jorge
> Esquivel de Sánchez, María
> Sánchez Esquivel, Juan
> Sánchez Esquivel, Juana

The two names that form the full surname are sometimes joined by *y* (and), but this does not affect use of the first element in alphabetization:

> Ortega y Gasset, José   Leguía y Salcedo, Agusto

18.107 Not all Spanish names precisely fit the pattern described. For example, some persons use only one surname, and two given names are not uncommon. José Murguía and Augustín Pedro Justo are alphabetized (again, by the father's name):

> Murguía, José   Justo, Agustín Pedro

Also, some surnames include particles that may make them look like married women's names to the uninitiated, as José María Fernández de Sandoval or Cristóbal de Torre Redondo, alphabetized

> Fernández de Sandoval, José María
> Torre Redondo, Cristóbal de

Finally, persons with the conventional compound surname are sometimes known to the world by the mother's name rather than the father's, a well-known example being the poet Federico García Lorca, called Lorca in the English-speaking world. The name, however, is alphabetized

> García Lorca, Federico

and in this instance one would insert a cross-reference under *Lorca*.

18.108 These are not the only complications presented by Spanish names, and an indexer who is not conversant with Hispanic culture should seek help before trying to index any but the most straightforward examples.

18.109 *Hungarian names.* In Hungarian, personal names appear with the surname first, followed by the given name (Bartók Béla). In English, however, Hungarian names are usually written in English order and reinverted—with the comma—in alphabetizing:

Bartók, Béla   Molnár, Ferenc

18.110   *Arabic names.* Most modern Arabic names consist of a given name plus a family name (e.g., Taha Husayn) or a given name plus the given name of the individual's father plus the family name (e.g., Ahmad Hamid Hmisi). Such names are alphabetized under the family name:

Husayn, Taha   Hmisi, Ahmad Hamid

Family names beginning with *al-* (the equivalent of *the*) are alphabetized under the element following this particle. The particle itself may be placed after the whole inverted name or (the more modern practice) retained before it:

Hakim, Tawfiq al-   Jamal, Muhammad Hamid al-
    or: *or:*
al-Hakim, Tawfiq   al-Jamal, Muhammad Hamid

In either case *al-* is ignored in alphabetizing. Elided forms of the article (*ad-, an-, ar-,* etc.) are treated the same way—though the practice of spelling in the elided form is discouraged by most orientalists (see 9.106).

18.111   Arabic names of earlier periods are indexed in the form in which they originally became familiar in the West. In the classical period names consisted of a given name plus one or more other names reflecting place of origin or residence, trade, sect of Islam, etc. And the given name was often followed by a word of relationship such as *ibn-, bin-,* etc. ("son of") or *abu-* ("father of") and the name of the individual referred to. Such names are alphabetized under the element by which the person is most commonly known, which may be the given name or any of the appended names (consult the catalog of a large reference library in doubtful cases). The familiar Western form of some classical names is often remote from the original: Averroës, for example, actually bore the name Abu al-Walid Muhammad ibn-Ahmad ibn-Rushd al-Qurtubi—the name by which we know him being derived through Spanish from ibn-Rushd, one of the patronymics. For later times, too, the principle often holds. The founder of Saudi Arabia, for instance, is indexed under his patronymic, capitalized as if it were a surname, Ibn-Saud, but his son and successor is indexed under his given name, Faisal; in both instances these happened to be the forms in which the names first became familiar in Europe and America.

18.112   *Chinese names.* In English-language texts Chinese names are spelled in Latin characters so as to suggest the Chinese pronunciation, sometimes according to no particular system (e.g., the *Soong* family), usually according to either the Wade-Giles or (especially since the mid-1970s) the pinyin system. The indexer should spell the names as given in the work, making no attempt to regularize them and adding no cross-references unless the author uses them in the text. Romanized Chinese names often appear in the forms in which they first became familiar to Western readers, so a mixture of systems in the same work is not uncommon.

18.113   Chinese personal names generally consist of three syllables, the one-syllable family name coming first, the two-syllable given name following. In romanized form both names are capitalized; in the Wade-Giles system the given name is hyphenated, in pinyin, closed up (see also 9.111–14):

Wade-Giles	Pinyin
Li K'o-jan	Li Keran
Ch'eng Shih-fa	Cheng Shifa
Tseng Yu-ho	Zeng Youhe
Chao Wu-chi	Zhao Wuji

When alphabetizing Chinese names that are written in traditional form, with family name first, do not invert, and use no commas.

18.114   Some Chinese names, particularly from earlier times, consist of only two syllables. In the romanized forms, there is little consistency about the use of hyphens. These names too should be alphabetized without inversion:

Lao-tzu
Li Po
Sun Fo

Many twentieth century Chinese with ties to the West adopted the practice of giving the family name last (Tang Tsou, H. H. Kung, T. V. Soong, etc.). These names should be inverted in alphabetizing:

Kung, H. H.
Soong, T. V.
Tsou, Tang

18.115   *Japanese names.* Japanese names normally consist of two elements, a family name and a given name—in that order. If the name is Westernized, as it often is by authors writing in English, the order is reversed. Thus:

Japanese Order	Western Order
Tojo Hideki (i.e., the famous, or infamous, General Tojo)	Hideki Tojo
Yoshida Shigeru	Shigeru Yoshida
Kurosawa Noriaki	Noriaki Kurosawa

547

In recent years, however, there has been a tendency among authors writing in English on Japanese subjects to use the traditional order for personal names. It is important, therefore, in alphabetizing Japanese names that the indexer make certain which order the author has used. If a name is in Japanese order, it is left as is, with no inversion and no comma; if in Western order, it is inverted, with a comma, like a Western European name.

18.116 *Vietnamese names.* Like Chinese names, Vietnamese names consist of three elements, the family name being the first (Ngo Dinh Diem, Vo Nguyen Giap). Similarly, the family name is used in alphabetizing, and no inversion is necessary:

> Ngo Dinh Diem
> Vo Nguyen Giap

18.117 Confusion about Vietnamese names arises from the fact that Vietnamese persons are usually referred to—correctly and politely—by the last part of the given name (Premier Diem, General Giap). An exception was Ho Chi Minh, who was originally named Nguyen Tat Tan and later took the Chinese name by which he became widely known. He was referred to both in Vietnam and abroad as President (or General) Ho. Although Vietnamese names should always be alphabetized as shown above, a cross-reference from the more familiar part of the name may be inserted for the benefit of readers unfamiliar with the Vietnamese custom.

18.118 *Indian names.* Modern Indian names, of whatever ethnic and linguistic origin, generally appear with the family name last, and this is the name used in indexing. As in other countries, the personal preference of the individual as well as national usage should be observed:

> Nehru, Jawaharlal   Narayan, R. K.
> Gandhi, Mohandas Karamchand   Bhattacharya, Bhabhani

18.119 *Burmese names.* Family names are not used in Burma. The name by which a person is known is a given name, of one or two elements, preceded by a term of respect (*U* is the commonest), or a title, used in alphabetic listing:

> Nu, U   Po Lat, U
> Thant, U   Than Tun, Dr.

18.120 *Javanese and other Indonesian names.* Indonesians of Javan origin use only a personal name, family names being nonexistent in Java:

> Suharto
> Sukarno

In other parts of Indonesia family names often exist, although the personal name may still be the one to use in indexing. Also, an additional name may be taken by a person (for Muslims of strong religious bent, often an Arabic name). And Indonesians resident in the West may adopt an additional name simply to conform to local custom. Except for Javanese names of the type described above, an indexer should seek expert help in dealing with Indonesian names.

18.121 *Thai names.* Family names are used in Thailand, but the person is normally known by, and addressed by, the personal name. (In Thai order, the personal name precedes the family name.) The personal name is usually used in alphabetizing, but practice varies among students of Thai culture, as shown by the following examples, from the index to the distinguished *Journal of Siamese Studies*:

Sut Saengwichian	Songsaengchan, Suphat
Damrong Rachanuphap, Prince	Thong-Urai, Prachap

18.122 *Other Asian names.* Throughout Asia, many names derive from the European languages and from Arabic, Chinese, and other, less widely known, languages, regardless of the places of birth of the persons bearing the names. And in some places, such as the Philippines, names follow a strictly Western order and the Western custom of giving precedence to the family name, although the names themselves are derived from local languages and cultures. In many parts of the Orient, also, names denoting status (like the Indian castes) and titles often form part of the name as it appears in written work, and must be dealt with appropriately. In all these instances an indexer's problems are best solved by querying the author whenever the more dependable rules of standard reference works do not answer a specific question.

PLACE NAMES

18.123 *Geographic names.* Geographic proper names beginning with *Mount, Lake, Cape, Sea,* and the like, which actually refer to the names of mountains, lakes, capes, and seas should be alphabetized according to the rest of the name following this element:

Everest, Mount	Mendocino, Cape
Japan, Sea of	Titicaca, Lake

If, however, this first element is thought of as part of the complete name, the name should be alphabetized according to the first element:

Cape of Good Hope
Lake of the Woods

Names of cities or towns beginning with these same elements should be alphabetized according to the first element:

Cape Girardeau, Mo.	Mount Vernon, N.Y.
Lake Forest, Ill.	Sea Girt, N.J.

549

18.124   *Names beginning with articles.* Names beginning with non-English articles are usually alphabetized under the article:

El Dorado	Le Bourget
El Ferrol	Le Havre
El Paso	Les Eyzies
La Coruña	Los Angeles
La Crosse	Los Michis
LaPorte	's Gravenhage

Names beginning with *the* are alphabetized under the principal element:

Dalles, the
Hague, The
Lizard, the

18.125   *Names with "Saint."* Place names beginning with the appellation *Saint* or *Sainte* (*St.* or *Ste*) should be recorded in the index as spelled in the text (Press preference is for the spelled-out form for most such names). The name is alphabetized as though the word were spelled out in full whether or not it actually is in text and index. Note that in French place names the saint's name is invariably hyphenated:

Ile Saint-Louis
rue Saint-Honoré
Saint-Cloud

EDITING AN INDEX COMPILED BY SOMEONE ELSE

18.126   Copyediting a well-prepared index can be a minor pleasure, an ill-prepared one, a major nightmare. You cannot, as editor, remake a really bad index yourself. You can often make minor repairs, as noted below, and you can usually impose some typographical and logical consistency, but you cannot turn a sow's ear of an index into a silk purse. If an index is so bad that even after improvement it cannot be used, you have two choices: leave it out of the book or have a new one made by a professional indexer—and thereby delay production by some significant increment of days or weeks. (One of the authors of this manual once received an index for a 128-page book on ancient Egypt that included a heading "Nile, River," followed by 89 unanalyzed page references. In this instance the latter course was taken.)

18.127   The following suggestions for editing an index are based on the experience of University of Chicago Press editors, augmented by a checklist that editors at a sister university press shared with us.

COPYEDITING TASKS

18.128 Copyediting (apart from markup) should include the following:

1. Check principal headings for strict alphabetical order.

2. Check the spelling of each heading, using your copy of the page proofs as necessary.

3. Check punctuation for proper style and underline any end-of-line hyphens that should be set.

4. Check cross-references to make sure they go somewhere and that headings are identical. Make sure that they are needed: if only a few page references are involved, add these to the original heading and delete the cross-reference. Also see that their placement within the entries is consistent.

5. Check the reasonableness of page numbers (no "12122" or "193–93"), and make sure that sequences of page references are in ascending order.

6. Check subentries for consistency of order, whether alphabetical, chronological, or other; if "mentioned" or some other such device is used, make sure that the use is consistent.

7. If some entries seem overanalyzed (many subentries with only one page reference each), try to combine some of them, and if subheadings are longer and more elaborate than necessary, try to simplify them.

8. If "false" sub-subentries appear, correct them by adding appropriate repeated subheadings or by using em dashes. (For the latter procedure you will probably have to retype parts of the copy.)

9. If necessary, delete any trivial entries that you recognize from your own work on the book, such as references to place or personal names used only as examples of something. (Be careful here. This can be dangerous. It can also involve you in a great deal more work than you bargained for.)

MARKUP

18.129 Marking up an index manuscript for typesetting should include the following:

1. Identify the job for the typesetter by author and title at the top of the first page—or by whatever device you have been using for earlier parts of the book—and indicate what page the index begins on (if you know).

2. Mark type specifications at the top of the first page of the copy. If setting is to be ragged right, indicate the maximum allowable end-of-line space.

3. Mark en dashes on continued numbers for the first few lines of copy (if that is your style), and write a note to the typesetter asking for this style throughout.

4. Mark copy for blank lines between alphabetic sections of the index (e.g., between the *A*'s and the *B*'s).

5. Make sure all pages are numbered and in order before sending them off for setting.

TYPOGRAPHICAL CONSIDERATIONS

GENERAL PRINCIPLES

18.130 *Type size and column.* Indexes are usually set in smaller-sized type than the body of a book, often two sizes smaller. That is, if the body copy is set in 10-on-11-point type and the extracts, bibliographies, and appendixes in 9 on 10, the index would probably be set in 8 on 9. Usually, too, indexes are set in two columns; if the type page is 27 picas wide, the index columns are 13 picas wide, with a 1-pica space between. In large-format books, however, the index is often set in three columns or even four.

18.131 *Justification.* Body copy for most books is set in a *justified* column; that is, the right side of the column is straight and even, just like the left. This effect is achieved by varying the amount of space between words to make all lines the same length. The shorter the lines the more awkward this is to do, and in a narrow index column the result is sometimes ludicrous. So it is increasingly the practice to set index columns *ragged right* (see the text examples in this chapter and the index to this book). This is not only better looking (according to many typographers) than a narrow justified column but is easier to set and to correct in proof (see 19.27).

18.132 *Indention.* The distinction between the indented and run-in styles of setting subentries was noted above (18.13). If the indented style is adopted, and if there are sub-subentries (perhaps even sub-sub-subentries), the editor or designer should figure maximum indentions before marking up copy for the typesetter. Subentries might be indented 1 em, sub-subentries 2 ems, sub-sub-subentries 3 ems, and runover lines 4 ems. This may mean, however, that the runover lines are too short for efficient setting and that something else must be done. Indentions could be reduced to 1 en (also called *nut space*), 1 em, 1½ ems, and 2 ems, or the index set in two columns instead of three, or the sub-sub-subentries run into the sub-subentries. Whatever the solution, the point is that problems like this should be solved before any type is set.

18.133   *Bad breaks.* What cannot be solved before setting type are the problems connected with page and column breaks. A line consisting of only one or two page numbers should not be left at the top of a column, for example. A single line at the end of an alphabetic section (followed by a blank line) should not head a column, nor should a single line at the beginning of an alphabetic section be allowed to stand at the foot of a column. Blemishes like these (called *bad breaks* by editors and typesetters) are eliminated by transposing lines from one column to another, by adding to the white space between alphabetic sections, and sometimes by lengthening or shortening all columns on facing pages by one line. Another kind of bad break is more easily corrected. In a long index, it often happens that an entry breaks in the middle at the foot of the last column on a right-hand page. Then the first column on the following (left-hand) page begins with the indented part of the entry, a confusing situation for the reader. This is corrected by repeating the main heading above the carried-over part of the entry followed by the word *continued* in parentheses:

Ingestive behavior, 65–71
    definition of, 13, 15
    in dog, 93–94
    in hydra, 20–21
    and manipulative ability, 61
    metabolic processes cause stimulation of, 71

Ingestive behavior (*continued*)
    network of causes underlying, 68
    physiology of, 69–70, 86–87
    in rat, 100
    in sheep, 22
    in starfish, 45, 52–62

18.134   *Special typography.* An index to a complicated book can often be simplified if special typography is used to differentiate headings, references, or both. If, for example, two kinds of personal names need to be distinguished in an index—perhaps authors and literary characters—one or the other might be set in caps and small caps. Page references to illustrations might be in italic and references to the principal treatment of a subject in boldface. Before settling on such a system, however, the author or editor should confer with a representative of the typesetter to make sure the scheme is practicable. One must also remember to provide a key to the significance of the different kinds of type at the head of the index (as in examples *B, C,* and *E*).

EXAMPLES

18.135   *Example A.* A typical scholarly index for a long (450-page) study of Soviet industrialization. Note the alphabetization of the run-in subentries. Note also what are essentially run-in sub-subentries under "Annual plans: functioning of." This can occasionally be done without confusion if the sub-subentries are all identical in construction (here, "for such-and-such year") and attach themselves obviously to the preceding subentry. In most circumstances, sub-subentries are possible only in an indented-style index, such as example *C*, or by using em dashes, as in example *D*.

A. An Extensive Scholarly Index

Agriculture, 6, 7, 35, 176, 308–58; during *All-out Drive*, 83–85, 96–97, 139; investment in, 84–85, 137, 191, 192, 238, 304; labor in, 310–12, 320, 384–86; during NEP, 41–42; during *Post-Stalin*, 329, 432–33; and price system, 287–88, 293; during *Purge Era*, 177, 195–98; during *Stalin Has Everything His Way*, 238, 239, 241–42, 309–10, 343–44; during *Three "Good" Years*, 139–42, 156–58, 176; during *Warming-up*, 55–56. *See also* Acreages, sown; Animal products; Crop production; Farm output; Farm products; Kolkhozy; Livestock; Peasants; Sovkhozy; *and names of individual commodities*

"All-citizen statistical ration," 282, 384, 410

Annual plans: functioning of, 27, 125–26; for 1931, 73, 77–79, 120; for 1932 and 1933, 120–21; for 1935 and 1936, 129–32; for 1937, 184–85; for 1947, 254–56; targets of, 120, 130–32, 183. *See also* Control figures

Arden Conference, 178 n

18.136   *Example B*. Index in run-in style for a book on animal behavior, showing the use of references in boldface and italic type to distinguish illustrative material.

B. Index Employing Boldface and Italic References

References to drawings are printed in boldface type. Numbers in italics refer to the photographic inserts; the first number is that of the location of the insert, the second that of the page in the insert

Goose: allelomimetic behavior of, **18**; imprinting in, 178, *148–2*
Grasshopper population fluctuations, 216
Gravity as related to tactile sense, 34
Ground squirrel. *See* Prairie dog
Group formation, 160–61
Growth curve, 224–26, **225**
Growth of populations, 224–32, *212–2*
Guinea pig: female sexual behavior of, 80–81; limited motor capacity of, 32–33; male sexual behavior of, 81–82
Gull: nesting territories of, 222; primary stimulus in, 142
Gynandromorph, behavior of, 126
Habitat selection in deermouse, 243–44, **243**

Habit formation, 98; decreases variability, 156; makes behavior consistent, 122; in organization of behavior, 150; versus variability, 108
Habrobracon, behavior of gynandromorphs of, 126
Hand-rearing, effects of, 113–15, 235–36; of chimpanzees, 197–98; of sheep, 24
Hands of vertebrates, 46–47
Hardy's law, 240–41; conditions seldom met in natural populations, 249; and human populations, 251
Harvard University Laboratory of Social Relations, 105

18.137   *Example C*. Index in indented style for a book on astronomy. Note the use of sub-subentries, as well as the use of italic type for references to pages upon which definitions occur (the index is called "Index to Subjects and Definitions").

C. Index in Indented Style

Page numbers for definitions are in italics

Brightness temperatures, 388, 582, 589, 602
Bright rims, 7, 16, 27–28. *See also* Nebular forms
B stars, 3, 7, 26–27, 647
Bulbs (in nebulae). *See* Nebular forms

Cameras, electronic, 492, 499
Carbon flash, 559
Cassiopeia A (3C461). *See* Radio sources; Supernovae
Catalogs
  of bright nebulae, 74
  of dark nebulae, 74, 120
    Lundmark, 121
    Lynds, 123
    Schoenberg, 123
  Herschel's (of nebulae), 119
  of planetary nebulae, 484–85, 563

Perek-Kohoutek, 484, 563
  Vorontsov-Velyaminov, 484
  of reflection nebulae, 74
  3C catalog of radio sources, revised, 630
Central stars. *See* Planetary nebulae
Cerenkov radiation, 668, 709
Chemical composition, 71. *See also* Abundances; *names of individual elements*
  of stars and nebulae, 405
Clark effect, *756, 758,* 765
Clouds. *See* Interstellar clouds
Cluster diameters, 170, 218
  angular, 184
  apparent, 167, 168
Cluster distances, 167, 168, 171, 173, 174, 215–16
Clusters, 172–73, 181–82
  absolute magnitudes, 181

18.138   *Example D.* The use of 1-em dashes before subentries in this index represents a compromise between indented and run-in styles. Each subentry under "Armor and weapons" starts a new line, but sub-sub-entries are run in, so the indention is no more than that for a normal run-in index such as example *A* or *B*, above. This style is most satisfactory for an index in which a few entries require rather elaborate breakdown, the rest being simple entries.

D. Use of the Dash

Argos: cremation at, 302; and Danaos of Egypt, 108; Middle Helladic, 77; Mycenaean town, 204, 233, 270, 309; painted tomb at, 205, 299; shaft graves at, 84
Arkadia, 4; Early Helladic, 26, 40; Mycenaean, 269, 306
Armor and weapons. *See also* Frescoes, battle; Metals and metal-working
—attack weapons (general): Early Helladic and Cycladic, 33; Mycenaean, 225, 255, 258–60; from shaft graves, 89, 98–100; from tholos tombs, 128, 131, 133
—body armor: cuirass, 135–36, 147, 152, 244, 258, 260, 311; greaves, 135, 179, 260; helmets, 101, 135, 147, 221, 243, 258

—bow and arrow, 14, 99, 101, 166, 276
—daggers, 33, 98, 255, 260
—shields, 98–99, 135, 147, 221, 260
—sling, 14, 101, 260
—spears and javelins, 33, 195, 210, 260
—swords: in Crete, 147; cut-and-thrust, 228, 278; Middle Helladic, 73; Mycenaean, 175, 255, 260, 279; from shaft graves, 98; from tholos tombs, 128, 131, 133, 135
Arne. *See* Gla
Asine: Early Helladic, 29, 36; Middle Helladic, 74; Mycenaean town and trade, 233, 258, 263; seals from, 38; shrine at, 166, 284–88; tombs at, 300

18.139   *Examples E, F, and G.* The first example, from a beautifully edited anthology, *Poetry of the English Renaissance, 1509–1660,* edited by J. William Hebel and Hoyt H. Hudson, combines indexes of authors, titles, and first lines. Such a combination, probably easiest of all on the reader, is less usual for an anthology than separate indexes—one of authors and titles, set narrow measure, and another of first lines, set wide measure, with leaders (examples *F* and *G*).

E. THREE TYPES OF ENTRIES COMBINED

Author's names are printed in CAPITALS, *titles of poems in italics, and first lines of poems in ordinary* roman *type*

Come, my way, my truth, my life, 743
Come over the bourn, Bessy, 408
Come, pass about the bowl to me, 872
Come sleep! O sleep, the certain knot of peace, 112
Come, sons of summer, by whose toil, 665
Come, spur away, 693
Come then, and like two doves with silv'ry wings, 647
Come, we shepherds whose blest sight, 768
Come, worthy Greek, Ulysses, come, 280
Come, you whose loves are dead, 394
Coming homeward out of Spain, 73
Commendation of her beauty, stature, behavior, and wit, 208
Compare me to the child that plays with fire, 224
Comparison of the sonnet and the epigram, 521

Complaint of a lover rebuked, 29
Complain we may, much is amiss, 47
Confined love, 463
Conscience, 739
CONSTABLE, HENRY, 229
Content, not cates, 661
COOPER, ROBERT, 42
Cooper's Hill, 844
CORBET, RICHARD, BISHOP OF OXFORD AND NORWICH, 633
Coridon and Melampus' song, 386
Corinna's going a-maying, 654
CORNISH, WILLIAM, 42
Corpse, clad with carefulness, 80
Corydon, arise my Corydon, 199
Could not once blinding me, cruel, suffice, 766
Country men of England, 426
Courage, my soul! now learn to wield, 859
COWLEY, ABRAHAM, 829
CRAIG, ALEXANDER, 228
CRASHAW, RICHARD, 758, 1025

F. AUTHOR-TITLE INDEX

McCord, David, 27, 51, 130
MacLeish, Archibald, 55, 62, 180
Man Is But a Castaway, 125
Man Said to the Universe, A, 139
Martial, 119
Masefield, John, 136
Masked Shrew, The, 105
Master, The, 185
Masters, Edgar Lee, 166
Mathematics or the Gift of Tongues, 72
Melville, Herman, 128
Men Say They Know Many Things, 124

Message from Home, 99
Metropolitan Nightmare, 115
Millay, Edna St. Vincent, 75, 133
Moore, Marianne, 67, 84, 147
Moss, Howard, 181
Motion of the Earth, The, 38
My Father's Watch, 24

Naked World, The, 69
Nash, Ogden, 120
Newton, 158
New York—December, 1931, 149
Nicholl, Louise Townsend, 26, 36, 52, 142

Nicholson, Norman, 38
Non Amo Te, 119
No Single Thing Abides, 9
Numbers and Faces, 91

Ode to the Hayden Planetarium, 29
Once a Child, 21
Our Little Kinsmen, 107

Physical Geography, 52
Plane Geometry, 87
Pleiades, The, 31
Point, The, 89
Pope, Alexander, 121, 157
Prelude, The; Book VI, 85
Princess, The, 33
Progress, 130

G. INDEX OF FIRST LINES

God sends his teachers unto every age 388
Good-bye, my Fancy 474
Good-bye, proud world! I'm going home 309
Gusty and raw was the morning 436
Hark! hark! the bugle's lofty sound 75
Has there any old fellow got mixed with the boys? 385

557

Part 3

Production and Printing

19 *Design and Typography*

Preliminary Planning 19.3
    Castoff 19.6
Prose Texts 19.10
    Typeface 19.10
      Alphabets 19.11
      Characteristics 19.13
    Type Page 19.16
      Width 19.17
      Length 19.19
    Spacing 19.20
      Between words 19.21
      Between letters 19.22
      Between lines 19.23
    Justification 19.26
    Subheads 19.28
    Extracts 19.31
      Reduced type 19.32
      Indention 19.33
    Notes 19.34
      Type size 19.35
      Space 19.37
      Hairline rules 19.38
      Continued notes 19.39
      Note numbers 19.40
      Paragraphing 19.41
    Indexes 19.42
Display Type 19.45
    Preliminaries 19.47
    Chapter Openings 19.52
    Running Heads 19.59
    Folios 19.60
Text Other than Prose 19.61
    Verse 19.61
    Plays 19.64
      Cast of characters 19.64
      Act and scene numbers 19.65
      Speakers' names 19.66
      Stage directions 19.67
      Line numbers 19.68
Layout 19.69
    Sample Layouts and Marked Manuscript 19.72
For Further Reference 19.73

19.1   The purposes of a chapter on design and typography in this manual are two. First, it is intended to give editors some basic facts about bookmaking so that they may work more knowledgeably with professional designers, production personnel, and typesetters. Second, it aims to give helpful suggestions to those editors, copywriters, and others who must plan the design and typography of a book, pamphlet, or brochure without the guidance of an expert. It is *not* intended to serve the needs of professional designers, typographers, or production people. For these reasons it deals only with the bare essentials of designing a book.

19.2   The design of a book ideally complements and enhances the subject of the book. A textbook usually requires a complex design (not to be undertaken by an amateur), a scholarly monograph a less complex design but one that will accommodate notes, bibliographies, glossaries, and other aspects of scholarly communication.

PRELIMINARY PLANNING

19.3   At the initial stage of planning a design the editor who has acquired the book can greatly assist the designer by explaining the nature of the work and the audience for whom it is intended. This editor should also stipulate the placement of notes, the kind and number of illustrations to be included, the number of tables, graphs, or charts, how many levels of subheads are necessary, what the running heads will consist of, what material is to be in the preliminary pages and what in the back matter, and any other special problems peculiar to the work. Many publishing houses, the University of Chicago Press among them, provide the acquisitions editor with a printed transmittal sheet upon which to list such information (see fig. 19.1);[1] the sheet goes with a copy of the manuscript to the production and design department. Such fact sheets are often not enough, however, and subsequent conferences between designer and editor are necessary.

19.4   Before designing a book, the designer must know not only the nature of the subject and the contents of the book but also its length. The editor's rough estimate of the number of words is not usually enough, nor is the number of manuscript pages. The designer must have an accurate *castoff* (or *character count*), prepared by the production department (in some publishing houses by the editor), giving the number of characters in (*a*) text, (*b*) extracts, (*c*) footnotes or endnotes, (*d*) appendixes, glossary, bibliography, etc. Physical size as well as the

---

1. Not to be confused with the transmittal sheet that later accompanies the edited manuscript to the production department and the typesetter (see fig. 2.3).

nature of the book will determine the width and length of the type page and the typeface, type size, and leading between lines to be specified.

19.5   It should be emphasized that the manuscript used by the designer should be *final* (at least so far as the title and the number and nature of

---

Book Transmittal

Date:
Acquisitions editor:

Author
Editor / Translator
Full title

General: Author's background and our reasons for publishing book:

Checklist	Herewith To come	**Contract**
	[x] [date]	Contract no.: Series: Series contract no.:
Half title		☐ Book represents all new work by one or more authors under contract to us.
Series title		☐ Category of book as follows:
Title page		
Copyright page . . .		**Manuscript Editing**
Dedication		Manuscript and proof to:
Epigraph		
Contents		Index to be done by:
List of illustrations		
List of tables		**Rights and Permissions**
Foreword		☐ We have world rights, all languages, all editions. ☐ Rights specified below
Preface		☐ Author(s), editor(s), translator(s) citizens of U.S. ☐ Specifics below
Acknowledgments .		☐ No permissions needed ☐ Permissions in, free to Press ☐ Details below
Introduction		
Complete text		**Design and Production**
Notes		☐ Duplicate MS attached No. words: If reprint, no. pages:
Appendix(es)		No. line drawings: No. maps: No. photos:
Glossary		☐ All straight composition ☐ Special sorts (see below) No. tables:
Bibliography . . .		☐ Standard trim size OK ☐ Special trim (see below) ☐ Offprints needed
Index . . .		Proposed del. date: Proposed print run: Bind (cloth/paper):
All illustrations		
Tables		**Marketing**
		Publishing season: Subject codes:
		Proposed price and discount— Cloth: Paper:

Remarks/Explanations

Fig. 19.1. Transmittal form to be filled in by the acquisitions editor and sent with a copy of the manuscript to the design and production department. A machine copy of the completed form goes to the manuscript editor with the copy to be edited.

the parts are concerned) and *complete* in all essentials. In some publishing houses it is the practice to complete the editing phase of preparation before turning the manuscript over for design. In others (including Chicago), to save time, the book is designed from a second copy of the manuscript while the master copy is being edited. If the latter system is used, the editor should quickly inform the designer of any editorial changes affecting the design of the book, such as the addition of a subtitle to the book title or an increase in the number of levels of subheadings.

CASTOFF

19.6 The most accurate way to estimate the exact length of a printed work from a typewritten manuscript is to count each *character,* meaning each letter, mark of punctuation, and space between words. With heavily edited material this may be the only way. The less time-consuming and more usual way is to count (*a*) the characters in an average line of the manuscript and (*b*) the number of lines, and then to multiply *a* by *b*. If different typewriters have been used in preparing the manuscript—one with elite type, another with pica, for example—the number of characters per line will of course also be different. A separate estimate should then be made for each type size in the manuscript and the results added together for the total number of characters.

19.7 Estimating the length of a manuscript prepared on a word processor may be simpler. Many word processors use systems able to count and record (*capture*) the characters in a "manuscript," thus providing a quick and accurate estimate of length. Such information should be furnished by the acquisitions editor along with a paper printout (*hard copy*) for the designer's use.

19.8 The designer needs, however, not just a total character count of the work but a count broken down by kinds of material in it. Each kind of material will be set in its own specified type size, in part determined by the amount of material in a given category. For material such as notes, bibliographies, and glossaries, where each item begins a new line, the number of lines, including runover lines, is often more helpful than a character count. A typical character count might read as follows:

	CHARACTERS	NUMBER OF LINES
Text	700,000	. . . .
Extracts	50,000	. . . .
Appendix	85,000	. . . .
Bibliography	. . . .	240

The number and any peculiarities of size of tables and illustrations should be included with the character count, although characters in tables and legends need not be counted.

19.9　The designer, with the manuscript and its character count in hand, will decide upon the typeface, the type sizes for each category, and the size of the type page, and will thus be able to determine how many characters of each type size will fit on a single printed page. Dividing the figures in the character count by the relevant number of characters per printed page will give an accurate estimate of the length of the finished book.

PROSE TEXTS

TYPEFACE

19.10　Which typeface and what sizes of type to use for text, notes, and other apparatus in a given book are perhaps a designer's most important decisions. These decisions rest partly on suitability of type to subject and partly on which typesetting process is to be used and the availability of particular typefaces in that process. Among questions to be considered are: Is the text peppered with foreign words requiring a variety of diacritical marks? Is it highly technical, containing mathematics or other material requiring symbols? In the field of mathematics, for example, only a few typefaces are available with all the necessary characters (Times Roman is perhaps the most widely available).

19.11　*Alphabets.* The usual font (all the type characters of one face and size, i.e., a complete *set* of all the characters) contains five alphabets: roman capitals, roman lowercase letters, italic capitals, italic lowercase letters, and small capitals. Some works, however, require seven alphabets, the additions being boldface capital and lowercase letters. For these works a typeface—such as Times Roman or Baskerville—with a related boldface in the appropriate sizes must be chosen.

19.12　Authors and editors will aid the bookmaking process, both economically and aesthetically, by avoiding wherever possible the use of boldface letters or other characters not commonly found in a five-alphabet font. It is not necessary, for example, to introduce boldface numerals in bibliographies or reference lists, or in section numbers or subheadings in the text. Where boldface numbers have a real function to perform—as in this manual, where they aid in indexing and cross-referencing—they may well be specified, but only after checking with the typesetter as to the feasibility and cost of adding them to the font.

19.13   *Characteristics*. The previous edition of this manual illustrated various typefaces by showing ten different specimens, all of them either Linotype or Monotype faces. With the advent of photomechanical and then electronic (CRT) composition, specimen typefaces can no longer serve a similar purpose because no one of them would be universally applicable. For example, this edition of the manual is composed electronically in Times Roman. The same typeface produced by a different typesetting system, though generally similar in appearance, will vary in many minor details.

19.14   Also, the measurement of characters per pica in a given typeface and type size is no longer a fixed number. In film setting, the "set"—i.e., how close together the characters appear—can range from moderately loose or *maximum* through standard or *optimum* to very tight or *minimum* (where the letters can actually touch each other).[2] The typesetting operation determining the set is called the *track*—one-track, two-track, three-track:

> Literature is the written expression of those who believe they have something to say that is worth recording and

> Literature is the written expression of those who believe they have something to say that is worth recording and reading by

> Literature is the written expression of those who believe they have something to say that is worth recording and reading by others. It has

19.15   Some of the typefaces most commonly available and widely used for bookwork today are Baskerville, Bembo, Garamond, Janson, Palatino, and Times Roman. The general contours of these faces, and usually the names, are the same as those of their metal counterparts of the previous generation; but, because of the many variations in the current versions of these typefaces, the amateur designer should consult the typesetter who is to produce the work before making a final decision on which typeface to use.

TYPE PAGE

19.16   The type page, also called *text page* or *text area,* is measured in picas. It includes the space occupied by the running head, text column, side heads (if any), footnotes (if any), and page number (or folio). In addition to the dimensions of the type page in picas, the number of text lines in a full page and in a chapter-opening page are commonly specified. *Trim size,* measured in inches, refers to the size of the whole page, including all margins.

2. The standard set is the one normally used for castoff and estimate when counting characters per pica.

19.17   *Width.* As a rule, text matter intended for continuous reading (as opposed to reference material) should be set in lines neither too wide nor too narrow for comfortable reading. Ideally the line should accommodate 65 to 70 characters. Depending upon the size of type chosen, this means a line 22 to 27 picas wide.

19.18   In addition to reference materials, such as dictionaries, various other kinds of books are more economically set in double columns—books of readings, lengthy proceedings, and the like. A double-column format will accommodate considerably more words per page. First, the text page may be wider than is practical for a single column. Second, the shorter reading line in a double-column format permits the use of smaller type and less leading, without impairing readability, than does a typical one-column line. The width of the type page in a double-column format will include the space necessary between the two columns, usually 1 pica. Thus, if the type page is 31 picas wide, each column will be 15 picas wide.

19.19   *Length.* The length of the type page is determined not so much by readability as by conventional relationships between width and length. Margins set off and enhance the type area in much the same way as does the mount for a drawing or picture. There should, generally speaking, be more margin at the bottom of a page than at the top to avoid the appearance of type falling off the page. The inner margins should be narrower than the outer margins, as a double-page spread is the entity and not two single pages. An old formula for the proportions of the four margins is 1½, 2, 3, 4 (inside, head, outside, bottom), but many well-designed books depart widely from this and other formulas.

SPACING

19.20   The following remarks apply to space between words, between letters, and between lines in the text.[3]

19.21   *Between words.* Spacing between printed words is partly a matter of the mechanics of composition. "Normal" word spacing is generally about one-third of an em. But when lines of type are justified—each line the same length (19.26)—spacing between words will vary slightly from line to line, though all word spacing in a single line should be the same. A line with narrow spacing is called a *close* line, one with wide spacing an *open* line. Excessively wide spacing detracts from readability, is unsightly, and is thus to be avoided. Also, a number of successive open lines may produce the printing phenomenon called a *river*—white spaces meandering vertically down the page and distract-

3. For vertical spacing with display type see 19.52 and sample layouts.

ing the eye of the reader. Modern composition methods in general, therefore, aim for close word spacing.[4]

19.22   *Between letters.* In display matter (title pages, chapter headings, etc.) and in anything set in full caps or caps and small caps, *letterspacing*—additional space between letters—is often specified by the designer. For subheads in the text the amount of space is likely to be standard; but for large display lines the designer may ask for *optical,* or *visual,* spacing. This means that the typesetter is to insert varying amounts of space between letters, depending upon their form: more, for example, between N and E, less (or none) between L and A. Except where so specified, letterspacing should be avoided by the compositor. All letters within words of a given typeface should be separated from each other by the same amount of space (but see 19.14). Authors and editors should be aware, however, that some combinations of letters, particularly in the italic alphabets, give the illusion of more space between them.[5]

19.23   *Between lines.* The space between lines of type is called *leading,* or *leads,* because originally in hand or Monotype composition it was created by strips of lead inserted between lines of type. To make more space between lines of text is to *lead it,* or to *lead it out.* To *close up* lines—less space between them—is to *delete leads.* Leading is measured in *points* and is always specified by a designer for each type size used in a book.[6] Where increased leading is necessary—before and after extracts, for example—the number of points is usually also specified. If extra leading is used to mark the divisions between sections, the words *blank line* circled in the margin or in the space itself will tell the compositor to insert space equivalent to one full line of type. A space mark (#) is usually sufficient to indicate extra space between alphabetic sections in indexes.

19.24   To determine an appropriate amount of leading requires consideration of a number of factors. The first of these, for text matter at any rate, is readability, and this is largely dependent upon the type measurements. The larger the type size, the more leading is required to prevent the eye from being distracted by the lines above and below the one being read. Also, the wider the line of type, the greater the leading needed, because the eye in moving from the end of one line to the beginning of the next takes a long jump, and in closely set material the

---

4. For word spacing in unjustified material see 19.27.
5. Garamond gives good examples of this.
6. If 2 points of leading are wanted between lines of a 10-point typeface, the usual designation is *10 on 12,* which in hot-metal composition meant a 10-point type letter cast on a 12-point body. The same designation is used for modern typesetting methods even though letters consist of film matrices or electronic impulses rather than blocks of metal.

eye may easily jump to the wrong line. Another factor often considered is economy. Use of a relatively small type size and reduced leading allows more words per page, making a thinner book and cutting costs of paper, mailing (weight), and so forth, although the cost of composition remains the same. The opposite of this is the desire to make a short work into a longer book. More than the usual number of points between lines will obviously result in fewer lines per page and thus more pages in the book.

19.25   The designer's ultimate concern, in specifying leading as in every other aspect of planning a book, is the nature of the material and the audience for whom it is intended.[7]

JUSTIFICATION

19.26   A column of type is conventionally rectangular, its left and right edges neatly aligned. To make a line of type, regardless of the words in it, exactly the same length as its fellows is to *justify* the line. This is still common practice in bookmaking. Since words in a language, unlike bricks in a building, are not all of the same length and since a word should not be divided at the end of a line without regard for the rules of word division, the spacing between words in justified lines cannot be exactly the same in each line. The shorter the line, the more acute the problem becomes for the compositor—or for the computer governing hyphenation and justification. In an index, for example, when an entry runs for two or more lines, the runover lines must be indented under the first line, thus making the runover line even shorter. Sometimes there is room for only two medium-sized words on a line. There may be enough space left over to accommodate another, shorter word, but the next word in the entry is too long to fit on the line and cannot be divided (*through* or *passed*, for example). A large, unsightly space must then be left between the two words to justify the line.

19.27   A solution to this problem, now not only acceptable but often desirable in bookmaking as in other kinds of printed material, is simply *not* to justify lines of type. The width of the type column is taken as the maximum. The left edge is even—that is, each line begins directly under the line above—but the right edge runs ragged (*ragged right*). Word spacing is the same in every line, and a line ends with the word falling nearest the maximum length of the type line. No word except a very long one has to be divided at the end of a line, and thus the reader is not distracted by vertical rows of hyphens. To avoid an excessively ragged look caused by one or more lines being set much

7. For examples of specifications appropriate to various kinds of material see sample layouts at the end of this chapter.

shorter than the rest, however, it is advisable to specify a *minimum* line length, usually 2 or 3 picas shorter than the maximum; thus for text set to a maximum of 24 picas, a designer might specify 22 picas as the minimum line length.

SUBHEADS

19.28   The typeface and type size used for all subheads (see 1.58–66) are ideally the same as those used for the text. Differentiation of levels is brought about by various combinations of the available five-alphabet font and by placement on the page. For example, *A*-level subheads might be set in caps and small caps (or in full caps), *B*-level in small caps, and *C*-level in italics (lowercase except the first word and proper names) at the beginning of a paragraph (often called *run-in side heads*). *A*- and *B*-level subheads may be letterspaced 1 to 3 points (see examples in 19.29 and subheads throughout this manual). *A*-level heads might be centered and *B*-level flush left, or both may be indented, say, 2 ems (or 2 picas) from the left. Space above and below each subhead should be inserted to set it off from the text.[8] A subhead should never be set at the bottom of a page with fewer than two lines following it on the page. Instead, the page should run short and the subhead should be set at the top of the following page. The first line of text following a subhead may begin flush left or be indented more than the usual paragraph indention.

19.29   The following examples illustrate a common design, described in 19.28, for three levels of subheads.

A-level:

NOMENCLATURE USED IN EASTERN AFRICA

B-level and text following:

BASIC ASSUMPTIONS
The first Pan-African Congress on Prehistory . . .

C- level:

The Kalomo industry. The Kalomo industry, which represents the Iron Age occupation of the Batoka Plateau . . .

19.30   In a work where the number of levels of subheads varies from chapter to chapter—for example, three levels in some chapters and only one or two in others—the designer will specify the type sizes and placement for all three levels but may suggest use of *B*-

8. Such spacing should be so specified that the subhead plus the white space above and below it exactly equals a whole number of text lines. If, for example, the text is being set on a 12-point body, a 12-point subhead might be leaded 8 points above and 4 points below. The subhead and its white space thus equal two lines of text.

level specifications for the most important level in chapters containing only one or two levels.

EXTRACTS

19.31   Extracts are commonly intended to illustrate points made in the text and are therefore considered part of the text proper.[9] They must, however, not only be identifiable as extracts but also be readable. There are various typographic ways to accomplish both purposes. Whichever method is used, extra space—at least 2 or 3 points—should be inserted both above and below each extract. The amount of space should be specified for the typesetter.

19.32   *Reduced type.* The traditional method for indicating extracts is to set them in a type size 1 point smaller than that of the text. Leading is also reduced at least 1 point. The extract is usually set to the same measure (width) as the text (except a verse extract, which is usually centered), the extra space above and the reduced type serving notice to the reader that this is quoted material. For example, if the text is set 11 on 13, the extracts may be set 10 on 12, or 10 on 11. Modern computer-assisted typesetting methods permit changing type size and leading while setting text, thus avoiding the extra expense of setting different sizes separately as older methods required.

19.33   *Indention.* An alternative way of indicating extracts is to set them in the same type size as the text but indented at least two picas from the left. They may also be indented from both left and right. The width of the type page and the length and number of the extracts are considerations here. The smaller the type page, the less feasible indention from both sides becomes.

NOTES

19.34   Notes documenting a text are now more commonly put in a section at the back of a book, although footnotes—notes at the bottom of the page—are still a fact of scholarly life. Where notes are to be placed in a given book is usually a decision to be made by the editor, with the author's consent; it is not to be arbitrarily changed by a designer without consultation.[10]

19.35   *Type size.* Footnotes are set in type at least two sizes smaller than that of the text, but no smaller than 8-point solid.[11] In most typefaces, 8 on 9 is a good and readable size for footnotes.

9. For length and nature of quoted material, here called extracts, see chapter 10.
10. For numbering and placement of endnotes see 1.71.
11. Notes to tables and the like are often set in 6- or 7-point.

19.36   Endnotes at the back of a book or at the end of a chapter are usually set in a type size smaller than that of the text but not so small as that of footnotes. The degree of difference between text and notes is not important here, since the two kinds of printed matter do not appear on the same page.

19.37   *Space.* There must be enough space between the footnotes and the text—at least 4 points—so that they are clearly differentiated. Spacing between notes and text is not an entirely rigid matter. In the same book it may of necessity vary, say, between 4 and 6 points to accommodate the exigencies of particular pages in makeup.

19.38   *Hairline rules.* In closely set text it is sometimes desirable to insert a 3- or 5-pica hairline rule flush left above the footnotes on each page. This device is optional. When a note must continue on a following page, however, a 3-pica or full-measure hairline rule should always be inserted above the continuation.

19.39   *Continued notes.* When a footnote is continued on a following page, not only should a hairline rule be used above it but the continuation should never begin with a full sentence because readers may very well think the note has finished on the first page and miss the continuation. This is of course a problem in page makeup and can be checked by the editor or proofreader only in page proofs. The length of the page or the footnote material itself can usually be adjusted easily to avoid such breaks.

19.40   *Note numbers.* Numbers in the text referring to footnotes or endnotes are always superior figures. Traditionally, the corresponding numbers introducing each footnote or endnote were also superior numbers, a practice still followed by many designers. The University of Chicago Press prefers the more modern and more convenient practice of setting note numbers on the line, in the same type size as that of the notes, and followed by a period. The larger number makes for easier identification by the reader. (For unnumbered notes see 15.70–73.)

19.41   *Paragraphing.* The paragraphing of footnotes or endnotes should be in keeping with the design of the rest of the book. They may be set flush (like the footnotes in this manual), in regular indented paragraph style, or even sometimes in *flush-and-hang* style.

INDEXES

19.42   Indexes are usually set in two or more columns. To determine the width of a column, subtract 1 pica from the width measurement of the type page (to account for the space between the columns) and divide by 2. For example, if the type page is 24 picas wide, the index will be set in columns 11½ picas wide, with a 1-pica space between them.

19.43 Index matter is usually set in 8- or 9-point type—8 on 9 (1-point leading) being a common specification in most typefaces. Indexes are almost always set ragged right (see 19.27).

19.44 Each main entry begins flush left, and runover lines are indented—flush-and-hang style. The amount of indention for runover lines should be specified. When the index contains no indented subentries, runover lines are indented 1 em. When subentries are separated from the main entry, they are indented 1 em and all runover lines are indented 2 ems. When sub-subentries are also set on separate lines, they are indented 2 ems and all runover lines are indented 3 ems. (See also 18.130–34 and examples in 18.135–39.)

DISPLAY TYPE

19.45 *Display type* means the typefaces used for preliminary pages (half title, series title, title page, copyright, dedication, epigraph, etc.), for part and chapter titles, for running heads, and sometimes for subheads. Display type used on the title and half-title pages and for chapter titles need not be the same typeface used for the text but should be compatible with it.

19.46 Like other art forms and fashions, type styles have changed radically over the years, as the most cursory comparison of eighteenth- and twentieth-century title pages will show. A good professional designer avoids faddishness while keeping abreast of current styles and possibilities of display type to enhance the aesthetic appeal of a book, and a nonprofessional will do well to follow suit. An article in a popular magazine may look more interesting with the title run vertically or dropped into the middle of the page, but a chapter title in a serious book—never.

PRELIMINARIES

19.47 Faced with planning a title page, an untrained person is well advised to keep it simple. Each item should be set on a separate line; all should be centered or all flush left or all flush right: main title, subtitle, author's name, publisher's imprint. The title on the half-title page (p. i) is usually set in the same type style as on the title page.

19.48 Material on the copyright page is set in the same typeface as the text but in a smaller type size—usually 8- or 9-point. The copyright notice may be centered or set flush left. The CIP information (see 1.23) should be set line-for-line as it appears on the library card replica received from the Library of Congress. It may be centered on the page or set flush left to match the placement of the copyright notice, and is set in the same typeface and size as the notice.

19.49 A dedication is normally placed on a recto page by itself (see 1.28). It is usually set in the same type size as the text (if only two words, it might be a size larger), either centered or flush left or right or indented to match other display matter, and placed on the page with the same sinkage (see 19.52) as the first line of text in a chapter.

19.50 An epigraph in the prelims is, like a dedication, usually on a page by itself (see 1.29–30). It may be set in the text type, indented two picas from each side (or flush left or right), and placed on the page with the same sinkage as the chapter text.

19.51 The table of contents (for title see 19.55) is best kept simple: chapter titles flush left, page numbers flush right, all set in text type size. Where subheads are given in the contents, they are usually indented one em under the chapter title. Part titles may be set in a larger type size or in the same size and separated from the chapter titles by extra space.

CHAPTER OPENINGS

19.52 Chapter display type generally is set lower than the top of the type page. The amount of space between it and the top of the page is called *sinkage*. The amount of sinkage (in picas) is specified by the designer, and, if possible, the chapter openings should be checked in page proofs for uniformity in this matter.

19.53 Some books carry only chapter titles, but in most books chapters are also numbered. Any book that contains cross-references in the text to other chapters (like this manual) must of course have numbered chapters. The University of Chicago Press prefers arabic figures to roman numerals for chapter numbers, and the figure alone, without the word *chapter,* should be sufficient. The figure should be at least as large as the type size used for the chapter title and is often set on the line above the title.

19.54 The chapter title should be set in a type size larger than that of the text but not so large as to dwarf the reading matter below it. The designer considers the length of each chapter title in a book before choosing a typeface and type size suitable for chapter titles. If titles require more than one line, as frequently happens, the designer should specify how many characters are allowed in each line and ask the editor to mark the breaks accordingly. But note that titles (and other display type) are never justified even where text lines are so treated, and word breaks should be avoided. When titles are set in full capitals, letter-spacing will make them easier to read. In books in which each chapter is by a different author the author's name is included in the display type.

19.55 Titles or parts of the book other than chapters—preface, contents, bibliography, index, etc.—may be set in the same type size as the chapter titles, but are more often set one or two sizes smaller. In special instances a designer may choose a different type style for them. Sinkage is generally the same for them as for the chapter openings.

19.56 An epigraph at the head of a chapter may be set in italics in the same size type as the text or in roman a size smaller than the text. It should be set to a shorter measure than the text: where the chapter title is centered, the epigraph may be indented two to three ems from each side; where the chapter title is flush left, the epigraph may be indented (2–4 ems) and set ragged right (19.27). (For examples of epigraphs see 10.35.)

19.57 The beginning of the text in each chapter is also a consideration in designing chapter openings. It is usual, for example, to omit the paragraph indention, setting the first line flush left. (This is often done after subheads also.) When the first line begins flush left, the first letter may be a display initial—either a *stickup initial* or a *drop initial* (if it is a three-line drop initial, for example, the second and third lines of text will be set shorter to accommodate it). If a display initial is used, the following word or two—article and noun, single long word, prepositional phrase, etc.—are often set in small capitals.

19.58 In a work with one appendix the word *Appendix* precedes the title (if any) of the appendix, usually on a line by itself and in smaller type than the title. Where there is more than one appendix, each is given a number or a letter (Appendix A, Appendix B, etc.) and the word *Appendix* is generally retained in the display type to avoid confusion with chapters and other parts of the book.

RUNNING HEADS

19.59 Running heads must be readable at a glance and distinct from the text.[12] In choosing the type size for running heads, the designer will consider the length of all possible running heads in the particular work, with the understanding that the editor may be able to shorten the overlong ones (see 2.151). There must also be allowance for sufficient space—at least 2 picas—between the running head and the page number.

12. For selection of material to be used in running heads see 1.77–82.

FOLIOS

19.60   Page numbers (folios) in the text are commonly placed at the top of the page, left on verso pages, right on recto pages. If the typeface provides a choice, old style (O.S.) or modern (lining or aligning) figures are specified. *Drop folios* (at the foot of the page) are used on the first page of a chapter and other opening pages (appendix, index, etc.) and may be used throughout the book. (Drop folios are common in books without indexes and in reference works, like this manual, that do not use page numbers in their indexes.)

TEXT OTHER THAN PROSE

VERSE

19.61   Works such as poems and verse plays differ from prose in that the length of a line is determined by the author, not, as in prose, by the designer. The designer must try to reproduce the author's intention within a stipulated width of the printed page.

19.62   The size of type, and the width of the type page, should wherever possible accommodate the longest line—allow it to be set on one line—so that the shape of the poem on the page helps the reader to understand its rhythmic nature; if more than a few lines must be run over, the shape of the poem may be lost.

19.63   In most books of poetry the individual poems will vary one from another in the length of lines, and, generally speaking, the best way to place them on the page is to center each poem optically within the given measure of the text. Blank verse and poems characterized by a preponderance of long lines are generally not centered but given a standard indention. No hard and fast rules can be laid down here; each book must be considered with its own characteristics in mind.

PLAYS

19.64   *Cast of characters.* For the reader's convenience a list of the characters appearing in a play (often called *dramatis personae*) is frequently given before the beginning of a play. This list usually appears on a page by itself, the verso of the title page introducing the play, facing the first page of the play proper. Such a list may be arranged either in alphabetical order or in order of appearance or in order of importance. Any identifying remark about a character, if less than a sentence, follows the name and is separated from it only by a comma (if a sentence or more, it is separated from the name and set as a sentence or several sentences). Both names and remarks are commonly set in the same typeface as the text of the play, in roman or in italics.

19.65   *Act and scene numbers.* Act and scene numbers may be designed in the manner described above (19.28) for setting the first two levels of subheads in prose works. A new act does not necessarily begin on a new page, but there should be at least 12 points above and 6 points below the new act number. A new scene should have about 8 points above and 6 points below the scene number. If an act or scene ends so close to the bottom of a page that at least two lines of the following act or scene cannot be accommodated on the page, the bottom of the page should be left blank (short page) and the new division should begin on the following page. Either arabic or roman (capitals for act, lowercase for scene) may be used to designate these divisions.

19.66   *Speakers' names.* Because the name of each speaker in a play must be easily identifiable, must stand apart from the words to be spoken, names are commonly set in a manner different from that of the text—for example, in italics or in caps and small caps or all in small caps—but in the same typeface as the text. They may be placed on a separate line, either centered or flush left, where they are most easily identified. This method, of course, takes more space, and when space is a consideration, especially if speeches are short and change of speaker frequent, it is better to set the name in the left margin of the text page, followed by a colon or a period (see fig. 15.5 and example in 19.67). Speakers' names may be abbreviated to save space, but abbreviations must be consistent throughout a volume and the speaker easily identifiable by the abbreviation used (an editorial consideration).

19.67   *Stage directions.* Like the speakers' names, stage directions must also be differentiated from the text by means of the type. They are usually set in italics and enclosed in brackets (sometimes parentheses). Introductory material setting the scene is also set in italics but not enclosed in parentheses.

Scene iii. Bohemia. A desert country
near the sea

Enter Antigonus, *with the* Babe, *and a* Mariner

Ant.   Thou art perfect then, our ship hath touch'd upon
The deserts of Bohemia?

Mar.   Ay, my lord; and fear
We have landed in ill time: . . .

Ant.   . . .
There lie, and there thy character; there these,
Which may, if Fortune please, both breed thee,
pretty,
               [*Laying down the babe, with a paper and a bundle*]
And still rest thine. . . .
Well may I get aboard! This is the chase;
I am gone for ever.
                      [*Exit, pursued by a bear*]

19.68   *Line numbers.* In verse plays, especially when there are notes or other references to particular lines, it is common practice to provide line numbers for every fifth or tenth line. These numbers are usually set flush right (see fig. 15.5).

LAYOUT

19.69   A *layout* is the designer's blueprint for a book. It shows the exact size of the trimmed page and of the type page and how the display type and text matter will fit within it. Specifications for the typeface and all type sizes and measurements are written by the designer on the layout.

19.70   A normal layout will include all the preliminary pages where display type is used; a chapter opening; two facing pages showing text, with extracts, subheads, footnotes if any, and running heads and page numbers; back matter, such as a page of an appendix, notes, glossary, bibliography or reference list, and index.

19.71   From the designer's layout the editor (or a production person) will mark the manuscript for the typesetter. The layout itself should accompany the edited, marked manuscript to the typesetter. Both production department and editor are well advised to keep machine copies of the layout in the files.

SAMPLE LAYOUTS AND MARKED MANUSCRIPT

19.72   Following this chapter are six pages showing (1) a layout for a chapter opening (p. 579), (2) a page of manuscript marked by an editor from specifications provided by the designer and an uncorrected proof of the same page set in type (pp. 580–81), (3) a layout for a two-page spread of text, with extracts, subheads, footnotes, and running heads (pp. 582–83), and (4) a layout for a page of text set in two columns (p. 584).

FOR FURTHER REFERENCE

19.73   Nonprofessionals seeking further help in book design may find it in *Bookmaking,* by Marshall Lee; the older, short work by Stanley Morison, *First Principles of Typography,* in the series of Cambridge Authors' and Printers' Guides is still useful. Both books are listed in the Bibliography.

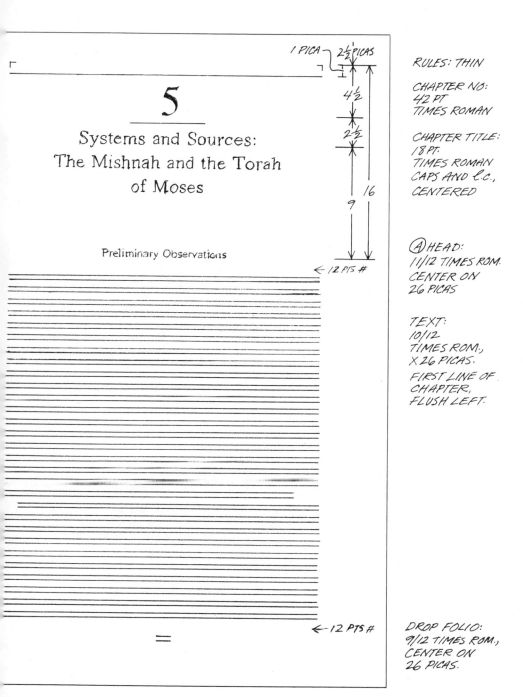

5

Systems and Sources:
The Mishnah and the Torah
of Moses

Preliminary Observations

RULES: THIN

CHAPTER NO:
42 PT
TIMES ROMAN

CHAPTER TITLE:
18 PT.
TIMES ROMAN
CAPS AND l.c.,
CENTERED

(A) HEAD:
11/12 TIMES ROM.
CENTER ON
26 PICAS

TEXT:
10/12
TIMES ROM.,
X 26 PICAS.
FIRST LINE OF
CHAPTER,
FLUSH LEFT.

DROP FOLIO:
9/12 TIMES ROM.,
CENTER ON
26 PICAS.

1 PICA — 2½ PICAS

4½

2½

16

9

← 12 PTS #

← 12 PTS #

New page·, verso or recto

Text: 10/12 Times Roman X 26

author's name Chap 5

42 Times Roman

24 Times Roman alc ctr. 3 lines

A head - 11/12 alc ctr.

flush par.

] 5 [

Chapter V

] SYSTEMS AND SOURCES: [

] The Mishnah and the Torah] of Moses [

Preliminary Observations. In the long unfolding of diverse versions of

Judaism, one form of Judaism will take up and revise materials of another

existing one, dropping some available elements, adapting others, as well

as inventing still others. But every sort of Judaism from the beginning

to the present has had to make its peace with the Scriptures universally

received as revealed by God to Moses at Mount Sinai or to the prophets,

or by the "Holy Spirit" to the historians and chroniclers, psalmists

and other writers. Insight into the modes and principles of selection

among all these candidates for authoritative and generative status

will therefore lead us far into the deepest structure and definitive

tension of a given kind of Judaism. From the formation of the Pentateuch

onward, framers of various sorts of Judaism have had to take

measure in particular of the Mosaic revelation and place themselves

in relationship to it. Each version has found it necessary to lay

claim in its own behalf to possess the sole valid interpretation of the

Torah of Moses. All have alleged that they are the necessary and logical

continuation of the revelation of Moses and the prophets. It is not

surprising, therefore, that in behalf of the Mishnah an equivalent claim

was laid down almost from the very moment of the Mishnah's completion

and closure.

The diverse versions of that claim in behalf of the Mishnah indeed

5

Systems and Sources:
The Mishnah and the Torah
of Moses

Preliminary Observations

In the long unfolding of diverse versions of Judaism, one form of Judaism will take up and revise materials of another, existing one, dropping some available elements, adapting others, as well as inventing still others. But every sort of Judaism from the beginning to the present has had to make its peace with the Scriptures universally received as revealed by God to Moses at Mount Sinai or to the prophets, or by the "Holy Spirit" to the historians and chroniclers, psalmists and other writers. Insight into the modes and principles of selection among all these candidates for authoritative and generative status will therefore lead us far into the deepest structure and definitive tension of a given kind of Judaism. From the formation of the Pentateuch onward, framers of various sorts of Judaism have had to take measure in particular of the Mosaic revelation and place themselves in relationship to it. Each version has found it necessary to lay claim in its own behalf to possess the sole valid interpretation of the Torah of Moses. All have alleged that they are the necessary and logical continuation of the revelation of Moses and the prophets. It is not surprising, therefore, that in behalf of the Mishnah an equivalent claim was laid down almost from the very moment of the Mishnah's completion and closure.

The diverse versions of that claim in behalf of the Mishnah indeed constitute one of the complex and interesting problems in the history of Judaism in the Mishnah's version both in the time in which the Mishnah was taking shape and afterward. But the analysis and historical evaluation of those efforts to lay down, in behalf of the Mishnah, a claim of the authority of revelation in the name of Moses and from the mouth of God just now need not detain us (see below, pp. 172–74). The reason is that these theological formations are post facto assertions. They are not data out of the inner history of the formation of the Mishnah itself and the unfolding of its ideas. Later

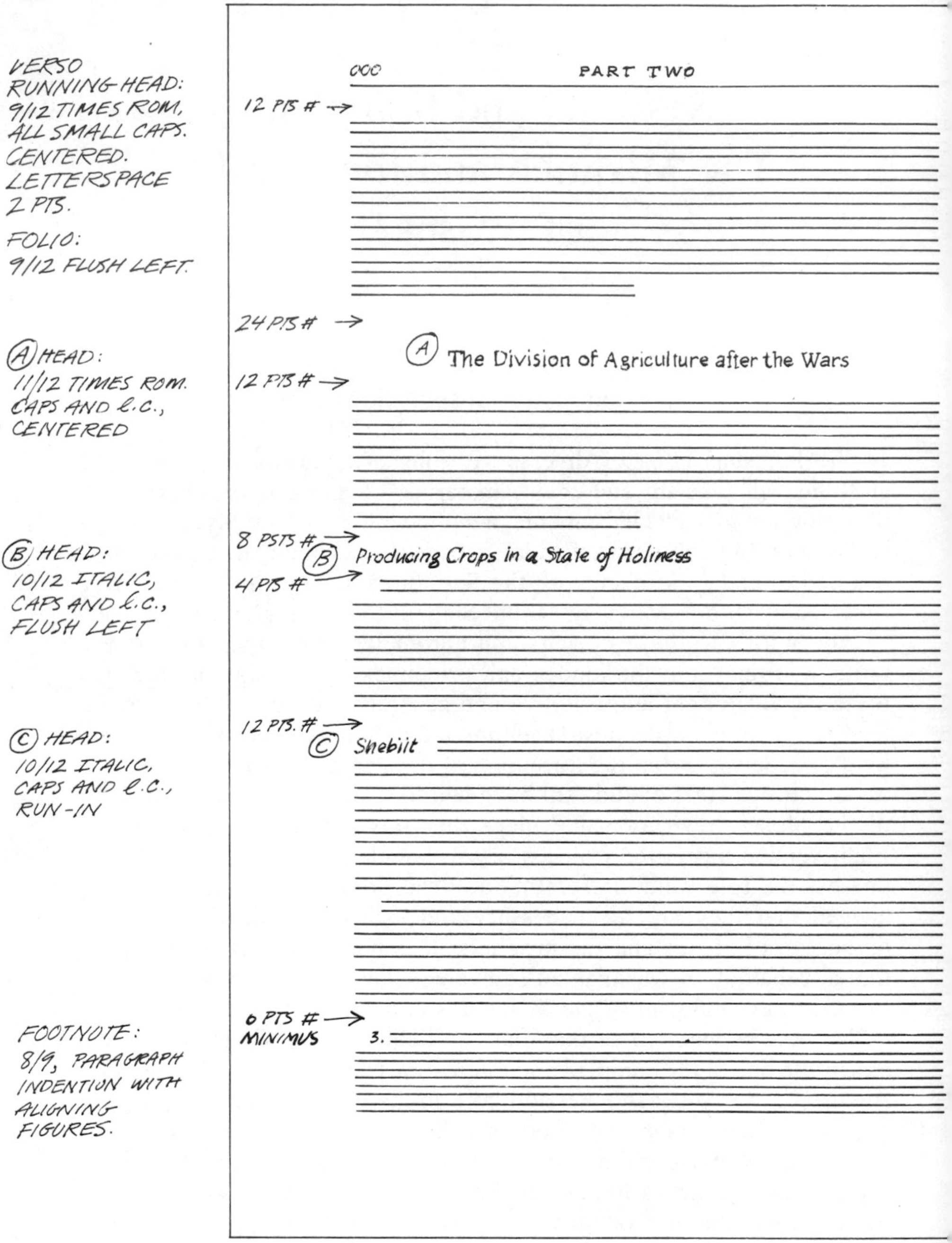

VERSO RUNNING HEAD: 9/12 TIMES ROM, ALL SMALL CAPS. CENTERED. LETTERSPACE 2 PTS.
FOLIO: 9/12 FLUSH LEFT.
000
PART TWO
12 PTS #
24 PTS #
A HEAD: 11/12 TIMES ROM. CAPS AND l.c., CENTERED
A The Division of Agriculture after the Wars
12 PTS #
8 PSTS #
B HEAD: 10/12 ITALIC, CAPS AND l.c., FLUSH LEFT
B Producing Crops in a State of Holiness
4 PTS #
12 PTS. #
C HEAD: 10/12 ITALIC, CAPS AND l.c., RUN-IN
C Shebiit
6 PTS # MINIMUS
FOOTNOTE: 8/9, PARAGRAPH INDENTION WITH ALIGNING FIGURES.
3.

RULES: THIN

RECTO
RUNNING HEAD:
9/12 TIMES ROM.
ITALIC, CAPS AND
l.c., CENTERED.

FOLIO: 9/12 FLUSH
RIGHT.

POETRY:
10/11, INDENT ONE
EM FROM LEFT

EXTRACT:
10/11, INDENT
ONE EM FROM
LEFT.

20 *Composition, Printing, and Binding*

The Hand Processes 20.4
   Type and Typesetting 20.4
   Printing with a Hand Press 20.7
   Binding 20.10
     Gathering, sewing, and trimming 20.11
     Rounding, backing, and headbanding 20.12
     Applying the cover 20.13
   Papermaking 20.14
     Making the pulp 20.15
     Forming and drying the paper 20.16
   Reproducing Illustrations 20.20
     Relief processes 20.21
     Intaglio processes 20.23
     Stone lithography 20.25
The Machine Processes 20.26
   Typesetting 20.27
     Monotype 20.28
     Linotype 20.29
   Proofing and Makeup 20.31
     Assembly in galleys 20.31
     Makeup 20.34
     Measurement 20.38
   Letterpress Printing 20.42
     Cylinder presses 20.44
     Vertical presses 20.46
     Rotary presses 20.47
   Gravure Printing 20.48
   Offset Lithography 20.49
   Case Binding 20.50
     Folding and collating 20.51
     Sewing 20.52
     Forwarding 20.53
     Casing in 20.54
     Boards and cloth 20.55
     Stamping and printing 20.56
   Papermaking 20.58
     Making the pulp 20.59
     Forming the pulp into paper 20.63
     Finishing 20.66
     Grain and sidedness 20.68
     Paper categories 20.70
     Measurement of paper 20.71
     Stock paper sizes 20.75
   Reproducing Illustrations 20.78
     Line work 20.80
     The halftone principle 20.81

Platemaking 20.86
  Letterpress plates 20.87
  Gravure plates 20.90
  Offset plates 20.92
Twentieth-Century Contributions: Composition and Makeup 20.96
  Strike-on Composition 20.97
    Text composition 20.98
    Composition for display 20.101
    Proofing and correcting 20.103
    Makeup 20.104
  Photocomposition 20.106
    First-generation typesetters 20.108
    Second-generation typesetters 20.109
  CRT Composition 20.112
    Character generation 20.113
    Output 20.114
  Typesetting Systems 20.115
    Input devices 20.117
    Computer storage and processing units 20.122
    Capabilities 20.125
  Proofing and Correcting 20.126
    Proofs 20.127
    Correcting 20.129
Twentieth-Century Contributions: Printing and Binding 20.130
  Four-Color Process Printing 20.130
  The Belt Press 20.134
  Web Offset 20.137
  Binding 20.139
    Saddle wiring and side wiring 20.140
    Perfect binding 20.141
    Mechanical binding 20.143
    Book jackets 20.144
For Further Reference 20.146

20.1   The processes of composition, printing, and binding, along with the allied arts of papermaking and platemaking, impose limitations on bookmaking that editors ought to understand if they are to play their parts well in the publishing enterprise. It is not necessary for us to understand these processes in all their detail, but some knowledge of what happens between the time an edited, marked-up manuscript leaves our hands and a finished book is placed in them is essential.

20.2   This chapter is not intended to serve as a history of the graphic arts: much that was of great importance in its time but has now disappeared is totally ignored. Nor is it intended to supply the technical detail and the terminology that a production controller must command to function effectively. It is intended only to supply a reader who knows little or nothing about the technology of bookmaking with enough information to picture what goes on, and to avoid making the worst mistakes. Unlike most other chapters in this volume, it is intended to be read straight through.

20.3 Our complicated modern processes all trace their origins to simpler, more ancient ones, and it will be best first to try to understand these.

THE HAND PROCESSES

TYPE AND TYPESETTING

20.4 The invention in the fifteenth century of *movable type*—individual bits of metal with the images of letters cast in reverse on their ends, which could be assembled into the lines and columns of a text—revolutionized bookmaking. Printing itself, from woodcuts or engraved metal plates, was much older and needed chiefly to be adapted to the use of movable type.

20.5 When handset type is used today, it is set in much the same way as it was five hundred years ago. The typesetter, or *compositor,* picks the individual pieces of type (*sorts*) one by one out of a case where they are arranged in some convenient order. He—she, perhaps—places the sorts one by one face up in a *composing stick,* a little two-sided box that will hold a dozen or so lines of type. After the last word in each line is set, the compositor gauges the amount of space left at the end of the line and inserts the requisite amount of space between words to *justify* the line—make it come out to a uniform length. When the composing stick is full, the compositor transfers the set lines to a shallow tray (*galley*) to await proofing and making up into pages. These processes are much the same for handwork as for machine work, and will be described later in the chapter (20.31–37).

Five pieces of type assembled in order and an impression made from them

20.6 Handsetting in the old way is still practiced, of course, both by private presses and by other noncommercial printers whose goal is the highest quality attainable, as well as by commercial houses when the work involved is too complex for machine setting. But mechanized ways of achieving a typeset page of copy have all but replaced handsetting.

In setting type by hand the typesetter picks the sorts one by one out of a type case and assembles them in a composing stick, adding space between words to justify the lines.

At this time in the city of Mainz in Germany, near the Rhine, and not as certain men say falsely, in Italy, the wonderful and hitherto unknown art of printing or lettering books was invented and devised by John Gutenberg, a citizen of Mainz, who when he had spent nearly all of his substance on the invention of this art, and worked in great poverty, lacking now this and now that, was almost at the point of giving up in desperation. Then with the advice and support of John Fust, also a citizen of Mainz, he completed the imperfect thing.

At this time in the city of Mainz in Germany, near the Rhine, and not as certain men say falsely, in Italy, the wonderful and hitherto unknown art of printing or lettering books was invented and devised by John Gutenberg, a citizen of Mainz, who when he had spent nearly all of his substance on the invention of this art, and worked in great poverty, lacking now this and now that, was almost at the point of giving up in desperation. Then with the advice and support of John Fust, also a citizen of Mainz, he completed the imperfect thing.

Copy set in justified and unjustified (ragged right) style

588

Whether set by hand or by machine, the lines of type are assembled in a galley as they are finished.

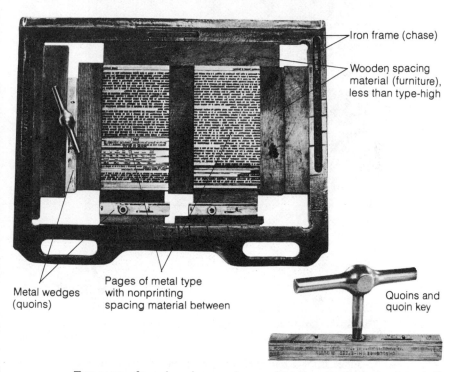

Iron frame (chase)

Wooden spacing material (furniture), less than type-high

Metal wedges (quoins)

Pages of metal type with nonprinting spacing material between

Quoins and quoin key

Two pages of type have been made up and are here seen locked up in a small chase. Furniture separates the pages and surrounds them on all four sides, and on two sides quoins lock type and furniture tightly together.

PRINTING WITH A HAND PRESS

20.7 When final corrections have been made, pages of type (and illustrations, if there are any) are placed face up in a metal frame (*chase*), surrounded by wooden spacing material (*furniture*), which will not print because it is lower than the surface of the type (less than *type-high*). Type and furniture are locked in place by metal wedges (*quoins*—pronounced *coins*), operated by a wrench (*quoin key*).

589

The Washington hand press, originally patented in 1821 and manufactured for many years, is still valued highly for the fine printing it is capable of producing.

20.8   In our example a hand press will be used, and two pages will be printed at the same time on a single sheet of paper. Because of the way the printed sheets will later be folded and sewn, a sheet must carry on each side at least two pages of the finished work—it could carry four, eight, sixteen, or more. The type pages that print together on one side of a sheet make up a *form*.

20.9   The chase with its two pages of type is clamped face up on the carriage of the press, and the type is inked by hand with a roller. (Printer's ink is thick and sticky—about like peanut butter—not thin like writing ink.) Hinged to the carriage is a paper- or parchment-covered board (the *tympan*), and hinged to the tympan is a light frame carrying a paper *frisket* with holes cut in it the size of each type page. The frisket

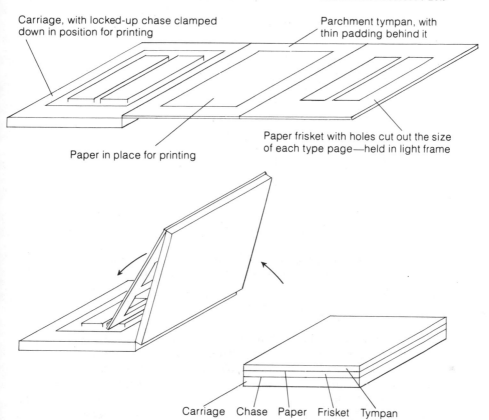

Carriage, with locked-up chase clamped down in position for printing

Parchment tympan, with thin padding behind it

Paper frisket with holes cut out the size of each type page—held in light frame

Paper in place for printing

Carriage   Chase   Paper   Frisket   Tympan

Above: The chase is in place on the carriage of a hand press, ready for printing. Type has been inked, paper is in place on the tympan, and a frisket, cut for the two pages to be printed, is held in the frisket frame. *Below:* The frisket is folded down over the tympan and the tympan over the type form before the carriage is run under the platen for printing.

serves to protect the paper from the ink that often gets on nonprinting parts of the form. A sheet of paper is fastened to the tympan, the frisket is flopped down over it, and both are folded down over the chase holding the type form. The whole sandwich is then cranked under the horizontal *platen* of the press, which is made to squeeze down on it with great pressure. Pressure is released, the carriage is cranked out from under the platen, and tympan and frisket frame are folded back. The sheet of paper, now printed as two pages, is removed from the tympan and set aside to dry. Later the sheet will be *backed up*—printed on the other side with two more pages. Eventually, the four-page sheets will be assembled for sewing and binding in book form.

591

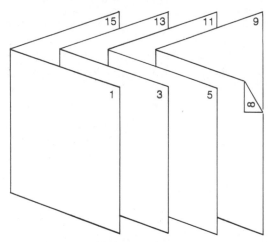

A signature made up of sheets printed and backed up two pages at a time. Note the numbers of the pages that have to be printed together.

BINDING

20.10 Whether binding is done by hand, as in the present example, or by machine, the pages of a book are so printed that groups (*signatures*), usually of no less than sixteen pages, can be sewn together in binding. Since we are printing in two-page forms (*folio imposition*), that means that a signature will consist of four sheets, each folded once down the middle and laid one inside another. The outside sheet will carry the first and last pages of the signature, say pages 1 and 16, on one side, backed up by pages 2 and 15. The next sheet will carry pages 3 and 14, backed up by 4 and 13. And so on to the middle of the signature, where pages 8 and 9 will form the center spread.

20.11 *Gathering, sewing, and trimming.* For hand binding, all the signatures of the book are first gathered in correct order. Then one by one they are sewn, with needle and linen thread, through the fold and around cords or over flat linen tapes held taut in a sewing frame. Small "kettle stitches" near the top and bottom of each signature link it to the adjacent ones. When all signatures have been sewn, they and the cords or tapes are removed from the sewing frame, and the endpapers (often decorative) are attached (*tipped*) to the outside signatures with a thin line of paste or glue. (Alternatively, the endpapers may have been sewn in with the signatures.) The spine is then knocked square and the book is trimmed, usually on all three exposed sides. A coating of flexible glue is commonly applied to the spine at this point, to help hold everything together.

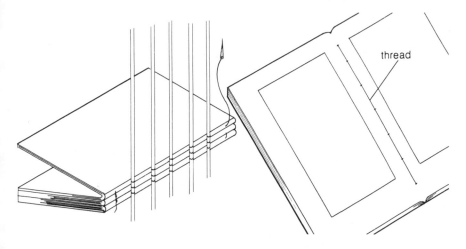

Left: In hand binding, signatures are sewn with needle and thread through the fold and around cords held vertically in a sewing frame. *Right:* Sewing threads can be seen in the middle of a signature when it is opened up flat.

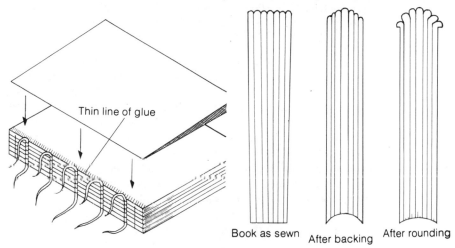

Thin line of glue

Book as sewn   After backing   After rounding

Left: Endpapers are tipped to the front and back signatures of a sewn book. *Right:* After the outer edges of the sewn signatures have been trimmed, rounding and backing compensate for the additional thickness given the spine in sewing.

20.12 *Rounding, backing, and headbanding.* The spine of the book, because of all the sewing, is now thicker than the fore-edge side, and the next two operations, *rounding* and *backing,* are designed to take care of this discrepancy. Held firmly in a vise (*backing press*), the book is hammered on the spine until it is *rounded* (convex) and the fore edge

593

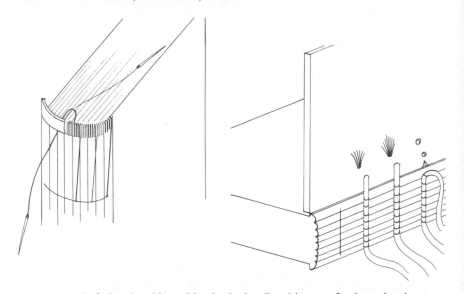

Left: In a hand-bound book, the headband is sewn firmly to the signatures themselves. *Right:* The cords around which the sewing was done are laced through holes drilled in the front and back boards.

is concave. Then the edges of the spine are flared outward (*backed*) toward the front and back to form a space that will later be taken up by the boards of the cover. Next a *headband,* a narrow strip of stout cord, vellum, or leather, is sewn to the top of the spine and anchored every few stitches to the kettle stitches below; the headband is intended to strengthen the spine where it is strained by a person's finger carelessly pulling the book from the shelf. A similar band is often sewn to the bottom of the spine also. At this point, if tapes have been used in sewing, a flattened tube of sturdy paper is often glued to the spine so that the cover, when it is pasted on, will stick to this and form a hollow spine; if cords have been used, the spine is usually lined with paper glued between the cords.

20.13   *Applying the cover.* Next, the boards (formerly thin wood but now usually *binder's board,* a heavy cellulose-fiber product) are attached to the book proper. This may be done by lacing the binding cords through holes made near the spine in the boards or by splitting the boards slightly at the spine and laying the raveled ends of the cords (or the cut-off ends of the tapes) in the clefts and gluing the boards back together. The cover for a fine binding, usually cut from thin leather, is often hand-tooled and hand-stamped with gold leaf on the spine area with the author's name and the title of the book and—when the binding is finished—on the front and back with decorative work.

The cover is pasted to the boards and to the spine (or to the paper tube over the spine if that has been used), and the edges turned in over the three exposed edges of the boards. At the spine, the leather is molded into thickened *head caps* over the headbands. Finally, the outside endpapers are pasted to the insides of the boards, thus concealing all but a thin border of the turned-in leather.

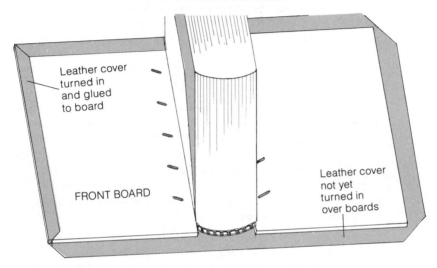

Leather cover turned in and glued to board

FRONT BOARD

Leather cover not yet turned in over boards

The leather cover is pasted to the outside of the boards and the edges are turned in all round.

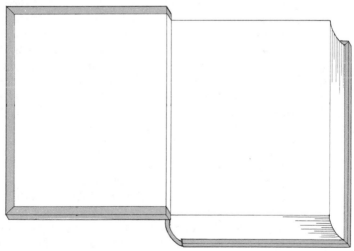

Finally, the outside endpapers are pasted to the inside surfaces of the boards, covering the ends of the cords and leaving a narrow margin of leather showing on three sides.

PAPERMAKING

20.14   Whether handmade or machine-made, paper consists of tiny, almost microscopic, cellulose fibers felted together into a thin sheet. The source of the fibers nowadays is chiefly wood, but formerly it was rags—originally linen, later cotton—and rags are still used in the manufacture of the very finest papers today. For papermaking the source materials are reduced to a slurry of fibers floating freely in water, and when the water is removed from a thin layer of this *pulp,* the end product is paper. In the paragraphs that follow, the old hand process for making paper (considerably simplified) will be described, and in later sections (20.58–77), the mechanical versions of that process.

20.15   *Making the pulp.* Rags to be made into paper are first sorted and unsuitable ones thrown out. Seams are opened, anything that doesn't belong in paper, like buttons, is removed, and the rags are chopped in small pieces. In any age rags have always been dirty, and an important part of the process is cleaning them, by boiling them with strong cleansing solutions. Thoroughly rinsed, they are beaten while damp until the threads disintegrate and the cellulose fibers are floating freely in water. This is now paper pulp.

20.16   *Forming and drying the paper.* Much diluted, the pulp goes to the *vat* where the paper will actually be made. The device used for forming the film of pulp is the *mold,* a rectangular frame containing wires running at right angles to each other. In the traditional form of mold, parallel wires, thin and closely spaced, run across the mold at the surface, and these are attached to thick, widely spaced wires running the opposite way beneath them. The *laid* paper formed on wire like this shows a typical ladderlike pattern when held up to the light. *Wove* paper is formed on a mold of plain woven wire screening, and shows a less distinct pattern. Thin wire formed into some design or other may be attached to the surface wires of the mold to produce a *watermark* in the finished paper. Used with the mold in forming the film of pulp is a rectangular frame (the *deckle*) which fits over the mold like a picture frame and converts it into a sort of tray.

20.17   To form the film of pulp the person handling the mold (*vatman*) dips it, with deckle in place, into the vat of dilute pulp and draws up a small quantity of pulp on the surface of the wire. The vatman tilts and shakes the mold until most of the water has drained through the wire and then removes the deckle while more drains through. A second worker (the *coucher*) takes the charged mold and transfers the film of pulp to a piece of damp felt, laying another piece of felt on top of it. Meanwhile the vatman is dipping a second mold. In this way a pile of alternating wet paper and felt is built up for the next operation.

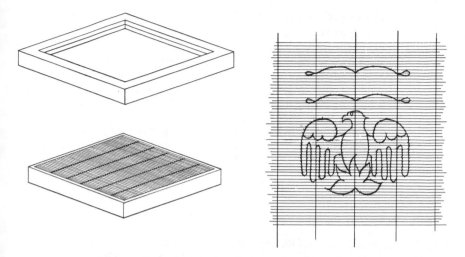

Left: The papermaker's wire-covered mold and framelike deckle fit together to form a tray. When mold and deckle are dipped in the vat of liquid pulp and drawn out, the wire of the mold holds the paper fibers on its surface as the water drains through. *Right:* A wire design sewn to the mold will thin the layer of pulp slightly, so that when the finished paper is held up to the light, the design, in the form of a watermark, shows through.

In this print of 1568 (by the artist Jost Amman), a vatman has lifted his pulp-laden mold from the vat and is tilting and shaking it to expedite drainage and to form the film of pulp. In the background are a wooden press with a stack of wet paper interleaved with felt and a waterpower hammer mill beating rags into pulp.

20.18   The wet pile is placed in a press (hydraulic nowadays, formerly a screw press) and a great deal more water is squeezed out. Then paper and felt are separated and the paper is pressed by itself again and hung up to dry. When dry, the sheets are dipped in a tub containing *size* (essentially gelatin or very dilute glue) and dried again: this gives the paper a harder and less absorbent surface than it would otherwise have.

20.19   All paper was made by hand until the early nineteenth century, and of course some still is. Most of this is used by artists, but some is used by hand printers, who consider it the finest printing surface ever produced.

REPRODUCING ILLUSTRATIONS

20.20   Printed books of the earliest period contained illustrations as well as text, and some of the processes used to make multiple copies of a drawing are considerably older than the art of printing from movable type. The old hand processes are still used by artists in their work, as are some other hand processes not quite so ancient. All have served as prototypes for the mechanized processes of later times.

20.21   *Relief processes.* Book printing of the kind described earlier in this chapter requires a *relief* printing surface, that is, a surface in which the parts that are to print are raised above the level of the parts that are not to print, just as in a piece of type the image of the letter is raised above the surface of the type body. This method of printing is known as *relief printing,* or, more familiarly, as *letterpress.*

20.22   Illustrations for letterpress books must be similarly prepared if they are to print along with the text. The earliest form of text illustration was the *woodcut.* To prepare a woodcut an artist draws the picture on the surface of a block of wood that is exactly as thick as the printer's type is high. The artist then carves away the wood around the parts that are to print. The woodcut can then be locked up in the form with the accompanying text. The linoleum block is a modern form of the same process and can be similarly used as a text illustration.

20.23   *Intaglio processes.* The *intaglio* (pronounced *in-TAL-yo*) processes are the reverse of relief printing. Here the parts that are to print lie below, not above, the general surface. For an *engraving* the drawing is rendered on a metal plate and the lines are cut into the plate as grooves in the otherwise flat surface. When the engraving is finished, the plate is inked and the plane surface is wiped clean with a piece of canvas or some other material, so that ink remains only in the grooves of the image. To take an impression, the artist lays a sheet of paper on

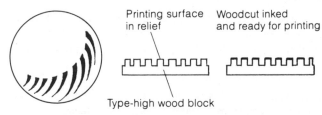

Printing surface in relief

Woodcut inked and ready for printing

Type-high wood block

A print from a woodcut. The sectional view at the right shows a slice through the middle of the wooden block from which the print was made. When the block is inked, only the high parts of the design receive the ink and transfer it to the paper.

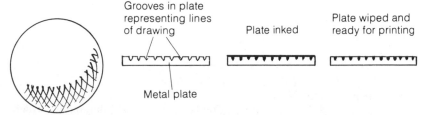

Grooves in plate representing lines of drawing

Plate inked

Plate wiped and ready for printing

Metal plate

A print from an engraving. The sectional view through the plate shows how, after inking and wiping, the ink remains in the engraved grooves, ready to be transferred to the paper.

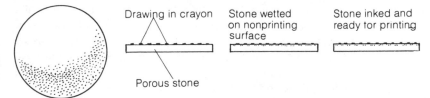

Drawing in crayon

Stone wetted on nonprinting surface

Stone inked and ready for printing

Porous stone

A lithograph made from an original on stone. The sectional view exaggerates the thickness of the drawing and the ink, which are essentially on the same plane as the stone (*planography* is another name for this kind of printing).

the plate and applies pressure to it. Then when the paper is lifted from the plate, it bears the image of what was engraved in the metal.

20.24   *Etching* is another intaglio process, one involving acids that attack metal. Here the metal plate is covered with a layer of wax or some other material (*resist*) that is not attacked by the acid used. The artist scribes the lines of the drawing through the wax with a needle-pointed tool, exposing the bare metal. When this work has been completed, the artist immerses the plate in an acid bath, which eats at the metal wherever it is not covered by the resist. The result is an intaglio surface that can be printed in the same way as an engraving.

20.25   *Stone lithography.* The surface from which a lithograph is made is neither relief nor intaglio but plane. The image and the surrounding nonprinting surface are essentially on the same level, and what separates the two in the printing process is the physical principle that oil and water repel each other. The artist draws the image on the surface of a slab of porous stone with a greasy crayon (*tusche*) and dampens the stone with water, which clings to the porous open surface of the stone but not to the greasy surface of the image. The lithographer then inks the stone with a greasy ink, which clings to the image but is repelled by the wet surface of the bare stone. Finally, as with the intaglio processes, paper is laid on the printing surface, pressure is applied, and the image is transferred from the stone to the paper.

THE MACHINE PROCESSES

20.26   The hand processes involved in setting type, printing and binding books, making paper, and reproducing drawings were largely developments of the Middle Ages and early Renaissance. (Among the processes described, the only notable exception is lithography, which was not invented until the closing years of the eighteenth century.) Efforts were constantly made to speed up and simplify the hand processes by using energy derived from sources other than human muscle. A few were successful, like the use, in the late Middle Ages, of a hammer mill driven by waterpower to beat rags into pulp for papermaking. But most applications of machine technology to bookmaking and the related arts were developments of the nineteenth century. All closely reflected the earlier arts they were designed to replace, and all survive in some form to the present time, in spite of the later development of more sophisticated ways of performing the same tasks.

TYPESETTING

20.27   Typesetting resisted mechanization until the 1880s, when the invention of the *Monotype* and *Linotype* machines revolutionized the way most type was henceforth set and assembled. The biggest problem in mechanizing typesetting was how to justify the right-hand margin of the type column, since justification had always been considered necessary to acceptable setting. (Now that we can do it so easily, of course, we often forgo justification and set type with a ragged right-hand margin.) The two processes both solved the problem, each in its own, equally ingenious, way. Monotype and Linotype together are often called *hot-metal* setting, because the end product of each is cast from molten type metal.

20.28   *Monotype.* The Monotype process employs two machines to produce justified composition that is virtually identical to handset type. The operator composes the work on a *keyboard* machine that produces a punched paper tape recording all keystrokes and other directions given it. Nearing the end of a line, the operator records on the tape the amount of space remaining in the line—space that must be distributed between words to justify that line. When a tape is completed, it goes to the *casting* machine, often located in another part of the shop. There the tape is run through the caster, which in response to the perforations on the tape casts individual pieces of type and spaces and assembles them line by line in a galley. Part of the ingenuity of the process lies in the fact that the punched tape is run *backwards* through the casting machine, so that the machine "knows" from the coding at the end of each line how much space to cast between the words of that line before it is set.

20.29 *Linotype*. The Linotype process combines keyboard and caster in one machine to produce not individual pieces of type but whole lines of type cast as column-wide *slugs*. (By one of the vagaries of industrial history there are actually two, virtually identical, linecasting machines, made by competing manufacturers, the Mergenthaler Linotype machine and the Intertype machine. Generically, however, the process is usually called by the name of the former.) As the Linotype operator keyboards the copy, brass *matrices* (colloquially, "mats"), or type molds, are assembled, with *spacebands* between words. As the operator reaches the end of the line, the spacebands, which are thin double wedges, push in from both sides and expand the word spacing so that the line is filled up. Then the whole line is cast in molten type metal, the slug drops into a galley to join its fellows, and the mats are put back where they came from, all automatically.

20.30 Linotype composition is cheaper than Monotype composition, but less satisfactory for work involving many type corrections. Monotype composition can be corrected like handset work, by picking out the incorrect characters and inserting the right ones. But any correction in Linotype, no matter how minute, involves resetting and replacing a whole line.

A Linotype or Intertype machine casts an entire line of type as a single slug.

PROOFING AND MAKEUP

20.31   *Assembly in galleys.* Whether set by hand or by machine, type is first assembled in long columns of text alone, still lacking any of the other type that the finished pages will have—chapter headings, subheads, running heads, page numbers, perhaps footnotes or endnotes and illustrations.

20.32   These other elements of the finished page are usually designed for different sizes and styles of type from the text itself. Chapter headings are normally set in a *display* face, which is sometimes a larger version of the *book*, or *reader*, face used for the text, sometimes a different, complementary face. Running heads and subheads are usually set in some variety of the book face—SMALL CAPS, **boldface**, *italic*, possibly a little larger or a little smaller than the text—or, again like the chapter heads, in a different but complementary face. *Extracts* (block quotations), appendixes, glossaries, and endnotes are often set in a smaller size of the book face, and footnotes always are.

20.33   When all the requisite type has been set, chapter headings, extracts, and subheads are inserted in the galleys of text material. If there are footnotes, they may be inserted in the columns of text after the appropriate reference numbers—for safekeeping, until the type is broken into pages—or they may be assembled in separate galleys. At this stage galley proofs are pulled and read, and corrections are made by the compositor. If the publisher has asked to see galley proofs, these are the proofs sent, usually several sets of them, including the *master,* or *working, set,* which has been read and marked for corrections by the supplier's proofreader. (Often, earlier stages of proof are pulled, but these never leave the supplier's proofroom and composing room.)

20.34   *Makeup.* When corrections have been made to the type standing in the galleys, it is then *made up* into pages. That is, it is divided into

Galley proofs are made of typeset material just as it has been assembled in the galleys. They show 20 inches or so of set matter and are pulled on long narrow sheets of paper.

Page proofs are sometimes made on the same kind of paper as that used for galley proofs and show three or four pages, one after the other. More convenient are the proofs that carry left- and right-hand pages opposite each other on the same sheet.

page-size chunks, footnotes (if any) are placed at the bottom of each page, and running heads and page numbers (*folios*) are added. Illustrations may also be inserted now. When *page proofs* have been pulled and compared with the galley proofs, and type corrections made, the pages are ready for printing.

20.35 Makeup is a highly skilled procedure. If galley material is simply divided mechanically into portions of equal length, without regard to where the divisions fall, some of the pages that result are bound to be unacceptable logically or aesthetically: they will incorporate *bad breaks*. Common examples of bad breaks are the following:

A widow, that is, a short line—one word or two or three little ones (some say anything less than a full line)—at the top of a page.

A page or column that ends with the first part of a broken word. (By some this is no longer considered a bad break unless it occurs at the foot of a right-hand page.)

A subhead falling at the foot of a page or column. A subhead should be followed by at least two lines of text.

A section break consisting of a blank line (or a type device in an otherwise blank line) falling at the head or the foot of a page or column. Such a section break should be preceded or followed by at least two lines of text.

An extract beginning on the last line or ending on the first line of a page or column. There should be at least two lines in either place.

A footnote that does not begin on the same page as its reference. At least two lines of the note should fall on the page containing the reference before the note continues onto the next page.

20.36   Bad breaks can often be eliminated without resetting type, by adjusting page lengths. Although a page is intended to have a standard number of lines, the designer usually permits the typesetter to let pages run one line long or one line short, so long as opposite pages match. By this means lines can be moved forward or backward to eliminate the bad break.

20.37   An alternate or ancillary method is to lengthen or shorten a paragraph in the vicinity of the bad break. Often a one-word paragraph ending can be pulled up by resetting a line tighter than it was originally set, or a full line can be reset looser to run it over. ("Save a line" and "Make a line" are the proofreader's directions for these operations.) Sometimes too a paragraph can be lengthened or shortened by slight rewording that does not change the meaning. This, of course, requires the cooperation of the author or editor or both, and the device can't be used with reprinted material. Again, if the subheads are set with a fair amount of white space above and below them, this space can sometimes be reduced or increased to save a line or make a line. This works particularly well when two subheads fall on the same page, and the stolen or added space can be split between them. (This is jumping ahead, but with computer-controlled typesetting, word spacing for a whole paragraph or page can be easily altered to avoid bad breaks— see 20.125.)

20.38   *Measurement.* Whether type is set by hand, by Monotype or Linotype, or by any of the processes yet to be described, it is measured in units that are peculiar to the trade. The size of a typeface is defined in terms of *points,* one point being approximately 1/72 of an inch. The *point size* of a particular face refers to the vertical measurement of the letters—historically, the body on which the characters were set. For most typefaces this is approximately the distance between the tops of the tallest letters—which may be either the capitals or the lowercase letters with ascenders, like *b* and *h*—and the bottoms of the letters with descenders, like *p* and *q*. The length of a line of type is measured in *picas,* one pica being equal to twelve points, or about 1/6 of an inch. Space between lines, called *leading* (pronounced *ledding*), is measured in points.

Style

approx. point size

The point size of type

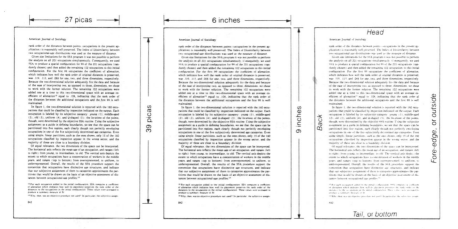

Left: The type page is a rectangle, measured in picas, enclosing all the typeset matter on the page. *Center:* The trim size of a book or journal is the dimensions of the bound sheets after trimming, measured in inches. *Right:* The margins of a page are the areas of white space surrounding the type page. Clockwise from the top of a right-hand page, they are called the head margin; fore-edge, or outside, margin; tail, or bottom, margin; and back, or inside, margin.

20.39 The *type page,* or *text page,* of a book is defined as the area that includes the running head at the top and the last line of a full page—or the folio, whichever is lower—at the bottom, and extends from the left edge to the right edge of any typeset matter, including side heads and folios but not including illustrations (which may *bleed* into the margins). The type page is measured in picas. Any internal measurement, such as the drop (*sinkage*) for chapter openings, is based on the type page.

20.40 The *trim size* of a book is the actual size of the page after the sheets have been printed, folded, sewn, and trimmed. In the United States and Canada it is measured in inches, in the rest of the world, in millimeters, because that is how standard sheet sizes for book papers are

605

measured. (Librarians, bibliographers, and those who produce publishers' catalogs often give the approximate size of a book in centimeters, but this is not the actual trim size.)

20.41   The page *margins*—the white space between the type page and the trimmed edges of the page—are specified in either picas or inches. But designers generally give the dimensions of only the back (inside, or gutter) and head margins, because picas, used for the type page, are not exactly compatible with inches, used for the trim size.

> A USEFUL RULE. A manuscript editor ought to possess a *pica rule* (also called *pica stick* and *line gauge*) for checking page and type measurements. A pica rule is always divided along one edge into picas and half-picas (that is, 12- and 6-point divisions) and along one other edge into inches. Along other edges (both sides are generally used) may appear scales for other common type sizes, such as 8- and 10-point, and often a scale for agate lines (exactly 14 to the inch), used to measure newspaper advertising space. A reader in possession of such a rule will easily find that this line of type measures 21 picas in width and that the regular text measures 23. From this or other pages the reader should also be able to determine that the type page of this book measures 27 by 45 picas and that the trim size is 6 by 9 inches.

LETTERPRESS PRINTING

20.42   So much has printing become a machine operation over the past two hundred years that it is often referred to simply as "machining," in distinction to the anterior process of composition and the following one of binding. Steam supplied the power for most printing machinery until the end of the nineteenth century, when the electric motor took over.

20.43   Power-driven printing presses developed along two different lines, and these resulted in two types of letterpress machines that are in use today. In one development the flat platen of the hand press was replaced by rolling pressure from a heavy cylinder, and in the other the flat platen and chase were kept but were made to open and close like the jaws of a pair of pliers. The first became the *cylinder press* of today, the second, the *vertical job press,* or *platen press*.

20.44   *Cylinder presses*. In a typical flatbed cylinder press, the form moves back and forth once for every impression made. As the form moves forward, it passes under inking rollers and then under the big rotating *impression cylinder* bearing a sheet of paper. When the impression is completed, the form starts back, and the impression cylinder lifts slightly to allow the form to pass beneath it. At the same time the cylinder sends the printed sheet to the *delivery end* of the press and on its next revolution picks up a fresh sheet from the *feed end*.

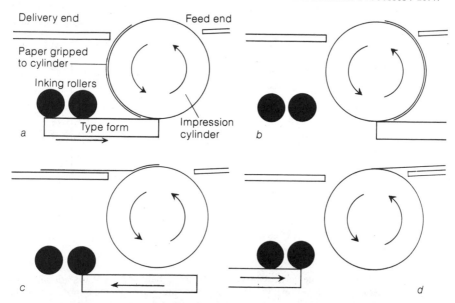

Principle of the cylinder press. In the most common type of cylinder press the impression cylinder makes two complete revolutions for every impression. *(a)* The bed carrying the form moves forward under ink rollers and meets the paper as it passes under the impression cylinder. *(b)* The impression completed, the cylinder continues to revolve as the bed stops and starts back. *(c)* The cylinder rises slightly to allow the bed to pass under it, while delivering the printed sheet. *(d)* The cylinder picks up another sheet as the bed starts forward again under the inking rollers, and the cycle repeats.

20.45   The printing surface employed in a cylinder press may be standing type in a chase, as described for the hand press, but it is more likely to be a *plate* of some kind made from the original type (see 20.86–89).

20.46   *Vertical presses.* The vertical job press is seldom if ever used for bookwork, but is often employed for printing leaflets, placards, and other small pieces. The stationary bed is vertical, and the flat platen presses the paper against the inked type in a kind of clamshell motion. As the press opens, the printed sheet is removed, and inking rollers pass down over the type. When the platen is fully open a fresh sheet of paper is placed on it and at that point the ink rollers are at the bottom of their travel. As the platen starts to close, the rollers move upward out of the way (and to receive a fresh supply of ink), and the paper is pressed against the inked type.

20.47   *Rotary presses.* The *rotary press* represents a further development of the cylinder principle. Here both the printing surface and the platen are cylindrical. Curved printing plates are clamped to the plate cylin-

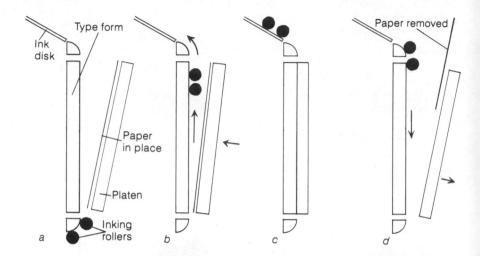

Principle of the vertical job press. The form, held vertically, is stationary, and the platen closes on it in a clamshell movement to make the impression on the paper. (a) The press is open, ink rollers are at the bottom of their travel, and a fresh sheet has just been laid in place on the platen. (b) The platen starts to close, and the ink rollers move upward out of the way. (c) The press is fully closed and the paper is pressed tight against the inked type to make the impression; ink rollers are on the ink disk picking up a fresh supply of ink. (d) The platen starts to open, the printed sheet is removed, and the ink rollers start downward to reink the type and begin a new cycle.

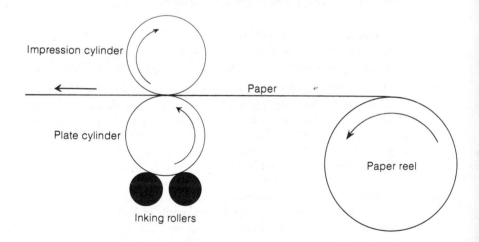

Principle of the web-fed rotary press. Paper is fed from the reel into the press, where it passes between pairs of cylinders that print first one side of the paper and then the other. The diagram shows one pair.

der, which is continuously inked and rotates in contact with the impression cylinder. A rotary press may print individual sheets of paper (a *sheet-fed* press), but more commonly prints a continuous roll of paper (a *web-fed,* or *reel-fed,* press). In the latter instance, the back of the paper is printed on a separate pair of cylinders before the web reaches the delivery end of the press, where it is cut into sheets and folded into signatures. Although letterpress printing has been largely replaced by other methods today, the web-fed rotary press is still the fastest printing machine, in terms of impressions per hour, ever developed.

GRAVURE PRINTING

20.48   *Gravure* printing employs the intaglio principle and is done on rotary presses, either sheet-fed or web-fed (*rotogravure*). In a gravure press the inked plate is constantly wiped by a metal *doctor blade* which squeegees the ink from the surface of the plate (gravure uses a very runny ink), leaving it only in the depressions that form the printing image. Much color printing is done by rotogravure, especially on newsprint in very long runs (200,000 to several million), for Sunday supplements and mail-order catalogs. See also 20.90–91.

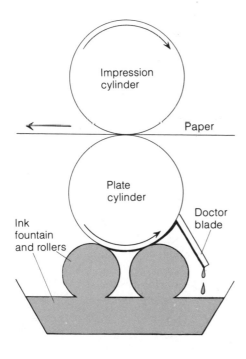

Principle of the rotogravure press. As the printing cylinder revolves, it is continuously inked, and the excess ink is continuously wiped from the surface and returned to the ink fountain. The paper passes between the printing cylinder and a soft impression cylinder, picking up ink left in the thousands of tiny wells etched in the surface of the printing cylinder.

609

OFFSET LITHOGRAPHY

20.49   Most book printing today is done by *offset lithography,* a process based on the principle of stone lithography, described earlier. Preparing the printing surface may begin with metal type, as with letterpress. When pages are made up, however, very clean proofs on special paper are pulled (*reproduction proofs,* or "repros"). These are then photographed, and the image is transferred to a grained metal plate that serves as the primary printing surface. In the printing process, the plate (wrapped around the plate cylinder) is continuously wetted, and the water adheres to the background area but not to the image of the type. After wetting, the rotating plate cylinder is inked, and the greasy ink sticks to the dry image of the type but not to the wet background. Continuing to revolve, the plate is pressed against another cylinder bearing a rubber blanket, which picks up the ink from the plate and transfers it (*offsets* it) to the paper. (Note that because the ink is transferred twice, not once, as in letterpress, an offset plate is *positive* and *right-reading,* like the original repro and the final printed page.) The soft, flexible rubber blanket, unlike a metal plate, tends to conform to the surface it is pressing against. Consequently, the offset process can be used for printing on rough-textured paper or cloth, and other materials with relatively uneven surfaces.

Principle of offset lithography. Five different kinds of cylinders and rollers are needed to complete the printing process. Offset presses can be either sheet-fed or web-fed.

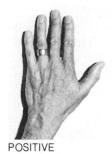

POSITIVE

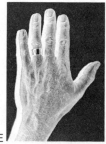

NEGATIVE

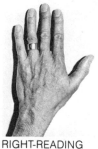

RIGHT-READING

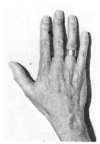

WRONG-READING

These four terms are sometimes confusing to people not trained in graphic arts work. Positive and negative refer to light values—whether light and dark areas appear in the image as in the original (a positive image) or reversed (a negative image). Right-reading and wrong-reading refer to orientation—whether the image is the same as the original with respect to right and left (right-reading) or a mirror image in which right and left are reversed (wrong-reading). An ordinary black-and-white camera negative is both negative and wrong-reading. When a photograph is reproduced in correct positive form but with right and left transposed (i.e., wrong-reading), it is said to be "flopped."

CASE BINDING

20.50   *Case binding* was the first fully mechanized method to be developed for binding books. The direct descendant of the hand-binding method described earlier, case binding (also called *edition binding* and *hardback binding*) is still employed for most trade and scholarly books. It produces a machine-bound book that superficially resembles a hand-bound one, although the binding differs structurally and is not as strong.

20.51   *Folding and collating.* Like all binding methods, case binding begins with folding the press sheets and gathering the signatures in order (*collating*), here done by machine. In book printing, 8, 16, or, more frequently, 32 pages are printed at one time on one side of the sheet and backed up with the same number on the other side, for signatures of 32 pages (large sheets are usually cut to 32-page size before folding). If separately printed plates are to be included in the book, they are added to the signatures by *wrapping, inserting,* or *tipping*.

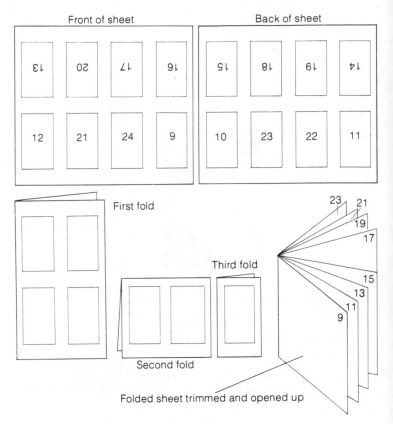

A press sheet is printed "eight pages to view," backed up, folded, and trimmed. Note how the arrangement of the pages in the form (the imposition) results in all pages being in numerical order after folding. For binding, this folded sheet would probably be slipped inside another 16-page folded sheet (bearing pages 1–8 and 25–32) to make a 32-page signature. The folding sequence (and corresponding imposition) shown here is only one of many variations used in bookmaking.

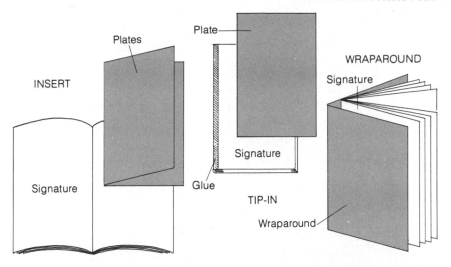

Three ways in which plates and text signatures of a book may be joined

20.52   *Sewing.* The signatures are then sewn, through the folds and to each other, but not around cords or tapes, as in hand binding. This is *Smyth* (rhymes with *blithe*) *sewing.* In *side sewing* the stitches go through all the signatures at once from the side. It is stronger than Smyth sewing, but the book will not open flat. After sewing, endsheets are tipped on, and the sewn book is *smashed* (squeezed in a press to remove air) and trimmed.

20.53   *Forwarding.* Next comes the sequence of operations collectively known as *forwarding.* These include a preliminary gluing of the spine, as in hand binding, rounding and backing, here performed by forcing the clamped sheets against steel rollers rather than by pounding, and finally, *lining.* Lining provides a hinge between the book and the cover. A piece of stout gauze (*super*) somewhat wider than the book is thick is glued to the spine with its edges extending outward. A strip of heavy paper is glued down over the super, with the headbands tucked between the two layers at the top and bottom. (Since the headbands are almost purely decorative in a case-bound book, they are sometimes left out to save money.)

20.54   *Casing in.* The book is now ready to be *cased in,* or enclosed in its cover. Unlike the cover of a hand-bound book, the case is completely preformed, with boards and paper *backstrip* pasted to the printed or stamped cloth, before it is joined to the book. Like all the other operations described, casing in is an automatic process in a modern bindery. The endpapers are given a coat of paste just before the case is

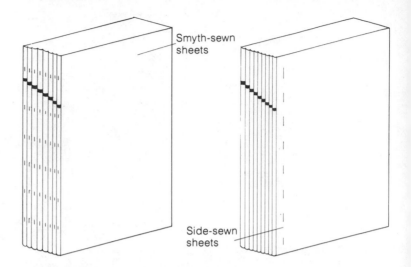

Smyth-sewn
sheets

Side-sewn
sheets

Two ways of sewing the signatures in machine binding. The black rectangles printed on the signature folds are collating marks. If a signature is missing, duplicated, out of order, or upside down, the error shows up as a variation in the straight slanted line of marks.

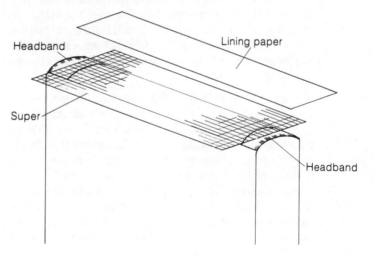

Headband

Lining paper

Super

Headband

After the attaching of endpapers, trimming, rounding, and backing, the book is lined, as shown here.

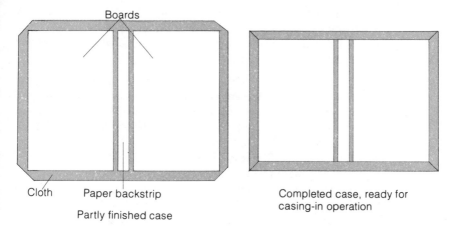

Boards

Cloth   Paper backstrip

Partly finished case

Completed case, ready for
casing-in operation

The case is completely finished before it is attached to the book.

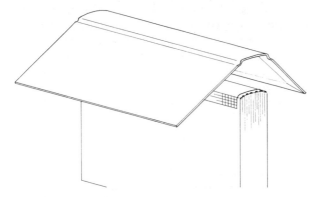

In casing in, the book rides spine side up through the machine, and endsheets
are covered with paste just before the case drops down from above, and the
whole book is squeezed together from the sides.

folded around the book and squeezed tight. The free edges of the super
are thus held between boards and endpapers and function as hinges.

20.55   *Boards and cloth.* The materials used in case binding and the ways in
which the case is imprinted and decorated vary widely. The board
used for most trade books, called *pasted board,* is a laminated stock
built up of several thicknesses of cardboard. *Binder's board,* mentioned earlier in connection with hand binding, is used for fine case
bindings, and inexpensive *chipboard* is chiefly employed when cost is
more of a consideration than quality. The cover material itself may be
binder's cloth, which comes in a wide range of qualities, colors, and
finishes. Binder's cloth is given body by a *filler,* either the traditional
starch or one of the more water-resistant plastic resins. Or the cover

615

may be made from one of the various *nonwoven* materials developed as substitutes for cloth. These include extruded synthetics and paper-backed vinyl, as well as paper itself which has been treated in various ways to give it some durability.

20.56 *Stamping and printing.* The cover is imprinted and decorated by *stamping, printing,* or a combination of the two processes. The dies used for stamping book covers are made of brass or other hard metal and have a relief surface like that of a woodcut or piece of type. Stamping is indeed identical to letterpress printing except that the pressure is greater, so that the cover is actually indented by the die. Ink may be applied to the die, in which case the cover is *cold-stamped.* Or *leaf* (powdered metal or pigment bonded to plastic film) may be placed between the die and the cover; for this kind of work the die must be heated and the cover *hot-stamped. Blind stamping* (no leaf or ink—just the impression of the die) must also be done hot.

20.57 Printed covers, often in more than one color, are usually achieved by offset lithography or by a process (not previously described) called *silk-screen* printing. This is a stencil process (something like mimeograph) in which ink is pressed through a sheer fabric on which the nonprinting areas of the design are blocked out. Both processes permit printing on relatively rough surfaces, and silk-screen is particularly well adapted to cover printing because of the opacity of the inks.

PAPERMAKING

20.58 Papermaking by machine is in outline a mechanization of the hand process, with many additions and often with different raw materials. The machine that forms the paper from the pulp is called a *fourdrinier* (pronounced *fore-dri-NEER*), after the English family that financed its development in the early nineteenth century.

20.59 *Making the pulp.* Very little paper for book printing is made from rags, and what little is made is extremely expensive. Wood is the main ingredient of paper pulp now, and it is converted into pulp by chemical or mechanical means, or by a combination of both. *Chemical pulp* starts with logs that have been peeled of their bark and reduced by machine into chips. The chips are boiled in strong caustic solutions that dissolve away those parts of the wood that are not cellulose, such as lignin and resin, and leave the cellulose fibers more or less free. There are two chief varieties of chemical pulp, called after the chemical compounds used in their manufacture. *Sulfate pulp,* also called *kraft,* is made from wood of either deciduous or coniferous trees and produces a very strong paper. Less widely used is *sulfite pulp,* which is made only from coniferous wood and employs an acid solution in its manufacture.

20.60   *Mechanical pulp,* or *groundwood,* is made chiefly by stone-grinding peeled logs in a stream of water so that the wood is broken up into fibers. Groundwood contains all the constituents of the original wood, including those considered impurities in chemical pulp. It is used mainly for newsprint because paper made from groundwood alone quickly discolors and becomes brittle, and is not very strong to begin with. A superior, stronger form of mechanical pulp, called *thermomechanical pulp,* is made from wood chips treated with steam under high pressure. In spite of its impurities and lack of strength, groundwood is often added to the chemical pulps used in making book papers because of its relatively low cost. A paper containing no groundwood is called a *free sheet.*

20.61   Before the pulp is ready to be made into paper it is mechanically beaten or refined and, for most purposes, bleached. (Unbleached kraft pulp is used for making grocery bags and heavy wrapping paper.) Other materials are also added to the pulp, depending upon the kind of paper to be made. For book papers, fillers such as white clay and titanium oxide may be added to give opacity and extra whiteness, and size to give stiffness and smoothness. For tinted papers dyes are also added at this point. The specific combination of pulps and other ingredients used in making a particular kind of paper is called the *furnish* for that paper.

20.62   For the better grades of paper, care is taken that the furnish be chemically neutral (registering pH 7 on the acid-base scale). For permanence, paper must be *acid-free,* and any work intended to enjoy a long life should be printed on this type of paper.

20.63   *Forming the pulp into paper.* In essence the fourdrinier machine takes (at its *wet end*) pulp that is 99 percent water and by draining it and subjecting it to suction, pressure, and, finally, heat, converts it into a continuous web of paper containing only a few percentage points of moisture at the *dry end* of the machine.

20.64   At the wet end the pulp is continuously flowed onto the surface of a moving endless belt of fine-mesh screening (called the *wire,* though now usually made of nylon). The liquid pulp is prevented from slopping over the sides of the wire by rubber *deckle straps* that move along with it. As the wire moves forward it is shaken from side to side to help the water drain through, much as the vatman shakes the mold in the hand process. Toward the end of the wire, suction boxes below the wire pull more water through, and a wire-mesh-covered cylinder (the *dandy roll*) presses on the web of pulp from above. The dandy roll may be covered with plain wire cloth, which imparts a *wove* effect, or with wire in a ladder pattern for the *laid* effect. If there is to be a watermark, the wire design for this is attached to the dandy roll.

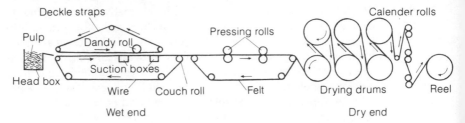

Deckle straps   Calender rolls

Pulp   Dandy roll   Pressing rolls

Head box   Suction boxes

Wire   Couch roll   Felt   Drying drums   Reel

Wet end   Dry end

A diagram can suggest the chief operating parts of the fourdrinier machine for making paper, but can give no sense of its enormous size—sometimes nearly a city block in length.

20.65   At the end of the wire the web of pulp, now the consistency of very soggy paper, is lifted by the *couch roll* onto an endless belt of wool felt and carried between a series of rollers that squeeze more water from it. It then passes over a series of very large, steam-heated, cast-iron drums that complete the drying process. During drying, the web is held tightly against the hot drums by endless belts of fabric above and below.

20.66   *Finishing.* After drying, the paper is usually run through a series of highly polished metal rollers (*calender rolls*) that further compact it and smooth the surface. The calender rolls are arranged in pairs, and the rolls of each pair run at somewhat different speeds from each other, thus tending to polish the paper as it passes between them. Depending upon how much if any calendering the paper is subjected to, a variety of finishes can be obtained, ranging from *antique* (the softest and dullest), through *eggshell, vellum,* and *machine finish,* to *english finish* (the hardest and shiniest obtainable without further treatment).

20.67   Further treatment may include *supercalendering, coating,* or *tub* (or *surface) sizing. Supercalendering* is a polishing process similar to calendering but done on a separate machine with rollers of different composition. The final finish of *coated* papers is brushed or rolled on in liquid form; the finish may be matte (as for reproduction typing) or glossy (as the *enamel* papers for high-quality halftone printing). Most papers include size in the furnish, but additional sizing may be applied to the surface for a harder finish after the paper is made.

20.68   *Grain and sidedness.* Machine-made paper has a definite *grain,* tending to fold and tear more easily in one direction than the other, as anyone discovers in trying to tear an article neatly out of a newspaper page. This is because the cellulose fibers tend to align themselves in the direction of travel as the pulp is laid down on the wire—the shaking promotes but does not fully achieve random alignment, as it exists in

618

handmade paper. In reeled paper the grain always runs the long way. In sheet paper it may run either the long way or the short way, depending upon how it is cut from the reel. For bookwork sheet paper should be ordered *grain long* or *grain short* so that (depending upon the particular printing and binding machinery) the spine fold will be with the grain and not across it. Books folded cross-grain have an unpleasantly springy feel and tend not to stay closed.

20.69   Like most fabrics, paper has a "right" and a "wrong" side. The bottom of the web—next to the wire at the wet end of the machine (and hence called the *wire side*)—is slightly rougher than the top (or *felt*) side. Consequently, if only one side of the paper is to be used, as is usually true in typing and sometimes in printing, the smoother, felt side is the one commonly chosen. Paper made on a *twin-wire* fourdrinier has either two felt sides or two wire sides, because two webs of pulp are laid down simultaneously and pressed together, same side in, as the paper is dried and finished. (For some purposes the wire side is preferred: though not as smooth as the felt side, it has fewer of the fiber clumps called *fines*, which tend to float to the surface as the paper is formed on the wire.) One-sided paper is more expensive than ordinary two-sided paper.

20.70   *Paper categories.* Paper is made in a bewildering variety of weights, colors, textures, and finishes for a multitude of purposes, including those of the publishing industry. What follows is a brief listing of the chief categories used in bookmaking:

> *Book papers* are intended for book and journal printing and are supplied in either roll or sheet form. Nearly all book papers are now surface-sized for offset lithography (the sizing resists penetration by the water used in offset printing, as well as the *picking* of surface fibers by the tacky offset ink). They are made mainly from sulfate pulp, often with the addition of some groundwood.
>
> *Text papers* come in many colors and textures, for use in advertising leaflets, endpapers, and the like. They are also sized for offset printing.
>
> *Cover papers* are heavier papers, made in a wide range of finishes, textures, and colors, for use as covers of pamphlets, journals, and paperback books.
>
> *Newsprint* is made for printing newspapers, advertising catalogs, inexpensive mass-market paperbacks, and other items that will be read once or twice (if at all) and thrown away. It is made from groundwood pulp, usually with some chemical pulp added for strength.
>
> *Bond* is made, mainly for office use, in a wide range of qualities,

from top-grade papers made from 100 percent rag pulp to low-grade stocks consisting largely of groundwood.

20.71 *Measurement of paper.* Paper varies from one kind to another in thickness and in relative weight, and both measurements are used in designating a given paper stock.

20.72 At the mill the thickness of a sheet is known as the *caliper* and is measured in thousandths of an inch (*mils*). For the purposes of publishers, however, this figure is usually converted into *pages per inch* (*ppi*), or *bulk*. Book papers may bulk anywhere from 200 to nearly 1,000 pages to the inch, but the commonly used "50-pound" (see below) machine-finished papers generally bulk in the neighborhood of 500–550 pages per inch. (Remember that each leaf equals two pages.)

20.73 Paper is sold by weight, and different grades of the same type of paper are distinguished by how much some standard quantity of that paper actually weighs. For most of the world the standard quantity is one sheet of paper one square meter in area. In this system the relative weight of the paper (called *grammage*) is given in grams per square meter (g/m^2, or *gsm*), and the same system is used for all categories of paper.

20.74 In the United States, however, an antiquated system of *basis weights,* now abandoned even in England, where it originated, is still used to compare the relative weights of papers. The standard quantity is one ream, or 500 sheets, but the standard sheet size varies from one category of paper to another. For book papers the standard, or *basis,* sheet measures 25 by 38 inches. So to describe a paper as "50-pound book paper" means that 500 sheets of that paper, if cut to 25 by 38 inches (never mind the actual size of the paper in hand) would weigh 50 pounds. For cover stocks, on the other hand, the basis size is only 20 by 26 inches, and consequently a 50-pound cover paper is nearly twice as heavy as a 50-pound book paper. For bond papers, basis weight is usually referred to as *substance* (note the label on a package of typing paper). The basis size is 17 by 22 inches (which, incidentally, cuts evenly into four standard 8½-by-11-inch sheets), and so a 20-pound bond is approximately equal to a 50-pound book paper. See table 20.1, which compares the common basis weights of the five categories of paper described above and gives metric equivalents, and table 20.2, which gives conversion factors for American and metric systems.

20.75 *Stock paper sizes.* Both in the United States and abroad, paper merchants stock the most popular grades of paper in certain standard sizes, although special sizes may be ordered. Here again, the metric system used in Britain and on the Continent is much simpler than the American system.

TABLE 20.1 Basis Weights Compared

	Book & Text (25 × 38)	Cover (20 × 26)	Newsprint (24 × 36)	Bond (17 × 22)	Grammage (g/m²)
Book & Text	**30**	16	27	12	44
	40	22	36	16	59
	45	25	41	18	67
	50	27	45	20	74
	60	33	55	24	89
	70	38	64	28	104
	80	44	73	31	118
	90	49	82	35	133
	100	55	91	39	148
	120	66	109	47	178
Cover	91	**50**	82	36	135
	110	**60**	100	43	163
	119	**65**	108	47	176
	146	**80**	134	58	216
	164	**90**	149	65	243
	183	**100**	166	72	271
Newsprint	31	17	**28**	12	46
	33	18	**30**	13	49
	35	19	**32**	14	52
	37	20	**34**	15	55
	38	21	**35**	15	57
Bond	33	18	30	**13**	49
	41	22	37	**16**	61
	51	28	46	**20**	75
	61	33	56	**24**	90
	71	39	64	**28**	105
	81	45	74	**32**	120
	91	50	83	**36**	135
	102	56	93	**40**	151

SOURCE: Table 20.1 is based in large part on a similar table in *Pocket Pal* (New York: International Paper Co., 1979), 158.

NOTE: Numbers in boldface are the common basis weights in pounds for the various categories of papers. Basis sheet sizes are given in the column headings.

TABLE 20.2 Conversion Factors, Metric and U.S. Basis Weights

Category and Basis Size	U.S. to Metric	Metric to U.S.
Book and text (25 by 38)	$1.480 \times$ lb. $=$ g/m²	$0.675 \times$ g/m² $=$ lb.
Cover (20 by 26)	$2.704 \times$ lb. $=$ g/m²	$0.370 \times$ g/m² $=$ lb.
Newsprint (24 by 36)	$1.627 \times$ lb. $=$ g/m²	$0.614 \times$ g/m² $=$ lb.
Bond (17 by 22)	$3.760 \times$ lb. $=$ g/m²	$0.266 \times$ g/m² $=$ lb.

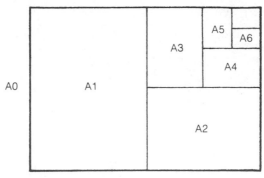

Area=1 square meter

In the metric *A* series of stock paper sizes, each size is half the area of the next larger, and all are the same shape.

TABLE 20.3   The *A* Series of Stock Paper Sizes

	Sheet Size	
	Millimeters	Inches (approx.)
A0	841 × 1,189	33⅛ × 46¾
A1	594 × 841	23⅜ × 33⅛
A2	420 × 594	16½ × 23⅜
A3	297 × 420	11¾ × 16½
A4	210 × 297	8¼ × 11¾
A5	148 × 210	5⅞ × 8¼

20.76   In Europe a series of mutually compatible stock sizes has virtually crowded out the old welter of stock sizes that was formerly offered. The metric *A* series is based on a standard sheet of paper, rectangular in shape (841 mm by 1,189 mm) and one square meter in area. This size is called *A0*. Cutting this sheet in half produces *A1*, and cutting *A1* in half produces *A2*, and so on down to *A5*, which is 1/32 the area of *A0*. (See diagram and table 20.3 for the dimensions of the *A* series.) An interesting feature of the series is that all sheets are the same shape; that is, the ratio of short side to long side is identical throughout the series of sizes. There is also a *B* series of sizes that are intermediate between the *A* sizes and two larger sheet sizes that are compatible with *A0*.

20.77   American stock sizes for book paper reflect the sizes of the presses commonly used for bookwork and the most popular trim sizes for books in the United States. See table 20.4 for some of these stock sheet sizes. Cover papers are generally stocked in smaller sizes, and paper on rolls for web-fed presses comes in various standard widths.

TABLE 20.4   Some American Stock Sizes for Book Paper (Inches)

Sheet Size	Number of Pages per Sheet	Folds to, before Trimming	Trim Size
Grain short:			
35 × 45	64	5⅝ × 8¾	5½ × 8½
38 × 50	64	6¼ × 9½	6⅛ × 9¼
Grain long:			
41 × 61	128	5⅛ × 7⅝	5 × 7⅜
44 × 66	128	5½ × 8¼	5⅜ × 8
45 × 68	128	5⅝ × 8½	5½ × 8¼
46 × 69	128	5¾ × 8⅝	5⅝ × 8⅜

REPRODUCING ILLUSTRATIONS

20.78   Another of the contributions of nineteenth-century technology to bookmaking was the ability to reproduce illustrations quickly, cheaply, and in large numbers. From the earliest days of printing, woodcuts had been printed along with text, and as illustrated books became more sophisticated, engravings and etchings (and later on, stone lithographs) were separately printed and bound or tipped into the text. But these modes of reproduction were essentially hand processes, and not very well adapted to the needs of the fast, inexpensive, machine printing that had come into being meanwhile. The invention that brought about the revolution in book illustration was *photoengraving*.

20.79   Photoengraving is a process whereby a relief printing surface is created photographically. The illustration, say a pencil sketch, is photographed, and the image is transferred to a metal plate in such a way that when the plate is immersed in acid, the background will be etched away and the image left in relief. (The term *photoengraving* is of course a misnomer: the process should have been called "photoetching"—but it's too late now.) For the purposes of photoengraving the artwork for illustrations falls into one of two categories, *line copy* or *continuous-tone copy*.

20.80   *Line work.* Line copy is work that consists only of pure blacks and pure whites—pen-and-ink or pencil drawings, bar charts, graphs, prints of engravings or etchings, impressions made from type, and the like. The copy is photographed on a sheet of zinc or magnesium and treated chemically to harden the image itself and to wash away the background. The hardened image then acts as a *resist* (see 20.24) when the plate is treated with acid. The result is a relief surface similar to that of a woodcut. When mounted on a wooden block to bring it up to type height, it can print along with typeset matter. In this form it is called a *line engraving, line cut, line block* (the latter chiefly British), or simply a *zinc*.

The halftone principle

20.81   *The halftone principle.* Continuous-tone copy may include pure blacks and pure whites, but it also includes gradations of tone between those extremes, a scale of grays that merges at one end into black and at the other end into white. For us the most familiar form of black-and-white continuous-tone copy is the photograph. For the purpose of printing, such copy is broken up into tiny round dots that vary in size according to the depth of the tone. If you look at a printed reproduction of a photograph through a magnifying glass, you will see that the black dots in the lightest areas are very small, those in the areas of medium gray are larger, and those in darker areas are so large that they merge into one another, leaving little white dots among them. This is known as a *halftone* reproduction.

20.82   Halftone photoengravings are made on metal (the finest on copper, rather than zinc or magnesium) and etched in much the same way as line cuts. But the image is first broken up into the requisite halftone dots by photographing the copy through a cross-ruled *screen*. The screen is positioned between the copy and the camera, and the openings between the cross-rules act as little pinhole cameras, bringing the light passing through them to focus on the photographic emulsion as round dots. Halftone screens for letterpress work are ruled at from 65 to 150 lines to the inch, the coarser screens being used for newspaper work. For offset work (more on this later), the ruling may run up to 300 lines to the inch.

20.83 Halftone engravings (also called *halftone cuts* and *halftone blocks*) do not print well on ordinary book paper, let alone newsprint. (That is why, when most newspapers were still printed by letterpress, 65- and 85-line screens had to be used for the news photos.) A hard-surface coated paper is needed for good reproduction of very fine-screen halftones, such as might be employed in reproducing photomicrographs in a medical text. Medium-screen halftones can be printed on a machine-finish or supercalendered sheet. Consequently, for a letterpress book illustrated with photographs or other continuous-tone copy, a paper has to be chosen that will accommodate the halftones, or the illustrations have to be gathered in one or more separate sections that are printed on special paper. When printed separately from the text, illustrations are known as *plates* (see 11.4).

20.84 One of the chief deterrents to printing halftone illustrations by letterpress is the problem of *makeready*. Try to visualize halftone dots of varying size from the side, in section as it were. The tiny dots in a highlight area rise from the etched background of the plate up to the printing surface as thin columns of metal, whereas the large dots, often merging into one another, are more like massive plateaus. In the printing process the small dots exert pressure (in terms of pounds per square inch) many times that exerted by the large ones. (Think what spike heels do to a cork floor in contrast to flat heels.) To even out the printing pressure, preventing the small dots from punching through the paper and the large dots from printing too light, the pressman causes more pressure to be exerted on the areas needing it by cutting out and pasting pieces of paper to the corresponding areas of the platen or impression cylinder. This procedure is called makeready. The extra thickness—several layers of paper may be used—increases the pressure in these areas and lessens it correspondingly in others. In a form printed from standing type, paper may also be placed under the halftone cuts.

20.85 Makeready is very expensive in terms of time—the pressman's time and down time on the press. And for an illustrated book or periodical every page may require as much as an hour of makeready time. Consequently, printing options that require little or no makeready are exceedingly attractive.

PLATEMAKING

20.86   When steam-powered printing presses first began to be developed, the need was felt for some way to duplicate the printing surface (see 20.42–47). Metal type holds up for only a certain number of impressions before it becomes so battered that it must be replaced, and this point was reached quickly with the new printing machinery that was coming into being to meet the demands of newspaper publishers.

20.87   *Letterpress plates.* The need for duplicate printing surfaces was met with the invention of the *stereotype.* This is an exact duplicate of the metal-type printing surface. In making a stereotype a mold is formed by pressing wet papier-mâché against the printing surface of the type and drying it with heat. It is then used to cast any number of type-metal printing plates—stereotypes—that are exact duplicates of the original type. Photoengravings did not exist when the stereotype was invented, but when they came along later in the nineteenth century, the technology was adapted to duplicating them as well as the type. Stereotypes came to be used chiefly (and to a much lesser extent still are) on high-speed rotary newspaper presses. For this purpose the papier-mâché mold (or *mat*) was held in curved form while the stereotype was cast. The result was a curved plate that could be clamped to the printing cylinder of the rotary press.

20.88   The *electrotype* was a later invention used mostly for long-run high-quality magazine and book printing. A wax (later plastic) mold was made of the printing surface, and the inside surface dusted with graphite. This was then electroplated with copper or nickel to produce a shell that could be pulled free of the mold and backed up with type metal. The resulting printing plate was very long-wearing and reproduced the detail of fine-screen halftones, which stereotypes cannot do.

20.89   To a limited degree the platemaking process allows the printing surface to be altered in ways that reduce the amount of makeready needed, and this is an advantage. There has never been any way to eliminate completely the need for fairly extensive makeready in letterpress printing, however.

20.90   *Gravure plates.* The printing surface in the gravure process (see 20.48) is copper, either a copper cylinder or a copper plate wrapped around a steel cylinder. In gravure work, unlike letterpress or offset lithography, the entire printing image, text as well as illustrations, is screened. The screen is a fine one, and difficult or impossible to see with the naked eye, but quite obvious under a magnifying glass. To see one, find a catalog from a large mail-order house like Burpee Seed Company or Sears, Roebuck, and put a pocket magnifier over the text.

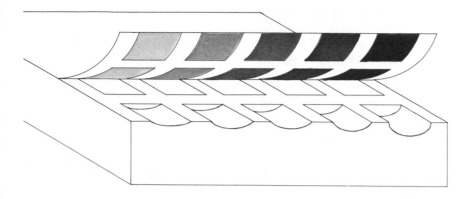

The square wells of a gravure plate vary in depth and consequently the amount of ink they will hold. Lighter tones are produced by the shallow wells, darker ones by the deeper wells.

20.91   Like letterpress photoengravings, gravure plates are made by a photochemical etching process. The photographic medium is a gelatin emulsion (called *carbon tissue*) that is first exposed to an allover screen and then to a film positive of the text and illustrations. After development, the gelatin, hardened wherever light struck it, forms a resist to the etching acid. The end result is a printing surface made up of thousands of tiny square wells, their walls formed by the image of the screen. The wells are deep where the image is dark, shallow where it is light and nonexistent (filled up) in the white, nonprinting areas. In printing, the sidewalls of the wells serve to support the doctor blade as it rides on the surface of the plate, wiping the unwanted ink from nonprinting areas. Then, when the plate is pressed against the paper, the deeper wells deposit more ink than the shallower wells, producing the effect of continuous tone. In light areas the ink is laid down in a dot pattern, but in dark areas the greater quantity of ink in the deep wells flows outward on the surface of the paper, obscuring the divisions between wells.

20.92   *Offset plates*. In contrast to letterpress and gravure plates, the plates used in offset lithography (see 20.49) are fairly simple affairs. An offset plate is typically a sheet of very thin aluminum (for short runs, even paper) carrying a positive printing image on its surface. Plates are made photographically, employing a medium that produces an image on the plate which will accept ink and repel water.

20.93   Printing plates carrying sixteen, thirty-two, or more pages are exposed in either of two ways. For the *stripping* method full-size line negatives of the text and screened negatives of the illustrations are assembled in individual pages. The page negatives are then taped down (stripped) on a large sheet of masking paper according to the printing layout (so that the printed sheet, when backed up and folded, will make a signature in correct page order). Finally, rectangular holes are cut in the masking paper so as to reveal the page images while masking out the nonprinting areas between them. This assemblage of masked negatives, called a *flat,* is next held down tightly on a photosensitive plate and exposed to light. When developed, the plate is ready for printing.

20.94 For the *projection* method of making offset plates, small negatives are made of the page materials in the order and orientation in which the printing images will appear on the plate. These are then projected one by one, at page size, onto the plate by a *step-and-repeat* enlarging device. The result, when developed, is a plate similar to that obtained by stripping.

20.95 The ease with which plates can be made and printed accounts for much of the popularity of offset lithography. The cost of using line illustrations is negligible: once they have been statted to correct size, they can be photographed along with the text at no extra charge. And good-quality halftones, made with 133- or 150-line screens, can print with the text on ordinary book paper. (High-resolution, 300-line halftones do, however, require smoother and denser stock.)

TWENTIETH-CENTURY CONTRIBUTIONS: COMPOSITION AND MAKEUP

20.96 Since all that is needed in offset lithography for making a printing plate is an image on paper or film, it doesn't really make any difference how the image gets there, so long as it is sharp and clear. There is no need to set metal type, if an image similar to that of a page of repro proof can be created by some other means. And that is what all modern, *direct-image* composition systems are designed to do. The simplest mode of direct-image composition—and the first in time to be used—is *strike-on* (essentially typewriter) *composition.* More complex and sophisticated are the various methods and systems known collectively as *photocomposition.* And still more sophisticated and versatile are the more recently developed systems employing *electronic,* or *digital,* typesetting machines controlled by computers—also called *CRT* (cathode-ray tube) composition.

STRIKE-ON COMPOSITION

20.97 When typewriter composition first began to be used in commercial printing, it was often referred to (originally, probably jocularly) as *cold type,* because reproduction copy was produced without the agency of

WWWWW MMMMM NNNNN aaaaa iiiii 11111 .....

WWWWW MMMMM NNNNN aaaaa iiiii lllll .....

The ordinary office typewriter allots the same amount of space to every character—capital, lowercase letter, or punctuation mark. "Real" type is designed so that characters vary in width according to the design of the letters, a capital *M* being three or four times as wide as a lowercase *l,* for example. This is the meaning of the term *proportional spacing.*

molten type metal. The name seems to have stuck, and has even been extended to cover other modes of direct-image composition. It is much more of a layman's term, however, than a professional's.

20.98   *Text composition.* The simplest form of strike-on composition is that produced by an ordinary office typewriter, and this method is sometimes used by scholarly publishers for special-interest monographs, where the cost of conventional typesetting cannot be justified by the probable sales revenue. The machine commonly used is the IBM Selectric, with its many interchangeable "golf ball" type fonts and carbon ribbon. Such composition lacks proportional spacing (*i*'s and *w*'s occupy the same space) and is usually unjustified.

20.99   Such typing is preferably done on a special matte-finish clay-coated paper that assures good contrast in reproduction. For long jobs, especially when a book is part of a series with a uniform format, the publisher often supplies the typist with specially prepared paper. This is printed with light blue lines (which are not picked up by the lithographer's camera) showing the position of the margins, chapter opening, page number, and the like.

20.100   More sophisticated is the MTST (magnetic-tape Selectric typewriter) system still in use in many small typesetting houses. It provides proportional spacing, mixing of fonts, justification, automatic centering of subheads, and some other refinements. MTST does this by storing on magnetic tape the record of up to 4,000 keystrokes, including function commands (such as font changes, line justification, etc.) and using the tape to drive an automatic typewriter. It produces a page or two of typeset matter at a time. Other strike-on systems have similar or greater capabilities.

20.101   *Composition for display.* Typewriter composition is unsuitable for anything larger than 12-point, so display work—title pages, chapter headings, part titles, and the like—must be composed in other ways. One possibility, seldom used but attractive if there is a calligrapher on the staff, is to write them out by hand. Another is to put them together with the press-on type sold in art-supply stores (Letraset is one ex-

629

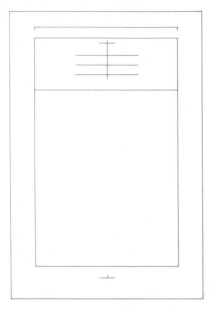

For common typewriter composition it is useful to provide the typist with ruled sheets, printed in "dropout" blue, showing the size of the type page, sinkage for chapter openings, placement of folios, and the like.

ample). This is printed on transparent vinyl backed with adhesive wax to make it stick down, and comes in a great variety of faces and sizes.

20.102 Or conventional modes of typesetting may be resorted to for the display lines only. They may be set in metal type and repro proofs pulled, or they may be set on any of the phototypesetters capable of display work. In either case the display lines are all set at the same time and then cut apart and pasted down on the appropriate pages for photographing.

20.103 *Proofing and correcting.* The strike-on mode of composition produces just one copy of the set matter, so conventional proofs are not available. Instead, it is customary to make copies of what has been set on an office copying machine. Since most typewriter-composed books are typed in page form, the machine copies are the equivalent of page proof. Corrections are marked on these, the typist retypes whatever needs to be corrected, whether words or whole lines, and the retyped copy is pasted over the original. Needless to say, corrections involving transfers of lines from one page to another are discouraged.

20.104 *Makeup.* If a book is typed in page form, most of the makeup decisions—avoidance of bad breaks, spacing of subheads, placement of footnotes, and the like—are made by the typist. If there are to be illustrations, space is left for these. Line work, such as graphs and diagrams, statted to appropriate size, may be pasted down directly on the typed pages. (Typewriter composition prepared on an office machine is ordinarily reduced from 10 to 20 percent when negatives for the printing plates are made; MTST and other similar composition is usually reproduced same size.) If photographs are to be used, the pages are *keylined* to show the positions and shapes of these, and the photographs, marked for cropping, are sent to the printer separately.

20.105 When offset negatives of the pages have been made and stripped up in position, the printer may make blueprints of the flats if the publisher asks for them and is willing to pay for them. These provide the editor with his or her only chance to check on the placement of halftone illustrations, and are useful for checking the positioning of typed material on the page and for making sure that everything intended for inclusion in the book is actually there (omitted pages and dropped halftones are not uncommon in offset work). Dirt, ink, or a piece of tape on the type area shows up as a blank on the blueprint, and can be caught and corrected at this time. A scratch shows as a black line.

PHOTOCOMPOSITION

20.106 Because of the high cost of hot-metal composition and the typographic limitations and slowness of strike-on composition, *photocomposition* accounts for most of the book, periodical, and newspaper typesetting done today. In photocomposition, or *phototypesetting*, the repro copy from which offset printing plates will be made is created by exposing photosensitive paper or film to light formed into the shapes of type characters, one by one. The paper or film is then processed like any other photograph.

20.107 All modern phototypesetting systems consist of three basic parts: an *input device* (such as a keyboard), a *computer* (for storage and retrieval of typographic information), and a *typesetter* (which actually creates the type images on the paper or film). The *photomechanical* typesetter forms light into the shapes of letters, numbers, and punctuation marks by passing light through a film negative of the character and onto the light-sensitive medium—something like projecting a slide on a screen.

20.108 *First-generation typesetters.* The earliest machines developed to produce *photoset* (or *filmset*—the terms are synonymous) composition were simply adaptations of already existing typecasting machines. Instead of brass matrices serving as type molds, film matrices were used to form the type images as light was projected through them. The Monophoto, Linofilm, and Fotosetter machines, for example, used the technology and much of the machinery of, respectively, the Monotype, Linotype, and Intertype metal-casting machines to produce paper photographic prints of the typography generated. Typesetting with these first-generation machines was slow, owing in part to the slow tungsten-filament light sources used, and few if any of them remain in use.

20.109   *Second-generation typesetters.* The next generation of photomechanical typesetters was based on new technology developed specifically for film composition. The fonts of type images are carried on film or glass in negative form in any of several configurations. One is a disk or segment of a disk that rotates to bring the negative for any particular character into position for projection. Another is a film strip wrapped around a drum that similarly rotates. Some typesetters employ several drums or disks simultaneously for enhanced typographic capacity.

20.110   The character image is projected by a brilliant flash of light from a stroboscopic xenon source through a lens system onto the light-sensitive paper or film that is the end product of the system. Many changes of point size are made optically, rather than by changing fonts. Some typesetters use several lenses, each for a particular enlargement or reduction of the type image, mounted in a turret that rotates to bring any particular lens into position. Others use a zoom lens (like that of a television camera) for the same purpose.

20.111   After passing through the lens system the beam of light either passes through a prism or reflects off a mirror at right angles to the beam, before it strikes the light-sensitive paper or film. An escapement system (similar in principle to that of a proportional-spacing typewriter) rotates the prism or mirror the right amount after each character is projected, so that the next character is projected to the right of the last. At the end of the type line a mechanism similar to the carriage return of a typewriter rotates the prism or mirror back to the beginning position, and advances the paper or film upward a notch to put it in position for the next line of type images.

CRT COMPOSITION

20.112   Phototypesetters of the third generation are entirely electronic. These typesetters use information stored in digital form to generate type images at great speed on the surface of a cathode-ray tube (CRT). The process is analogous to the way a television set uses signals received over the air or from a videotape to generate images on the picture tube.

20.113   *Character generation.* Any CRT is in essence an evacuated glass bottle. The screen, at the bottom end, is coated on the inside with phosphors, chemical substances that emit light when bombarded with electrons. A mechanism at the neck end generates and controls a stream of electrons that constantly sweeps the inside of the screen in a pattern of closely spaced lines. If the stream of electrons is continuous, the screen is completely lighted, but if the electrons are emitted in controlled bursts rather than a steady stream, the beam can be made to build up an image on the screen. This is what happens inside a TV picture tube and inside the character-generating CRT of an electronic typesetter. The typesetter's "picture" is much finer, of course: the scan lines forming the type image generally run 1,000–5,000 to the inch, whereas the picture tube of a medium-sized TV receiver produces a picture with scan lines spaced about 200 to the inch.

20.114   *Output.* In some digital typesetters the image of a character is projected through an optical system similar to that of a photomechanical typesetter, onto photosensitive paper or film. In other machines the front surface of the CRT is a fiber-optic plate, and the paper or film is held in contact with this. The image is thus transmitted directly to the paper or film exactly as it is generated, with no magnification or reduction.

TYPESETTING SYSTEMS

20.115   A typesetter is itself only one part of an integrated system that includes one or more other units that function with the aid of computers. Any second- or third-generation typesetter has a small computer built into it which governs its basic internal functioning. Such a machine is far from self-governing, however. In the main it is a "slave," making no decisions on its own but responding to commands from outside. Here "outside" means what industry people refer to as the "front end" of the system—one or more input devices and various computer storage-and-retrieval and processing units.

20.116   Typesetting systems vary greatly in capability and in how their various units integrate with one another. The most sophisticated systems can be programmed to produce completely made-up pages that need no further attention before they are photographed for offset printing. Indeed, some can be made to produce offset negatives of the pages, ready for stripping. Less sophisticated systems produce only the basic typography for a page, which then must be cut up and pasted down on boards, as with strike-on composition.

20.117   *Input devices.* The most usual form of input device in modern integrated typesetting systems is an *input and editing terminal,* also called a *video display terminal,* or *VDT.* This consists of (1) a keyboard that includes all the usual typewriter keys plus a number of other keys controlling special functions and (2) a CRT viewing screen on which computer-stored copy can be displayed. As the operator keyboards ("types") the material to be set, keystrokes are recorded in digital form on magnetic tape or disks and appear as typed copy on the screen above the keyboard. Copy can be "edited"—additions, corrections, cancellations made—as it is being recorded, or it can be called up later and edited then.

20.118 Along with the copy itself the operator inputs other information that will be needed for typesetting. The amount of information needed varies according to the capabilities of the system in use. It always includes *codes* (arbitrary sequences of letters and numbers) directing a change of typeface, as from roman to italic or from 10-point to 8-point, or changes of alignment, as at the beginning and end of indented material. It may also include end-of-line decisions about hyphenation. The keyboard is then characterized as *counting* and the input *justified*. But many typesetting systems are capable of making justification decisions on their own, and when keyboarding material for such a system, the operator simply types along, without regard to line endings. In that instance a *noncounting* keyboard can be used and the input is *unjustified*. (Tape containing unjustified copy is sometimes called *idiot tape*.)

20.119 Systems differ in how the keyboard integrates with the rest of the system. A *direct-input* keyboard or terminal is connected directly to the typesetter. An *off-line* keyboard or terminal is connected to an intermediate storage-and-retrieval unit.

20.120 One of the most ingenious input devices is the OCR (for *optical character recognition*) device. This machine scans the lines of a typewritten manuscript and records the characters in digital form on magnetic tape for use in driving a typesetting system. Appropriate input codes may be included in the original manuscript, or they may be inserted later in the digital input. OCRs are now capable of interpreting digitally a number of different typewriter faces.

20.121 The word processors manufactured by business-machine companies are also capable of producing input for typesetting systems. The computer language they employ, however, is designed primarily for office and scientific use, and it usually has to be "translated" for use as typesetting input.

20.122 *Computer storage and processing units.* Between keyboard and typesetter an integrated typesetting system includes a great deal of computer capacity for the storage and retrieval of information and for manipulating input in such ways as to produce acceptable typeset material. These functions (hyphenation and justification, for example, or basic page makeup) may be performed by individual "stand-alone"

The operator of this video display terminal can check input as it is recorded or call it back for subsequent "editing." At the left are two floppy disks in their paper sleeves.

units connected electronically, or they may be combined in a *central processing unit* (CPU), which stores all the information and performs all the command functions needed to drive the typesetter.

20.123 Part of the information stored in a central processing unit is in permanent storage (the *master file*) and is seldom, if ever, altered. This might include the following:

Kerning records (for example, "when *T* is followed by *a, e, o,* or *u,* set the word so the crossbar of *T* overhangs the next letter by so many units").

Logical hyphenation routines—a series of instructions that answers many word-division questions.

Exception dictionary—acceptable division given for many words to which the logical hyphenation routines do not apply.

Justification program, for spacing out words to fill the line.

Makeup instructions on adjusting spacing, number of lines to the page, etc., to avoid bad breaks.

For driving a digital typesetter, all the characters in all the fonts the machine is capable of setting, in digitized form.

20.124 Information in temporary storage (the *job file*) would probably include the following:

The text itself in digital form.

Specific commands concerning font and point size.

635

Specific makeup instructions—line length, page length, indention of various elements, etc.

20.125   *Capabilities.* Modern computer-controlled typesetting systems offer opportunities to control the appearance of the type images in the line—whether the typesetter driven by the computer is photomechanical or electronic—to a far greater degree than was ever possible with metal. Word spacing ranging from maximum to minimum may be specified for a line or two, a paragraph, or a whole manuscript by giving the simplest of instructions. Space between letters, which formerly could be no closer than the width of the metal type body permitted, can now be made so close that the letter forms are actually tangent. And any letter (not just a few specially designed "kerned" type sorts) may overhang any other when the forms of the letters permit:

> Total control is often sought but seldom attained.
> Total control is often sought but seldom attained.
> Total control is often sought but seldom attained.

PROOFING AND CORRECTING

20.126   Because of the completely different way that typeset material is created in a phototypesetting system, the ways the proofs are made and corrections entered are quite different from the ways familiar to us in hot-metal days.

20.127   *Proofs.* The most usual form of proof from a modern system is a machine copy of the typesetter output. This may be a first proof (the equivalent of a galley proof), showing the typeset material in long columns. Or if the typesetting system is one that produces made-up pages on its own, it may be the equivalent of page proof. In either case it is read by author and editor in the same way as conventional proof from metal type.

20.128   If the system includes a *lineprinter,* an initial proof may be produced in the form of computer printout. The magnetic record of the text as keyboarded and processed can be retrieved from where it is stored, and typed out by the lineprinter. This typed record can be proofread and used as the basis for making corrections. A disadvantage of the procedure is that the printout seldom *looks* very much like the finished product. An ordinary printout contains the text, with end-of-line hyphenation shown, but the lines are not spaced out to full measure. It shows no variations in type style—chapter headings, text, and extracts look the same, as do roman and italic. It also contains all the coded commands to the typesetter, which tend to get in the way if you aren't used to them (but once you are, they can help you to visualize the text in final form). If author and editor are willing to read proof in this form, a good deal of time and money can often be saved.

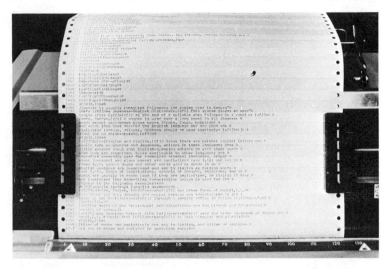

This lineprinter reproduces magnetic input intended for typesetting just as it is recorded, including encoded computer commands. The copy is some intended for chapter 9 of this book (9.116).

20.129   *Correcting.* The least sophisticated typesetting systems require corrections to be made in the least sophisticated way—by resetting words or lines and pasting these down on the typesetter output, as is done with strike-on composition. With more sophisticated systems the operator simply calls up on the screen of the VDT whatever parts of the text require correction and makes the needed changes directly on the digital magnetic record. If the changes necessitate lengthening or shortening the text, a system with page-makeup capability will then remake any pages as necessary, just as a printer would do with metal composition.

TWENTIETH-CENTURY CONTRIBUTIONS: PRINTING AND BINDING

FOUR-COLOR PROCESS PRINTING

20.130   As the developments in typesetting just described were a product of the middle and late twentieth century, the development of modern color printing was a product of the early days of the century. *Process printing* is a method of printing from three or more halftone plates, each inked with a different color, to obtain a result resembling a color photograph or painting. Just as an ordinary halftone gives an illusion of continuous tone in black and white and shades of gray, so process printing gives an illusion of continuous tone in natural colors. If you

637

The Cameron belt press produces finished paperback books by the letterpress process in relatively short runs at relatively low cost.

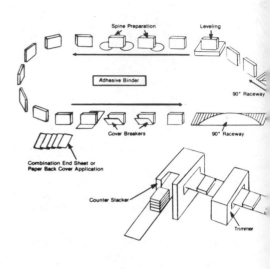

look at a color illustration in a magazine under a magnifying glass, you will see that the image is composed of tiny dots of pure primary colors, some overlying others but most of them adjacent to one another. The dots of each color vary in size and number across the face of the image, and our eyes, unable to distinguish the individual dots, interpret the patterns they make as natural colors.

20.131   The primary colors used in process printing are not the familiar red, blue, and yellow of a kindergartner's paint box. The yellow is more or less a pure yellow (and so named), but the blue, called *cyan,* is a greenish blue, and the red, called *magenta,* is a purplish red. In color theory, these three hues can be combined in varying proportions to make all the colors of the spectrum, as well as black. But printer's inks are not, and cannot be, perfect theoretical primaries, so a fourth "color," black, is added to the three primaries to help produce the darker shades and the pure black of shadows. Hence "four-color" process printing.

20.132   The halftone plates used in process printing are made from *color-separation negatives,* one for each color plus black. These may be made

638

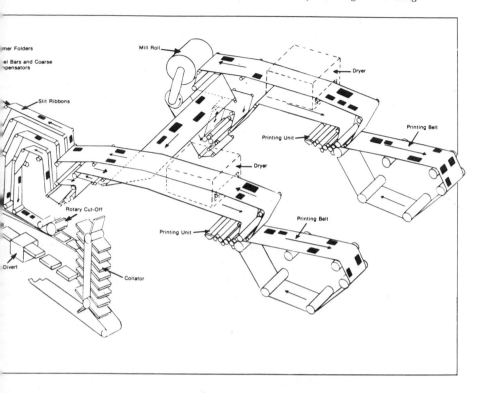

Labels on diagram: mer Folders; el Bars and Coarse npensators; Slit Ribbons; Rotary Cut-Off; Divert; Collator; Mill Roll; Dryer; Printing Unit; Dryer; Printing Belt; Printing Unit; Printing Belt

by shooting the color artwork through filters that blank out all but the one color wanted for that plate or by scanning the artwork on an electronic *color scanner* that separates the colors. As with all halftones, the printing surface is made by shooting through a screen that breaks the image up into dots. For each color, however, the screen is rotated a certain number of degrees so that the resulting dots do not all superimpose on one another or line up in the shimmering, wavy pattern called *moiré* (*mwa-RAY,* colloquially *maw-RAY*).

20.133 Four-color process work is done by all three of the major printing techniques. As noted earlier, a great deal of four-color work is done on newsprint, by rotogravure.

THE BELT PRESS

20.134 Just as the early demise of letterpress printing was being confidently predicted, the *belt press* (often called the *Cameron belt press* after one of its manufacturers) made its appearance and changed the outlook for letterpress. The belt press is web-fed and prints from plastic plates carried not on a cylinder but on an endless belt. It prints a complete book in one pass through the press. Belt presses are particularly suitable for paperback books in runs of from 2,000 to 5,000.

20.135   The plastic plates (whose development made possible the belt press) are made from a light-sensitive synthetic material and are acid-etched in much the same way as metal photoengravings. The plates, which are themselves flexible, are attached to an endless flexible belt that can be lengthened or shortened to suit the job. Usually the plates for several books of ordinary length can be accommodated at the same time. The press has two plate belts, one for each side of the web. With the plastic plates that are used, very little makeready is needed.

20.136   As the web of paper goes through the press it is first printed on one side by passing between the rotating plate belt and an impression cylinder, and then the ink impression is dried by heat. Continuing through the press, the other side of the web is printed and dried in the same manner. It is then slit into ribbons of paper two pages wide, and these are folded down the middle and chopped into four-page signatures, which are collated at the delivery end of the press. In some installations the collated signatures are fed into an automatic perfect-binder (see 20.141), and the end product is finished books, ready for shipping.

WEB OFFSET

20.137   A great deal of printing for publishers today is done by web-fed offset lithography, called "web offset" for short. Presses are generally similar to those used for sheet-fed offset and employ the same five kinds of rolls—plate cylinder, blanket cylinder, impression cylinder, dampening rollers, and ink rollers. The paper, however, is supplied to the press in the form of a continuous reel rather than as individual sheets. The web is printed first on one side, then on the other, and cut into press sheets as it leaves the press. With one form of web-offset press, the two sides of the web are printed simultaneously. The *blanket-to-blanket* press has no impression cylinder, but a pair of blanket cylinders tangent to each other print the web on both sides as it passes between them, each blanket cylinder acting as an impression cylinder for the other.

20.138   Web-offset printing is extremely fast and generally uses paper some 36–38 inches wide (some take webs more than 60 inches wide). As a consequence, web offset is useful to book publishers chiefly for textbooks, dictionaries, encyclopedias, and reference works, where press runs of 20,000 or more are usual. Development of the *miniweb* press, however, with a web less than 30 inches wide, sometimes makes relatively short runs (5,000 or even less) practical.

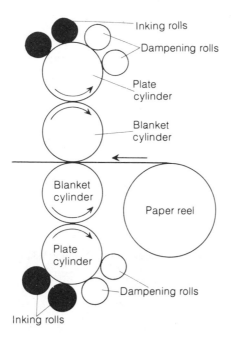

Inking rolls

Dampening rolls

Plate cylinder

Blanket cylinder

Blanket cylinder

Paper reel

Plate cylinder

Dampening rolls

Inking rolls

The blanket-to-blanket web-offset press dispenses altogether with an impression cylinder, printing both sides of the web at the same time.

BINDING

20.139 A number of different binding techniques have come into prominence in the twentieth century as substitutes for, or supplements to, the traditional case binding. Also a phenomenon of this century is the modern book jacket, a cover for a cover.

20.140 *Saddle wiring and side wiring.* Publications of pamphlet size, such as many popular magazines, are usually held together by *saddle wiring* (also called *saddle stitching*); that is, they are stapled two or three times from the outside to the inside of the fold. In *side wiring* (or *side stitching*) the staples go through the pages from the side, as in side sewing. Side wiring, unlike saddle wiring, permits more than one signature to be held together, and a separate paper cover may be pasted on near the spine so that the staples do not show. With either type of binding the pages are trimmed after the wiring operation.

20.141 *Perfect binding.* The method by which most paperback books and city telephone directories are held together is known as *perfect binding*. When the signatures have been folded and collated, they are held tightly and about an eighth of an inch is sliced off the spine, reducing the book to a series of separate pages. The trimmed spine is then

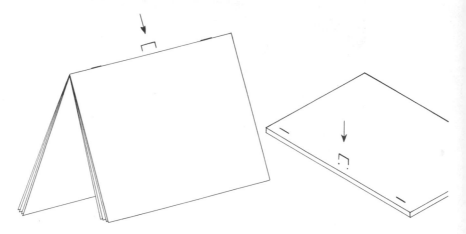

In saddle wiring, staples go in through the fold, and in side wiring they go in from the side.

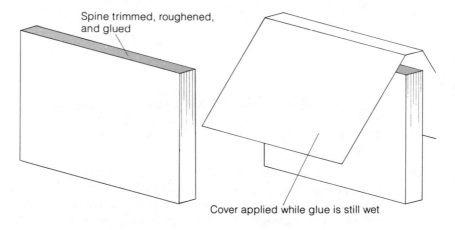

Spine trimmed, roughened, and glued

Cover applied while glue is still wet

Perfect binding involves gluing a paper cover to the specially prepared spine of the book. The book is trimmed on the other three sides after binding.

roughened or notched and coated with a flexible glue, and a paper cover is wrapped round the book. Stacks of books are then trimmed on the other three sides. Perfect binding has become much more dependable in recent years and is widely used both for original trade books (with a hardback case) and for quality magazines that formerly were side-wired.

20.142   Paperback covers are generally printed on flexible stock 10 to 15 *points* (same as *mils,* thousandths of an inch) in thickness, coated on

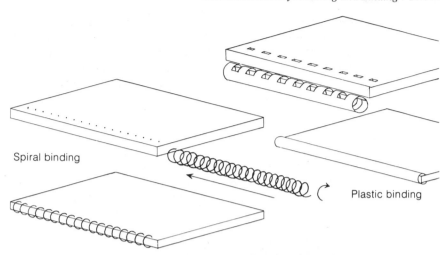

Spiral binding

Plastic binding

These two types of mechanical binding involve punching covers and sheets (trimmed on all four sides) with a row of holes in the back margin. For spiral binding the holes are small and round, and a corkscrewlike wire is threaded through them. For plastic binding, the holes are rectangular, and claws of springy plastic go through them from both back and front.

one side (the side that will carry the printing). The surface is usually protected by a transparent coating of some kind—*varnish,* applied with a cylinder printing press; "*liquid laminate,*" a synthetic resin applied in liquid form; *film laminate,* a transparent plastic film bonded directly to the printed surface; or any of various other coatings.

20.143 *Mechanical binding.* For several types of binding, collectively known as *mechanical binding,* the signatures are trimmed close to the fold (as for perfect binding), and a series of holes is punched through the pages at the back margin. Something is then run through the holes to hold the pages in order. The familiar three-ring notebook and the post binder are types of mechanical binding. But those commonly used for books (cookbooks, workbooks, and the like) are *spiral* and *plastic bindings.* Spiral and plastic binding are both fully automated processes, but because of the cost of the materials they are considerably more expensive than perfect binding.

20.144 *Book jackets.* Originally a simple wrapper provided to keep a cloth binding clean, the book jacket has become in modern times an advertising poster to attract attention to the book in a display and a vehicle for promotional copy intended to help sell the book once it is in a prospective buyer's hands. Even scholarly books are now quite generally given jackets, to attract attention to them at professional meetings and in college bookstores.

20.145 Jackets are printed in one, two, three, or four colors, generally on a small offset press. Printing is often "two up" or "three up"—meaning that the plate cylinder bears the images for two or more jackets, which then print together on one sheet of paper. The printed jacket may be left as is, but is more frequently given a protective coating like those given paperback books.

FOR FURTHER REFERENCE

20.146 Readers will find further information about many of the topics discussed in this chapter in *Bookmaking,* by Marshall Lee, and the International Paper Company's little paperback, *Pocket Pal.* Both are listed in the Bibliography.

Glossary of Technical Terms

Words set in SMALL CAPS are defined elsewhere in the Glossary

---

AAs. *See* ALTERATION.

ACCESS. In computer terminology, *access* refers to the ability to find a particular location in a body of stored data. Data stored on magnetic tape is subject only to *sequential* access, whereas data stored on disks or drums permits *random* access.

ADDRESS. Digitally coded label for a particular location in computer STORAGE.

AGAINST THE GRAIN. Feeding paper to a printing press in a direction across the grain of the paper fibers is said to be feeding *against the grain*. So also is folding paper in that direction for binding. The latter is also called folding, or binding, *cross-grain*. *See also* GRAIN.

AGATE LINE. A unit of measurement for newspaper advertising space, 1/14 of a column inch.

ALPHABET LENGTH. The horizontal measurement, in POINTS, of the lowercase alphabet set in type of a particular face and size.

ALPHANUMERIC. Consisting of letters, numbers, and symbols (generally, those available on a typewriter)—as an *alphanumeric code* for a computer command.

ALTERATION. A change from the manuscript copy introduced in proof, distinguished from a *correction* made to eliminate a printer's error. Alterations are billed as a separate item (above the charge for original composition). Alterations made by the author (*author's alterations*—colloquially, "AAs"), or some part of them, are customarily charged against royalties.

AMPERSAND. The name for the character "&."

ARABIC NUMERALS. The familiar digits used in arithmetical computation. In many type fonts they are available in two forms: *lining,* or *aligning* (1 2 3 4 5 6 7 8 9 0)—invariably used in tabular matter—and in *old style,* abbreviated *O.S.* (1 2 3 4 5 6 7 8 9 0)—the latter characterized by ASCENDERS and DESCENDERS.

ARTWORK. (1) Illustrative material (photographs, drawings, etc.) intended for reproduction. (2) Additions or corrections made by hand on etch proofs (*see* PROOF) or other reproduction copy.

ASCENDER. The part of such letters as *d, f, h,* and *k* that extends above the X-HEIGHT, or top of the letter *x.*

A SERIES. Series of stock paper sizes, widely used in Europe, based on a rectangular sheet one square meter in area. Throughout the series stock sizes have the same proportion of short side to long side, namely, one to the square root of two. A supplementary *B series* is cut in sizes between successive *A* sizes.

AUXILIARY STORAGE. Means for storing data in digital form outside the main computer memory—on magnetic tape, disks, etc.

BACKBONE. The SPINE of a book.

BACKING. In case binding, applying the BACKSTRIP.

BACK MARGIN. Inside MARGIN of a page.

BACKSTRIP. In case binding, a strip of paper pasted to the back of the sewn sheets after they have been rounded.

BACK UP. To print the back side of a sheet already printed on the front.

BAD BREAK. In page makeup, any of various unsightly or misleading arrangements of type occurring at the bottom or top of a page or column, as a paragraph ending consisting of only a word or two at the top of a page or column (called a *widow*), a subheading falling on the last line of a page or column, starting a page (especially a verso page) with a hyphenated word, etc.

BASE LINE. In type, a line connecting the bottoms of the capital letters. *See also* X-HEIGHT.

BASIS WEIGHT. The weight in pounds of a ream (500 sheets) of paper cut to a standard size (25 by 38 inches for book papers); or, when the letter *M* is used in the designation, the weight of 1,000 such sheets. Book papers generally run in the range of 40 to 80 pounds. *See also* GRAMMAGE.

BED. Flat surface of a FLATBED PRESS, to which the locked-up CHASE or printing plates are clamped.

BELT PRESS. A fast web-fed letterpress machine employing endless belts bearing flexible plastic printing plates in place of plate cylinders. Often called the *Cameron belt press* after the developer.

BENDAY PROCESS. A method of laying a screen (dots, lines, or other textures) on line plates by the use of gelatin films, to give the printed image an appearance of tone. Named for the inventor, Benjamin Day (1838–1916). Similar effects can be produced by an artist working directly on the original artwork with a MECHANICAL SCREEN. *See also* HALFTONE; HALFTONE SCREEN.

BEVEL. The sloping edge of an ELECTROTYPE or STEREOTYPE, by which the plate is attached to the base with catches while being printed.

BIBLE PAPER. Very thin opaque paper often used for Bibles and other books with a great many pages where easy portability is desired. Also called *India paper.*

BINARY. The *binary* system of numbers, which employs only the digits 1 and 0, is the basis for all modern digital computers.

BINDER'S BOARD. *See* BOARDS.

BINDER'S DIE. *See* DIE, STAMPING.

BINDING. (1) A covering for the pages of a book. (2) The process by which such a covering is attached. Materials include leather, cloth, paper, and plastic. Processes include CASE BINDING, PERFECT BINDING, and MECHANICAL BINDING.

BINDING CLOTH. *See* COVER MATERIALS.

BIT. In computer terminology, a *bi*nary digi*t,* the smallest possible unit of information, resulting from a choice between 0 and 1. *See also* BINARY; BYTE.

BLACK LETTER. *See* TYPE STYLES.

BLANKET. In OFFSET LITHOGRAPHY, the resilient rubber covering of the *blanket cylinder,* which receives the ink impression from the plate cylinder and offsets it onto the paper.

BLEED. An illustration that continues off the page when the edge of the paper has been trimmed away in binding is said to *bleed.*

BLIND FOLIO. A page number counted but not actually expressed in the makeup of a book.

BLIND KEYBOARD. A keyboard lacking the ability to produce HARD COPY of what is typed on it.

BLIND STAMP. An impression from a die on a cover, letterhead, certificate, or other piece of printing without the use of color.

BLOCK. A CUT.

BLOCK LETTER. *See* TYPE STYLES.

BLOW UP. To enlarge photographically. A photograph, chart, figure, etc., subjected to such treatment is termed a *blowup.*

BLUEPRINT. *See* PROOF.

BMI SPECIFICATIONS. *See* NASTA.

BOARDS. Stiffening material used in bookbinding, to which the cover is attached. Formerly wood, now generally a paper product such as *binder's board* (the finest quality), *pasted board* (often used in CASE BINDING), or *chipboard* (low quality). *Redboard* is used for flexible bindings.

BODY. The part of a piece of metal type that serves as a base for the raised printing surface. *Body size* (measured in points) is the dimension corresponding to the height of the printed letter and is the same for all characters in the font. In machine composition type may be cast on a larger body than that of the font (as a 10-point face on a 12-point body—"10 on 12") to obtain an effect of leading between lines. *Body width* is the dimension corresponding to the width of the printed letter and varies from character to character. *See also* FONT; MEASUREMENT; SORT; TYPE SIZES.

BODY TYPE. The type used for the text of a work, as distinguished from the DISPLAY TYPE used for chapter openings, subheadings, etc.

BOLDFACE. *See* TYPE STYLES.

BOND PAPER. Paper made chiefly for use in offices and as writing paper.

BOOK CLOTH. Cotton cloth, sized, glazed, or impregnated with synthetic resins, used for book covers and available in a large variety of weights, finishes, colors, and patterns. *See also* COVER MATERIALS.

BOOK PAPER. Paper made principally for the manufacture of books, pamphlets, and magazines as distinguished from newsprint and from writing and cover stock.

BOX. A printed rectangle enclosing typeset matter or an illustration.

BRACKETS. A device for enclosing material [thus]. In British usage, ( ) are known as brackets, [ ] as *square brackets*.

BREAK UP. In letterpress printing, to separate a form that is no longer needed into its component parts—type, furniture, engravings, etc.—and to dispose of each appropriately.

BROADSIDE. A broadside page is one designed to read normally when the book is turned 90 degrees (also called *landscape*). Wide tables and illustrations are often run broadside. In University of Chicago Press practice the *left* side of a broadside table or illustration is at the *bottom* of the page.

BRUSH-COATED. *See* COATED PAPER.

B SERIES. *See* A SERIES.

BUCKRAM. A heavy book cloth much used for library bindings or for binding large, heavy books.

BUG. In computer technology, something that causes a system to malfunction, such as a mechanical defect or a programming error. *See also* DEBUG; GLITCH.

BULK. The thickness of paper in number of pages per inch; also used loosely to indicate the thickness of a book, excluding the boards. *See also* CALIPER.

BULKING DUMMY. Resembles the finished book in every respect except that the pages and cover are blank. Such a dummy is used by the designer as a final check on the appearance and "feel" of the book, as a guide for the size and position of elements on the jacket, and as a positive indication of the width of the spine (for the stamping).

BUTT SLUGS. To join two short Linotype slugs with no space between them, making one long line of type or spacing material.

BYTE. A sequence of binary digits (bits), less than an entire WORD, processed by the computer as a whole. *See also* BIT.

CALENDER. Part of a papermaking machine, consisting of pairs of steel rollers that smooth the dried web of paper before it is reeled up. *Calendering* is the process of running paper through a calender to achieve varying degrees of smoothness. *See also* FINISH.

CALIFORNIA JOB CASE. *See* CASE, TYPE.

CALIPER. The thickness of a sheet of paper or board, measured in thousandths of an inch (referred to as *mils* in connection with paper and *points* in connection with board).

CAMERA-READY COPY. Artwork, type proofs, typewritten material, etc., ready to be photographed for reproduction without further alteration.

CAMERON BELT PRESS. *See* BELT PRESS.

CANCEL. A new leaf or signature replacing a defective one or one containing errors; any material substituting for deleted material. To cancel is to cut out blank or printed pages.

CAPS. An abbreviation for "capital letters."

CAPS AND SMALL CAPS. Two sizes of capitals (as used for subject entries in this glossary) constituting parts of the same FONT.

CARBON TISSUE. Light-sensitive material used in preparing GRAVURE plates.

CARDING. Inserting strips of heavy paper or extra leads between lines to lengthen a page or column; sometimes called *faking*. In PHOTO-COMPOSITION called *feathering*.

CARET. A sign directing the typesetter to insert the correction or additional material written immediately above the line (in manuscript) or at the side (on proofs).

CASE. A cover or binding, made by a casemaking machine or by hand and usually printed, stamped, or labeled before it is glued to a book. The process of applying such a ready-made cover is called *casing in*.

CASE, TYPE. A container with individual compartments for each SORT of a font of type. In older cases, capitals were kept in the upper rows of compartments, lowercase letters in the lower rows (hence the terms *uppercase* and *lowercase*). In the *California job case* they are kept side by side.

CASE BINDING. In case binding, sewn signatures plus endpapers are enclosed in a rigid cover. *Smyth sewing* passes the thread through the fold of each signature and locks it at the back. *Side sewing* passes the thread through the entire book from the side. *Side wiring* is essentially the same, except that wire staples are used instead of thread. At this stage the book is referred to as *unbound signatures*. A hinge of heavy gauze (*super*) is glued to the spine, and the last step, *casing in,* sees the signatures attached to the rigid case by the endpapers and the flaps of the hinge.

CASTING OFF, *or* CASTING UP. *See* COPYFITTING.

CATHODE-RAY TUBE. A vacuum tube with a screen at one end, illuminated by means of an electron beam controlled by magnetic devices at the other end. A television picture tube and the video screen of a word processor are common examples. Abbreviated *CRT. See also* CRT COMPOSITION; VIDEO DISPLAY TERMINAL.

CENTERED DOT. A heavy dot, •, used as an ornament before a paragraph. Familiarly called a *bullet*. A lighter centered dot is used in mathematical composition as a multiplication sign.

CENTRAL PROCESSING UNIT. A computer, or division of a computer, that performs all the chief functions of the system and generally contains the main data-storage area. Abbreviated CPU.

CHARACTER. A letter, numeral, symbol, or mark of punctuation. In printing type, characters vary in width, as they do on a *variable-spacing* typewriter. On an ordinary typewriter characters are all the same width.

CHARACTER COUNT. In COPYFITTING, a character count is made by computing the number of characters and spaces in an average line of the manuscript and multiplying by the number of lines in the manuscript.

CHARACTER GENERATION. In CRT COMPOSITION, the formation of type characters on the face of the cathode-ray tube from stored digital information. In PHOTOCOMPOSITION, the projection of type images from film matrices.

CHASE. A metal frame in which type and engravings are locked up for letterpress printing.

CHEMICAL PULP. Pulp for papermaking made from cellulose-containing substances (in the United States, generally wood chips) by chemical means. Distinguished from MECHANICAL PULP, or *groundwood. See also* SULFATE PROCESS; SULFITE PROCESS.

CHIPBOARD. *See* BOARDS.

CHROMALIN. Four-color proof made from COLOR SEPARATIONS to check color before printing.

CHUNK MAKEUP. Makeup, in either metal or direct-image composition, whereby portions of the page are made up by the compositor and proofed, to be fully made up later by other workers.

CLEAR. In computer technology, to erase stored data and to restore circuits to their beginning state.

CLOTHBOUND. A book protected by a rigid cover, usually cloth wrapped around boards, is called *clothbound* (sometimes the wrapping is paper of a distinctive pattern). *See also* PAPERBOUND.

COATED PAPER. Paper to which a surface coating of clay or other opaque material has been applied. Papers may be *coated one side* (abbreviated *C1S*) or *coated two sides* (*C2S*). *Machine-coated* papers are coated with rollers as they come off the papermaking machine; *brush-coated* papers are run through a special brush-coating machine. Coated papers range from matte finishes (*dull-coated*) to very shiny (*gloss enamel*).

CODES. In computer-assisted composition, combinations of letters, numbers, and symbols representing instructions to the computer, entered through a keyboard.

COLD TYPE. A popular term for strike-on, or TYPEWRITER COMPOSITION.

COLLAGE. An illustration made by pasting photographs, line cuts, type, etc., in combination.

COLLATE. In bookmaking, to arrange the folded signatures of a book in proper sequence for binding.

COLLATING MARK. A short rule is positioned on the press so as to print the collating mark on the outside of the fold of each SIGNATURE. When the signatures are collated in the proper order, these marks align diagonally. A miss means an omitted signature; two side by side mean a duplication. Instead of a rule, letters, figures, or a shortened book title may be used. Sometimes a small letter or figure is printed at the bottom of the first page of each signature (chiefly a British practice).

COLLOTYPE. A method of printing from a plane surface of hardened gelatin treated so that a greasy ink adheres to the parts of the plate bearing the image and from there is transferred to paper. The process embraces the principle of LITHOGRAPHY, the nonprinting areas retaining moisture which repels ink, leaving the printing areas ink-receptive. Collotype is used principally for the reproduction of pictorial copy.

COLOR PRINTING. *See* PROCESS COLOR PRINTING.

COLOR SEPARATION. Analyzing color copy for reproduction in terms of the three colors (plus black) to be used in printing; separation is achieved by shooting through filters or by electronic scanning. Also, a film negative or positive so produced.

COLUMN BREAK. *See* BAD BREAK.

COLUMN INCH. A unit of measurement for newspaper advertising space, one inch deep and one column wide.

COMBINATION PLATE. A printing plate combining HALFTONE matter with line ENGRAVING, as when lettering appears on a photographic illustration.

COMMAND. *See* INSTRUCTION.

COMP. Short for *comprehensive layout,* as for an advertisement or a book jacket. Also for COMPOSITOR.

COMPOSE. To set type, whether by HOT-METAL COMPOSITION, PHOTOCOMPOSITION, or TYPEWRITER COMPOSITION.

COMPOSITION, COMPUTER-ASSISTED. Text rendered in digital form is recorded on a magnetic medium (tape or disks) and run through a computer, where line-ending, hyphenation, justification, and other typographic decisions are carried out. The resulting record is used to drive a photomechanical or CRT typesetter. *See also* CRT COMPOSITION; PHOTOCOMPOSITION; PHOTOMECHANICAL COMPOSITION; VIDEO DISPLAY TERMINAL.

COMPOSITOR. Colloquially, "comp," a highly skilled person who makes corrections in metal type by hand and performs other hand operations, particularly in constructing tables and other technical matter. *See also* OPERATOR.

COMPUTERIZED TYPESETTING. *See* COMPOSITION, COMPUTER-ASSISTED.

CONDENSED. The characters of a condensed typeface are narrower than normal, permitting more material to be set in a line of the same width.

CONTINUOUS TONE. A continuous-tone image, such as a photograph, has gradations of tone from dark to light, in contrast to an image formed of pure blacks and whites, such as a pen-and-ink drawing or page of type (*see* LINE COPY).

COPY. Typescript, original artwork, photographs, etc., to be used in producing a printed work.

COPY BLOCK. A number of contiguous lines of type treated as a unit in design or in makeup.

COPYFITTING. The process of estimating the space required to print a given quantity of copy in a desired type size or of producing a quantity of manuscript which, when printed, will fill a given space. The former process is also called *casting off* copy. The usual method is to estimate the number of characters in the manuscript (*see* CHARACTER COUNT) and divide (1) by the *characters per pica* for the typeface and size to be used (this information appears with the sample in the printer's specimen book), (2) then by the measure of the typeset line, and (3) finally by the number of lines of type per page. The result is an estimate of the number of printed pages the manuscript will occupy when set and made up.

COVER. The two hinged parts of a book binding, front and back; also the four surfaces making up the covers in this sense, when used to carry printed matter. In a journal or magazine these are often designated *covers 1, 2, 3, and 4;* cover 1 carries the journal's name and sometimes the contents; covers 2, 3, and 4 may carry information about the journal or advertising.

COVER MATERIALS. Flexible materials, such as leather, cloth, paper, or plastic, used to form the cover in CASE BINDING.

COVER STOCK. Paper, generally thicker than book paper, used for the covers of pamphlets, brochures, paperbacks, etc.

CPU. CENTRAL PROCESSING UNIT.

CRASH. Same as SUPER.

CROP. To cut down an illustration, such as a photograph, in size to improve the appearance of the image by removing extraneous areas. Cropping is performed not by physical cutting but by masking, and *crop marks* are placed on the photograph or drawing as a guide to the printer's cameraman.

CRT. CATHODE-RAY TUBE.

CRT COMPOSITION. A CRT typesetter, driven by a computer, generates type images on the surface of a cathode-ray tube from digital records of the letter forms and transfers the images to photographic paper or film.

CUT. A LETTERPRESS PRINTING term originally referring to a *woodcut* but now generally used to denote a zinc etching, halftone engraving, or other illustrative matter (*see* ENGRAVING).

CYAN. A greenish blue, one of the three colors used in PROCESS COLOR PRINTING.

CYLINDER PRESS. *See* FLATBED PRESS.

DANDY ROLL. Roller of metal gauze which presses down on the web of pulp as it moves through a papermaking machine. When a WATERMARK is desired, the dandy roll carries the wire design for this on its surface.

DATA BANK. Information stored in a computer for later retrieval and use.

DATA BASE. (1) In statistical work, the total number of responses upon which a percentage is based, indicated by N or N. (2) A discrete body of information in computer storage.

653

DATA PROCESSING. In computer technology, handling stored information so as to produce some intended result, as combining keyboarded text copy and makeup instructions with font data to produce a typeset page.

DEAD COPY. Manuscript copy from which type has been set and corrections made on proofs, hence no longer needed.

DEBUG. To trace and correct defects in an electronic system such as a computer. *See also* BUG; GLITCH.

DECISION. In computer technology, a choice, or series of choices, between alternatives, made by comparing new data with stored instructions, such as a hyphenation-and-justification program for typesetting.

DECKLE. In hand papermaking, a frame that keeps the liquid pulp from flowing over the side of the wire mold; in machine papermaking a moving rubber *deckle strap* serves the same purpose.

DECKLE EDGE. The untrimmed edge of paper as it comes from the machine or the rough natural edge of handmade paper. A deckle edge is sometimes artificially produced on machine-made paper to give a handmade effect.

DEEP-ETCH PLATE. In OFFSET LITHOGRAPHY, a working plate on which the image is etched very slightly below the nonprinting surface. Deep-etch plates give high-quality reproduction of fine detail and permit very long press runs.

DESCENDER. The part of such letters as *p, q,* and *y* that extends below the *base line,* or bottom of the capitals.

DICTIONARY. In computer-assisted typesetting, an EXCEPTION DICTIONARY.

DIE, STAMPING. A die of brass or other hard metal used to STAMP the CASE of a book.

DIE-CUTTING. The process of cutting regular or irregular shapes out of paper by the use of specially fashioned steel knives. The result may be a "door" that can be folded back or a hole in the paper.

DIGITIZE. To describe something, such as a letter form, in terms of BINARY digits, so that it can be entered in, and retrieved from, computer storage.

DIRECT-IMAGE COMPOSITION. Any form of typesetting that produces an image directly on paper without the setting of metal type, such as typewriter, filmset, or CRT composition.

DIRECT-INPUT KEYBOARD. A keyboard connected directly with a typesetting device. The term is commonly used in connection with computer-assisted composition, but it applies equally to a typewriter or Linotype keyboard. *See also* OFF-LINE KEYBOARD.

DISK. Because disks offer random access to information stored on them, they are widely used in modern composing systems. A number of photomechanical typesetting machines use disks for the film matrices of their type fonts. And in the computer systems used to drive modern type-setters, digitized information for permanent storage is usually carried on rigid magnetic disks, whereas temporarily stored information (such as the text of a book) is generally carried on flexible ("floppy") disks. *See also* COMPOSITION, COMPUTER-ASSISTED.

DISPLAY. Telling the printer to *display* part of the copy means that it will be set on its own line, apart.

DISPLAY TYPE. Type that is larger than the body type used for setting the text of a printed work. Display faces are used for title pages, chapter openings, subheadings, etc., in a book or journal, for headlines in advertising, and so on.

DISTRIBUTE. To distribute type formerly meant to take the individual pieces of type out of the CHASE one by one and distribute them to their proper compartments in the CASE to be used again; foundry type is still treated in this fashion. Used in connection with machine-set metal type, the expression now means the same as *kill,* that is, to melt down type and Linotype slugs after they have served their purpose.

DROP FOLIO. A page number printed at the foot of the page.

DRUM. Magnetic-surface drums are used, like disks, for the storage of information in many computers.

DRY OFFSET. A combination of the letterpress and offset methods of printing wherein a relief plate cylinder (like that of a rotary press) prints on a blanket cylinder, which then offsets the image onto the paper. Also called *letterset.* Of little importance in book and periodical work.

DULL-COATED. A paper FINISH.

DUMMY. An unprinted or partially printed or sketched sample of a projected book, pamphlet, book cover, or other material to suggest the final appearance and size of the completed work. *See also* BULKING DUMMY.

DUOTONE. A two-color HALFTONE reproduction from a black-and-white photograph.

DUST WRAPPER. *See* JACKET.

EDITING TERMINAL. A VIDEO DISPLAY TERMINAL that permits correcting and rearranging copy stored in digitized magnetic form.

EGGSHELL. A paper FINISH.

ELECTROTYPE. A metal printing plate cast from a wax, lead, or plastic mold of type or illustrations, on which has been deposited by electrolysis a copper, nickel, or steel shell, which thus forms a hardened metal face on the softer backing. Because of durability and ease of storage, electrotypes are used instead of original type and cuts for printing a large edition or subsequent impressions of a book.

ELITE TYPE. Typewriter type that runs twelve characters to the inch (also called *twelve-pitch*). *See also* PICA TYPE.

EM. In printing, a unit of linear measurement equal to the point size of the type in question; i.e., a 6-point em is 6 points wide. An *en* is equal to half an em. *See also* MEASUREMENT; SPACING.

ENAMEL. A type of paper FINISH.

ENDPAPER. A folded sheet pasted or, rarely, sewed to the first and last signatures of a book, one leaf of which is pasted down to the inside of the front and back covers for the purpose of securing the book within the covers. Also called *endsheet*.

ENGLISH FINISH. *See* FINISH.

ENGRAVER'S PROOF. *See* PROOF.

ENGRAVING. (1) In fine arts, a print from an *intaglio plate* prepared by cutting below the surface with a graver, or burin. (2) In the graphic arts, short for *photoengraving,* a metal plate with a relief printing surface prepared by acid etching. (Here the term is a double misnomer because etching rather than engraving is used, and the result is a relief rather than an intaglio surface.) (3) Also, an illustration printed from such a plate.

A photoengraving is classified as a *line engraving (zinc,* or *zinc etching),* used for reproduction of material containing only solid blacks and whites (*see* LINE COPY), or a *halftone engraving,* used for reproduction of CONTINUOUS-TONE copy. *See also* HALFTONE.

ETCH PROOF. *See* PROOF.

EXCEPTION DICTIONARY. In computer-assisted typesetting, a list of words acceptably divided, consulted by the computer if the HYPHENATION ROUTINE does not supply the answer to an end-of-line hyphenation problem.

EXTENDED. The characters of an extended typeface are wider than normal ("fatter"), so that less material is set in a line of the same measure.

FACE. *See* TYPE STYLES.

FELT SIDE. The top side of a sheet of paper as it comes from the papermaking machine (the other side is the WIRE SIDE).

FIGURE. (1) An illustration printed with the text (hence also called a *text figure*) in distinction to a PLATE, which is printed separately. (2) An ARABIC NUMERAL.

FILE. In computer terminology any body of related, digitally stored information, as the text of a book.

FILM LAMINATE. A plastic film bonded to a jacket or paperback cover to protect the surface.

FILMSET. Same as *photoset,* i.e., set by means of a PHOTOTYPESETTER.

FINES. In paper, blemishes formed of clumps of fibers that remain stuck together through the papermaking process.

FINISH. The character of the surface of paper, generally achieved by calendering, supercalendering, and sometimes coating. The roughest finish regularly used in bookwork is *antique*. Calendered finishes, in increasing order of smoothness, are *eggshell, vellum,* and *english finish;* generically, calendered papers are called *machine-finished* (*MF*). Supercalendered papers are smoother and harder. In coated papers, the finish is determined by material, such as white clay, applied to the surface. *See also* CALENDER; COATED PAPER; SUPERCALENDER.

FLAT. In offset printing, a large sheet of paper with the negatives or positives taped into position for printing. The offset plate is made from it (*see* OFFSET LITHOGRAPHY).

FLATBED PRESS. Printing press with a flat surface (horizontal or vertical) to hold the type. In a cylinder press *ink rollers* and the *impression cylinder* carrying the paper pass alternately over the type. In old screw-type presses, the paper was laid on the inked type and a flat platen was pressed down from above.

FLOPPY DISK. A flexible disk coated with magnetically sensitive material, widely used for temporary storage of information in computer technology.

FLUSH. In typesetting, lines set *flush left* are aligned vertically along the left-hand margin. *Flush right* means the opposite. *See also* PARAGRAPH; RAGGED RIGHT.

FLUSH AND HANG. To set flush and hang is to set copy with HANGING INDENTION, as the entries in this glossary.

FLUSH BLOCKING. Mounting a CUT on a wooden block with a double-sided adhesive. This replaced the older method of tacking, which required a margin of wood all around.

FLYLEAF. Any blank leaf at the front or back of a book, except the endsheet pasted to the inside of the cover.

FOIL. Metallic LEAF used in stamping.

FOLDER. A machine that folds printed sheets into signatures for binding, often attached directly to the press at the delivery end.

FOLDOUT. An oversize leaf, often a map, an illustration, or a table, folded to fit within the trim size of the book and tipped in.

FOLIO. (1) In printing, a page number, often placed at the outside of the running head at the top of the page. If placed at the bottom of the page, the number is a *drop folio*. A folio counted in numbering pages but not printed (as on the title page) is a *blind folio;* any folio printed is an *expressed folio*. (2) In descriptive bibliography, a leaf of a manuscript or early printed book, the two sides being designated *r* (*recto,* or front) and *v* (*verso,* or back). (3) Formerly, a book made from standard-size sheets folded once, each sheet forming two leaves, or four pages.

FONT. A complete assortment of a given size of type, including capitals, small capitals, and lowercase, together with figures, punctuation marks, ligatures, and the commonly used signs and accents. Many special signs and accents are available but are not included in the regular font. The *italic* of a given face is considered a part of the equipment of a font of type but is spoken of as a separate font.

FORE EDGE. The trimmed outer edge of the leaves of a book. The outer MARGIN of a page is called the *fore-edge margin*.

FORM. (1) In most methods of book printing, all the pages that print together on one side of the sheet. (2) The printing surfaces—type, cuts, metal plates, offset plates, etc.—so ordered as to produce the foregoing. (On a BELT PRESS, forms as such do not exist.) *See also* IMPOSITION; SIGNATURE; STRIP.

FORMAT. The shape, size, style, and general appearance of a book as determined by type, margins, etc. Formerly, the size and proportion of a book as determined by the number of times the sheets have been folded, as FOLIO, QUARTO, OCTAVO, etc.

FORWARDING. In bookbinding, the processes between folding the sheets and casing in, such as rounding and backing, putting on headbands, reinforcing backs, etc.

FOUL PROOFS. Type proofs from which corrections have been made and approved by the author or the editor.

FOUNDRY PROOF. *See* PROOF.

FOUNDRY TYPE. Certain metal typefaces are available only from a foundry—that is, the printer cannot order matrices but must buy the pieces of type. Foundry type, set by hand, is reserved for display material or other small jobs.

FOUR-COLOR PROCESS. *See* PROCESS COLOR PRINTING.

FOURDRINIER. A papermaking machine.

FOUR-UP. *See* TWO-UP.

FRACTION. The printer will have the commoner fractions (e.g., $\frac{1}{2}$, ½) set on one SORT or MATRIX; these are called *piece fractions*. Others may be *built up,* either with full-size lining figures and a solidus (7/8) or with SUPERIOR and INFERIOR FIGURES (split fractions) (^{1}, -, $_{2}$, $\frac{1}{2}$).

FRAKTUR TYPE. *See* TYPE STYLES.

FREE SHEET. Paper free of MECHANICAL PULP.

FRISKET. In hand printing, a piece of paper with holes cut in it placed between the inked form and the paper, to keep unwanted ink from getting on the paper. Also, a paper or plastic film stencil used in preparing artwork.

FULL MEASURE. *See* MEASURE.

FUNCTION KEY. On a keyboard, a key that gives an instruction to the machine or computer, as opposed to keys that govern letters, numbers, marks of punctuation, etc. On an ordinary typewriter the shift and backspace keys are function keys.

FURNISH. The specific combination of materials, including the type of pulp, fillers, size, pigments, etc., that goes into the making of a particular type of PAPER.

FURNITURE. Wood spacing material used with metal type. Thin pieces of furniture are called *reglets*.

GALLEY. *See* PROOF.

GATEFOLD. A FOLDOUT leaf in a book or periodical.

GILDING. The application of gold leaf to the edges of book paper for the purpose of decoration. *See also* STAINING.

GLITCH. In computer terminology, something that causes a system to malfunction, such as a mechanical defect or a programming error. Same as *bug,* the older term. *See also* DEBUG.

GLOSSY. Short for *glossy print,* a photograph with a hard, very shiny finish, preferred for reproduction work.

GOTHIC. *See* TYPE STYLES.

GRAIN. In machine papermaking the fibers tend to align themselves longitudinally with the web as it moves through the machine, thus establishing the *grain* of the paper. For paper supplied in reel form, the grain is always in the direction of the web. Paper supplied in sheets may be cut *grain long* (grain running the long way of the sheet) or *grain short* (grain running the short way).

GRAMMAGE. In the metric system for specifying the BASIS WEIGHT of paper, the weight in grams of one square meter of the paper, i.e., *grams per square meter,* abbreviated g/m^2 or *gsm*.

GRAVURE PRINTING. A method of printing in which the impression is obtained from etched INTAGLIO plates, differing from letterpress plates in that the image to be printed lies below the surface of the plate in ink-filled depressions or wells. When the inked plate is wiped clean, the ink remaining in the depressions is left for transfer to the paper by adhesion. *See also* ROTOGRAVURE.

GRAY GOODS. Undyed, unfinished book cloth as it comes from the loom (*gray* is a mild misnomer for *greige*).

GRIPPERS. On a printing press, fingers that seize the edge of the paper and pull it through the press. The *gripper edge* of a printed sheet is the edge that goes through first.

GROUNDWOOD. Same as MECHANICAL PULP.

GUTTER. The two inner margins (back margins) of facing pages of a book.

HAIR SPACE. In hot-metal composition, a very thin piece of horizontal spacing material, variously defined as ¼ point, ½ point, or ⅕ of an em; or an analogous space in other modes of composition. Sometimes (incorrectly) called a *thin space* (¼ em).

HALFTONE. A process whereby a CONTINUOUS-TONE image, such as a photograph, is broken up into a pattern of dots of varying size from which a printing plate is made. When printed, the dots of the image, though clearly visible through a magnifying glass, merge to give an illusion of continuous tone to the naked eye. Reproductions of photographs in printed matter, whether letterpress or offset, are called *halftones*.

HALFTONE SCREEN. A grid used in the HALFTONE process to break the image up into dots. The fineness of the screen is denoted in terms of lines per inch, as *a 133-line screen*.

H & J. Hyphenation and justification, sometimes so abbreviated in connection with computer programs for typesetting.

HANGING INDENTION. The first line of a paragraph or item set flush left and subsequent lines indented. *See also* PARAGRAPH.

HARD COPY. Eye-readable typescript or printed copy, artwork, and the like, in contrast to copy recorded on magnetic tape, disks, etc.

HARDWARE. In computer terminology, machinery, circuitry, and other physical entities, in distinction to SOFTWARE, or programming.

HEADBAND. Decorative band at the top (and usually also the bottom) of the spine of a book, originally intended to take the strain of a person's finger as a book is removed from the shelf.

HEAD MARGIN. Top MARGIN of a page.

HICKEY. In offset lithography, a blemish in the impression caused by dirt, a blob of ink, etc., on the plate or blanket.

HINGE. In a bookbinding, the connection between the covers and the book proper; in hand binding its strength is due to the tapes or cords to which the signatures are sewn, in a case binding, to a strip of gauze (SUPER).

HOT-METAL COMPOSITION. Cast metal type set either by hand or by machine.

HYPHENATION ROUTINE. In computerized composition, a set of instructions for hyphenating words at the end of a line, usually supplemented by an EXCEPTION DICTIONARY.

660

IDIOT TAPE. In computerized typesetting, magnetic tape bearing only the keyboarded text itself—hyphenation, justification, and other instructions being added by a computer programmed to perform these functions.

IMPOSITION. The process of arranging the made-up pages of a FORM so that, when the sheets are printed and folded, the pages will be in the proper order. In OFFSET LITHOGRAPHY usually called *stripping*.

IMPRESSION. The inked image on the paper created during a single cycle of a press; the speed of a printing press is given in terms of *impressions per hour*. Also, in book publishing, a *printing*, i.e., all the copies of a book printed at the same time ("third impression" and "third printing" are synonymous).

IMPRESSION CYLINDER. In various methods of printing, a cylinder that backs up the paper as the impression is made.

INDENT. To set a line of type so that it begins or ends inside the normal margin. In *paragraph-style* indention the first line is indented from the left-hand margin and the following lines are set full measure. In *hanging* indention the first line is set full measure and the following lines are indented.

INDIA PAPER. Same as BIBLE PAPER.

INFERIOR FIGURE. A small numeral that prints partly below the base line: A_2. *See also* SUBSCRIPT.

INITIAL. A large letter used to begin a chapter or section. A *two-line* or *three-line* initial cuts down into the text two or three lines; a *stickup* initial aligns at the bottom with the first line of text but sticks up into the white space above. *Swash* initials are available in some faces. They are a florid version of the standard italic capital letters.

INK-JET PRINTING. In this process the printed image is formed as the paper moves past a row of minute jets that squirt ink in response to electronically controlled signals.

INPUT. *To input* is to enter information, instructions, text, etc., in a computer system; *input* is the data so entered. *Input devices* include the DIRECT-INPUT KEYBOARD, OFF-LINE KEYBOARD, OCR reader, and others.

INSERT. An extra printed leaf, sometimes folded, usually of different paper from the text, which is tipped in or placed loosely between the text pages. Also, additional matter typed on a separate page and pinned to the proof, to be set in type and run in.

INSTRUCTION. A command to a computer in digitally coded form to perform some function in connection with data supplied to it. A computer PROGRAM consists of many such instructions.

INTAGLIO. Term used to describe a printing surface in which the image is incised or etched below the nonprinting background. *See also* GRAVURE PRINTING.

INTERFACE. The junction point between two parts of a computer system, as between the operator and the input device, or between keyboarded tape and a central processing unit.

INTERTYPE. A slug-casting machine, similar to the LINOTYPE but manufactured by a different company. Matrices for the two machines are interchangeable.

ITALIC. *See* TYPE STYLES.

JACKET. A protective wrapping, usually paper, for a clothbound book; it carries the *blurb* on its *flaps,* which fold around the front and back covers. In the rare-book trade usually called *dust wrapper* (*abbr.* d.w.).

JOB PRESS. A small letterpress machine, usually a vertical platen press, used for printing letterhead, circulars, and other small jobs.

JUSTIFY. To space out lines of type to a specified measure.

KEEP TYPE STANDING. *See* STANDING.

KERN. In metal type, the part of a letter that extends beyond the edge of the type body and overlaps the adjacent sort. In phototypesetting *kerning* is adjusting the spacing between characters.

KEYBOARD. To *keyboard* reading matter is to copy it by means of a machine with a keyboard resembling that of a typewriter, or of a Monotype or Linotype machine. The end product may be HARD COPY, hot-metal type, or machine-readable magnetic tape, magnetic disks, or punched paper tape. *See also* DIRECT-INPUT KEYBOARD; OFF-LINE KEYBOARD.

KEYLINE. Copy for offset reproduction, with outlines showing the placement of halftones and type, as well as which parts print in which colors. *See also* MECHANICAL.

KILL. To omit, purposely, text or illustrations in revision of manuscript or printed matter. Also, an order to a letterpress printer to break up pages and melt down type (*see also* STANDING).

KISS IMPRESSION. In letterpress printing, an impression just hard enough to produce a fully inked image. In offset lithography any impression is a kiss impression.

KRAFT. Brown paper, used chiefly for wrapping paper, made from unbleached sulfate pulp (*see* CHEMICAL PULP).

LAID. Machine-made *laid* paper shows a characteristic pattern of widely spaced vertical lines and closely spaced horizontal lines when held up to the light. The laid effect (in imitation of handmade paper) is produced by the DANDY ROLL. *See also* WOVE.

LATIN ALPHABET. The ancestor of our alphabet, consisting of twenty-one letters (*j, u, w, y,* and *z* lacking). It is the parent of alphabets used in printing western European languages, including the Old English, German *Fraktur,* and Irish forms of letters. *Latin* is also used to distinguish an alphabet like ours from such forms as the Greek, Cyrillic, and Semitic alphabets.

LAYOUT. A designer's conception of the finished job, including spacing and type specifications; for interior or jacket also called "COMP."

LEADERS. A row of dots, evenly spaced, designed to carry the reader's eye across the rows of a table, from the chapter title to its page number in a table of contents, etc. Seldom used now.

LEADING. Extra spacing between lines of metal type, in addition to that provided by the shoulders of type sorts. A *lead* (pronounced *led*) is a thin strip of metal the length of the line, 1, 2, or 3 points thick. Ordinarily the word *lead* alone means a 2-point lead, and *leaded matter* therefore refers to matter in which there are 2 points between lines. A *slug* is a strip of metal 6 or 12 points thick, used where wider blank spaces are necessary. Spacing material of greater thickness than 12 points is known as *furniture* and is ordinarily made in multiples of 12 points.

The amount of space appearing between lines is called *visual space.* For a typeface that is *small on its body* this may be considerable and should be taken into consideration when leading is specified.

By extension, the spacing between lines set by means other than casting in metal is often referred to as leading, although the term is a misnomer.

LEAF. (1) One of the hinged pieces of paper making up a book or pamphlet, consisting of two pages. (2) Plastic film to which pigment or metallic powder has been bonded, used in stamping book covers (*see* STAMP).

LETTERPRESS PRINTING. Printing from raised surfaces, such as type, photoengravings, and wood or linoleum cuts. The paper is pressed against the inked surface to form an impression.

LETTERSPACING. *See* SPACING.

LIGATURE. Two or more connected letters cast on the same body, such as æ, fi, ff, etc. Older, more decorative forms (as ct) are known as *quaint characters. See also* LOGOTYPE.

LIGHTFACE. The ordinary variety of roman or italic type, in distinction to boldface. *See also* TYPE STYLES.

LINE. *See* HALFTONE SCREEN.

LINECASTING MACHINE. A typesetting machine that casts metal type in line-length slugs, specifically the Linotype or Intertype machine.

LINE COPY. Copy for reproduction which contains only solid blacks and whites, such as a type proof or a pen-and-ink drawing.

LINE NEGATIVE. *See* NEGATIVE.

LINEPRINTER. A machine, driven by a computer, which prints out stored data one line at a time.

663

LINING FIGURES. *See* ARABIC NUMERALS.

LINOTYPE. A typesetting machine invented by Ottmar Mergenthaler (1854–99) and developed in the decade before 1886. By use of a keyboard, *matrices* of various letters and signs are arranged and spaced out automatically in a line. The line of matrices is then brought in contact with molten type metal, and the entire line is cast as one *slug*. *See also* INTERTYPE.

LIQUID LAMINATE. A liquid coating for book jackets and paperback covers that when dry gives an effect similar to film laminate.

LITHOGRAPHY. (1) Stone lithography, an art medium whereby a number of impressions can be made from an image drawn with a greasy crayon on porous stone, which is then wetted and inked. (2) A generic designation for machine processes similar in principle to stone lithography (*see* OFFSET LITHOGRAPHY).

LOCATION. In computer terminology a location is the particular place in a storage medium where specific data are to be found, identified by an ADDRESS.

LOCK UP. In letterpress, to wedge the type pages firmly within the CHASE, or frame, by means of QUOINS.

LOGIC. The configuration of computer circuits for data processing; also the circuits themselves.

LOGOTYPE. Familiarly, "logo"; one or more words, or other combinations of letters, made available as one SORT. Often used for company names, trademarks, etc.

LONG PAGE. In makeup, a page that runs longer than provided for in the design.

LOWERCASE. The uncapitalized letters of a FONT (*abbr.* lc).

LUDLOW. A slug-casting machine for composing lines of type—principally in display sizes of 18 points or larger. Matrices are assembled by hand and locked in a frame, then placed over a slot in the machine; molten metal is brought in contact with the matrices, thereby casting a solid line, or slug.

MACHINE-COATED. A type of COATED PAPER.

MACHINE COPY. A copy of anything made on an office copying machine, such as a Xerox machine; often used as proof with DIRECT-IMAGE COMPOSITION.

MACHINE-FINISHED. In papermaking, same as calendered (*see* CALENDER).

MACHINE READABLE. Said of a text or of data that are recorded in digital form with codes appropriate to the particular computer as programmed.

MACHINING. *See* PRESSWORK.

MAGAZINE. In Linotype or Intertype, a case holding the particular fonts of matrices available at any one time.

MAGENTA. A bluish red, one of the three colors used in PROCESS COLOR PRINTING.

MAINFRAME. In computer terminology, a large CENTRAL PROCESSING UNIT, as distinct from input and other devices attached to it. The term is commonly reserved for powerful scientific and business-oriented computers.

MAKEREADY. In letterpress printing, a series of operations, performed by highly skilled workers, designed to ensure that all parts of a form print evenly. This process requires a varying amount of time, from a comparatively short period for plain type forms to many hours when halftone illustrations are involved. In offset lithography, the analogous operations are simpler and less time-consuming.

MAKEUP. The arranging of type lines and illustrations into page form.

MARGINS. The white space surrounding the printed area of a page, called the *back,* or *gutter, margin;* the *head,* or *top, margin;* the *fore-edge,* or *outside, margin;* and the *tail, foot,* or *bottom, margin. See also* TYPE PAGE.

MARKUP. The process of marking manuscript copy for typesetting with directions for use of type fonts and sizes, spacing, indention, etc.

MASTER PROOF. *See* PROOF.

MATRIX (MAT). In Linotype and Monotype, the mold in which the letters are cast; in phototypesetting processes, the image of the character is sometimes referred to as the *mat.* Also, the paper mold from which a STEREOTYPE is made.

MEASURE. The length of the line (width of the column) in which type is set. *Full measure* refers to copy set full width. *Narrow measure* refers to a block of copy (such as a long quotation) indented from one or both margins to distinguish it from surrounding full-measure copy, or to copy set in short lines for two-column makeup.

MEASUREMENT. The printer's basic unit of measurement is the *point,* approximately $\frac{1}{72}$ of an inch; 12 points equal 1 pica, approximately $\frac{1}{6}$ of an inch.

Within a font of type of one size the printer commonly measures by *ems.* In 9-point matter, to mark the copy for 1-em paragraph indention means to indent each paragraph 9 points (*see* EM).

665

MECHANICAL. Board prepared for offset reproduction with all type, artwork, photographs, etc., statted to size and pasted down. Differs from a KEY-LINE in that all camera-ready materials are supplied in place.

MECHANICAL BINDING. Category of bindings for books and pamphlets in which the spine fold is trimmed off and the leaves punched to accept some device that holds them together. Spiral, plastic (or comb), post, and ring bindings are examples.

MECHANICAL PULP. Pulp for papermaking made by grinding debarked logs. Also called *groundwood,* it contains all the impurities removed from CHEMICAL PULP and is used chiefly for newsprint.

MECHANICAL SCREEN. Thin transparent film printed with white or black dots, placed over artwork to simulate halftone work.

MEMORY. In computer terminology, part of a CENTRAL PROCESSING UNIT in which digitized information is permanently stored in magnetic form. Also, less strictly, any medium for permanent or temporary storage of information.

MIL. One-thousandth of an inch, term used for the measurement of paper thickness (*see* CALIPER).

MISPRINT. *See* TYPOGRAPHICAL ERROR.

MNEMONIC. Pertaining to (human) memory. Mnemonic computer codes are those that are easily memorized, like *TR9* for "9-point Times Roman type."

MODERN. *See* TYPE STYLES.

MOLLY. Printer's term for an EM. *See also* NUT.

MONOTYPE. A composing machine invented by Tolbert Lanston (1844–1913) and developed about 1890. In this machine a ribbon of paper, which is perforated on a keyboard, operates a casting machine by bringing the single matrices in contact in the proper order with a mold, so that the letters are cast one at a time and arranged in lines automatically spaced to the proper length.

MONTAGE. A photograph in which several images are combined photographically. Often mistakenly used for COLLAGE.

MORTISE. A space cut into a mounted printing plate so that type matter may be inserted.

MTST. For *magnetic tape Selectric typewriter,* a widely used typewriter-composing machine manufactured by the IBM Corporation.

MULTILITH. A printing machine, often used as an office duplicator, which operates on the offset principle.

MULTIPLE-INPUT. In computerized typesetting, characterized by permitting several input terminals (such as video display terminals) operating simultaneously to serve the same system. Also called *multiple-access* and *multiterminal.*

NASTA. National Association of State Textbook Administrators. *NASTA specifications,* revised periodically, cover manufacturing standards (particularly those pertaining to bindings) required of books intended for sale to schools. Formerly called *BMI* (Book Manufacturers' Institute) *specifications.*

NEGATIVE. (1) A photographic image in which light values are reversed (i.e., black appears as white); *see also* POSITIVE; RIGHT-READING. (2) Film used in PHOTOENGRAVING and in PHOTO-OFFSET.

NONWOVEN MATERIAL. Class of synthetic cover materials for bookbinding made by extrusion or felting rather than weaving.

NUMERALS. *See* ARABIC NUMERALS; ROMAN NUMERALS.

NUT. Printer's term for an EN (*See* EM).

OCR. For *optical character recognition.* In computerized typesetting, an OCR input device is capable of scanning a typescript and interpreting the typed characters in digital form, recording them on a magnetic medium for computer input.

OCTAVO. An old term for a book made from sheets which have been folded three times, each sheet forming eight leaves or sixteen pages. Sometimes applied to any book measuring about 6 by 9 inches.

OFF ITS FEET. Metal type knocked askew on the proof press is said to be off its feet.

OFF-LINE KEYBOARD. A keyboard not connected directly with a typesetter or central processing unit. Material from such a terminal is stored temporarily for later processing. *See also* DIRECT-INPUT KEYBOARD.

OFFPRINT. An article, chapter, or other excerpt from a larger work printed from the original type or plates and issued as a separate unit; also called *reprint.*

OFFSET. The accidental transfer of an impression from a freshly printed sheet to the back of the next sheet; an alternative term is *setoff.* Also, short for OFFSET LITHOGRAPHY.

OFFSET LITHOGRAPHY. An adaptation of the principles of stone lithography in which the design or page is photographically reproduced on a thin flexible metal plate. For photo-offset, a *negative* is used. If especially fine quality is wanted, a *positive* is used to prepare a DEEP-ETCH PLATE. The plate is curved to fit one of the revolving cylinders of the printing press. The design on this plate is transferred to, or *offset* on, the paper by means of a rubber blanket that runs over another cylinder. Other terms for this process are *planograph* and *lithoprint.*

OLD ENGLISH. Layman's term for *text* type. *See* TYPE STYLES.

OLD STYLE. *See* TYPE STYLES.

OLD STYLE FIGURES. *See* ARABIC NUMERALS.

OPAQUE. In photoengraving, to paint out on the negative those areas that are not wanted on the plate.

OPERATOR. The person who sets copy at the keyboard in any of the various typesetting processes. Often called COMPOSITOR.

OUTLINE HALFTONE. A HALFTONE engraving in which all or part of the background has been eliminated.

OUTPUT. Whatever comes out of a computer system, or any division of a system, as opposed to what goes in. The output of a keyboard terminal may be digitized information recorded on magnetic tape or disks, and these may become input for a central processing unit or typesetter, whose final output is finished typography.

OVERLAY. A hinged flap of paper or transparent plastic covering a piece of artwork. It may be there merely to protect the work, or it may bear type or other artwork intended for reproduction along with what lies underneath. Often used with a MECHANICAL or a KEYLINE.

OVERRUN. More than what was ordered, pertaining especially to paper from a mill and presswork from a printer. According to trade custom, usually mentioned in the order, overruns and underruns to a specified maximum are considered acceptable in fulfillment of a contract. The cost of an overrun is added to the customer's bill, that of an underrun subtracted from it.

PAGE. The pieces of paper making up a book are called *leaves*. One side only of such a leaf is called a *page*.

PAGE BREAK. *See* BAD BREAK.

PAGE PROOF. *See* PROOF.

PAGINATION. In the terminology peculiar to computerized typesetting page MAKEUP is sometimes referred to as pagination.

PAPER. Paper is made from cellulose fibers derived mainly from wood. Printing papers are described in terms of their FINISH, the process by which they are made (*see* CHEMICAL PULP; SULFATE PROCESS; SULFITE PROCESS), their relative weight (*see* BASIS WEIGHT), their thickness (*see* BULK; CALIPER), whether cut into sheets of various standard or nonstandard sizes or delivered in the form of rolls (*see* WEB), as well as of their color—principally white, but shading into *warm* (tannish) or *cool* (grayish) tones.

PAPERBOUND. Bound with a paper rather than a cloth-and-board cover (*see* CLOTHBOUND). A paperbound book is often called a *paperback*.

PARAGRAPHS. A *plain* paragraph has the first line indented and the other lines flush. A *hanging* paragraph, or paragraph with *hanging indention,* has the first line set flush and all others indented. A *flush* paragraph has all lines set flush and extra space is used between paragraphs to separate them.

PASTED BOARD. Stiffening material used for the covers of most casebound books (*see* CASE BINDING).

PASTEUP. The assembling of the various elements of type and illustration as a guide to the printer for makeup. Also, preparing CAMERA-READY COPY.

PE. Abbreviation for *printer's error,* used in correcting proof (*see* TYPOGRAPHICAL ERROR).

PENALTY COPY. Copy difficult to compose (heavily corrected, faint, much in a foreign language, etc.) for which the typesetter charges a certain percentage over the regular rate.

PERFECT BINDING. A method of holding together the pages of a book without stitching or sewing. After folding and collating, the backs of the signatures are cut off; the cut edges are then roughened to produce a surface of intermingled fibers to which an adhesive is applied. The books are usually finished with a wraparound paper cover.

PERFECTOR PRESS. A press designed to print both sides of the paper in one pass through the press. Also called *perfecting press.*

pH. Designation, on a scale of 14, of the acidity or alkalinity of a substance; pH 7 is neutral, lower numbers progressively acidic, higher numbers progressively alkaline. Paper with a pH value of 7 is desirable for any artwork or printed matter intended to have a long life.

PHOTOCOMPOSITION. Typesetting performed through the agency of light, as distinguished from HOT-METAL and TYPEWRITER COMPOSITION. Historically, the term has been used to include both PHOTOMECHANICAL COMPOSITION and CRT COMPOSITION, but is now often considered to be synonymous with the former and to exclude the latter.

PHOTOENGRAVING. *See* ENGRAVING.

PHOTOMECHANICAL COMPOSITION. PHOTOCOMPOSITION performed by a typesetting machine employing film matrices, as distinct from CRT COMPOSITION.

PHOTO-OFFSET. An offset printing process in which a negative print of the copy is used in the photochemical preparation of the metal plate. Photo-offset is known also as OFFSET LITHOGRAPHY, *photolithography,* and, loosely, as *planography* and *lithography.*

PHOTOSET. Set by a photocomposing method; synonymous with *filmset.*

PHOTOSTAT. A photographic copy made on a Photostat machine; familiarly, STAT.

PHOTOTYPESETTER. Usually, a typesetting machine that operates by projecting light through film matrices of the type characters upon light-sensitive paper or film. *See also* PHOTOCOMPOSITION.

PI. To mix up type accidentally.

PICA. Twelve points.

PICA EM. Twelve-point em.

PICA TYPE. Typewriter type that runs ten characters to the inch (also called *ten-pitch*). *See also* ELITE TYPE.

PICK. *Picking* is the pulling loose of paper fibers by heavily inked type; such fibers collectively are called *pick*.

PICK UP. To reuse previously printed matter as part of a new work, either by printing from the original type or by PHOTO-OFFSET. As a direction to the printer or artist, sometimes abbreviated *P.U.*

PLANOGRAPH. *See* MULTILITH; OFFSET LITHOGRAPHY; PHOTO-OFFSET.

PLASTIC BINDING. Type of MECHANICAL BINDING; also called *comb binding*.

PLATE. (1) An image-bearing surface that, when inked, will produce one whole page or several pages of printed matter at a time; used in OFFSET LITHOGRAPHY and (as ELECTROTYPES or STEREOTYPES) in LETTERPRESS PRINTING. (2) A printed illustration, usually of high quality and produced on special paper, tipped or bound into a book; when so printed, plates are numbered separately from other illustrations in the book.

PLATEN. In a printing press, a flat surface that presses the paper against the inked type to produce the impression.

PLATEN PRESS. Same as JOB PRESS.

PLATE PROOF. *See* PROOF.

POINT. (1) The printer's basic unit of type measurement—0.0138 inch (approximately $\frac{1}{72}$ of an inch). (2) One-thousandth of an inch, a unit used in measuring paper products employed in printing and binding. *See also* CALIPER.

POSITIVE. A photographic image on paper or film which corresponds to the original subject in values of light and shade.

PREPRESS. In OFFSET LITHOGRAPHY, the processes between completion of individual offset negatives of the pages and printing are referred to as *prepress*. They include stripping (*see* STRIP), platemaking (*see* PLATE), and MAKEREADY.

PREPRINT. Part of a book printed and distributed before publication for promotional purposes.

PRESS RUN. The number of copies printed. Also called *print run*.

PRESSWORK. In bookmaking, the actual printing of the book, as distinct from *composition (see* COMPOSE) and MAKEUP, which precede, and BINDING, which follows. Also called *machining.*

PRINTER'S ERROR. *See* TYPOGRAPHICAL ERROR.

PRINTOUT. Output of a LINEPRINTER or other device that produces normal-reading copy from computer-stored data.

PRINT RUN. Same as PRESS RUN.

PROCESS COLOR PRINTING. Halftone reproduction of full-color art or photographs through use of several plates (usually four), each printing a different color. *Process colors* are yellow, magenta, cyan, and black.

PROGRAM. A set of data-processing instructions for a computer. To *program* is to devise and enter such a set of instructions.

PROGRESSIVE PROOFS. Proofs of PROCESS COLOR plates, showing the colors individually and progressively combined, as the plates will print. Colloquially called "progs."

PROOF. A *galley proof* is an impression of metal type as it stands in a long, shallow metal tray known as a *galley.* Such proofs are used by the proofreader and author for reading, and errors are corrected by the compositor while the type remains in this form. After corrections have been made in a galley, a *revised proof* is taken for checking them. N.B.: Although the term is a misnomer, first proofs of matter set by other modes of composition, such as photocomposition and typewriter, are often called galley proofs or simply "galleys."

A *page proof* is an impression of typography after it has been made into page form.

A *foundry proof* is an impression taken of a page of metal type after it is locked up for the casting of book plates. The black border on such proof is made by the *bearers* in which the type is enclosed in locking up.

A *plate proof* is an impression taken of a completed plate for final checking before printing.

An *etch proof* (or *reproduction proof*—"repro") is the proof of a type page or other matter to be reproduced by photo-offset.

Master proof is the set of galley or page proofs carrying all corrections and alterations, both printer's and author's; it is usually so stamped by the printer.

An *engraver's proof* is a proof of a line or halftone engraving.

Blueprints, vandykes, and *silver prints* are photographic prints prepared from text or art copy intended for offset reproduction. They serve the same purposes as page proof and engraver's proof in letterpress work.

PROOF PRESS. A small, hand-operated press for pulling letterpress proofs.

PROOFREADERS' MARKS. A system of marking errors on proofs evolved over many years and (with minor variations) internationally understood.

P.U. *See* PICK UP.

PULP. Material from which paper is made, consisting mainly of cellulose fibers and water, formerly obtained chiefly from rags, now from wood (*see* CHEMICAL PULP; MECHANICAL PULP; RAG PAPER).

QUAD. (1) A large space to be used in setting a line of type; if not otherwise designated, an *em quad,* equal in width to the point size of the type. *En quads* are half that width and 2- and 3-em quads are also available. (In printer's parlance, a *3-to-em space*—that is, one-third of an em—is abbreviated to *3-em space,* and an en quad is called a *nut,* to avoid confusion with "em quad.") (2) In machine-set type to *quad* is to fill out a line with spacing material, as when a heading has been set flush left, centered, or flush right. This and the analogous procedure in photocomposition are accomplished automatically.

QUAINT CHARACTERS. *See* LIGATURE.

QUARTO. An old term for a book made from sheets which have been folded twice, each sheet forming four leaves or eight pages. Sometimes applied to any book measuring about 9 by 12 inches.

QUERY. On manuscript or proof, a question addressed to the author or editor (abbreviated *qy*).

QUOINS. Metal wedges (pronounced *coins*) used to lock up printing material in the CHASE. Opened and closed with a *quoin key.*

RAGGED RIGHT. Set with the right-hand margin unjustified. *See also* JUSTIFY.

RAG PAPER. High-quality paper made from cotton (formerly linen) rags chopped, boiled, and beaten to pulp.

RANDOM ACCESS. *See* ACCESS.

RANGE. *Range right* and *range left* are equivalent to *flush right* and *flush left*—chiefly a British usage. *See also* FLUSH.

RAW DATA. (1) Statistical results not yet examined to eliminate incomplete, unresponsive, and other flawed data (*see* DATA BASE). (2) Information, usually in digital form, that has not yet been processed by a computer.

REAM. The number unit on the basis of which paper is handled—now usually 500 sheets. *See also* BASIS WEIGHT; PAPER.

RECTO. The front side of a LEAF; in a book, a right-hand page. To "start recto" is to begin on a recto page, as a preface or an index normally does. *See also* VERSO.

REDBOARD. *See* BOARDS.

REEL-FED. *See* WEB-FED.

REGISTER. To print an impression on a sheet in correct relationship to other impressions already printed on the same sheet, e.g., to superimpose exactly the various color impressions in PROCESS COLOR PRINTING. When such impressions are not exactly aligned, they are said to be *out of register.*

REGLET. Thin piece of FURNITURE.

REMAKE. To alter the MAKEUP of a page or series of pages.

REPRO. Short for *reproduction proof,* a fine-quality type proof pulled for use in photoengraving or in offset lithography. Now often means final, corrected photocomposed typography.

REVERSE OUT. When an image of type or of a drawing appears in white surrounded by a solid block of color or black, the copy is said to be *reversed out.* This technique makes possible the use of the white paper as a "color."

REVISE. A corrected (*revised*) PROOF.

RIGHT-READING. Said of a photographic image in which right-to-left orientation appears as in the original subject; *wrong-reading* is the opposite, i.e., a mirror image. The terms are not to be confused with POSITIVE and NEGATIVE, which refer to light values.

RIVER. In widely spaced composition an undesirable streak of white space running down through several lines of type, breaking up the even appearance of the page.

ROMAN. The ordinary type style, distinguished from *italic.*

ROMAN NUMERALS. Numbers formed from traditional combinations of roman letters, either capitals (I, II, III, IV, etc.) or lowercase (i, ii, iii, iv, etc.). *See also* ARABIC NUMERALS.

ROTOGRAVURE. Web-fed gravure printing, typically used for long runs of material involving many illustrations. Rotogravure is capable of producing good-quality images on uncoated paper, especially newsprint, and so is employed for mail-order catalogs, newspaper weekend supplements, and the like.

ROUNDING. In bookbinding, imparting a convex curve to the spine.

ROUT. To cut away or deepen the blank, or nonprinting, areas in a metal printing plate with a special engraver's tool, so that they will not become inked and make a mark on the paper during printing.

ROUTINE. In computer technology, a set of instructions to be followed in a particular order, such as a HYPHENATION ROUTINE in computerized typesetting.

673

RULE. A strip of brass or other metal, type high, used with metal type to produce a printed line. Also the printed line so produced, and analogous lines produced by DIRECT-IMAGE COMPOSITION.

RUN. (1) PRESS RUN. (2) Material produced at the same time by a paper or cloth mill. (3) Processing of a given body of data by a computer.

RUNAROUND. Type set in narrow lines to fit around an illustration or a box.

RUN BACK. In reading proof, to move material from the beginning of one line to the end of the one above it (*abbr.* rb).

RUN DOWN. In reading proof, to move material from the end of one line to the beginning of the next (*abbr.* rd).

RUN IN. (1) To merge a paragraph with the preceding one. (2) To insert new copy (whether an omission of the operator or an author's addition) into the text.

RUNOVER. (1) In FLUSH-AND-HANG material (*see* INDENT), all lines after the first of a particular entry; (2) the continuation of a heading on a second line; (3) a large amount of reset material.

SADDLE-WIRED. Said of printed sheets that are stapled through the middle of the fold—like *Time* or *Newsweek*. Also called *saddle-stitched*.

SANS SERIF. *See* TYPE STYLES.

SCALE. To *scale* an illustration is to calculate (after cropping) the proportions and finish size of the reproduction, and the amount of reduction needed to achieve this size.

SCANNER. Device for producing film color separation negatives or positives for PROCESS COLOR PRINTING by electronically scanning the copy. Also, any device that senses alternation in light and dark, such as an OCR input device, or in magnetized and unmagnetized state of a medium, such as various parts of a computer system.

SCREEN. (1) A HALFTONE SCREEN; also the dot pattern in the printed image produced by such a screen. (2) A MECHANICAL SCREEN. (3) A screen used in the BENDAY PROCESS. (4) The face of a CATHODE-RAY TUBE.

SCRIPT. A variety of type (*see* TYPE STYLES). Also, short for *manuscript* or *typescript*.

SELF COVER. A cover for a pamphlet, offprint, etc., made of the same paper as the text.

SEPARATION NEGATIVE. *See* COLOR SEPARATION.

SERIF. A short, light line projecting from the top or bottom of a main stroke of a letter; originally, in handwritten letters, a beginning or finishing stroke of the pen. Gothic and sans serif faces lack serifs.

SET. The horizontal dimension of type. It is expressed in units on composing machines and is generally spoken of as *condensed* or *extended, thin* or *fat.*

SETOFF. *See* OFFSET.

SEWING. *See* BINDING.

SHEETWISE. A method of printing in which a different form is used for each side of the sheet, as distinct from WORK-AND-TURN.

SHILLING MARK. *See* SOLIDUS.

SHINGLE. For a SADDLE-WIRED periodical or pamphlet with a great many pages, to vary slightly the placement of the type image from page to page, so that, after binding and trimming, the outside margins will be equal in width.

SHORT PAGE. In makeup, a page that runs shorter than provided for in the design.

SHOW-THROUGH. An undesirable aspect of printed matter in which what is printed on the back of the sheet shows through the front.

SIDE-SEWN. Side-sewn books are sewn straight through the signatures from the side, close to the spine, before they are bound. Libraries typically rebind books in this manner. A side-sewn book is more durable than a SMYTH-SEWN book but will not open flat.

SIDE-WIRED. Said of signatures of printed matter that are stapled through the side before the cover is glued on.

SIGNATURE. A sheet of a book as folded ready for sewing. It is often 32 pages but may be only 16 or even 8 pages if the paper stock is very heavy, or 64 pages if the paper is thin enough to permit additional folding. The size of the press also regulates the size of the signature.

SILK-SCREEN PRINTING. A stencil process in which ink is forced through the pores of a fabric screen bearing a reverse image of the design to be printed.

SILVER PRINT. *See* PROOF.

SINGER-SEWN. Same as SIDE-SEWN.

SINKAGE. The amount type is dropped downward on a display page such as a chapter opening.

SIZE. Gluelike material added to paper, either in the FURNISH or on the surface, to make it stiffer and more resistant to moisture.

SLANT. *See* SOLIDUS.

SLASH. *See* SOLIDUS.

SLAVE. In computer terminology, a device operated wholly by data input and programmed from another part of the system. In computerized typesetting the typesetting machine itself is commonly operated as a *slave* to the software program of the CENTRAL PROCESSING UNIT.

SLIPCASE. A protective box in which a book or set of volumes fits. When shelved, the spines of the books are visible.

SLIP SHEET. A sheet of paper placed between printed sheets as they come off the press to prevent SETOFF from one sheet to another.

SLIT ON PRESS. To cut printed sheets or web longitudinally before they reach the FOLDER.

SLUG. A line of type or spacing material cast by a Linotype machine; also similar spacing material used with other kinds of composition. *See also* LEADING.

SMALL CAPS. Capital letters that are smaller than the regular caps of a font (*abbr.* sc). Small caps are usually equal to the X-HEIGHT of the font.

SMYTH-SEWN. The signatures of a Smyth-sewn book are individually sewn through the fold before being bound. A Smyth-sewn book has the advantage of lying flat when open, unlike a SIDE-SEWN or *perfect-bound* book (*see* PERFECT BINDING).

SOFTWARE. Computer programs. *See also* HARDWARE.

SOLID. To set type *solid* is to set with no additional space between lines (LEADING).

SOLIDUS. A type sort consisting of a slant line (/), used between the parts of a fraction (5/8), to separate lines of poetry when quoted in run-in fashion, as an abbreviation for the shilling in predecimalized British currency (2/6), etc. Also called *virgule, shilling mark, slant,* and *slash.*

SORT. Body of metal with a character in relief cast at one end. Each sort is *type high to paper*—that is, 0.9186 inch high, wide in proportion to the width of the character (*i* is narrow, *m* wide, and *a* intermediate), and a certain number of points deep. The nonprinting area (less than type high) of the sort above and below the character is called the *shoulder.* Part of the character extending beyond the body of the sort is called a *kern.*

By extension, whatever produces the image of a particular character, such as a film negative (in phototypesetting) or digital sequence (in computerized setting) can be termed a sort.

SPACEBAND. In a linecasting machine, a sliding wedge used for word spacing; at the end of a line the wedges slide forward and force the words apart to JUSTIFY the line.

SPACING. By spacing is meant lateral spacing between words, sentences, or columns, and paragraph indentions. (Vertical spacing between lines is called LEADING.) Two systems of measurement, based on old methods of hot-metal typesetting, are in common use. One employs the terminology and rationale of handset foundry type, the other that of the Monotype system of machine setting.

The first system uses the *em quad* as its basic unit, a block of type metal as wide as it is high, varying in dimensions from one type size to another. Thus in 12-point type, an em quad (or simply *em*—the word *quad* being understood) is 12 points square, and in 8-point type, it is 8 points square. Other spacing is measured in multiples and fractions of the basic em: *2-em, 3-em, 4-em quads,* etc.; also the *en* (½-*em*) *quad* and other spaces such as *3-to-em, 4-to-em,* and *5-to-em* (⅓, ¼, and ⅕ of an em, respectively). In this system a *thin space* is usually defined as a *4-to-em space,* and a *hair space* a *5-to-em space.* Minimum word spacing, depending on the needs of justification, is about that of a thin space.

The second system employs a unit that is ¹⁄₁₈ of a *quad*. For most faces the quad is an actual em quad, but some faces use a slightly wider quad ("fat" faces) and others a slightly narrower one ("thin" faces). There are always 18 units in a quad, however. Thus for a regular-size face a *9-unit space* is exactly the same as an *en quad,* and *6-unit, 5-unit,* and *4-unit* spaces approximate the *3-to-em, 4-to-em,* and *5-to-em* spaces of the first system.

Two caveats may be in order. (1) Actual shop terminology often differs from that just given. Thus an *em quad* and an *en quad* are usually called a *molly* and a *nut space,* respectively; and *3-to-em, 4-to-em,* etc., commonly are spoken of as *3-em, 4-em,* etc. (2) Also, elements of a third system sometimes appear, with horizontal spacing given in terms of *points,* down to ½ *point* and even ¼ *point,* the latter the hairiest of hair spaces available in any system.

SPEC. Short for specification (plural, *spex*).

SPINE. The part of a book binding visible when the book is shelved. In University of Chicago Press practice the spine title reads either across the short dimension of the spine or from top to bottom (so that it reads normally when the book is lying face up on a table).

SPIRAL BINDING. A type of MECHANICAL BINDING.

STAINING. The coloring of the edges of book pages for decorative effect. *See also* GILDING.

STAMP. In CASE BINDING, to imprint the spine of the case and sometimes the front cover with hard metal dies. Stamping may be done blind or with foil (*hot stamping*) or with ink. *See also* BLIND STAMP; FOIL; LEAF.

STANDING. *Standing type* is metal type that has been set and is (more or less) ready for printing. To print from standing type is to print from the type that was set, in distinction to printing from an ELECTROTYPE or STEREOTYPE made from that type, or printing by PHOTO-OFFSET. "Keep type standing" (*abbr.* KTS) is an order to the printer to hold the made-up pages for a possible subsequent printing (*see* KILL).

677

STAT. Short for PHOTOSTAT. To "stat up" is to enlarge a piece of copy photographically and to "stat down" is to make it smaller, usually in connection with producing CAMERA-READY COPY for OFFSET LITHOGRAPHY.

STEP AND REPEAT. Used to describe a camera or projector that advances one step (frame, page, etc.) horizontally or vertically for every exposure, according to a preset sequence.

STEREOTYPE. A printing plate cast from a papier-mâché matrix ("mat") made by forcing the latter into the face of type matter and drying it by baking.

STOCK. Paper to be used for printing.

STORAGE. To put data in computer *storage* is to record the data in digital form on a magnetic medium, such as tape, disks, or drums, either inside or outside the computer itself.

STRAIGHT COPY. Material that can be set in type with no handwork or special programming—i.e., copy that contains no math, tables, unusual accents, or special display work.

STRIKE-ON COMPOSITION. Same as TYPEWRITER COMPOSITION.

STRIP. To join offset negatives in a FLAT for the purpose of producing the printing plate. Also, to correct a negative by cutting out an incorrect line or passage and taping in a corrected one.

STYLE. Rules of uniformity in matters of punctuation, capitalization, word division, spelling, and other details of expression—many of which may vary according to custom. *House style* is the set of rules adopted by a particular publishing or printing house.

SUBSCRIPT. In mathematics, a small numeral, letter, fraction, or symbol that prints partly below the BASE LINE.

SUBSTANCE. Same as BASIS WEIGHT. Used usually of BOND PAPER.

SULFATE PROCESS. A process of papermaking in which wood chips from both deciduous and coniferous trees are cooked in a solution of caustic soda and sodium sulfide to produce the pulp from which the paper is made. Kraft paper is made from unbleached sulfate pulp.

SULFITE PROCESS. A process of papermaking in which wood chips from coniferous trees are cooked in a solution of lime and sulfurous acid to produce the pulp from which the paper is made. Paper made from sulfite pulp generally has fewer impurities and is more permanent than paper from sulfate pulp.

SUPER. Heavy gauze used to form the hinge in a casebound book (*see* CASE BINDING).

678

SUPERCALENDER. A machine, similar to a CALENDER but separate from the papermaking machine, used to give additional smoothness and hardness to paper.

SUPERIOR FIGURE. A small numeral that prints partly above the X-HEIGHT: A^2. *See also* SUPERSCRIPT.

SUPERSCRIPT. In mathematics, a small numeral, letter, fraction, or symbol that prints partly above the X-HEIGHT.

SWASH LETTERS. Capital letters of peculiar or unusual character introduced into a font of type for ornamental purposes.

TAIL MARGIN. Bottom MARGIN of a page.

TEARSHEET. A page cut or torn from a book or periodical.

THIN SPACE. In typesetting, a space usually defined as ¼ em ("4-to-em" or "4-em"). *See also* HAIR SPACE.

THREE-UP. *See* TWO-UP.

TIP-IN. A separately printed leaf pasted, or *tipped*, into a book. *See also* WRAPAROUND.

TRANSPOSE. In proofreading and editing, to switch the positions of two words, sentences, paragraphs, etc. Also, simply to move copy from one position to another.

TWO-UP. In OFFSET LITHOGRAPHY, to duplicate the printing image on the plate so that two copies of the piece are printed at the same time. The terms *three-up, four-up,* etc., are analogous.

TYPEFACE. A named type design, such as Baskerville or Times Roman, produced as a complete font.

TYPE HIGH. Exactly as high as a piece of metal type (0.9186 inch).

TYPE PAGE. The area of a page occupied by the type image, from the running head to the last line of type on the page or the folio, whichever is lower, and from the inside margin to the outside margin, including any area occupied by side heads. The type page, also called *type area*, is measured in picas.

TYPESCRIPT. A typewritten manuscript.

TYPESETTER. A person, firm, or facility that sets type. Also, especially in PHOTOCOMPOSITION, a typesetting machine.

TYPE SIZES. Before the adoption of the point system, which became general about 1878, type sizes were known by distinguishing names. The sizes to which these names referred lacked uniformity among different type-founders, particularly in different countries; this confusion led to the immediate popularity of the point system, which originated in France and was developed in the United States (*see also* MEASUREMENT). Types of various sizes formerly bore names, such as Great Primer for

679

18-point type. For a complete list of these see any large dictionary under "Type."

The designation of type sizes by points refers to the vertical size of the SORT and has no definite reference to the size of the typeface itself. All the different styles of 12-point faces, for instance, are approximately the same size, but there is considerable variation. The designation *12-point,* as referring to a particular typeface, means that it is ordinarily cast on a 12-point body. In Monotype and Linotype composition the size of the body is often increased to enlarge the space between the lines without having to insert leads for that purpose. Thus a face ordinarily cast on a 10-point body may be cast on a 12-point body to give the appearance of 2-point leading; it is then referred to as "10 on 12." In photocomposition the same effect is achieved by regulating the spacing of the successive lines of optical images, and the same terminology is used.

TYPE STYLES. The type commonly used in books and all classes of ordinary reading matter is known as *roman.* Although all roman types are essentially the same in form, there are two fairly well-defined divisions or styles. The older form is called *old style* and is characterized by strength and boldness of feature, with strokes of comparatively uniform thickness and with an absence of weak hairlines. The serifs are rounded, and the contour is clear and legible. Caslon is an example of an old-style face. The other style is called *modern* and is characterized by heavier shadings, thinner hairlines, and thin, straight serifs. Bodoni is an example. Although a few typefaces combine certain characteristics of the two styles, and are thus called *transitional,* it is usually comparatively easy to classify any particular face as *old style* or *modern.* Aside from the *roman,* there are four general classes, known as *italic, script, gothic,* and *text. Boldface* versions of all the commonly used faces (sometimes in both roman and italic) are also available, and many faces are also available in both *extended* and *condensed* versions.

The slanting letter mainly used for emphasis and display is known as *italic.* It is cut to match all roman typefaces, and a font of roman type for book and magazine work would be considered incomplete without a corresponding font of italic.

Script types are imitations of handwriting. Their widest use is in the printing of announcements, invitations, and stationery.

Gothic or *sans serif* is perfectly plain, with lines of uniform thickness and without serifs. It is sometimes known as *block letter.*

Text is a survival of the first types cast and was originally an imitation of the hand lettering which prevailed before movable types were invented. It is often known as *black letter.* German *Fraktur* resembles it closely.

Body type is a common name for type used for reading matter as distinguished from *display type,* which is used for advertisements, title pages, part and chapter headings, etc.

TYPEWRITER COMPOSITION. Text matter produced by typewriter for OFF-SET LITHOGRAPHY. The typewriter may be a hand-operated office machine or a highly sophisticated proportional-spacing machine with automatic justification, driven by punched-paper or magnetic tape. Good typewriter composition employing "book" typefaces may closely resemble machine work. Also called *strike-on composition.*

TYPOGRAPHER. A type designer. Also, more loosely, someone who sets type.

TYPOGRAPHICAL ERROR. Colloquially, "typo," an error made by the compositor or operator; also called *printer's error (PE).* The layman's term is *misprint.* When proof is being corrected, typos (PEs) are strictly distinguished from author's alterations.

UNDERRUN. *See* OVERRUN.

UNJUSTIFIED. Of lines of type, not justified; i.e., with an uneven right-hand margin. Also called *ragged right.*

VANDYKE. *See* PROOF.

VARNISH. A shiny protective coating applied to printed matter, such as a paperback cover, to protect it.

VDT. VIDEO DISPLAY TERMINAL.

VERSO. The back side of a leaf; in a book, a left-hand page. *See also* RECTO.

VERTICAL. Often refers to a *vertical platen press,* or JOB PRESS.

VIDEO DISPLAY TERMINAL. In computer technology, an input keyboard with a video screen on which the keyboarded material can be viewed in typed-out form. If previously keyboarded material can be retrieved and altered, it is often called an *editing terminal.*

VIRGULE. *See* SOLIDUS.

WATERMARK. Design, maker's name, etc., on paper, produced by thinning the paper slightly so that the design shows when the paper is held up to the light. *See* DANDY ROLL.

WEB. On a printing press using paper in reel form the paper is referred to as the *web.* The same term is also used for paper as it is being made by machine.

WEB-FED. Applied to printing presses using paper in reel form rather than in sheets. Also called *reel-fed.*

WEB OFFSET. Short for *web-fed offset lithography. See also* OFFSET LI-THOGRAPHY.

WIDOW. A short line ending a paragraph at the top of a page, avoided when possible by changes in wording or spacing which either remove the line or lengthen it; also, less strictly, a word or part of a word on a line by itself at the end of any paragraph.

WINDOW. A rectangle (of red acetate or black paper or any other material that has a smooth edge when cut and photographs as black) pasted on a REPRO page in the blank space left for a HALFTONE illustration. When a negative is made of the page, the rectangle becomes a clear opening, or *window,* in the film, into which the halftone negative is stripped, thus combining the type and halftone components onto one FLAT.

WIRE SIDE. The "back side" of a piece of paper, opposite the "top" or FELT SIDE. It often shows an impression of the wire on which the paper is formed from pulp.

WOODCUT. *See* CUT.

WORD. In computer terminology, a sequence of binary digits (bits) conveying meaning in combination, often processed as a whole by the computer. *See also* BIT.

WORD DIVISION. Dividing words at the end of a line.

WORD PROCESSOR. A general term for a variety of electronic machines upon which text consisting of words and figures can be keyboarded ("typed"), displayed on a video screen, edited, and recorded in magnetic form .

WORK-AND-TURN. To print *work-and-turn,* a form is arranged (imposed) so that a sheet may be printed on one side, turned right for left, and printed on the other side, to give two copies of the pages when cut in half. In printing *work-and-tumble* the sheet is turned end for end. *See also* SHEETWISE.

WORK-UP. A mark or smudge on a printed page, caused when a piece of spacing material in an improperly locked letterpress form works up into printing position.

WOVE. Machine-made *wove* paper shows a faintly discernible woven-fabric effect when held up to the light. The effect is produced by the metal screening of the DANDY ROLL as it passes over the wet web of paper during manufacture. *See also* LAID.

WRAPAROUND. A folded sheet of paper bearing printed illustrations, slipped around the outside of a signature before sewing as a means of adding such illustrations to a book without the necessity of tipping in single leaves. Thus, when a wraparound is placed on a 16-page signature, the two leaves of the wraparound sheet appear 16 pages apart in the finished book. *See also* TIP-IN.

WRONG FONT. A type of different size or face from that of the context in which it accidentally appears (*abbr.* wf).

WRONG-READING. *See* RIGHT-READING.

X-HEIGHT. In type, a vertical dimension equal to the height of the lowercase letters (such as *x*) without ascenders or descenders. *See also* BASE LINE.

ZINC ETCHING. *See* ENGRAVING.

Bibliography

American Institute of Physics. *Style Manual for Guidance in the Preparation of Papers.* 3d rev. ed. New York: American Institute of Physics, 1978.

Intended to assist authors in the preparation of articles published by the American Institute of Physics and its member societies.

American Medical Association. Scientific Publications Division. *Style Book and Editorial Manual.* 6th ed. Chicago: American Medical Association, 1976.

Written for authors preparing copy for the *Journal of the American Medical Association,* this manual is often helpful to editors working on medical copy.

American Men and Women of Science: Physical and Biological Sciences. 14th ed. 8 vols. Edited by Jaques Cattell Press. New York: R. R. Bowker, 1979.

American Men and Women of Science: Social and Behavioral Sciences. 11th ed. Edited by Jaques Cattell Press. New York: R. R. Bowker, 1978.

American Psychological Association. *Publication Manual of the American Psychological Association.* 2d ed. Washington, D.C.: American Psychological Association, 1974.

Style manual for APA journals; useful for all writers in the field.

Anglo-American Cataloguing Rules. 2d ed. Prepared by the American Library Association, the British Library, the Canadian Committee on Cataloguing, the Library Association, and the Library of Congress. Edited by Michael Gorman and Paul W. Winkler. Chicago: American Library Association; Ottawa: Canadian Library Association, 1978.

Intended for library catalogers but useful to editors, especially for the forms and alphabetization of proper names.

Ashley, Paul P. *Say It Safely: Legal Limits in Publishing, Radio, and Television.* 5th ed. rev. With Camden M. Hall. Seattle: University of Washington Press, 1976.

A readable discussion of the laws of libel in the field of communications. Revised frequently.

Bartlett, John. *Familiar Quotations: A Collection of Passages, Phrases, and Proverbs Traced to Their Sources in Ancient and Modern Literature.* Edited by Emily Morison Beck. 15th ed. revised and enlarged. Boston: Little, Brown & Co., 1980.

The traditional source to consult in checking a familiar quotation.

685

Barzun, Jacques. *On Writing, Editing, and Publishing: Essays Explicative and Hortatory.* Chicago: University of Chicago Press, 1971.

Cogent, previously published essays addressed primarily to writers.

Barzun, Jacques, and Henry F. Graff. *The Modern Researcher.* 3d ed. New York: Harcourt Brace Jovanovich, 1977.

Although addressed primarily to historians, the practical advice on how to turn research into well-organized, literate exposition goes well beyond the field of history.

Bernstein, Theodore M. *The Careful Writer: A Modern Guide to English Usage.* New York: Atheneum, 1965.

An alphabetically arranged list of usages, good and bad, with graceful discussion of why they should be embraced, tolerated, or shunned. A particularly helpful ally of the manuscript editor.

————. *Miss Thistlebottom's Hobgoblins: The Careful Writer's Guide to the Taboos, Bugbears, and Outmoded Rules of English Usage.* New York: Farrar, Straus, and Giroux, 1971.

A wealth of excellent advice for overzealous editors, by a very careful writer with a delightful sense of humor.

Bookman's Glossary. 5th ed. Edited by Jean Peters. New York: R. R. Bowker, 1975.

Covers English language terminology of the book trade and of the graphic arts.

Books in Print: Authors and *Books in Print: Titles.* 2 vols. each. New York: R. R.Bowker. Published annually.

The standard annual listing of books published by American publishers. An editorial office should have the current edition plus at least a selection of earlier volumes for reference. Published from a computerized data base and not to be used as final authority for spelling or dates.

British Books in Print: The Reference Catalogue of Current Literature. London and New York: J. Whitaker & Sons and R. R. Bowker. Published annually.

Serves the same purpose for British books as *Books in Print* (which see) does for American books. Supplemented by *The Bookseller,* a weekly periodical published in the United Kingdom by J. Whitaker & Sons.

Brooks, Philip C. *Research in Archives: The Use of Unpublished Primary Sources.* Chicago: University of Chicago Press, 1969.

A manual for researchers in archives, especially United States presidential papers, with helpful suggestions for citing references.

Butcher, Judith. *Copy-editing: The Cambridge Handbook.* Cambridge: Cambridge University Press, 1975.

A well-organized, lucid account of what a copyeditor does in Great Britain by the chief subeditor (copyeditor) of Cambridge University

Press. Highly recommended for American copyeditors as well. Contains many helpful lists but few examples.

Chemical Abstracts Service Source Index. 2 vols. Washington, D.C.: American Chemical Society.

Published every five years, with quarterly and annual cumulations. Carries a comprehensive list of abbreviations of journal titles.

Cockerell, Douglas. *Bookbinding and the Care of Books.* New York: Taplinger Publishing Co., 1978.

Paperback reprint of a standard work, with many useful illustrations of the techniques of bookbinding.

Collison, Robert L. *Indexes and Indexing: Guide to the Indexing of Books, and Collections of Books, Periodicals, Music, Gramophone Records, Films, and Other Material, with a Reference Section and Suggestions for Further Reading.* London: Ernest Benn, 1959.

As the baroque subtitle indicates, this book covers a good deal more than the indexing of scholarly books and may usefully be consulted by an indexer with problems of indexing nonbook materials. Regarding the mechanics of indexing, the method taught by Collison here is ingenious, fast, and economical but should not be attempted by anyone lacking experience in indexing.

―――. *Indexing Books.* Rev. ed. Tuckahoe, N.Y.: John de Graff, 1967.

A fuller treatment of book indexing than that included in the preceding entry. Most of the preferences of the University of Chicago Press are reflected at least as alternatives.

Columbia Lippincott Gazetteer of the World. Edited by Leon E. Seltzer. New York: Columbia University Press, 1952. Supplement 1961.

Sometimes supplies information not found in *Webster's Geographical Dictionary* (which see).

Concise Dictionary of American History. Edited by Thomas C. Cochran and Wayne Andrews. New York: Charles Scribner's Sons, 1962.

A convenient desk book for editors of historical works. Authoritative articles carefully selected and abridged from the five-volume original.

CBE Style Manual Committee. *CBE Style Manual.* 5th ed. Bethesda, Md.: Council of Biology Editors, 1983.

The standards of the "CBE *Manual*" are followed by a great many journals and are acceptable to most publishers of scientific books. Except in a few details its recommendations and those of *The Chicago Manual* are identical. A good feature is a discussion of effective writing that could be studied profitably by authors in any field.

Dictionary of American Biography. 20 vols. and 6 supplements to 1980. Published under the auspices of the American Council of Learned Societies. New York: Charles Scribner's Sons.

A standard reference work (does not list living persons).

Dictionary of National Biography. Edited by Leslie Stephen and Sidney Lee. 21 vols. with supplement. London: Oxford University Press.

A standard source book for British biography.

Directory of American Scholars. 7th ed. 4 vols. Edited by Jaques Cattell Press, Tempe, Ariz. New York: R. R. Bowker, 1978.

Biographies of scholars in history, English, languages and linguistics, philosophy, religion, and law.

Follett, Wilson. *Modern American Usage: A Guide.* Edited and completed by Jacques Barzun and others. New York: Hill and Wang, 1966; Grosset and Dunlap, 1970.

An excellent dictionary of usage, with illuminating essays on a number of questions of concern to authors and editors.

Fowler, H. W. *A Dictionary of Modern English Usage.* 2d ed. revised by Sir Ernest Gowers. Oxford: Clarendon Press, 1965.

The classic work on English usage for discriminating writers. A necessity in any university press editorial office.

Gowers, Sir Ernest. *The Complete Plain Words.* Revised by Sir Bruce Fraser. Baltimore: Penguin Books, 1973.

An elegant and witty guide to precise writing by the eminent reviser of Fowler's *Modern English Usage.*

Guide to the National Archives of the United States. Washington, D.C.: National Archives and Records Service, General Services Administration, 1974.

An indispensable tool for anyone working with archival materials in United States history. Includes a numerical list of the record groups by which materials are classified in the National Archives. Quarterly supplements are issued in *National Archives Accessions.*

Guide to Reference Books. 9th ed. Compiled by Eugene P. Sheehy. Chicago: American Library Association, 1976. Supplement 1980.

Standard guide to how to look things up.

Hamer, Philip M., ed. *Guide to Archives and Manuscripts in the United States.* New Haven: Yale University Press, 1961.

A standard guide to archival materials in the United States

Harman, Eleanor, and Ian Montagnes, eds. *The Thesis and the Book.* Toronto: University of Toronto Press, 1976.

A series of articles, which appeared originally in *Scholarly Publishing,* offers much useful advice to those who aspire to turn Ph.D. theses into publishable books.

Hart's Rules for Compositors and Readers at the University Press, Oxford. 38th ed. London: Oxford University Press, 1978.

Reflects the typographical usages of a prestigious and conservative scholarly press. It is much briefer than the present manual and sometimes at variance with it, but it is nonetheless useful to American editors. The section on setting foreign languages is particularly helpful.

Harvard Guide to American History. Rev. ed. Edited by Frank Freidel, with the assistance of Richard K. Showman. 2 vols. Cambridge: Harvard University Press, Belknap Press, 1974.

Authoritative lists of titles in American political, social, constitutional, and economic history; especially useful for government publications.

Hopkins, Jeanne. *Glossary of Astronomy and Astrophysics*. 2d ed. Chicago: University of Chicago Press, 1980.

Compilation of scientific terms used in the *Astrophysical Journal*.

Index Medicus. Bethesda, Md.: National Library of Medicine.

Cumulative index of titles in clinical medicine; every January carries a list of abbreviations of journal titles recommended for medical reference lists.

International Who's Who. London: Europa Publications. Published annually.

Biographical information on currently eminent personalities throughout the world.

Johnston, Donald F. *Copyright Handbook*. New York: R. R. Bowker Co., 1978.

Good introduction to the subject.

The Language of the Foreign Book Trade: Abbreviations, Terms, Phrases. 3d ed. Edited by Jerrold Orne. Chicago: American Library Association, 1976.

Alphabetical lists in fourteen European languages with translations into English.

Latman, Alan. *The Copyright Law: Howell's Copyright Law Revised and the 1976 Act*. 5th ed. Washington, D.C.: Bureau of National Affairs, 1979.

New edition of a standard work on copyright law.

Lee, Marshall. *Bookmaking: The Illustrated Guide to Design, Production, Editing*. 2d ed. New York: R. R. Bowker, 1979.

A well-written, clearly illustrated, and easily understood book on the mechanics of bookmaking (composition, engraving, platemaking, printing, etc.) for authors, editors, designers, and production people. The best book on the subject. The second edition adds a section on editing and much useful information on the recent revolutionary changes in the technology of typesetting.

The Librarian's Practical Dictionary in Twenty-two Languages. 6th ed. Edited by Zoltán Pipics. New York: R. R. Bowker, 1974.

689

List of bibliographical terms in English translated into major foreign languages, with an index in each language.

Literary Market Place (LMP). New York: R. R. Bowker. Published annually.

A handy, paperback directory of current publishing personnel and services, including lists of book publishers, book clubs, literary awards, reviewers, translators, and trade events of the year.

Manual of Foreign Languages, for the Use of Librarians, Bibliographers, Research Workers, Editors, Translators, and Printers. 4th ed. Edited by Georg F. von Ostermann. New York: Central Book Co., 1952.

Somewhat outdated but still useful for spelling, capitalization, diacritics, and basic grammatical forms of the major languages of the world.

Menzel, Donald H., Howard Mumford Jones, and Lyle G. Boyd. *Writing a Technical Paper*. New York: McGraw-Hill, 1961.

An excellent brief treatment of the subject.

Miller, Casey, and Kate Swift. *The Handbook of Nonsexist Writing*. New York: Lippincott and Crowell, 1980.

A guide to what constitutes sexism in language and sensible advice on how to avoid it.

Modern Language Association. *MLA Handbook for Writers of Research Papers, Theses, and Dissertations*. New York: Modern Language Association, 1977.

Based on the well-known *MLA Style Sheet* compiled by William Riley Parker in 1951 and revised by John H. Fisher and others in 1970. Useful for notes and bibliographies in the humanities. Many examples.

Morison, Stanley. *First Principles of Typography*. Cambridge Authors' and Printers' Guides, no. 1. Cambridge: Cambridge University Press, 1951.

A still useful pamphlet offering assistance to the nonprofessional faced with designing a piece of printed matter or selecting typefaces.

The New York Times Manual of Style and Usage: A Desk Book of Guidelines for Writers and Editors. Revised and edited by Lewis Jordan. New York: Quadrangle/New York Times Book Co., 1976.

A dictionary of names and terms primarily for newspaper writers. Useful for spelling and capitalization.

Nimmer, Melville B. *Nimmer on Copyright: Literary, Musical, Artistic Property*. 4 vols. New York: Matthew Bender. Continually updated.

Indispensable for keeping up with the latest developments in copyright.

O'Neill, Carol L., and Avima Ruder. *The Complete Guide to Editorial Freelancing*. New York: Dodd, Mead & Co., 1974.

Out-of-date in some respects but contains advice still useful to freelancers.

Pemberton, John E. *British Official Publications*. 2d rev. ed. Oxford and New York: Pergamon Press, 1973.

Useful source of information, particularly about command papers.

Perrin, Porter G. *Writer's Guide and Index to English*. 5th ed. Revised by Wilma R. Ebbitt. Glenview, Ill.: Scott, Foresman, 1972.

A widely used college textbook on expository writing, including chapters on sentence and paragraph construction, spelling, punctuation, and various types of papers.

Pocket Pal: A Graphic Arts Production Handbook. New York: International Paper Co. Paperback, revised every few years to reflect late developments.

A succinct compendium of information on typesetting, printing, binding, and papermaking, with emphasis on contemporary methods and equipment. Useful to both editors and production people.

Rodgers, Frank. *A Guide to British Government Publications*. New York: H. W. Wilson, 1980.

Very thorough, well-organized account of a complex subject.

Schellenberg, Theodore R. *Modern Archives: Principles and Techniques*. Chicago: University of Chicago Press, 1956.

A work on archival principles and techniques that contains a helpful explanation (pp. 195–204) of the classification systems of the British, French, and German archives.

Schmeckebier, Laurence F., and Roy B. Eastin. *Government Publications and Their Use*. 2d ed. Washington, D.C.: Brookings Institution, 1969.

Helpful in citing U.S. government publications.

Scholarly Publishing. Published quarterly by the University of Toronto Press.

Full of valuable information for editors and authors of university press books.

Schwartz, Robert J. *The Complete Dictionary of Abbreviations*. New York: Thomas Y. Crowell Co., 1955.

A long (194 three-column pages), extremely inclusive list of abbreviations alphabetically arranged. Useful for identifying a rare or unfamiliar abbreviation in copy.

Seltzer, Leon E. *Exemptions and Fair Use in Copyright: The Exclusive Rights Tensions in the 1976 Copyright Act*. Cambridge: Harvard University Press, 1978.

A fine discussion of a complicated subject.

The Statesman's Year-Book: Statistical and Historical Annual of the States of the World. Edited by S. H. Steinberg. New York: St. Martin's Press. Published annually.

Particularly valuable to the editor for its up-to-date information on

Commonwealth countries and international organizations, including the United Nations.

Strong, William S. *The Copyright Book: A Practical Guide*. Cambridge: MIT Press, 1981.

A succinct and well-written analysis of the law and a practical guide to its application.

Strunk, W., Jr., and E. B. White. *The Elements of Style*. 3d ed. New York: Macmillan, 1979.

A short classic offering excellent, practical advice on achieving a clear and graceful expository style; should be required reading for all authors and editors.

Swanson, Ellen. *Mathematics into Type: Copyediting and Proofreading of Mathematics for Editorial Assistants and Authors*. Rev. ed. Providence, R.I.: American Mathematical Society, 1979.

Includes instructions on all phases of producing a book or an article in the field of mathematics: preparation and submission of manuscript, editing and marking, design and typesetting, proofreading and page makeup, and more.

Turabian, Kate L. *A Manual for Writers of Term Papers, Theses, and Dissertations*. 4th ed. Chicago: University of Chicago Press, 1973.

Intended for students and other writers of papers not written for publication. Useful material on notes and bibliographies.

Ulrich's International Periodicals Directory. 18th ed. New York: R. R. Bowker, 1979–80. Supplemented by *Ulrich's Quarterly*.

A listing by subject of serials published throughout the world. Indexed.

A Uniform System of Citation. 13th ed. Cambridge: Harvard Law Review Association, 1981.

Citation forms and abbreviations used by many law reviews.

United Kingdom. Public Record Office. *Guide to the Contents of the Public Record Office*. 3 vols. London: H. M. Stationery Office, 1963, 1968.

The standard guide to British archival materials.

U.S. Geological Survey. *Suggestions to Authors of the Reports of the United States Geological Survey*. 6th ed. Washington, D.C.: Government Printing Office, 1978.

Useful to editors of geological material of any description.

U.S. Government Printing Office. *Style Manual*. Rev. ed. Washington, D.C.: Government Printing Office, 1973.

An exhaustive treatment of typographical style as practiced by the Government Printing Office. The "GPO *Manual*" is most useful as a supplement to manuals such as this one, particularly in the handling of governmental material and foreign languages.

Webster's Biographical Dictionary. Springfield, Mass.: G. & C. Merriam, 1976.

Indispensable for checking spelling and alphabetization of personal names.

Webster's New Collegiate Dictionary. Springfield, Mass.: G. & C. Merriam, latest edition.

Based on *Webster's Third New International Dictionary,* the *Collegiate* is the best desk dictionary for author or editor to have at elbow. Actually, the *Collegiate* rather than the big dictionary should be followed for word division whenever possible: prepared after the parent work, it represents the later thinking of the editors on the principles of word division and frequently departs from the divisions given in the unabridged dictionary.

Webster's New Geographical Dictionary. Rev. ed. Springfield, Mass.: G. & C. Merriam, 1977.

The first source to consult in checking the spelling or alphabetization of place names.

Webster's Third New International Dictionary of the English Language, Unabridged. Springfield, Mass.: G. & C. Merriam, 1964.

The standard for spelling of English words and a basic reference work for any editorial library. "Webster 3" has been criticized for abandoning the attempt to define the "standing" of English words (bookish, colloquial, substandard, etc.) and to suggest that usages are "good" or "bad." Whether it is the province of a dictionary to do so is a separate question, but the 1935 *Second International* did and is still useful for those purposes.

Who's Who: An Annual Biographical Dictionary. New York: St. Martin's Press.

A useful listing of living notable persons, mainly British.

Who's Who in America. Chicago: A. N. Marquis. Published biennially.

A useful listing of living Americans.

Wincor, Richard. *Literary Rights Contracts: A Handbook for Professionals.* New York: Law & Business; Harcourt Brace Jovanovich, 1979.

Useful on various kinds of contracts; written for publishers and agents as well as for professional legal advisers.

Words into Type. Based on studies by Marjorie E. Skillin, Robert M. Gay, and other authorities. 3d ed. Englewood Cliffs, N.J.: Prentice-Hall, 1974.

An excellent manual of printing practice for authors and editors. The sections on grammar and use of words are particularly helpful.

The World Almanac and Book of Facts. Published annually by Newspaper Enterprise Association, Inc. (hardbound edition, Doubleday & Co.).

An enormous compilation of names and facts about the world—gov-

693

ernment agencies, population figures, laws, events, etc.—with a comprehensive general index.

Zinsser, William. *On Writing Well: An Informal Guide to Writing Nonfiction.* 2d ed. New York: Harper and Row, 1980.

Useful pointers on style, usage, and organization for the professional writer.

Zweifel, Frances W. *A Handbook of Biological Illustration.* Chicago: University of Chicago Press, Phoenix Books, 1961.

A highly useful guide for authors, editors, and nonscientific artists on preparation of various kinds of illustrative materials for scientific publication.

Index

References are to paragraph numbers except where specified otherwise (tables and figures are listed by page number). Running heads in the text include paragraph numbers. Definitions of technical terms are found in the Glossary (pp. 645–83), which is not indexed here.

A, an, 6.49. See also *The*
  in alphabetizing, 16.23, 18.89, 18.100
  in titles, 7.123, 7.130–31, 17.11, 18.89
Abbreviations, 14.1–56. *See also* Acronyms
  with addresses, 14.17, 14.21–22
  of agencies and organizations, 14.15, 18.87
  alphabetizing, 18.97, 18.103, 18.125
  in author-date citations, 15.21–23
  of bibliographic terms, 10.59–60, 14.32, 17.16–21, 17.58
  in bibliographies, 14.13, 16.6, 16.24, 16.25, 16.27, 16.53, 16.101–2
  of books and versions of Bible, 14.34–35, 17.63
  capitalizing, 7.152–53, 14.15, 17.17
  chap., 7.136
  of chemical elements, 14.54
  in classical references, 17.65
  commercial, 14.55
  with company names, 14.12–14, 16.76
  of compass points, 14.23–25
  of computer terms, 7.152–53
  of countries, 14.19–20
  cross-references with, 18.13, 18.97
  with dates, 8.41–42, 14.3, 14.27
  of degrees (academic), 14.3, 14.8, 14.11
  of directions, 14.18, 14.21–22, 14.23–25
  dividing, 6.45
  ed., comp., trans., 14.32, 16.24–27, 16.53, 17.10, 17.35–37
  of edition, 16.54
  of eras, 8.41–42, 14.3, 14.27
  fig., 11.8, 11.31, 14.32
  of geographical terms, 14.17–25
  in indexes, 18.87, 18.97, 18.103, 18.125
  of journal titles, 15.76, 15.80, 16.101–2
  Latin, 6.59, 14.31–32
  of latitude and longitude, 14.24–25
  in legends, 11.33
  in mathematics, 13.42
  with measurements, 14.36–53
  of months, 14.28, 17.55, 17.57, 17.80
  with musical works, 7.146
  with names, 14.4–11, 14.16, 15.67, p. 415
  n.d., for date of publication, 16.75, 16.93, 16.95
  in notes, 2.98, 14.13, 14.15, 15.66, 15.67, 17.10, 17.12–13, 17.15, 17.16–25, 17.36, 17.95, p. 414
  n.p., for place of publication, 16.74–75
  with numbers, 6.45, 8.15, 14.48–49
  periods with, 5.5, 14.2, 14.15, 14.43, 14.54
  plurals of, 6.9–10, 14.36, 17.16
  with publisher's name, 16.76
  roman for, 6.59, 13.42
  of *saint,* 14.16, 14.18, 18.103, 18.125
  scholarly, 6.59, 14.31–32
  scientific and technical, 7.99–101, 14.41–49, 14.50–54
  of *section* and *article,* 14.56, 17.58
  with ships and aircraft, 7.96–97
  of SI units of measure, 14.41–49
  of source citations, 10.60, 15.66, 15.67
  spacing within, 14.2
  of speakers' names, 10.34, 19.66
  spelling out, 2.79, 3.29, 18.97, pp. 53, 94, 95
  of state names, 14.2, 14.17, 14.21–22, 16.70
  with sums of money, 8.27, 8.29
  in tables, 12.28, 12.77, 14.14, 14.15
  with taxonomic names, 7.99–101
  in text, 14.1–3, 14.31
  of time units, 14.26, 14.40
  of time zones, 7.73
  of titles of persons, 14.3, 14.5–11
  of titles of works, 15.67, 15.80, 16.101–2, 17.15, 17.64
  of years, 8.35, 8.40
Abbreviations, list of
  checking against text, 2.50
  with notes or bibliography, 10.60, 15.22, 15.67, 15.76, 16.102, pp. 414–15
  placement of, 1.45, 15.67, 15.76, 16.102
  typing, 2.28
Academic degrees and honors, 1.11, 7.26, 14.3, 14.8, 14.11, 18.81
Academic titles, 7.17n, 7.21, 7.26, 14.8, 14.11, 18.81
Academic years, 7.25

Accents, 2.14, 9.11, 9.32, 9.54, 9.67, 9.79. *See also* Diacritical marks
Accordingly, punctuation with, 5.69
-ache, compounds with, p. 177
Acknowledgments, 1.39–42. *See also* Permission to reprint; Source notes
  content of, 1.39, 1.40, 4.12, 4.54
  on copyright page, 1.27, 1.28, p. 12
  in notes, 15.71–72
  placement of, 1.1, 1.39
  title of, 1.39
Acronyms, 14.15. *See also* Abbreviations
  alphabetizing, 18.97
  in author-date citations, 15.22
  computer terms, 7.152–53, 16.182
  cross-references with, 18.13, 18.97
  full caps for, 7.152–53, 14.15
  in indexes, 18.87
  list of, 15.22, p. 415
  plurals of, 6.9–10
Act and scene. *See* Plays
Acts and treaties, 7.67–68
A.D., 8.41, 14.3, 14.27
  in titles, 7.123
Additions. *See also* Corrections
  in manuscript, 2.35, 2.36, 2.62
  in proof, 3.16, 3.37
  in quoted material, 10.50–53
Address, direct, 5.41, 7.30
Addresses
  abbreviations in, 14.17, 14.21–22
  capitalization in, 9.20
  French, 9.20
  numerals in, 8.60–62
  punctuation with, 5.57, 5.59
Adjectival phrases, 5.36
Adjectives
  compound, 5.94, 6.31, pp. 176–81
  coordinate, punctuation with, 5.45
  derived from names of sacred books, 7.86
  derived from proper names, 7.34, 7.46
Administration, 7.53
Administrative bodies, 7.47, 7.49, 7.53
Admiral, 7.19
Adverbial phrases, 5.29–35
Adverbs
  with adjective or participle, p. 177
  transitional, 5.39, 5.69
Æ, œ, 6.50, 9.42. *See also* Diacritical marks
Affiliations, authors', 1.47–48, 1.53, 2.171, 15.71–72, 16.11
African languages, 9.84
Age, of persons
  plural of, 8.63
  spelled out, 8.3
Agencies
  as authors, 15.20–23, 15.97, 16.29–30

names of, 7.47, 7.49, 9.108, 14.15, 17.54, 18.87
Ages, historical, 7.61, 7.63–64, 7.109
Agreement, publishing. *See* Contract, publishing
Aggregation, signs of, 13.27–28
Aircraft, 7.96–97
Alignment. *See also* Indention; Spacing
  marking for, 2.81–82, 3.25–27, pp. 53, 94, 95
  in tables, 2.23, 12.41–43, 12.65, 12.71
All-, compounds with, p. 179
Alliances, 7.54
"All rights reserved," 1.14
Alphabetizing
  abbreviations, 18.97, 18.103, 18.125
  accented letters, 18.99
  with articles, 16.23, 18.88–89, 18.100, 18.124, 18.139
  bibliographies, 2.30, 2.104, 15.82, 15.87–92, 16.23, p. 422
  checking, 2.104, 2.114, 18.128
  cross-references, 18.13
  glossaries, 2.27, 2.28
  hyphenated terms, 18.43
  index cards, 18.38, 18.40–44
  indexes, 2.114, 18.59, 18.92–125, 18.128, 18.135
  index subentries, 18.100
  initials, 18.96–97
  letter-by-letter vs. word-by-word, 18.43, 18.92–94
  names, 2.104, 9.109, 15.82, 15.87–92, 16.23, 18.95–96, 18.102–25, p. 422
  numbers, 18.98
  with punctuation, 18.43
  St., 18.125
  titles of works, 16.23, 18.88–89, 18.139
Alphabets. *See also* Special characters
  Cyrillic, p. 266
  Greek, p. 276
  Latin, p. 254
  in type font, 19.11–12
Alterations. *See* Author's alterations; Corrections
A.M., 8.48, 14.2, 14.3, 14.30
Ambassador, 7.18
Amendment, 7.67
Ampersand
  in author-date citations, 15.15
  in company names, 14.12–13
  in publishers' names, 16.78–79
  punctuation with, 15.15
  in titles, 7.125
And
  in author-date citations, 15.15
  in publishers' names, 16.79
  in titles, 7.123, 7.126

Animal names, 7.98–107
Anonymous works
  in bibliographies, 16.21–23
  copyright on, 4.12
  in notes, 17.33
Anthologies
  copyediting, 2.166–68
  permissions for, 2.165, 4.57–58
  preparing manuscript for, 2.158–62
  source notes in, 2.163–65, 15.70
Antithetical elements, punctuation with,
  5.46–49
Apostles, 7.78, 14.16
Apostrophe
  in German, 9.34
  for hamza, 9.102, 9.104
  in Italian, 9.47, 9.53
  marking, 2.67, 3.34, pp. 53, 94, 95
  with plurals, 6.5, 6.10
  with possessives, 6.12–23
  for prime, p. 369
  with time span, 6.14
Appendixes
  content of, 1.67
  indexing, 18.25
  numbering, 1.68, 19.58
  placement of, 1.1, 1.68–69
  tables in, 12.19, 15.64
  titles of, 1.68, 19.58
  type specifications for, 1.70, 2.140, 19.58,
    20.32
Appositives, punctuation with, 5.43–44, 5.64
Arabic, 9.102–9
  capitalization, 9.107–8
  names, 7.11, 9.105–6, 9.109, 18.110–11
  particles, 9.106–9, 18.110–11
  special characters, 9.102, 9.104
  transliteration, 9.102–6
Arabic numerals. *See also* Numbering; Num-
    bers; Roman numerals
  for chapter numbers, 7.136, 19.53
  in classical references, 17.70–71
  for page numbers, 1.86, 1.88, 2.148, 8.32
  for volume numbers, 16.10, 16.43, 16.103,
    17.23
Aramaic, transcribing, 9.102
Archaeology, 6.4, 6.50
Archbishop, 7.20
Archives. *See also* Manuscript collections;
    Unpublished material
  abbreviations for, 15.67, p. 415
  in bibliographies, 15.29, 16.134–40, p. 433
  government, 16.158–59, 16.171–72, 16.174,
    17.93–96
  names of, 7.142, 15.29, 15.70, 16.35
  rights governing use of, 4.43–44
Arctic, 7.34

Armed forces, 7.93, 8.57
Art, styles of, 7.66
Art, works of, 7.144–48
  exhibitions, 7.65
  in indexes, 18.90
  titles of, 7.144–48
Article, 14.56
Articles. See also *A, an; The*
  foreign, 9.4n, 18.124 (*see also* Particles)
  with titles of works, 7.123, 7.130–31, 16.23,
    17.11, 18.88–89, 18.139
Articles, journal. *See also* Journals; Maga-
    zines, popular
  in bibliographies, 15.80, 15.83, 16.6,
    16.98–127, pp. 424, 426
  contracts for, 4.29, p. 118
  date of publication, 16.104–5, 16.109–14
  foreign, 16.121–23, 17.54
  in notes, 17.2, 17.8, 17.51–56
  in parts, 16.116
  series number with, 16.47, 17.51, 17.52
  titles of, 7.134–36, 15.80, 16.6, 16.114,
    16.115, 16.121, 17.54, p. 424
  titles of, omitted, 15.80, 16.6, 16.115, p. 424
  in two places, 16.117
  volume and page numbers of, 16.103–14,
    16.119, 16.124–25, 17.53
Artwork, 11.6–24. *See also* Illustrations
  corrections on, 11.23–24
Asian names, 18.112–22. *See also* Chinese;
    Japanese
Associations, 7.58–59. *See also* Organizations
Asterisk
  for levels of probability, 12.51
  as note reference, 12.49, 12.51, 15.68, 15.69
  not used in ellipses, 10.36
Astronomical terms, 7.110–14, 14.51–53
Audiovisual material, 16.177–81
Author. *See also* Author's name
  affiliation of, 1.47–48, 1.53, 15.71–72, 16.11
  biography of, 1.7, 1.43, 1.47
  correspondence with, 2.59, 2.122–26
  as indexer, 18.20
  queries to, 2.1, 2.87, 2.116–23
  responsibilities of, in publishing, 2.3,
    2.171–73, 4.36–58, 11.35
Author-date citations, 15.4–35. *See also* Ref-
    erence lists
  abbreviations in, 15.21–23
  and in, 15.15
  author's name in, 15.7, 15.13–23
  checking against reference list, 2.44, 2.104,
    15.33
  cross-references with, 15.21–22
  dates in, 15.4, 15.7–9, 15.18, 15.25, 15.27,
    15.28, 15.29, 15.33, 15.79, 15.90–92 (*see
    also* Date of publication)

Author-date citations (*continued*)
  editor's name in, 15.13
  et al. in, 15.17–19
  multiauthor books in, 15.14–19, 16.16
  multiple references, 15.24–26
  with notes, 15.34–35, 15.68
  page numbers with, 15.8–12
  parentheses with, 15.7, 15.31–32
  placement of, 15.31–32
  punctuation with, 15.7–9, 15.11, 15.15, 15.24, 15.25
  unnumbered notes with, 15.72
  unpublished material in, 15.28–29, 16.143
  volume numbers in, 15.11–12
Author's affiliation, 1.47–48, 1.53, 2.171, 15.71–72, 16.11
Author's alterations, 3.35–37. *See also* Corrections; Proofreading
  cost of, 2.125, 3.36, 3.52
Authorship, guarantee of, 4.27, 4.36
Author's name
  in author-date citations, 15.7, 15.13–23
  in bibliographies, 2.30, 15.79, 15.89–97, 16.11–30, 16.99, p. 423
  in chapter display, 1.48, 1.53, 19.54
  coauthors' names, 15.14–19, 15.95–96, 16.15–17, 17.10, 17.27–31
  in collection of letters, 1.57
  editor as author, 16.24–27 (*see also* Editor's name)
  with foreword, 1.38
  in indexes, 18.2, 18.90–91, 18.134, 18.139
  initials with, 1.11, 16.11–13, 16.99
  inversion of, 1.47, 16.14–15, 17.3, 17.27
  in legal references, 17.76
  in list of contributors, 1.5, 1.47, 1.53, 7.16, 15.71
  with multiauthor books, 1.5, 1.33, 1.47–48, 1.53, 15.14–19, 15.76, 15.95–96, 16.15–17, 17.10, 17.27–31
  in notes, 15.66, 17.6–8, 17.10, 17.13, 17.27–34
  organization as author, 15.20–23, 15.97, 16.29–30
  with preface, 1.41, 1.42
  in table of contents, 1.33, 1.48
  3-em dash for, 2.30, 5.96, 15.94–97
  title in place of, 16.23
  in title of work, 17.32
  on title page, 1.11, 1.13, 19.47
  translator as author, 16.24–27 (*see also* Translator's name)
Awards, 7.70, 7.95
ʿAyn, 9.102, 9.104

Back matter. *See also names of individual elements*

content of, 1.67–76
indexing, 18.25
page numbers of, 1.89, 1.91, 2.8
part title with, 1.55
references to, in text, 7.135
running heads to, 1.81–82, 15.56–57, p. 409
sequence of, 1.1
in table of contents, 1.32, pp. 14–16
type specifications for, 1.70, 1.73–75, 2.140–44, 16.10, 18.130–39, 19.34, 19.36, 19.42–44, 19.55, 19.58, pp. 13–16
Backnotes. *See* Endnotes; Notes
Bastard title. *See* Half title
Battles, 7.94
B.C., 8.41–42, 8.68, 14.3, 14.27
  in titles, 7.123
Besides, 5.69
Bible
  abbreviations of books and versions, 14.34–35, 17.63
  names of books and versions, 7.84
  references to, 7.84, 14.33–35, 17.63
Bibliographical terms. *See also* Parts of book
  abbreviations of, 10.59–60, 14.32, 17.16–21, 17.58
  in notes, 17.16–25
  numbers with, 8.32
  translation of, 16.121, 17.22
Bibliographies. *See also* Reference lists
  abbreviations in, 14.13, 16.6, 16.24, 16.25, 16.27, 16.53, 16.101–2
  alphabetizing, 2.104, 15.82, 15.87–92, 16.23, p. 422
  annotated, 1.73, 15.77, 15.84, 15.86, pp. 429, 432
  anonymous works in, 16.21–23
  archival material in, 15.29, 16.134–40, p. 433
  arrangement of, 1.73, 2.29–30, 15.82–92
  audiovisual material in, 16.177–81
  author's name in, 2.30, 15.79, 15.89–97, 16.11–30, 16.99, p. 423
  bibliographical essay, 1.73, 15.77, 15.85–86, p. 430
  book reviews in, 16.126
  books in, 16.11–97
  capitalization in, 16.6, 16.31–32, 16.37, 16.44, 16.100–101, 16.114, 16.121, 16.139
  chapter titles in, 16.49, 16.51
  checking notes against, 2.43, 2.103
  checking text citations against, 2.44, 2.104, 15.33
  chronological order in, 15.83, 15.90–92, p. 428
  classical works in, 16.55–56
  computer programs in, 16.182
  content of, 1.73, 15.76–77, 16.2–4

copyediting of, 2.104
cross-references in, 15.81
date of publication in, 15.92, 16.6, 16.55,
    16.57–58, 16.61–62, 16.64–66, 16.74–75,
    16.88–97
dissertations in, 16.129
edited volumes in, 15.81, 15.92, 16.49–53
edition in, 16.54–58, 16.89
editor or translator in, 16.24–27, 16.44–45,
    16.49–50, 16.53
estimating length of, 19.8
facts of publication in, 16.29, 16.61–97
foreign works in, 9.4, 16.38–39, 16.121
initials with names in, 16.6, 16.11–13, 16.99
journal articles in, 15.80, 15.83, 16.6,
    16.98–127, pp. 424, 426
manuscript collections in, 15.29, 15.83,
    15.86, 16.134–40, p. 432
in multiauthor books, 15.75
multiauthor books in, 15.89, 15.95–96,
    16.15–17
multivolume works in, 16.25, 16.41–42,
    16.90–92
newspapers in, 15.83, 16.127
nonbook materials in, 16.176–82
notes compared with, 17.3, 17.26–61
    passim
not indexed, 18.25
numbered items in, 15.6
page numbers in, 16.50, 16.106–14, 16.119,
    16.124–25
parts of book in, 16.49–53
physical facts omitted in, 16.4
placement of, 1.1, 1.72, 15.75
public documents in, 16.134–40, 16.141–75
punctuation in, 2.30, 16.7, 16.15, 16.44,
    16.62–63, 16.64, 16.107, 16.114, 16.124
relation to notes, 2.103, 15.46, 15.77, 17.2,
    17.6
reprints in, 16.48, 16.57–58, 16.86
selected, 1.73, 15.74, 15.76
shortened citations in, 16.1, 16.37
style of, 1.74, 15.77, 15.82–97, 16.5–10
subdivision of, 1.73, 15.77, 15.78, 15.83,
    15.84, 15.85, pp. 426–27
3-em dash in, 2.30, 5.96, 15.94–97
title of, 2.103, 15.74
titles of works in, 16.31–40, 16.44, 16.52,
    16.100–101, 16.114, 16.121, 16.139, p. 422
type specifications for, 1.74, 2.142, 16.10,
    19.12, 19.55
typing of, 2.16, 2.29–30
unpublished material in, 15.83, 16.61,
    16.97, 16.128–82
volume numbers in, 16.10, 16.42–43, 16.46,
    16.103, 16.107–14, 16.119
works by same author in, 2.30, 5.96,
    15.90–97
Billion, 8.3, 8.7, 8.25, 8.26
Binding
    case binding, 20.51–57, pp. 612–15
    checking, 3.56
    hand process, 20.10–13, pp. 592–95
    machine process, 20.50–57, 20.139–45,
        pp. 612–15
    materials for, 20.55
    mechanical, 20.143, p. 643
    perfect binding, 20.141, p. 642
    saddle and side wiring, 20.140, p. 642
    stamping and printing, 20.56–57
Biographies, of authors, 1.7, 1.43, 1.47
Bishop, 7.20, 18.80
Black (race), 7.32–33
"Blackboard bold," 13.15
Blank lines (as divisions). *See* Line space
Blank pages, 1.1, 1.3, 1.54, 2.112, 2.148
Blind entries, 18.11, 18.57. *See also* Cross-
    references
Block quotations. *See also* Quotations
    beginning in text, 10.20
    capitalization in, 10.13
    defined, 10.8
    indention of, 2.83, 19.33
    interpolations in, 10.20
    marking for typesetter, 2.83, 2.134
    in notes, 15.52
    paragraphing, 10.19, 10.30
    poetry, 2.20, 2.135, 10.10, 10.21–23, 10.68,
        19.61–63
    quotation marks in, 10.29
    source citations with, 2.135, 10.21, 10.23,
        10.63, 10.66–68
    spacing with, 2.16, 2.20, 2.83–84, 19.23,
        19.31–32
    typesetting, 20.32
    type specifications for, 2.16, 2.134–36,
        19.23, 19.31–33, 20.32
    typing, 2.16, 2.20
    when to use, 10.9–10
Blueprints, 3.52, 3.55, 20.105
    of illustrations, 11.49
    in typewriter composition, 20.104
Board, 7.49, 7.57
Boldface type
    in bibliographies, 16.10n, 19.12
    in indexes, 18.134, 18.136
    marking for, 2.77, 3.32, 13.15, pp. 53, 94, 95
    in mathematics, 13.15, 13.32, 13.43–44,
        p. 372
    for section numbers, 19.12
    for table titles, 12.66
    in type font, 13.44, 19.12, p. 372
-book, compounds with, p. 177
Book club rights, 4.33

Book design. *See also* Type specifications
    copy of manuscript for, 2.4, 2.6, 19.3
    layouts for, 19.69–72, pp. 579, 582–84
    planning, 19.3–5
Book reviews, 16.126, 17.56
Book titles. *See* Titles of works
Botanical names, 7.98–107
Box credits, 11.36. *See also* Credit lines
Boxheadings. *See* Column headings
B.P., 8.41, 14.27
Braces, in mathematics, 13.6, 13.27–28
Brackets, square, 5.102–6
    with anonymous works, 16.21–22
    with author's name, 16.12, 16.18–20, 17.33
    with capitals in quotations, 10.12–15, 10.49
    with *continued,* 5.105
    with date of publication, 16.93
    with editor's notes, 15.69
    with interpolations in quotations, 2.96,
        5.14, 5.102, 10.20, 10.50–53
    with *italics added,* 10.52–53
    in legal works, 10.15, 10.49
    marking for, 2.69, p. 53
    in mathematics, 13.6, 13.27–28
    with missing letters or words, 10.48
    within parentheses, 5.103
    with phonetic transcript, 5.104
    with pseudonyms, 16.12, 16.18–20, 17.33
    punctuation with, 5.10, 5.15, 5.23, 5.67,
        5.73, 5.81, 5.101
    with *sic,* 5.14, 5.102, 6.59, 10.51
    for stage directions, 19.67
    with translation, 10.50, 16.39
    type style of, 5.4
Breaks. *See also* Makeup, page; Word
        division
    equation, 13.35–38
    page and column, 18.133, 19.28, 19.39,
        20.35–37
    in thought, 5.12, 5.38, 5.83, 5.97–99, 9.26,
        9.46, 9.70, 9.91
Breathing marks, Greek, 9.104, 9.122–25
Breve, 9.11, 9.60
British spelling, 6.3, 7.54n
Broadside tables, 12.54–55, 12.78, 12.81
Broken type, 3.13, 3.33, pp. 94, 95
Buildings
    names of, 7.43–45, 9.20, 14.21
    numbers of, 8.62
Burmese names, 18.119

Ca., 6.59, 14.32
Cabinet, 7.53
Cabinet offices, 7.18
Calendar designations, 7.71–73. *See also*
        Dates; Time; Years
Cambridge, 16.72

Camera copy. *See* Artwork; Illustrations; Re-
        production proofs; Typewriter composi-
        tion
Canada, public documents of, 16.174, 17.92
Capitalization. *See also* Caps and small caps;
        Full caps; Small caps
    of abbreviations, 7.152–53, 14.15, 17.17
    in Arabic, 9.107–8
    in bibliographies, 16.6, 16.31–32, 16.37,
        16.44, 16.100–101, 16.114, 16.121, 16.139
    of chapter titles, 2.18
    in Chinese, 9.116
    after colon, 5.74, 5.75, 5.80
    of compounds, 7.124, 9.20, pp. 177, 180
    of computer terms, 7.152–53
    in Czech, 9.12
    in Danish, 9.14
    in Dutch, 7.7, 7.9, 9.4, 9.16
    of *figure* and *table,* 11.8, 12.15
    in Finnish, 9.18
    following ellipsis points, 10.49
    of foreign titles, 9.4, 9.88, 9.107–8, 9.117,
        16.38–39, 16.121, 17.42–43, 17.54
    in French, 7.7–8, 9.4n, 9.20
    in German, 6.58, 7.7, 7.9, 9.4, 9.33
    in glossaries, 2.27
    headline style, 11.45, 12.67
    of historical and cultural terms, 7.60–70
    in Hungarian, 9.43
    of hyphenated terms, 7.124, 7.128, 9.20,
        p. 180
    in indexes, 18.58
    for irony, 6.51
    in Italian, 7.7, 7.9, 9.45
    in Japanese, 9.116
    in Latin, 9.55
    in legal style, 10.15, 10.49
    in legends and captions, 11.25, 11.33
    in list of illustrations, 11.45
    marking for, 2.74, 2.75, 3.32, pp. 53, 94, 95
    of military terms, 7.93–95
    of mottoes and inscriptions, 7.150
    of musical notes and keys, 6.74–77
    of nationalities and tribes, 7.32–33
    in Norwegian, 9.61
    in notes, 17.41, 17.54, 17.68
    of organizations, 7.47–59, 9.20, 9.108, 17.54
    of parts of book, 7.134–36, 11.8, 12.15
    of personal names, 7.2, 7.6–9
    of place names, 7.34–46, 9.20
    within poem, 7.139
    in Polish, 9.63
    in Portuguese, 7.7, 7.9, 9.66
    of question, 5.18–19, 5.66
    in quotations, 10.6–7, 10.12–15, 10.49
    of religious names and terms, 7.20, 7.74–92
    in Russian, 9.87–88

of scientific terms, 7.98–120
of seasons, days, etc., 7.71–73
sentence style, 2.139, 12.25, 12.67, 12.68,
  16.6, 16.100
of series and edition, 7.137, 16.44
of signs and notices, 7.149
in Spanish, 7.7, 9.68
styles of, 7.2–4, 7.74
of subheads, 2.18, 2.139
in Swedish, 9.80
in tables, 2.23, 12.25, 12.31, 12.38, 12.67
of table titles, 12.25, 12.66, 12.67
of titles and offices, 7.15–27
of titles of works, 7.122–24, 7.128, 9.4, 9.55,
  9.88–89, 9.107–8, 9.117, 16.31–32, 16.37,
  16.44, 16.100–101, 16.114, 16.121,
  16.139, 17.41, 17.54, 17.68
in Turkish, 9.82
Capitol, 7.43
Caps and small caps. *See also* Small caps
  in bibliographies, 16.10n
  for captions, 11.25
  in indexes, 18.134, 18.139
  in legal references, 17.76
  marking for, 2.75, 3.32, pp. 53, 94, 95
  for *section* and *article,* 14.56
  for speakers' names, 10.7, 10.34, 19.66
  for subheads, 2.137, 2.139, 19.22, 19.28–
  29
  in table titles, 12.66
  for theorems, etc., 13.45
Captions, 11.25–43. *See also* Legends;
  Tables, titles
Cardinal, 7.20
Caret, 2.62, 2.66, 2.69, 3.15, 3.16, 3.34
Caret, inverted, 2.67, 2.69
Case. *See* Binding; Covers, book
Case histories, 2.16
Cases, legal, 7.69, 16.157, 17.76
Castoff, 19.4, 19.6–9
Cataloging in Publication (CIP) data
  examples of, pp. 8–13
  explained, 1.25n
  obtaining, 1.24
  placement of, 1.1, 1.23, 19.48
Cathode-ray-tube (CRT) composition, 20.96,
  20.112–14. *See also* Photocomposition
Cedilla, 9.11, 9.32
  typing, 2.14
Celestial coordinates, 14.52
Celestial objects, 7.110–14
Cells, empty, in tables, 12.40, 12.71
Census, 7.49
Centering, marking for, 2.81, 2.135, pp. 53,
  94, 95. *See also* Type specifications
Central, 7.34–35
Cents, 8.23–24

Century
  with A.D., etc., 8.41–42
  capitalization of, 7.60
  spelled out, 8.40
  in titles, 7.125
Cf., 14.31, 14.32, 15.53
Chairman, 7.21
Chapter, 7.136
Chapter numbers, 1.52–54, 1.63
  arabic numerals for, 7.136, 19.53
  within parts, 1.54
  as subheads with endnotes, 1.71, 15.55,
    17.16, p. 409
  in text references, 7.136, 19.53
Chapter one, numbering, 1.1, 1.88
Chapter opening
  author's name in, 1.48, 1.53, 19.54
  note references with, 1.52, 15.42
  paragraph indention with, 19.57
  punctuation in, 1.52, 5.11, 5.42
  type specifications for, 2.18, 2.131–32,
    19.52–59, 20.32
  typing, 2.17, 2.18
Chapter titles. *See also* Chapter opening
  in bibliographies, 16.49, 16.51
  capitalizing of, 2.18
  changes in, 2.38
  content of, 1.51
  punctuation with, 1.52, 5.11, 5.42
  quotation marks with, 7.134, 16.49
  as running heads, 1.51, 1.79, 2.151
  as subheads with endnotes, 15.55, 17.16
  in table of contents, 1.32, 1.33, 1.51, 2.38,
    3.46
  type specifications for, 2.18, 19.53–54,
    20.32
  typing, 2.18
Character count, 19.6–9
Characters, cast of, 19.64
Charts. *See* Illustrations; Line drawings;
  Maps
Checklist, editor's, 2.156–57, p. 79
Chemical terms, 7.118–20, 14.54
  spelling of, p. 178
Chinese
  capitalization, 9.116
  characters, 9.118
  italics in, 9.116
  names, 7.12, 9.111–12, 9.114, 9.116,
    18.112–14
  romanization of, 7.12, 9.111–14, 18.112–14,
    p. 272
Chords, musical, 6.77
Chronological order. *See also* Chronologies
  in bibliographies, 15.83, 15.90–92, p. 428
  in indexes, 18.51, 18.101
  for letters and diaries, 1.57

Chronologies, 1.49, pp. 23, 24
Chronology, systems of, 14.27. *See also*
　　Dates
Church. *See also* Religious names and terms
　　capitalization of, 7.44, 7.53, 7.80–82, 9.20
　　fathers, 7.78, 14.16
　　numbers with, 8.58
CIP. *See* Cataloging in Publication
Circumflex, 9.11, 9.32, 9.67
Citations, text, 15.6. *See also* Author-date
　　citations; Source citations
City, 7.36, 7.37
City name. *See also* Place names; Place of
　　publication
　　with newspapers, 18.88
Civil titles, 7.15–17, 7.18, 14.5
Civil War, 7.94
Class
　　academic, 7.25
　　taxonomic, 7.102
Classics
　　in bibliographies, 16.55–56
　　notes to, 15.73, pp. 418–20
　　references to, in notes, 17.65–75
Close-up marks, 2.62, 2.65, 2.70, 2.72–73,
　　3.20, 3.21, pp. 53, 94
Coast, 7.41
Coauthors, names of, 15.14–19, 15.95–96,
　　16.11, 16.15–17, 17.10, 17.27–31. *See
　　also* Contributors, list of; Multiauthor
　　books
Coding. *See also* Color coding
　　in photocomposition, 2.15, 2.130, 3.12,
　　20.118, 20.128
Coined words, 6.5
Collections, manuscript. *See* Manuscript
　　collections
Colon, 5.74–81
　　in author-date citations, 15.9, 15.11
　　in biblical references, 17.63
　　capitalization after, 5.74, 5.75, 5.80
　　between clauses, 5.74
　　in index entries, 18.54
　　introducing list or series, 5.75–78
　　introducing quotation, 5.75, 5.80, 10.16–18
　　introducing speech or formal statement,
　　5.75, 5.79, 5.80
　　in legends, 11.32
　　marking, 2.68, 2.69, 3.34, p. 94
　　with other punctuation, 5.81, 10.41
　　with parentheses or quotation marks, 5.81
　　with place of publication, 16.62, 16.64
　　spacing after, 16.62, 16.107
　　with time, 8.47
　　in titles, 1.9, 7.126, 7.128, 16.31–32
　　between volume and page numbers,
　　16.107–14, 16.119, 17.20

Colophon, 1.13, 1.76, p. 30
Color, for marking manuscript, 2.86–87
Color-coding
　　in manuscript, 2.87, 2.136, 2.140
　　in mathematics, 13.43
　　in proofs, 3.15, 3.17, 3.35
Color printing, 20.130–33
Colors, compound adjectives for, p. 178
Column headings, 5.11, 12.26–31, 12.64–67,
　　12.74, 12.77, 12.81, 12.84
Columns
　　in indexes, 2.144, 18.130–39, 19.42
　　in newspapers, 17.57
　　in tables, 2.25
Comma, 5.24–67
　　with addresses, 5.57, 5.59
　　with antithetical elements, 5.46–59
　　with appositives, 5.43–44, 5.64
　　with author-date citations, 15.7–8, 15.11,
　　15.15, 15.25
　　in classical references, 17.69–71
　　in compound sentences, 5.25–29
　　with coordinate adjectives, 5.45
　　with dash, 5.67, 5.88–89
　　with dates, 8.36, 8.39, 8.41, 8.64
　　as decimal point, 8.22, 14.49
　　with dependent clauses or phrases, 5.29–37
　　with direct address, 5.41
　　with display lines, 1.52, 5.42
　　with ellipsis points, 5.12, 10.41
　　with elliptical constructions, 5.61–62
　　with *etc.,* 5.53
　　between identical words, 5.56
　　in index entries, 18.54
　　with interjections, 5.39
　　marking, 2.66, 2.69, 3.34, pp. 53, 94, 95
　　with names, 16.15, 18.109, 18.113, 18.115
　　in numbers, 2.106, 8.41, 8.64–66, 12.42,
　　14.49
　　with *oh* and *O,* 5.40
　　with page numbers, 16.124
　　with parenthetical elements, 5.38, 5.97
　　with places, 5.57, 5.59
　　to prevent mistaken junction, 5.55
　　with question, 5.66
　　with quotation marks, parentheses, brack-
　　ets, 5.67, 6.63
　　with quotations, 5.63–65, 5.67, 5.89, 6.63,
　　10.12, 10.18
　　with restrictive elements, 5.29–31, 5.36,
　　5.44, 5.64
　　in series, 5.26, 5.50–53, 7.126, 8.72
　　with *that is,* etc., 5.54
　　with titles of persons, 5.43, 5.58, 8.54
　　with titles of works, 7.126, 7.128, 17.20
　　with transitional adverbs, 5.39
　　between unrelated numbers, 5.56

with volume number, 16.119, 17.20
Commander in chief, 7.19
Command papers (United Kingdom), 16.168, 17.89
Commercial abbreviations, 14.55
Commission agreement, 4.10, 4.30, p. 119
Committee, 7.48
Communist (-ism), 7.54, 7.56
Company names, 7.57, 14.12–14, 16.76
Compass points, 14.23–25. *See also* Directions
Compilations. *See* Anthologies; Edited works; Multiauthor books
Compiler's name, 16.24–27, 17.10, 17.35–37
Composition. *See* Photocomposition; Typesetting; Typewriter composition
Compound names, 18.104, 18.106–7
Compounds. *See* Adjectives, compound; Noun compounds; Sentence, compound; Words, compound
Computers. *See also* Photocomposition
  indexing by, 18.24
  information storage by, 20.122–24
  typesetting controlled by, 2.15, 13.8–9, 20.96, 20.115–25
  word division by, 3.11, 20.123
Computer terms, 7.151–53
  dates, 8.46
  programs, 16.182
Computerized composition. *See* Computers; Photocomposition
Conferences, 7.58–59. *See also* Multiauthor books; Symposia papers read at, 16.130, 17.59
Congress, 7.48, 8.55
Congress, documents of, 16.146–54, 17.85–86. *See also* Public documents
Congressman, 7.18
Conjunctions
  capitalizing, 2.23, 7.123
  in index subentries, 18.100
  punctuation with, 5.25–26
Consent-to-publish form, 2.171, 4.30, pp. 118–19
Constellations, 7.110, 7.113
Constitutions, 7.67, 14.56
Contents, table of
  authors' names in, 1.33, 1.48
  chapter titles in, 1.32, 1.33, 1.51, 2.38, 3.46
  checking against text, 2.38, 2.111, 3.46
  content of, 1.32–33
  copyediting, 2.38, 2.111
  examples of, pp. 14–16
  page numbers in, 1.32, 2.39, 3.45
  part titles in, 1.32, 19.51, p. 15
  placement of, 1.1, 1.31
  subheads in, 1.32, 3.46, 19.51, p. 16

title of, 1.31
type specifications for, 19.51
Continent, 7.34
Continued, 5.105
  in indexes, 18.133
  with tables, 12.80–81, 12.84
Continuing numbers, 5.92–93, 8.67–70, 16.108, 17.24–25, 18.9
  examples of, 8.67–68
Continuous-tone copy. *See* Halftones
Contract, publishing, 4.26–30
  contributors' ("consent to publish"), 2.171, 4.30, pp. 118–19
  and copyright notice, 1.15
  and credit lines, 11.40
  editor's consulting of, 2.59, 2.110
  examples of, pp. 118–19
  for multiauthor books, 4.27, 4.29–30
  and permissions, 4.57, 4.58
  for works made for hire, 4.10–11, 4.30, 11.40
Contributors, list of, 1.47–48, 1.53, 2.171, 7.16, 15.71. *See also* Multiauthor books
  example, p. 22
  placement of, 1.1, 1.5, 1.47
Contributor's agreement, 4.29–30, p. 119
Conversation. *See* Dialogue; Personal communication
Coordinate adjectives, 5.45
Coordinate clauses, 5.26–28
Copies, machine
  of artwork, 2.32, 2.162
  citation of, 7.142, 16.61, 16.131, 17.59
  and color of editing, 2.86
  and copyright, 4.24–25
  of layout, 19.71
  of legends, 2.107, 11.47
  of manuscript, 2.4–6, 2.31, 2.32, 2.86, 2.127, 2.158, 2.159, 2.161, 18.60, 19.3, 19.5
  of previously published material, 2.32, 2.158, 2.161–62
Copy. *See* Artwork; Manuscript
Copyediting, 2.51–157. *See also* Copyeditor
  bibliographies, 2.104
  color used for, 2.86–87, 2.136, 13.43
  correspondence with author, 2.59, 2.116, 2.122–26
  editorial marks, 2.61–85, p. 53
  estimating time for, 2.60
  extent of, 2.51–52, 2.59–60
  illustrations, 2.108, 2.111
  indexes, 2.114, 18.126–29
  legends, 11.46
  list of illustrations, 11.44–46
  marking type specifications, 2.129, 2.131–44, 19.71, pp. 580–81

Copyediting (*continued*)
mathematics, 13.41–52, p. 366
mechanics of, 2.61–88
multiauthor books, 2.174–76
notes, 2.97–103
preliminary work, 2.59
previously published material, 2.158–60, 2.166–68
queries to author, 2.1, 2.87, 2.116–23
quotations, 2.96, 10.29, 10.36
sequence of, 2.89–115
tables, 2.105–6, 12.62–84
text, 2.89–96
Copyeditor. *See also* Copyediting
and author, 2.116–28
functions of, 2.51–57, 2.174–76
responsibility of, 2.110, 2.174–76, 3.43, 11.44–46
and typesetter, 2.129–57
Copyholder, 3.2, 3.9
Copyright, 4.3–25. *See also* Permission to reprint; Source notes
author's responsibilities concerning, 4.36–58
changes in United States law, 1.14, 4.3–18, 4.22–23, 4.24
date of, 1.15–17 (*see also* Date of publication)
duration of, 4.4–12, 4.42
and fair use, 4.22–25, 4.41, 4.45–47
original, 4.36–37
in part of work, 4.19
publisher's responsibility for, 4.26–35
registering, 4.20–21, 4.31, p. 114
renewal of, 1.17, 4.5, 4.7, 4.14, 4.31
rights, defined, 4.1–2, 4.4
subsidiary rights, 4.2, 4.32, 4.33–34
transfer of, 1.17, 4.1, 4.2, 4.13
and unpublished works, 4.43
Copyright notice, 4.16–19
changes in, 1.17
copyright symbol, 1.14–15, 4.16
form and content of, 1.14–17, 4.16
in legends, 11.38
mistakes in, 4.18, 4.21
placement of, 1.1, 4.17, 19.48
publisher's responsibility for, 4.31
in source note, 2.163, 15.70
for translations, 1.18, 1.21, 4.10
Copyright page, 1.14–27
acknowledgments on, 1.27, 1.28, p. 12
checking proofs of, 3.48, 3.57
content of, 1.4, 1.14–27
examples of, pp. 8–13
placement of, 1.1, 1.14
publisher's responsibility for, 2.3, 2.110, 4.31

type specifications for, 19.48
Corrections. *See also* Author's alterations; Copyediting; Proofreading
on artwork, 11.23–24
author's, 2.33–36, 2.128
editor's, 2.61–88, p. 53
in manuscript for scanning, 2.15, 2.52
in photocomposition, 3.13, 20.129
in previously published material, 2.160
in proof, 3.16, 3.35–37
in quotations, 10.6
by typesetter, 20.30, 20.33, 20.129
on typewriter, 2.13, 2.15
in typewriter composition, 20.103
Correlation, statistical, 8.20
Correspondence. *See* Letters (correspondence)
Councils, religious, 7.83
Countries, abbreviations for, 14.19–20
Country, 7.37
Court, 7.50–52, 7.53
Court cases, 7.69, 16.157, 17.76
Courtesy, 11.41
Covers, book. *See also* Binding; Jacket, book
copy for, 2.149, 2.150, 3.56
paperback, 20.139–42, p. 642
Credit lines. *See also* Legends; Permission to reprint; Source notes
on copyright page, 1.27, p. 13
with illustrations, 4.53, 11.34–43
with tables, 12.46, 12.72, 12.83
Creeds, 7.88
Cropping, of illustrations, 11.15–16, p. 308
Cross-, compounds with, p. 179
Cross-references
with abbreviations, 18.13, 18.97
alphabetizing, 18.13
with author-date citations, 15.21–22
in bibliographies, 15.81
checking, 2.37, 2.40–41, 2.94, 18.57, 18.128
in indexes, 18.10–17, 18.46–47, 18.55, 18.57, 18.59, 18.64, 18.67, 18.72, 18.74, 18.97, 18.107, 18.117, 18.128
to notes, 2.40, 15.44, 15.47
to page numbers, 2.41, 2.94
with personal names, 18.11, 18.107, 18.117
placement of, 18.14–16
with pseudonyms, 16.20, 18.11, 18.72
to sections, 1.62–63
supplying in proof, 2.41, 3.35
to tables, 2.40
Crown, 7.48
CRT composition, 20.96, 20.112–14. *See also* Photocomposition
Cultural terms, 7.60–66
events, 7.65–66
movements and styles, 7.66

periods, 7.60–64
Currency, 6.44, 8.23–31, 14.57
Cut-in heads, in tables, 5.11, 12.30, 12.31, 12.65
Cuts. *See* Halftones; Illustrations; Line drawings
Cyrillic alphabet, 9.86–89, 10.70n, p. 266
Czech, 9.12–13

Dagger, for note reference, 12.49, 15.68, 15.69
Danish, 9.14–15
Dash, em, 5.82–91
  with appositives, 5.43
  with break in thought, 5.12, 5.38, 5.83, 5.97–99
  comma with, 5.67, 5.88–89
  with dialogue, 5.12, 9.25, 9.48, 9.69, 9.90
  for emphasis, 5.84
  exclamation point with, 5.90
  with explanatory elements, 5.84–87
  in French, 9.25
  in indexes, 18.53, 18.128, 18.135, 18.138
  in Italian, 9.48
  marking, 2.70, pp. 53, 94, 95
  number per sentence, 5.91
  with parentheses, 5.98
  with parenthetical elements, 5.38, 5.85, 5.90–91, 5.98
  question mark with, 5.90
  spacing with, 2.70, p. 369
  in Spanish, 9.69
  with summary, 5.87
  in tables, 12.40, 12.71
  with *that is,* etc., 5.54
  in titles, 7.126, 7.128
  typing, 5.92, p. 369
Dash, en, 5.92–94
  compared with hyphen, 5.92
  in compound words, 5.94, p. 180
  with continuing numbers, 2.71, 5.92, 8.67–70, 18.9
  with dates, 5.92–93, 16.91
  marking, 2.70, 2.71, 3.34, 18.129, pp. 53, 94, 95
  with time, 5.92
  typing, 5.92
Dash, 3-em
  in bibliographies, 2.30, 5.96, 15.94–97
  for missing words, 5.96
  spacing with, 5.96
Dash, 2-em
  for missing letters, 5.95
  for name, 6.78
  spacing with, 5.95
Date lines, 5.11, 5.42
Date of publication
  in author-date citations, 15.4, 15.7–9, 15.18,

15.25, 15.27, 15.28, 15.29, 15.33, 16.95
  in bibliographies, 15.92, 16.6, 16.55, 16.57–58, 16.61–63, 16.64–66, 16.74–75, 16.88–97, p. 422
  checking against reference list, 2.44, 2.104, 15.33
  on copyright page, 1.14, 1.15, 1.19, 1.21, 16.88–89
  defined, 3.4–5, 16.88
  forthcoming, 16.94–95
  of incomplete works, 16.91
  of journal articles, 16.104–5, 16.109–14
  letters used with, 15.91
  month with, 16.105, 16.110, 16.113, 16.121
  of multivolume works, 16.90–92
  n.d. for, 16.75, 16.93, 16.95
  of newspapers, 15.83, 17.57
  in notes, 17.2, 17.50
  original, 15.27, 16.57–58
  in reference lists, 15.29, 15.33, 15.79, 15.90–91, 16.6, 16.63, 16.64, 16.93–95, pp. 422–24
  of reprints, 16.57–58, 17.48
  on title page, 1.13, 16.88
  unknown, 16.93–97
  as volume number, 17.53
Dates, 8.33–46. *See also* Date of publication; Time; Years
  abbreviations with, 8.41–42, 14.3, 14.27
  all-figure, 8.43–46
  alphabetizing, 18.98
  beginning sentence, 8.9–10, 14.3
  centuries, 8.40–42
  dash with, 5.92–93, 16.91
  day of the month, 8.36–38
  decades, 8.40
  in diaries, 1.57
  inclusive, 5.92–93, 8.68–69
  military system, 8.45
  with preface or foreword, 1.41
  punctuation with, 5.60, 5.92–93, 8.36–39, 8.41, 8.64, 17.38
  questionable, 5.16
  sequence of elements in, 8.36–38
  in titles, 7.126, 7.128, 8.69, 17.38
Day, 7.72
Days
  of the month, 8.36–38, 8.43–46
  of the week, 7.71, 14.29
Dead copy. *See* Manuscript, dead; Proofs, foul
Deadlines. *See* Schedules
Debates, 16.150–52, 16.166
  speakers' names, 10.34
Decades, 8.40
Decimal fractions, 8.17–22, 8.24
  aligning, in tables, 12.42

Decimal fractions (*continued*)
 with celestial coordinates, 14.52
 punctuation of, 8.22, 8.64, 14.49
 zero with, 8.19–21, 8.24, 12.42, 13.20
Decimal point, 8.22, 12.42, 14.49
Decked heads, in tables, 12.28–29, 12.31
Dedication page, 2.3
 content of, 1.28
 placement of, 1.1, 1.28
 type specifications for, 19.49
Definitions. *See also* Glossary; Translation
 in mathematics, 13.45
 quotation marks with, 6.56, 6.57, 6.61
 of special terms, 2.92
Degrees (academic), 1.11, 7.26, 18.81
 abbreviation of, 14.3, 14.8, 14.11
Degrees (of arc), 8.11, 8.16, 14.52, p. 368
Degrees (temperature), 8.11–12, 8.16, 14.50
Deities, 7.75–77
Deletions
 marking, 2.62, 3.20, pp. 53, 94, 95
 in proofs, 3.20, 3.37, pp. 94, 95
Delivery date, 3.4–5, 3.58
Denominations, 7.81
Department, 7.49, 7.57
Dependent clause, punctuation of, 5.29–35
Depositories. *See* Archives; Manuscript collections
Design. *See* Book design; Layouts; Type specifications
Diacritical marks, 9.10–11, p. 254. *See also* Special characters
 in African languages, 9.84
 alphabetizing words with, 18.99
 in Arabic, 9.102, 9.104
 and book design, 19.10
 with capitals, 9.32, 9.54, 9.79
 in Czech, 9.13
 in Danish, 9.15
 in Dutch, 9.16
 in Finnish, 9.19
 in French, 9.32
 in German, 9.42
 in Greek, 9.125–27
 handwritten, 2.14
 in Hungarian, 9.44
 in indexes, 18.64, 18.99
 in Italian, 9.54
 in Latin, 9.60
 with Latin alphabet, p. 254
 names of, 9.11
 in Norwegian, 9.62
 omitting, 9.32, 9.54, 9.79
 in Polish, 9.64
 in Portuguese, 9.67
 in South Asian languages, 9.110
 in Spanish, 9.79
 in Swedish, 9.81
 in Turkish, 9.83, 9.102
 typing, 2.14
Diaeresis, 9.11, 9.67, 9.79, p.254
 typing, 2.14
Dialogue
 dash with, 5.12, 9.25, 9.48, 9.69, 9.90
 faltering speech, 5.12, 9.26, 9.46, 9.70, 9.91
 in French text, 9.22–26
 in Italian text, 9.48
 paragraphing, 10.30, 10.31
 punctuation of, 5.41, 5.75, 5.80, 10.30–31, 10.34
 quotation marks with, 9.22–24, 9.48, 9.69, 10.30–31, 10.33, 10.34
 in Spanish text, 9.69
Diaries. *See also* Archives; Manuscript collections
 arrangement of, in book, 1.57
 in bibliographies, 16.135, 16.137
 in notes, 17.77
Diary, 7.142, 17.77
Dictionaries
 for alphabetizing, 18.102–3
 cited in notes, 17.62
 for classical abbreviations, 17.65
 for hyphenation, 6.24, 6.29
 for personal names, 7.6, 18.102–3
 for spelling, 6.1
 for trademarks, 7.121
Die copy, checking proofs of, 3.56
Digital typesetting, 20.96, 20.112–14. *See also* Photocomposition
Digraph, in Old English, 6.50
Diphthongs, in word division, 6.35, 9.56
Direct address
 names in, 7.30
 punctuation with, 5.41
 titles in, 7.16
Direct discourse. *See* Dialogue
Directions
 abbreviation of, 14.18, 14.21–22, 14.23–25
 capitalization of, 7.34–35
Discussion, speakers' names with, 10.34
Diseases, 7.115–16
Disks, floppy, 2.2, 2.5, 2.51, 2.53, p. 635. *See also* Photocomposition
Display matter. *See also* Chapter opening; Chapter titles; Preliminaries
 letterspacing in, 19.22, 19.54
 note references with, 1.52, 1.64, 15.42
 page numbers of, 1.1, 1.87–89
 proofreading, 3.48, 3.57
 punctuation of, 1.52, 5.11, 5.42
 quotation marks with, 10.35
 quoting, 10.7
 running heads omitted with, 1.52, 1.78, 1.83

spacing of, 19.22, 19.54
typesetting, 20.32
type specifications for, 19.22, 19.45–60
in typewriter composition, 20.101–2
Dissertations
footnotes in, 2.21n
rights governing use of, 4.44
titles of, 7.142, 16.129
Distances, 8.11–12, 8.15–16
Ditto marks, 12.35
Divinity, 7.75–77
Division of words. *See* Word division
Documentation. *See* Author-date citations; Bibliographies; Notes; Reference lists
Documents. *See* Archives; Manuscript collections; Public documents
Dollars, 8.23–25, 8.30
in tables, 12.24, 12.28, 12.42
Dots. *See* Ellipsis points
Double-column format, 19.18
for indexes, 2.144, 18.130–39, 19.42
Double-numeration system, 1.63, 2.176, 11.9, 12.18
in mathematics, 13.25–26, 13.39
Double spacing
of indexes, 2.31, 18.31, 18.33, 18.58, p. 532
of tables, 2.16n, 12.14
of text, 2.16, 2.20, 2.21, 2.29, 13.19
Dr., 14.3, 14.6, 14.10
Dramatis personae, 19.64
Drawings. *See* Artwork; Illustrations; Line drawings
Drop, chapter, 2.131, 19.52, 19.55, 20.39
Drop folios, 1.52, 1.84, 1.87–89, 19.60
Drugs, 7.117
Duplicated material, 7.142, 16.131, 17.59. *See also* Copies, machine
Dutch
capitalization, 7.7, 7.9, 9.4, 9.16
names, 7.7, 7.9, 18.102
special characters, 9.17
Dynasties, 7.60, 8.55, 9.114

Earth, 7.113
East(ern), 7.34–35
Economic organizations, 7.54–56
Edited works. *See also* Multiauthor books
in bibliographies, 15.81, 15.92, 16.49–53
contributions to, 4.30, 16.49–53, 17.46
copyrighting, 4.9–10, 4.30
unnumbered notes with, 15.73, pp. 418–20
Editing. *See also* Copyediting; Copyeditor
of index cards, 18.45–57, p. 527
types of, defined, 2.55, 2.57
Edition
abbreviation of, 16.54
in bibliographies, 16.54–58, 16.89

with classical references, 16.55–56, 17.67
in copyright notice, 1.16, 1.21, p. 8
new, citing of, 15.27, 16.89
with newspapers, 17.57
in notes, 10.58, 17.47–48, 17.62, 17.64
of reference books, 17.62
reprints, 16.48, 16.57–58, 16.86, 17.48
title of, 7.137, 16.54
on title page, 1.10
Editor. *See* Copyeditor; Editor's name; Series editor; Volume editor
Editor, abbreviation of, 14.32, 16.24–27, 16.53, 17.10, 17.35–37
Editorial marks, 2.61–85, p. 53
"Editor's checklist," 2.156–57, p. 79
Editor's name
as author, 16.24–27
in author-date citations, 15.13
in bibliographies, 16.24–27, 16.44–45, 16.49–50, 16.53
in classical references, 17.67, 17.72, 17.74
in notes, 17.10, 17.35–37
on title page, 1.12
Editor's notes, 15.69, 15.73, pp. 418–20
Editor's preface, 1.42
E.g., 14.31, 14.32
punctuation with, 5.54, 5.72, 5.76, 5.86, 5.99
in text, 14.31
-elect, compounds with, p. 177
Electronic typesetting, 20.96, 20.112–14. *See also* Photocomposition
Electrotype, 20.88
Elements, chemical, 7.119–20
Elisions. *See* Ellipses
Ellipses, 10.36–49. *See also* Ellipsis points
Ellipsis points
beginning paragraph, 10.19
beginning sentence, 10.38, 10.47
capitalization following, 10.49
centered, 13.24
at end of sentence, 10.38, 10.42–44, 10.47
in faltering speech, 5.12, 9.26, 9.46, 9.70, 9.91
in French, 9.26
full line of, 10.45–46
with incomplete sentence, 10.44
in Italian, 9.46
in mathematics, 13.24
for missing words, 10.36, 10.48
number of, 2.96, 10.36–46
for omission of paragraph, 10.46
omitted with interpolation, 10.50
with other punctuation, 5.12, 10.6, 10.41, 10.42–43
with poetry, 2.20, 10.45
in Russian, 9.91

Ellipsis points (*continued*)
within sentence, 10.38, 10.40–41
with short titles, 16.37
spacing of, 10.36
in Spanish, 9.70
when to omit, 10.47–48, 10.50
Elliptical constructions, punctuation of,
5.61–62
Embellishments, in mathematics, 13.14
Emperor, 7.15, 7.18, 7.22
Emphasis
dash for, 5.84
italics for, 6.52, 6.53, 10.52–53
Emphasis added, 10.52–53
Empire, 7.37
Encyclopedias, cited in notes, 17.62
End matter. *See* Back matter
Endnotes, 15.54–57, 15.65–66, p. 409. *See
also* Footnotes; Notes
abbreviations in, 15.66, 15.67, p. 414
advantages of, 15.64, 15.65
arrangement of, 1.71, 15.55, p. 409
author's name in, 15.66
defined, 15.36
footnotes with, 15.68–69
ibid. in, 15.66
indexing, 18.26
numbers of, 19.40 (*see also* Note references)
page numbers in, 15.66
placement of, 15.54
running heads with, 1.71, 1.82, 15.54,
15.56–57, p. 409
titles of works in, 15.66
type specifications for, 19.34, 19.36, 20.32
unnumbered, 15.70, p. 420
unnumbered notes with, 15.70, 15.72
Endpapers. *See* Binding
Engravings, 20.23, p. 599. *See also* Halftones;
Illustrations; Line drawings
Entries, index. *See* Indexes, headings in; Indexes, subentries in
Enumerations, 8.72–75. *See also* Lists; Numbers; Series of items
parentheses with, 5.8, 5.100, 5.101, 6.46,
8.72, 8.74–75
Epigraph, 1.30, 2.3
placement of, 1.1, 1.2, 1.29, 1.52, 19.56
quotation marks with, 10.35
type specifications for, 19.50, 19.56
Epithets, 7.24, 7.28, 7.61
Epochs, geological, 7.108–9
Equations. *See also* Mathematics
breaking, 13.35–38
difficult, 13.29–34
displayed, 13.6, 13.26, 13.29–31, 13.33,
13.35–38

handwritten, 13.19
in line, 13.29–31, 13.33–34
numbering, 13.25–26
solidus in, 13.30–31
Equator, 7.34
Eras, 7.108, 8.41–42, 14.3, 14.27
Errata sheet, 1.92–93, p. 35
Errors. *See also* Corrections; Errata sheet;
Typographical errors
of fact, 2.119, 3.14
printer's, 3.35
Esq., 14.9
Estimating
editorial time, 2.60
illustrations, 2.9, 19.8
length of book, 2.4, 2.6, 19.4, 19.6–9
length of index, 18.61–62
tables, 2.9, 19.8
Et al., 14.32
in author-date citations, 15.17–19
in bibliographies, 16.16
in notes, 17.10, 17.27, 17.31
roman for, 6.59
Etc., 5.53, 14.31
Ethnological terms, 6.57
Et seq., 14.32, 18.9
Eucharist, 7.90
Events, historical and cultural, 7.65–66
Ex-, compounds with, p. 177
Excerpts. *See* Block quotations
Exclamation point, 5.13–15
as editorial protest, 5.14, 10.50, 10.51
with ellipsis points, 10.42
marking, 2.68, 2.69, 3.34
with *oh,* 6.48
with other punctuation, 5.90, 17.38
with quotation marks, parentheses, brackets, 5.15, 5.101
in Spanish, 9.71
with titles of works, 17.38
Executive departments, documents of,
16.155. *See also* Public documents
Exhibitions, art, 7.65
Expletives deleted, 5.96
Exponents, 13.34. *See also* Subscripts and
superscripts
Extracts. *See* Block quotations

F., ff.
in indexes, 18.9
in notes, 17.24
Facing page, 1.34, 11.45
Facing pages, length of, 3.44, 20.36
Factor loadings, 8.20
Facts of publication. *See also* Date of publication; Place of publication; Publisher's
name

in bibliographies, 16.29, 16.61–97
with classical references, 17.67
in notes, 17.50
parentheses with, 16.104, 17.50
for public documents, 16.146
punctuation with, 16.62–63, 16.64
translation of, 16.121
Fair use, 4.22–25, 4.41, 4.45–47
Faltering speech, 5.12, 9.26, 9.46, 9.70, 9.91
Family names, 7.30, 14.8
in indexes, 18.73, 18.82, 18.102–22
numbers with, 8.52–54
"f and g's," checking, 3.57
Federal, 7.53
Fees, permission, 4.52, 4.55–56, 11.36
Fellow, compounds with, p. 176
Fences, in mathematics, 13.27–28
Festschrifts, 17.38
Fictitious names, 7.29. *See also* Pseudonyms
Figure
abbreviation of, 11.8, 11.31, 14.32
capitalization of, 11.8
Figures. *See* Illustrations; Numbers
Films and slides, 16.179–81
Finnish, 9.18–19
Flap copy, 1.7, 1.25, 2.150, 3.56
Fliers (query slips), 2.120–21
Flush-and-hang style
in bibliographies, 2.142
in indexes, 2.143, 18.18, 18.132–39, 19.44
in notes, 19.41
Flush left and flush right, 2.80, 2.132, 19.57.
See also Indention; Justification
-fold, compounds with, 2.79, p. 179
Folded sheets, 3.57
Foldout tables, 12.55
Folios. *See* Drop folios; Page numbers
Following, punctuation with, 5.78. See also
F., ff.
Font. *See* Type; Typefaces; Type specifications; Wrong font
Footnotes, 15.58–66. *See also* Endnotes;
Notes
abbreviations in, 15.67
with author-date citations, 15.35
author's name in, 15.66
continued, 19.39
copyediting, 2.97–103
defined, 15.36
difficulties with, 15.58–60
discursive, 2.100
in dissertations, 2.21n
endnotes with, 15.68–69
how many, 15.61–63
indexing, 18.26, 18.91
length of, 2.100, 15.48, 15.60–61
in mathematics, 13.16

numbering, 2.22
numbers of, 2.22, 19.40 (*see also* Note references)
and page makeup, 15.58–60
paragraphing, 2.21, 2.141, 15.48, 19.41
in previously published material, 2.159
punctuation with, 2.21, 2.22
rules with, 19.38–39
for sources, 1.53, 2.163–64, 12.46, 12.72, 15.70
spacing with, 2.141, 19.37
substantive, 15.68
to tables, 2.26, 2.106, 12.45, 12.46–52, 12.72–73, 12.83, 15.43, 15.45, 19.35n
titles of works in, 15.66
type specifications for, 2.141, 19.34–35, 20.32
typing, 2.3, 2.21–22
unnumbered, 1.48, 1.53, 2.141, 2.163–64, 15.70, 15.76, pp. 418–19
Foreign languages. *See also* Foreign words;
Translations (works); *and names of individual languages*
capitalization in, 7.7, 9.4–6
with Latin alphabet, 9.3–84
personal names in, 7.8–14, 18.102–22
place names in, 6.55, 7.42, 7.45, 9.20, 9.87, 18.124–25
punctuation in, 9.7–8
quotations in, 10.69–71
special characters in, 9.10–11, p. 254
titles of works in, 9.4, 9.88–89, 9.107–8, 9.117, 16.38–40, 16.87, 16.121, 17.42–43, 17.54
transliterated and romanized, 9.85–135
word division in, 9.9
Foreign words, 6.54–59
as adjectives, p. 178
bibliographical terms, 16.121, 17.22
division of, 9.9 (*see also* Word division)
in ethnological studies, 6.57
familiar, 6.58
in italics, 6.54–59
plurals of, 6.8
in roman, 6.54–59
translation with, 6.56
Foreword
author's name with, 1.38
in bibliographies, 16.28
content of, 1.38
indexing, 18.25
place and date with, 1.41
placement of, 1.1, 1.38
For example (*e.g.*), punctuation with, 5.72, 5.76, 5.86, 5.99
in text, 14.31
Fort, 14.18

Forthcoming, 16.94–95
Foul proofs, 3.38–39
Fractions
    breaking, 13.37
    decimal, 8.17–22, 8.24, 8.64, 12.42, 13.20,
        14.49, 14.52
    difficult, in text, 13.30–31
    figures for, 8.11, 8.13, 8.14
    hyphenation of, pp. 177, 179
    solidus with, 13.30–31
    spelled out, 8.11, 8.13–14, 8.16, pp. 177, 179
    split, p. 373
Fragments, classical, 17.74
French
    capitalization, 7.7–8, 9.4n, 9.20
    dialogue, 9.22–26
    ligatures, 6.50
    personal names, 6.6, 6.18, 7.7–8, 18.102
    place names, 6.6, 7.45, 9.20, 18.124, 18.125
    punctuation, 9.21–26
    special characters, 9.32
    titles of works, 9.4n, 16.38, 16.121–22,
        17.42, 17.54
    word division, 9.27–31
Frontispiece, 1.1, 1.8, 1.34
Front matter. *See* Preliminaries
Führer, 7.18
Full caps
    for abbreviations, 7.152–53, 14.15
    in book titles, 7.122n, 7.123
    for chapter titles, 19.54
    for subheads, 19.22
    for table titles, 12.25, 12.66
    in typed material, 2.18, 7.122n, 12.25

Gallery, of illustrations, 2.48, 11.4–5
Galley proofs. *See also* Page proofs; Proof-
        reading; Proofs
    checking page proofs against, 3.38–39
    as first proofs, 3.6–7, 20.127
    foul, 3.38–39
    indexing from, 18.30, p. 523
    marking figure placement in, 3.51
    marking folios in, 2.148
    master set, 3.7, 3.18, 20.33
    number of sets, 2.125, 3.7
    in photocomposition, 20.127
    production of, 20.33, p. 602
    schedules for, 2.125, 3.4–5, 3.36
    transferring author's corrections, 3.7
    transpositions in, 3.18
Genealogical tables, 12.60
General
    compounds with, p. 176
    rank, 7.19
Genetic tables, 12.61, p. 340
Genus and species names, 7.99–101

Geographic names, 7.38–42, 18.123. *See also*
        Place names
    abbreviations with, 14.17–25
Geological terms, 7.108–9
German
    capitalization, 6.58, 7.7, 7.9, 9.4, 9.33
    names, 7.7, 7.9, 18.102
    punctuation, 9.34–35
    special characters, 9.42
    titles of works, 16.38, 17.42
    word division, 9.36–41
German type, 9.42, 13.43–44, p. 372
Gerunds, compounds with, p. 176
Glossary
    capitalization in, 2.27
    content and arrangement of, 1.72, 2.27,
        2.28, 6.57
    estimating length of, 19.8
    not indexed, 18.25
    placement of, 1.1, 1.72
    punctuation in, 1.72, 2.27
God, 7.75–77
Gospel, 7.84
Gothic letters
    in mathematics, 13.43–44, p. 373
    for shape, 6.79
Government
    archives, 16.158–59, 16.171–72, 16.174,
        17.93–96
    bodies, as "author," 15.97, 16.29–30
    bodies, names of, 7.47–53, 8.55–57
    officials, 7.18
    programs, 7.67
    publications (*see* Public documents)
Government Printing Office, 16.146, 16.155
Governor, 7.18
Grand-, compounds with, p. 176
Grants, acknowledging, 15.71
Graphs. *See* Illustrations; Line drawings
Gravure printing, 11.5, 20.48, 20.90–91
Great-, compounds with, p. 176
Great Britain. *See* United Kingdom
Greek, 9.119–35. *See also* Greek letters
    accents, 9.125–27
    alphabet, 10.70n, p. 276
    breathing marks, 9.104, 9.122–24, 9.127
    ligatures, 6.50
    names, 6.20
    numbers, 9.129, p. 278
    punctuation, 9.128
    transliterating, 9.120–21, p. 275
    typesetting, 9.119–20
    word division, 9.130–35
Greek letters, p. 276
    identifying, 2.14, pp. 368–69
    in mathematics, pp. 368–69, 372
    names of, 11.33, 14.3

Groups. *See* Organizations
Guillemets
  in French, 9.21–26
  in German, 9.35
  in Italian, 9.48
  in Russian, 9.90
  in Spanish, 9.69

Hair space, 17.21, 17.24, 18.26, p. 94
Half-, compounds with, p. 179
Half title (bastard title), 2.3, 2.110
  content of, 1.2, 1.4, 1.29
  placement of, 1.1, 1.88
  second, 1.1, 1.50n, 1.85, 1.88, 2.148
  type specifications for, 19.47
  verso of, 1.3–8
Halftones. *See also* Illustrations; Plates
  defined, 11.2–3
  placement, 2.48, 11.4–5
  printing, 11.21–22, 20.81–84
  screening, 11.3, 11.13–14, 20.81–84, 20.90,
    20.132
Hamza, 9.102, 9.104
Hausa, 9.84
Headbands, 20.11, 20.53
Headings. *See also* Subheads
  in indexes, 18.3, 18.5–8, 18.11–13, 18.66–67
    (*see also* Indexes, subentries in)
  in tables, 12.14, 12.26–31, 12.64–67, 12.74,
    12.77, 12.81, 12.84
Headline style of capitalization, 11.45, 12.67
Heavenly bodies, 7.110–14
Hebrew, transcribing, 9.102
Hebrew letters, in mathematics, p. 372
Hemisphere, 7.34
Hence, punctuation with, 5.69
High-, compounds with, p. 178
Highways, 8.60
Hire, works made for, 4.10–11, 4.30, p. 119
Historical, etc., *a* or *an* with, 6.49
Historical terms
  events, 7.65–66
  periods, 7.60–64
Holidays, 7.72
Holy days, 7.72
Homonyms, distinguishing, p. 180
Honorable, 14.7
Honorific titles, 7.27, 14.8, 14.11
Hotel, etc., *a* or *an* with, 6.49
Hours. *See* Time
-house, compounds with, p. 177
House style, 2.57, 2.96, 2.99, 2.116
However, punctuation with, 5.39, 5.69
Hundred, 8.3
Hungarian
  capitalization, 9.43
  names, 7.14, 18.109

special characters, 9.44
Hyphen, 6.24–42. *See also* Hyphenation;
  Word division; Words, compound
  in alphabetizing, 18.43
  capitalization with, 7.124, 7.128, 9.20,
    p. 180
  compared with en dash, 5.92
  end-of-line, 2.73, 3.11, 3.39, 18.128, 18.133
  marking, 2.70, 2.71, 2.72, 2.73, 3.34, pp. 53,
    94, 95
  in names, 9.20, 18.125
  in titles, 7.124
Hyphenation, 6.24–42. *See also* Hyphen;
  Word division; Words, compound
  of compound adjectives, pp. 177–79
  of compound words, 6.24, 6.26, 6.30, 6.31,
    pp. 176–81
  by computer, 20.118, 20.122–23
  in manuscript for scanning, 2.15
  of noun compounds, pp. 176–77
  with prefixes, pp. 180–81
  of proper names, 18.104, 18.110–11, 18.114,
    18.125

Ibid.
  in notes, 14.31, 15.43, 15.66, 17.13, 17.69
  roman for, 6.59
  in text references, 10.56, 10.59
Ice Age, 7.109
Ideas, Platonic, 7.79
Idem, 14.32, 17.13, 17.14
I.e., 14.31, 14.32
  punctuation with, 5.54, 5.72, 5.76, 5.86,
    5.99
  in text, 14.31
Illustrations, 11.1–24, 11.47–49. *See also* Captions; Halftones; Legends; Line drawings; Plates
  checking against text, 2.108
  copyediting, 2.108, 2.111, 11.23
  corrections on artwork, 11.23–24
  credit lines with, 4.53, 11.34–43
  cropping, 11.15–16, p. 308
  defined, 11.1–5
  estimating, 2.9, 19.8
  identifying, 2.47–48, 2.146, 2.176n,
    11.10–11, 11.30
  identifying parts of, in legend, 11.32–33
  indexing, 18.27, 18.134, 18.136
  for jacket, 4.52, 4.56
  lettering on, 13.39
  machine copies of, 2.32, 2.162
  marking for printer, 2.47–48, 11.12–20
  in mathematics, 13.39–40
  in multiauthor books, 1.36, 2.176, 11.9
  notes to, 15.45
  numbering of, 2.9, 2.47–49, 2.107, 2.176,

Illustrations (*continued*)
  8.32, 11.7–9, 11.29–30, 13.39
  orientation of, 2.48, 11.11
  page numbers of, 1.34, 1.89, 3.41, 3.47,
    11.45
  permission to reproduce, 4.40, 4.51–52,
    4.56, 11.35
  physical handling, 11.10–12
  placement of, 2.47–49, 2.108, 3.51–52, 3.55,
    11.4–5, 11.7
  preparing for letterpress, 11.21–22
  preparing for offset, 11.6–20
  in previously published material, 2.162
  printing of, 1.8, 11.5, 20.20–25, 20.78–85,
    20.130–33, p. 599
  proofs of, 2.107, 3.50–52, 11.47–49, 20.105
  redrawing, 2.109
  running heads omitted with, 1.83, 3.41
  scaling, 11.17–20, p. 310
  space allowance for, 2.146, 3.50–52, 20.104
  text references to, 2.40, 11.8–9
  tipped-in, 1.8, 20.78
  in typewriter composition, 20.104
Illustrations, list of, 1.34–36, 11.44–46
  capitalization in, 11.45
  checking against text, 2.49, 3.47
  content and arrangement of, 1.34–35,
    11.45–46, pp. 18–19, 319
  copyediting, 11.44
  page numbers in, 1.34, 3.47, 11.45
  placement of, 1.1, 1.34, 11.45
  relation to legends, 1.35, 2.49, 11.46
  title of, 1.34, 11.45
  when to include, 1.36, 11.44
Impression, new, 1.16, 1.19, 1.21, 16.57n,
    16.89, p. 8
Imprint, publisher's, 1.13, 16.86, 19.47
Inc., Ltd., etc., 14.12, 16.76
Inclusive numbers, 5.92–93, 8.67–70, 16.108,
    17.24–45, 18.9
  examples of, 8.67–68
Indeed, punctuation with, 5.69
Indention. *See also* Outline style; Paragraph-
    ing; Runover lines; Type specifications
  in bibliographies, 2.142
  of block quotations, 2.83, 19.33
  of chapter openings, 19.57
  of footnotes, 2.21, 19.41
  in indexes, 2.143, 18.18, 18.132–39, 19.44
  marking for, 2.82–83, 2.132, 2.134–36,
    2.139, 2.141, 2.142–44, 3.24
  with poetry, 10.22
  after subheads, 2.139, 19.28, 19.57
  in tables, 12.34–36, 12.69–70
Index, plural of, 6.11
Index cards
  alphabetizing, 18.38, 18.40–44
  checking page numbers on, 18.38
  editing, 18.45–57
  number of, 18.29, 18.61–62
  preparing, 18.37–39, p. 524
  saving, 2.31, 18.60
  typesetting from, 18.31
  typing, 18.29
Indexer, qualifications of, 18.19–23
Indexes
  abbreviations in, 18.87, 18.97, 18.103,
    18.125
  alphabetizing, 2.114, 18.59, 18.92–125,
    18.128, 18.135
  alphabetizing subentries, 18.51, 18.100
  authors' names in, 18.2, 18.90–91, 18.134,
    18.139
  author's responsibility for, 2.3n
  capitalization in, 18.58
  chronological order in subentries, 18.51,
    18.101
  column width in, 18.130–32, 19.42
  computer-generated, 18.24
  copies of, 2.4, 2.31, 18.60
  copyediting, 2.114, 18.126–29
  cross-references in, 18.10–17, 18.46–47,
    18.55, 18.57, 18.59, 18.67, 18.72, 18.74,
    18.97, 18.107, 18.117, 18.128
  dashes in, 18.53, 18.128, 18.135, 18.138
  definitions of terms, 18.2–18
  diacritics in, 18.64, 18.99
  editing cards for, 18.45–57
  equipment for making, 18.28–29
  estimating length of, 18.61–62
  of first lines, 18.2, 18.139
  first page number of, 2.115, 3.45, 18.129
  format of, 2.144, 18.130–39, 19.42
  grammatical relationships in, 18.6–7
  headings in, 18.3, 18.5–8, 18.11–13,
    18.66–67 (*see also* Indexes, subentries in)
  inversion of headings, 18.5, 18.109, 18.110,
    18.113–14, 18.115, 18.116, 18.121–22
  justified lines in, 18.131, 19.26
  key words in, 18.11, 18.66–67
  making cards for, 18.37–39, p. 524
  marking manuscript for typesetter, 18.129
  marking proofs for, 18.30–36, p. 523
  mechanics of indexing, 18.24–63
  in multiauthor books, 2.171
  multiple, 18.2, 18.139
  to multivolume works, 1.90–91
  name, 1.75, 18.2
  numbering manuscript pages, 2.10, 2.115,
    18.58
  page numbers in, 2.114, 18.3–4, 18.9, 18.26,
    18.38, 18.48–49, 18.128, 18.134,
    18.136–37
  passim in, 18.9

placement of, 1.1, 1.75, 2.115
plans for, 2.125
proofs of, 3.49, 18.60
proper names in, 18.64, 18.68–86, 18.95–96, 18.102–25, 18.134
pseudonyms in, 18.72
punctuation in, 18.13, 18.54–56, p. 532
references to illustrations, 18.27, 18.134, 18.136
references to notes, 18.26, 18.91
references to preliminaries, 18.25
references to tables, 18.27
runover lines in, 2.143, 18.18, 18.132, 19.26, 19.44
schedule for, 2.114, 2.125, 3.5, 3.49, 18.22–23
spacing within, 2.16, 2.31, 18.58, 18.129, 18.133
styles of, run-in and indented, 18.15, 18.18, 18.132, 18.135–39
subheadings in, 18.4–9, 18.11, 18.18, 18.47–53, 18.100–101, 18.128, 18.135–39
subject, 1.75, 18.2
titles of persons in, 18.76–84
titles of works in, 18.88–91, 18.139
type specifications for, 1.75, 2.143–44, 18.15, 18.18, 18.130–39, 19.42–44, 19.55
typing, 2.31, 18.31, 18.58–60, p. 532
typography in, 18.134–39
variant forms in, 18.70–91
Indian names, 18.118
Indirect discourse, 5.17–19, 5.66, 10.32–33
Indonesian names, 18.120
Inferior characters. *See* Subscripts and superscripts
Infinitives, in titles, 7.123
Information storage, 20.122–24
-ing, dividing words with, 6.42
Initials. *See also* Acronyms
    alphabetizing, 18.96–97
    in bibliographies, 16.6, 16.11–13, 16.99
    display, 2.132, 19.57
    in legal references, 17.76
    period with, 14.4
    with personal names, 1.11, 6.43, 7.6, 14.2, 14.4, 16.6, 16.11–13, 16.99, 18.96
    spacing of, 7.6, 14.2, 16.12
    used alone, 6.78, 7.6, 14.4
-in-law, compounds with, p. 176
In press, 16.94–95
Input, 7.151
Inscriptions
    capitalization of, 7.150
    collections of, 17.71
    missing letters in, 10.48
Insertions. *See* Additions; Corrections
Institutions. *See* Organizations

Intaglio process, 20.23–24, p. 599
Integral sign, 13.5–6, 13.29–30, 13.34, 13.36, pp. 367, 371
Intellectual movements, 7.66
Interjections, punctuation with, 5.39, 5.40
International Standard Book Number (ISBN), 1.24–25
International Standard Serial Number (ISSN), 1.26
International System of Units, 14.41–49, 14.50–51
Interpolations, in quotations, 2.96, 5.102, 10.20, 10.50–53
Interrogation point. *See* Question mark
Interruptions in speech or thought, 5.12, 5.38, 5.83, 5.97–99
    in foreign languages, 9.26, 9.46, 9.70, 9.91
Intertype. *See* Linotype
Interviews, 16.132, 17.61
Introduction
    content of, 1.40, 1.44
    indexing, 18.25
    page numbers of, 1.44
    placement of, 1.1, 1.44, 1.55
    references to, 16.28
Inversion
    of authors' names, 1.47, 16.14–15, 17.3, 17.27
    of index headings, 18.5, 18.88, 18.109, 18.110, 18.113–14, 18.115, 18.116, 18.121–22, 18.139
Iron curtain, 7.36
Irony, 6.51, 6.52, 6.68
ISBN (International Standard Book Number), 1.24–25
ISSN (International Standard Serial Number), 1.26
Issue numbers, 16.105, 16.110, 16.112–13, 16.119–20
Italian
    apostrophe in, 9.47, 9.53
    capitalization, 7.7, 7.9, 9.45
    dialogue, 9.48
    names, 7.7, 7.9, 7.45
    punctuation, 9.46–48
    special characters, 9.54
    titles of persons, 9.45
    word division, 9.49–53
Italics
    added in quotations, 10.52–53
    in Chinese and Japanese, 9.116
    for *continued,* 5.105
    deleting, 2.78
    for emphasis, 6.52, 6.53, 10.52–53
    for foreign words, 6.54–59
    for genus and species, 7.99–102
    in indexes, 18.134, 18.136–37

Italics (*continued*)
  for key terms, 6.60
  for legal cases, 7.69
  in legends, 11.32–33
  for letters as letters, 6.72
  for letters in enumerations, 8.72
  in manuscript for scanning, 2.15
  marking for, 2.76, 3.32, 13.41, pp. 53, 94, 95
  in mathematical expressions, 13.41, 13.43, 13.45–46, p. 368n, pp. 372–73
  plural of words in, 6.8
  possessive of words in, 6.17
  punctuation, 5.4, 6.60
  for question, 5.19
  for rhyme schemes, 6.81
  for ships, etc., 7.96–97
  for *sic*, 6.59
  for stage directions, 10.7, 19.67
  for subheads, 19.28–29
  in tables, 12.66, 12.69
  for technical terms, 6.61
  for theorems, etc., 13.45–46
  for titles of books, 7.5, 7.129–30, 16.31–32, 16.52
  for titles of journals, 7.129, 7.131, 16.101
  for titles of motion pictures, 7.143
  for titles of musical works, 7.5, 7.144, 7.147
  for titles of paintings, etc., 7.148
  for titles of plays, 7.140, 16.52
  for titles of poems, 7.5, 7.138, 16.52
  in type font, 19.11
  underlining for, 2.12, 2.15, 10.53n, 13.43
  for whole sentence, 6.53, 6.54
  for words as words, 6.66

Jacket, book, 20.144–45
  flap copy for, 1.7, 1.25, 2.150, 3.56
  illustrations for, 4.52, 4.56
  proofs of, 3.56
Japanese
  capitalization, 9.116
  characters, 9.118
  italics in, 9.116
  names, 7.42, 9.116, 18.115
  romanization, 9.115
Javanese names, 18.120
Joint works. *See* Coauthors, names of; Contributors, list of; Multiauthor books
Journals. *See also* Articles, journal; Diaries; Magazines, popular
  abbreviation of titles, 15.76, 15.80, 16.101–2
  foreign, 16.121, 17.54
  issue numbers, 16.105, 16.110, 16.112–13, 16.119–20
  place of publication, 16.118
  series numbers, 16.47, 17.51, 17.52
  the with titles of, 7.130–31, 18.89

titles of, 7.129–33, 9.4, 15.76, 15.80, 16.101–2, 16.114, 16.121, 18.89
  volume numbers, 16.103, 16.107–14, 16.119, 17.53
Jr., 8.52, 8.54, 14.8, 16.15, 18.82
Judicial organizations, 7.47, 7.50–52
  documents of, 16.56–57
Justice (office), 7.18
Justification, 19.21, 20.5, 20.27–29, p. 588. *See also* Ragged-right style
  by computer, 20.122–23
  defined, 19.26
  in indexes, 18.131

Kaiser, 7.18
Keys, musical, 7.145
Key words
  in indexes, 18.11, 18.66–67
  italics for, 6.60
King, 7.22. *See also* Monarchs
Kingdom, 7.37
Kinship names, 7.30. *See also* Family names

l (letter)
  identifying, pp. 366, 368
  typing, 17.16, p. 368n
Labor unions, 7.58, 8.59, 14.15
Lacunae in texts, 5.95, 10.48, 10.50
Lakes, 7.38, 7.40, 18.123
Latin
  abbreviations, 6.59, 14.31–32
  alphabet, 9.3, p. 254
  capitalization, 9.55, 17.68
  ligatures, 6.50
  special characters, 9.60
  titles of works, 9.55, 17.68
  word division, 9.56–59
Latitude and longitude, 14.24–25
Laws, 7.67–68, 16.156, 16.169–70, 17.90. *See also* Public documents
Laws, physical, 7.118
Layout, designer's, 19.69–72. *See also* Book design; Type specifications
  copies of, 19.71
  marking manuscript from, 2.129, 2.131–44, 19.71, pp. 580–81
  sample, pp. 579, 582–84
  for spine, 2.150
Leaders, in tables, 12.37, 12.40, 12.71
Leading, 2.133–34, 3.22, 19.23–25, 20.38. *See also* Spacing
Lectures, titles of, 7.142
Legal cases, 7.69, 16.157, 17.76
Legal works
  brackets in, 10.15, 10.49
  capitalization in, 10.15, 10.49
  idem in, 17.14

in notes, 15.53, 17.14, 17.76
Legends, 11.25–43
  abbreviations in, 11.33
  capitalization in, 11.25, 11.33
  checking against list of illustrations, 2.49,
    3.47
  copy for, 2.3, 2.107, 11.11
  copyediting, 11.46
  credit lines in, 4.53, 11.34–43
  defined, 11.25–26
  editor's copy of, 2.107, 11.47
  identifying parts of illustration in, 11.32–33
  italics in, 11.32–33
  to maps, 11.25
  numbering, 2.47–49, 11.29–31
  proofs of, 2.107, 3.52, 11.47–48
  punctuation in, 5.11, 11.28, 11.32, 11.37
  relation to list of illustrations, 1.35, 11.46
  symbols in, 11.33
  type specifications for, 11.27
  typing, 2.47, 2.107
Legislation, 7.67–69
Legislative bodies, 7.47–48, 7.53. *See also*
    Congress, documents of
Letterpress printing, 1.8, 11.5, 20.21–22,
    20.42–47, 20.87–89, 20.134–36
  preparing illustrations for, 11.21–22
Letters. *See also* Mathematics, signs and
    symbols; Special characters; Subscripts
    and superscripts
  with enumerations, 8.72
  identifying, pp. 366, 368–69
  in legends, 11.33
  as letters, 6.72
  missing, 5.95, 10.48, 10.50
  as musical notes, 6.74–77
  names of, 6.73, 6.80
  as names of persons, 6.78
  plurals of, 6.9–10
  for rhyme schemes, 6.81
  as shapes, 6.79–80
  superior, in classical references, 17.73
  superior, as note references, 2.26, 12.48,
    12.50, 12.73, 15.45
  as words, 6.71–81
Letters (correspondence). *See also* Archives;
    Manuscript collections
  arrangement of, in book, 1.57
  in bibliographies, 16.133, 16.137
  collections of, 17.77–84
  copyright in, 4.44
  from editor to author, 2.59, 2.116, 2.122–26
  personal communication, 15.28, 16.133,
    17.61
  quotation marks with, 10.27
  references to, 15.28, 17.61, 17.77
  signature with, 5.42, 14.4

Letterspacing, 19.22, 19.54
  marking for, p. 94
Library of Congress, 1.23–24, 4.20
Ligatures, 6.50
-like, compounds with, p. 179
Line drawings. *See also* Illustrations
  defined, 11.2
  preparing for reproduction, 11.21–24
  printing, 1.8, 11.4–5, 20.20–25, 20.79–80
Line numbers
  abbreviation with, 17.16
  cited in text, 15.66
  in notes, 17.16, 17.64
  notes keyed to, 15.73, pp. 418–19
  in plays, 19.68
Lineprinter, 20.128, p. 637
  printout from, as manuscript, 2.2, 2.5, 2.53
Line space
  in indexes, 18.58, 18.129, 18.133, 19.23
  for text divisions, 1.66, 2.84, 19.23
Linguistic groups, 7.32
Linguistics
  abbreviations used in, 14.32
  definitions, 6.56
  phonetic transcripts, 5.104
Linotype, 3.1, 13.4, 20.27, 20.29–30
List of illustrations. *See* Illustrations, list of
List of tables. *See* Tables, list of
Lists. *See also* Outline style; Series of items
  colon introducing, 5.75
  dash introducing, 5.85
  numbering of, 8.72–75
  parentheses with, 5.8, 5.100, 5.101, 6.46,
    8.72, 8.74–75
  punctuation of, 5.8–9, 5.71, 5.75, 5.76–78,
    5.100
  word division in, 6.46
Literary movements, 7.66
Lithography
  offset, 1.8, 11.5, 20.49, 20.92–95, p. 610
  stone, 20.25, 20.26, p. 599
Loc. cit., 14.32, 17.12
Lodges, 8.59
Low-, compounds with, p. 178
Lowercase, marking for, 2.74, 3.32, pp. 53,
    94, 95
-ly, compounds with, p. 177

Mac, Mc, names with, 18.105
Machine copies. *See* Copies, machine
Macron, 9.11, 9.60
Magazines, popular, 16.124–25, 16.127, 17.55.
    See also Journals
Makeready, 20.84–85, 20.89, 20.135
Makeup, page, 3.16, 15.58–60, 19.28, 19.39,
    20.34–39. *See also* Proofs, page
  in photocomposition, 15.58, 20.122–24,

Makeup, page (*continued*)
20.129
and proofs, 3.40–44, 3.50–52, 19.52,
20.34–39, p. 603
in typewriter composition, 20.104
Manuscript. *See also* Copyediting
author's corrections on, 2.33–36, 2.128
checking author's changes, 2.128
copies of, 2.4–6, 2.31, 2.32, 2.86, 2.127,
2.158, 2.161, 18.60, 19.3, 19.5
correlating parts of, 2.37–50
dead, 3.8
design and production copy, 2.4, 2.6, 19.3,
19.5
editor's changes on, 2.61–88, p. 53
estimating length of, 2.4, 2.6, 18.61–62,
19.4, 19.6–9
identifying parts of, 2.145–46, 2.176n
index, 2.31, 18.31, 18.58, 18.60, p. 532
mailing, 2.127
marking for typesetter, 2.129, 2.131–44,
19.71, pp. 580–81
numbering, 2.7–10, 2.35, 2.112, 2.115,
2.147–48, 18.58, 18.129
paper printout as, 2.2, 2.5, 2.53
preparing, 2.3–50, 13.17–40
previously published material used as,
2.158–68
ribbon copy of, 2.4, 2.6
for scanning, 2.6, 2.15, 2.52
schedule for returning, 2.125
sequence of parts, 1.1, 2.145–48
typing, 2.11–31, 13.18–19, 18.31, 18.58–60
Manuscript collections. *See also* Archives;
Letters (correspondence); Unpublished
material
abbreviations for, 15.67, p. 415
in bibliographies, 15.29, 15.83, 15.86,
16.134–40, p. 432
government, 16.158–59, 16.171–72, 16.174,
17.93–96
names of, 7.142, 17.78
in notes, 17.2, 17.9, 17.77–84
page numbers in, 17.78, 17.79
references to, 15.29
restrictions on use of, 4.43–44
Manuscript editor. *See* Copyediting; Copyeditor
Maps. *See also* Illustrations
checking against text, 2.94
legends to, 11.25
in list of illustrations, 11.45
numbering, 11.9
placement of, 2.47
typing names for, 2.109, 11.23
Margins
in manuscript, 2.17, 13.19

of type page, 19.19, 20.41, p. 605
Marked proofs, 3.7, 3.18, 3.38, 20.33
Marks, editorial, 2.61–88, p. 53
Marks, proofreaders', 3.3, 3.15, 3.19–34,
pp. 94, 95
Markup for typesetter, 2.129, 2.131–44, 19.71,
pp. 580–81
of indexes, 18.129
of mathematics, 13.41–52, p. 366
Married women's names, 18.11, 18.74–75,
18.106–7
Mass, 7.90
Mass number, 7.120
Master-, compounds with, p. 176
Master proofs, 3.7, 3.18, 3.38, 20.33
Mathematics. *See also* Equations
abbreviations, 13.42
ambiguous expressions, 13.47–52,
pp. 368–69
and book design, 19.10
color-coding in manuscript, 13.43
difficult expressions, 13.29–34
embellishments, 13.14
illustrations, 13.39–40
italic letters, 13.41, 13.43, 13.45–46,
pp. 368n, 372–73
list of special characters; 2.154, 13.11–13
marking copy for typesetter, 13.41–52,
p. 366
nonitalic type, 13.43–44, pp. 372–73
preparing manuscript, 13.17–40
punctuation, 13.23–28
signs and symbols, 13.4–16, 13.47–52,
pp. 368–73 (*see also* Subscripts and
superscripts)
spacing in, pp. 368–69
style and usage, 13.20–28
theorems, etc., 13.45–46
typefaces used in, pp. 372–73
typesetting, 13.3–16, 13.49–50
type specifications for, 13.16
typing, 13.4–5, 13.18–19
Matrix
in Linotype, 20.29
mathematical, 13.38, 13.43
type of table, 12.58, p. 337
Mayor, 7.18
M.D., 1.11, 16.11
Measurements
abbreviations with, 14.36–53
English system, 14.37–40
international system, 14.41–49, 14.50–51
numbers with, 8.11–16
of type and type page, 2.84–85, 20.38–41
Mechanical editing, 2.61–88
defined, 2.55
Medals, 7.70, 7.95

Medical terms, 7.115–17
Medieval works, 17.75
Meetings. *See* Conferences; Symposia
Metric system, 14.41–49, 14.50–51
Microform material
  in bibliographies, 16.29, 16.59–60, 16.61
  dissertations, 16.129
  in notes, 17.49, 17.84, 17.129
Middle English, 9.136
Military terms
  capitalization of, 7.93–95
  dates, 8.45
  time, 8.49
  titles, 7.15–17, 7.19, 14.5
  units, 8.57
Million, 8.3, 8.7, 8.25
Mimeographed material, 7.142, 16.131, 17.59.
  See also Copies, machine
Ministers. See *Reverend*
Minus sign
  spacing with, p. 369
  in tables, 12.42
Minutes. *See* Time
Missing words or letters, 5.95–96, 10.48, 10.50
Monarchs, 7.11, 7.15, 7.22, 8.50, 18.76–77
Money
  British currency, 2.14, 6.44, 8.26–28
  foreign currency, 8.26–31
  fractional sums, 8.24, 8.26, 8.27
  symbols with, 8.23, 8.26, 8.27, 8.29, 8.30,
    14.57
  United States currency, 8.23–25
Monotype, 20.27–28, 20.30
  leading in, 19.23
  for mathematics, 13.6, 13.10, pp. 372–73
Month
  abbreviation of, 14.28, 17.55, 17.57, 17.80
  capitalization of, 7.71
  with date of journal article, 16.105, 16.110,
    16.113, 16.121
  in dates, 8.36–39
  day of, 8.36–38, 8.43–46
Monuments, 7.43
Moon, 7.113
Motion-picture rights, 4.33
Motion pictures, names of, 7.143
Mottoes, 7.150
Mount, 14.18, 18.123
Mountains, 7.38–40, 7.42
Mr., Mrs., Ms., 14.3, 14.6, 14.10
MS. (manuscript), 17.78
Multiauthor books. *See also* Edited works;
  Symposia
  appendixes in, 1.69
  author-date citations to, 15.14–19
  author's affiliations in, 1.47–48, 1.53, 2.171,
    7.16, 15.71–72
  authors' names, 1.5, 1.33, 1.47–48, 1.53,
    15.14–19, 15.76, 15.95–96, 16.15–17,
    17.10, 17.27–31
  bibliographies in, 15.75
  in bibliographies, 15.81, 15.89, 15.95–96,
    16.15–17
  chapter openings in, 1.48, 1.53, 19.54
  contracts for, 4.27, 4.30, p. 119
  copyeditor's responsibility, 2.174–76
  copyright on, 4.8–9
  illustrations in, 1.36, 2.176, 11.9
  list of contributors in, 1.47–48, 1.53, 2.171,
    7.16, 15.71
  in notes, 17.10, 17.27–31
  note style in, 2.99
  permissions for, 2.163–65, 2.171
  planning for, 2.170
  problems of, 2.169
  proofs of, 2.171
  running heads in, 1.79
  schedule for, 2.172, 2.176
  table of contents in, 1.33
  tables in, 2.176, 12.18
  unnumbered notes in, 1.48, 1.53, 2.163,
    15.70, 15.71–72
  volume editor's responsibility, 2.170–73
Multiplication sign
  dot for, p. 369
  identifying, 2.14, pp. 368, 369
Multivolume works
  in bibliographies, 16.25, 16.41–42, 16.90–92
  date of publication, 16.90–92
  editorial style, 2.59
  incomplete, 16.91
  indexes, 1.90–91
  ISBN for, 1.25
  in notes, 17.44
  number of volumes, 16.41
  page numbers, 1.90–91
  in series, 16.46
  titles of, 16.41–42
Music
  chords, 6.77
  notes and keys, 6.74–77
  styles, 7.66
Musical works
  abbreviations with, 7.146
  scores, 16.176
  titles of, 7.5, 7.144–47, 16.36
Mutilated texts, 10.48, 10.50

N (number), 12.5, 12.10–11, 12.24, 12.45
  small cap for, 12.66
N.; nn. (for notes), 14.32, 17.16, 17.21, 18.26
Namely, 5.54, 5.72, 5.76, 5.86, 5.99
Names. *See* Author's name; Editor's name;

Names (*continued*)
    Family names; Personal names; Place
    names; Proper names; Publisher's name;
    Titles of persons; Titles of works
Nationalities, 7.32–33
Navy, 7.93
n.d., for date of publication, 14.32, 16.75,
    16.93, 16.95
New series (*n.s.*), 14.32, 16.47, 17.52
Newspapers
    in bibliographies, 15.83, 16.127
    city name with, 18.88
    date of publication, 15.83, 17.57
    foreign, 18.88
    in indexes, 18.88
    in notes, 17.57–58
    page numbers of, 17.57–58
    the with, 7.131, 18.88–89
    titles of, 6.8, 7.129, 7.131, p. 415
Nicknames, 7.28
No and *yes*
    punctuation with, 5.40, 5.41
    quotation marks with, 10.33
Nobility, 7.11, 7.15, 7.22–23, 18.77–79
Non-, compounds with, p. 180
Nonbook materials, in bibliographies,
    16.176–82
Nonrestrictive clauses, punctuation of, 5.29,
    5.31, 5.36, 5.44
North(ern), 7.34–35
Norwegian, 9.61–62
Not, punctuation with, 5.47–48
Note numbers (with note), 2.22, 2.141, 19.40.
    See also Note references
    checking, 2.42, 2.101
Note references (in text), 12.48–51, 12.72–73,
    15.38–45
    checking, 2.42, 2.101
    letters for, 2.26, 12.48, 12.50, 12.73, 15.45
    marking, 2.67, 15.57
    number of, 15.62–63
    omitted with display type, 1.52, 1.64, 15.42
    placement of, 2.22, 2.141, 15.39–42, 19.40
    with quotations, 10.6, 15.41
    symbols for, 12.49, 12.51, 15.68, 15.69
    in tables, 2.26, 12.48–50, 12.73, 15.43, 15.45
    typing, 2.22
Notes, 15.36–73, 17.2–96. *See also* Endnotes;
    Footnotes; Note references; Unnum-
    bered notes
    abbreviations in, 2.98, 14.13, 14.15, 15.66,
        15.67, 17.10, 17.12–13, 17.15, 17.16–25,
        17.36, 17.95
    acknowledgments in, 15.71–72
    adding and deleting, 15.44
    arrangement of, 1.71, 15.55, p. 409
    author-date citations with, 15.34–35, 15.68

author's name in, 15.66, 17.6–8, 17.10,
    17.13, 17.27–34
book reviews in, 17.56
capitalization in, 17.41, 17.54, 17.68
chapter numbers as subheads to, 1.71,
    15.55, 17.16, p. 410
chapters and parts of books in, 17.46
checking against bibliography, 2.43, 2.103
checking against text, 2.42, 2.101
classical references in, 17.65–75
compared with bibliographies, 17.3,
    17.26–61 passim
content of, 15.46–52, 17.2–4, 17.6–9
copyediting, 2.97–103
cross-references to, 2.40, 15.44, 15.47
date of publication in, 17.2, 17.50
defined, 15.36
discursive, 2.100
in dissertations, 2.21n
dual system of, 15.68–69
ed., comp., trans. in, 17.10, 17.35–37
edition in, 10.58, 17.47–48, 17.62, 17.64
editor's name in, 17.10, 17.35–37
editor's or translator's, 15.69, 15.73,
    pp. 418–20
endnotes vs. footnotes, 15.36, 15.58–60,
    15.64–66, 19.34
facts of publication in, 17.50
form of, 2.99, 15.48–50, 15.63, 17.2–96
full references in, 15.46, 17.2–5, 17.13
how many, 15.61–63
ibid. in, 14.31, 15.43, 15.66, 17.13, 17.69
idem in, 17.14
to illustrations, 15.45
indexing, 18.26, 18.91
journal articles in, 17.2, 17.8, 17.51–56
keyed to lines, etc., 15.73, pp. 418–20
legal style, 15.53, 17.14, 17.76
length of, 2.100, 15.48, 15.60–61, 15.65,
    19.8
manuscript collections in, 17.2, 17.9,
    17.77–84
in mathematics, 13.16
microform material in, 17.49, 17.84, 17.129
multiauthor books in, 17.10, 17.27–31
multivolume works in, 17.44
newspapers in, 17.57–58
numbering of, 2.22, 2.42, 2.101, 2.166,
    12.48–51, 12.72–73, 15.38–45, 19.40 (*see
    also* Note references)
op. cit., loc. cit. in, 17.12
page numbers, etc., in, 15.66, 17.16–25
paragraphing, 2.21, 2.141, 15.48, 19.41
placement of, 1.1, 1.71, 15.54, 15.70, 15.72,
    19.34
plays and poems cited in, 17.64
in previously published material, 2.159
public documents in, 17.85–96

punctuation in, 2.21, 2.22, 15.50, 15.51, 15.62, 17.20, 17.41, 17.63, 17.69–71
quotations in, 15.51–52
reference books in, 17.62
references to, 17.21
relation to bibliography, 2.103, 15.46, 15.77, 17.2, 17.6
renumbering, 2.42, 2.101, 2.166
repeated, 15.43
reprints in, 17.48
rules with, 19.38–39
running heads to, 1.71, 1.82, 15.54, 15.56–57, p. 409
see, cf. in, 15.53
series in, 17.45
shortened references, 2.43, 2.97–98, 15.46, 15.67, 17.6–15, 17.68, 17.69
source citations in, 15.49, 15.51, 15.62–63, 15.66
source notes, 1.53, 2.163–64, 12.46, 12.72, 15.70
spacing of, 2.16, 2.21, 2.141, 19.37
substantive, 15.68
to tables, 2.26, 2.106, 12.45, 12.46–52, 12.72–73, 12.83, 15.43, 15.45, 19.35n
tables in, 2.100, 15.64
titles of works in, 15.66, 17.2, 17.6–8, 17.11, 17.38–43, 17.68, 17.69
translator's, 15.69, 15.73
translator's name in, 17.10, 17.35–37
type specifications for, 2.141, 19.34–41, 20.32
typing, 2.3, 2.21–22
unpublished material in, 17.2, 17.9, 17.59–61, 17.77–96
volume numbers in, 17.16, 17.20, 17.53
Notes, musical, 6.74–77
Notices, 7.149
Noun compounds, spelling of, pp. 176–77
n.p., for place of publication, 14.32, 16.74–75
n.s. (*new series*), 14.32, 16.47, 17.52
Numbering
of chapters within parts, 1.54
double numeration, 1.63, 2.176, 11.9, 12.18, 13.25–26, 13.39
of equations, 13.25–26
of illustrations, 2.9, 2.47–48, 2.107, 2.176, 8.32, 11.7–9, 11.29–30, 13.39
of manuscript, 1.1, 2.7–10, 2.35, 2.112, 2.115, 2.147–48, 18.58, 18.129
of notes, 2.22, 2.42, 2.101, 2.166, 12.48–51, 12.72–73, 15.38–45, 19.40 (*see also* Note references)
of pages (*see* Page numbers)
of paragraphs, 1.63, 19.12
of tables, 2.9, 2.23, 2.46, 2.176, 8.32, 11.9, 12.15–20

Numbers. *See also* Chapter numbers; Dates; Fractions; Numbering; Page numbers; Roman numerals; Volume numbers
with abbreviations, 6.45, 8.15, 14.48–49
in addresses, 8.60–62
alignment, in tables, 12.41–43
alphabetizing, 18.98
beginning sentence, 8.9–10, 14.3
for centuries and decades, 7.125, 8.40
comma in, 2.106, 8.41, 8.64–66, 12.42, 14.49
comma to separate, 5.56
compounds with, pp. 177, 178, 179, 180
consistency in style of, 8.8
continuing (inclusive), 5.92–93, 8.67–70, 16.108, 17.24–25, 18.9
decimals, 8.17–22, 8.24, 8.64, 12.42, 13.20, 14.49
dividing at end of line, 6.44
with enumerations, 8.72–75 (*see also* Lists)
with *-fold,* p. 179
with governmental designations, 8.55–57
Greek, 9.129, p. 278
issue, 16.105, 16.110, 16.112–13, 16.119–20
large, 8.6–7, 8.25, 8.65, 8.66
line, 15.66, 15.73, 17.16, 17.64, 19.68, pp. 418–19
mass, 7.120
with measurements, 8.11–16
with military units, 8.57
money, 8.23–31, 14.57
N, in tables, 12.5, 12.10–11, 12.24, 12.45, 12.66
with names, 6.43, 8.50–54
nonscientific usage, 8.12–14
note, 2.22, 2.141, 19.40 (*see also* Note references)
with *-odd,* p. 178
ordinals, 8.4, 8.50
with organizations, 8.58–59
with parts of book, 8.32
percentages, 8.17–18, 12.5–11, 12.23, 12.45
for physical quantities, 8.11–16
plurals of, 6.9, 8.63
prefixes with, p. 180
round, 8.5–7, 8.25
in scientific text, 8.11, 8.66
section, 1.62–63, 19.12
spelled out, 7.125, 8.2–9, 8.12–13
spelling out (marking), 2.79, 3.29, pp. 53, 94
with subheads, 1.62–63
superior, in classical references, 17.73
with symbols, 8.16 (*see also* Symbols)
with time, 8.47–49
in titles, 7.125, 17.38
typing, 2.14
Numerals. *See* Numbers

O (letter), identifying, p. 368
O and *oh,* 5.40, 6.48
Oceans, 7.38
O'clock, 8.47, 8.48
OCR (optical character recognition device), 2.2, 2.6, 2.15, 20.120. *See also* Scanning
-odd, compounds with, p. 178
Officials, government, 7.18
Offprints (reprints)
    and arrangement of book, 1.53n, 1.69, 15.75
    in multiauthor books, 153n, 1.69, 2.171, 15.54, 15.75
    of journal articles, 4.29
Offset lithography, 1.8, 11.5, 20.49, 20.92–95, p. 610
    illustrations printed by, 1.8, 11.5, 20.95
    preparing artwork for, 11.6–20
Oh and *O,* 5.40, 6.48
Old English, 6.50, 9.136–37
Omissions. *See* Deletions; Ellipses; Ellipsis points
One (numeral)
    identifying, pp. 366, 368
    typing, 2.14
Op. cit., 14.32, 17.12
Operational signs
    copyeditors', 2.74–85, p. 53
    mathematical, 12.42, 13.21, 13.24, 13.35–36, pp. 368–69, 370
    proofreaders', 3.20–31, pp. 94, 95
Opposition, 7.55n
Optical character recognition device (OCR), 2.2, 2.6, 2.52, 20.120. *See also* Scanning
    typing for, 2.15
Optical spacing, 19.22
Opus number, 7.146
Or
    in appositives, 5.43
    in titles, 7.123, 7.127, 17.41
Ordinal numbers, 8.4, 8.50
Organizations, 7.47–58
    abbreviation of, 14.15, 18.87
    as author, 15.20–23, 15.97, 16.29–30
    capitalization of, 7.47–59, 9.20, 9.108, 17.54
    foreign, 9.108, 17.54
    in indexes, 18.88
    numbers with, 8.58–59
    the with, 7.57–58
Ornaments, type, 1.66
Outline style, 8.73–75. *See also* Lists
Output, 7.151
Overbars, in mathematics, 13.33
Overlay, for corrections on artwork, 11.24
Ozalids, 3.55

P., pp., 10.67, 14.32, 15.10, 17.16–20, 17.18n, 17.49, 17.79. *See also* Page numbers

Page breaks. *See also* Makeup, page
    with continuing footnotes, 19.39, 20.35
    in indexes, 18.133
    with subheads, 19.28, 20.35
Page length, 3.16, 3.44, 20.35–36
Page makeup. *See* Makeup, page
Page numbers (folios), 1.84–91. *See also* Numbering
    arabic numerals for, 1.86, 1.88, 2.148, 8.32
    with author-date citations, 15.8–12
    of back matter, 1.89, 1.91, 2.8
    in bibliographies, 16.50, 16.106–14, 16.119, 16.124–25
    of blank pages, 1.1, 1.3, 2.112, 2.148
    boldface for, 18.134, 18.136, 19.12
    changes in, in proof, 3.16, 3.37
    checking, 3.41–42, 18.38, 18.128
    cited in text, 1.88–89, 10.57, 10.67, 15.66
    in classical references, 17.66
    continuing, 5.92, 16.108, 17.24–25, 18.9, 18.36–37
    cross-references to, 2.41, 2.94
    of display pages, 1.1, 1.87–89
    drop folios, 1.52, 1.84, 1.87–89, 19.60
    of first text page, 1.1, 1.88, 2.148
    of illustrations, 1.34, 1.89, 3.41, 3.47, 11.45
    of index, 2.10, 2.115, 3.45, 18.58, 18.128
    in indexes, 2.114, 18.3–4, 18.9, 18.26, 18.38, 18.48–49, 18.128, 18.134, 18.136–37
    italics for, 18.134, 18.136–37
    of journal articles, 16.106–14, 16.119, 16.124–25, 17.53
    in list of illustrations, 1.34, 3.47, 11.45
    in list of tables, 3.47
    of manuscript, 2.7–10, 2.35, 2.112, 2.147–48, 18.129
    in manuscript collections, 17.79
    in multivolume works, 1.90–91
    with newspapers, 17.57–58
    in notes, 15.66, 17.16–20
    notes keyed to, 15.73, p. 420
    omitting, 1.1, 1.84, 1.87–89, 3.41
    p., pp. with, 10.67, 14.32, 15.10, 15.66, 17.16–20, 17.49, 17.79
    placement of, 1.52, 1.84, 1.87–89, 2.151, 19.60
    of plate section, 1.34, 11.4–5, 11.45
    of prelims, 1.1, 1.85–87, 1.88, 1.91, 2.112, 8.32
    punctuation with, 16.107–14, 16.119, 16.124, 17.20
    recto and verso, 1.1, 17.19, 17.79
    roman, 1.1, 1.85–86, 1.88, 1.91, 2.148, 8.32
    in running heads, 1.71, 1.82, 3.42, 15.56–57, p. 409
    supplying in proof, 2.41, 3.35, 3.42, 3.45, 3.47

in table of contents, 1.32, 2.39, 3.45, 3.47
with text-fiche material, 17.49
type specifications for, 2.151, 18.134,
    18.136–37, 19.60
with volume number, 16.107–14, 16.119,
    16.124–25, 17.20, 17.53
zeroes for, 1.32, 1.34, 2.39, 2.41, 11.45
Page proofs. *See also* Proofreading; Proofs
additions and deletions, 3.16, 3.20, 3.37
checking repros against, 3.53
as first proofs, 3.6–7, 3.40, 20.127, 20.129
foul, 3.38
of illustrations, 3.50–52, 11.47–49, 20.105
of index, 3.49, 18.60
indexing from, 18.30–36
makeup of, 3.40–44, 3.50–52, 20.34–39,
    20.104–5, 20.129, p. 603
master set, 3.7, 3.18, 3.38
in multiauthor books, 2.171
number of sets, 2.125, 3.7
in photocomposition, 20.127, 20.129
revised, 3.38–39
schedules for, 2.215, 3.4–5, 3.36, 3.49
as second proofs, 3.38–39, 3.40
transferring author's corrections, 3.7
transpositions in, 3.18, pp. 94, 95
in typewriter composition, 20.103–5
Pages. *See also* Makeup, page; Page num-
    bers; Page proofs
blank, 1.1, 1.3, 1.54, 2.112, 2.148
manuscript, added, 2.35
manuscript, numbering, 1.1, 2.7–10, 2.35,
    2.112, 2.115, 2.147–48, 18.58, 18.129
manuscript, size of, 2.35, 2.158
saving, 1.1
type, 19.4, 19.9, 19.16–19, 20.39, p. 605
Pagination. *See* Page numbers
Paintings, 7.148. *See also* Art, works of; Illus-
    trations
Pamphlets, 7.129
Paper. *See also* Papermaking
grain and sidedness, 20.68–69
for printing halftones, 11.21, 20.83
size of, 20.75–77, p. 622
types of, 20.66–67, 20.70
for typewriter composition, 20.99, p. 630
for typing manuscript, 2.11, 13.19, 18.31,
    18.58
weight of, 20.71–74, p. 621
Paperbacks
binding, 20.140–42, p. 642
reprint editions, 16.48, 16.57–58, 16.86,
    17.48
rights to, 4.33
Papermaking
hand process, 20.14–19, p. 597
machine process, 20.58–77

Papers, collected, 17.77–84. *See also* Ar-
    chives; Manuscript collections; Unpub-
    lished material
Papers, symposium, 7.142, 16.130, 17.59. *See
    also* Symposia
Paragraphing. *See also* Paragraphs
block quotations, 10.19, 10.30
chapter openings, 19.57
dialogue, 10.30, 10.31
marking for, 2.80, 3.23, pp. 53, 94, 95
notes, 2.21, 2.141, 15.48, 19.41
after subheads, 2.139, 19.28, 19.57
Paragraphs. *See also* Paragraphing
numbering, 1.63, 19.12
omitted from quotations, 10.36, 10.45
quotation marks with, 9.23, 10.25–28,
    10.30
running in, 2.80, pp. 53, 94
spacing between, 10.19
Parentheses, 5.97–101
with appositives, 5.43
with author-date citations, 15.7, 15.31–32
with brackets, 5.103, 13.27–28
colon with, 5.81
comma with, 5.67
with credit lines, 11.36
with dash, 5.98
with enumerations, 5.8, 5.100, 5.101, 6.46,
    8.72, 8.74–75
exclamation point with, 5.15, 5.101
with facts of publication, 16.104, 17.50
function of, 5.97
with *italics added,* 10.52–53
marking, 2.69, 3.34, p. 53
in mathematics, 13.27–28, 13.30
in notes, 15.51
other punctuation with, 5.101
with parenthetical elements, 5.38, 5.85,
    5.97–98
period with, 5.7, 5.8, 5.10, 5.101
question mark with, 5.23, 5.101
semicolon with, 5.73
with source citations, 10.54–68, 15.51,
    15.66
with species names, 7.100
with tables, 12.24, 12.28
with *that is,* etc., 5.54, 5.99
with translations or definitions, 6.56, 16.39
type style of, 5.4
Parenthetical elements, punctuation of, 5.38,
    5.85, 5.90–91, 5.97–98
Parliament, 7.18, 7.48, 7.53
documents of, 16.165–72, 17.88
Participles
compounds with, pp. 178, 179
dividing, 6.42
Participial phrase, punctuation with, 5.37

Particles 234
  in Arabic, 9.106–9
  names with, 7.7–11, 9.106–9, 18.102,
    18.107, 18.110–11
Parts, 1.54–55. *See also* Parts of book; Part
    title
  chapter numbering within, 1.54
  introductions to, 1.55
  references to, in text, 7.134
Parts of book, 1.1–93. *See also* Bibliographi-
    cal terms; *and names of individual ele-
    ments*
  abbreviations for, 10.59–60, 14.32,
    17.16–21, 17.58
  author's responsibility for, 2.3
  back matter, 1.67–76
  in bibliographies, 16.49–53
  capitalization of, 7.134–36, 11.8, 12.15
  in notes, 17.46
  numbers with, 8.32, 10.59–60
  page numbers of, 1.1, 1.84–91
  preliminaries, 1.1–49
  quotation marks with, 7.134–35
  references to, 7.134–36, 10.59–60
  running heads for, 1.77–83
  sequence of, 1.1–76, 1.84–91
  text, 1.50–66
Part title
  for back matter, 1.55
  content of, 1.54
  inclusion of, 1.55
  numbering of, 1.1, 1.32, 1.54, 1.88, 2.148
  placement of, 1.1, 1.54
  with poetry, 1.56
  in table of contents, 1.32, 19.51
Party, 7.54
Passim, 6.59, 17.25, 18.9
Pedigree (table), 12.60
Penalty copy, 13.1
Pen-and-ink drawings. *See* Line drawings
Pencil, color of, 2.86–87. *See also* Color-
    coding
Peninsula, 7.38, 7.41
Percentages, 8.17–18
  beginning sentence, 8.9
  in tables, 12.5–11, 12.23, 12.42, 12.45
  when to use % sign, 8.18
Period, 5.6–12. *See also* Decimal point; Ellip-
    sis points; Periods (time)
  with abbreviations, 5.5, 14.2, 14.15, 14.43,
    14.45
  in bibliographies, 16.7
  with display lines, 5.11
  with ellipsis points, 10.42–43
  at end of sentence, 5.6–7
  in index entries, 18.55
  with initials, 14.4

  in large numbers, 8.65
  in legends, 5.11, 11.28, 11.37
  in lists, 5.8–9, 8.73, 8.75
  marking, 2.66, 2.69, 3.34, pp. 53, 94, 95
  omission of, 5.7, 5.8–9, 5.101
  with quotation marks, parentheses, brack-
    ets, 5.7, 5.8, 5.10, 5.101, 6.63
  with running heads, 5.11
  with subheads, 1.60, 5.11
Periodicals. *See* Journals; Magazines, popular
Periods (time)
  geological, 7.108–9
  historical and cultural, 7.60–64, 7.108
Permission to reprint. *See also* Source notes
  acknowledging, 4.36, 4.53–54, 11.34–38,
    15.70
  in acknowledgments, 1.27, 1.39, 4.12
  for anthologies, 2.165, 4.57–58
  asking, 4.38–52, 4.57–58, p. 126
  author's responsibility for, 2.3, 4.38–58,
    11.35
  on copyright page, 1.25, 1.27, p. 11
  and fair use, 4.22–25, 4.41, 4.45–47
  fees for, 4.52, 4.55–56, 11.36
  granting, 4.2, 4.31, 4.35
  for illustrations, 4.51–52, 4.56, 11.35
  material requiring, 4.41–47
  in multiauthor books, 2.163–65, 2.171
  in source notes, 2.163–65, 15.70
  unpublished material, 4.43–44
Persian, transcribing, 9.102
Personal communication, 15.28, 16.133, 17.61
Personal names, 7.6–21. *See also* Author's
    name; Pseudonyms
  abbreviations with, 14.4–11, 14.16, 15.67,
    p. 415
  alphabetizing, 2.104, 9.109, 15.82,
    15.87–92, 16.23, 18.95–96, 18.102–22,
    p. 422
  authorities for, 7.6, 18.102–3
  capitalization of, 7.2, 7.6–9
  compound, 18.104, 18.106–7
  cross-references with, 18.11, 18.107, 18.117
  dividing at end of line, 6.43
  family, 7.30, 8.52–54, 14.8, 18.73, 18.82,
    18.102–22
  fictitious, 7.29 (*see also* Pseudonyms)
  first names, supplying, 2.92, 16.6, 16.11–13,
    18.71, 18.85
  foreign, 7.7–14, 18.102–22 (*see also under
    individual languages*)
  hyphenated, 18.104, 18.110–11, 18.114
  identifying, 2.92, 18.72–76, 18.80, 18.84–85
  in indexes, 18.11, 18.64, 18.70–86,
    18.95–96, 18.102–22, 18.134
  initials only, 6.78, 7.6, 14.4
  initials with, 1.11, 6.43, 7.6, 14.2, 14.4, 16.6,

16.11–13, 16.99, 18.96
  inversion of, 18.109, 18.110, 18.113–14,
    18.115, 18.116, 18.121–22
  letters for, 6.78
  with *Mac, Mc,* 18.105
  of married women, 18.74–75, 18.106–7
  numbers with, 6.43, 8.50, 8.52–54
  order of, 7.10, 7.12, 7.14
  with particles, 7.7–11, 9.106, 9.109, 18.102,
    18.107, 18.110–11
  plural of, 6.5–7
  possessive of, 6.15–23
  punctuation in, 5.57, 18.109, 18.113, 18.115
  religious, 7.78 (*see also* Saints)
  of rulers, 7.11, 7.15, 7.22, 8.50, 18.76–77
  with *Saint,* 14.16, 18.103 (*see also* Saints)
  signatures, 1.41, 1.42, 5.42, 14.4
  spelling of, 18.64, 18.102–3
  titles with, 7.15–22, 7.24, 14.5–11, 18.76–83
    (*see also* Titles of persons)
  2-em dash for, 6.78
  variants of, 18.64
Personifications, 7.29, 7.31
Philology. *See* Linguistics
Philosophical
  movements, 7.66
  terms, 6.63, 7.79
Photocomposition, 20.96, 20.106–29. *See also*
    Computers; Scanning; Typesetting
  coding in, 2.15, 2.52, 2.130, 3.12, 20.118,
    20.128
  computer-controlled systems, 2.15, 13.8–9,
    20.96, 20.115–25
  corrections in, 3.12–13, 20.129
  manuscript for, 2.2, 2.5
  marking type specifications for, 2.52, 2.130,
    2.133
  of mathematics, 13.3–4, 13.7–9, 13.16,
    13.49
  page makeup in, 15.58, 20.122–24, 20.129
  proofs in, 3.33, 20.126–28
  typefaces in, 19.13–15
  word division in, 3.11, 20.123
Photocopies. *See* Copies, machine
Photoengraving, 20.78–85, 20.87
Photographs. *See* Halftones; Illustrations
Physical terms, 7.118–19
Physics
  abbreviations used in, 14.50
  laws of, 7.118
Pica rule, 20.41
Picas, measurements in, 2.85, 20.38–39
Pictures. *See* Art, works of; Illustrations
Pinyin system, 7.12, 9.111–14, 18.112–13,
    p. 272
Place names, 7.34–45
  abbreviation of, 14.17–25

alphabetizing, 18.95–96, 18.123–25
  Arabic, 9.105–6
  with articles, 18.124
  capitalization of, 7.2, 7.34–46, 9.20
  Chinese, 9.111–12, 9.114, 9.116
  compounds with, p. 177
  foreign, 6.55, 7.42, 7.45, 9.20, 9.87,
    18.124–25
  French, 6.6, 7.45, 9.20, 18.125
  hyphenated, 18.125
  identifying, 18.85, 18.86
  in indexes, 18.64, 18.68–69, 18.85–86,
    18.95–96, 18.123–25
  Japanese, 9.116
  political divisions, 7.35, 7.37
  popular, 7.36
  punctuation with, 5.57, 5.59
  regions of the world, 7.34
  with *Saint,* 14.18, 18.125
  spelling of, 2.94, 18.64
  structures and public places, 7.43
  topographical, 7.38–42, 18.123
Place of publication
  in bibliographies, 16.61–63, 16.64–66,
    16.68–75
  of journals, 16.118
  of newspapers, 18.88
  in notes, 17.50
  n.p. for, 14.32, 16.74–75
  placement in book, 1.1, 1.13
  on title page, 1.13
  translation of, 16.73
Planets, 7.110
Plants
  scientific names, 7.98–103
  vernacular names, 7.104–7
Plates. *See also* Halftones; Illustrations;
    Plates, printing
  in list of illustrations, 1.34, 2.49, 11.43
  numbering, 2.48–49, 11.4–5, 11.29–31
  placement of, 2.48, 11.4–5
  references to, 11.8
Plates, printing, 20.86–95
  gravure, 20.90–91, p. 627
  letterpress, 20.87–89
  offset, 20.92–95
  plastic, 20.135
Platonic ideas, 7.79
Plays
  act and scene, 7.141, 10.59–60, 10.68, 19.65
  dramatis personae, 19.64
  line numbers with, 17.64, 19.68
  references to, in notes, 10.60, 17.64
  references to, in text, 10.59–60, 10.68
  speakers' names, 10.7, 10.34, 19.66
  stage directions, 19.67
  titles, 7.138, 7.140–41

Plays (*continued*)
  type specifications for, 10.7, 19.64–68
Plurals, 6.5–11
  of abbreviations, 6.9–10, 14.36, 17.16
  of acronyms, 6.9–10
  apostrophe with, 6.5, 6.10
  of foreign words, 6.8
  of *index,* 6.11
  of italicized words, 6.8
  of letters, 6.9–10
  of numbers, 6.9, 8.63
  possessive of, 6.12, 6.15
  of proper names, 6.5–7
  of titles of works, 6.8
  -ums vs. *-a,* 6.11
P.M., 8.48, 14.3, 14.30
Poems
  alignment of, 2.20, 10.21–23
  books of, 1.56
  capitalization in, 7.139
  centering on page, 2.20, 2.135, 10.21
  first lines of, 7.139, 18.2, 18.139
  indexing, 18.2, 18.139
  line numbers with, 17.64, 19.68
  lines omitted from, 2.20, 10.45
  parts of, 7.141
  permission to reprint, 4.40, 4.47
  quotation marks with, 10.23, 10.26
  quoting, 10.10, 10.21–23, 10.26
  rhyme schemes of, 6.81
  source citations with, 2.135, 10.21, 10.23,
    10.63, 10.68, 17.64
  titles, 7.5, 7.138–41
  type specifications for, 2.135, 19.61–63
  typing, 2.20
Points, measurements in, 2.84, 20.38
Polish
  capitalization, 9.63
  special characters, 9.64
  word division, 9.65
Political divisions and organizations, 7.35,
    7.37
  capitalization of, 7.54–56
  numbers with, 8.56
Popes, 7.20, 8.50, 18.76
Portuguese
  capitalization, 7.7, 7.9, 9.66
  names, 7.7, 7.9
  special characters, 9.67
Possessive, 6.12–23
  formation of, 6.12
  in German, 9.34
  of Greek names, 6.20
  of *Jesus* and *Moses,* 6.19
  of plurals, 6.12, 6.15
  of proper names, 6.15–23
  of titles, 6.17

  of words ending in sibilants, 6.12, 6.15,
    6.18–23
  of words in italic, 6.17
Pound sign (British), 2.14
Prayers, 7.87
Predicate, compound, punctuation with, 5.28
Preface, 1.39–42
  author's name with, 1.41, 1.42
  content of, 1.38, 1.39, 1.40, 1.46
  contrasted with foreword, 1.38
  editor's, 1.42
  indexing, 18.25
  to new edition, 1.42
  place and date with, 1.41
  placement of, 1.1, 1.39, 1.42
  relation to acknowledgments, 1.39
  title of, 1.42
  type specifications for, 19.55
Prefixes
  spelling words with, pp. 180–81
  and word division, 6.41
Preliminaries (front matter), 1.2–49. *See also*
    Display matter; *and names of individual*
    elements
  blank pages in, 1.1, 1.3, 2.112, 2.148
  checking proofs of, 3.48
  content of, 1.1–49
  copyediting, 2.110–13
  indexing, 18.25
  missing material in, 2.113
  numbering manuscript pages of, 2.7, 2.112
  pagination of, 1.1, 1.85–87, 1.88, 1.91,
    2.112, 8.32
  references to, in text, 7.135
  responsibility for, 2.3, 2.110–11, 2.171
  roman numerals for, 1.85–87, 1.88, 2.112,
    8.32, 17.23
  running heads for, 1.78
  sequence of, 1.1–49, 2.112
  in table of contents, 1.32
  type specifications for, 1.9–11, 19.45,
    19.47–51, 19.55
Prepositions
  compounds with, p. 176
  in index subentries, 18.100
  title as object of, 7.132
  in titles of works, 7.123
President, 7.15, 7.16, 7.18, 7.21
Press, 16.77. *See also* Printing presses; Pub-
    lisher; Publisher's name
Press sheets, checking, 3.57
"Press style," 2.57, 2.96, 2.99, 2.116
Previously published material
  copyediting, 2.166–68
  illustrations in, 2.162
  manuscript assembled from, 2.158–62
  notes in, 2.159

source notes for, 2.163–65
Priests. *See* Reverend
Primary sources. *See* Archives; Manuscript collections; Unpublished material
Prime ('), 13.49, p. 369
Prime minister, 7.18
Printed material used as manuscript, 2.158–68
Printer's errors, identifying, 3.35
Printing, place of, on copyright page, 1.1, 1.20
Printing history, on copyright page, 1.1, 1.16
Printing methods. *See also* Printing presses
    four-color printing, 20.130–33
    gravure, 11.5, 20.48, 20.90–91
    hand process, 20.7–9, pp. 589–91
    for illustrations, 1.8, 11.5, 20.20–25, 20.78–85, 20.130–33, p. 599
    letterpress, 1.8, 11.5, 11.20–22, 20.21–22, 20.42–47, 20.87–89, 20.134–36
    machine processes, 20.42–49, 20.134–38
    offset lithography, 1.8, 11.5, 20.49, 20.92–95, p. 610
    platemaking, 20.86–95
Printing presses
    belt, 20.134–35
    cylinder, 20.43–45, p. 607
    gravure, 20.48, p. 609
    hand, 20.7–9, pp. 589–91
    rotary, 20.47, 20.48, p. 608
    vertical, 20.43, 20.46, p. 608
    web offset, 20.137–38, p. 641
Printout, paper, as manuscript, 2.2, 2.5, 2.53
Prizes, 7.70
Probability, statistical, 8.20, 12.46, 12.51, 13.20
Proceedings. *See* Symposia
Production schedules. *See* Schedules
Product sign, 13.29–30, pp. 367, 369, 371
Professional titles, 1.11, 7.15–17, 7.21
Professor, 7.16, 7.17n, 7.21
Proofreader, printer's, 3.2, 3.9, 3.13, 3.35, 20.33
Proofreaders' marks, 3.3, 3.19–34, pp. 94, 95
    placement of, 3.15
Proofreading, 3.9–37. *See also* Author's alterations; Galley proofs; Page proofs; Proofreaders' marks; Proofs
    for broken type, 3.13, 3.33, pp. 94, 95
    for coding errors, 3.12
    color-coding in, 3.15, 3.17, 3.35
    with copyholder, 3.2, 3.9
    of copyright page, 3.48, 3.57
    of display matter, 3.48, 3.57
    identifying PEs and AAs, 3.35
    of indexes, 3.49, 18.60
    mechanics of, 3.15–34
    methods of, 3.1–3, 3.9
    for page makeup, 3.40–44, 3.50–52, 19.52

page proofs, 3.40–48
    by printer's proofreader, 3.2, 3.9, 3.13, 3.35, 20.33
    responsibility for, 3.2
    second proofs against first proofs, 3.38–39
    for sense, 3.14
    supplying page numbers, 2.41, 3.35, 3.42, 3.45, 3.47
    for typographical errors, 3.9–10, 3.35
    for word division, 3.11
    for wrong font, 3.13, 3.33, pp. 94, 95
Proofs, 3.1–58. *See also* Proofreading; Proofs (mathematical)
    blueprints, 3.52, 3.55, 11.49, 20.105
    of book jacket, 3.56
    of die copy, 3.56
    first proofs, 3.6–8, 3.40, 20.127, 20.129
    foul, 3.38–39
    galleys (*see* Galley proofs)
    of illustrations, 2.107, 3.50–52, 11.47–49, 20.105
    of index, 3.49, 18.60
    of legends, 2.107, 3.52, 11.47–48
    master set, 3.7, 3.18, 3.38, 20.33
    pages (*see* Page proofs)
    in photocomposition, 3.1–3, 3.33, 20.126–28
    press sheets, 3.57
    producing, 20.33
    reproduction proofs, 3.33, 3.54, 13.7, 20.49, 20.106
    revised, 3.38–39
    schedules for, 2.125, 3.4–5, 3.36, 3.49
    second proofs, 3.38–39, 3.40
    typesetter's queries on, 2.120
    in typewriter composition, 20.103–5
Proofs (mathematical), 13.46
Proper names. *See also* Personal names; Place names
    compounds with, pp. 177, 179, 180
    foreign, 6.55
    plural of, 6.5–7
    possessive of, 6.15–23
    words derived from, 7.46, 7.86
Protestant, 7.80
Pseudonymous works, copyright in, 4.12
Pseudonyms, 16.18–20, 17.33
    cross-references with, 16.20, 18.11, 18.72
    in indexes, 18.11, 18.72
Publication. *See* Date of publication; Facts of publication; Place of publication; Publisher's name
Public documents
    in bibliographies, 16.134–40, 16.141–75
    in Canada, 16.174, 17.92
    facts of publication for, 16.146
    government archives, 16.158–59, 16.171–72, 16.174, 17.93–96

Public documents (*continued*)
  of international bodies, 16.175
  in notes, 17.85–96
  numbers of, 16.148, 16.153, 16.155
  reference elements needed, 16.141–44
  state and local, 16.160
  of United Kingdom, 16.161–73, 17.87–91,
    17.94–95
  of United States, 16.146–60, 17.85–86
  unpublished, 16.158–59, 16.171–72, 16.174,
    17.93–96
Public domain, 4.19, 4.41–43, 11.39. *See also*
  Copyright
Public places, names of, 7.43–45
Publisher
  address of, 1.22
  agents of, 1.1, 1.22
  responsibilities of, 2.3, 2.110, 2.170, 3.2,
    4.26–35
Publisher's name
  abbreviations with, 16.76–77
  ampersand or *and* with, 16.79
  in bibliographies, 16.61–63, 16.64–67,
    16.76–87
  copublishers, 16.82–84
  foreign, 16.80, 16.87
  in notes, 17.50
  spelling of, 16.78
  the with, 16.76
  on title page, 1.13
Publishing agreement. *See* Consent-to-publish form; Contract, publishing; Works
  made for hire
Publishing history, on copyright page, 1.19
Pulp, paper, 20.15, 20.59–62
Punctuation. *See also* Punctuation marks;
  and names of individual marks
  with adverbial clauses or phrases, 5.29–35
  in alphabetizing, 18.43
  with antithetical elements, 5.46–49
  with appositives, 5.43–44, 5.64
  in author-date citations, 15.7–9, 15.11,
    15.15, 15.24, 15.25
  of biblical references, 17.63
  in bibliographies, 2.30, 16.7, 16.15, 16.44,
    16.62–63, 16.64, 16.107, 16.114, 16.124
  with brackets, 5.10, 5.15, 5.23, 5.67, 5.73,
    5.81, 5.101
  in classical references, 17.69–71
  between clauses, 5.74
  close vs. open, 5.1–2
  of compound sentences, 5.25–28, 5.30,
    5.68–70
  with coordinate adjectives, 5.45
  with dates, 5.60, 5.92–93, 8.36–39, 8.41,
    8.64, 17.38
  with dependent elements, 5.29–35

  of dialogue, 5.41, 5.75, 5.80, 10.30–31,
    10.34
  with direct address, 5.41
  with display lines, 1.52, 5.11, 5.42
  with ellipsis points, 5.12, 10.6, 10.41,
    10.42–44
  of elliptical constructions, 5.61–62
  with enumerations, 5.8–9, 5.71, 5.76–78,
    8.72–75
  with facts of publication, 16.62–63, 16.64
  with faltering speech, 5.12, 9.26, 9.46, 9.70,
    9.91
  in French, 9.21–26
  function of, 5.1–2
  in German, 9.34–35
  in glossaries, 1.72, 2.27
  in Greek, 9.128
  in index entries, 18.13, 18.54–56, p. 532
  with interjections, 5.39, 5.40
  in Italian, 9.46–48
  in legends, 5.11, 11.28, 11.32, 11.37
  marking, 2.66–73, 3.34, pp. 53, 94, 95
  of mathematics, 13.23–28
  modernizing, 10.6
  with names, 5.57, 5.59, 18.109, 18.113,
    18.115
  in notes, 2.21, 2.22, 15.50, 15.51, 15.62,
    17.20, 17.41, 17.63, 17.69–71
  in numbers, 2.106, 8.41, 8.64–66, 12.42,
    14.49
  with page numbers, 16.107–14, 16.119,
    16.124, 17.20
  with parentheses, 5.7, 5.8, 5.10, 5.15, 5.23,
    5.67, 5.73, 5.81, 5.101
  of parenthetical elements, 5.7, 5.85,
    5.90–91, 5.97–98
  of questions, 5.19–22, 5.66
  with quotation marks, 5.10, 5.15, 5.23, 5.67,
    5.73, 5.81, 6.63, 9.22, 9.35
  of quotations, 2.96, 5.63–65, 5.67, 5.73,
    5.75, 5.89, 10.6, 10.12, 10.16–18
  of restrictive elements, 5.29–31, 5.36, 5.44,
    5.64
  with running heads, 5.11
  in Russian, 9.90–92
  of sentence within sentence, 5.7
  of series, 5.8, 5.26, 5.50–53, 5.71, 5.76–77,
    5.100, 5.101, 7.126, 8.72
  with single quotation marks, 5.10, 6.63
  with source citations, 10.61–68
  in Spanish, 9.69–71
  with speakers' names, 10.34
  with subheads, 1.60, 2.19, 2.139, 5.11, 5.42
  in tables, 2.23, 5.11, 12.38
  with *that is*, etc., 5.54, 5.72, 5.76, 5.86, 5.99
  of time, 5.92, 8.47, 8.49
  of titles of persons, 5.42, 5.43, 5.58

726

in titles of works, 1.9, 7.126–28, 7.146, 16.31–32, 16.37, 17.38, 17.41
with transitional adverbs, 5.39
with volume and page numbers, 16.107–14, 16.119, 17.20
Punctuation marks. *See also* Punctuation; *and names of individual marks*
following italic word, 5.4, 6.60
multiple, 5.5, 5.67, 5.81, 5.88–90
type style of, 5.4

Quad marks, 2.82–83, 2.143, 3.24
Quantities
abbreviations with, 14.36–53
numbers for, 8.11–16
Quasi, compounds with, pp. 176, 179
Queen, 7.22, 7.23. *See also* Monarchs
Queries to author, 2.1, 2.87, 2.116–23
Query slips, 2.120–21
Question. *See also* Question mark
capitalization of, 5.18–19, 5.66
indirect, 5.22
polite request, 5.21
punctuation of, 5.17, 5.19–22, 5.66
rhetorical, 10.32
within sentence, 5.17–19, 5.66, 10.32
single word, 5.19
Question mark, 5.16–23. *See also* Question
with dash, 5.90
as editorial comment, 5.16, 10.50
with ellipsis points, 10.42
at end of sentence, 5.16, 5.20–22
marking, 2.68, 2.69, 3.34, p. 94
omitting, 5.19, 5.21–22
with other punctuation, 5.90, 17.38
with quotation marks, parentheses, brackets, 5.23, 5.101
in Spanish, 9.71
with titles of works, 17.38
Quotation marks, 10.24–35. *See also* Quotations
in block quotations, 10.29
with chapter titles, 7.134, 16.49
colon with, 5.81
comma with, 5.67, 6.63
with definitions, 6.56, 6.57, 6.61
with dialogue, 9.22–24, 9.48, 9.69, 10.30–31, 10.33, 10.34
with display matter, 10.35
double and single, 10.24, 10.29
exclamation point with, 5.15
in French, 9.21–26
in German, 9.35
for irony, 6.52, 6.68
in Italian, 9.48
marking, 2.67, 2.69, 3.34, pp. 53, 94, 95
with paragraph, 9.23, 10.25–28, 10.30

with parts of book, 7.134–35
period with, 5.10, 6.63
for philosophical terms, 6.63
with phrases, 6.64–65
with poetry, 10.23, 10.26
punctuation with, 5.10, 5.15, 5.23, 5.67, 5.73, 5.81, 6.63, 9.22, 9.35
question mark with, 5.23
within quotations, 10.6, 10.24, 10.29
with radio and television programs, 7.147
in Russian, 9.90
single, 2.69, 5.10, 6.56, 6.63, 10.6, 10.24
with slang, 6.69
in Spanish, 9.69
for special usage, 6.52
for technical terms, 6.62
with titles of articles, 7.134, 16.6, 16.114
with titles of musical works, 7.5, 7.144, 7.147
with titles of poems, 7.5, 7.138–39
with titles of works, 7.5, 7.134, 16.25, 16.31–32, 16.33–36, 16.100, 16.138–39, 17.38
for titles within titles, 16.25
with translations of foreign words, 6.56
with unpublished material, 7.142, 16.128
for words as words, 6.67
Quotations, 10.1–70. *See also* Block quotations; Dialogue; Permission to reprint; Quotation marks
accuracy of, 2.96, 10.4–5
capitalization in, 10.6–7, 10.12–15, 10.49
colon introducing, 5.75, 5.80, 10.16–18
copyediting, 2.96, 10.29, 10.36
direct discourse, 10.30–31, 10.33, 10.34
display, 10.35 (*see also* Epigraph)
ellipsis in, 10.6, 10.36–49
foreign language, 2.96, 10.69–71
integration with text, 10.11–14
interpolations and alterations in, 2.96, 10.6–7, 10.20, 10.50–53
introductory phrases with, 10.16–18
italics in, 10.52–53
note references with, 10.6, 15.41
in notes, 15.51–52
permissions for, 1.27, 10.2
of phrases, 6.64–65
poetry, 10.10, 10.21–23, 10.26
punctuation of, 2.96, 5.63–65, 5.67, 5.73, 5.75, 5.89, 10.6, 10.12, 10.16–18
run into text, 10.8–18
sic with, 5.14, 5.102, 6.59, 10.51
source citations with, 1.30, 2.102, 10.2, 10.54–68
spelling in, 2.96, 10.6
in titles of works, 17.38
translation of, 2.96, 10.70–71

Quotations (*continued*)
  typography in, 10.7
  use of, 10.1–3
  what not to quote, 10.3

Rabbi, 7.20
Racial connotations, 2.92
Racial groups, 7.32–33
Radical sign, 13.33, 13.37, p. 371
Radio stations and programs, 7.143, 14.15, 18.97
Ragged-right style, 19.27, 20.27, p. 588. *See also* Justification
  defined, 6.47
  for display matter, 19.55
  for epigraphs, 19.56
  in indexes, 18.131, 19.43
  in manuscript for scanning, 2.15
  marking for, 6.47
  word division in, 6.47, 19.27
Record group numbers, 16.158, 17.93
Recordings, sound, 16.177–78
Recto page
  for chapter openings, 1.52, 1.53n
  defined, 1.1
  marking in manuscript, 2.112
  for new section, 1.68–69, 1.75, 2.112
  page references to, 17.19, 17.79
  in preliminaries, 2.112
  running head on, 1.79
Reference books, in notes, 17.62. *See also* Dictionaries
Reference lists, 15.74–81, 15.87–97, 16.2–4, pp. 422–24. *See also* Author-date citations; Bibliographies
  alphabetizing, p. 422
  authors' names in, 15.79, p. 423
  checking text citations against, 2.44, 2.104, 15.33
  content of, 15.77, 16.2–4
  copyediting, 2.104
  cross-references in, 15.81
  date of publication in, 15.29, 15.33, 15.79, 15.90–91, 16.6, 16.63, 16.64, 16.93–95, pp. 422–24
  form of, 15.78–81, pp. 422–24
  multiauthor books in, 15.81
  numbered items in, 15.6
  placement of, 1.1
  shortened form, 15.80
  type specifications for, 2.142
  works by same author in, 15.90–91
Reference matter. *See* Back matter
Reference numbers, 17.16–25. *See also* Bibliographical terms; Note references
References, note. *See* Note references

Regions of the world, 7.34–35. *See also* Place names
Relief process (of printing), 20.21–22, p. 599
Religions, 7.80–81
Religious names and terms
  capitalization of, 7.20, 7.74–92
  deities, 7.75–77
  events and concepts, 7.89
  holidays, 7.72
  objects, 7.92
  quotation marks with, 6.63
  religious bodies, 7.32, 7.80–83, 9.20
  revered persons, 7.78
  rites and services, 7.90–91
  saints, 5.57, 7.78, 14.16, 18.83, 18.103
  titles of persons, 7.15–17, 7.20, 7.78, 14.7, 18.80
  writings, 7.84–88 (*see also* Bible)
Reprint editions, 16.48, 16.57–58, 16.86, 17.48. *See also* Offprints; Permission to reprint
  rights to, 4.33
Reproduction proofs (repros), 3.33, 3.54, 13.70, 20.49, 20.106
Republic, 7.37, 8.55
Responsibility
  of author, 2.3, 2.171–73, 4.36–58, 11.35
  of copyeditor, 2.110, 2.174–76, 3.43, 11.44–46
  of publisher, 2.3, 2.110, 2.170, 3.2, 4.26–36
  of volume editor, 2.170–73
Restrictive elements, punctuation of, 5.29–31, 5.36, 5.44, 5.64
Reverend, 7.20, 14.7, 18.80
Rhyme schemes, 6.81
Rights. *See* Copyright; Permission to reprint
River (in type), 19.21
Rivers, names of, 7.38–39, 7.41–42
Romanization, 9.85. *See also* Transliteration
  of Chinese, 7.12, 9.111–14, 18.112–14, p. 272
  of Japanese, 9.115
Roman numerals
  for act and scene, 10.59n
  avoiding, 16.10, 16.43, 16.103, 19.53
  for back matter, 1.91
  for classical references, 17.71
  in dates, 8.44
  formation of, 8.71
  for musical chords, 6.77
  with names, 8.50–53
  in outline style, 8.75
  for page numbers, 1.1, 1.85–86, 1.88, 1.91, 2.148, 8.32
  for preliminaries, 1.85–87, 1.88, 2.112, 8.32, 17.23
  for volume numbers, 16.10, 16.43, 16.103

Roman type
  for foreign words, 6.54–59
  marking for, 3.32, pp. 94, 95
  in mathematics, 13.42–43
Rounding, in tables, 12.42, 12.45
Round numbers, 8.5–7, 8.25
Royalties, 4.2, 4.27, 4.55
Rulers, names of, 7.11, 7.15, 7.22, 8.50,
  18.76–77
Rules
  with footnotes, 19.38–39
  in tables, 2.25, 2.106, 12.13, 12.29, 12.31,
    12.42, 12.44, 12.58, 12.74
Run-in style, in indexes, 18.15, 18.18, 18.132,
  18.135–39
Running heads, 1.77–83
  in back matter, 1.81–82, 15.56–57, p. 409
  chapter titles as, 1.51, 1.79, 2.151
  checking in proof, 3.41–43
  content of, 1.78–81, 2.151, 2.153
  copy for, 2.3, 2.149, 2.151–53, 19.59
  to endnotes, 1.71, 1.82, 3.42, 15.54,
    15.56–57, p. 409
  in multiauthor books, 1.79
  omitting, 1.52, 1.77–78, 1.83, 3.41, 12.75
  in preliminaries, 1.78
  punctuation with, 5.11
  recto and verso, 1.78–82
  subheads as, 1.79–80, 3.43
  in text, 1.79–80
  type specifications for, 2.151, 19.59, 20.32
Runover lines. *See also* Flush-and-hang style
  in bibliographies, 2.29, 2.142
  in equations, 13.36
  in glossaries, 2.27
  in indexes, 2.143, 18.18, 18.132, 19.26,
    19.44
  in outline style, 8.73
  in tables, 12.69–70
Russian
  alphabet, 9.86–89, 10.70n, p. 266
  capitalization, 9.87–88
  names, 7.13, 9.86
  punctuation, 9.90–92
  titles of works, 16.39–40, 17.43
  transliteration of, 9.86–89, 10.70n, p. 266
  word division, 9.93–101
Russian letters, in mathematics, p. 373

Sacred writings, 7.84–87
Saint
  abbreviation of, 14.16, 14.18, 18.103, 18.125
  names with, 14.16, 14.18, 18.103, 18.125
Saints
  appellations of, 7.78
  indexing, 18.83, 18.103
  names of, 5.57

Sans serif type
  in mathematics, 13.43–44, p. 373
  for shape, 6.79
Satellites, 7.96, 7.110
Scaling of illustrations, 11.17–20, p. 310
Scanning, 20.120
  coding of manuscript for, 2.15
  corrections in, 2.52
  editing material for, 2.52
  number of manuscript copies needed, 2.6
  typing for, 2.15
Schedules
  affected by author's alterations, 3.36, 3.52
  for edited manuscript, 2.125
  for index, 2.114, 2.125, 3.5, 3.49, 18.22–23
  for multiauthor books, 2.172, 2.176
  for proofs, 2.125, 3.4–5, 3.36, 3.49
School, 7.57, 7.66
Scientific terms
  abbreviation of, 7.99–101, 14.50–54
  astronomical, 7.110–14
  capitalization of, 7.98–120
  geological, 7.108–9
  names of plants and animals, 7.98–107
  physical and chemical, 7.118–20, 14.54
Screening of halftones, 11.3, 11.13–14,
  20.81–84, 20.90, 20.132
Script letters, in mathematics, 13.43–44,
  p. 373
Scriptures, 7.84–87. *See also* Bible
Sculpture, 7.148
Seasons, 7.31, 7.71
Second (2d), 8.4
Sections. *See also* Parts; Subheads
  abbreviation of *section,* 14.56, 17.58
  cross-references to, 1.62–63
  numbering of, 1.62–63, 19.12
See, see also
  in indexes, 18.10–17, 18.55
  in notes, 15.53
Self-, compounds with, pp. 176, 178
Semicolon, 5.68–73
  in author-date citations, 15.24, 15.25
  in bibliographies, 16.15
  in compound sentences, 5.27, 5.68–70
  in elliptical constructions, 5.61–62
  in index entries, 18.13, 18.54–55
  marking, 2.68, 2.69, 3.34, pp. 53, 94
  in notes, 15.50, 15.62
  with quotation marks, parentheses, brack-
    ets, 5.73
  with series of items, 5.52, 5.71, 8.72
  with *that is,* etc., 5.54, 5.72
  in titles of works, 17.41
  with transitional adverbs, 5.69
Sentence. *See also* Question
  compound punctuation of, 5.25–28, 5.30,

Sentence (*continued*)
5.68–70
incomplete, 10.44, 10.47
italics for, 6.53, 6.54
within another sentence, 5.7
Sentence-style capitalization, 2.139, 12.25, 12.67, 12.68, 16.6, 16.100
Serial numbers, with public documents, 16.153, 16.155
Serial rights, 4.33
Series. *See also* Series of items
International Standard Serial Number, 1.26
journals, 16.47, 17.51, 17.52
new series, 14.32, 16.47, 17.52
number, 16.44, 16.47
reprint, etc., 16.48
series title page, 1.1, 1.2, 1.4, 2.110
title, 7.137, 16.44–48, 17.45
volume number with, 16.46
Series editor, 1.4, 16.44–45
Series of items. *See also* Enumerations; Lists
colon introducing, 5.75–78
parentheses with, 5.8, 5.100, 5.101
punctuation of, 5.8, 5.26, 5.50–53, 5.71, 5.100, 5.101, 7.126, 8.72
in titles, 7.126
Sexist connotations, 2.92
Shapes, letters as, 6.79–80
Sheets, press, 3.57
Shilling mark. *See* Solidus
Ships, 7.96–97, 8.51
Short titles
in author-date citations, 15.18
in bibliographies, 16.6, 16.37
in classical references, 17.68, 17.69
in notes, 2.97–98, 15.67, 17.6–8, 17.11, 17.68, 17.69
in text, 10.56
Sibilants
plural of words ending in, 6.7
possessive of words ending in, 6.12, 6.15, 6.18–23
Sic, 5.14, 5.102, 6.59, 10.51
Side heads, run-in, 1.60, 2.138, 2.139. *See also* Subheads
Signature. *See also* Binding
with letter, 5.42, 14.4
with preface, 1.41, 1.42
punctuation with, 5.11
Significance, levels of, 8.20, 12.46, 12.51, 13.20
Signs, mathematical. *See* Symbols, mathematical
Signs (notices), 7.149
Silver prints, 3.55, 11.49
Single spacing, 2.16, 2.21n, 12.14. *See also* Double spacing

Sinkage, 2.131, 19.52, 19.55, 20.39
SI units, 14.41–49, 14.50–51
Slang, 6.69
Slant line. *See also* Solidus
for deletions, 3.20, pp. 94, 95
for lowercasing, 2.74, 3.32, pp. 53, 94, 95
Slash. *See* Solidus
Small caps, 2.75n. *See also* Caps and small caps
for A.D., etc., 7.123, 8.41, 14.3, 14.27
for A.M., etc., 8.48, 14.3, 14.30
for chapter opening, 2.132, 19.57
marking for, 2.75, 3.32, pp. 53, 94, 95
for N (number), 12.66
in quotations, 10.7
in titles, 7.123
So, punctuation with, 5.69
So-called, 6.70
Social titles, 14.3, 14.6
Societies, 7.58, 9.4. *See also* Organizations
Solidus
with dates, 5.93
with fractions, 13.30–31
for *per,* 14.55
with poetry, 10.10
Songs, 7.144, 7.147
Source citations. *See also* Source notes
abbreviations for, 10.60, 15.66, 15.67
with block quotations, 2.135, 10.21, 10.23, 10.63, 10.66–68
in notes, 15.49, 15.51, 15.62–63, 15.66
parentheses with, 10.54–68, 15.51, 15.66
placement of, 2.135, 4.53–54, 15.51
with poetry, 2.135, 10.21, 10.23, 10.63, 10.68, 17.64
punctuation with, 10.61–68
in text, 10.54–68
Source notes. *See also* Credit lines; Permission to reprint; Source citations; Unnumbered notes
copyright notice in, 2.163, 15.70
with previously published material, 2.163–65
to tables, 12.46, 12.72, 12.83
unnumbered, 1.53, 2.163–64, 12.46, 12.72, 15.70
South(ern), 7.34–35, 7.36
South Asian languages, 9.110
Spacecraft, 7.96–97, 8.51
Space mark, 2.65, 2.72, 2.84, 3.21, 3.22, pp. 53, 94, 95
Space programs, 7.97
Spacing. *See also* Alignment; Double spacing; Indention; Type specifications
within abbreviations, 14.2
with block quotations, 2.16, 2.20, 2.83–84, 19.23, 19.31–32

with colon, 16.62, 16.107
with dash, 2.70
in display matter, 19.22, 19.54
of ellipsis points, 10.36
with *f., ff.,* 17.24
hair space, 3.22, 17.21, 17.24, 18.26
within indexes, 2.16, 2.31, 18.58, 18.129,
  18.133
of initials, 7.6, 14.2, 16.12
between letters, 3.22, 19.22, 20.125, p. 629.
  (*see also* Letterspacing)
between lines, 2.133–34, 3.22, 19.23–25,
  20.38
in manuscript, 2.16, 2.17, 2.28, 2.29
marking for, 2.65, 2.81–85, 3.21–22, 19.23,
  pp. 53, 94, 95
in mathematics, pp. 368–69
with *n., nn.,* 17.21, 18.26
with notes, 2.16, 2.21, 2.141, 19.37
optical, 19.22
between paragraphs, 10.19
in proofs, 3.21–22
in running heads, 19.59
between sections of text, 1.66, 2.84, 19.23
with subheads, 2.139, 19.22
with tables, 2.16n, 2.23–25, 12.14, 12.31,
  12.52, 12.54
vertical, 1.66, 2.84–85, 2.131, 19.23–25,
  20.37–38
between words, 3.22, 19.21, 19.26–27, 20.5,
  20.37, 20.125, p. 588 (*see also* Justification)
Spanish
  capitalization, 7.7, 9.68
  dialogue, 9.69
  personal names, 6.7, 6.18, 7.7, 7.10,
    18.106–8
  place names, 7.42, 7.45, 18.124
  punctuation, 9.69–71
  special characters, 9.79, 9.81
  word division, 9.72–78
Spanner heads, 12.29, 12.31, 12.65, 12.74
Speaker of the House, 7.18
Speakers' names, in plays, discussions, etc.,
  10.7, 10.34, 19.66
Special characters, 9.10–11, p. 254. *See also*
  Diacritical marks; Symbols
  in African languages, 9.84
  in Arabic, 9.102, 9.104
  in Danish, 9.15
  in Finnish, 9.19
  in French, 9.32
  in German, 9.42
  in Hungarian, 9.44
  in Italian, 9.54
  in Latin, 9.60
  in mathematics (*see* Symbols, mathemati-
    cal)
  in Norwegian, 9.62
  in Portuguese, 9.67
  in Spanish, 9.79
  in Swedish, 9.81
  in Turkish, 9.83, 9.102
Special characters, list of, 2.149, 2.154,
  13.11–13
Species names, 7.99–101
Specifications. *See* Type specifications
Speech. *See also* Dialogue
  colon introducing, 5.75, 5.80
  faltering, 5.12, 9.26, 9.46, 9.70, 9.91
Spelling, 6.3–50
  in Arabic, 9.105–6
  British vs. American, 6.3, 18.64
  checking, 2.89
  of compound words, 6.24–32, pp. 176–81
  dictionary for, 6.1
  on illustrations, 2.108
  in indexes, 18.64
  ligatures, 6.50
  modernizing, 10.6
  of personal names, 18.64, 18.102–3
  plurals, 6.5–11
  possessives, 6.12–23
  of publishers' names, 16.78
  in quotations, 2.96, 10.6
  special preferences, 6.3–4
  in titles of works, 7.125, 16.31–32
  variant, 6.4, 18.64
  words with prefixes, pp. 180–81
Spelling out
  abbreviations, 2.79, 3.29, 18.97, pp. 53, 94,
    95
  numbers, 2.79, 3.29, 7.125, 8.2–9, 8.12–13,
    pp. 53, 94
Spine copy, 2.149, 2.150, 3.56
Sr., 14.8
Stage directions, 10.7, 19.67
Stars, 7.110
State, 7.36, 7.37, 7.53. *See also* State names
Statement, formal, punctuation of, 5.75
State names, abbreviations of, 14.2, 14.17,
  14.21–22, 16.70
Statistical material, 8.20, 12.51. *See also*
  Tables
Statues, 7.43n, 7.148
Statutes, 7.67–68, 16.156, 16.169–70, 17.90.
  See also Public documents
Stet, 3.30, pp. 53, 94, 95
Stories, titles of, 7.134
Streets, 7.43–45, 8.60–61, 14.21–22
Strike-on composition, 20.96–105
Structures, 7.43–45
Stub, in tables, 12.27, 12.32–38, 12.44,
  12.68–71, p. 332

Style
  of capitalization, 7.2–4, 7.74
  defined, 2.56, 2.57
  house, 2.57, 2.96, 2.99, 2.116
  of punctuation, 5.1–2
  regularizing, 2.90–91
Style sheet, editor's, 2.90–91, 2.116, 2.149,
    2.155, p. 61
Subentries, index, 18.4–8
  alphabetizing, 18.51, 18.100
  arrangement of, 18.51–53, 18.100–101,
    18.128
  with dash, 18.53, 18.128, 18.135, 18.138
  number of, 18.48–50, 18.128
  punctuation of, 18.54
  relation to main entry, 18.6–7, 18.46–47
  run-in or indented, 18.15, 18.18, 18.132,
    18.135–39
Subheads. *See also* Subentries, index; Tables,
    column heads; Tables, subheadings
  capitalization of, 2.18, 2.139
  content of, 1.58, 2.93
  copyediting, 2.93
  indention following, 2.139, 19.28, 19.57
  levels of, 1.59–61, 2.19, 19.28–30
  note references with, 1.64, 15.42
  numbers with, 1.62–63, 19.12
  and page makeup, 19.28, 20.35
  placement of, 1.60–61, 2.18, 2.19, 2.81,
    2.139, 19.28–30
  punctuation with, 1.60, 2.19, 2.139, 5.11,
    5.42
  as running heads, 1.79–80, 3.43
  spacing with, 2.139, 19.22
  in table of contents, 1.32, 3.46, 19.51, p. 15
  text following, 1.65, 2.93
  type specifications for, 1.60–61, 2.137–39,
    19.28–30, 20.32
  typing, 2.18–19
Subscripts and superscripts. *See also* Letters,
    superior; Numbers, superior
  alignment of, 13.48–49
  italics for, 13.41
  marking, 2.67, 2.141, 13.48
  solidus with, 13.30
  typefaces for, pp. 372–73
  typing, 13.4, 13.18n
Subsidiary rights, 4.2, 4.32–34
Substantive editing, 2.57
Substantive notes, 15.68
Subtitles
  in bibliographies, 16.31–32, 16.100
  or with, 7.123, 7.127, 17.41
  punctuation with, 1.9, 7.126, 7.128,
    16.31–32, 17.41
  type specifications for, 1.9, 19.47
Summation sign, 13.5–6, 13.29–31, pp. 367,

  371
Sun, 7.113
Superior characters, 2.67, 2.141. *See also*
    Note references; Subscripts and super-
    scripts
  in classical references, 17.73
Superscripts. *See* Subscripts and superscripts
Surnames. See Personal names
Suspension points. *See also* Ellipsis points
  in French, 9.26
  in Italian, 9.46
  in Russian, 9.91
  in Spanish, 9.70
S.v., 14.32, 17.62
Swahili, 9.84
Swedish
  capitalization, 9.80
  special characters, 9.81
Syllabication. *See* Hyphenation; Word divi-
    sion
Syllabus style, 8.73, 8.75
Symbols. *See also* Abbreviations; Special
    characters; Symbols, mathematical
  beginning sentence, 14.3
  chemical, 7.119, 14.51
  commercial, 14.55
  in computer typesetting, 2.15
  editorial, 2.61–85, p. 53
  identifying, 2.14
  in legends, 11.33
  monetary, 14.57
  for note references, 12.49, 12.51, 15.68,
    15.69
  with numbers, 8.16
  for percent, 8.18
  proofreaders', 3.3, 3.19–34, pp. 94, 95
  repeating, 8.16
  with sums of money, 8.23, 8.26, 8.30
  in tables, 12.28, 12.42
  typing, 2.14
Symbols, mathematical
  ambiguous, 13.47–52, pp. 368–69
  handwritten, 13.15, 13.18–19, 13.48, 13.51,
    pp. 368–69
  in illustrations, 13.39
  list of, 13.11–13, 13.16
  operational signs, 12.42, 13.21, 13.24,
    13.35–36, pp. 358, 369
  substitutions for, 13.14, 13.32–34
  typefaces for, pp. 372–73
  typesetting, 13.5–9
  typing, 13.4–5, 13.18–19
Symposia. *See also* Multiauthor books
  authors' affiliations, 1.47–48, 1.53, 15.71–72
  in bibliographies, 16.49–53, 16.130
  contracts for, 4.30
  handling, 2.169–76

illustrations in, 2.176, 11.9
papers read at, 7.142, 16.130, 17.59
place and date of, 1.6
tables in, 2.176, 12.18
titles of, 7.59
Syndromes (medical), 7.115

Table, capitalization of, 12.15
Table of contents. *See* Contents, table of
Tables
abbreviations in, 12.28, 12.77, 14.14, 14.15
alignment in, 2.23–25, 12.41–43, 12.65, 12.71
in appendix, 12.19, 15.64
arrangement of elements, 12.12–52
blank cells, 12.40, 12.71
body, 12.39–45
brief, in run of text, 2.24
broadside, 12.54–55, 12.78, 12.81
capitalization in, 2.23, 12.25, 12.31, 12.38, 12.67
column headings, 5.11, 12.14, 12.26–31, 12.64–67, 12.74, 12.77, 12.81, 12.84
column numbers, 12.28
consistency in, 2.106, 12.33
constructing, 12.3–11
continued, 12.79–84
copyediting, 2.105–6, 12.62–84
cross-references to, 2.40
cut-in heads, 5.11, 12.30, 12.31, 12.65
dashes in, 12.40, 12.71
decimal point in, 12.42
decked heads, 12.28–29, 12.31
doubling up, 12.56
estimating, 2.9, 19.8
examples of style, 12.85, pp. 345–50
foldout, 12.55
genealogical, 12.60, p. 339
genetic, 12.61, p. 340
indentions in, 12.34–36, 12.69–70
indexing, 18.27
labeling, 2.146, 2.176n
leaders in, 12.37, 12.40, 12.71
levels of probability in, 12.46, 12.51
matrix, 12.58, p. 337
in multiauthor books, 2.176, 12.18
N (number) in, 12.5, 12.10–11, 12.24, 12.45, 12.66
note references in, 2.26, 12.48–50, 12.73, 15.43, 15.45
notes to, 2.26, 2.106, 12.45, 12.46–52, 12.72–73, 12.83, 15.43, 15.45, 19.35n
in notes, 2.100, 15.64
numbering, 2.9, 2.23, 2.46, 2.176, 8.32, 11.9, 12.15–20
numbers of (typing), 2.9, 12.20

page numbers omitted with, 1.89, 3.41
parentheses in, 12.24, 12.28
percentages in, 12.5–11, 12.23, 12.42, 12.45
placement in book, 2.45–46, 2.105
placement in manuscript, 2.3, 2.23, 2.46, 2.105
punctuation in, 2.23, 5.11, 12.38
references to, in text, 2.40, 2.45, 12.15–16
rules in, 2.25, 2.106, 12.13, 12.29, 12.31, 12.42, 12.44, 12.58, 12.74
running heads omitted with, 1.83, 3.41, 12.75
size and shape, 12.53–56, 12.75–84
sources, 12.46, 12.72, 12.83
spacing with, 2.16n, 2.23–25, 12.14, 12.31, 12.52, 12.54
spanner heads, 12.29, 12.31, 12.65, 12.74
stub, 12.27, 12.32–38,. 12.44, 12.68–71
subheadings, 2.23, 12.24–25, 12.28, 12.34, 12.70, p. 332
symbols in, 12.28, 12.42
titles, 2.23, 2.46, 12.21–25, 12.63–67
totals in, 12.36, 12.44–45, 12.69, 12.74, 12.82
type specifications for, 12.63–64, 12.68–70, 12.77, 12.85, pp. 345–50
typewriter composition of, p. 350
typing, 2.23–26, 12.14, 12.20, 12.25, 12.31, 12.52, 12.53–54, p. 350
of words, 12.14, 12.42, 12.44, 12.59, p. 338
zero in, 12.40, 12.42
Tables, list of
checking against tables, 2.46, 3.47
content of, 1.37
inclusion of, 1.37
placement of, 1.1, 1.37, 11.45
Tape, transparent, 2.35n
Tape recordings, in bibliographies, 16.177–78
Tapes, computer, 2.2, 2.5, 2.51, 2.53. *See also* Photocomposition
Taxonomic names, 7.98–103, 7.116
Technical terms. *See also* Scientific terms
abbreviations for, 14.50–54
italics for, 6.61–62
quotation marks for, 6.62
Television programs, 7.143
Temperature, 8.11–12, 8.15–16, 14.50
Territory, 7.37
Text. *See also* Manuscript
copyediting, 2.89–96
numbering, 1.1, 2.8
organization of, 1.1, 1.50–66
page numbers of, 1.88–89
running heads to, 1.79–80
type specifications for, 2.131–44, 19.16–27
Text-fiche, 16.59–60
Thai names, 18.121

That is (*i.e.*)
punctuation with, 5.54, 5.72, 5.76, 5.86, 5.99
in text, 14.31
The
in alphabetizing, 16.23, 18.88–89, 18.100, 18.124, 18.139
with organizational names, 7.57–58
with place names, 18.124
with publishers' names, 16.76
with titles of works, 7.123, 7.130–31, 17.11, 18.88–89, 18.139
Theology. *See* Religious names and terms
Theorems, etc., 13.45
Therefore, punctuation with, 5.39, 5.69
Theses, 7.142, 16.129. *See also* Dissertations
Third (*III* or *3d*), 8.52–54, 14.8, 18.82.
Thousands
comma in, 2.106, 8.41, 8.64–66, 14.49
spelling out, 8.3
Thus, punctuation with, 5.69
Tilde, 9.11, 9.79
Time, 7.71–73, 8.47–49. *See also* Dates; Eras
abbreviations with, 14.26–30, 14.40
A.M. and P.M., 8.48, 14.2, 14.3, 14.30
apostrophe with span of, 6.14
colon with, 8.47
of day, 8.47–49, 14.30
days, months, seasons, 7.71, 8.36–38, 8.43–46, 14.29
en dash with, 5.92
punctuation with, 5.92, 8.47, 8.49
twenty-four-hour system, 8.49
zones, 7.73
Tip-ins
errata sheet, 1.92
illustrations, 1.8, 20.78
Title page
author's name on, 1.11, 1.13, 19.47
content of, 1.9–13, 1.29
copyediting, 2.111
placement of, 1.1, 1.9
type specifications for, 1.9–11, 19.47
Titles of persons, 7.15–25
abbreviation of, 14.3, 14.5–11
academic, 7.17n, 7.21, 7.26, 14.3, 14.8, 14.11, 18.81
in acknowledgments, 7.16
capitalization of, 7.15–24
civil, 7.15–17, 7.18, 14.5
degrees and honors, 1.11, 7.26, 18.81
in direct address, 7.16
epithets, 7.24, 7.28
following name, 7.17
honorific, 7.27, 14.8, 14.11
in indexes, 18.76–84
Italian, 9.45

in list of contributors, 1.47, 7.16
military, 7.15–17, 7.19, 14.5
named professorships, 7.17n
with names, 7.15–22, 7.24, 14.5–11, 18.76–83
of nobility, 7.11, 7.15–17, 7.22–23, 18.77–79
professional, 1.11, 7.15–17, 7.21
punctuation with, 5.42, 5.43, 5.58
religious, 7.15–17, 7.20, 7.78, 14.7, 18.80
social, 14.3, 14.6
on title page, 1.11
in toasts, 7.16
used alone, 7.17
Titles of works, 7.122–48. *See also* Articles, journal; Title page
abbreviation of, 15.67, 15.80, 16.101–2, 17.15, 17.64
alphabetizing, 16.23, 18.88–89, 18.139
articles with, 7.123, 7.130–31, 16.23, 17.11, 18.88–89, 18.139
as "author," 16.23
in bibliographies, 16.31–40, 16.44, 16.52, 16.100–101, 16.114, 16.121, 16.139, p. 422
books, 7.129–33
capitalization of, 7.122–24, 7.128, 9.4, 9.55, 9.88–89, 9.107–8, 9.117, 16.31–32, 16.37, 16.44, 16.100–101, 16.114, 16.121, 16.139, 17.41, 17.54, 17.68
classical, 17.67–69
comma following, 17.20
dash in, 7.126, 7.128
dates in, 7.126, 7.128, 8.69, 17.38
descriptive, 7.147, 7.148
foreign, 9.4, 9.88–89, 9.107–8, 9.117, 16.38–40, 16.87, 16.121, 17.42–43, 17.54, 17.68 (*see also under individual languages*)
hyphenation in, 7.124, 7.128
in indexes, 18.88–91, 18.139
italics for, 7.5, 7.129–31, 16.31–32, 16.52, 16.101
journal articles, 7.134–36, 15.80, 16.6, 16.100, 16.114, 16.115, 16.121, 17.54, p. 424
journals, 7.129–33, 9.4, 15.76, 15.80, 16.101–2, 16.114, 16.121, 18.89
in legal references, 17.76
medieval, 17.75
multivolume works, 16.41–42
music, 7.5, 7.144–47, 16.36
in notes, 15.66, 17.2, 17.6–8, 17.11, 17.38–43, 17.68, 17.69
numbers in, 7.125, 17.38
as object of preposition, 7.132
older titles, 16.37, 17.40–41
or in, 7.123, 7.127, 16.22, 17.41
paintings and sculpture, 7.148

parts of book, 7.134–36
plays, 7.138, 7.140–41
plurals of, 6.8
poems, 7.5, 7.138–41
punctuation in, 1.9, 7.126–28, 7.146,
  16.31–32, 16.37, 17.38, 17.41
quotation marks with, 7.5, 16.25, 16.31–32,
  16.33–36, 16.100, 16.138–39, 17.38
quotations within, 17.38
series titles, 7.137, 16.44–48, 17.45
shortened (*see* Short titles)
as singular nouns, 7.133
spelling of, 7.125, 16.31–32
subtitles with, 7.126, 7.128, 16.31–32,
  16.100, 17.41
title within title, 16.25, 16.31–32, 16.33–36,
  17.39
translation of, 16.39–40, 16.87, 16.122,
  17.43
typography for, 7.123, 16.31
unpublished, 7.142, 16.128
works of art, 7.144–48
To (infinitive), in titles, 7.123
Toasts, 7.16
Topographical names, 7.38–42, 18.123. *See
  also* Place names
Totals, in tables, 12.36, 12.44–45, 12.69, 12.74,
  12.82
Trademarks, 7.107, 7.117, 7.121
Trains, 7.97
Transitional adverbs, punctuation with, 5.39,
  5.69
Translation. *See also* Translations (works)
  of bibliographical terms, 16.121, 17.22
  brackets with, 10.50, 16.39
  of facts of publication, 16.121
  of foreign titles, 16.39–40, 16.87, 16.122,
    17.43
  of quoted material, 2.96, 10.70–71
  of words in text, 6.56
Translations (works). *See also* Translator's
  name
  copyright for, 1.18, 1.21, 4.10
  facts of publication with, 16.73, 16.87
  notes to, 15.69, 15.73
  rights to, 4.33
Translator, abbreviation of, 16.24–27, 16.53,
  17.10, 17.35–37
Translator's name
  as author, 16.24–27
  in classical references, 17.67
  in notes, 17.10, 17.35–37
Translator's notes, 15.69, 15.73
Transliteration, 9.85. *See also* Romanization
  of Arabic, 9.102–6
  of Greek, 9.120–21, p. 276
  of Russian, 9.86–89, 10.70n, p. 266

of South Asian languages, 9.110
Transmittal sheet
  acquisitions editor's, 19.3, p. 563
  copyeditor's, 1.149, 2.156–57, p. 79
Transposition, marking for, 2.63–64, 3.28,
  pp. 53, 94, 95
Treaties, 7.67
Tribes, 7.32–33
Trim size, 19.16, 20.40, p. 605
Tropics, 7.34
Turkish
  capitalization, 9.82
  special characters, 9.83
  transcribing, 9.102
Twenty-four-hour clock, 8.49
Type. *See also* Boldface type; Italics; Type-
    faces; Type specifications; Wrong font
  alignment of, 3.25–27, pp. 94, 95
  broken, 3.13, 3.33, pp. 94, 95
  justified, 18.131, 19.21, 19.26, 20.5,
    20.27–29, 20.122–23
Typefaces. *See also* Type specifications
  in bibliographies, 16.10
  in film setting, 19.13–15
  for mathematics, pp. 372–73
  point size of, 20.38, p. 605
  for text, 19.4, 19.10–15
  on typewriter, 2.12, 13.18n, 20.98, 20.100,
    p. 350
Type page
  defined, 20.39, p. 605
  measurement of, 19.4, 19.9, 19.16–19
Typescript. *See* Manuscript
Typesetter
  coding of manuscript, 2.52, 2.130
  instructions to, 2.145 (*see also* Type specifi-
    cations, marking manuscript with)
Typesetting
  computerized (*see* Computers; Photo-
    composition)
  corrections, 3.13, 20.30, 20.33, 20.103,
    20.129
  direct-image, 20.96–129
  hand process, 20.4–6, pp. 587–89
  Linotype, 3.1, 13.4, 20.27, 20.29–30
  machine process, 2.2, 20.27–30
  of mathematics, 13.3–16
  Monotype, 3.1, 13.6, 13.10, 19.23,
    20.27–28, 20.30, pp. 372–73
  page makeup, 3.16, 15.58–60, 19.28, 19.39,
    20.34–37, 20.122–24, 20.129
  photographic (*see* Photocomposition)
  strike-on composition, 20.96–105
  typewriter composition, 13.5, 13.18n,
    20.96–105, p. 350
Type specifications. *See also* Book design;
  Layouts; Typefaces

Type specifications (*continued*)
    for appendixes, 1.70, 2.140, 19.58, 20.32
    for bibliographies, 1.74, 2.142, 16.10, 19.12,
        19.55
    for block quotations, 2.16, 2.134–36, 19.23,
        19.31–33, 20.32
    for chapter openings, 2.18, 2.131–32,
        19.52–59, 20.32
    coding of, 2.15, 2.130, 3.12, 20.118, 20.128
    for display matter, 19.22, 19.45–60
    for indexes, 1.75, 2.143–44, 18.15, 18.18,
        18.130–39, 19.42–44, 19.55
    for legends, 11.27
    marking manuscript with, 2.129, 2.131–44,
        19.71, pp. 580–81
    in mathematics, 13.16
    for notes, 2.141, 19.34–41, 20.32
    for page numbers, 2.151, 18.134, 18.136–37,
        19.60
    in photocomposition, 2.52, 2.130, 2.133
    planning of, 19.3–5
    for plays, 10.7, 19.64–68
    for poems, 2.135, 19.61–63
    for preliminaries, 1.9–11, 19.45, 19.47–51,
        19.55
    for running heads, 2.151, 19.59, 20.32
    for subheads, 1.60–61, 2.137–39, 19.28–30,
        20.32
    for tables, 12.63–64, 12.68–70, 12.77, 12.85,
        pp. 345–50
    for text, 2.131–44, 19.16–27
Typewriter
    for typewriter composition, 13.18n, 20.98,
        20.100
    for typing manuscript, 2.12–15
Typewriter composition, 20.96–105
    corrections in, 20.103
    display type with, 20.101–2
    illustrations in, 20.104
    of mathematics, 13.5, 13.18n
    page makeup in, 20.104
    paper for, 20.99, p. 630
    proofs in, 20.103–5
    reduction of copy, 20.104
    of tables, p. 350
    typewriter for, 13.18n, 20.98, 20.100
Typing. *See also* Typewriter composition
    correcting errors, 2.13, 2.15
    dashes, 5.92, p. 369
    diacritics and symbols, 2.14
    index cards, 18.29
    index manuscript, 2.31, 18.31, 18.58–60,
        p. 532
    legends, 2.47, 2.107
    manuscript, 2.11–31, 13.18–19
    mathematics, 13.4–5, 13.18–19
    notes, 2.3, 2.21–22

    numbers, 2.14
    paper for, 2.11, 13.19, 18.31, 18.58
    spacing, 2.16, 2.20, 2.21, 2.29, 2.31, 12.14,
        13.19, 18.31, 18.33, 18.58, p. 532
    subheads, 2.18–19
    tables, 2.23–26, 12.14, 12.20, 12.25, 12.31,
        12.52, 12.53–54, p. 530
    typewriter, 2.12–15, 13.18n, 20.98, 20.100
    word division, 2.15
Typographical errors
    correcting in second impression, 1.92, 3.58
    found by indexer, 18.63
    in proof, 3.9–10, 3.35
    in quotations, 10.6
Typographical signs, proofreaders', 3.32–33,
    pp. 94, 95
Typography. *See also* Type specifications
    in indexes, 18.134–39
    in quotations, 10.7
    for tables, 12.63–64, 12.85, pp. 345–50
    in titles, 7.123, 16.31

Umlaut, 9.11, 9.42
    alphabetizing, 18.99
    typing, 2.14
Underlining
    deleting, 2.78
    for italics, 2.12, 2.15, 10.53n, 13.43
    in typing manuscript, 2.18
Unions, 7.58, 8.59, 14.15
United Kingdom, public documents of,
    16.161–73, 17.87–91, 17.94–95
United States
    abbreviation of, 14.2, 14.19–20
    public documents of, 16.146–60, 17.85–86
University, 7.57, 16.77
Unjustified lines. *See* Justification; Ragged-
    right style
Unnumbered notes
    with author-date citations, 15.72
    for authors' affiliations, 1.48, 1.53, 15.71–72
    with endnotes, 15.70, 15.72
    keyed to line or page, 15.73, pp. 418–20
    labeling, 2.141
    in multiauthor books, 1.48, 1.53, 2.163,
        15.70, 15.71–72
    placement of, 2.141, 15.70, 15.72
    source notes, 1.53, 2.163–64, 12.46, 12.72,
        15.70
    to tables, 12.46–47, 12.72, 12.83
Unpublished material. *See also* Archives;
        Manuscript collections
    in bibliographies, 15.83, 16.61, 16.97,
        16.128–82
    in notes, 17.2, 17.9, 17.59–61, 17.77–96
    permission to use, 4.43–44
    public documents, 16.158–59, 16.171–72,

16.174, 17.93–96
references to, in text, 15.28–29, 16.143
titles of, 7.142, 16.128
Uppercase. *See* Capitalization; Caps and
small caps; Full caps; Small caps
Urdu, transcribing, 9.102
U.S., 14.2, 14.19–20
USSR, 7.37, 14.19
Utopia, 7.36

Valley, 7.38, 7.41
Vandykes, 3.55, 11.49
Variables, in tables, 12.4–11, 12.32
VDT. *See* Video display terminal
Vectors, 13.32, 13.43
Vehicles, 8.51
Verse. *See* Poems
Verso page
blank, 1.1, 1.3, 2.7
for chapter opening, 1.52, 1.53n
defined, 1.1
page references to, 17.19, 17.79
running head on, 1.79
verso of half title, 1.3–8
Vice-, compounds with, p. 176
Video display terminal (VDT), 2.52, 20.117,
p. 635. *See also* CRT composition; Photocomposition; Scanner
Videorecordings, 16.179–81
Vietnamese names, 18.116–17
Virgule. *See* Solidus
Volume editor, responsibilities of, 2.170–73.
See also Editor's name; Multiauthor
books
Volume numbers. *See also* Multivolume
works
arabic numerals for, 16.10, 16.43, 16.103,
17.23
in author-date citations, 15.11–12
in bibliographies, 16.10, 16.42–43, 16.46,
16.103, 16.107–14, 16.119
of journals, 16.103, 16.107–14, 16.119, 17.53
in notes, 17.16, 17.20, 17.53
with page numbers, 16.107–14, 16.119,
16.124–25, 17.20, 17.53
punctuation with, 16.107–14, 16.119, 17.20
of series, 16.46
years as, 17.53
Volumes, number of, 16.41. *See also* Multivolume works

Wars, 7.65, 7.94
Weight. *See* Measurements
Well-, compounds with, p. 178
West(ern), 7.34–35
White (race), 7.32–33

-wide, compounds with, p. 179
Widows (in type), 20.35
Woodcuts, 20.22, p. 599
Word division, 6.33–47. *See also* Hyphenation
abbreviations, 6.45
American system of, 6.34
bad breaks, 18.133, 20.35–37
compound words, 6.40–41
by computer, 3.11, 20.123
in French, 9.27–31
in German, 9.36–41
in Greek, 9.130–35
in Italian, 9.49–53
in Latin, 9.56–59
marking in manuscript, 2.73, p. 53
numbers, 6.44
personal names, 6.43
in Polish, 9.65
principles of, 6.34–46, 9.9
in proofs, 3.11, 3.39
in ragged-right style, 6.47, 19.27
in Russian, 9.93–101
in Spanish, 9.72–78
in typing, 2.15
words with *-ing,* 6.42
words with prefixes, 6.41
Word processors
castoff from, 19.6
for typesetting input, 20.121
Words. *See also* Words, compound
coined, 6.5
distinctive treatment of, 6.51–81
foreign (*see* Foreign words)
letters as, 6.71–81
missing, 5.95, 10.48, 10.50
tables of, 12.14, 12.42, 12.44, 12.59, p. 338
as words, 6.66–67
Words, compound, 6.24–32, pp. 176–81
capitalizing, 7.124, 9.20, pp. 177, 180
dividing, 6.40–41
hyphenating, 6.24, 6.26, 6.30, 6.31,
pp. 176–81
with proper names, pp. 177, 180
spelling, 6.24–32, pp. 176–81
temporary, 6.29, 6.31
in titles, 7.124
types of, defined, 6.25–29
Word spacing, 19.21, 19.26–27. *See also* Justification; Ragged-right style
Working proofs, 3.7, 3.18, 3.38, 20.33
Works made for hire, 4.10–11, 4.30, p. 119
World, parts of, 7.34–36. *See also* Place
names
Wrong font, marking in proof, 3.13, 3.33,
pp. 94, 95

Xerox copies. *See* Copies, machine

Years. *See also* Dates
  abbreviations for, 8.35, 14.27
  academic, 7.25
  alphabetizing, 18.98
  centuries, 7.125, 8.40–42
  comma in, 8.41, 8.64
  decades, 8.40
  figures for, 8.33–39, 8.41, 8.43–46
  inclusive, 5.92–93, 8.68–69
  plurals of, 6.9, 8.63
Yes and *no*
  punctuation with, 5.40, 5.41

  quotation marks with, 10.33
Yet, punctuation with, 5.69

Zero
  in decimal fractions, 8.19–21, 8.24, 12.42,
    13.20
  identifying, p. 369
  for page number, 1.32, 1.34, 2.39, 2.41,
    11.45
  in tables, 12.40, 12.42
  typing, 2.14

The Chicago Manual of Style

Designed by Cameron Poulter
Diagrams by R. Williams
Photographs by Ted Lacey
Composed at
The University of Chicago Printing Department
in Linotron Times Roman by the PENTA system
Printed by the Maple Press Company
on Warren's 1854 Cream Regular text stock
Bound by the Maple Press Company
in Holliston Roxite Linen
with Permacolor Smoke endsheets